Many Peoples, Many Faiths

Women and Men in the World Religions

Seventh Edition

Robert S. Ellwood
University of Southern California

Barbara A. McGraw
Saint Mary's College of California

Prentice
Hall

Upper Saddle River, New Jersey 07458

Library of Congress Cataloging-in-Publication Data

Ellwood, Robert S.
   Many peoples, many faiths : women and men in the world religions /
Robert S. Ellwood, Barbara A. McGraw.—7th ed.
     p. cm.
   Includes bibliographical references and index.
   ISBN 0-13-034172-X
   1. Religions   2. Religion.   I. McGraw, Barbara A. II. Title

BL80.3 .E44 2002
291—dc21

2001054579

Editorial director: *Charlyce Jones Owen*
Editorial/production supervision: *Joe Scordato*
Acquisitions editor: *Ross Miller*
Manufacturing buyer: *Sherry Lewis*
Manufacturing manager: *Nick Sklitsis*
Cover art: *Norman Rockwell,* "The Golden Rule," *UN/DPI*
Cover design: *Bruce Kenselaar*
Editorial assistant: *Carla Worner*

This book was set in 10/12 Cheltenham by Stratford Publishing Services and was printed and bound
by Hamilton Printing Company. The cover was printed by Phoenix Color Corporation.

Photo credits are listed on page xx.

 © 2002, 1999, 1996, 1992, 1987, 1982, and 1976 by Pearson Education, Inc.
Upper Saddle River, New Jersey 07458

Printed in the United States of America
10 9 8 7 6 5 4 3 2 1

ISBN 0-13-034172-X

Pearson Education Ltd.
Pearson Education Australia Pty. Ltd.
Pearson Education Singapore, Pte. Ltd.
Pearson Education North Asia Ltd.
Pearson Education Canada, Ltd.
Pearson Educación de Mexico, S.A. de C.V.
Pearson Education–Tokyo, Japan
Pearson Education Malaysia, Pte. Ltd.
Pearson Education, Upper Saddle River, New Jersey

For Richard Scott Lancelot Ellwood
May your faith be always adventurous

For Erin Eklund Roddy and Echo Anne McCollum,
Daughters not of my body, but of my heart,
May the world greet you with a door wide
open to the fulfillment of all your potential.

CONTENTS

PREFACE

For nearly three decades this introduction to the world's religions, *Many Peoples, Many Faiths,* has endeavored in various ways to combine factual information with empathetic writing that tries to convey something of the flavor of our planet's diverse religions and cultures. While striving for accuracy and depth, it is neither an encyclopedic compilation of data nor a survey of alternative philosophies. Instead, it seeks to present something of the total human experience, made up as it is of an inseparable mingling of conceptual, worship, and social factors, of religious life from past to present. The authors hope that their efforts will implant in many readers a sense of the richness and fascination of the areas of scholarship that lie behind the presentation of this experience, and that it will inspire at least some to explore these areas more deeply.

Barbara McGraw, Associate Professor, St. Mary's College of California, joined with the original writer, Robert Ellwood, Emeritus Professor, University of Southern California, as coauthor for the sixth edition of *Many Peoples, Many Faiths,* and continues to have a large part in the rewriting of all sections of the seventh edition of the book. In particular, Professor McGraw has contributed nearly all of the material that was added in the sixth edition on women in the world religions. The growing interest in this issue and its own intrinsic importance have led both of us to believe that world religions textbooks must now give substantial amounts of space and detail to the role and experience of women in religion. And we hope that the effort to combine factual information with empathetic writing has been carried over into the material on women in the world's faiths, while recognizing at the same time that sometimes shedding light on a subject at all may call its basic tenets into question.

In general, this seventh edition of *Many Peoples, Many Faiths* seeks to continue the balanced and empathetic approach to the religions of the world toward which previous versions have striven. Additions made to earlier editions have been maintained and, where appropriate, updated. For example, in the sixth edition new material was added throughout on the presence of the world religions in the United States. Further, it was previously recognized that in a world increasingly faced with very difficult choices and with a growing awareness of current injustices, no human institution, religion included, can avoid challenge and criticism. New material was previously added to the introductory chapter on critical approaches to religion, and a new final chapter was then appended on religion in the context of present and future crises, which has been substantially revised for the seventh edition. Readers will be challenged to think about how religion has responded to present developments in ecology, technology, globalization and other trends, and what possible futures for religion there may be in light of them.

Further, this seventh edition has been substantially edited in many places and additional headings have been added as "pointers" to make the material even more accessible to students than it was before—without, however, losing any of the beauty and flow of Robert Ellwood's original words. Also, the first person narratives that this book has been known for in the past have been restored. In this regard, notations have been provided to indicate which of the authors is speaking—an asterisk (*) indicating Robert S. Ellwood, a dagger (†) indicating Barbara A. McGraw.

The glossary for the seventh edition has been substantially expanded so that it can be used more effectively as a teaching and learning tool. The authors suggest that students be instructed to use the glossary as a study guide for each chapter. In addition, updated material has been added throughout the book, including the addition of recent books to the lists of suggested readings at the end of each chapter. As before, it must be emphasized that these lists are by no means exhaustive. In many of the categories, there are hundreds, even thousands, of valuable books. What we have tried to do is suggest a few books in each subject area, not so much for advanced research as for broader familiarization with the area. Most, therefore, are books written at a level accessible to beginning or middle-level students. Many are textbooks with good further bibliographies. Books footnoted in the text but not cited in the reading lists are generally recommended too. In many cases, the books in the suggested reading lists have gone through a number of editions; the dates given may not represent the earliest or latest printing. Again, these are only books representative of the wealth of material available in the study of the religious world; the inclusion or exclusion of a book should not be taken to reflect the authors' own critical judgment of a particular book.

In this edition, new material has been added to Chapter 10, "Spirits Rising," on new religious movements in the hope that appreciation of the dynamic, changing quality of religion will be enhanced. New material has also been added to Chapter 8 to reflect the growth and impact of Christianity in Asia, Africa, and Latin America, and to Chapter 9 to reflect the developments of Islam around the world. In addition, it is hoped that teachers and students will be aided by the Appendix, which gives practical suggestions on how to write papers for classes using this text. In addition, maps have been updated and improved.

As always, true understanding of the many faiths of the many peoples of earth requires a mixture of knowledge and empathy. As you read this book keep the necessary facts in mind, but read it also with that human empathy that alone can furnish an understanding of what those facts mean to human beings for whom they are gateways to ultimate meaning.

We are indebted to many people who have helped to make this seventh edition possible. First, we would like to thank everyone at Prentice Hall who has worked on this book. Unfortunately, we cannot name them all here, but we would like to thank Ross Miller, the Acquisitions Editor for Religion, who has overseen this project, and whose diligence and guidance have contributed immensely to a successful result, and Joseph Scordato, the Production Editor, whose efficiency and generally pleasant manner of communication certainly have made an invaluable contribution to this book and made its production a pleasant experience, as well. In addition, special thanks is given to our copy editor, Stephen Hopkins, whose attention to detail and copy suggestions were much appreciated.

We also wish to acknowledge the reviewers who offered suggestions for the improvement of this seventh edition. Our thanks and appreciation to: Araminta Johnston of Queens College and Randal Cummings of California State University, Northridge. And we also wish to acknowledge the work of Professor McGraw's research assistant, Andrew J. Gibson, who contributed to the updating of the "Suggested Readings" sections throughout this book.

Further, Barbara McGraw would like to acknowledge her former professor and now colleague and friend, Professor Elizabeth Say, Director of Women's Studies, California State University at Northridge, for her continuing inspiration, especially with regard to the study of women in religion, and Professor Robert S. Ellwood for opening the doors that count.

ABC NEWS
ABC News/PH Video Library
Issues in World Religions

Video is the most dynamic of all supplements you can use to enhance your class. But the quality of the video material and how well it relates to your course still makes all the difference. Prentice Hall and ABC News are now working together to bring you the best and most comprehensive video ancillaries available in the college market.

Segments from award-winning ABC News programs, including *20/20, World News Tonight, Primetime Live,* and *Nightline* cover issues related to text concepts and applications. The programs have extremely high production quality, present substantial content, and are hosted by well-versed, well-known anchors.

PHOTO CREDITS

CHAPTER ONE

Understanding the World's Religious Heritage

CHAPTER OBJECTIVES

After studying this chapter, you should be able to

❋ **Talk about what you mean by religion, and what a religion includes.**

❋ **Discuss religion in terms of the human experience of a split-level universe—as conditioned and unconditioned reality.**

❋ **Cite and interpret Joachim Wach's Three Forms of Religious Expression.**

❋ **Discuss other methods for approaching the study of religion: descriptive, critical, and historical.**

A New Day of Religious Encounter

The religions of the world—the words themselves may evoke a panorama of images, perhaps drawn from a host of movies and novels with east-of-Suez settings. Incense and temple gongs, yogis in strange contorted postures, ancient and enigmatic chants—all these and more sweep past our inner eyes and ears. Most often, what fascinates us is that which is far away or long ago.

But the study of the religions of the world is no longer a matter of reading about exotic lands to which only the most intrepid travelers have voyaged. In today's **pluralism** and world community, almost any faith from anywhere is a presence and an option throughout the world. The temples of Hindu Americans and the mosques of Muslim Americans embellish larger American cities. American Zen centers, quiet with the great peace of the Buddha, teach Eastern meditation. Christianity and Judaism in all their manifold forms have long existed here side by side, just as Christianity has been carried by American missionaries to the homelands of Hinduism and Buddhism.

All of this makes "now" an exciting time to study religion. We who come to the study of religion today bring with us expectations shaped by these times. The presence of many options, and ferment within most of them, is something we sense inside ourselves as well as in the outside world.

A glance at virtually any morning paper or evening TV news reminds us that now is also an important time to study religion, though often for grimmer reasons than its color and diversity. Especially in the post–Cold War world, religion, generally linked to passionate nationalism, appears to be a major factor in many of the planet's tragic conflicts. Reports from India, Ireland, the Middle East, the Balkans, and, after September 11, 2001, New York and Washington, remind us of this distressing reality over and over. While the religions invoked in these oft-bloody disputes cannot usually be solely blamed for them, no full comprehension of the earth's current crises is possible without an in-depth understanding of the faiths involved. In assessing our own attitudes toward religious belief, we are forced to deal with the fact that it is not always a good thing by ordinary human values.

On a happier note, our increasingly global world and economy means that the adult careers of many of today's students will bring them in close contact with, perhaps even residence in, societies like India, China, or Japan. Whether one's primary interests are in law, business, diplomacy, or academic study, the greatest success in these endeavors requires a deep understanding of how a society works, including sensitivity to its religious heritage. In this book we will see, for example, how a sense of enduring Confucian values helps one to grasp how both Japanese corporations and the Chinese People's Republic really work.

All of this also indicates how complex religion is. It is now time to try to sort out this complexity by introducing some categories through which we can try to understand it. We shall first suggest ways of looking at the religion of another culture. Next we describe three forms of religious expression, discuss descriptive and critical approaches, and finally outline the basic stages of religious **history**. In the process we shall, among other things, be working toward a definition of religion, but we may not reach that point even by the end of the book.

Doors and Windows to the Ultimate

What is religion, then?

Suppose you were taking a trip to a country whose culture was completely foreign to you, and you wanted to determine the religion of that culture. Suppose, further, that because you cannot speak the language of the country well enough to ask anyone about it, you have to look for clues in what you see around you and in what people do. What would you look for?

Most of what you see, of course, has an obvious explanation. Most aspects of culture apparently meet understandable human needs for shelter, food, drink, security, and pleasure in this world. Most buildings up and down the streets are houses where people live or shops where craftspeople work or merchants sell. Most of the people scurrying about are out on business or seeking recreation.

Once in a while, though, you may perceive something that offers no such "ordinary" interpretation. A structure may be neither home nor shop, yet is obviously important, set apart, and perhaps elaborately ornamented. A human activity may be neither work nor play in the usual sense. It may not produce food nor exercise the body nor challenge one's skill in any ordinary way, yet clearly it is of great importance and marked by a solemn or festive air. Both the building and the activity may be associated with symbols and gestures that make no sense in terms of the usual affairs of this world, yet are of deep significance to these people.

You suspect that these are places and practices connected to the religion of the land. You know that you could be wrong, of course; without considerable background information, certainty would be impossible. The special building might be a court instead of a temple; the activity a game or dance instead of a rite. Indeed, the rites of state and of religion are often intermingled, and in many societies, games and dances have been done for reasons that combine their own intrinsic excitement with the sacred. On the other hand, even activities that do offer an "ordinary" interpretation may have a special sense of the sacred associated with them by the people of that land. For example, the particular method used for the harvesting of crops may have a ritualized significance that points to something more than providing food.

But still you are aware of one other thing: Traditional religion in innumerable different cultures affirms that human life has relationships and objectives beyond the ordinary, basic physical and emotional needs of individual people—beyond ordinary labor and frolic. Certain structures, doings, and gestures have a special relation to invisible realities they express or into which they "fit." They may well be what is commonly called religion. They may vary from the rhetoric of preaching to the quiet of meditation, from the ornate garb and carefully stylized motions of elaborate ritual to the gladsome tones of gospel music, but in any case they point to a belief that reality has more to it than the everyday, and that this extraordinary reality, this "something more" impinges on human life and can be touched, channeled, and made manifest by special means. The something more may be experienced as an otherness that stands outside the "this-worldly" plane. Or, it may be experienced as giving a special significance to the world or the universe as a whole. In either case, rites and symbols are reminders of, and methods for participating in, that something more.

Basic to religion is the assumption that we live in a split-level universe or, to use the expression of the historian of religion Mircea Eliade, that reality is non-homogeneous. As we have said, for the religious person, there is ordinary reality and something more. Certain visible places, people, and events are more in touch with that something more than others. They are sacred places, persons, and rites.

Using relatively neutral terms derived from Buddhist thought, we may think of the two sides of this split-level universe—the ordinary and the something more—as conditioned and unconditioned reality, respectively. Let us start by talking about **conditioned reality**. To say something is conditioned simply means that it is limited or restricted. We are obviously conditioned in time and space. If we are living in the twentieth century, we are not also in the ninth with Charlemagne or in the twenty-third with Star Trek. If we live in Ohio or Oklahoma, we are not also in Hong Kong or on the planet Neptune. Further, we are conditioned by the limitations and habits of our minds. We can think about only one thing at a time, and we forget far more than we remember. Even the greatest genius can only know the tiniest fragment of what there is to know or think more than the minutest fraction of what there is to think. Moreover, we continually build limits around ourselves when we, in effect, say such things as, "I'm a person who does this but not that," "I believe this but not that," or "I like this but not that."

Consider now what **unconditioned reality**, the opposite of all the above, would be like. It would be equally present to all times and all places. Its knowledge, wisdom, and mental power would be unlimited and would embrace all that could possibly be known or thought. If it (or he or she) had preferences as to doing, believing, or liking, they would be based on omniscient wisdom, not the bundle of ill-informed fears and prejudices by which we too often act and react. Unconditioned reality would, in fact, be no different from the Divine or Ultimate Reality of religion and philosophy. It goes by different names and has varying degrees of personality, but in most religions, some unconditioned pole of reality stands over our very-much-conditioned everyday lives. Even the legions of secondary sacred entities that also inhabit the religious world—polytheistic gods, buddhas, bodhisattvas, angels, spirits—have their significance because they are in a special relationship to and in some particular way refract bits of light or energy from unconditioned reality. We can illustrate conditioned and unconditioned reality and its names in various religions like this:

Unconditioned Reality
Brahman (philosophical Hinduism)
Nirvana (Buddhism)
Dao (Daoism)

Gold Hill Mahayana Buddhist temple in Zhenjiang, China.

Worship of Durga in Calcutta.

Heaven (Confucianism)
God (Judaism, Christianity, Islam)
Awareness of Presence of Spirits (Shamanism)

Conditioned Reality[1]
Maya (philosophical Hinduism)
Samsara (Buddhism)
Under Heaven (Daoism, Confucianism)
Choice of Death (Judaism)
The World (Christianity)
Realm of War (Islam)
Experience of Absence of Spirits (Shamanism)

One point remains to be added. For religion, the line between unconditioned and conditioned reality is not seen as solid, as though the two realms were hermetically sealed off from each other. Instead, the main idea behind any religion (whether it views unconditioned and conditioned reality as conterminous and concurrent or as actual separate spheres) is that it is full of doors and windows and that much commerce passes between the two. Words and people pass through those invisible doors, and the world is full of places and occasions that are like windows to the other side. This porous borderline, where the action is, is the sphere of the religious.

Crossings are diverse. Revelations, angels, gods, saviors, and spirits are envoys from unconditioned to conditioned reality. All religions believe that certain teachings, practices (such as prayer or meditation, rites, and services), and modes of ethical behavior best express or fit in with the nature of ultimate reality and so are in themselves like the doors and windows. Certain persons or institutions are also held to be in especially close touch with unconditioned reality and so are also like those portals. In a somewhat different sense, so are works of religious art, music, or literature. It is also possible for people themselves to move through the windows or doors, so to speak, and enter the infinite, the ultimate, the entirety of unconditioned reality, whether through prayer, mystical experience, or death.

Some will object that not all of what is ordinarily called religious, or which has to do with gods and the like, is really concerned with unconditioned reality. People go to church or temple or conduct rituals for social reasons or merely because they like the music. Yet, we think that understanding religion should not always be limited by the conscious intention of the religionist (often hard to judge in any event) or by the explicit language of the example under study. Even if a person goes to church only to meet someone, or if a particular hunting chant is a tradition that bonds the tribe, something more is implied by the very existence of church and chant. In the church or temple, God will probably be spoken of and things done that make no sense if there is no God, and the hunting chant tells us there is more to the hunt than just human beings hunting.

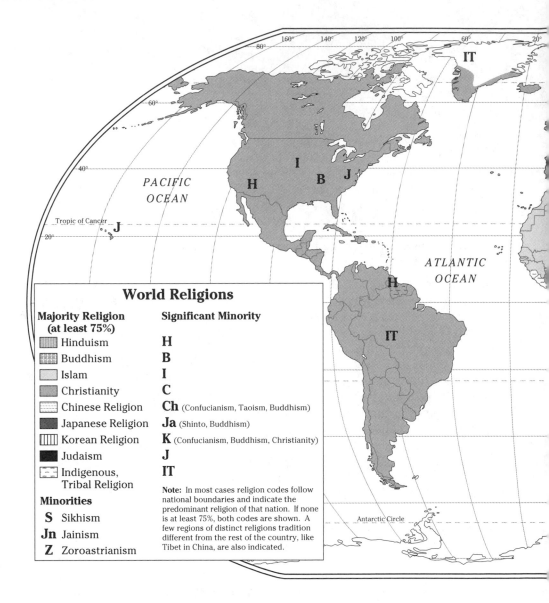

World Religions

Majority Religion (at least 75%)

		Significant Minority	
▦	Hinduism	**H**	
▦	Buddhism	**B**	
▢	Islam	**I**	
▨	Christianity	**C**	
▨	Chinese Religion	**Ch**	(Confucianism, Taoism, Buddhism)
■	Japanese Religion	**Ja**	(Shinto, Buddhism)
▥	Korean Religion	**K**	(Confucianism, Buddhism, Christianity)
■	Judaism	**J**	
▤	Indigenous, Tribal Religion	**IT**	

Minorities

S Sikhism
Jn Jainism
Z Zoroastrianism

Note: In most cases religion codes follow national boundaries and indicate the predominant religion of that nation. If none is at least 75%, both codes are shown. A few regions of distinct religions tradition different from the rest of the country, like Tibet in China, are also indicated.

Both chant and church open up in back, so to speak, to that invisible realm, which is something more than the world of ordinary existence. For the thoughtful, it probably begins with a notion of unconditioned reality, whose power all gods, saints, spirits, and shrines engage in some particularized way. Even for those who give it little thought, their experience tells them there is more than the ordinary. In

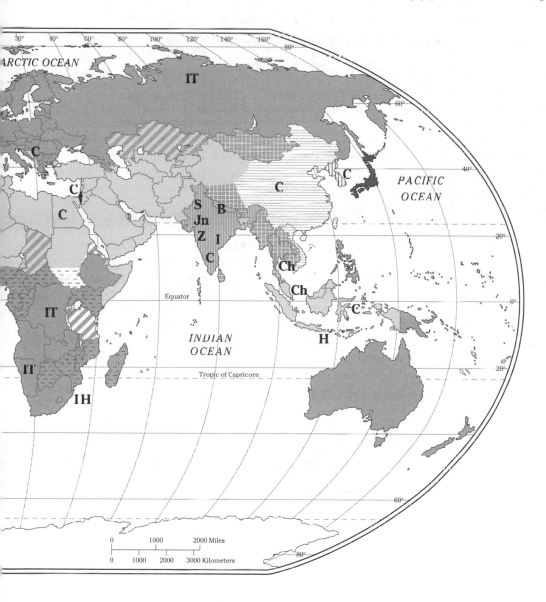

either case, participation in something more is expressed as religion in almost countless variations that are the doors and windows between unconditioned and conditioned reality. Yet, while the particulars of religion have many variations, there are constants in the *kinds* of expression that the religious consciousness takes.

Three Forms of Religious Expression

The sociologist of religion Joachim Wach (1898–1955) has provided one useful description of these constants. While the essence of religion may be beyond words, the religious experience, he tells us, expresses itself in human life in three ways. These three forms of religious expression he called theoretical, practical, and sociological.[2] These categories will be referred to from time to time in this book in order to show the place and interrelationship of the various human religious activities of which we shall speak. It will be helpful now to get a preliminary idea of what is meant by each.

Theoretical Expression: What Is Said in Religion?

The first level of religious expression, the **theoretical**, embraces essentially the verbal expression: what is said. Religions say things about certain basic, ultimate issues—how the spiritual universe is set up, what ultimate reality is, where the world came from and where it is going, and where humans came from and where we are going. Religions talk about how we know ultimate truth and how we are helped to get from here to the ultimate. They say these things in two fundamental ways: **myth**, or narrative story, and **doctrine**. In the history of religions, the term *myth* is

The Three Forms of Religious Expression

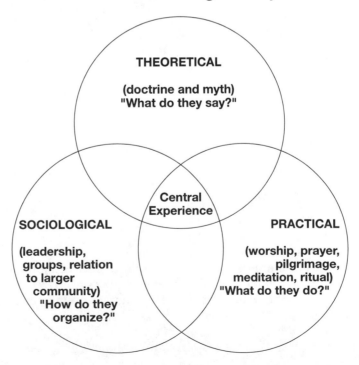

used in a special way to denote stories that express in narrative form the central values of the society and the way it views what the world is and means. This is a usage different from the popular denotation of the word *myth* as a fable or story that is not true. In the history of religions, the use of this word is only a statement of its function, and no judgment is passed on its truth.

Practically all religions have stories that encapsulate the basic perception of the world and the human place in it in narrative form. The most important are often creation stories. They state an important view of the nature of the cosmos by, for example, telling of a God like that of the Judeo-Christian tradition, who created the universe from nothing and stands outside it, or like that of other traditions, where the creation of the world is by the division of a Divine being in a primal sacrifice, signifying that the Divine is in creation. These examples imply very different relationships between the Divine and the world.

Another important type of myth is the hero story, the story of the individual who is able to find the way back to the ideal state of the world at its beginning. This person shows us the way from here to there and helps us along the way. He or she undertakes a mighty quest and experiences great anguish. But whether the model hero is a suffering savior like Jesus Christ, a profound meditator like the Buddha, or a persevering pacifist like Anne Lee, the founder of the Shakers, an American communal movement, says much about the central values of the community that cherishes the figures. Religions also have model stories of miracles, saints, and conversions, as well as stories of the activities of gods or goddesses, that express unconditioned reality and help to bring others to it.

Practical Expression: What Is Done in Religion?

The practices of religion—worship, rite, pilgrimage, forms of devotion or meditation, and other personal or group activities—constitute the form of religious expression Joachim Wach referred to as the **practical** expression of religion. This form of religious expression covers the visible and performed side of faith. To stand out as especially religious actions, things done have to have an appearance that makes their religious character evident, and this is likely to be the case only if they follow patterns recognizable in the culture as "religious," neither just meeting ordinary needs in an ordinary way nor being merely peculiar. In other words, it will have to be a gesture that is traditionally religious and so something that comes out of the religious past. Even the simplest religious services are generally performed in special places and employ a few set words and phrases that mark them as religious according to that tradition.

One important dimension of the practical expression is the experience of religion as something that has persisted through time to the present; part of the sense of expansiveness it gives is a sense of free access to the past. Even religion's visions of the future tend to be put in language that suggests a renewed past: the descent of the heavenly Jerusalem, the coming of a future Buddha, the return to the inherent balance of nature. Religious rites often carry over from the past vestments, language, and the like that are obsolete in the rest of the culture. Thereby, they give people a larger world and, indeed, a sense of unboundedness, by getting them outside the narrow confines of the present. At the same time this perpetuation of an idealized past serves to reinforce the values of the culture it celebrates.

Another dimension of the practical expression is the experience of religion as a method for getting outside the ordinary and into unconditioned reality in the immediate present. A rite may create a context that is extraordinary in its emotional tone, color, and activity, such as a special dance or chant created solely for the occasion. Meditation may focus the mind so as to leave behind all the distractions of the world.

Sociological Expression: What Kinds of Groups Are Formed by Religion?

Forms of organization, and the way they relate to the broader social context, are also part of religion, the **sociological** expression of religion. Generally, religion's structures fall into two types. These may be called the "church type" and the "withdrawal-group" type. The church, in this sense, is the broadly based religion that represents the normative spiritual values of a society, and in which most people are involved by virtue of their membership in the society—Hinduism in India or Catholicism in Spain. This is the faith a person in a society belongs to if he or she has not made a self-conscious, deliberate choice to be something else. The church type of structure is often a comprehensive system allowing for individual variations and in practice not making extremely rigorous demands on anyone. (An exception would be when the dominant religion has real political power and uses it to enforce its strictures or impel social change, as in Puritan New England or countries affected by Islamic fundamentalism, such as Iran.) In America, we would have to think of the church role being played in effect by a number of major denominations, which tacitly but effectively support a general American religious consensus in the minds of the majority.

In contrast to this consensus are the withdrawal groups, which express the experiences of those for whom personal commitment and experience are more important than the family and functions of religion involved in the larger societal community. They meet the needs of those who feel the faith or unfaith of the majority is not for them and want to define themselves more sharply by making a separate choice. Such groups are of two types. Some groups, such as the Amish or Jehovah's Witnesses in the Christian tradition, represent a more intense and unbending commitment than the average to the religion that is the general tradition. These are often called **sects**. Other groups combine separation with new ideas and an emphasis on mystical experience and are often called **cults**, although that word should be used with caution since it has acquired a negative connotation.

The relation of a religion to the broader society tells its own story about the meaning of humankind's relation to the spiritual world, whether it is a faith widely if diffusely known or an esoteric wisdom well known by only a few intensely dedicated people. Other aspects of the collective life also tell a religion's stories. There is a message about both the Divine and humanity in whether the group is open or authoritarian; whether the leadership is charismatic, acting out of the radiant power of the leader's own experience, or whether it works through traditional, constitutional, or rational channels.

The Interrelationship of the Forms of Expression

In any religion, the three forms of expression work together to form a unified experience. It is usually a mistake to think that one comes first and the others follow after. Children learn about their mother-faiths more or less through all forms of expression at once—they hear the stories, see the special atmosphere of church, temple, or religious rite when taken by parents, and pick up the tone of its social life as they play with friends and relatives who share it. Even an adult convert will probably be drawn by all three forms and will participate in all three simultaneously. They unite to form a single, almost indefinable experience, which points to the ultimate nature of the sacred and becomes a part of the inner life of each person touched by it.

Descriptive and Critical Approaches

But, you may ask, is it enough just to talk, in a neutral way, about the shape of a religion's doors and windows as they open toward unconditioned reality?

It is not the purpose of a study such as this to decide on the ultimate truth or falsity of any religion. We are simply trying to know and understand them better. Even so, does one look on everything in the religious world—from a human sacrifice to the healing work of a Mother Teresa—with exactly the same understanding gaze? Can we not at least consider the social and cultural roles of religions from a critical as well as an appreciative perspective?

Important questions are now being raised around the world about religion and the oppression of women, about its role in maintaining exploitative family and economic systems, about ways in which religion impedes rational attacks on current problems, like overpopulation, through allegedly outmoded beliefs. In each case, both sides—the tradition and its critics—have much to say. But too much empathy can certainly get in the way of even seeing where the problems are, and world religion scholars are coming to realize that they need to be a part of this discussion.

The role of women in most traditional religions has generally been obscured by outward male dominance of the religion. For the most part, men have written the scriptures and doctrines and have been the faith's priests and spokespersons. Criticism of that reality has led us to inquire what role women have in religion and how it has affected their lives. Such questions have opened up perceptions of things we probably would not have seen before, leading many to the view that religion, despite its claim that it manifests the sacred, has been and can continue to become a tool of oppression, just as religion's critics like Karl Marx have argued.[3]

Furthermore, beneficial change will not occur unless questions are asked and criticisms made. But fair and effective change also requires the most accurate information and authentic insight that can be garnered. For this reason, there remains a vital place for the phenomenologist's goal of attempting to present a clear and unvarnished account of things just as they are, even if she or he inevitably falls short of the mark. Empathetic insight into the meaning of practices in a cultural context that may be quite different from the one of the observer remains a valuable contribution to interpreting religion.

If an attack is made, for example, on a certain religion's endorsement of war, one needs to be sure that there is an appreciation of the policy under question, as it is understood by believers, and its place in the framework of the faith's total life and practice. (It would also be helpful to analyze to what extent it differs from the practice of one's own and other religions.) Only then would one properly be able to make a critical statement—that is, a responsible statement challenging the religion to reassess its position. One would also need to be clear as to what values one is appealing to in making the criticism, and why she or he believes those values should be considered superior to those of the religion itself.

Our goal in this book is to be mostly descriptive. It is primarily a work on the level of getting information and attempting empathetic insight. But we must recognize that empathy with the dominant figures in a religion may not be empathy with those not in positions of power. We must continually remind ourselves not to mistake a bare description of a particularly disturbing phenomenon for a balanced or empathetic approach.

Criticism made honestly on the basis of knowledge and insight is ultimately necessary if we are to come to our own conclusions about the validity or rightness of a religious expression that is foreign to us in our own cultural context. Criticism is essential in any open and honest interfaith discourse; we must be prepared to deal not only with our criticism of religions other than our own but also with their criticism of ours. Readers of this book are challenged to reflect on what their critical judgments might be about their own and others' religions.[4]

Periods in Religious History

Religion is never static. We are now going to look at some broad periods in religious history from the beginning. These will help us to understand the history of particular religions. We must bear in mind, though, that people in traditional religions did not and do not always think of their religion in this way. For them the important thing is whether a particular hymn or practice or ritual is what is usually done in their community, or is meaningful to them personally, not whether it is old or new. But in studying we tend to think historically. Following are some periods in religious history worldwide, starting with the earliest society. (It must be remembered, however, that variations of the religions of all of these periods still persist today in many parts of the world.)

Hunting and Gathering Religion

The earliest human society of which we can speak is that of hunters and gatherers. Typically, spiritual power was focused in the sky, the world of animals, and the ecstatic individual. Often a "high god" above made the world and sustained it. A very deep relation existed between humans and animals; beasts had spirit, as did humans, and to take them required that they be enchanted, propitiated, and respected. The human custodian of spiritual power may have been the **shaman**, an individual who had gained mastery over spirits and who knew the paths of the dead by means of a great initiatory experience. Commonly, the initiation of all members of society was important too; life was seen as a series of stages through which one passes, gaining appropriate power at each stage. Birth and death were likewise stages in this endless cycle, and the land of the dead was thought of as similar to this, though the ghosts of ancestors were potent and feared.

Agricultural Religion

The development of agriculture is generally viewed as a great landmark in religion, as it is in economic history. The transfer of attention from the forest to the planted field meant that the earth goddess grew in significance and was revered as a principal deity. Moreover, the development of agriculture brought home the relation of death to life, in the seed that seems to be dead but is born anew—generating a belief in human renewal after death as well. Animal and human sacrifice to the powers of fertility and initiatory mysteries reached a high point in archaic agricultural society. Spiritual life became more and more tied to the cycle of the seasons, marked by spring planting rites and the autumn harvest festival. The sedentary nature of agricultural life brought vast changes in human society that were to profoundly affect religion as well.

Ancient Empires

One result of agriculture was a great increase in the number of people who could be sustained by a given tract of land in fertile areas. Moreover, the population was sedentary, bound to the soil and the seasonal round. This in turn made possible and inevitable trade on a large scale, the growth of towns, and the unification of large areas into great political units, each of which could be controlled by a small but mobile elite based in a major urban center. These were the ancient agricultural empires, such as those of Egypt, Mesopotamia, India, or China. Their first religious results were the formalization of motifs of archaic agricultural religion. The earth as the goddess who gives birth to the plants to be harvested, and to whom the dying return, was a prominent deity. The relationship between the earth and human society was often symbolized as the sacred marriage of the king to the earth goddess herself—the marriage thus establishing the sovereignty of the king. The sacred king, such as the pharaoh of Egypt, acquired an immensely exalted spiritual position as one in special relationship to the Divine, who was initiated through a mystery of death and rebirth parallel to that of the plant, and who performed the rites of spring and harvest. Polytheism reached an apex during this period, for it was really a result of the union of a number of tribes (each with its own patronal goddess or god) into a single society, and also of heaven being made to imitate the increased compartmentalization of human labor in the city and the bureaucracy of earthly government.

Religion Responding to History

Other forces were also at work. The growth of trade and new imperial social organization led to writing, chronicles, and intercultural contact. Out of all this arose glimmerings of historical awareness—the view that time seems to move irreversibly in one direction, that things have changed and will not change back. This "discovery" of history is always a crucial challenge to religion. Because religion points toward self-transcendence, it must somehow show that historical change is not the last word—that even if the old timeless world of the hunter or the planter's seasonal round is passing, something stands above history. Responses to history follow the four main strands listed below, sometimes separated and sometimes intertwined.

Epic.   One possible response is to accept history but to see in it the unfolding of a purpose implanted in it from the beginning—the triumph of a particular people or dynasty, for example, the defeat of the powers of darkness by the true God. Much of the great narrative literature that grows out of the era of the discovery of history has this basic motif: the Old Testament, the Kojiki in Japan, the *Aeneid*. In these, the historical experience of wars and conquests, empires and disasters, are part of a narrative with a beginning and an ending.

Ritual.   Another response is to keep certain rites, especially those of a court, a city, or an official priesthood, unchanged as a sort of frozen perpetuation of the past before the discovery of history and as a symbolic area of experience untouched by it. In ancient Rome, the institution of the Vestal Virgins and the sacrifices of the city's priesthood remained virtually unchanged through all the historical vicissitudes of the empire. In ancient Japan, an imperial princess was sent far away from the court, to the vicinity of the Grand Shrine of Ise, where she avoided all Buddhist practice and even words. She represented the court before the great ancestral deities at Ise, not as it was but as it would like to be seen by the Shinto gods, as she took her place in the classic, purely Shinto rites of the Grand Shrine.

The Religious Founders.   The most consequential event of this era, however, was the emergence in the ancient world of the great international and national religions built upon the work of individual founders. Only a half-dozen or so persons have filled this awesome vocation, which has made their names more powerful in history than those of countless kings. They are Moses, Zoroaster, the Buddha, Confucius, Laozi, Jesus, and Muhammad. Out of the hundreds of thousands of years humanity has lived on this earth, all the major religious founders have lived within a span of less than two millennia—between Moses in the thirteenth century B.C.E. and Muhammad in the seventh century C.E.[5] At the same time, the shift from oral tradition in religion to reliance on the written word in this period is likely to have had a profound impact on what and who is remembered from prehistory to the present. Nonetheless, in each case, the work of the founders, sometimes only after several centuries during which a transformation of values was quietly permeating an older society, resulted in a new state, empire, or cultural wave that greatly impacted vast populations.

The founder-religions—Judaism, Zoroastrianism, the Chinese faiths, Buddhism, Christianity, and Islam—have in common that they see in the life and words of the founder the exemplification and perfect statement of the ideal human life, and also in some way see him as empowering his followers to live it. Buddhism, Christianity, and Islam, especially, view the founder's religion as being transnational and transcultural and have demonstrated this by spreading it across many boundaries and seas through missionary activities, as well as, in the case of Christianity and Islam, by conquest. The founder-religions are a unique response to the "discovery-of-history" experience. By making the life of a single individual the pivot of history, they acknowledge its irreversible movement and at the same time give it a sharply focused central axis. By emphasizing the drama of a single and unique life as the bearer of revelation, they show that now, in the more complex, diversified, and chancy life of a modern society, the individual and not just the immemorial custom of a tribe is what counts.

Yet at the same time, they are religions that emerged in a time when traditions were still strong. They provided foci around which all manner of things new and old were consolidated—they all have expression on many levels, from folkways to philosophy to eccentric individualism. They could only have come into being in their historical form after or along with the development of writing, large political systems, and international trade. These have been their bearers. All make much of scriptures and political implications. Yet the founder-religions have come to be greater than particular times and places.

Wisdom. Another path to transcending the onslaughts of history is through an absolutizing of the state of consciousness or angle of philosophical vision in which the timeless shows its incomparable superiority over time. In India, at approximately the same time as the emergence of the founders, the tradition that was to become Hinduism produced texts such as the **Upanishads** and **Bhagavad-Gita**; in them the central theme is the unity of the individual self, who seems to suffer the vicissitudes of time and space, with the absolute, who changes not. These books, representing the composite wisdom of many sages, derive from much the same era as do the founders in other traditions.

Even in the founder-religions, a reaction in favor of **mysticism** and wisdom tended to set in a few centuries after the founder's day, and the same was true where polytheistic worship persisted. In either case, the wise urged a perspective that saw unity beyond the many gods or the comings and goings of founder-teachers. In the West, Neoplatonic, Stoic, and Epicurean philosophy fulfilled this role. In Judaism, books such as Proverbs and the apocryphal Wisdom of Solomon personified wisdom as a maiden greatly to be desired and through whom God made the world; to know her is to know the inner mystery of the way things work. In the same manner, from around the first century C.E., Mahayana Buddhism personified wisdom, Prajnaparamita, or the "wisdom that has gone beyond," a sort of perfect intuitive insight, as a goddess to be worshipped and desired. Christianity, especially in the Greek theologians and mystics, and Islam also went through a stage in which the deepest emphasis was on understanding with mystically illumined insight the eternal realities of God and God's relation to humanity and the creation that underlay the particulars of the revelation through Jesus or Muhammad.

The wisdom movements all had in common a highly sophisticated restatement of the motifs of the shamanism and initiatory rites of the earliest religion—belief that through proper psychological procedures one can obtain perception into the inner laws of the cosmos and thus obtain power over them, or wisdom to live in harmony with them. For this reason, wisdom religion is also an ancestor of modern science.

Medieval Devotion

Wisdom mysticism, however profound, did not allow for a full expression of emotional feelings. The Middle Ages in both Asia and Europe brought to flower a piety in which feelings of rapturous love and identification with god or savior were preeminent. We speak of the love of Christ and the Virgin Mary in the devotion of medieval Europe, of passionate Sufi mysticism in Islam, of devotion to Krishna and other Hindu gods in India, and of pure faith in the compassion of Kannon and Amida in East Asian Buddhism. These movements, in which romantic love and religion interfuse, bespeak a new individualism and sensitivity in their stress on the feelings of the devotee. They were generally accompanied by rich artistic expression in images and paintings of the beloved deity.

Modernism

The roots of modernism in religion go back as far as the end of the Middle Ages and are typified by such developments as the emergence of Pure Land Buddhism in Japan and the Protestant Reformation in Christianity. In both cases, emphasis was put on salvation not by involved spiritual practices or feelings but by a simple act of faith, which could be made as effectively by the laity as by monk or priest. What this really implied was a new exaltation of the **secular** world and the individual in it. The gradual breakdown of peasant culture based on the agricultural round meant a loss of the spiritual unity of communities. Now religion was something an individual could do wherever he or she was—in the fields or the shop or the home.

Later reform movements in Islam and Hinduism went the same direction as those in Christianity and Buddhism in rejecting the wisdom and medieval devotional approaches in favor of the supposedly plain and nonpriestly original teachings of the faith. One reason for the early modern reaction in the direction of simplicity and faith certainly is the modern realization that we can do much to control and exploit the world through trade and technology, but to do so we must have a religion that can be practiced in the midst of worldly work and so can validate it. The modern faith cannot be too tied to a peasant outlook, or be too demanding of time or emotional energy, or too appreciative of mystical or emotional rather than rational and pragmatic states of mind.

As a result, modernism sought to explain the complexity of the diverse world that trade and technology presented in terms of a rational unifying "absolute" foundation. In the West in this period, philosophy and science split from theology as separate disciplines also seeking to provide a universal ground for the diverse influences modernism was encountering. These new disciplines, combined with the new secular freedom, led to what is called "liberalism" in religion, essentially the restatement of religious "absolutes" so as to fit with the normative social and scientific values of the cultural context.

Yet modernism led, perhaps inevitably, to a crisis of modernity. The very trade and technological departures liberated by the religions of faith eventually began to undermine them, for the intercultural contact and scientific discoveries that resulted made people wonder about the ultimate basis of faith. In non-Western cultures this crisis of modernity was exacerbated by the fact that it meant coping not only with new social and scientific ideas and the changing conditions of life brought about by industrialization and urbanization but also with an alien dominant culture—that of the West—often brought by colonial overlords. Traditional religions in the West and East have responded in ways ranging from rigid rejection of the new to reformism based on traditional principles, like that of Gandhi or Reformed Judaism; to undergirding militant nationalism, as in the Japan of the 1930s and 1940s or in Khomeini's Iran; to lending support to radical revolution, as did some Buddhists in Communist China and Catholic priests in Latin America.

Postmodernism

The crisis of modernity and the concomitant shaking of the foundations of faith, and any other absolute ground, has led to skepticism as to whether the search for absolutes itself has any intrinsic validity for faith, philosophy, science, or any other discipline, for that matter. This skepticism is the core of what has been termed "postmodernism." Instead of seeking absolutes, postmodernism embraces the relative truth of subjective experience. It eschews all attempts to categorize things, such as religion, in terms of "-isms," like Buddhism, liberalism, or even postmodernism itself, as contrary to the actual richness and complexity of human experience. It sees too much labelling, claims of objectivity, and the search for absolute values as mere power plays on the part of the elite. Moreover, postmodernists reject modernism because, in the wake of the many atrocities of the modern period, modernism's failure to fulfill its implied promise that it would conquer ignorance and assert rationality in its place has undermined its credibility for them.[6]

Yet out of postmodern consciousness there flourishes a new wave of religious activity—one focused not so much on "absolutes" as on the enrichment of the particular lives of people. Here there is renewed interest in, appreciation of, and respect for the particular and the diverse. There is a return to custom, magic, the primitive, the aesthetic, and meaning found in the particulars of traditional narratives, while at the same time a recognition of something unifying in each unique human particularity participating in the complexity and fragmentary nature of human experience, including religious experience. It is in this context that a postmodernist may assert that the relative may in fact be the absolute and that, therefore, a statement like the Dalai Lama's that there is a "possibility of different absolute truths existing simultaneously" may begin to make sense. Not surprisingly, postmodern religious consciousness has generated an interest in developing an interfaith discourse that seeks to move beyond the "my god is better than your god" arguments of the late modern period to a willingness to be present to one another in all our multifarious beauty.[7]

But postmodernism is controversial because it challenges all of the assumptions of modernism, not least of which is that there can be certainty in religious faith. This has generated its own set of reactions, such as Protestant fundamentalism and the neo-Orthodox movements of Judaism and Islam. Critics assert that postmodernism's willingness to be satisfied with uncertainly, a lack of unifying explanations, and relativism leaves no credible foundation on which to ground human society. Consequently, they assert, it leads potentially to an "anything-goes" morality, which easily can be criticized as contributing to the decline of the civilized world.

Looking Forward

It is clear, then, that religion is today in a state of flux and transition. Yet this has always been the case, although it has not always been quite so readily apparent. Each stage has always been melting into the next; there are always constant themes in religion, but their ways of expression shape themselves anew to some extent in each generation. The process is a complex interaction of tradition and new ideas, working through expression in word, act, and group formation, expressed through symbols or concepts that may be as old as cave art or as inspired and imaginatively created as something made only yesterday. And it should be remembered that virtually nothing of significance that appears in the long history of a religion is ever really lost. Some whiff or savor will survive to keep it a putative part of every subsequent configuration of that tradition: Vedic rites can still be seen in India; Protestant churches still sing medieval hymns; and postmodern religious movements, like the New Age and Goddess movements of the West, borrow from the archaic as well as Eastern and Western motifs of today.

Women in the World Religions

One of the most significant ways in which religion today is in a state of flux and transition involves the role of women. Every major world religion we will be studying in the pages ahead is asking the "woman question": What are the proper roles, rights, and status of women in religion and society? Each religious tradition is struggling to find the proper balance between the traditional ways in which that question has been answered and modern ideas about women's equality. Because this is such a central question for each tradition, we cannot come to an understanding about any religious tradition without addressing it. To leave it out is to leave a "blind spot" in the study of religion.

When we look at the "woman question," however, we see that the line between descriptive and critical approaches to the study of religion is not so clear. Sometimes describing something raises critical issues, and that often is the case when the descriptive approach is used in the study of women in religion. Just to shed light on the subject is to call it into question. Still, it is important to look specifically at the issue, especially in terms of its historical context, so we can see where it has been and where it is headed and be better able to assess our own views about what we think its future should be.

There are many parallels in the history of women in the various religions around the world. Generally, early in the evolution of the major religions—Hinduism, Buddhism, Confucianism, Judaism, Christianity, and Islam—regardless of what their founders may have intended, **patriarchy**, that is, a patriarchal social pattern, developed. In other words, the rulers in any social subunit were men—the patriarch or father. Because of this, women lived under the authority of male religious leaders, fathers, husbands, and even sons in societies based on religious tenets that did not permit individual status and authority for women. Generally, but with some exceptions, as we shall see, women's participation in the official religious practice was very limited and secondary to that of men.

Women were not without religious outlet, however. Often they were very involved in religious folk myths and practices that were intermingled with officially sanctioned doctrines and practices. This **little tradition** often emerged alongside the official tradition and provided a place of considerable participation for women. Further, many women proved to be so spiritually adept that their authenticity could not be denied by the authorities. Accordingly, through the centuries some women have been able to attain positions of status, authority, and respect, despite official doctrine advancing notions to the contrary.

One might ask: Why have the authors included special sections on women in the chapters about the major world religions and not a complementary one on men? The reason is that most of what we study about religion is a generalization of human experience using men's experience as the norm. In other words, religion, just as many other subjects of study, traditionally has been developed and studied from only a male point of view. This is exacerbated because men have been the record-keepers of the official tradition in every major world religion. This is called being **androcentric**. The study of women in religion is an effort to undo this androcentric perspective and shed light on the other side. In this way, we are beginning to talk about human experience that includes women.

Today, to greater and lesser degrees, all of the world's religions are engaged in discourses about the role and rights of women. This presents a difficult crossroad for each religious tradition because much of what reform-minded women and men challenge as patriarchal and, therefore, inappropriately biased against women's full participation is considered by traditionalists to be central to the religion's identity. As we shall see in the chapters to follow, how this "woman question" is answered in each religio-cultural context shapes the daily lives of women.

Fundamental Features of Religions

The fact that each of the world's religions has a history and encompasses each of the three forms of religious expression means that they all have common patterns. They usually ask and answer certain questions. All have a basic worldview, ideas about the Divine or Ultimate Reality, ideas about the origin and destiny of the world

---

FUNDAMENTAL FEATURES OF RELIGIONS

THEORETICAL

Basic Worldview	How the universe is set up, especially in its spiritual aspect—the map of the invisible world.
God or Ultimate Reality	What the ultimate source and ground of all things is.
Origin of the World	Where it all came from.
Destiny of the World	Where it is going.
Origin of Humans	Where we came from.
Destiny of Humans	Where we are going.
Revelation or Mediation between the Ultimate and the Human	How we know this and how we are helped to get from here to our ultimate destiny.

PRACTICAL

What Is Expected of Humans: Worship, Practices, Behavior	What we ourselves must do.

SOCIOLOGICAL

Major Social Institutions	How the religion is set up to preserve and implement its teaching and practice; what kind of leadership it has; how it interacts with the larger society.

and of individual humans, a revelation or authority or mediation between the Ultimate and humankind, standards about what is expected of humans (that is, patterns of worship, spiritual practices, and ethics or behavior), and an institutional or sociological expression.

In order to provide a convenient guide to these fundamental features, a chart has been prepared for each religion discussed in this text. An introductory outline is presented here so that the reader can see what will be covered in each of the categories used.

It should be remembered that these charts are able to present only the dominant or traditional interpretation of the religion; variations often exist but cannot be taken into account in the charts, although they may be in the text.

It is now time to turn to the religions themselves.

✸ Summary

This chapter has tried to present some basic perspectives for understanding the religions of the world comparatively. We discussed religion as the "doors and windows" between conditioned and unconditioned reality. We presented the three forms of religious expression: theoretical (narrative and doctrine), practical (styles of worship), and sociological (forms of group life). We reflected on ways in which both descriptive and critical approaches to religion are valid and important. We talked about the problems and possibilities inherent in discussing religion in terms of its history and summarized the major historical periods of human religion. We also discussed the "woman question" in the world religions and how the answer to that question impacts women's lives. Finally, we indicated that each actual, living religion contains tensions and seemingly conflicting motifs that it tries to resolve into a pattern.

This may all make religion appear very complex and difficult; but if you will look within yourself, you will see that your own life is ordered in much the same way. By increasing your understanding of yourself as a human being, you will grow in your ability to understand the complexity of human religion.

✸ Questions for Review

1. Discuss whether or not you agree with the contention that today is a particularly exciting time to study world religions.
2. Describe some of the problems in today's world that seem to be involved with religion and some ways religion can help intergroup and international understanding.
3. Explain the difference between conditioned and unconditioned reality and religion's role regarding them.
4. Name and explain Joachim Wach's three forms of religious expression.

5. Describe how religious doctrine develops from myths and narratives.

6. Compare "cosmic" and "historical" views of time.

7. Discuss what sort of messages might be transmitted nonverbally by the practical (style of worship) and sociological expressions of a religion.

8. Explain how the three forms of religious expression interact.

9. Present the values of both descriptive and critical approaches to the world religions. Give examples of both based on your own observation.

10. Discuss the advantages and possible pitfalls of a historical approach to understanding a religion.

11. Summarize the main periods in the history of human religion.

12. Indicate the main ways in which religion has responded to the experience of the "discovery of history."

13. Describe some common characteristics of founder-religions, especially Buddhism, Christianity, and Islam.

14. Explain some of the major characteristics of the modern experience and how religion has responded to them.

15. Discuss some of the issues raised by postmodern consciousness and how religion has responded to them.

16. Discuss the "woman question" in the world religions and how an androcentric point of view might provide only a limited perspective of religion.

17. Discuss how religions both contain and try to resolve the tensions common to human existence.

❋ Suggested Readings on the Study of World Religions

Carmody, Denise Lardner, *Women and World Religions*. Englewood Cliffs, NJ: Prentice Hall, 1989. A helpful beginning investigation of the roles of and beliefs about women in the religions of the world.

——, and John Tully Carmody, *How to Live Well: Ethics in the World Religions*. Belmont, CA: Wadsworth, 1988. A helpful survey of this important area of religious life throughout the world of faiths.

Eliade, Mircea, *Cosmos and History*. New York: Harper Torchbooks, 1959. A good basic approach to the history of religions; compares concepts of time in different types of religion.

——, *From Primitives to Zen*. New York: Harper & Row, 1967. A useful collection of texts and description arranged thematically.

——, *Patterns in Comparative Religion*. Cleveland, OH: Meridian Books, 1963. A substantial cross-cultural treatment of basic religious symbols and themes, such as sun, moon, and agriculture.

——, *The Sacred and the Profane*. New York: Harper Torchbooks, 1961. An excellent basic introduction to the history of religions, elucidating such matters as the meaning of the temple, the festival, initiation, and myth.

Falk, Nancy A., and Rita M. Gross, eds., *Unspoken Worlds: Women's Religious Lives*. New York: Harper & Row, 1980. As the title suggests, a view into religious spheres in which women have, for too long, lived in silence.

Gross, Rita M., "Androcentrism and Androgyny in the Methodology of History of Religions" in *Beyond Androcentrism: New Essays on Women and Religion*, Rita M. Gross, ed. Missoula, MT: Scholars Press, 1977. An important essay discussing the methodological problems found in approaching the history of religions from an androcentric perspective and providing insights on how to correct them.

———, *Feminism and Religion: An Introduction*. Boston: Beacon Press, 1996. An excellent introduction on the subject.

Haddad, Yvonne Yazback, and Ellison Banks Findly, eds., *Women, Religion and Social Change*. Albany: State University of New York Press, 1985. A collection of important and often-cited articles regarding women in the world religions.

James, William, *The Varieties of Religious Experience*. New York: Longman, Green, 1902 (many later editions). A classic work in the psychology of religion.

Lerner, Gerda, *The Creation of Patriarchy*. New York: Oxford University Press, 1986. An important book on economic, social, and political influences on the Patriarchal Revolution.

Lessa, William A., and Evon Z. Vogt, *Reader in Comparative Religion: An Anthropological Approach*. New York: Harper & Row, 1965 (later editions). A useful collection of primary sources in this field.

Lévi-Strauss, Claude, *Structural Anthropology*. Garden City, NY: Doubleday, 1967. An important modern anthropologist's treatment of how myth, ritual, and shamanism create symbolic worlds.

MacDonald, Margaret Read, *The Folklore of World Holidays*. Detroit, MI: Gale Research, 1992. An encyclopedic study with useful bibliographies that gives invaluable insight into the folk dimensions of the world's faiths.

Morgan, Peggy, and Clive Lawton, eds., *Ethical Issues in Six Religious Traditions*. Edinburgh, U.K.: Edinburgh University Press, 1996. A very readable and well-organized discussion of ethics in six of the world religions.

Morris, Brian, *Anthropological Studies of Religion*. Cambridge: Cambridge University Press, 1987. A survey of twentieth-century views from the perspective of this discipline.

Otto, Rudolf, *The Idea of the Holy*. London & New York: Oxford University Press, 1958. A classic statement of the experience of the "numinous" from which religion begins.

Pals, Daniel L., *Seven Theories of Religion*. New York: Oxford University Press, 1996. An excellent introduction to the major modern psychological and social scientific views of religion: Freud, Marx, and others.

Sharma, Arvind, ed., *Today's Woman in World Religions*. Albany: State University of New York Press, 1994. A collection of excellent essays on the issues facing contemporary women in the world religions.

———, *Women in World Religions*. Albany: State University of New York Press, 1987. A collection of readable essays on women in particular religions by an expert on each.

Sharpe, Eric J., *Comparative Religion: A History*. New York: Scribners, 1975. A useful story of the study of world religions.

Smith, Huston, *The World's Religions*. New York: HarperSanFrancisco Publishers, 1992. A very readable and insightful survey.

Smith, Jonathon Z., *Imagining Religion*. Chicago: University of Chicago Press, 1982. An engrossing critical look at several theories and issues in the history of religions.

Smith, W. C., *The Meaning and End of Religion*. New York: Harper & Row, 1962, 1978. A fresh approach to understanding religion as a phenomenon of human history.

Stocking, George W., Jr., *Victorian Anthropology*. New York: The Free Press, 1987. This work discusses the nineteenth-century founders of the science in the context of their times.

Swidler, Arlene, ed., *Homosexuality and World Religions*. Valley Forge, PA: Trinity Press International, 1993. A pioneering presentation of attitudes on this topic in the major faiths.

van der Leeuw, Gerardus, *Religion in Essence and Manifestation,* 2 vols. New York: Harper & Row, 1963. A classic thematic study containing a succinct statement of the phenomenological method.

Wach, Joachim, *The Comparative Study of Religion*. New York: Columbia University Press, 1958. A brilliant treatment of the major concepts and problems in comparative religious studies from the author's point of view.

————, *Sociology of Religion*. Chicago: University of Chicago Press, 1944. A classic statement of the different kinds of religious groups, leaders, and forms of expression.

Weber, Max, *The Sociology of Religion*. Boston: Beacon Press, 1963. A collection of basic writings by one of the seminal thinkers in this area.

The student is also referred to good encyclopedic treatments of particular topics, such as those in the Encyclopedia Britannica; Keith Crim, ed., *Abingdon Dictionary of Living Religions* (Nashville, TN: Abingdon Press, 1981); and Mircea Eliade, ed., *The Encyclopedia of Religion* (New York: Macmillan, 1987).

CHAPTER TWO

The Sacred in Nature

Cosmic Religions of Prehistoric and Tribal Peoples

CHAPTER OBJECTIVES

After studying this chapter, you should be able to

❋ **Discuss common features of primal and tribal religions.**

❋ **Explain shamanism.**

❋ **Interpret the transition from hunting-gathering to agricultural religion, including the contribution of women.**

❋ **Talk about how religious symbolism is influenced by economic forces in a society.**

❋ **Discuss the importance of understanding early religion for human life today, including ways in which its themes can still be found.**

The First Human Faiths

Behind the panorama of the great religions with their founders and scriptures, behind even the world of the ancient empires with their writing systems and sprawling political-economic entities out of which the founder religions mostly emerged, hangs the backdrop of the religious world that went before all. That was a religious world without written texts but rich in art, myth, and dance. It was the religious world of the ancestors of all living human beings for hundreds of thousands, perhaps millions, of years between the emergence of human culture as a distinct way of life on earth and the appearance of writing, large political units, and the rest of what makes up the form of human culture we call civilization. As such, it may be called "prehistoric religion," for written history had to await the invention of writing.

Away from the centers of civilization, forms of religious life continuous with the prehistoric have persisted—though in diminishing numbers—down to the present. We are speaking of societies characterized by two determinative features: They are nonliterate (that is, they do not have reading and writing), and they are organized in very small political units, such as tribes or clans. They may subsist by hunting and gathering only, or practice an archaic form of agriculture, or live as nomadic pastoralists. To further clarify the type of society of which we are speaking, let us note that it would not include nonliterate peasants within a large social unit, such as ancient Egypt or medieval England, in which a literate elite also existed; nor would it include tribal peoples such as Eskimos or Arab Bedouins, who have embraced a scriptural religion (Christianity for Eskimos, Islam for Bedouins) and are to that extent literate.

As late as the nineteenth century, vast stretches of the earth, from Siberia to Africa, from Australia to the Americas, still supported such tribal societies, though under steadily increasing pressure. Their traditional forms of religion also flourished, though they were giving way to the efforts of missionaries even as the traditional ways of livelihood and social organization fell before the incursions of "civilized" traders, settlers, and colonial rulers. Today only remnants of tribal, nonliterate society and religion survive. But there is enough to provide a picture of what it was like. We must also note that among some tribal peoples now embraced by modern states, such as the Maori in New Zealand or Native Americans in the United States, there has recently been a trend toward reviving features of their spiritual heritage and a growing interest in it on the part of some others.

To extrapolate from present-day tribal religion back to worldwide prehistoric religion is risky. Sometimes influences from the great religions have slipped in unostentatiously; sometimes the very fact that tribal religion was probably under siege by the time observers arrived has made a difference. Nonetheless, it seems safe to assume that at least the major themes of today's tribal religions are continuous with those of prehistoric religion, and in a single chapter we can do little more than examine major themes. So we will consider prehistoric and tribal religions together.

This type of religion has gone by many names among the literate. It has been called primitive, primal, basic, or archaic religion; it has been referred to as **animism** and **shamanism**. Problems exist with all these terms. Terms in the first set, of which primitive has been the most widely used, are acceptable insofar as they simply point to the fact that this is the style of religion that appeared first among humans. But the term primitive in particular has also acquired unjust and inaccurate connotations of crudity and barbarism, and "firstness" in any case is not the only characteristic of the religions in question. Having persisted down to the present, they have as long a sequence of development as any other faith; this development has just gone in a different direction from that of religions employing writing and scripture and interacting with kingdoms and empires. Animism, or belief that everything in nature— stones, trees, mountains, lakes, as well as human beings—has a **soul** or spirit, and shamanism (to be discussed later) allude to beliefs and practices widespread in prehistoric and tribal religions but of varying importance and also questionable as definers. Avoiding a single term for such an immense and diverse collection, we shall merely speak of prehistoric and tribal religions.

The substance of these religions is tremendously varied, for the roster of prehistoric and present-day tribes and nonliterate cultures, each with its own gods and rites, is almost endless; very many have undoubtedly been forgotten forever. Because of the immense variety, this chapter cannot hope to cover the subject in a systematic or culture-by-culture way. Our discussion is impressionistic and rather nonhistorical, although we shall take note of the religious significance of one important event in prehistoric "history"—the emergence of agriculture. Generally, however, our approach will be thematic, drawing from cross-cultural data to illustrate certain of the great motifs of nonliterate spirituality. Not all of these motifs are shared by all such cultures, of course. For specific data on particular cultures, the reader is referred to the literature of anthropology.

Mircea Eliade has used the expression **cosmic religion** to refer to a religious outlook largely coextensive with the religion of archaic hunters and farmers but with continuations down to the present.[1] Cosmic religion, he tells us, has little sense of history or of what was discussed in the last chapter as linear time. It finds and expresses sacred meaning in aspects of nature and human life—seasons, sacred rocks or trees, the social order, birth and death—without linking them to historical personalities or written documents as do founder-religions. Although the situation is full of ambiguities, reflecting on the cosmic religion experience is a good way to start meeting the prehistoric and tribal spiritual world.

Cosmic religion includes festivals of hunting, seedtime, and harvest, and the sacred trees and mountains around which the earth seems to pivot. It is the interplay of ordinary daily life with the extraordinary experience of the natural world as being full of gods and goblins, of elves, and spirits of the returning dead. It is the rites of hunting and archaic agriculture where there is no sharp division between the phenomenal world and an "Other" world; instead this world—here and now— is fundamentally sacred, and everything is alive with spirit. It is the ecstasies of shamans who are believed to be able to travel in trance to heaven or the underworld to recover strayed or stolen souls or to intercede with the gods. It is the performance of ritual to remind the participants of the fundamental sacredness of nature and human beings' part in it—its ultimate connection to cosmic reality.

At first glance, the world of cosmic religion seems very remote to those of us steeped in worldviews defined by Judaism, Christianity, or Islam. Yet many of the motifs of cosmic religion, when communicated in fairy tales or African masks, come across as hauntingly beautiful or nightmarishly powerful. They hit one unexpectedly with all the impact of a half-remembered but very important scene from a dream or early childhood. Then again, countless survivals from the world of cosmic religion—from Christmas trees to the Muslim pilgrimage to Mecca—continue to flourish as much as ever, albeit with somewhat transmuted meanings. It could be argued that most **popular religion** of ordinary people, whether in Buddhist, Christian, or Muslim lands, is only a partially altered cosmic or primitive religion under another name. Our holidays are, after all, bits and pieces of forgotten faiths.

Christmas, for example, is a festival of Christianity, which derives from the era of the discovery of history and commemorates an historical event, around which all history is believed to turn. But consider the Christmas symbolism. It is a celebration of light at the darkest time of the year—the Winter Solstice—the inauguration of a new year, an ornamented tree representing a "cosmic tree" symbolizing the mystical center of the earth and a way of access to the Divine world. This is not only pre-Christian in origin but also expresses the cosmic religion kind of emphasis: the spiritual experience produced by the turn of the seasons, the sacred meaning of landmarks of nature like trees and mountains, the sheer immediate evocative power of symbols like light and glitter, the perennial importance to spiritual life of family and the sacred, set-apart time of festival.

Then there is our orange-and-black feast, with its atmosphere of jack-o'-lanterns and tales of witches amid frost and falling leaves. Perhaps the oldest holiday that is a part of general American culture is Halloween. It is almost a pure momento of cosmic religion, and it incorporates no small number of its themes. On this night, children masked and costumed as ghosts, witches, and devils, or as pirates, cowboys, or monsters visit homes to receive candy with the threat of "tricks or treats."[2] Pranks ranging from soaping windows to putting a farmer's wagon on top of his barn have also sometimes been part of Halloween. There are costume parties with spooky decorations and traditional games like bobbing for apples.

Perpetuated into Christian times as the eve of All Hallows or All Saints' Day, Halloween was originally the autumn festival of the ancient Britons and their Druid priests, called Samhain. It was the Celtic and Anglo-Saxon New Year. Like festivals of harvest and the new year everywhere, Samhain had motifs of settling accounts, the harvest moon, the celebration of the last harvest before winter, the return of the dead to visit the living, and the kindling of a new fire to light the way and warm the spirit as the darkest, coldest time of the year looms near. It suggested a temporary return to the chaos before the world was created and thereby the release of the dark and uncanny denizens of chaos. Behind children's masks of monsters and witches, behind "tricks or treats" and bobbing for apples, lies the ancient cosmic religious orientation toward the turn of the seasons, rather than a historical event, as the time when reality is revealed.

An important motif of cosmic religion is a feeling that the turn of the year is like a clock running down and coming virtually to a stop just before it is wound up

A symbol of fertility, Venus of Willendorf (c. 15,000–10,000 B.C.E.)

again on New Year's Day. New Year's Day is like a recurrent Day of Creation to cosmic religion, and so the preceding eve is like replunging into that precreation flux when there were no controls. This is illustrated by dark, grisly entities coming out on Halloween, the ancient New Year's Eve, and our tradition of getting drunk on the modern New Year's Eve. In ancient Rome, the end-of-the-year festival was the Saturnalia, when masters and slaves exchanged roles in a gesture of turning upside down the ordinary structures of society.

May Day, another holiday celebrated mainly by children, continued the pre-Christian spring festival of ancient Britain, known as Beltane. As Halloween in the fall bore a mood of night, moon, the dead, and unwholesome visitants, so May Day is a celebration of day, sun, flowers, and all that is bright, warm, and fresh, although also supernatural. Dancing around the Maypole was an ancient practice to encourage fertility; May baskets were gifts of the bounty of the enchanting White Lady who rode through the land awakening the miracle of spring. A center of this belief was the town of Banbury in central England; until modern times the visit of the White Lady was enacted on May Day in a pageant culminating at the ancient market cross in the town square. As the old rhyme has it:

> *Ride a cock-horse to Banbury Cross,*
> *To see a fine lady upon a white horse,*
> *With rings on her fingers and bells on her toes,*
> *She shall have music wherever she goes.*

Long after Christianity came, in fact, May Day celebrations were held in Banbury in which youths would gather boughs and make garlands, a maypole would be set up, and a girl would be chosen as May Queen (in pagan times representing the goddess of fertility), who would ride to the festivities on a white horse.

It is interesting that the most colorful survivals of cosmic religion, May Day and Halloween, are practiced mainly by children. Part of the world of nonliterate religion indeed seems childlike: wearing masks; keeping special days; and believing in spirits, magic places, and gestures. Moreover, there is a sense in which the culture of children is always conservative. It retains lore in fairy tales, games, and holidays that have lost power in adult culture.

It would, however, be a grave mistake to think of peoples practicing cosmic religions as children. Adults among them are adult; their myths and symbols are full of evidence that people have passed through adolescence, experienced adult sexuality, married, and had children of their own. All these experiences are marked by rich ceremonies and permeate the rites of spring and harvest and the tales of the gods. Tribal people can think as rationally, and handle ideas as complex, as any other adults. Their symbol systems often convey as much complex information and insight as pages of writing or even mathematical equations.

Moreover, survivals such as Halloween and May Day contain only a few of the themes of early religion in its fullness. They suggest a typical (at least in temperate climates) seasonal emphasis, but the pantheon of gods and the full relation of the religion to society in these holidays is less evident as those relations recede from memory and into the realm of fantasy.

But we must now approach the world of prehistoric and tribal religion in its fullness. Although these religions do have rational worldviews expressed through rite and symbol and society, they do not have the formal written ideological statements that in other religions are all-too-tempting pegs for interpretation. We have to see what the unified experience and the particulars alike are saying themselves.

What we shall be examining, then, is images, and it is images—symbols, gestures, sacred art, and the mighty figures of myth—that stand out in the world of cosmic religion. It is from the accounts of heroes in story, from masks, from priests in the midst of a hunting rite, from carvings of ancestors, and from paintings on rocks and caves that cosmic religion is learned. All of these go together to make up a cosmos in which spirit and matter are thoroughly interwoven, and everything is more than it seems, as myth, rite, and art make the invisible visible. In this cosmos, human life is only complete in its total relationships—with family, tribe, ancestors, and all that is spirit.

Gods, Spirits, and the World

Prehistoric and tribal religion has its demarcations between conditioned and unconditioned reality. Yet, as Clifford Geertz has pointed out, they generally seem complex, only semiordered, and deeply intermingled with all of life. The images they imprint on the mind, however, borne by the powerful languages of myth and ritual, are unforgettable.[3]

Most prominent of these images may be those of the time of human origins and the gods of that time, for there, if anywhere, is mastery of time and death. At the same time, humans are aware that the world is far from perfect and that if the creation was meant to be good, something must have gone wrong. Often an original or ultimate god will be portrayed as having made the world, but then seeming to have little concern for humankind except perhaps to enforce the moral law. A deity like this is spoken of as a **deus otiosus**, a "hidden god."

Sometimes a myth, comparable to the Garden of Eden narrative, accounts for the separation of humankind from primordial closeness to the creator. With the separation, death enters the world. The natives of Poso, Sulawesi (Celebes) Island, Indonesia, said that originally the sky where the creator dwelt was very near the earth, and he would lower gifts down on a rope to his children. Once he thus let down a stone, but the first men and women were indignant at such a useless gift and refused it. So the creator pulled it back up and lowered instead a banana. This they took. But the creator called to them, "Because you have chosen the banana, your life shall be like its life. Had you taken the stone, you would have been like it, changeless and immortal."[4]

Or the creation itself may have been accomplished by lesser deities. Among the Semang, a simple hunting culture in Malaysia, it is said the **high god**, Karei, lives in the sky and his wife, Manoid, in the earth. Their children are sons: Ta Pedn,

Begreg, and Karpgen and a daughter Takel; the thunder is Karei playing with his children. Karei's son, Ta Pedn, created everything; Karei himself made nothing. Karei merely enforces, as a firm and inexorable father-judge, the moral law. He requires that transgressors make a blood expiation. It is said, in fact, among the Semang that Ta Pedn is good, but Karei is evil.[5]

But though the creator high god (if there is one) may be far removed from ordinary human affairs, many much more involved spiritual entities inhabit the world. Lesser gods, perhaps offspring of the creator, like the children of Karei, may be closer presences in sacred mountains or the forests the hunter enters. **Ancestral spirits** are likely to be especially loved and feared, for they stay near their families to impart the strength that goes with the lineage, but they also punish individuals whose faults dishonor it.

Indeed, the concept of the soul as a separable, undying part of oneself is extremely widespread. But ideas as to what happens to it after death are mixed. In fact, a notion of several souls to accommodate the different prospects is common.

One idea is that the departed spirit remains close to hearth and home, becoming an ancestral soul that must be propitiated at a nearby grave or shrine. Sometimes these spirits are personified by dancers in ceremonies, often with masks. Another idea is that they go to a distant land of the dead, perhaps a known but remote island or mountain, perhaps a more mythical place like the Australian "Dreamtime" world. But usually this place is less a fanciful paradise than a mirror image of this world, where life goes on much the same as here though perhaps more pleasantly, with days always mild and food always abundant. Finally, it is also sometimes thought that the dead reincarnate in the same tribe or family, perhaps after a stay in the alternative world. Sometimes one finds a concept of several souls evoked to deal with these varied destinies, one to become an ancestral spirit and another to go to the other world.

But tribal religion is acted as much as it is thought. Among its best-known and most significant acts are **initiations**, scenarios that enact views concerning birth and death as stages through which the soul passes; and ancestors living and dead are seen as custodians of enabling power.

Initiation Rites of Men and Women

For most tribal cultures, life is a series of initiations, and it is through them that its most meaningful signs of status are bestowed, as well as the deepest mysteries of the ultimate meaning of human existence revealed. Birth and death are themselves initiatory experiences and so are a part of the series; the great ceremonial initiations enhance, ratify, recapitulate, and prepare one for what is imparted by these two deepest of all sacred mysteries.

Appropriately, initiation is a painful trial, like birth and death. Among the Papuans about Finsch Harbor in New Guinea, the traditional initiation ceremony for all male youths was held every ten to eighteen years, and the boys who underwent it ranged in age from four to twenty. The central feature, as in many such rites around the world, was circumcision or, more exactly, a ritual death and redemption of which circumcision is a lasting token.

At the appointed time, the young candidates were taken by the men of the tribe into the forest. The bull-roarers—flat elliptical pieces of wood, which when twirled make an unearthly roaring sound—were booming. (Significantly, the word *balum* means both "bull-roarer and ghost.") The women of the tribe looked on from a distance, anxious and weeping, for they had been told the boys were to be eaten by a balum or ghostly monster, who would release them only on condition of receiving a sufficient number of pigs. The women had therefore been fattening pigs since the ceremony was announced and hoped they would be adequate to redeem their sons and lovers—or at least they pretended to believe all this. One pig was needed for each initiate.

Deep in the forest, the boys were taken to a secret lodge designed to represent the belly of the monster. A pair of eyes was painted on the entrance, and roots and branches betokened the horror's hair and backbone. As they approached, he "growled"—the voice of more hidden bull-roarers.

The pigs were sacrificed and eaten by the men and boys, for the monster demanded only their "souls." The boys entered the lodge and underwent the circumcision operation. They remained in seclusion three or four months, living in that long hut inside the "monster." During this time they wove baskets and played two sacred flutes, said to be male and female and to be married to each other. No women were allowed to see these flutes, which were employed only during such sacred seasons as this.

At the end of the seclusion period, the boys returned to the village, but they returned in a special manner that bespoke festival and rebirth. They were first taken to bathe in the sea, and then were elaborately decorated with paint and mud. As they went back to the village, they had to keep their eyes tightly shut. An old man touched each on the forehead and chin with a bull-roarer. They were then told to open their eyes and then were allowed to feast and talk to the women.[6]

In the New Hebrides island of Malekula, where a similar Melanesian culture prevails, the men spend their lives undergoing a series of higher and higher initiations, as they are able to obtain the requisite pigs (raised by the women) for sacrifice and feast. These achievements are memorialized in the imperishable tusks of the boars and by wooden markers like **totem** poles in the courtyard of the men's lodges; these become ancestral gods. By the spiritual power of the pigs, a man is enabled to pass the lair of Lehevhev, the terrible spider-woman who guards the road to the spirit world. In the highest of these degree-rites, the initiates are garbed in masks and ghostly white webbing, as though they were already sacred ancestors with the dread power of one who has passed from death into unearthly life.

Besides these tribal rites, there are also special individual initiations. For some peoples, in fact, the initiation of all young men was more individualized than in New Guinea; the Native American Pawnee young man was expected to remain alone in the bush until he personally received a dream or vision of his guardian spirit. There are also particular sacred individuals, especially kings and shamans (men or women), who are set apart by distinctive movements of the sacred.

By no means are initiation rites solely the province of men in tribal religions. Aboriginal women of Australia, for example, have a role in male initiatory rites, albeit in ways differing from that of the men. Women may participate in dramatic separation enactments that precede the circumcision rite of a young man and perform sacred dances during the circumcision itself at a place adjacent to but removed from that of the men. Further, Aboriginal women have their own rites marking important passages in their lives. A young woman's first menstruation, probably the most important passage, marks her coming of age, and the ritual that comes at this time is parallel in many ways to that for young males. (In fact, it is probably the case that the male initiation rite, with its birthing imagery and the shedding of blood through circumcision, mirrors women's life processes.) The women of the tribe take the girl to a sacred, secluded location, separate from the men. Her menstrual blood, **taboo** for the men, is sacred to her as a source of great magic and power, and secret rites are performed by the women in recognition of this. The return to the community is a celebration that is an acknowledgment of her new status as a mature and fertile woman who provides for the tribe.

Part of a totem pole

> *She is brought triumphantly into the main camp in formal procession, followed by an old woman who jokes and dances, clowning, stamping her feet, throwing her arms about, in contrast to the solemnity of the others: the girl's mother especially, is crying and wailing . . . The girl steps ritually over a row of food . . . then sits down while more food is heaped beside her. Afterward she distributes this.*[7]

Such tribal rites reflect the interplay of spiritual forces in the affairs of human life. They emphasize that the spirits of nature work through the natural processes of the human body (particularly in the case of women whose bodily processes are, therefore, mimicked in the men's rites), and celebrate that which sustains the tribe as coextensive with ultimate cosmic reality.

Shamans

There are persons singled out by the Divine to receive special ecstatic powers for dealing with spiritual things. These are the men or women called *shamans* or, less precisely, medicine men or witch doctors. The **shaman** above all is one who, on subtle planes of perception or soul travel, moves freely among the spirits. The shaman knows the geography and dynamics of the invisible spirit world that overlays and is present in this world. Thus, the shaman can serve as guide of the souls of the dead, as healer and intercessor, and counselor to the tribe—for all matters are matters of the spirit.

The word *shaman* is Siberian, and it is in that land of endless birch and evergreen forests, broad rivers, wide skies, and dark subzero winters that its classic form is found, although shamanism or closely related phenomena appear in most parts of the earth. Indeed, it has been argued that shamanism is the prototype of much of the religious world.

Let us look at a few shamanistic practices and try to understand the common features of shamanism.

The Altaic shaman in Siberia wore brown leather and elaborate decorations of metal disks, bird feathers, and colored streamers. He entranced himself by sitting astride a horsehide-covered bench or a straw goose and beating a drum rhythmically for hours, the beat being the pounding of the hooves or wings of these spirit-steeds as they bore him to the parallel realm of the spirits. Finally, the shaman would dismount and, flushed with **ecstasy**, climb nine steps notched in a tree trunk. At each stage in the ascent he would relate the difficulties of his journey, address the gods of that level, and report what they were telling him about coming events. Some of the episodes were comic, such as a burlesque hare hunt on the sixth level. The shaman's scenario was generally enacted with a rich dramatic sense for the right combination of spectacle, mystery, suspense, comic relief, and exalted sentiments. When the Altaic shaman had gone as high as his power permitted, he concluded with a reverent prayer of devotion to Bai Ulgan, the high god, and then he collapsed, exhausted.[8]

Peter Freuchen in his *Book of the Eskimos* describes a shaman's seance he attended.[9] He emphasizes that the shaman, named Sorqaq, prepared seriously for the exercise by fasting and meditation on the cliffs. Sorqaq was to contact a god who dwelt beneath the earth to find out why the tribe had been suffering a series of accidents. Nonetheless, he opened the session by telling those who attended that they were a bunch of fools for coming, that nothing he did would have any truth in it. The audience responded with cries of belief and encouragement. The shaman then sat naked upon a sealskin on a ledge in the igloo, and his assistant bound him tightly with sealskin thongs. His drum was placed beside him. The lights, except for one small flame, were put out.

Then Sorqaq began to sing, and his voice grew louder and louder. Soon it was accompanied by the beat of the drum and the rustle of the sealskin, which seemed to be flying about the room. The awful din rose to a crescendo, with everyone joining in the singing. Sorqaq's own voice then became fainter and seemed to be coming from farther and farther away.

The assistant suddenly put on the lights. Freuchen noticed that the audience was ecstatic—eyes gleaming, bodies twisting to the music of the shaman's song like participants at a revival. Even more remarkable, the shaman himself was gone, his place on the ledge empty save for the drum and sealskin! Among the crowd the spiritual intensity grew, with people experiencing seizures and speaking in strange words, including a special seance language in which persons and objects are referred to by alternative terms.

Then the assistant announced that the shaman was returning. People went back to their seats and the lights were put out. The assistant told with what difficulty Sorqaq was swimming through the rocks beneath. His voice was heard growing in volume, once again the drum sounded louder and louder, and the sealskin crackled in the air. The room quieted after Sorqaq returned, and he was seen again seated on the ledge tightly bound in straps. He told what he had learned: "To avoid more tragedies, our women must refrain from eating of the female walrus until the winter darkness returns!" After the performance, Sorqaq said to Freuchen, "Just lies and tricks. The wisdom of our ancestors is not in me. Do not believe in any of it!"

These accounts should make evident that the shaman is distinguished from other types of religious specialists, such as the priest or the sorcerer, in part by the dramatic quality of his or her performance, with its semispontaneous appearance and the fact that the shaman seems to, and often does, undergo the psychic and physical changes attendant upon altered states of consciousness. Anthropological work has brought to light that taking hallucinogenic plants, such as the fly agaric mushroom in central Asia and plants of the datura family in the Western Hemisphere, is a part of shamanism in many cultures.[10] The altered state of consciousness and the visions of the shaman, however valid spiritually in the context of the culture, are often facilitated by the well-known effects of these drugs.

That is not the case with all shamanism, however. Trance-induced altered states of consciousness in which radically nonordinary perception and audition are obtained are quite possible without the aid of drugs. Trances of this sort are often accompanied by violent trembling, swelling, discoloration, and berserk behavior, as well as Divine utterance. Sometimes seemingly superhuman strength is attained; Tibetan shamans have been reliably reported to be able to twist strong steel swords into knots while in this state. Afterward the performer will be so exhausted as to sleep for days, and such shamans are said, in fact, to be generally short-lived.

The shaman is also distinguished by a related factor, the nature of her or his "call." Other religious functionaries may have entered into their role by heredity, choice, or apprenticeship. But in the case of the shaman, although these factors may play a part, the important point will generally be that he or she has passed through a powerful spiritual ordeal of selection, testing, and "remaking" by divine beings themselves. Above all, he or she will probably receive an assisting spirit, who gives the shaman supernormal powers and control over other spirits.

Here is a vivid account of the manner in which an Eskimo shaman received his power:

> *The angakok consists of a mysterious light which the shaman suddenly feels in his body, inside his head, within the brain, an inexplicable searchlight, a luminous fire, which enables him to see in the dark, both literally and metaphorically speaking, for he can now, even with closed eyes, see through darkness and perceive things and coming events, which are hidden from others: thus they look into the future and into the secrets of others.*
>
> *The candidate obtains this mystical light after long hours of waiting, sitting on a bench in his hut and invoking the spirits. When he experiences it for the first time "it is as if the house in which he is suddenly rises; he sees far ahead of him, through mountains, exactly as if the earth were one great plain, and his eyes could reach to the end of the earth. Nothing is hidden from him any longer; not only can he see things far, far away, but he can also discover souls, stolen souls, which are either kept concealed in far, strange lands, or have been taken up or down to the Land of the Dead."*[11]

Navajo Indian Shaman

The process of becoming a shaman is sufficiently violent to cause Mircea Eliade to speak of it as an "initiatory psychopathology." The future shaman's career begins typically with a "call" from a god or spirit, perhaps the primordial master shaman, in the form of "voices" or strange impulses or seizures. For a time, unable to escape from a supernatural world for which the future shaman is not prepared, he or she may be tormented by cruel spirits in the head and body. Extremes of anxiety and rapture may be suffered. The future shaman may wander about the village in a dissociated manner, have fits, be unable to eat or drink, even become criminal. The future shaman is, in a word, what we in our culture would call insane.

In terms of the future shaman's own culture, however, she or he is one marked by the gods as a possible candidate for a mighty vocation. However much the future shaman may want merely to be "normal," that can never be; the gods will not let the one they have designated to be scorned. One must either serve them or face the unspeakable terrors of their punishment in mind and body.

Even so, success is not inevitable. There is a great test that lies ahead. The future shaman is already in the spiritual world. Now power must be acquired to master it. There is no choice; it must be mastered, or it will destroy the tormented one. This power can only be acquired with the help of one who has it. An initiator must be found, either a great shaman in this world or a supernatural ally in the parallel spirit world, who will impart to him or her the techniques of control. In our terms, the future shaman, now novice, must conquer this "sickness" and make it work for him or her. It must continue to produce knowledge-giving visions of the spiritual world, or the subjective world if one prefers, but only when requested by the novice to do so. This must become an insanity that can be turned on and off at will, so one can learn the things only this state can teach, yet not be enslaved by it.[12]

To arrive at this kind of control, the novice must pass through a catharsis that is virtually a death and rebirth. Alone in the wilderness, in sickness, as aide to a senior shaman, the novice meets this crisis. Among the Eskimos, it is said that the future shaman must take out all his bones and count them; among the Australians, that the soft viscera must be replaced by organs of quartz.

But however exclusive the call, shamanism is not lacking the social dimension of religion. The future shaman's spiritual attack, private as it is, is also a phenomenon expected in the society and has a conventional interpretation and resolution. Moreover, the shaman who has passed through the initiation has a role that is traditional in the society, which frequently has great prestige.

However genuine the call, the role—partly because of the conventional expectations—is not without an element of showmanship or even fraud, as the Eskimo shaman Sorqaq intimated. Perhaps his point of view was the same as that of Quesalid, a shaman of the Kwakiutl Indians of British Columbia, who told the anthropologist Franz Boas the story of his life.[13] Quesalid said that he started out as a skeptic and associated with shamans to learn their tricks and expose them. Invited to join with them, he learned plenty: sacred songs, how to induce trances and fits, how to produce seemingly magical feats by sleight of hand, and much else. In the meantime, knowledge of his training spread, and he was invited by a family to heal a sickness.

Despite Quesalid's disbelief, he felt constrained to accept the offer, and the healing was a success. As more triumphs followed, word spread that he was a great shaman. Knowing such things as that the "sickness" he pretended to suck out of the ill person's body was actually made of down he had previously concealed in his mouth, Quesalid was at a loss how to interpret to himself what he was actually doing. Finally, he came to feel that the healings worked because the sick person "believed strongly in his dream about me," and he apparently felt that the deceptions were justifiable insofar as they helped people believe. Nonetheless, he proved the superiority of his method in competition with shaman colleagues and was contemptuous of most other shamans as charlatans, saying he had known only one he thought was a "real shaman," who employed no trickery he could detect and who would not accept pay.

There are variations in shamanism. One major distinction is between the "traveling" shaman, such as the Altaic and Eskimo already presented, who goes to the spirit world or underworld in his or her trance. The other is the "possession" shaman who, as it were, draws the gods to her or him rather than going to them, being possessed like a medium by gods and spirits and letting them speak through her or him.

A good example of the latter are the *miko,* or shamanesses, of Japan. Now disappearing, they played a substantial part in the popular religion of Japan in the past. They are found today mostly in the far northern part of the island of Honshu; every summer they gather there for a sort of convention on Mount Osore at the upper tip of that island. The Japanese shamans of this type are all female and, what is more, are all blind or nearly so. All are initiated into the vocation of shamanizing as young girls. While it precludes marriage (unlikely for a blind girl in any case in traditional society), it does provide a respected place in the village for girls who otherwise would have had slim prospects.

Blind girls become apprentices of older shamanesses at six or eight years of age. After a strict training involving fasts, undergoing cold-water ablutions, observing taboos, and learning of shamaness songs and techniques of trance and divination, they are initiated.

For this rite, the novice wears a white robe called the death dress. She sits facing her mistress and other shamanesses; these elders sing and chant formulae and names of deities. Suddenly the mistress cries, "What deity possessed you?" When the candidate gives the name of a Shinto god or Buddha or bodhisattva (who will thereafter be her main supernatural patron), the mistress throws a rice cake at her, causing her to fall onto the floor in a faint. The elders then dash water onto her head as many as 3333 times. Then they lie beside her and revive her with body heat. When she comes to, she is said to be reborn; she exchanges the death dress for wedding apparel, and a traditional Japanese wedding—with the traditional exchanges of cups of sake nine times—is performed. The new shamaness is the bride; her deity, the groom. Next a great feast of celebration follows, shared by relatives and friends of the new medium; she demonstrates her proficiency at communicating with spirits of the dead. For a week following, as a sort of Divine honeymoon, she may live alone in a shrine of her deity.[14]

While doing field work in Japan in 1966, I* visited a shamaness who consented to give me a "reading." One wall of the main room of her small house was taken up with altars—Shinto and Buddhist alike—reflecting the syncretistic nature of popular religion around the world. She sat on the floor facing the altars and sang in a sleepy, mystical tone as she swayed back and forth, going into a light trance. Then she called on the help of the sovereign gods, giving out a list of popular Shinto and Buddhist figures and calling on the patrons of the local mountains and districts. Next she received her modest payment and worked the 500-yen note in her hands slowly and placed it on an altar.

After this, she called down the guardian deity of the author's family, whom she said was Fudo, a **bodhisattva** prominent in popular Buddhism. He gave me such warnings as that I was in danger of having a cold in the next ten days, that my wife would become ill in the middle of the year, and a doctor from the South would help her to recover. This directional emphasis was doubtless due to the influence of Taoist geomancy (the plotting of auspicious and unlucky directions), on folk belief in both China and Japan.

*Robert Ellwood.

Next, the spirit of my grandmother was summoned. The *miko* had some diffidence about this request, since she had never before summoned a non-Japanese spirit. But she proceeded, and the shade of my American grandmother spoke in Japanese and as though she were an oriental ancestral spirit.

She started by saying, "Except when it is difficult, offer me water. In this matter I am not happy. The good faith my grandson would show in offering me water as a parting gift would make me happy." She continued, however, to say that although a good doctor was not called when she died, she had had a long enough life and had no regrets; she was now happy in heaven but wanted to be remembered more by offerings of water, presumably at the small shrines of Buddhas and ancestral spirits found in a corner of a traditional Japanese home. She inquired about relatives, gave such advice as to watch out for pickpockets on busses and trains, made a few minor prophecies, and promised to be with her grandson.

The shamaness said nothing of much evidential value, but the session did provide a vivid insight into the shaman's role; to serve as a meeting ground between the living and the dead and as a reinforcer of popular spiritual lore. The altars and references to many faiths indicated that she was not tied to the systematic beliefs of any faith but was rather alive to the presence and powers of gods and spirits of any sort. She knew, so to speak, the secret shortcut paths to the parallel spirit world and seemed able to link them. One got a feeling that the real value of what she did was in the performance, with its atmosphere of mystery and belief in the survival of the deceased, rather than in the somewhat banal things the departed was purported to have said. In all this she was in the great tradition of shamanism.

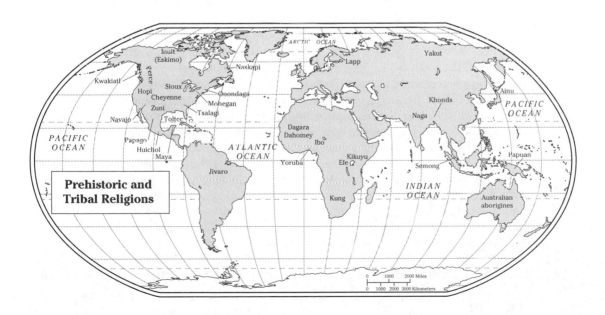

Prehistoric and Tribal Religions

Archaic Hunters

Religion past and present concerns itself not only with crossing the bar to contact ancestors and spirits, but also with ordinary human needs. Modern churches not only talk about salvation but also offer prayers for harvest and good industrial relations. People have always viewed the object that is the source of their lives materially and subjectively to be the very presence or at least a symbol of the Divine: the animal for hunters, the plant for agriculturalists, the king as giver of order for the ancient city and empire, the psychological sense of selfhood in the great ethical and salvation religions of individual decision and experience.

Thus, the relation of the archaic hunter to the game makes it more than mere killing. It is an important part of religious life. Going into the field, tracking, and taking the animal is, so to speak, an act of interplay with spiritual forces and in this respect is comparable to going to church or temple. Even though some tactics of the archaic hunter may seem cruel and ruthless and can be as exploitative as those of any other people, the relation to the animal is seen as that of one power or soul with another. To take the animal requires in some sense the consent of the animal or that of its Divine masters, due propitiation for the wrong done to it, and proper magic to make anything happen at all.

It is necessary to prepare spiritually for a great hunt. Ceremonies set the hunters apart. Rites such as drawing a picture of the animal sought and charming it strive to attract the game, even as apologies to the animal may be offered. As the hunters leave for the field, a sacred silence may be observed. While out, they may observe taboos of diet, remain continent, and talk in a special vocabulary. They may stir up the animal's attention with a ritualized dance to draw it into an ambush or wait for it by a watering hole with a yogalike quietude. When it is taken and devoured, the remaining bones may be treated with respect, for the animal's soul may return to see how its remains were treated, or the bones may be mystically animated to make them magical instruments of great potency. Killing, in other words, entails all sorts of responsibilities. This is a different world of human–animal relations from that of the modern slaughterhouse or of many a modern sportsman with his high-powered rifle, telescopic sight, and desire for a "trophy."

Archaic hunters frequently believe in a Divine "master or mistress of animals" who has control over the forest or a major species and is able to "open" or "close" the forest, making game available or impossible to find. Among the Naskapi Indians of Labrador, for example, the Caribou Man is said to live in a world of caribou hair white as snow and deep as mountains. These mountains comprise the immense house of the Caribou Man, who is white but dresses in black. He is surrounded by thousands of caribou two or three times normal size, both live caribou and caribou ghosts. The animals pass in and out of his caribou paradise, along paths lined several feet deep with hair, and shed caribou horns, as the Caribou Man releases them into our ordinary world for the proper use of humankind.

No human is allowed within 150 miles of the Caribou Man's house. But yet it is said that a hunter who really comes to know the ways of the caribou—virtually thinking like one and sharing its life, observing all the proprieties in his hunting, not taking too much game and respectfully using every part of an animal he does kill— becomes almost one with the Caribou Man and is always given what he needs.

When the Naskapi shamans address the animals, they say, "You and I wear the same covering and have the same mind and spiritual strength." This attitude governs their understanding of the animals that are so crucial to their survival in a harsh climate. Souls of animals circulate; the ghosts dwelling with the Caribou Man are waiting to be sent back into the world in fleshly bodies to be killed once again. It is therefore important that humanity live in reverent harmony with the biological and spiritual ecology of nature. Animals treated rightly will cooperate and return to offer themselves as game to hunters again; those who are not will be enemies, now and hereafter.[15]

A comparable view of life was reflected in the bear sacrifice of the Ainu, formerly a hunting people who live on Hokkaido, the northernmost island of Japan.[16] They believe that a spirit world reflects this one virtually as a mirror image; life circulates between there and here. When it is night here it is day there, and so forth. From time to time the Ainu took a small bear cub, which they raise in their village and treated with great affection, like a spoiled child. When it had nearly reached adulthood, it was killed and sent back to the spirit world in a long and elaborate rite, which was the greatest event in Ainu religious life. Before being sacrificed, the young bear was solemnly addressed. It was told that it had been sent into the world to be hunted and to remember how much care and love was showered upon it. They begged it not to be angry but to realize what an honor was being conferred upon it. They said that it was being sent back to its parents in the spirit world, and they asked it to speak well of the Ainu before them. Finally, they begged the bear to come back into the world to be sacrificed again.[17]

Archaic Gatherers

Hunting is not the only spiritually charged economic activity of such tribes. The relation of the archaic gatherer to the land also reveals an especially rich center of spiritual life. Here, too, there is an interplay of ordinary activities for the well-being of the tribe with spiritual forces. Recent archeological and anthropological evidence indicates that for many prehistoric and tribal groups, the main diet consisted not of large game (an occasional and special food) but of plant-foods and small animals gathered, for the most part, by women. The gatherers had special knowledge of the earth spirit (or spirits) who provided these "gifts" out of her (or sometimes his) bounty.

The important role of women as gatherers is reflected in the high status accorded them in hunter-gatherer societies where there appears to be an egalitarian bent exhibited by a great degree of complementarity in the roles of men and women. Although not universally so, this remains so today in many extant hunter-gatherer societies, such as the !Kung of the Kalahari desert in Southern Africa.[18]

Archaic Farmers

The beginning of agriculture, perhaps at several places, some 10,000 years ago, and the subsequent spread of the practice of planting and harvesting produced probably the most far-reaching religious changes of any transition in the history of religion. In many ways we are still living in the age set in motion by the development of agriculture. The modern city is an extension of the village of the first sedentary planters. At least until the twentieth century, the average person almost anywhere in the world was a peasant who lived close to the soil and seasons and whose life and values were more like the life and values of the archaic, **Neolithic** agriculturalists than those of the workers in contemporary technological society. It may be that today, as we finally move away from the world shaped culturally by the peasant farmer's way of life into a truly urban world of computers and space travel, religious changes as marked as those that separate the archaic farmer from the hunter will eventuate.

What was the development of agriculture, and why was it so important? First of all, it may seem strange that it should have taken us something like a million years to make the seemingly simple and obvious observation as that seeds could be planted in the spring to produce plants in the fall when and where one wanted them, and that animals could be kept around the house. Second, it may seem just as strange that such a clearly mundane, economic matter should have such far-reaching religious significance as appears to be the case. In fact, these paradoxes are very instructive of the profound relation between religion—or, if one prefers, worldview—and culture, and conversely of the deep impact such things as economic system and social organization have on religious forms. Each does much to determine what is, at least psychologically, available in the other sphere.

That it took people so long to develop such a simple thing as planting, despite the fact that we always needed food and that trees and herbs were setting examples by "planting" themselves all around every year, reveals a vastly different worldview than what those in developed countries today hold.

Probably, earlier peoples ignored the possibilities of planting and domesticating animals because they may not have wished to disturb the natural flow of things—as being sacred in its own right. The worldview of the hunter-gatherers made possible a deep appreciation of the mysteries of animal life, the life-giving earth source, and our spiritual as well as material interaction with them. They saw the human state as that of a being who wanders about the face of the earth under the sky, going whither the guardians of the forest directed and accepting what they chose to give. Holding such a worldview, it would not occur to them to consider the possibilities of sedentary habitation on one small piece of land deliberately worked for all it could produce. The difference in attitude is well expressed in the words of a Native American who, when urged by the United States government to take up farming on a reservation, refused in these words:

> You ask me to plow the ground! Shall I take a knife and tear my mother's bosom?
> Then when I die she will not take me to her bosom to rest. You ask me to dig for

stone! Shall I dig under her skin for her bones? Then when I die, I cannot enter her body to be born again. You ask me to cut grass and make hay and sell it, and be rich like white man! But how dare I cut off my mother's hair?[19]

These words were spoken in the nineteenth century, but they are an echo of the **Paleolithic** mind. They come from the world that was before the discovery of agriculture. As such they give us a hint of why for many peoples the introduction of agriculture seemed to be a kind of loss of innocence, or "fall," and its practice a way of life that, though more productive than hunting, was also somehow haunted by a sense of guilt that agricultural human beings felt but could never quite express save in myth and rite.

And, in any event, time-consuming and laborious agricultural work may not have been thought worth the trouble by those in hunter-gatherer tribes who found no difficulty finding food. As Margaret Ehrenberg in *Women in Prehistory* points out, there are many advantages to gathering food that are lost when society shifts to agriculture. The !Kung of the Kalahari desert, knowing that other tribes in their area practice agriculture, do not think it worth the considerable effort required to undertake agriculture: "Why bother to grow crops when there are so many mongongo nuts in the world?"[20]

We do not know exactly how the discovery of planting took place, although it is thought by many anthropologists that it was developed by women as an extension of their work as gatherers. With the development of agriculture, the religious

Farmers' planting and harvesting dance in Seoul, Korea.

focus shifted even more to earth and tilled field for its metaphors. It shifted to the plant, which "dies" in the autumn to provide life for others, and then through the surviving seed comes back to life after a sort of burial in the spring.

The introduction of agriculture resulted in considerable advancement in human living standards and culture for some, though for vast numbers of those who sunk to peasant class as tillers of the fields it probably meant a more impoverished diet, depending on only a few staples, and certainly a life of more monotonous labor than that of the hunter-gatherer. Indeed, the discovery of agriculture seems often to have been half-consciously regarded as an unlocking of forbidden knowledge or to have involved a crime, a murder, which although it may have brought humankind wealth was spiritually a second "fall," putting humanity still farther away from the gods and primal innocence. (The second offense in the Bible, after that of Eden, was committed by Cain, tiller of the soil.) It will be said that the first plants were "stolen," or that the one who introduced agriculture was a trickster or rebel against the primal gods, or that the first plants came from the body of a slain but innocent maiden. Many myths of archaic origins reflect these themes.

Thus in the Kojiki, the ancient Japanese mythology, it is related that the moon god, Tsukiyomi, came down to earth and, going to the home of the food goddess, requested something to eat. She gave him a meal, but he considered it all repulsive food. In his anger he slew the food goddess and found in her body all sorts of food plants of a new sort—rice, beans, and so forth. These Tsukiyomi took back to heaven, and the High Goddess Amaterasu said they would be for planting in the broad and narrow fields of heaven and earth.

A myth from Ceram, in Indonesia, relates the same experience to the *dema,* Divine creators and helpers who lived with human beings in mythical times. It tells us that a hunter long ago found a coconut on the tusk of a boar he slew. That night he was commanded in a dream to plant it. Immediately it grew into a great tree, and, shortly after, a girl-child was born out of the tree after the hunter had spilled blood on it accidentally. He named her Hainuwele; in three days she was of marriageable age. Hainuwele then attended a great dance. For nine days she stood in the midst of the dancing area and passed out gifts to the dancers. Nonetheless, on the ninth day the dancers dug a grave, put Hainuwele in it, filled it in, and continued by dancing on it.

When Hainuwele did not come home the next morning, the hunter sensed that she had been murdered. He found the body, cut it into pieces, and buried the pieces in different places. The interred pieces gave birth to previously unknown food plants. The hunter carried Hainuwele's arms to a leading *dema,* Satane, who took them into the dancing ground, drew a nine-spiral figure with them on the ground and went to the middle of it. She said, "Since you have killed, I will no longer live here. I shall leave this very day. Now you will have to come to me through this door." Satane vanished through the mystic spiral into another mode of existence, and since then humans have been able to meet her only after death. After the agriculture-giving murder, the *dema* have no longer lived in companionship with humankind.[21]

Through stories such as this, a grim basic principle came to affect the agricultural worldview even more than the hunter's: the principle of death for life. Agriculture seems to have brought out a new and darker sense of the interconnection of death and life. This interconnection was not unknown to the hunter; the Naskapi believed that by a reverent treatment of the bones of a slain beast, the soul of the animal could be influenced to return and offer itself again. The Ainu believed that by sacrificing the precious bear cub, they could persuade it and its relatives in the spirit world to return and replenish the supply of game.

But in agricultural society, all of this becomes more accentuated, often reaching a point that seems a grisly preoccupation with ritual death, whether animal or human. Religious headhunting, human sacrifice, and large-scale animal sacrifice are not genuinely primitive but are usually associated with agricultural societies and are a part of the mentality to which it gave rise. The meaning of sacrifice for early agricultural society can be ascertained by a few examples.

The Naga tribes of northeast India, archaic agriculturalists, were famous as headhunters. Heads from neighboring tribes were sought on several occasions— to grace the funeral of a chief, to settle blood feuds, and as an aspect of attaining manhood. A male could not marry until he had taken a head. Heads were presented at the harvest festival to placate the ancestral ghosts, and in some Naga tribes heads were placed on poles in the fields of growing crops, so that the life-power of the severed head would flow into the food plants. Headhunting was always undertaken with religious preparation; men performed special rituals and remained apart from women both before and after a hunt.[22]

The relationship of headhunting to agriculture is even clearer in the case of the Jivaro of the upper Amazon. A Jivaro male who had taken and shrunk a head would perform a dance with it and two female relatives, usually his sister and his wife. He would hold the head in his outstretched hand, and they would hold on to him as they danced; this would empower these women to gain greater productivity from the crops and animals it was their province to tend. The dance seemed to make power flow from the head through the husband and then through his sister and his wife into the crops. After this rite, the head was no longer powerful and could be discarded like a squeezed lemon.[23]

The Khonds, a tribe in Bengal, offered a human victim to the earth goddess. The sacrificed person was supposed to be a volunteer but was often bought from his parents as a child. After he had been set apart for this grim vocation, he lived happily for years. Like the Ainu bear cub, he was well treated and looked upon as especially consecrated. Finally, at a great festival, also marked by an orgy to promote fertility (another important aspect of agricultural religion), the victim was decked with butter and flowers. The tribesmen danced around him, praying loudly for good crops and weather. After he was drugged with opium and killed, the priests cut his body carefully into pieces; these were buried with great ceremony in the fields to promote fertility.[24]

In many places, captives taken in battle were killed as sacrifices. Archaic peoples often considered it auspicious to place a human sacrifice under the foundations of a new building or to kill a victim in connection with the launching of a new boat. In all of this, it is clear that human sacrifice meant a transfer of power from the victim to the sacrificer or his or her works, a concept prefigured in the murders that mark the beginning of agriculture in myth.

The sedentary character of agriculture in itself effected extensive changes in religion and culture. Because cultivation can sustain far more people than hunting and gathering on the same acreage, the advent of agriculture led to a marked increase in population in fertile regions. Inevitable results of this and related factors were the emergence of towns and cities, elaborate trade relationships, and an extensive division of labor. A flourishing agricultural economy could support not only the farmers, but also various traders, artisans, rulers, priests, and even a few scholars and philosophers. Finally, the susceptibility of the agricultural routine to commerce, taxation, and control, and its need in many lands for large-scale public works such as market roads and irrigation systems, led to writing and the ancient empires in which civilization as we know it emerged. The religious products of this new economy were far-reaching: Elaborate polytheism mirrored in the heavens the new extensive division of labor and the coming together of many tribes; sacred scriptures were a first result of writing; even more far-reaching were the fruits of the leisure of priests, scholars, and philosophers. We must return to more immediate products of the discovery of the plant as miraculous lifegiver. The sedentary farmer's closeness to the cycle of the plant made the farmer extremely aware of the turning of seasons, especially planting and harvest. Out of this came such festivals as May Day and Halloween, associated with seedtime and harvest.

Women in Early Agrarian Societies and the Reassertion of Masculine Interests

Some have speculated that life in archaic agricultural communities made the role of women important as symbol of place, home, and social continuity. Certain of these societies were matrilineal, tracing descent through women, and matrilocal, meaning that men moved into the homes of the women they married. The common association of earth and plant with mother and child made the spiritual power of the symbolic feminine increase with the growing importance of the soil and plant. Feminists, such as the late Marija Gimbutas and others, have theorized that considerable evidence of pervasive female symbolism during this time reflects the prominence of women and perhaps matriarchal societies.[25] Such ideas are very controversial, however, because the academy in general holds that there is very little evidence that there were societies where women ruled, and there appear to be no such societies extant today.[26] The common view is that pervasive goddess symbolism did not reflect the holding of power on the part of earthly women but rather represented the importance of fertility to the archaic community. While many of the great goddesses of later antiquity—Isis, Demeter, Ishtar, Kali, Amaterasu—clearly stem from the powerful agricultural mother of archaic farming culture, the societies that held them sacred moved toward social conventions that proved more limiting for women than had been the case for the earlier archaic women. These were times when women, though perhaps inventors of agriculture, were increasingly domesticated and even virtually enslaved.

In this regard, the continued development of agriculture was marked by significant and long-ranging reactions on the part of the men. Some of the men's initiations that are kept most secret from the women and that most obviously imitate women's mysteries, such as those from New Guinea, emerge from archaic planting societies. Sometimes these movements take extreme shape in their reassertion of the remaining masculine virtues of group loyalty, strength, warlikeness, and spiritual skill, such as headhunting or the Leopard Society of West Africa. One men's society in Melaesian, New Britain, the Dukduk, traveled from place to place with the function of enforcing the law in a rough-and-ready way wherever they landed.

An interesting penultimate reaction is **megalithism**—the erection of giant stone monuments such as those at Stonehenge. A period of making bigger and bigger constructions of this type as temples, observatories, or tombs occurred in many parts of the globe just before the breakthrough to ancient civilization. They are found in England, Malta, China, and Japan, and they are succeeded by even greater edifices, such as the pyramids and ziggurats of Egypt, Mesopotamia, and Meso-America. It is as though the megalith were an extension of the custom in many men's lodges of erecting great totemlike figures as memorials of initiatory feasts and of ancestors.

The last archaic stage has been called the "Patriarchal Revolution." At the onset of the ancient civilizations—whether in Egypt, Mesopotamia, India, or China—we see a vigorous assertion of male primacy in powerful sovereigns and a corresponding suppression of female religious figures, whether queens, goddesses, or shamanesses. In China and Japan, early edicts may be found forbidding or limiting the work of various sorts of priestesses. The sexless **asceticism** of early yogis and Buddhist monks says the same thing, in different words, as does the ascendancy of the pharaoh who made Isis, the great goddess, his throne, but who identified himself with the male Ra and Osiris. We may ask ourselves whether now,

Stonehenge, built about 1400–800 B.C.E. from bluestones up to 30 feet high in two concentric circles with astronomical significance.

after thousands of years of patriarchy, the pendulum is swinging again toward egalitarian values in religion and culture.

FUNDAMENTAL FEATURES OF PREHISTORIC AND TRIBAL RELIGIONS

THEORETICAL

Basic Worldview	The universe is a place animated by many spirits, some friendly and some not. Humans have a real place in the cosmos, which works by rules and cycles that can be known.
God or Ultimate Reality	Many gods and spirits; but perhaps a high god or unifying force over them.
Origin of the World	Either no point of origin or created by the gods or a high god who may subsequently have withdrawn from activity.
Destiny of the World	Usually not clear.
Origin of Humans	Often children of gods or semidivine primal parents.
Destiny of Humans	Frequently we go after death to another world, not unlike this world, sometimes also to be reborn here in this world.
Revelation or Mediation between the Ultimate and the Human	Myth, often told and enacted at festivals and by shamans; benign gods and ancestral spirits as helpers.

PRACTICAL

What Is Expected of Humans	Worship, practice, behavior to undergo initiation; to honor and sacrifice to gods and ancestors; to observe tribal norms of behavior and taboos.

SOCIOLOGICAL

Major Social Institutions	Tribe as a spiritual unit; shamanism.

✦ Summary

Prehistoric and tribal religion, the backdrop of all later religion, is a vast and complex phenomenon. But it possesses certain basic themes which, in modified forms, appear centrally in later religion as well. It is, first of all, cosmic religion—concerned with showing the relation of humankind to nature and the cosmos, it celebrates the turn of the seasons and places of special sacred power. It has myths telling of the creation of the world by Divine powers but often also adds a mythic account of a "fall" that explains why humanity is no longer as close to the creative powers as at the time of creation.

Second, primitive religion is concerned with soul or spirit. Endeavoring to explain the diverse feelings people have within them, it sometimes tells of two or more souls. Confronting the eternal human dread of death, it describes the destiny of the soul in the afterlife: Sometimes different souls have different destinies, sometimes one at least goes to an alternative world, sometimes another aspect of the self remains around its familiar haunts as a ghost, sometimes one is reincarnated in this world. The spirits of ancestors or unappeased ghosts are usually feared and propitiated.

Initiations are very important for many primitive peoples. They serve the end of social cohesion by inducting adults into the tribe after proper training and a potent shared experience, and they often serve the end of individual fulfillment as well by giving status and perhaps secrets of value in the soul's journey after death. Initiations involve a process of separation, marginality when one is separated from the social structure but close to Divine powers, and reincorporation of the individual into the social order. Such initiations also emphasize that the spirits of nature work through the natural processes of the human body (particularly the female body, the processes of which are mimicked in men's initiations rites) and celebrate what sustains the tribe as coextensive with ultimate cosmic reality.

The shaman is usually a person with a very special and personal, often lonely, initiation. She or he is believed to have powers of controlling spirits, healing, and confronting the gods, expressed through dramatic scenarios of trance and dance.

The religion of hunter-gatherer peoples expresses the hunter's sense of dependence on the animal, as well as the gatherer's dependence on the natural world to provide the staples of the diet of the tribe. The hunter knows that the hunted animal, and often a "master or mistress of animals" deity in charge of a species must be kept as a benign spirit if game is to be taken; the gatherer knows that the secrets of nature must be unlocked in order to receive the gifts of the earth spirit's bounty.

Agriculture gave a tremendous impetus to human culture but seems often to have been perceived as a sort of "fall" from a purer state. The religion of agriculturalists tends to involve more blood and sacrifice, and more antagonism between the sexes, than that of the hunters and gatherers. Agriculture tore the earth deeply but also allowed the rise of sedentary societies, great increases in population, and finally the ancient empires.

❀ Questions for Review

1. Explain the meaning of "cosmic religion."

2. Be able to show how some features of early religion are related to individual needs and others to tribal needs; some to humanity's relation to the cosmos or nature and others to the destiny of the individual soul. Notice that some features more than others combine an interest in two or more of these motifs, as indicated by their placement on the chart.

3. Discuss what human problems and experiences lie behind common myths of gods and spirits.

4. Talk about what early myths may be trying to say through their accounts of the soul, its often multiple character, and its destiny in the afterlife.

5. Explain the scenarios of initiation and their meaning in terms of the archaic interpretation of human life.

6. Understand shamanism, and describe how a shaman characteristically acquires special powers and what he or she is believed able to do.

7. Present the main features of hunter-gatherer religions, the worldview that lies behind them, and how this worldview is reflected in the relations between men in women.

8. Explain what impact agriculture had on ancient societies, transforming them and leading to the Patriarchal Revolution.

9. Following the chart, explain some fundamental features of prehistoric and tribal religion.

❀ Suggested Readings on Prehistoric and Tribal Religions

American Museum of Natural History, *The First Humans: Human Origins and History to 10,000 B.C.,* Goran Burenhult, ed., *The Illustrated History of Humankind* series. San Francisco: HarperSanFrancisco, 1993. Presents views alternative to those of Marija Gimbutas, cited below.

Blakely, Thomas D., Walter E. A. van Beek, and Dennis L. Thomson, eds., *Religion in Africa: Experience & Expression.* London: James Currey; and Portsmouth, NH: Heinemann, 1994. A very interesting collection of articles on the subject but may be a difficult read for undergraduate students.

Caillois, R., *Man and the Sacred.* New York: The Free Press of Glencoe, 1960. A sparkling essay, including treatment of such topics as the sacred meaning of play and war in archaic societies.

Douglas, Mary, *Purity and Danger.* Baltimore, MD: Penguin Books, 1966. A classic study of pollution and taboo beliefs and practices. Although to some degree outdated, it is nevertheless a pivotal work.

Ehrenberg, Margaret, *Women in Prehistory.* London: British Museum Publications, 1989. A very interesting and consummately readable survey of archeological and anthropological findings about prehistorical woman.

Eliade, Mircea, *A History of Religious Ideas,* Vol. I: *From the Stone Age to the Eleusinian Mysteries*. Chicago: University of Chicago Press, 1978. A highly literate outline of prehistoric and ancient religion as viewed by a distinguished historian of religion.

———, *Shamanism: Archaic Techniques of Ecstasy*. New York: Pantheon Books, 1964. A masterful overview of the data and its meaning from the perspective of a historian of religions.

Evans-Pritchard, Edward E., *Nuer Religion*. Oxford: Clarendon Press, 1956. A very influential study of the religion of one African people.

Gill, Sam D., *Beyond 'The Primitive': The Religions of Nonliterate Peoples*. Englewood Cliffs, NJ: Prentice Hall, 1982. A good introduction.

———, *Native American Religions: An Introduction*. Belmont, CA: Wadsworth, 1982. An excellent beginning survey of the field.

Gimbutas, Marija, *The Civilization of the Goddess: The World of Old Europe*. San Francisco, HarperSanFrancisco, 1991. A beautiful and persuasive account of the subject, which has engendered much debate as it challenges generally accepted scholarship in the field.

Gross, Rita M., "Tribal Religions: Aboriginal Australia" in *Women in World Religions,* Sharma, Arvind, ed. Albany: State University of New York Press, 1987. A fascinating study from the women's point of view.

James, E. O., *Prehistoric Religion*. London: Thames and Hudson, 1957. An orderly overview of the data.

Leslie, Charles, ed., *Anthropology of Folk Religion*. New York: Random House, 1960. A collection of fascinating essays on topics ranging from the Krishna cult in India to Haitian voodoo.

Lowie, Robert H., *Primitive Religion*. New York: Grossett & Dunlop, 1952. A classic text.

Maringer, Johannes, *The Gods of Prehistoric Man*. New York: Knopf, 1960. Authoritative summary of what is known about the religion of Stone Age humanity.

Miller, Christine, and Patricia Chuckryk, eds., *Women of the First Nations: Power, Wisdom, and Strength*. Winnipeg: The University of Manitoba Press, 1996. Women's experience among Native Americans.

Peters, Virginia Bergman, *Women of the Earth Lodges: Tribal Life on the Plains*. North Haven, CT: Archon Books, 1995. Native American women's ritual and social life.

Radin, Paul, *Primitive Religion*. New York: Viking Press, 1937. A book providing an important perspective; it emphasizes the place of individual differences and doubt among primitive people.

Ray, Benjamin, *African Religions: Symbol, Ritual, and Community*. Englewood Cliffs, NJ: Prentice Hall, 1976. A competent overview of traditional religion on the African continent.

Redfield, Robert, *The Primitive World*. Ithaca, NY: Cornell University Press, 1953. A basic book by a great anthropologist; gives much attention to religion.

CHAPTER THREE

Life against Time

The Spiritual Paths of India

CHAPTER OBJECTIVES

After studying this chapter, you should be able to

❁ Discuss the major features of Hinduism as a religion, including basic terms and common concepts.

❁ Present the central message of the Hindu classics, such as the Upanishads and the Bhagavad-Gita.

❁ Be able to recognize the chief Hindu gods and goddesses and their myths.

❁ Discuss the importance of Hinduism and other religions of India in the contemporary world.

❁ Understand the impact of Hindu ideology on attitudes toward and practices with respect to women in India.

❁ Discuss Hinduism's impact on the American religious landscape.

Tribal religious scene.

Tribal ceremonialist.

The Face of India

I* first entered India by plane from Kabul, Afghanistan, and followed, at jet speed, the track over the famous Khyber Pass of countless invaders and pilgrims from the hard but exhilarating highlands of central Asia. With them, I dipped down into the heat-thick air of the Ganges River basin. Long before, at the dawn of history, Indo-European cattle herders had perhaps taken the same trail, and after them Alexander and his Greeks, then Huns, Turks, and the cavalry of the opulent Mughul emperors. Others had come over the passes for reasons other than physical spoils, for India has never failed to draw seekers of all sorts: Chinese monks seeking authentic scriptures of the Buddha, son of India, who became the Enlightened One; and God-intoxicated mystics of Islam who were partly to conquer India in turn.

Like me, most international travelers today arrive in India by air, landing at Delhi, Bombay, or Calcutta. The air terminal will be located some miles out of the city, and the visitor will get his or her first impression of this fabled land riding in a bus or cab through a brief patch of countryside and then the messy environs of the metropolis.

At first, visitors may be quite disappointed if their expectations about India were shaped by that genre of literature and art in which India emerges closer to Oz than this earth. They will see a dull flat land of green fields and brown dust or mud, depending on the season. The landscape will be suffused, if it is clear, with glaring heat and light. Yet for all the brilliance, the scenery seems to give a drained, faded impression, as though too much sun had leached it of the brighter colors. The monotony of the softly verdant fields is broken only by clumps or rows of stolid trees, or slow muddy rivers, or the dull white of humped cattle, or tiny homes and shops all drab with dust, rust, and water stains.

As the visitor enters the city, another experience unfolds: She or he is lost amid labyrinthine crooked streets, open-air shops, houses of earth and corrugated metal, and rain-browned official buildings. The narrow ways are thronged with oxcarts, horse-drawn wagons, countless bicycles, ancient buses and trucks, and once in a while a chauffered auto. On the most important streets as well as the byways, traffic may be backed up as a whitish inviolable cow ambles along or stands still, staring at the bustle of the human world with placid, indifferent eyes.

Above all there are people—women in many-hued saris, men in pants and pastel shirts, half-naked children. People are jammed into the streets like water being forced through a narrow funnel, jammed into buses and trains until they hang onto the railings and windows, crowding in and out of buildings, sometimes flaring up at each other, sometimes moving as though it were all a great dance.

On the surface, then, India may give an impression of drabness and grubbiness, not to mention the depressing signs of extreme poverty and hunger that are too often apparent. Families live and die in culverts or pallets on the streets; there are emaciated children and animals, thin adult faces deeply lined with toil and malnutrition, and hawkers and beggars in public places. India is indeed a harsh land,

*Robert Ellwood.

given to cruel extremes of flood and drought, heat and cold. The fierce climate racks the tired, overworked soil year after year and wastes the far too many humans who swarm over it.

But for all that, one does not get the feeling of a sad, listless land or people. As soon as one's eyes and ears truly focus, vitality pops up everywhere like bright eyes from behind veils: craftsmen vigorously hammering metal, the glint of copper and brass in shops, lurid movie posters, the shining faces of children running and playing. Rather than listless, India is a country of strange and violent extremes. Everything—beauty and horror, life and death, rapture and anguish, love and callousness—seems to run to unbridled extremes; the beauty is more extravagant and the horror more terrible than in more temperate lands.

Ganesha

When I* first left India after three weeks, I felt emotionally exhausted, as one does after passing through a major personal joy, crisis, or grief. India had been, in a real sense, all three. For life and beauty, there were warm eyes, flashing smiles, festivals full of colored streamers, bejeweled elephants and palanquins, and vigorous and sinuous dances. For grief, there was a madwoman lying ranting in the middle of the highway, ignored or left to her dream by the passersby; the ragged begging children; the indigents sleeping on streets by the thousands night after night. India was not so much an interesting experience, in the casual sense, as an intense and unforgettable vision. As in a high dream, a door had opened a crack to let me glimpse something of an alternative world where the extreme potentials of human life in all directions—ecstasy, beauty, madness, depravity—extremes over which we in the West so often draw a veil—were starkly revealed.

Understanding Hinduism

The religion of approximately 80 percent of the people of India is Hinduism, a religion with a very distinctive flavor. The first real Hindu temple I* visited was not in India but on the island of Fiji, where many people from India have settled. The air was humid and heavy; the place of worship was by the side of a road and was largely open air. The first thing seen was a large *lingam,* the phallic pillar, which is the expression of Shiva, set in an oval base called the *yoni* (a name for the female organ), which is the expression of Shakti. **Shiva** is the absolute cosmic Being, sheer life force, and **Shakti** is the absolute power of the phenomenal universe, creative and destructive. Like sexuality, the Shiva-Shakti dynamic is able to give the most stupendous joy and excruciating pain, to make and to rip apart. In the presence of the *lingam* and *yoni,* one has the feeling that the Indian worldview is deeply biological, tending always in the end to see the cosmos as a great living organism.

Betty Heimann has suggested that it is the biological flavor of Hinduism to which one must turn for understanding.[1] This is a deep insight because Hinduism presses biology beyond the point where other religions set humankind and nature, or mind and body, over against each other. But as is represented in the lingam and

*Robert Ellwood.

yoni of Shiva and Shakti, in Hinduism the biological and the Divine are one unity. I* have written elsewhere:

> *Hindu society is not a contractual state, but a great organism. By means of the* **caste**
> *system, every individual finds his place through the biological process of birth and*
> *contributes to the whole like a cell of the body. . . . The numinous Hindu gods, [dwell]*
> *in the dark cavelike interior of the temple (called the* garbha, *"womb"). . . .* **Yoga** *[a*
> *Hindu practice] requires a skillful and persistent combined engineering of physiological*
> *and psychological forces. It says these two are ultimately one. It suggests the goal,*
> **samadhi,** *blissful unconditioned awareness, is the epitome or ultimate objective of the*
> *unceasing biological process. . . . To Hinduism, the meaningful dualism is not of man*
> *and nature, or of mind and body, but of the infinite or unconditioned and the finite or*
> *conditioned. Mind, the unconscious, human society, and nature are all part of a*
> *biological continuum, all on one side of the dualism, because they are all alike*
> *conditioned; only the breakthrough which sees them all at once and so makes the*
> *many one moves to the other side.*[2]

This polarity is expressed in the basic polarity throughout Hindu thought and life—between **dharma** and **moksha**. Within the union that is life and the cosmos, these are the two lenses through which it ideally can be seen: as *dharma*, or the social order; and from the perspective of *moksha*, or the state of liberation or unconditionedness.

The word *dharma* is one of those terms so broad as to require more an intuition than a precise definition. But basically it can be understood as the social order of human civilization when it is righteous, that is, in accord with the cosmic order, called **rita**, and it is the rites of the priests that sustain both. But *dharma* also implies the righteousness and duty of the people, themselves, in the sense that it means moral behavior that upholds the social order. Finally, *dharma* includes ritual usages that uphold the great cosmic–social order by demarcating one's place in society or *caste* and sustaining the work of creation by "fueling" the Divine forces that move it.

Actually, seeing the world as *dharma* means regarding life as ritual. It means that one suppresses one's individualistic predilections in order to harmonize with the swing of the total pattern, so that the world becomes like a great dance. There are rituals for rising, for brushing one's teeth, for bathing, for eating, for love, for study, for worship. One's personal *dharma,* **svadharma**, his or her particular steps in the great dance, are determined by individual birth and **karma**.

Humans and even the gods of nature can live in accordance with or rebel against *dharma,* but they cannot escape the consequences that *dharma* imposes through *karma. Karma,* related to our word "car," means basically action or activity, as in **Karma-yoga**, which we shall see means the way of union with God through right actions. But action always implies cause and effect, for nothing in this world acts or moves without an impelling cause. Therefore, *karma* also refers

*Robert Ellwood.

to that chain of cause and effect set in motion by one's deeds in the world. Sooner or later, through inexorable laws of justice built into *dharma,* they rebound to affect one's own future as retribution or reward. As one sows, so one reaps. One could just as well attempt to defy nature by jumping off a cliff and trying to fly, but would be met by the consequences. Retribution or reward will include (but is not limited to) the state in which one is reborn—as a monarch or slave, a god or a dog.

This is the realm of endless and ultimately self-correcting change driven by striving and cause and effect in which we dwell. It is an interesting level but in the end wearisome. However, it is not necessary to remain forever running with its tides and tossed hither and yon by the self-made waves of *karma.* There is always the possibility of leaping aboard a raft and skimming to a different level altogether, to a state as opposite to it as land is to water. This is *moksha,* "leaping out," finding liberation. It is the final quest, after all other quests have run out. The quest for *moksha* is undertaken under the guidance of a **guru**, a spiritual guide who initiate s the seeker into the path he is qualified to impart and direct him along. Later we will examine some of these paths.

According to the Laws of Manu (c. 100 C.E.), there are four basic goals that motivate humanity, also known as the "Four Ends of Human Life": pleasure (*kama*), gain (*artha*), righteousness (*dharma*), and liberation (*moksha*). Each has its own place and, indeed, its own "rituals," such as those for *kama* in the well-known **Kama-sutra**. But all except *moksha* finally exhaust themselves in craving for something beyond that level.

We may imagine a young man (since the pattern was designed with the male in mind) starting out in life motivated mainly by *kama*—a playboy, a hedonist. But after a whirl at this he finds that pleasure alone, without direction or purpose beyond today, gives one a sense of disintegration. He feels that if he keeps up that way of life he will just keep wanting more and more to provide the same satisfaction, and that he will finally end up enslaved, more anxious to avoid losing pleasures and their symbols than enjoying them.

So next he decides to try instead for some real goals: getting ahead, making money, getting a big house and car (or, in ancient India, a chariot). This is the second stage, *artha,* and in time this goal is increasingly well met.

But still the man senses a certain inner disquiet. There is a quality of self-respect, or of desire for the respect of others, that he does not have. He wants not only to be successful, but also to be substantial; a solid, respectable citizen; a community leader. He wants to exemplify and uphold *dharma* in this world. So he becomes active in organizations that address social issues, and perhaps even gets into politics—highly motivated, of course. (Or, in ancient India, he is active in the *panchayat,* the local governing body of his caste, or is a faithful ritualist, or even a gracious and just king.)

Yet, when a busy day is done and he goes to bed, he may later wake in the middle of the night with an empty, despairing feeling, as though he were all straw, with gnawing rats inside. What he is doing is good, yet somehow it means nothing, or rather it would mean nothing if it is all that people do, age after age, generation after generation, getting nowhere because it all has to be done time and time again, for all eternity. The big questions are now unavoidable: Why does nothing fully meet the unquenchable yearning in a person? What will become of me in the end? What is the real purpose of life, and why is it so hard to discover? Who am I, anyway? He is now ready to tackle the last goal—*moksha*.

In India, these developments ideally would be in tandem with the four **ashramas**, also known as the "Four Stages of Life": student, householder, hermit or forest dweller, and renunciant. But the first three goals—pleasure, gain, and dharma—would be dealt with in the householder stage, since the student was expected to practice continence and application and was under obedience to his father and teacher. Then, after he had seen his first grandchild or his hair had begun to turn gray, he could retire to a hermitage to begin the quest for *moksha* and culminate it by becoming a **sannyasin**, or renunciant, a wandering monk free from all ties. His wife could accompany him if he desired and if they maintained celibacy. Of course, not more than a small percentage of the people of India, largely upper caste, have followed this regimen, and frequently the "retirement" of the last two stages is actually to a private room within the house. But the tradition is still alive and answers to something universal; one feels many Westerners would be happier by accepting that in the last half of life pleasure and gain should be put aside in favor of another quest, which can be repressed but deep inside becomes more and more insistent.

The goal of Hinduism may be given many labels—God-realization, identification with the absolute, supreme bliss, cosmic consciousness—but it is perhaps best spoken of by more negative terms such as release, liberation, or freedom. For it is really beyond all concepts and labels. It is simply freedom. Not freedom in any political or individualistic sense but inner freedom from everything that circumscribes or conditions the sense of infinity one has within; that is, freedom from all relation to the cause and effect of *karma* within or without. One is to rise above and master all this, to become as lithe and free as sunlight and clouds in the sky. Then one knows the answer to the secret of who one really is.

The prevailing Hindu answer is that, in the great quiet of meditation, in hearing the sonorous words of scripture, in the joy of devotion, the realization comes through that there is only One—**Brahman**, Universal Being, God beyond all personalities—and that "Thou art that."

There are many paths to *moksha*, bespoken by the many gods and goddesses, temples and teachers of Hinduism—many of which we will be encountering in the pages to follow. But before we begin that exploration, it is important to recognize that Hinduism is not so much a "religion" in the sense we think of it in the West as it is a general term covering all those religions and spiritual paths that have a common base in the *Vedas*—Hinduism's ancient scriptures. In fact, the culture and religion of India is neither monolithic nor divided into watertight compartments. Like America, but more so, it is a mix of many colors. Individual components can be distinguished, but, in a sense, the mixture always has been slowly stirring, blending, and receiving new inputs throughout history. As we now turn to that history, we also will be identifying distinct religious trends that have been stirred into the mixture known as Hinduism through the centuries. Let us begin with the ancient Aryans and their Vedic scriptures.

Major Influences on and Developments in Hinduism through Time

The Religion of the Ancient Aryans

The Indus Valley, in what is now Pakistan, was the scene of a remarkable civilization around 2500 to 1500 B.C.E. Two cities some 400 miles apart, Harappa and Mohenjo-Daro, together with some smaller towns and villages, constituted it. Each city was laid out on a grid plan, and the houses, although often identical and severely functional, were technologically advanced; the plumbing has been equaled only by that of the Romans and the modern world. The writing of this culture has not been deciphered, and many mysteries about it remain, not least its religion. The cities contained no obvious temples, though on high ground above each was a cloisterlike complex, with a pool perhaps used for ritual bathing, which may have been the stronghold of a powerful priestly order. Enigmatic religious motifs appear on many of the seals and small art objects that have been found; these suggest a mother goddess (as one would expect in a highly sedentary agricultural society like this), phallic gods, sacred bulls, and in one case a deity in perhaps a yogic meditation posture. Some scholars have theorized that the sides of Hinduism that center around Shiva and Shakti, bulls, the mother goddess, water ablutions, and yoga come out of indigenous cultures of the Indus Valley.[3]

But around 1500 B.C.E. a new people arose in India, and around this time the cities of the Indus Valley declined into ruins. Being simple nomads, the new people did not establish a comparable material culture for many centuries, although spiritually they brought a different but equally impressive religious complex that was to provide the formal foundation of intellectual Hinduism. These were the Aryans, cattle herders who have long been thought to have come out of central Asia across the famous Khyber Pass into the hot plains of India. Recently a few scholars have questioned the notion of an Aryan "invasion," suggesting instead that the Aryan peoples were long a part of, or identical with, the Indus Valley civilization. In any case, these peoples came to be known as Indo-Europeans, as they eventually populated Europe as well, and their Sanskrit language is related to Greek, Latin, Irish, German, and English. We have already seen cognates in our language, such as he word "car," to Sanskrit words, such as *karma*.

The Aryans in India are chiefly known as the people of the **Vedas**, the fundamental official scriptures of Hinduism. On their earliest level, they are dominated by the hymns and rituals of their priests. Their poetic style splendidly reflects freshness of vision, heroic virtues, and ritual precision. The oldest and most important of the Vedic scriptures is the *Rig Veda,* hymns to the gods sung while sacrifices were being presented. Parallel to it are sets of songs and chants for auxiliary groups of priests and of charms called the *Sama, Yajur,* and *Atharva Vedas,* respectively. These in turn have sets of commentaries called the *Brahmanas, Aranyakas* ("Books of the Forest Schools"), and **Upanishads**. They offer ritual instructions but also, over the centuries, present more and more philosophical reflection on the meaning of the rites. The *Vedas* were transmitted orally and not actually committed to writing until recent centuries.

The original gods of the Aryans were vital, flashing, brilliant beings of sky and storm. They dwelt in the three levels of the known cosmos—sky, atmosphere, earth—and those of the middle atmospheric level acted most vigorously.

The most popular deity was Indra, prototype of the Indo-European warrior and comparable to Thor (after whom Thursday is named) in European mythology. He wielded a thunderbolt and dwelt in the atmosphere, where the action is. He was accompanied by the Maruts, a boisterous band of warrior-companions who rode in chariots like the armies of ancient India. Every dawn was a victory for Indra. Abetted by the morning sacrifices of the priests, he and his Maruts would arise and defeat the demonic powers of darkness. Indra consumed countless cattle and, in preparation for heroic exploits, vast lakefuls of the sacred drink, Soma. Indeed, it was he who had originally found and taken Soma from high in the mountains. Indra slew the monster Vritra in mythical times but finally, as his age gave place to another, he was superseded by other gods closer to the heart of wisdom.

The *Vedas* speak of Dyaus—whose name is obviously cognate to the Latin *Deus* and Greek *Zeus*—as sky-father, but he is shadowy and remote, virtually a **deus otiosus**. Equally mysterious is the vague but profound-seeming figure of Aditi, light (or mind) beyond shadow or stain, and mother of the gods. Then there are two sky gods of somewhat more concrete personality, Varuna and Mitra, kingly figures whose main task is the upholding of *rita*, the cosmic laws. There are few female figures. And the ones that are referenced, like Aditi and Ushas (the Dawn), seem passive and indistinctly conceived although they are the subject of lovely hymns. It is as though the Vedic people thought naturally in the ways of the masculine world (unlike the Indus Valley with its fertility goddesses), and so the feminine appears as beautiful but rare.

In a sense, however, all the bright gods and goddesses of the *Vedas* are elusive; all are described interchangeably as shining and benevolent, and each is addressed in turn as though he or she were the only deity, until finally we come to wonder if there is just one god who bears a series of names and parts. Yet a tremendous vitality and sense of Divine force is at work in the *Vedas*. Nowhere is this paradox more apparent than in two further deities, Agni and Soma.

These are deities of the rituals. They are only barely personified but extremely important. Agni, whose name is cognate with the Latin *ignis* and the English "ignite," is fire. Fire is the crucial mystery in the cycle of conception and consumption that keeps life in process; all its transitions, from sex through eating to death (in which we are eaten in turn, whether by microbe, worm, or tiger) are various gradations of oxidation, that is, of fire. This lively magician of life and death is Agni, and he is the central actor in the drama of the sacrifice. On earth, it is said, he is fire; in the atmosphere, lightning; in the sky, the sun. Existing in principle in all strata, he is also the quick messenger of the gods; he bears prayer and sacrifice to them.

Soma is the sacred drink of power and immortality that the gods consumed, especially Indra, and that was also manufactured, offered, and consumed in the sacrifices. It has an exhilarating, empowering effect: Indra fortified himself with

HISTORY OF RELIGION IN INDIA

GENERAL HISTORICAL CONTEXT

End of Indus Valley
civilization

Consolidation of Indo-
European supremacy
in north

Kashi (Benares) prominent

Urban civilization
beginning in Ganges
basin

Invasion by Alexander 326
Mauryan Empire 321–185
Gupta Empire in N. 320–540
classic Hindu period

PERSONALITIES AND MOVEMENTS

The Buddha 536–483

Mahavira c. 540–468

First Buddhist Council
c. 480

Buddhism prestigious

Ashoka r. 273–232

SACRED LITERATURE

Rig Veda

Brahmanans

Early Upanishads

Buddhist Tripitaka
Later Upanishads

Heart Sutra and
other early
Mahayana
writings

Yoga Sutras

| 1500 B.C.E. | 1000 B.C.E. | 500 B.C.E. | 1 B.C.E./C.E. |

Small states, largely
Hindu

Delhi sultanate (Muslim) 1211–1398

Small states, many Muslim ruled
Mughul Empire 1526–c. 1765

18th century–1947
Independent India,
Pakistan 1947–
Bangladesh 1971–

Nagarjuna c. 150
Decline of Buddhism
in India
Rise of Bhakti
Growth of Hindu Tantrism
Shankara c. 8th century
and Advaita Vedanjta

Kabir 1440–1518
Nanak 1470–1540 fdr.
of Sikhs

Akbar r. 1556–1605

Ramakrishna 1836–1886

Ramanuja d. 1137 Gandhi 1869–1948

Laws of Manu

Bhagavad-Gita

Lotus Sutra and other
later Mahayana sutras

Puranas

Tantras

Guru Granth Sahib

500 C.E.   1000 C.E.   1500 C.E.   2000 C.E.

Soma for his battle with Vritra and on one occasion he felt frenzied, exalted, as though he had passed beyond earth and sky, and asked himself rhetorically if he had been drinking Soma. The **brahmins**, or priests, also sang:

> *We have drunk the Soma, we are become Immortals,*
> *We have arrived at the Light, we have found the Gods,*
> *What now can hostility do to us, what the malice of mortals,*
> *O immortal Soma!*

The question arises, what was Soma? The juice that is presently used in *brahmin* ceremonies under the same name does not produce any such effects. Many suggestions have been made. R. Gordon Wasson has argued that Soma was made from the fly agaric mushroom, a hallucinogenic plant still employed by shamans in central Asia to induce altered states of consciousness. He points out that the cryptic Vedic allusions to the plant from which Soma is made do not speak of root or leaf, and in other respects seem compatible with the mushroom. Wasson also suggests intriguingly that the reason the secret of the original Soma was lost is that the fly agaric only grows high above sea level; as the Aryans penetrated farther and farther into India, it was necessary to substitute for it.[4]

To understand Vedic thought, we must glance at what actually went on in the *brahmin* rites. The group of words related to *brahmin* appear to come from a root meaning a magical force or spell.[5] From the earliest times, shamans and wizards have employed words of power that encapsulate the essence of a god or line of force in the cosmos and so such words can be used to control that power or force. The *brahmins* used them in connection with their sacrificial rites. Just as through words of power and sacrifice the gods made the world, *brahmins* said, so by words and sacrifice the gods could themselves be controlled. Thus, the sacrifices controlled the gods, and the *brahmin* priests controlled the sacrifice, becoming like higher gods themselves.

It would be a great misconception to imagine these rites as being like a gorgeous ceremonial along the lines of a high mass or the processions and offerings of later devotional Hinduism. For while the *brahmin* rites required much preparation and many priests, outwardly they were quite plain. They were performed out of doors but often under a temporary shelter, in a quiet place with only the priests and the lay patron who was paying for them present. Three fire pits of different shapes—representing earth, atmosphere, and sky—and a grass-lined pit for preserving offerings and utensils were dug. Offerings of butter, vegetables, or flesh were placed into the fires; the plainest offering was just slowly pouring melted and strained butter (*ghee*) from two spoons into the fire. While the offerings were being presented, other priests would chant the proper hymns; sometimes still another would just stand in the center, meditating on the whole procedure, unifying it in his thought. Yet these relatively undramatic acts had to be done precisely right. The fuel and the fires were built with immense care as to detail and if a single syllable of the hymn was mispronounced or a single gesture wrong, the rite might be stopped and started all over again from the beginning. All was crisp, sharp, and exact. It had the atmosphere of a modern laboratory experiment.

Indeed, the Vedic rites were a sort of science; while the premises may have been different from ours, the old *brahmins* saw themselves less as enthusiastic lovers of their gods than as technicians making precise adjustments in the cosmic order to correct an imbalance or produce some desired result. For the sacrifice was nothing less than "making the world" and calling into life the gods who rule over it; the purpose then was to meditate on what the cosmos is like and to make adjustments in it in such a way as to keep it on course or direct its power in desired directions: prosperity, the inauguration of a king's reign, a son, long life, immortality in heaven.

It was as though a reducing lens had been held up to the cosmos. The sacrificial spread was a miniaturization of the universe as a whole, made much smaller and its processes correspondingly speeded up. The fire was the destruction and transmutation of material—food—through heat that keeps the universe going. The words of the chants, the **mantras**, or "thought-forms," were sounds whose "vibrations" were in tune with the gods and the subtle currents of reality itself. On this "laboratory" world the priests performed their delicate technical operations. The rites to keep the universe on course and to help humans were like making tiny adjustments in a tremendously huge and intricate machine—perhaps only turning a single screw a quarter of a turn. But a trained technician, who knows exactly what he is doing, can by such minute modifications make the difference between whether the machine works as desired or not. Or so the *brahmin* priests understood their ritual activities.

But as time went on, as the *brahmin* sages pondered over and over the meaning of the rites, new questions arose. They thought of the web of vibrations, which the mantras and the miniaturization process seem to suggest, as orchestrating the universe. The whole was like a magic web that held the universe of humans, gods, and substance together, "the thread stretched out on which these creatures are strung together" (*Atharva Veda* 10:8:37). Within even this was "the thread of the thread," the fundamental unity, subtle beyond all sight yet inextricably there, beneath the world's multiplicity—Brahman, originally the power of the *mantras* or sacred words that held the world in course. Upon this secret the *brahmin* priest, who supervised and by his thought unified the sacrifice, was to meditate.

Other questions concerned Agni, the sacred fire. Fire is at the center of the world and so of the sacrifices—but is it only the fire that burns visibly? What of the fire that burns within a person's own body—the fire of joy, of concentration, even of fever? Does this make the person also an altar, and a world?

In *brahminical* thinking, the sacrifices of their rites were, in effect, "interiorized." Tapas—interior heat—was generated by the real sacrifice, which was within one. And this interiorization of the sacrifice, in time, paved the way for philosophy and yoga.[6] Through the **asceticism** of fasting and concentration, one built up *tapas,* and this power could be used by the **adept** to bless or curse or to gain cosmic vision. For the person was now the cosmos; one replaced with oneself the cosmic sacrifice; all without was also within, the greater in the smaller and the smaller in the greater. This is the secret of the ***Upanishads,*** the last and most philosophical commentary of the *Vedas.*

The Upanishads

The *Vedas* called the *Upanishads* are a collection of texts that attempt through words to point its adherents to the inner or final meaning of things. These words would be imparted by a father or master to his most advanced pupils as the culminating stage of their learning. They are not for beginners, for until one has had enough experience of life or has matured enough to ask the right questions, the highest wisdom would be only empty sounds. Far from preaching it to everyone, the wise jealously preserved Upanishadic wisdom for those ready for it. The ten to sixteen principal Upanishadic treatises, composed in the centuries after 500 B.C.E., were not published or taught widely but were passed on orally in secret at the right times.

Thus, the *Chandogya* Upanishad tells of a *brahmin* father who sent his son to study in a forest school. When the son returned, full of pride in his Vedic scholarship, the father deflated his son's ego and increased his wisdom by telling him of a further knowledge, "that knowledge by which we hear the unhearable, by which we perceive the unperceivable, by which we know the unknowable."

This arcane knowledge was that, as different things made of clay or gold go by different names, yet are still clay or gold, so all things are One Existence under many names. At the beginning, this One Existence thought to himself, "Let me grow forth." "Thus out of [itself] it projected the universe; and having projected out of itself the universe, [it] entered into every being. All that is has [itself] in it alone. Of all things [it] is the subtle essence."

And the father adds the crucial words about the One to his son: That Art Thou.

Other analogies are used in this passage: One honey is made from nectar gathered by bees from many flowers; all rivers flow into one sea. The One Existent is the invisible essence of all things, like the "nothingness" at the heart of a seed of a giant tree. And after each example of the essence, the father repeats: That Art Thou.

This essence is Brahman. The great inner knowledge to which the wise ones of the Upanishads came is "Atman is Brahman." **Atman** is the innermost self, the "soul"; Brahman is the universal One Existent. "He is pure, he is the light of lights." All persons and all things are really Brahman, taking many shapes like fire taking the shape of every object it consumes or air taking the shape of every vessel it enters.

As the *Svetasvatara Upanishad* puts it beautifully:

O Brahman Supreme!
Formless art thou, and yet
(Though the reason none knows)
Thou bringest forth many forms;
Thou bringest them forth, and then
Withdrawest them to thyself.
Fill us with thoughts of thee!
Thou art the fire,
Thou art the sun,

Thou art the air,
Thou art the moon,
Thou art the starry firmament,
Thou art Brahman Supreme:
Thou art the waters—thou,
The creator of all!
Thou art woman, thou art man,
Thou art the youth, thou art the maiden,
Thou art the old man tottering with his staff;
Thou facest everywhere.
Thou art the dark butterfly,
Thou art the green parrot with red eyes,
Thou art the thundercloud, the seasons, the seas.
Without beginning art thou,
Beyond time, beyond space.
Thou art he from whom sprang
The three worlds.[7]

The movement from *Veda* to *Upanishad* is well expressed in the *Katha Upanishad*. It begins with the account of a young man named Nachiketa. Nachiketa's crusty old *brahmin* father presented a sacrifice of the Vedic sort in which he was supposed to offer all his possessions but was careful to present only old and scroungy cattle. The boy, shocked by this, told his father he also was one of his possessions and asked him to whom he would give his son. The irritated parent responded that he would give him to Yama, the ancient King of the Dead.

Nachiketa, taking this very seriously, proceeded to the home of this king, Death. Death was not at home, forcing Nachiketa to wait. When he returned, Death in compensation offered the sincere young brahmin three wishes, which he agreed to fulfill.

Om Symbol

The first two wishes were clearly rooted in the traditional Vedic world. Nachiketa asked that his father's anger would be appeased; this wish concerned the worldly social obligations of patriarchal society. Second, he asked to know the fire sacrifice that led to heaven, for as we have seen, the power of the sacrifice extends from this world to the next. But this was only a worldly matter, too, for life in the Vedic heavens extended only as long as the warping of cosmic energy by the rite lasted. Depending on one's skill and power, it might assure bliss for a very long time; but being just a matter of technical craft, it would ultimately wear down, for within the cosmos there is no such thing as perpetual motion or energy.

But the third question was a shift to another level of discourse. Nachiketa said, "When a man dies, there is this doubt: Some say, he is; others say, he is not. Taught by thee, I would know the truth. This is my third wish."

Understanding the thrust of the question, that Nachiketa is probing the fringes of an entire new spiritual world from that of the Vedic rites and might well be ready to enter it, Death parried with him. He went through the time-honored conventions of the master seeming to frustrate and discourage the novice in order to test him. He informed Nachiketa that the gods themselves find the answer hard to understand and urged him to select some other favor. He urged him to select sons, cattle, elephants, gold, a mighty kingdom, or celestial maidens so beautiful as not to be meant for mortals.

But Nachiketa stood fast, pointing out that these things are only grasped for a fleeting day, then vanish like smoke . . . in the process, they wear away the senses. How can one desire them, he asked Death, who has once seen Death's face? There is a secret of imperishability and immortality that is beyond them, he insisted, and would not yield till Death had imparted it.

Inwardly well pleased, Death confirmed that there is another secret, one that cannot really be taught at all, but can be caught from a true teacher by the student who is truly prepared: that the Self within is the imperishable, changeless Brahman, the One beyond and, at the same time, in all these forms and changes. The *mantra,* or sound, that expresses Brahman himself, and whose recitation can give rise to his consciousness, is "OM." The King of Death continues:

> *The Self, whose symbol is OM, is the omniscient Lord. He is not born. He does not die. He is neither cause nor effect. This Ancient One is unborn, imperishable, eternal: though the body be destroyed, he is not killed.*
>
> *If the slayer think that he slays, if the slain think that he is slain, neither of them knows the truth. The Self slays not, nor is he slain.*
>
> *Smaller than the smallest, greater than the greatest, this Self forever dwells within the hearts of all. When a man is free from desire, his mind and senses purified, he beholds the glory of the Self and is without sorrow.*
>
> *Though seated, he travels far; though at rest, he moves all things. Who but the purest of the pure can realize this Effulgent Being, who is joy and who is beyond joy.*
>
> *Formless is he, though inhabiting form. In the midst of the fleeting he abides forever. All-pervading and supreme is the Self. The wise man, knowing him in his true nature, transcends all grief.*
>
> *The Self is not known through study of the scriptures, nor through subtlety of the intellect, nor through much learning; but by him who longs for him is he known. Verily unto him does the Self reveal his true being.*
>
> *By learning, a man cannot know him, if he desist not from evil, if he control not his senses, if he quiet not his mind, and practice not meditation.*[8]

Brahman and Atman Diagram

The Self—Atman, who is really Brahman—is the only Being, the Sole Existent, the One Mind. He is everywhere yet indivisible. Brahman alone exists; all else floats insubstantial on the face of the shoreless ocean of his being, wisdom, and bliss, like reflections in an unstained mirror. Yet the ordinary consciousness grasps only the things and not Brahman, for the simple reason that Brahman is consciousness. In the same way, the eye cannot see itself or a pair of pliers grab itself. Brahman plays hide-and-seek with itself in the world, dwelling in the myriad things while elusive to human thought and dream. Why? None of us groping about in the world of the many can fully know, just as those inside a house can only know incompletely the whole plan and shape of the structure. They would have to step through the door and look at it from outside as well.

The sages of India tell us there are doors that the wise and intrepid can find. As the end of the above passage tells us, it is through meditation, that is, quieting the senses and the mind, that the door to the infinite dimension can be unlatched. For it is the play of the senses and the mind that turn one away from one's true nature—Brahman—to the phantasmagoria of many things to which feeling and thought attach themselves like leeches.

It is as though a play had been going on for a very long time—not weeks and weeks but countless years. It has been going on for so long that the actors have forgotten they are merely playing parts and have come to identify themselves with the parts. They think that when one actor murders another, the victim is really dead, and the red gore on the floor is not ketchup but real blood. They think that when two members of the cast fall in love or break up with tears and angry words, these are absolute and final realities of life, not just events woven into the web of a greater drama with higher purposes beyond their ken. So the show becomes so mad, with the actors' involvement and anxiety rising out of control, that the prompter behind the stage must send out messengers to remind them that it is only a play, to remind them who they really are.

This is like the Upanishadic view of the world. The messengers are like the great sages who remind us of how things really are; the *rishis,* or seers, who composed the *Vedas,* are the God-realized teachers who bring students into Brahman consciousness in all ages. But the difference is that in the Upanishadic vision there are not many actors but one actor—the One Mind—who is playing all the parts and is also the prompter. He who is playing the part of the one you love and also the one you hate and the stranger to whom you are indifferent is none other than the Self, of whom our outward-directed thoughts have been forgetful.

One other message from the *Upanishads:* The *Mandukya Upanishad* tells us that the Self, as consciousness, has three aspects—and beyond them, a fourth.

The first is the "ordinary waking consciousness." It is you or I walking down the street, perceiving other objects and people as outside of oneself, and thinking of oneself as separate from them, while enjoying the pleasures of the senses.

The second aspect is the mental nature turned upon itself, enjoying a mental world created within the head. It is the "dreaming state of consciousness" and, by extension, the worlds of imagination, fantasy, and the deep archetypes of the unconscious. The images that dance behind the curtains of the mind in this state derive from things remembered by the senses and so come from outside, and except in advanced yogic states they are more or less out of control—we cannot usually tell ourselves what to dream. Yet, although the second is not a divine state of consciousness but rather an inward turning of the first, it does have some similarity to Brahmanic consciousness; it is one mind growing a whole world of bright and transient forms, which do not exist elsewhere, out of itself.

The third aspect is the self in the state of "deep sleep without dreams." When all forms external and internal vanish into formlessness and mind and sense are still, like a windless lake in the midst of night, one enters the third state. Significantly, it is called the *prajna* state. **Prajna** means wisdom, not in the sense of factual knowledge about all sorts of things, which obviously would not apply, but that sharp, intuitive insight that simply knows, without the confusion of words or ideas from the world of the many. And what is known in this way, all that is known in this way, is Brahman.

In an important sense, then, the "deep-sleep-without-dreams state is closest of these three to Brahman-consciousness. A fundamental principle of Hindu and Buddhist philosophy is that all outward, particularized perceptions and concepts, such as one has in the waking state, are really limitations. If you are thinking about one thing or a thousand, there are still millions of things you are not thinking about; and the very things you are thinking about cut you off from them and so limit you. Only when this part of thought is quieted does the mind become like Brahman's—thinking of nothing in particular, and thus horizonless, infinite, in tune with the All. In deep sleep one is functioning just on the biological plane and so becomes an integrated part of the dance of the atoms and galaxies, without being cut off by any individualizing thoughts from this infinite play of Brahman.

This is really the fulfillment attained in the fourth state. For the *Mandukya Upanishad* tells us that the true Self, OM or AUM, is the unification of all three other states. It is the state of a person who walks through the world bearing the gifts of all three. That person has the fearlessness and sense of oneness of one at ease in our universe-home, or of one dead, or of Brahman. He has under control all the delights and occult powers of the inner dream world yet lives and works with acute capability in the outer world, for he knows things as they really are, down to their roots. In the vision of the *Upanishads,* such a person alone is a complete human being.

Spiritual Ferment and the Rise of Buddhism

The Upanishadic vision is the epitomizing expression of the classic lore of the most prestigious scholarly class, the brahmins. It enjoys a unique status and is accepted as authoritative, along with the rest of the Vedic literature, by all who consider themselves orthodox. But to think that it is the tool by which Hindu culture is to be interpreted, or that it plays a role in Hinduism exactly parallel to the Qu'ran in Islam or the Bible in Christianity, would be to oversimplify.

Although reference to the *Upanishads* greatly illuminates the mentality that underlies India's gods, art, and institutions, one who tried to understand what was happening in an average Hindu village temple or pilgrimage center solely on the basis of the *Upanishads* would be quickly at sea. It must be borne in mind that, through the centuries, the great majority of the people of India, illiterate and provincial, doubtless never heard much of the teaching of the *Vedas* directly. Indeed, as we have seen, these scriptures were considered unsuitable for any but advanced upper-caste students, and they were restricted until quite modern times. Chinks of their light must have reached the peasants through the lips of wandering holy men or veiled in myth or song, but the people would know them as treatises no more than they knew the Sanskrit language to which the Vedas were traditionally confined, unwritten but passed privately by rote from brahmin teacher to disciple.

So it was that the spiritual movement of India around the fifth century B.C.E., which produced the "interiorization of sacrifice" of the *Upanishads,* produced other equally important results. At the time the Upanishadic vision was crystallizing, much else was happening as well across the dusty face of India. Although the Indus Valley cities were shattered, much of the indigenous culture persisted, with its religious emphasis on fertility, the mother, purity, and (presumably) mystic states of consciousness attained by techniques of the yogic sort. Doubtless this heritage did much to influence the direction which the Upanishadic culmination of Vedism took. Not only did the Aryan thinkers in India move toward mystical **monism** rather than **monotheism**, as in Iran, but the doctrine of **reincarnation**, central to later Hinduism and Buddhism, appears first in the *Upanishads.* In the earlier *Vedas,* it is in very rudimentary form and can be supposed to be largely a contribution of the indigenous culture.

It was a time when the Aryan rulers were pressing across northern India and had established control virtually to the Ganges Delta. No great unified empire had as yet arisen, although the sub-Himalayan plain was a patchwork of Aryan kingdoms large and small. Material civilization was still scanty, but spiritual and philosophical cultures were vigorous and moving ahead rapidly.

Spiritual teachers strolled from village to village in the company of bands of disciples, even as do **sadhus**, or "holy men," in India today. Typically, they would walk in the morning, arriving at their destination by noon, when they would beg for food. In the afternoon they would rest and meditate; in the evening the townsfolk would gather around. The visitors—intriguing and the subject of much local talk because they came from "outside"—would pay for the hospitality they had been afforded with spiritual instruction, and doubtless also by telling news. The next day, unless a local magnate persuaded them to stay on as his guest, they would leave, possibly taking with them a local lad or two who had been impelled by a combined itch for adventure and hunger for higher things to leave home in the company of the peripatetic master.

Their teachings were wide-ranging and circumscribed by few dogmatic presuppositions, for these teachers were not *brahmins* defending the Vedic tradition, performing the sacrifices, and interpreting them now on Upanishadic lines. The *brahmins* were still mostly priests retained by courts or living in their own communities, hardly likely to go wandering among the common folk. But the new teachers, from other ranks of society, were looking for truth everywhere. One might be saying the world was created, another that it is eternal; one might be saying all is mind, another that there is nothing but matter.

One assumption that they shared in common, however, was that philosophical teaching was not to be merely abstract but was to aid in attaining a state of inner liberation. Each one should imply a spiritual path that could be tested empirically. Most advocated methods involving extremely rigorous self-denial and self-control.

Many wanderers are now forgotten; but two, Vardhamana, called Mahavira ("Great Hero"), c. 540–468 B.C.E., who was the founder of the Jain religion, which we shall look at in more detail later, and Siddhartha Gautama, of the Sakya clan and a contemporary of Mahavira, called the **Buddha** ("Enlightened One"), 563–483 B.C.E., are not. Both founded faiths that have persisted through twenty-five centuries; both have symbolized for many the highest conceivable human state; both have structured the lives and blessed the deaths of innumerable spiritual children through the ages. Moreover, both were of similar background; each was the son of a minor non-Aryan, indigenous ruler afforded more or less honorary warrior-caste status; each was considered by his followers to be the last of a great chain of mighty teachers. Indeed, similar legends are told about the nativity and life of both, so much so that scholars once wrongly concluded they were the same person going by different names in two different religions. They did, however, roam the Eastern Ganges River Valley contemporaneously.

Beyond this, however, their destinies differ, and far more so do the destinies of the two faiths. **Jainism**, profoundly Indian, has remained remarkably unchanged in teaching and practice through the ages, but at the price of remaining small and restricted to India. Buddhism has reached hundreds of times more adherents than Jainism, has spread over vast continental areas, has exfoliated into incredible diversities of sect and practice—and, again in contrast to Jainism, essentially died out in its homeland (although it has had something of a modern revival there) while spreading from Siberia to Ceylon, and from the Caspian Sea to China and Japan, not to mention its influence in the West.

While Mahavira taught a way of stern denial and control, the Buddha called his path the "Middle Way," for it was a spiritual tack of dwelling in the calm spot of equilibrium between all polarities, such as asceticism and indulgence, love of life and desire for death, even being and nonbeing. The Buddha, we are told, had been brought up in luxury and had tried the extremes of fasting and asceticism, but he came to see both sides as forms of egotism. It should not be supposed, however, that Buddhism is any sort of easy-going, moderation-in-all-things philosophy. To hit the exact spot of equilibrium where one is in precise balance with the universe and so has all power is no easy act of spiritual archery. It involves neutralizing all the outward and subtle desires that keep us shooting impulsively this way and that, scarcely seeing the target, much less hitting the bull's-eye.

Although the Buddha and Buddhism are discussed in detail in the next chapter, it is important here to place the inception of Buddhism in its historical time and place. Initially, Buddhism prospered in India, doubtless because of its close relation to the indigenous tradition and the moderation and attractiveness of its monks. They found favor in the homes of the mighty. In particular, the Buddhists won the support of the Emperor Ashoka (r.c. 273–232 B.C.E.), one of the noblest rulers of all time.

Ashoka unified northern India and then, under Buddhist influence, ceased to make war, proclaimed tolerance for all beliefs, and promulgated noninjury to life. He reportedly sent the first Buddhist missionaries outside India to Ceylon, Southeast Asia, and the West. While Ashoka was personally nonsectarian, supporting and

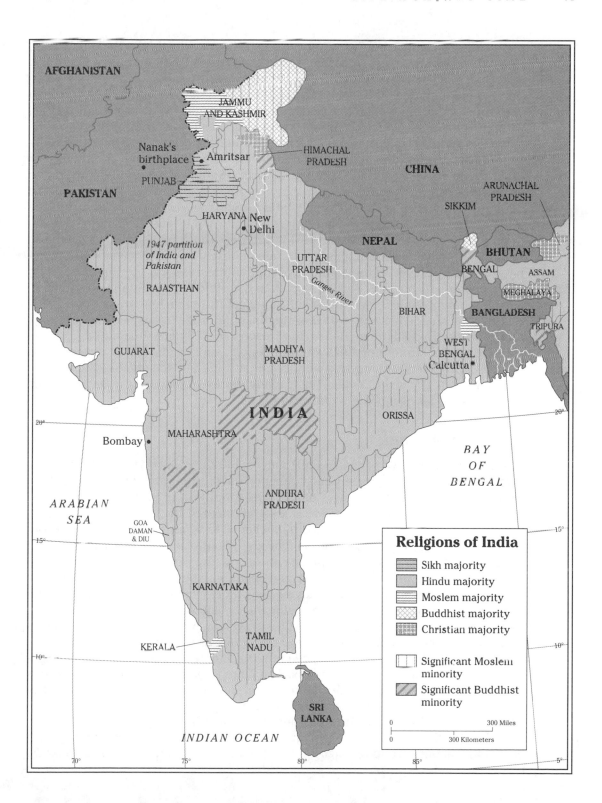

AFGHANISTAN

JAMMU
AND KASHMIR

Nanak's
birthplace • Amritsar

HIMACHAL
PRADESH

CHINA

PAKISTAN

ARUNACHAL
PRADESH

SIKKIM

PUNJAB

HARYANA New
• Delhi

NEPAL

*1947 partition
of India and
Pakistan*

UTTAR
PRADESH

BHUTAN

BENGAL

ASSAM

Ganges River

MEGHALAYA

RAJASTHAN

BIHAR

BANGLADESH

TRIPURA

GUJARAT

MADHYA
PRADESH

WEST
BENGAL
Calcutta •

INDIA

ORISSA

Bombay •

MAHARASHTRA

20°

20°

*BAY
OF
BENGAL*

*ARABIAN
SEA*

ANDHRA
PRADESH

GOA
DAMAN
& DIU

15°

15°

KARNATAKA

TAMIL
NADU

KERALA

10°

10°

SRI
LANKA

INDIAN OCEAN

70°   75°   80°   85°   5°

Religions of India

Sikh majority
Hindu majority
Moslem majority
Buddhist majority
Christian majority

Significant Moslem
minority

Significant Buddhist
minority

0   300 Miles
0   300 Kilometers

approving worthy teachers of whatever persuasion, evidently the Buddhists were closest to his heart. His patronage, extended by various later kings, gave Buddhism a prestige that it was to enjoy in India for several centuries.

To understand Buddhism it is helpful to realize that there is a sense in which one can say that Buddhism has seldom been *the* religion of a society, for it deals with personal liberation and not much with religion's role of legitimizing social institutions such as family and government. In countries where Buddhism is prominent, these legitimizing roles are often taken care of by other traditions, for example, in India by Hindu traditions. Nor is Buddhism intolerant of Hindu or other gods; it is glad to acknowledge them so long as they are seen as pupils of the Buddha, "teacher of gods and men." Rather, Buddhism is really the **samgha**, the order of Buddhist monks, dwelling within a society, but in a sense standing outside it, providing guidance for those ready for Buddha's teachings—quietly available.

Yet Hinduism and Buddhism were also consciously or unconsciously competitive in India. Even in the high tide of the Buddhist period, the Hindu tradition was providing responses and alternatives to the Buddha's way that would eventually help it supersede Buddhism in India itself, at the same time tremendously enriching and broadening the appeal of Hinduism in order to answer the questions raised by the Buddhist experience. But in so doing, Hinduism capitalized on the older religion's strong points as a total religious expression: Hindu concern was not only with liberation but also with the organization of society, the pluralism of spiritual paths and stages implicit in its many representations of the Divine. Let us now examine this new post-Buddhist Hinduism.[9]

The Laws of Manu

One Hindu response was the Laws of Manu (c. 100 C.E.), which were a systematization of the Hindu view of society and contained the teaching about the "Four Ends of Human Life" and the "Four Stages of Life," described earlier in the "Understanding Hinduism" section. The Laws of Manu also rationalized the caste system of India, which places one in the great social order believed to be prescribed by *dharma*. The Laws of Manu, therefore, speak of the four great divisions of society, called **varnas** (literally "colors")—*brahmins* or priest-scholars, *kshatriyas* or rulers and warriors, *vaishyas* or merchants and craftsmen, and *shudras* or peasants. It is said that they come from different parts of the body of the primal man: *brahmins* from the head, *kshatriyas* from the arms, *vaishyas* from the thighs, and *shudras* from the feet.

This pattern makes clear that the caste system, with all its attendant evils, is a product of Aryan dominance. The top three **varnas** are the original three Aryan social groups, the *shudras* are descendants of indigenous peasant peoples conquered and subjugated by the Aryans. The large population outside the four *varnas* altogether, popularly called *harijans* or untouchables—now about twenty percent of the whole and often living miserable lives even today—seem in large part descended from tribal groups brought into the Hindu system.

In all of this, the Laws of Manu are clearly trying to deal in a unified way with the two great but hard-to-reconcile poles of Hindu experience, *dharma* and *moksha* (or one's duty in society and liberation). So the two are seen as appropriate concerns for different stages of life, and through the caste system the social many is made manifestly compatible with oneness through the image of the great social organism, with each cell and organ playing its part, but some with much better roles than others.

FUNDAMENTAL FEATURES OF HINDUISM

THEORETICAL

Basic Worldview	The universe is profoundly one. Even though it goes through surface changes and cycles, its ultimate nature as expression of the divine does not change.
God or Ultimate Reality	Brahman, the one Mind or Life, is the one reality. It expresses itself in all that is like a flame taking many shapes.
Origin of the World/ Destiny of the World	The world goes through endless cycles of creation and destruction but has no real beginning or end.
Origin of Humans	Like the world, the individual has no known beginning. It goes through countless lifetimes, the nature of which is determined by karma.
Destiny of Humans	The series of lifetimes continues and may include episodes in heavens and hells. Finally, one transcends karma through God-realization.
Revelation or Mediation between the Ultimate and the Human	The Vedic scriptures; the brahmin priesthood; the gods and God-realized Saints as expressions of the One; following one's *guru* as spiritual guide.

PRACTICAL

What Is Expected of Humans; Worship, Practices, Behavior	To follow *dharma* through rituals, behavior, and righteous deeds. If one seeks *moksha,* or liberation, one would practice *yoga,* meditation, or devotion under the guidance of a guru.

SOCIOLOGICAL

Major Social Institutions	The caste system; temples as places of the worship of gods; holy men; the family; the brahmin priesthood.

The Yoga Sutras

What would one do during the course of seeking liberation? Can Hinduism compare with Buddhist meditation on this count? One important answer was given by yoga, which was synthesized in the *Yoga Sutras* of Patanjali (c. 300 C.E.)—another response to the rise of Buddhism in India.[10] Buddhism had emphasized introspective meditation, with analysis of sensation and consciousness; the *Yoga Sutras* returned to India's deeply biological, psychosomatic understanding of human nature as the background for liberation. Thus, **hatha-yoga**, the physical yoga of postures and breathing exercises, plays a major role in the spiritual quest. Rightly understood, breath and body are indispensable tools. Brought under control of spirit as precision instruments, they can facilitate states of consciousness that evoke the goals of spirit.

The goal of the *yogi,* the practitioner of yoga, is control of the modulations of the mind; in other words, *kaivalya,* "isolation," independence of the anxiety and limitations imposed by interaction with the changing world of sight and feeling and fantasy. This is done by getting the mind and body strictly under control by the exercises and then using this control to withdraw attention from the outer world, so that the inner light shines unimpeded.

According to the *Yoga Sutras,* the process is comprised of eight steps, called "limbs." The first two steps, *yama* and *niyama,* are positive and negative moral rules aimed at a life of quietness, gentleness, and purity, for one's manner of life must be prepared and purified before yoga can hope to succeed. Releasing yoga's potent spiritual forces into an unworthy vessel can, in fact, be most dangerous both to the individual and to society. Then come the two steps of *asana* (posture) and *pranayama* (breath control) in which the psychosomatic powers are lined up to move in the one direction of liberation.

After the *yogi* gains control of his or her own bodily and emotional house in this way, *pratyahara,* the stage of the disengagement of the senses and attention from outer things, becomes possible. This makes for acute inner, subtle ways of awareness. Just as a blind person develops especially sharp touch and hearing, so yoga tells us that when all the gross senses are withdrawn, other undreamed-of capabilities latent in the human being begin to stir. When they come to be mastered, the *yogi* has awareness of things near and far and the ability to use occult forces, beside which the ordinary senses and capacities are as an oxcart to a rocketship. The Yoga Sutras tell us how to read minds, walk on water, fly through the air, make oneself as tiny as an atom, and be impervious to hunger and thirst.

But these powers called *siddhis,* doubtless tempting to many, are to be given up for an even greater goal—true liberation of the true self. This is the work of the last three steps, which are interior: *dharmana,* concentration; *dhyana,* meditation; and **samadhi**, the absolutely equalized consciousness of perfect freedom.

The Bhagavad-Gita

Both of these responses to Buddhism—the way of society (Laws of Manu) and the way of the *yogi* —are brought together in the greatest Hindu statement of the period, the **Bhagavad-Gita**. Also composed somewhere around 100 C.E., it is really a section of the mighty epic called the *Mahabharata*, which has to do with a great war between cousins over the succession to the throne of an Aryan state. But the *Bhagavad-Gita,* or "Song of the Lord," can stand by itself once its setting is understood.

The *Bhagavad-Gita* tells the story of Prince Arjuna, whose charioteer is the heroic god **Krishna** in human form. Arjuna is setting out to lead his army into bloody battle against the foe. Appalled at what he is about to do, Arjuna pauses in deep moral distress. The book is a series of answers that Krishna gives the prince in answer to his irresolution. It discourses on why Arjuna can and must fight, but its implications go much further than this. The pacifist Mahatma Gandhi (to be discussed later) greatly treasured this book, taking it as an allegory of nonviolent struggle against injustice and for spiritual purity.

Krishna's first answer is along the lines of Upanishadic thought. He emphasizes that there is no reality behind the talk of life and death, killing and being killed:

> Some say this Atman   Unborn, undying,
> Is slain, and others   Never ceasing,
> Call It the slayer: Never beginning
> They know nothing.   Deathless, birthless,
> How can It slay. . .   Unchanging forever.
> Or who shall slay It?   How can It die
> Know this Atman. . .   The death of the body?[11]

But if it does not make any difference, the question could be asked: Why kill instead of not killing? This Krishna answers, in effect, "Because you are a *kshatriya,* a warrior, by birth and caste, and therefore fighting is your role in the drama of the universe; there is no honorable way you can shirk it, and right is on your side since the enemy has gone against *dharma.*"

Further questions arise. Does this mean, then, that one born a warrior has no hope for salvation comparable to that of the *brahmin* whose hands are unstained with blood and who enacts the mystic sacrifices? Does it mean that he whose place in society makes it almost mandatory that he stay in the world cannot compete with one who is able to become an **ascetic** or a yogi?

No, replies Krishna. It is all a matter of how one lives in the world. The object is to become one with the Absolute, so that nothing in one's thoughts or deeds causes separation. But if Brahman is truly All, the world of the activist is just as much God as that of the recluse. Brahman is expressed through *dharma* as much as *moksha* if it is truly All—in the caste laws and all of life's stages together. One can realize God in acting as much as in meditation, if one's actions are as selfless as meditation and as passionless. Thus, Krishna gives his second answer and teaches Arjuna the secret of *karma-yoga,* yoga in the midst of doing. The point is to be in the world impersonally, objectively—doing not out of personal desire for the fruits of one's actions but fearlessly and dispassionately, as it were by proxy for someone else, motivated solely by the duty and righteousness of the act. Then, with one's feelings not getting in the way, one's actions are a part of the great dance of the cosmos, of the life of the whole social and natural organism, and are as quiet and far-reaching as meditation.

> *You have the right to work, but for the work's sake only. You have no right to the fruits of work. Desire for the fruits of work must never be your motive in working. Never give way to laziness either.*
>
> *Perform every action with your heart fixed on the Supreme Lord. Renounce attachment to the fruits. Be even tempered in success and failure; for it is this evenness of temper which is meant by yoga.*
>
> *Work done with anxiety about results is far inferior to work done without such anxiety, in the calm of self-surrender. Seek refuge in the knowledge of Brahman. They who work selfishly for results are miserable.* [12]

Traditionally, *karma-yoga* was interpreted in a highly conservative way to mean that one must accept the role given by caste. Some modern Hindus, however, see it instead as a view that liberates one for bold and selfless acts of service to humankind, however risky, unpopular, or likely to fail—if one is acting out of impersonal righteousness, rather than for the gratification of pocket or ego, which do not matter.

A philosophy like this does not satisfy all the spiritual needs of most people. However noble it may be, by itself it has a quality of dry resignation that does not answer one's thirst to know God. Yet something like *karma-yoga* can be an invaluable preparation for what seems to be its opposite, a religion of deeply felt awe and love in the presence of God. Only the person whose ego-self is unobtrusive can truly know God in any case.

This reflects the spiritual progression of the *Bhagavad-Gita.* After the *Upanishadic* and *karma-yoga* stages, the dialogue moves more and more into a sense of a mystical presence.

> *Now I shall tell you*
> *That innermost secret:*
> *Which is nearer than knowing,*
> *Open vision*
> *Direct and instant.*
> *Understand this*
> *And be free for ever*
> *From birth and dying*
> *With all their evil.* [13]

Who burns with the bliss
And suffers the sorrow
Of every creature
Within his own heart,
Making his own
Each bliss and each sorrow:
Him I hold highest
Of all the yogis.[14]

Something else begins to arise in the tradition, a sense that the relationship of the individual and this mystical presence can be one of love, and that love is greater than success or failure in keeping the formal obligations of law and rite.

Great is that yogi who seeks to be with Brahman,
Greater than those who mortify the body,
Greater than the learned,
Greater than the doers of good works:
Therefore, Arjuna, become a yogi.
He gives me all his heart,
He worships me in faith and love:
That yogi, above every other,
I call my very own.[15]

The greatest spiritual explosion, however, is yet to come. Nearness and love, in place of philosophy and duty, lead to a radically different relationship between humankind and God, and one far more analogous to the relationship between people than between persons and natural law. Moving into this spiritual sphere, Arjuna culminates the discourse by asking to see Krishna in his full splendor and glory. Krishna obliges:

Then . . . Sri Krishna, Master of all yogis, revealed to Arjuna his transcendent, divine form, speaking from innumerable mouths, seeing with a myriad eyes, of many marvelous aspects, adorned with countless divine ornaments, brandishing all kinds of heavenly weapons, wearing celestial garlands and the raiment of paradise, anointed with perfumes of heavenly fragrance, full of revelations, resplendent, boundless, of ubiquitous regard.

Suppose a thousand suns should rise together into the sky: such is the glory of the Shape of Infinite God.

Then the son of Pandu [Arjuna] beheld the entire universe, in all its multitudinous diversity, lodged as one being within the body of the God of gods.

Then was Arjuna, that lord of mighty riches, overcome with wonder. His hair stood erect. He bowed low before God in adoration, and clasped his hands, and spoke.

Arjuna:

> *Ah, my God, I see all gods within your body;*
> *Each in his degree, the multitude of creatures;*
> *See Lord Brahma throned upon the lotus;*
> *See all the sages, and the holy serpents.*
> *Universal Form, I see you without limit,*
> *Infinite of arms, eyes, mouths, and bellies—*
> *See, and find no end, midst, or beginning.*
> *Crowned with diadems, you wield the mace and discus,*
> *Shining every way—the eyes shrink from your splendour*
> *Brilliant like the sun; like fire, blazing, boundless.*
> *You are all we know, supreme, beyond man's measure,*
> *This world's sure-set plinth and refuge never shaken,*
> *Guardian of eternal law, life's Soul undying,*
> *Birthless, deathless; yours the strength titanic,*
> *Million-armed, the sun and moon your eyeballs,*
> *Fiery-faced, you blast the world to ashes.*[16]

Here Arjuna sees Krishna (as **Vishnu**, to be discussed later), brighter than a thousand suns, express through endless multiplicity the same infinity that can also be expressed as the One, Brahman. God is here represented by the myriad things, and among them he is as an enthroned sovereign. But God as infinite series or infinite multiplicity also brings out the dark side of God: infinite series expressed through time as well as space; and in time all things perish, so God appears as destroyer—"By me these men are slain already," Krishna says a little later of Arjuna's foes. Hence, this vision too is a justification of Arjuna's fighting, and of much more as well. Yet God as personal being, with whom one can have a relationship of knowledge and love, and who moreover comes among people as friend and brother like Krishna, engenders a new spiritual sensitivity too.

Advaita Vedanta

The tradition of Hindu philosophy that has generally been most prestigious in India and is best known outside that country is **Vedanta**. The word literally means "the end (i.e., culmination) of the *Vedas*"; the school essentially centers itself on the teaching of the *Upanishads,* the last and most philosophic of the *Vedas,* concerning Brahman as one with Atman and as the Sole Existent. Other texts, such as the earlier *Vedas* and the *Bhagavad-Gita,* are interpreted in this light.

The most influential school of Vedanta among intellectuals, however, has been **Advaita Vedanta**, which may be rendered "nondualism in the Vedic tradition." Its leading exponent was Shankara (?700–732 C.E.), who argued forcefully and uncompromisingly for radical oneness in a universe of apparent manyness. Commenting on the *Upanishads,* Shankara brought home in metaphysical language its intuition that there is only one reality, Brahman. Only Brahman exists; all else—every idea, form, and experience—is "superimposed" on Brahman owing to our *avidya,* ignorance of the true nature of reality. What we see ordinarily is **maya**, often translated "illusion," but illusion that has to be understood in the right sense, for *maya* is an appearance of Brahman and so is not unreal. The world is really there; it is not on a level with the pink elephants of the proverbial drunk. But it is *maya* when the world is not seen for what it is. Shankara liked to use the simile of a man who saw something lying on the ground and jumped, thinking it was a snake; he looked again and saw it was only a piece of rope. In the same way, we really see something when we see the world, but we misapprehend what it is we see; we think it is really many separate things, when actually it is but one "thing," Brahman.

Shankara's influence on the practical side of Hinduism was comparable to his philosophical influence. He reformed and promoted **monasticism**, establishing four great monastic centers of learning in the quarters of India. He tried to modify the harshness of caste distinction and encouraged devotion to the Hindu gods as aspects of the One. In all this, although he would not admit it was a goal, he was establishing Hindu parallels to the intellectual monasticism, subtle nondualist philosophy, and conditional devotion to Buddhas and bodhisattvas of Buddhism.[17]

Tantrism

Another movement starting in these centuries cut across both Hinduism and Buddhism and deeply affected the course of both. It is the complex and mysterious set of spiritual attitudes and practices called **Tantrism**—a road to enlightenment through powerful initiations, "shock therapy" techniques, the negation of conventional morals and manners, magical-seeming acts and chants, and the use of sexual imagery and ritual. Tantrism seeks through radical means to induce powerful consciousness-transforming experience, while preserving something of the technical aura of the old Vedic rites.

One reason why Tantrism's origins and teachings are so hard to trace is that it has often attracted persons in reaction against the current religious establishment of *brahmins,* princely rulers, and Buddhist monks. Tantrism presented itself to people who were marginalized in society as a secret, underground path far more potent than the official teaching, if one were bold enough to reject conventionality by accepting it. If the adept, it says, do not shrink back or go mad at its "steep path," then, in a single lifetime, Tantrism can bring them to a state of realization and power that would take countless lifetimes by ordinary means.

Roughly, the procedures of Tantra are this: The novice is initiated into the practice of a particular Tantric path by a *guru* (spiritual teacher); this impartation of power is said often to be physically felt and is extremely important. Being empowered, the aspirant then seeks identity with a deity like Shiva or Kali (a manifestation of Shakti) through magical evocations of the god's visible presence, visual fixation on diagrams (**mandala** and **yantra**) of his or her powers, and recitation of *mantra* that encapsulate his or her nature. By becoming one with the divinity, the aspirant hopes to share the divinity's cosmic realization and omnipotence.

In this process, the Tantrist seeks to experience the totality, the unity beyond all opposites. To do this, one may liberate oneself from "partiality" by getting outside of structure—living independent of caste and morality. In some Tantric traditions, "forbidden" things—such as meat, alcohol, and sex outside of the social conventions of marriage and caste—are partaken of, either symbolically or actually, in specific rites. The male Tantrist identifies himself with a male deity like Shiva, the absolute, and his female partner with Shakti, who is the phenomenal universe; as the Tantric couple unites, they mystically unite the absolute and the universe in a flash of ecstasy. Thus, sexuality, in particular, is important to Tantrism, not only because of the "shock therapy" effect of sexual rites, but also because it is a tremendous evoker of energy (which the skilled practitioner can then sublimate to the spiritual quest), and a symbol and sacrament of the Tantrist view of reality.

But the rite cannot do this sacramentally, nor can moral reversal be spiritually efficacious, nor the sexual energies transmuted to spiritual realization, until the novice is well advanced in a tantric *sadhana,* or path. Unless one has truly negated self and identified with the god, sex is merely lust and not participation in Divine mysteries.

Tantrism had an influence far beyond the schools that taught it in its strictest form. All Hindu worship on a serious level is now likely to show some influence of Tantra, if only in the use of *yantra* and the repetition of the name of a deity and *mantram* over and over. It has also had a substantial impact on Indian art.

The important concepts of **kundalini** and the **chakras** come out of the Tantric tradition, although they are represented today in most yoga. They are an interiorization of the Shiva/Shakti dynamic. The *kundalini,* or "serpent power," is a feminine energy believed to dwell, coiled three and a half times, below the base of the spine. Through *yogic* techniques of posture, breathing, and concentration, the *kundalini* is awakened and aroused to be drawn up the spinal column. In the process it "opens" seven *chakras,* "circles," or lotus-centers of dormant psychic energy located along the spinal column at the base of the spine, lower abdomen, solar plexis, heart, throat, and forehead ("third eye"), culminating in the *sahasrara* or thousand-petaled lotus at the top of the head.

This, together with the withdrawal of senses from the outer world incumbent upon yogic practice, is said to produce remarkable states of awareness. The final objective, however, is only achieved when the *kundalini* reaches the inside of the skull where, with a psychic explosion at the crown *chakra,* it awakens a thousand-petal lotus that grants cosmic consciousness and God-realization. The awakening brings into the light an entire world within the head, replete with its own miniature mountain, lake, sun, and moon, and in its midst Shiva is enthroned.[18]

Devotional Hinduism

The early Middle Ages were times of realization of both the social and devotional promise of the Hindu reactions to Buddhism. In the process, Hinduism became a system integrating all the population of India into a loosely knit organism providing for a multitude of spiritual drives and social needs. New tribes and peoples throughout the land were brought into the system by being recognized as branches of major castes; thus thousands of subcastes, or *jati,* were created. The folk-gods of all these people were recognized as representations, or aspects, of one of the great gods of Hinduism—which by now owed as much or more to the indigenous traditions as to the *Vedas*. To these gods, devotion, the service of a loving heart, weighed more than legal righteousness, caste, or ritual.

Accounts of these gods, their myths and words and methods of worship, are presented in books called **Puranas,** deriving from the early Middle Ages. The devotional gods, some many-armed or animal-headed, rejoice in colorful images and pictures; they enjoy lavish temples and dramatic processions. It is this Hinduism that most moves the average Indian and is most conspicuous to today's tourist.

In Hinduism, **devotionalism** is the spiritual path of **bhakti**—the way to liberation or *moksha* through losing one's egocentricity in love for the chosen god. Love is, for most people, the human drive in which one most readily forgets (if only now and then) self-centeredness. In these moments, one's feelings go outside of one's self to share in the subjective life of another human being through caring and empathy. Why not, then, *bhaktists* say, utilize this drive to propel the ultimate quest, for loss of self in the Divine? Through the love of gods, whom one can visualize and adore, but who are themselves not separate from the absolute, one shares their nonseparateness, for one becomes what one loves.

Nondevotional Hinduism may take very austere forms In the case of renunciants who "interiorize" It all and worship without priest or temple. But it has never entertained much the Puritan idea that there is something virtuous about making ordinary worship drab. Rather, India (outside Buddhism) tends to feel that genuineness is found at extremes; whatever path a person takes, it should be taken all the way, with the abandon of the mystic. **Ascetics** may starve their eyes and ears as they starve their bellies, striving to find God in the all by negating God in any particular form. The *bhakta,* the devotionalist, goes the other way and characteristically follows that path without restraint, using particular gods as stepping-stones to love of the All. This is the Hinduism of the temple, where nothing is spared of lights, music, flowers, jewels, pomp, incense, and offerings to create an atmosphere of kingship (God as king), love, and heavenly delight, which takes the worshipper out of the ordinary and into the transforming circle of the sacred. Images of the god may be sheathed in gems worth a royal ransom; on festivals the bejeweled deities may be taken through the streets on festooned elephants or giant chariots.

The greatest theologian of *bhakti* was Ramanuja (born C.E. 1017). Although trained in Shankara's nondualist Vedanta, Ramanuja was of strong religious bent and a devotee of Vishnu. He criticized Shankara's system as being both inconsistent and spiritually unsatisfying. If everything is Brahman, he argued, but this is not known because of *avidya*, ignorance, then this would mean that the ignorance lies in Brahman himself. Better to postulate a different model for the relation of universe and God than veiled identity—an organic model in which God is like the head and the cosmos the body, the two inseparable and interacting but having distinct modes of life. In this theistic system, God is personal and loving. Souls, in lifetime after lifetime, can respond to his love and grace, and by purifying themselves through bhaktic worship, draw near to him until they gain blissful eternity with him in a paradisal heaven. Through highly sophisticated philosophical argument, Ramanuja defended the religion of the love of a personal god, which was and is the faith of the great majority of his countrymen.

The devotional gods are best thought of as belonging to two families—the Vishnu family and the Shiva family. The difference can be thought of in this way: Vishnu and his religious system are somewhat like the Western concept of God, in that the masculine figures are heroic and dominant and the feminine figures rather demure; Vishnu as God represents not so much the cosmic totality as the forces on behalf of order or righteousness. He descends from highest heaven in incarnate form whenever righteousness declines, working to restore good in the world. Krishna of the *Bhagavad-Gita* is one such descent of Vishnu.

In the Shiva system, God is, above all, simply the Absolute, and so the union of all opposites—creation and destruction, male and female. Shiva and Shakti thus have equal prominence, and she is far from unassertive. But although they may appear in visions, they are not usually claimed to be born incarnate among humans. Shiva is like the Brahman of the *Upanishads* personified.

The Vishnu Family of Devotional Gods.   Vishnu, it is said, slept over the cosmic ocean on a great serpent made up of the remains of the last universe before this one was formed; time is immense cycles of Divine sleep and waking. When it came time for the cosmos to be made again, a lotus grew out of Vishnu's navel, and on the lotus appeared Brahma, the creator god (not to be confused with Brahman). Brahma defeated the imps of chaos and fabricated the world. Then Vishnu uprose, seated himself in high heaven on a lotus throne with his consort goddesses Lakshmi (Fortune) and Bhu-Devi (the Earth). The serpent arched his hoods over the divine sovereign to make a canopy; the lesser gods attended him.

But as time progresses, the set moral order of the world—*dharma*—declines and the power of demons grows. To counteract the latter, Vishnu periodically enters the world in bodily form; these are called his **avataras** (descents or **incarnations**). The most popular list gives ten: as a fish, a tortoise, a boar, a man-lion, a dwarf, Parasurama (a brahmin hero), Rama, Krishna, Buddha, and Kalkin, who is the incarnation yet to come.

The most important are Rama and Krishna. Rama is the hero of the Ramayana, a great epic very popular among all classes in India and Southeast Asia. It relates that Rama was a prince of the ancient city of Ayodhya but, owing to intrigue, was wrongly exiled from court. His brother and his faithful wife, Sita, accompanied him as he went to live a simple life deep in the forest. But Sita was abducted by the demon Ravana and carried off to his palace in Lanka (Ceylon). Assisted by a monkey-army, especially the mighty monkey-hero Hanuman, Rama waged war against Ravana and prevailed. He received back his wife, was reconciled to his father, and finally presided over a long reign of peace and paradisal prosperity. This was not, however, until after he had considered it necessary to send Sita away because many people thought she may have been unfaithful to him while with Ravana. She finally called on the Earth-goddess to take her if she were pure. This the Earth-goddess did, appearing on a golden throne, embracing Sita and disappearing with her.

While Rama does not seem to have been considered Divine at first, and his devotion did not become really popular until fairly recent times, he is now firmly established as an incarnation of Vishnu. He remains, however, essentially God as supreme human ideal: gentle, brave, devoted. Sita, regarded as an incarnation of Lakshmi (Vishnu's consort), is the supreme model of the traditional Hindu wife, utterly pure and loyal. Hanuman's loyalty is also extolled; in North India his shrines are quite common, and in some cases he is shown with his breast torn open to reveal Rama and Sita reigning in his heart.

Krishna's languid poses, his impudent charm, his effortless omnipotence fascinate India because they are like the beguiling paradoxes of God. He is God himself, and when he came to earth long ago to counter the decline of righteousness, he brought with him the whole sensuous and rapturous ambience of his highest heaven—slow rivers; gemlike flowers cascading everywhere; the frolics of the *gopis,* or milkmaids, who eternally love him—all under a moon as big as one remembered from a childhood summer evening.

His name means "The Dark One," and much of his worship, especially the agricultural and erotic elements, derives from the culture of the darker indigenous peoples. His commonest title is Govinda, popularly regarded as meaning "Cowherd" or "Cow-finder." Because of attempts of the king, Kansa, to kill him, Krishna was brought up by a plain cowherd family. The homely tales of his youth are full of milk, butter, and the warm smells of cattle barns. In this simple and relatively innocent world, Krishna is delightfully naughty and much beloved.

Krishna appears in three basic modes: the marvelous infant, the Divine lover, and the great hero of the *Bhagavad-Gita*.

As an adorable but mischievous infant Krishna was given to transcendent pranks. He once ate some dirt, and when his irritated mother opened his mouth to check on it, she saw there the entire universe. He once stole some butter, but when his exasperated mother sought to tie him up in punishment, no matter how much rope she used, it was never quite enough.

Legs flexed and eyes half-closed, Krishna, as divine lover, would sound his flute deep in the woods, and the *gopis* (milkmaids) burning with intermingled human and divine love, would leave their legitimate husbands and dash into the forest of delights to revel with the young god. For the devotees of Krishna agreed with the troubadours of the Age of Chivalry in the West that extramarital love is a closer simile for the love of the worshipper for God than the nuptial tie, since the former is a passion freely given for the beloved's sake with no heed for the cost in shame and suffering, while the latter was (in old India and medieval Europe) probably a legal bond arranged in childhood by the families without regard for the individual's feelings.

Deep in the forest, Krishna would dance with the *gopis,* miraculously multiplying himself so that each would think she alone was his partner. Or he would hide himself and make the *gopis* seek for him—pining, that the celebration might be all the greater when he was found. Or he would steal the devotees' clothes

Brahma

while they were bathing in the river, to have them show their pure trust by emerging naked. In all this Krishna was as capricious and infatuating as a coy lover, for God also seems capable of playing cruel tricks on humans; yet we, like the *gopis*, continue to run after God, accept his changing moods, and feel something in us lifeless till we have once danced in abandon with him.

The *Srimad Bhagavatam*, the classic text of the life of Krishna that beautifully combines luminous simplicity with hints of the Divine profundity beneath its surface, tells us:

> *Sri Krishna is the embodiment of love. Love is divine, and is expressed in many forms. To Yasoda his foster-mother, the God of Love was her own baby Krishna; to the shepherd boys, Krishna was their beloved friend and playmate; and to the shepherd girls, Krishna was their beloved friend, lover, and companion.*
>
> *When Sri Krishna played on his flute, the shepherd girls forgot everything; unconscious even of their own bodies, they ran to him, drawn by his great love. Once Krishna, to test their devotion to him, said to them, "O ye pure ones, your duties must be first to your husbands and children. Go back to your homes and live in their service. You need not come to me. For if you only meditate on me, you will gain salvation." But the shepherd girls replied, "O thou cruel lover, we desire to serve only thee! Thou knowest the scriptural truths, and thou dost advise us to serve our husbands and children. So let it be; we shall abide by thy teaching. Since thou art in all, and art all, by serving thee we shall serve them also."*
>
> *Krishna, who gives delight to all and who is blissful in his own being, divided himself into as many Krishnas as there were shepherd girls, and danced and played with them. Each girl felt the divine presence and divine love of Sri Krishna. Each felt herself the most blessed. Each one's love for Sri Krishna was so absorbing that she felt herself one with Krishna—nay, knew herself to be Krishna.*
>
> *Truly has it been said that those who meditate on the divine love of Sri Krishna, and upon the sweet relationship between him and the shepherd girls, become free from lust and from sensuality.*[19]

This is the very heart of Krishna *bhakti* devotion—this loss of self in the Divine through the rapture of passionate love, until oneself, others, and the whole world become Krishna. His favorite among the milkmaids was the lovely Radha, whose image often stands beside his. However, he could not continue forever on earth—although he does in his heavenly world—in these pastimes of a divine youth. The time came for him to take up arms, slay the wicked king Kansa, take over his and later another kingdom, and work against the forces of evil. He slew demons all over India, took part (as we have seen) in the great battle of the *Mahabharata,* during which he delivered the *Bhagavad-Gita.* He was a worthy and magnificent ruler. Rukmini, a princess of Berar, became his chief queen among 16,000 wives, and he had 180,000 sons.

This happy estate, however, was not to last. In a scenario reminiscent of European mythology but oddly unique in India, Krishna's chief men fell into a drunken brawl and soon had the whole capital city in a tumult. Krishna's brother, chief son, and best friends were all slain in the rioting. Unable to stop this disintegration into chaos, Krishna left to wander dejectedly alone in the woods. There a hunter accidentally killed him as he sat meditating. Like Achilles, his heel was his only vulnerable spot, and there an arrow struck. He then returned to his eternal spiritual world.

Krishna's story, then, begins with a Divine Infancy, flight, and murder of innocents, reminiscent of Christianity, and ends on a note more suggestive of Greek tragedy or some bleak Nordic myth than mystic India. But, in between, the aura of Divine mystery about the pranks of infancy and the dalliance of love evokes the warm maternalism and poetic passions of India.

Above all, in the worship of Krishna, devotees lose themselves in graceful dance and chanting to exciting music. Women place images of the infant Krishna in tiny cribs and, calling themselves "mothers of the god," rock him back and forth as an expression of love. In devotional services, images of Krishna and Radha are often put together on the swing the bride and groom share in Hindu weddings, and are rocked back and forth. Always, the motive is put in terms of casting aside self-restraint and just asking, "What more can I do to show my love? What more can I do to please the beloved god, to make myself his indulgent mother, lover, or companion?"[20]

Devotion to Vishnu and Krishna takes equally expressive form. *Vaisnavas,* devotees of Vishnu or one of his forms, tend to be vegetarian, and flesh offerings are not used in their worship, only plant and dairy products. Some mark themselves with a V-shaped symbol on the forehead and perhaps upper arm.

The Shiva/Shakti Family of Devotional Gods.   The Shiva/Shakti family has a different feel about it. Instead of sunny Vishnu and playful Krishna, here is a fierce ascetic crowned with the mysterious moon, or a wild dancer whose hair is serpents, or one whose presence is simply the heavy stony pillar of the *lingam.* Rama was allied to an army of monkeys, but Shiva is companioned by a retinue of ghosts, and instead of the decorous Lakshmi or the charming Radha, his consort is Shakti who may manifest as the grim Kali, with bulging eyes and tongue hanging out to lap the blood of her victims.

Yet the Shiva/Shakti family are also deities of immense power, mystic depth, and ultimate goodness. The difference is that while the Vishnu family, like the Western monotheistic God, represents in the Divine all that is good, the Shiva/Shakti family represents simply the All, the totality, the union that lies beyond all dualities of matter and spirit, creation and destruction—their "goodness" is in the wisdom that comes from initiation into this ultimate unity.[21]

Shiva is descended from the deity of the *Vedas* named Rudra. A cross-grained god who lived off to himself in the mountains and who sang and danced in his solitude, Rudra could capriciously bestow healing herbs or send an epidemic. Worshippers called him Shiva ("Auspicious One") more in fearful hope than trusting love, for his lonely power was great. Shiva seems then to have assimilated much of the mystic and yogic divinity of non-Aryan religion. By the latest of the *Upanishads,* he already is the All—and, indeed, to those who lack the eye of wisdom, the universe itself does seem to sing and dance like a mountain madman with more zest than moral precision.

Shiva, serpent-entwined, is a much more enigmatic figure than Vishnu; one is less sure how to read his subtle, ambivalent smile. His four most important representations are as the Lord of the Dance, the Master Yogi, the Ultimate Teacher, and the Lingam. As Lord of the Dance, he dances with perfect equilibrium and pounds his drum down through all the changes of the world until the time comes for an age of the world to end; he then beats the drum louder and louder until its vibrations shatter the cosmos into its primal elements.

As the Master Yogi, he is seated high in the Himalayas, on skull-faced Mount Kailas, his body covered with the white ash that is a symbol of the ascetic's burning away of passion. He is seated on a tiger-skin pallet; his symbol, the trident staff, is in place beside him; the holy Ganges River leaps off the topknot of his long matted hair. He is sunk deep in meditation, and his concentrated thought is what sustains the world; if he were to cease his meditation for even a moment, the world would begin to vanish like a dream and leave not a trace behind. The story is told, in fact, that once his wife, Parvati, came up behind him and playfully put her hands

Dancing Shiva or "Auspicious One" representing the Absolute Being as "Lord of the Dance."

over her husband's eyes—but removed them in a hurry when she saw the mountains and forests fade and the sun and stars start to blink out.

Or as the cosmic Being, the sheer life-force and sole reality that underlies all that is, Shiva can be simplified and abstracted still further, to the still upright column of the *lingam* . . . the pivot on which the wheel of the universe turns or the phallus of an unquenchable will to live.

As Shiva represents absolute Being, Shakti (or Power) is the whole of the phenomenal world, in all its bounty, danger, and change, forever wedded to the Absolute. She is thus a being of fierce splendor and power, equal to Shiva just as in an even deeper sense the two are one. She is the fullness of the Eternal Female Divine, the Great Mother and Mistress in all her moods, and she goes by countless names.

As Parvati, she is the world at rosy dawn, nature at its gentlest and loveliest. As Annapurna, she is the bountiful mother, the goddess of food and abundant harvest. But as Durga, the coloration shifts a bit; Durga is good, for she slew a mighty demon, but the Great Goddess in this form is more chancy-looking: she proudly rides a lion and wields a great sword.

Finally, in the form of Kali, she is also good and the object of the devotion of mild and wise saints. But she is good in a dark way that only the wise can understand—for on the face of it she is time and death. She bears a sword and carries the severed head of a victim said to be a demon, killed out of mercy lest his bad *karma* become too weighty. Her tongue hangs out; around her waist are the arms of other victims, and their severed heads are garlanded around her neck. She is dark, often standing or dancing on the prostrate white body of Shiva, the passive Absolute whose being she draws upon. She is worshipped with offerings of male goats slain in her temples and in the past was presented with human sacrifice.

Kali standing on Shiva from whom she draws energy.

All of this expresses that Kali is the phenomenal world of time, change, and multiplicity. In it, all that comes into being is sooner or later destroyed. So it is said that Kali will give birth to a child, fondle it at her breast, and then wring its neck. The ways of Kali are not pleasant to contemplate, and one may wonder why such a goddess would be worshipped. Although the deities of other traditions, including the Western, also have their dark sides, India is unrivaled in exuberance of expression of both the light and dark colors of the sacred.

But there are those who say that until Kali is fully understood and loved, one cannot truly find peace or know God, for peace and God are beyond the vicissitudes of creation and destruction, and one must confront them and pass through them first. They say Kali is standing there with her blood and her victims, and one cannot simply go around her; one day a person on the way to liberation must face her squarely, if not embrace her.

Devotees of Shiva, called *Shaivites,* live austere lives. They cover themselves with white ash to symbolize the ascetic burning away of the passions, and they wear three white horizontal bars across the forehead as a symbol of the god to whom they ae devoted. Devotees of Shakti (as Kali), called *Shaktas,* focus on the worship of the Great Mother. Forgetting Shiva, *Shaktas* hold that in Kali alone is the power of the universe and the wellspring of bliss.[22] And, as we have seen, in Tantric practices Shiva and Shakti are worshipped together in a unique way.

Devotionalism in the Meeting of Hinduism and Islam

Another style of devotionalism emerged at the very end of the Middle Ages on the spiritual frontier between Hinduism and Islam. The faith of Muhammad was then coming into India in force together with Muslim rulers. Eventually as many as a fifth of the people of India—the present populations of Pakistan and Bangladesh, plus a scattered minority in the Republic of India—became Muslim, drawn by Islam's practical advantages, the greater simplicity of this faith without image or caste, and the attractiveness of many of its Sufi preachers and mystics.

However, the majority of Hindus, especially those of higher caste, remained Hindu and indeed became very conservative about it. The meeting of two cultures alien to each other, like Islam and Hinduism, produces two kinds of reaction. Some, generally the great majority, will respond with a conservative withdrawal into their own culture or faith. Especially if also politically subjugated, they will say, "They can take everything else from me; they will not take my faith," and they cling to it all the more tenaciously and inflexibly. The ultratraditionalism for which Hindu society was famous until recently—rigid adherence to caste, rite, and the authority of past models of life and relationships of the people—was not so much the heritage of the great creative periods of ancient India as it was a response, understandable in context, to the more recent centuries of Muslim and British rule, when it was the only possible vehicle for a Hindu sense of identity.

For others, the confrontation of faiths effects a different reaction. These are sensitive souls who say, "If one faith claims one truth and another a different truth, then is not everything we have taken for granted thrown into question? Perhaps reality is instead a truth beyond them both." There are some, from the great Mughul emperor Akbar (r. 1556–1605) to lowly weavers and washerwomen, who out of this situation were driven to adore a God beyond all particular places and rigidities of orthodoxy. The wandering ecstatic of a God in all persons and places, who is loved in a *bhaktic* way, became a new and attractive style of pilgrim. A good example is the poet Kabir (1440–1518). Alluding to the Kaaba in Mecca, the center of Muslim devotion, and Mount Kailas in Tibet, venerated as the abode of Shiva and a place of Hindu pilgrimage, he sings:

> *O servant, where dost thou seek Me?*
> *Lo! I am beside thee.*
> *I am neither in temple nor in mosque: I am neither in Kaaba nor in Kailash:*
> *Neither am I in rites and ceremonies, nor in Yoga and renunciation.*
> *If thou art a true seeker, thou shalt at once see Me; thou shalt meet Me in a moment of time.*
> *Kabir says, "O Sadhu! God is the breath of all breath."*
> *It is needless to ask of a saint the caste to which he belongs;*
> *For the priest, the warrior, the tradesman, and all the thirty-six castes, alike are seeking*
>   *for God.*
> *It is but folly to ask what the caste of a saint may be;*
> *The barber has sought God, the washerwoman, and the carpenter . . .*

Hindus and Moslems alike have achieved that End, where remains no mark of
*   distinction.*
If God be within the mosque, then to whom does this world belong?
If Ram be within the image which you find upon your pilgrimage, then who is there to
*   know what happens without?*
Hari is in the East: Allah is in the West Look within your heart, there you will find both
*   Karim and Ram;*
All the men and women of the world are His living forms.
Kabir is the child of Allah and of Ram: He is my Guru, He is my Pir.[23]

A comparable mystic poet was Nanak, founder of the Sikh religion, which today numbers some 8 million. Nanak (1470–1540) had, like Kabir, strong ties to both the Muslim and Hindu traditions. He had an ordinary upbringing and marriage, but when he was about 30 he left his family to heed a call to the renunciant life. Then, when he was about 50, a decisive special vision was granted him. God above and beyond human places and faiths came to him, Nanak said, and pledged him to worship and teach faith in his Divine Name.

The god of this revelation was neither the god exclusively of Islam or Hinduism but the one all-powerful, loving God who is above them both, who makes no unfavorable distinctions among humanity as to creed or caste but rather looks into the heart. He may be called by any name—Brahma, Rama, Hari, or Allah—so long as the worshipper recognizes that he is not limited to any of them. Sikhs love, above all, just to call the Lord *Sat Nam,* the True or Absolute Name. The repetition of his name is itself true devotion and equal to any pilgrimage to Mecca or Benares—in submission to it lies freedom. Here we see a fruitful combination of the fervent, loving devotion to one God of *bhaktic* Hinduism with the strong concept of submission to a personal and sovereign God, found in Islam.

Nanak spent a number of years, surrounded by disciples, as an itinerant poet and minstrel of this God. Here is one of his most expressive poems:

Those who believe in power,
Sing of His power;
Others chant of His gifts
As His messages and emblems;
Some sing of His greatness,
And His gracious acts;
Some sing of His wisdom
Hard to understand;
Some sing of Him as the fashioner of the body,
Destroying what He has fashioned;
Others praise Him for taking away life
And restoring it anew.
Some proclaim His Existence
To be far, desperately far, from us;

Others sing of Him
As here and there a Presence
Meeting us face to face.
To sing truly of the transcendent Lord
Would exhaust all vocabularies, all human powers of expression,
Myriads have sung of Him in innumerable strains.
His gifts to us flow in such plenitude
That man wearies of receiving what God bestows;
Age on unending age, man lives on His bounty;
Carefree, O Nanak, the Glorious Lord smiles.[24]

Nanak believed he had been called to serve as the guru, or teacher, of this faith in the true God. After him, a succession of nine more gurus bore his authority. Following the tenth and last, the Holy Granth, the Sikh scripture comprised of poems of Nanak, Kabir, and others took the place of a living teacher. The story of how **Sikhism** became inevitably another religion, instead of a faith beyond all religion, is a colorful and fascinating one. It will be told later.

The Practice of Hinduism Today

The long past we have looked at is still present in India. Much has been poured into the melting pot of Indian culture over the centuries and millenia, but little (except Buddhism) has been lost. The earliest continues alongside the latest. As jet planes whine over modern Delhi or Bombay, *brahmin* priests still chant the Vedas and prepare the ancient fire rites. Hindu worship and social expression, while capable of change, move at a slower rate than intellectual or historical forces. Let us look at some of these phenomena.

In a devout Indian household, especially of the upper castes, the day begins early. It is understandable that dawn should seem the most apt time for worship in India. Not only is it natural that one should turn to God at the beginning of a day's activities, but the Indian dawn has a special quality. Except in winter, the day soon enough becomes wearisomely hot, muggy, or dusty. But for a short time, just before and during sunrise, it is as though an enchantment had fallen over the ancient land. The air is limpid, fresh, and inviting; dew gems the grass; all is as still and hopeful as the deep meditation of Shiva just before a new world streams forth from his thoughts. At this hour, the head of the household arises, splashes himself with water, and going out on his porch or rooftop says the Gayatri mantram, the morning hymn to the sun. He may place on his body sacred marks, indicating the deity of which he is a devotee, who represents his "chosen ideal."

He then proceeds to the household shrine of the chosen deity. There he presents morning worship: He ritually chants praise and mantra of the deity, presents cups of water, washes the image, and offers food cooked by his wife. He may also study and meditate. If the household can afford it, the rites may be performed by a retained *brahmin;* otherwise, they must be done by the head of the household.

The household, in fact, is the real center of Hinduism, although, of course, its religious life is rarely seen by the foreign visitor, unlike that of the spectacular temples. But many devout Hindus never go to public temple. They express their faith through home customs and rites. To follow the home rites of one's caste and lineage is expected for social standing, at least in such matters as coming-of-age and marriage; worship at the temple is much more a matter of personal preference.

In the upper castes, there are **samskaras**, or sacraments, that mark the stages of life for boys, and would be marked by appropriate family ceremonies with a *brahmin* officiating: the child's birth, first eating of solid food, first haircut, and his attainment of manhood, when he is invested with the sacred cord.

Weddings

No occasion is greater in Hindu family life than a wedding. For a woman, it is the decisive event in her life. She has no separate sacramental initiations; her marriage is the great initiation that sets up her spiritual framework. After marriage, it is with and through her husband that she formally worships the patron of the household—although women also worship in the temples with other women. The wife does not present formal offerings at the household shrine, but prepares the offerings the husband presents, and in a deeper sense worships, in her husband, the god of whom her husband is family priest, since priest and god become identified.

A Hindu marriage is a long, exhausting ceremony lasting several days. There are offerings, formal meetings of the two families and of the bride and groom (who if they are of very traditional families would not have seen each other prior to the wedding day). There are vivid rites, such as the bride and groom sitting together on a swing and later binding their hands to each other, as the groom says, "I am heaven, thou art earth."

Funerals

Funerals, on the other hand, are not generally performed by *brahmins,* at least not by those of high status. Although a member of a class of funeral priests may officiate, the chief functionary at a funeral of a man is the deceased's eldest son, who lights his father's funeral pyre, and when the skull becomes red hot cracks it with a stick. Bodies are brought from all over India to the banks of the Ganges, especially at Benares, to be burned; the ashes are thrown into the sacred river. Even if it is not possible to bring the body to Benares, the ashes may later be brought to that site.

All these rites suggest some of the great themes of Indian thought and point to both unities and tensions in Indian culture. The funeral fire reminds us of the Vedic sacrificial fire and tells us that death is but another stage in the cycle of conception and consumption through which the sacred fire dances. The sacramental structure of life and the role of the eldest son suggest the organic, biological view of life of which we have also spoken.

Caste

Another usage that suggests the biological view of life is the caste system. Caste presents its own paradox: On the one hand, it suggests the organic unity of life, while on the other, a desire for symbols of separateness with each group in its own place, not eating or mating outside a small unit. Although the ancient classification of society had only four great orders, the practical division of modern society is into thousands of *jati,* literally "births," with their own caste rules. They range from various types of *brahmins* through bankers, silversmiths, and farmers down to the "untouchables," to whose lot falls tasks such as sweeping, washing, and tanning hides.

The real principle of division is not occupation, as many think, but commensality—who can cook food for whom, who can eat with whom, and by extension, who can marry whom, or, for that matter, who can even come near whom without pollution. It is a question of relative purity and impurity. One is made impure by contact with a member of a lower caste—sharing water or food, being touched by the lower one's spittle. These contacts would require ritual purification. A basic principle is that products of the body pollute; thus barbers and washermen, handling hair and grime from human bodies, are low on the caste scale.

Caste has been legally abolished in modern India, though attitudes based on it remain in many places.

Devout Hindus bathing in the sacred river, the Ganges.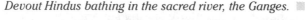

Water and Cows

So far we have dealt with aspects of the organic, *dharma* side of Hindu life—birth, marriage, death, caste. But even here, since caste itself is founded on a sense of the pure versus the impure, we get a glimmer of that basic thinking in terms of dualisms or polarities that carry up to the distinction of *dharma* and *moksha*. The *moksha* possibility is exemplified in other highly visible aspects of Hindu society: the holy man and the temple. But some things are simply pure and purifying in themselves; they stand as symbols of transition, on the borderline between the realm of *dharma* and that of *moksha,* and probably go back to days before the dichotomy of the two levels went beyond thinking of the impure and the pure. Two examples are water and the sacred cow.

Water has great symbolic and spiritual power in India as a purifier and as a transformative medium. There is a tank of fresh water near every temple that is not by a stream, river, or ocean. The main places of pilgrimage, like Benares, are near rivers or the sea. The Ganges, flowing past Benares, is the most sacred water of all, streaming from the head of Shiva, and Hindus in the millions throng to it to bathe.

An unforgettable sight confronting every traveler to India is that of innumerable white humpbacked cows wandering freely about streets, marketplaces, and all but the busiest sections of cities. The gentle-eyed beasts, often no better fed than the masses of Indians but safe from slaughter, frustrate one as their slow ambling holds up traffic. But they are as much a part of India as the dust itself. The sensitive observer may see in their warm and much-beloved frames, which appear in the most unlikely places, a different concept of the relation of human and animal from the Western, one of living together rather than of superiority of human over beast. The cows all belong to someone, to whom they supply milk and dung for fuel and plaster, but they seem also a public symbol, which indeed they are. They suggest the warm maternalism that India adores. Mohandas Gandhi, with his keen, non-Western perception, once remarked that the cow is really the most universal Hindu symbol, and cow protection its most expressive principle. Hindus, he said, may agree on nothing else, but they unite on the veneration and protection of the cow, a token of maternity, simplicity, nonmaterialism, and nonviolence. The products of the cow—its milk, urine, and even dung—are purifying and used in purificatory rites.

Sadhus

Visible reminders of the *moksha* side of things are the numerous *sadhus,* the holy men of India. Virtually every Hindu village and homestead may from time to time have strange, yet familiar, visitors. They may be sons from the house or village or from far away, but they will no longer be bound by family ties or have any claim other than charity upon the support of anyone.

The *sadhu* has in principle cut himself loose from society to be free for the greatest of quests. For what he represents—even if personally unworthy—he is welcomed and fed, his blessing sought and his curse feared. *Sadhus* have no centralized discipline like that of Western monastics, although most do acknowledge the absolute authority of their own *guru,* or in a few cases of an order. A *sadhu* may in turn establish his own "family," for disciples may join him, and devout lay people may seek him out and become his spiritual pupils. To these, the *sadhu* becomes formally a *guru*; he initiates them into his method, be it Vedantic, Tantric, or devotional. He takes on the burden of the disciples' karma and becomes their means of grace; followers worship the "lotus feet" of their *guru*. As the means to God for them, he becomes their personification and presence of God.

The way of life among *sadhus* varies greatly. Some wander as of old from village to village, teaching and begging. Some frequent temples and pilgrimage sites, where they seek alms and instruct in the appropriate devotions. Many are childlike, jovial spirits, going in merry bands from festival to festival. Others are unspeaking recluses deep in the woods, known only to a few who supply their meager needs. Some are charlatans, some are crazed, some are wise and learned, and some are true saints. Some were born to the holy life and have really followed no other. Some were prominent in business or civic affairs and only made the renunciation late in life. Some are devotees of Vishnu, wearing the V-shaped marks; others wear the three bars of Shiva and cover themselves with white ash. Traditionally, the ochre robe is the token of asceticism; some wear it, while others wear rags or nothing at all. Some shave their heads; others wear hair and beard as long and matted as old vines. But all are part of the pageant of Hinduism and are venerated by traditional Hindus. Insofar as they are God-realized, they are God, for they have become transparent to the God within, who is as much God as God anywhere. God is believed to be nowhere more present and visible than in Great Souls: To venerate them is to venerate God. Their diversity, and the strangeness of some of them, only bespeaks the mystery and infinity of the Divine Sea, whose waves crest in its lovers.

Temples

The temple, through the medium of art and architecture rather than of a human life, also bespeaks the Divine. Even as one approaches it, one senses the approach of another kind of realm. Here are lively people approaching in festive mood, and here are special shops selling flowers for offerings. The temple may be alive with monkeys and birds, with sacred cows grazing on the lawn, but it is also a throne room, and a brilliant image of the deity or a *lingam* and *yoni* stands toward the back. The arrangement and schedule of the temple are those of a king in his court, and the sanctuary containing the main Divine image is called the *garbha* or womb. The deity is awakened in the early morning with conch trumpets, given his meals with regal ceremony, and presented entertainments of music and dance. There is even a siesta at midday when the curtains about his throne are closed. At regular hours he holds court; then his subjects come with their gifts, most commonly wreaths of flowers, which are handed to a priest, naked from the waist up, who takes them and tosses them over the image. The priest receives a token payment and often bestows a blessing on the worshipper by placing a touch of color on the forehead.

The interior of the temple is splendid and colorful, suggesting the heavenly delights of the pure realms of the gods, who in turn shatter like prisms the clear light of the Absolute into these gay colors. The gods too suggest that beyond mere purity is the playful delight of the Divine, rolling out world after world. This warm and vivid atmosphere, of a piece with India's rain and sun, remains deeply impressed on a visitor long afterward.

The Western church is usually dead but for cut flowers, and it is tightly sealed against all nonhuman life. But through feast, sacrifice, or offering, the throbbing and dying life of the universe flows in and out of the Hindu temple like a vast tide of monkeys, cows, birds, flowers, and fruit. Indeed, the temples themselves, with their knobby unconventional shapes, seem almost more botanical than architectural. Like Hindu society itself, they grow out of the soil of India like prodigious plants, reaching away from nature yet still linked to its maternal arteries.

Modern Hinduism

A Clash of Values—East and West

Hinduism has undergone slow changes in modern times, as it has all through its long history. Just as the meetings of Aryan and indigenous cultures, and of Hinduism and Islam, were earlier problems, so the basic problem of thinking Hindus in the nineteenth and twentieth centuries has been the meeting of Hindu and Western values. How can the ancient faith respond to Western science, education, democracy, and the economic and social dislocations they bring? How does Hinduism fit in among the religions of the world? Dealing with questions like these while living in two worlds at once has led Hindu intellectuals to produce a fascinating array of new philosophical and spiritual options, some of which have had considerable influence in the West.

One great influence was Ramakrishna (1836–1886). Not an intellectual himself, this Bengali was in many ways a traditional Indian saint and mystic, deeply devoted to Kali, the Great Mother, able to go into deep ecstatic trance, profoundly aware of God in all things. Yet he was also aware of modern religious pluralism, and after experiencing from within several religious traditions, including Islam and Christianity, to his own satisfaction, he taught that all religions are of the same essence and are paths to God-realization. Disciples of his, particularly Swami Vivekananda (1862–1902), brought his message to the West. In his writings and in the work of the Ramakrishna Order, Vivekananda did much to make Vedantic Hinduism and the mysticism of Ramakrishna an intellectually vigorous and compassionate faith relevant to the modern world both in India and the West.

Mohandas K. Gandhi, Indian Independence, and Its Aftermath

Undoubtedly the most significant of all modern Hindus is Mohandas K. Gandhi (1869–1948), who led the movement for Indian independence through "truth force." Gandhi drew the theory behind his nonviolent resistance by noncooperation, demonstrations, and fasting from yoga and Jainism's **ahimsa** (harmlessness) and the *Bhagavad-Gita's karma-yoga.*

In the life of Gandhi, we see the Indian religious tradition working once again to weave together in a new pattern the two realms where it has seen and known the one God—the social order and the infinite within the self.

He was the son of a politician and a deeply religious mother. Though Hindu, he was raised in a part of India where Jainism was influential, and he studied law in England, where he also came in touch with the Christian "Sermon on the Mount" and the *Bhagavad-Gita* of his own religion. Upon his return to India, he met with little success in his practice of law until 1893, when he undertook to represent a Muslim firm in South Africa. He stayed there until 1915, increasingly involved in struggles with his countrymen against racial prejudice and discrimination in that country. Upon his return to India, he took up the cause of India's independence from Britain.

Gandhi became convinced that this was a spiritual as well as a political struggle. He opposed abuses within Hinduism, such as caste-discrimination and particularly ill-treatment of women and the "untouchables," or *harijan*—"children of God" as he called them, as much as he opposed foreign rule. Ancient Indian values, he asserted, were superior to European, but they needed to be affirmed through spiritual self-purification. This he called *satyagraha,* "holding to Truth." It was the basis of his well-known methods of "fighting"—by fasting, by nonviolent demonstrations, and by selected acts of deliberate disobedience of laws believed to be unjustly imposed or enforced. On other levels, by his simple, ascetic living, including strict vegetarianism, and the self-reliance shown by his famous spinning wheel, and by wearing only homemade cloth (which also was an afront to British manufacturing), Gandhi set an example of inner, spiritual freedom alongside political and economic emancipation. Moreover, he showed they were related; India could be truly free only if it lived simply and self-reliantly enough to eschew outside entanglements. And its people could fight in Gandhi's way effectively only if they were inwardly purified by such ascetic means, together with meditation and the practice of compassion to all beings.

Nonviolent combat is the supreme form of struggle, Gandhi taught, because it is equally accessible to everyone, rich or poor, strong or weak, male or female, and above all because it recognizes the truth of the Divine within one's opponent as well as within oneself—honors it by doing its physical vessel no harm and by appealing to its moral sense. With this principle Gandhi and his followers confronted the apparent might of the British Empire, marching to the sea to make salt in defiance of a government monopoly and lying down on the tracks in front of troop trains. Gandhi himself fasted on several occasions until he got his way. Rather than let him die on their hands or permit India to become totally ungovernable, the British rulers made many concessions to Gandhi and Indian self-rule, until, in 1947, weary from the World War II and India's incessant demands, London granted the former dependency complete freedom.

Gandhi and his followers not only achieved their political goal, they also successfully demonstrated a new method of political activism. The Hindu politician/saint profoundly influenced Martin Luther King, Jr., in the United States; land reformers in India like Gandhi's disciple Vinoba Bhave; and many others. At the same time, he showed the continuing vitality and adaptability of the ancient Hindu religion.

Tragically and ironically, however, independence initially brought great suffering to India. The country was partitioned between two states, the predominantly Hindu India and the Islamic state of Pakistan. The resulting bitterness between the two faiths, especially as people on the wrong side of the new borders tried to make their way to the other or were driven out, produced terrible riots and many deaths. Gandhi, who had opposed partition and who had always tried to care for Muslims as well as Hindus and enlist their support, was deeply saddened. He fasted for the sake of peace with some success. Then, early in 1948, he was assassinated by a Hindu extremist who thought he had gone too far in making concessions to the Muslims.

India has now been independent for over half a century. During this time religion has generally flourished, despite some inroads from **secularization**. However, Hindu–Muslim conflict has continued, culminating in 1992 with a dispute over a mosque in the ancient city of Ayodhya, reportedly the capital of Lord Rama, the god and king of the *Ramayana*. Hindus claimed that this mosque had been built on the site of a temple marking Rama's birthplace and wanted the site back. The movement to regain it, obviously laden with social and political symbolism, became militant and led to the destruction of the edifice in December 1992 by tens of thousands of Hindus. Today the events of 1992 remain a source of considerable animosity and continued violence. This has been exacerbated by the rise of Hindu nationalism in India and a corresponding intolerance in many quarters toward India's largest minority, despite the efforts of some otherwise, as well as Islamic resurgence around the world, which has emboldened Muslims in India, as it has elsewhere.

There was also conflict between Sikhs and the central government; Prime Minister Indira Gandhi (no relation to Mohandas K. Gandhi) was assassinated in 1984 by two of her Sikh bodyguards, following government suppression of a Sikh uprising that included government troops storming the Golden Temple in Amritsar, Sikhism's holiest shrine. Today, although Sikhs are a minority in India as a whole, they remain the majority in the state of Punjab at approximately sixty-five percent of the population. There considerable tensions remain as Sikhs continue to strive for political power.

But religion in contemporary India is not solely a matter of contention. India remains famous as the land of saints and wise spiritual teachers, of spectacular temples and colorful religious festivals, and of millions whose lives are lived in awareness of God in many forms.

Women in Hinduism

Sources of Classical Hindu Ideals of Womanhood

The earliest Vedic scripture, the *Rig Veda,* establishes the family as the central component of the socio-religious structure of Hinduism. Consequently, although the society was patriarchal and patrilineal, women held an important position in the social structure as wives and mothers. Because home was the center of religious worship and the gods were understood to bless the family as a collective, women were considered a necessary presence in rituals. High-caste women experienced relative freedom in comparison with their counterparts in later periods with respect to marriage, divorce, remarriage, and education.[25]

Later, however, the *Brahmana* texts reveal a shift in the religious orientation of the Vedic peoples, which was to have a profound effect on the status of women in the society. Religious rites became complicated, and the knowledge required to conduct them gave rise to specialists. As a consequence, religious education became a growing necessity. Education became the province of men, while women remained focused on the home. The result was a visible disparity in the education of women and men and a greater separation in their social roles.

Women's participation in religious rites declined, and certain social trends resulted that were to become problematic for women as such trends became exaggerated in later periods. For example, young women were married to older men. Women were deemed eligible for marriage soon after puberty—at 15 or 16 years old—while men needed to complete their studies, which could take up to 16 years.[26] Significantly, the status of *brahmin* men was tied to education and related abilities. Because women were denied this education, their status was lowered, and this resulted in their denigration in writings by men. Such attitudes were no doubt internalized by the women themselves. At the same time, however, women were permitted a derivative status by producing sons who would be educated and, therefore, qualified to perform rites for the family.

The ascetic ideal developed with the writing of the *Aranyakas* and the *Upanishads* and its ultimate focus of Hindu life as the realization of the One—Brahman. **Asceticism**, an option foreclosed to women, brought a further attitudinal shift toward them. Women were perceived by ascetics as an impediment on the road to liberation. "Many misogynist passages in the texts can be traced to the perspective of an ascetic-in-the-making who stereotyped women as temptresses before he had conquered his passions so that he was truly indifferent to the world." Even the order of Shankara, the great nondualist master of *Advaita Vendanta,* was open only to men, and it represented the feminine principle only as *maya,* which you will recall is the way the universe is seen by the ignorant.[27]

Attitudes toward women shifted with social change, and so did the doctrinal authority of the religion. While one may find favorable passages regarding women in the Hindu texts, generally they express an extremely negative stance, proclaiming that women are pervaded with countless vices and faults.[28] In addition, authoritative works memorialized the subordination of women. You may recall the four stages of the ideal Hindu life set forth in the Laws of Manu (c. 100 C.E.): student, householder, forest dweller or hermit, and renunciant. It is interesting to note that this ideal was the province of men, and only one of the stages—householder—relates men's lives to women's. On the other hand, women's lives were centered completely on and subordinated to men's. Most important, women's lives were oriented toward marriage. As a consequence, their stages of life revolved around this concern: maidenhood (eligible for marriage), wifehood (the married life), and widowhood (having been married).[29] Moreover, the Laws of Manu dictated the standards that were to govern women's lives for nearly two millennia:

> *In childhood a female must be subject to her father, in youth to her husband, when her lord is dead to her sons: a woman must never be independent. . . .*
>
> *Though destitute of virtue, or seeking pleasure (elsewhere), or devoid of good qualities, (yet) a husband must be constantly worshipped as a god by a faithful wife. . . .*[30]
>
> *Day and night, women must be kept in dependency by the males (of) their (families), and if they attach themselves to sensual enjoyments, they must be kept under one's control. . . .*
>
> *Through their passion for men, through their mutable temper, through their natural heartlessness, they become disloyal towards their husbands, however carefully they are guarded in this (world).*
>
> *Knowing their disposition, which the Lord of creatures laid in them at the creation, to be such, (every) man should most strenuously exert himself to guard them.*[31]

It is clear, then, that there was a perceived need to control women, in particular their sexuality. Many have speculated as to how this may have developed. One theory relates back to the Goddess Shakti—the universal power, both creative and destructive, from which all things derive. Just as Shakti became Parvati, devoted wife of Shiva, so women should be transformed. In other words, through the stabilizing force of Shiva, the unbounded Shakti power would produce a structured universe, otherwise "if the goddess were not controlled by her male consort, her energy would go to excess and produce chaos."[32] This model became a model for male control of women, who were perceived by men to embody Shakti, which must be controlled. Another theory is that any perceived threat to ethnic purity results in the subjugation of women to male control. This may result from warfare or occupation by an outside authority or merely the desire of the patriarchal head of the household to ensure that the children of the marriage are his own. Here one finds a possible source for the feminine ideal of purity, chastity, and unflinching loyalty.

All these various influences in some combination gave rise to the classical Hindu ideal of womanhood. She is married with at least one son and preferably more. She is chaste, humble, and devoted to the point of self-sacrifice for the welfare of the family, in particular her husband, as was exemplified in the myth of Sita who followed her husband, Rama, into exile and steadfastly defended her chastity. The ideal Hindu wife bathes, sleeps, and even eats only after her husband. She is uneducated (this fact having become a status symbol among those of the higher castes), and she is to contribute to three of the four goals of life of her husband. She is to provide pleasure (*kama*) by providing sexual pleasure and contributing aesthetic richness by maximizing personal desirability in appearance and manner, as well as beauty in the home. The husband's gain (*artha*) is advanced by providing him with sons who add to the auspiciousness of the home by their achievements and who also are able to perform the funerary rites that ensure safe passage for their father into the next life. The wife also contributes to righteousness (*dharma*) by generally fulfilling her duties in her role as wife, including fasting, making vows and sacrifices to the gods for the well-being of the family, and exhibiting all of the characteristics of the ideal Hindu wife. In this way, she participates in upholding the social and cosmic order.[33] Because a woman was oriented to the this-worldly aspects of her husband's life, her own highest goal was to fulfill her role as wife so as to be considered a good woman, who had gained sufficiently good *karma* by attending to her husband as a god so that she would be reborn as a man in the next life. Only then would she be eligible for the ultimate goal of Hinduism—*moksha*.

The Subordination of the Ideal Hindu Wife in the Classical Period

Classical attitudes toward women dictated the shape of women's lives at that time and resulted in a series of religio-cultural practices that came under severe attack in the nineteenth century both inside and outside India. One such practice was child marriage. Initially, the age of marriage was linked to puberty, perhaps to ensure virginity in marriage. By the time of the Laws of Manu (c. 100 C.E.), however, it had become the practice to marry girls as children, sometimes no more than five years old.[34] Presumably this was to limit a girl's social context extremely so as to guarantee her sole devotion to her husband. In some cases, however, physical injury from sexual relations at too early an age resulted in deformities in adult life.[35] Even if this did not occur, it was common for a young woman of 15 to have many children, which restricted and shortened her life.

Other practices came into vogue that severely limited women's lives and led to abuses. One such practice, which became popular in the North where there had been considerable Muslim influence, was **purdah**. This was the practice of confining the wife to the home, thus isolating her from society. Another much criticized practice, for which there is considerable evidence of abuse, is the custom of the bride's family providing a dowry to the family of the groom. There have been cases where a man has married and collected several dowries, each of the wives having died under mysterious circumstances, referred to commonly as "kitchen accidents." Furthermore, the dowry is a considerable financial burden on a girl's family, while at

Worshippers at the Jain temple of Palitana, India. Note the offering plates and the reliefs representing the outer sensuous world of illusion, in contrast to the eternal reality of liberation represented within.

Holy men devoted to Vishnu (note V-shaped forehead markings) at a Hindu festival.

the same time providing a means for attaining wealth for the family of the groom. This has, for obvious reasons, added to the Hindu preference for sons.

Other practices evolved out of the ideals of purity and chastity. Woman were not permitted to divorce; and if a woman's husband died before her, she was not permitted to remarry (although this was permitted for men).

Most criticized of all, however, have been the attitudes and practices associated with widowhood itself. Because a woman's focus is the well-being of her husband, if he dies before her, it is, in effect, her fault. Her in-laws, others in the family, and society consider such an unfortunate event to be the result of the widow's own bad *karma*. When one considers that women were to be self-sacrificial and otherwise live a severely restricted and controlled life, including many childbirths, one can discern that her early demise, in advance of her husband, was evidence that she had been properly performing her duties as a wife. The practice of childhood marriage, however, sometimes to men well advanced in age, made widowhood more likely than it might have been otherwise. As a result there were many young widows, many of whom were under ten years old.[36]

The widow was (and remains today in many parts of India) the most scorned figure in Hindu society, forced to live an extremely austere life; the red dot on her forehead, which signified wifehood (her only source of status), was removed. Ramabai Sarasvati, writing in the nineteenth century, described the situation:

> Among the Brahmans of Deccan, the heads of all widows must be shaved regularly every fortnight. . . . The widow must wear a single coarse garment, white, red or brown. She must eat only one meal during the twenty-four hours of a day. She must never take part in family feasts and jubilees, with others. She must not show herself to people on auspicious occasions. . . . A man or woman thinks it unlucky to behold a widow's face before seeing any other object in the morning. . . .
>
> A widow is called an "inauspicious" thing. The name "rand," by which she is generally known, is the same that is borne by . . . a harlot. . . . There is scarcely a day of her life on which she is not cursed by [the relatives and neighbors of the widow's husband] as the cause of their beloved friend's death. . . . [These practices are] part of the discipline by which to mortify her youthful nature and desire. She is closely confined to the house. . . . Her life then, destitute as it is of the least literary knowledge, void of all hope, empty of every pleasure and social advantage, becomes intolerable, a curse to herself and to society at large.[37]

There was, however, another, more "auspicious" way out of the predicament of widowhood. In some parts of India and among some castes, women could choose to become a **sati** (or **suttee**) in the ritual by the same name in which she was burned alive on the funeral pyre of her dead husband. This was the noble choice, which permitted the wife certain status as the "good wife," who was deserving of the good karma needed to join her husband in the next life or to be reincarnated as a man eligible for *moksha*. No doubt there have been many women for whom the practice of *sati* really was voluntary. Yet, one wonders what kind of choice this was considering the enormous social burden of the alternative. At the same time, however, there may have been women so devoted to their husbands that this supreme sacrifice actually was experienced by them as recognition of, or transformation into, the exalted ideal, the self-sacrificing and devoted wife that the practice was intended to exemplify. Yet, in other cases, the shame and burden of having a widow in the family may have provided incentive for the family to impose *sati* when it was not actually chosen. A case was reported in 1796

> *in which a widow escaped from the pyre during the night in the rain. A search was made and she was dragged from her hiding place.*
>
> *She pleaded to be spared but her own son insisted that she throw herself on the pile as he would lose caste and suffer ever-lasting humiliation. When she refused, the son with the help of some others present bound her hands and feet and hurled her into the blaze.*[38]

As Katherine K. Young has noted, "[i]t is significant that *sati* became common in regions where a wife could inherit her husband's property."[39]

Places of Power and Participation

It is important to remember, however, that we must not assume that the authoritative texts written by men for women accurately portray the full extent of women's lives. Although extremely difficult to trace, it is possible to make some assumptions based on the little evidence there is and by looking to the contemporary experiences of Indian women to discover places of divergence from orthodoxy. First, it must be remembered that what we have been describing so far is the *brahminical* ideal. Most of India consists of the lower castes. Scholars have noted that there is more equality between men and women as one descends the caste hierarchy.[40] On the other hand, since the practices we have been discussing were associated with status, those who sought to elevate themselves would be drawn to perform them. Second, the popular practice of a religion often differs in large degree from the orthodox canon. Undoubtedly, there always have been rituals associated with women's lives, such as for childbirth; and women's rites and festivals in contemporary India's popular religion are evidence that women's religious lives may have been richer in the past than the texts indicate.[41] In addition, because the home has always been the center of Hindu religious practices, rather than the temple, it is likely that women have been more involved in family ritual than one might think from reading only the texts.

More significant, however, there were religious movements within Hinduism that provided opportunity for the participation of women. As previously discussed, the advent of Buddhism led to the development of *bhakti,* the path of devotion, which, like Buddhism, was subversive to caste. Not noted earlier, however, is that *bhakti* was also subversive to the role restrictions for women as well. Here was a woman's path to liberation that was denied by the *brahminical* ideal. Since women had already been prepared for a devotional life at home, it was an easy transition to complete devotion to a chosen deity. So It is no surprise that women have been acknowledged as *bhakti* saints. Examples are Andal of South India (sixth century C.E.) and Mirabai (sixteenth century C.E.), both Krishna devotees. Upon the death of her husband, Mirabai refused widowhood or *sati* and declared herself to be the wife of Krishna himself.[42]

Often *bhakti* devotional gods are male. Hence, the model worshiper is female, which is exemplified, for example, in the myths of Krishna and the devoted *gopis* who chase after and dance with him in the forest. As a consequence, even male devotees are considered "spiritually female" and may "suspend their masculinity" by taking on feminine devotional behavior and even dressing like women, as did Ramakrishna, the great saint and teacher discussed earlier, in order to identify as the devoted lover of the beloved god.[43]

On the other hand, Hindu popular religion, which incorporates *bhakti* devotionalism, often focuses on female representations for the Divine, such as Shakti (phenomenal power), *prakriti* (primordial nature), Kali (*creatrix* and destroyer), or the Great Goddess as Mother. In some areas, such as Bengal, *bhakti* devotion to the Goddess is dominant.[44] Although this did not always translate into improved status for human women, such goddesses were exemplars that may have influenced attitudes toward women as well as provided sources of self-esteem and models for the empowerment for women.

Myths of the gods and goddesses also illustrate that sometimes it is appropriate for a wife to complain. When a husband does not perform adequately as a husband or otherwise unduly disrupts her life, she can insist that he right the situation. "Though Shiva was Lord of the Worlds, Parvati could nag at him for his neglect of her and their material welfare. She could accuse him of making her and their children pay the price of his idealism. And the god was willing to admit the rightness of her complaints."[45]

Tantrism (beginning about the sixth century C.E.), with its practice of societal reversals, offered leadership opportunities to women as well, who became *gurus* to men. On the other hand, Tantrism also may have resulted in the sexual use of women only for the purposes of the man's enlightenment or to legitimize prostitution at the expense of women. Yet, Tantrism's exaltation of the female Divine must have provided a source of power and esteem at least for some women practitioners. Its cosmology, contrary to Hindu religious tradition, does not elevate God over Goddess as the supreme expression of the Divine. Instead, Tantrism adheres to an ideology and practice that is intended to promote balance between the male and female principles of the universe. In some forms of Tantrism, identification with and immersion in the Goddess is the supreme goal of Its practice, whether by male or female adepts. This apparently is to reverse the unbalancing effects of mainstream religion. Some Tantric texts and practices also sought to reverse the prevailing social order by teaching men to recognize that the Goddess is in every woman and, therefore, women should be venerated, not subjugated. In Bengal, for example, women have been recognized Tantric teachers.[46]

Women and Reform in India

British colonial rule in India for some two centuries up to 1947 initially was slow in bringing reform for women. Western history has generally credited the British with reforms for Indian women. Although some of the British pushed for reforms, foreign rule in India actually had exacerbated the problem for Hindu women, resulting in a more insistent cry for reform from some within Indian society itself.[47] Not wanting to interfere with the *status quo* of long-held custom and religious practice, the British enforced Hindu laws regarding women in their courts. As a consequence, *sati* was not made illegal until 1829, when an educated Indian man, Raja Ram Mohun Roy, was successful in convincing the British that *sati* was not sanctioned by the *Rig Veda* as the *brahmin* priests had contended.[48] Furthermore, intending to provide uniform laws, the British imposed *brahminical* standards and practices regarding the family on the Indian population as a whole. The severe restrictions of the *brahminical* ideal for Hindu women, which primarily had been confined to the higher castes, were now imposed on Indian women regardless of caste. For example, where women had once been permitted divorce or remarriage, these practices were abolished. As the greater Indian female population was subjected to the severe restrictions of the *brahminical* ideal, a backlash resulted against the British. The British, who had claimed that one of the primary justifications for their occupation of India was to improve the lowly status of Hindu women, appeared hypocritical to reform-minded Indians, and the nineteenth-century Hindu reform movement was born, which included women, such as Pandita Ramabai (1858–1922). The British reversed course and passed several reforms, such as prohibiting marriage under the age of 12 and permitting remarriage.

In the early 1900s, the Indians, including the Women's Indian Association (founded in 1917), pushed for reforms beyond that which the British had envisioned. In many parts of India, for example, Indian women won the right to vote in advance of British women. As a consequence, the Indians were able to argue that their own attitude toward reform ran against the British contention that India's women needed British imperialism; therefore, they argued, Indian independence from British rule was in order.

Reforms for Hindu women, then, were inextricably bound up with the Indian independence movement. Gandhi, although he held to traditional roles for women, made a call to Indian women to join him in the struggle for independence. Having fully integrated the idea of self-sacrifice for the benefit of others, many Hindu women turned their attention from the home and directed their efforts toward the broader context of the Indian homeland. Sometimes their peaceful protests found them, with babes in arms, standing up to British authority. Many made the supreme sacrifice by giving their lives when fired upon by the British.

A large presence of women in the campaigns upset British stereotypes of Indian women and exposed police brutality. More significantly, it laid bare British hypocrisy over Indian men's maltreatment of women, since British police and army officers and government officials were quite prepared to intimidate, beat and shoot women demonstrators. These actions undermined the legitimacy of Britain's rejection of Independence, since the very women whom the British had claimed they were there to liberate from the abuses of Indian men, were taking up the fight against their foreign protectors.[49]

After independence was won (1947), women's rights were memorialized in the new constitution, in which women, such as Kitty Shiva Rao, had considerable input. In addition, enabling legislation was passed that, for example, provided equal pay for equal work; outlawed polygamy; raised the age of marriage to 18 and 21 for women and men, respectively; permitted divorce; provided maternity benefits; prohibited sexual harassment; and the like. As a consequence, the legal context for women was radically altered. The new secular state took hold, and in 1954 Jawaharlal Nehru, India's first prime minister, called on women to become full partners with men in the development of a new India.[50]

Implementation of reform in the actual villages of the vast Indian countryside has proven to be a daunting task, however, leaving most Indian women unaware of their rights—a problem that continues to this day. What has been granted by law is easily taken back by custom and tradition with a firm hold on the minds of the people. For example, female literacy rates continue to be lower than men's, and there appears to be a continuing decline in the ratio of females to males in the Indian population. This latter trend has led many to ask why. Some cite dowry murders as a possible reason. The dowry custom continues through much of India, and there is evidence that it is increasing. Others cite the related problem of the preference for sons. Because dowry imposes a financial burden on a girl's family, it may lead to female infanticide, another custom that has endured despite reforms. Another possibility is the neglect of female children with respect to nutrition and health care.[51]

Traditional attitudes have been difficult to change. The notion of the ideal Hindu wife is well imbedded in Hindu culture; and the practices and attitudes associated with widows continue to be a source of severe subjugation of women in today's India, never having been eradicated completely from Indian society, despite reforms.

On the other hand, the ideals of *lokasangraha* ("acting for the welfare of the world") and *satyagraha* ("grasping/insisting on the truth," or as Gandhi put it, "soul force") help women to move forward in their work to improve the status of women in India.[52] Hence, women's movements in India remain active, although there appears to be some decline since the fervor associated with the Independence Movement.[53]

The Political and Religious Forces Shaping the Lives of Today's Hindu Women

Today we find the Indian people in a similar struggle to that of the American people. Those who wish to continue the development of a secular state are pitted against those (liberal and conservative) who fear the loss of traditional culture in the wake of the elimination of religion from participation in the determination of the laws of the land. The most vocal of the latter group in India are the fundamentalists, who promote the return to Hindu tradition and seek to impose Hindu ideals on the Indian peoples as a whole. Citing the fact that Hindus constitute 82 percent of the population, they claim that Hindu tradition and culture should not be forsaken for the concerns of the minority, which in any event would be shown tolerance within the bounds of Hindu moral authority.

Along with other Hindu ideals, they desire a return to some of the laws that reflected and protected the ideal Hindu family. The traditional family had remained a stabilizing foundation for Hindu society for many centuries, they assert. With the advent of supposed reforms, however, the Hindu family is breaking down. As a consequence, fundamentalists are advocating a return to some of the more restrictive laws, for example, those regarding divorce and remarriage.

There are also cultural-economic trends resulting in a return to tradition. For example, because it is legally abolished, the caste system is breaking down, although it nevertheless continues to affect the attitudes of the people. As India develops economically, those who once had little opportunity are finding themselves upwardly mobile. In order to elevate their status, they are adopting practices with respect to women that were traditionally associated with status, such as *purdah* and limiting a women's access to education.

Even more puzzling for feminists in the West, however, is the call by some fundamentalist Hindu women to remove the legal ban on *sati*. Such women argue that *sati* should be a matter of choice for religious women who are devoted to their husbands and that governmental interference amounts to an infringement on their free speech rights. One such woman has written:

> [Feminists] should not pose to be holding a brief for all women of India and the approach towards men in this country. . . . [T]he West, which claims to have "liberated" women have fettered women with drug-addiction, alcoholism, and have made them libertine and even lewd. It will be a worthwhile study for [the protesters of sati] to know how many young girls, possessed with the fever of "liberation" phenomenon, have fallen victims to smoking, alcoholism and sensualism and have developed a hatred towards males. Such advocates of liberation described above, are free to pursue their own life style but they should not interfere in affairs of those women who want to marry and lead a compatible life with their husbands. Only women who enjoy a life of "conjugal love" alone can understand and appreciate the psyche of "Sati" and not women for whom marriage is a "slavery," and a "burden."[54]

On September 4, 1987, in defiance of the law, a woman named Roop Kanwar performed *sati,* an act which has become a symbol in the debate. Apparently, there have been other cases as well.

While some fundamentalist women argue for a return to such traditions as *sati,* one should not assume that many are not working to improve the status of women in Indian society. In discussing her work to improve the conditions of women in her native village (her *lokasangraha*), Uma Bharati, a member of a political party generally characterized as fundamentalist, said:

> *Women are inherently superior as a created species. Men are not such noble beings that women should fight for equality. Instead they should fight to be treated with respect. . . . If Indian women combine the madhurya (sweetness), their femininity, with self-pride and political awareness, they can teach the whole world the path of liberation.*[55]

Women of all political and religious stripes are forging ahead in India. Exceptional Indian women have opened the doors to education and have taken prominent positions in the professions, business, and government (although these avenues effectively are closed to ordinary women, who still live under the influence of the ancient religious laws). Indira Gandhi (1917–1984), prime minister of independent India (1966–1977; 1980–1984), served as a reminder of the many opportunities now open to women in India. Similarly, religious women are also finding doors opened to them that were previously closed. Many monasteries in India now welcome women ascetics into their folds, and many women have become spiritual teachers in their own right. Further, many respected Hindu masters have worked for gender parity and have hand-picked women successors for their movements, such as Gurumayi Chidvilasananda, successor to Swami Muktananda, and Mathru Sri Sarada, successor to Swami Lakshmana. Moreover, the worship of the Divine Mother is a growing phenomenon and is seen by many Hindus as reflected in women saints such as Sarada Devi, wife of Ramakrishna, who took over the order after his death, and Anandamayi Ma (1896–1982), who is considered to have been an incarnation of the Goddess Kali. This has led some to believe that women will be an even greater political and religious force in the years to come.

The outcome of these contemporary political and religious struggles in today's India is uncertain. One thing is certain, however, Hindu women can be heard loud and clear at the forefront of the debate.

Other Religions of India

We now shall present brief accounts of two smaller religions of India, Jainism and Sikhism. Like the other religious minorities in the predominantly Hindu Republic of India—Zoroastrianism, Islam, Buddhism, Judaism, and Christianity (to be considered in other contexts in this book)—they are not Hindu because they do not accept the authority of the Vedas or of the *brahmin* priesthood, even though they may accept some values associated with Hinduism.

Jainism

As we have already noted, **Jainism** was established in its historic form by Vardhamana, called Mahavira, an approximate contemporary of the Buddha, in the fifth century B.C.E. Mahavira is believed by his followers to have been the last in a series of *Tirthankaras* ("Crossing-Makers") who attained full liberation and taught the way to it. These men are honored as the greatest of *jinas* ("victors" or "conquerors"), from which the word "Jain" is derived. The ideal of conquering through great struggle is pervasive in Jain literature. But it is not a triumph over a human enemy that is lauded, for the foe is oneself and one's own material nature, which can be defeated by perseverance in asceticism or self-denial. This mood is often reflected in Jain art, which may portray the *Tirthankaras* as heroically rigid, immobile figures over which vines have extended their tendrils, in contrast to dancing or flute-playing Hindu deities.

Jainism teaches that sentient, feeling life dwells in all that exists—gods, humans, animals, plants, even stones, dust, and air. These *jivas,* souls or particles of life, are entrapped in the material shells of these substances as a result of *karma.* The Jain view of *karma* is somewhat different from the Hindu or Buddhist; for Jains it is more like a material coating that covers souls as a consequence of action based on desire and thereby condemns them to the suffering incumbent upon material existence.

One can look at it this way: *Karma* or action is inevitably directed toward some particular object and so "grows" the material form it needs to attain that object. If you want a piece of candy, you need an arm to reach out and grab it and a mouth with which to eat it. *Karmic* law says that in such matters you get what you want—but then you have to live with it. You now have a body so that you can enjoy candy, but you are also trapped inside that body, with all its limitations and capacity for pain—and you will have a very hard time getting out of it. According to Jainism, since it was action that got us into the material predicament, it must be its opposite—quietness and abstention—that begins to reverse it, as well as suffering induced by asceticism that wears down the *karmic* shell until the soul can break free, floating up to the top of the universe to enjoy an eternity of bliss and omniscience.

Inflicting suffering on another soul, whether through cruelty or indifference or even apparent necessity, adds to one's burden of *karma.* For this reason, Jains go to great lengths to counter the callousness of the world toward life. Virtually all Jains are strict vegetarians and go so far as to put screens around lamps to keep insects from flying into them. Many Jain temples maintain homes for unwanted animals and hospitals for injured birds.

Practice differs, however, between laity and monks. The former essentially live so as to add no more to the burden of *karma,* in the hope of becoming a monk in some future life and ultimately attaining *kaivalya,* or liberation.

*Women praying in a Jain
temple.*

Monks, however, are determined to make real headway toward that goal in this lifetime. They not only practice the great Jain virtue of *ahimsa,* harmlessness, but undertake great asceticism—fasting, meditating in the hot sun, enduring discomfort—to wear down the *karmic* shell. Jain monks are divided into two orders: the *Digambaras,* who are "sky-clad" or naked in many settings, and the *Svetambaras,* who wear a thin white robe.

The high value placed on asceticism, however, has not inhibited a respect for learning and beauty among Jains. Monks go among Jain communities as teachers and preachers; a great number of the laity are well educated in the faith. Historically, Jain monks have played a very creative role in the letters and philosophy of India. As we have seen, Mohandas K. Gandhi and through him such Americans as Martin Luther King, Jr., were deeply influenced by Jain teachings about harmlessness and nonviolence.

The Jains, typically merchants and bankers, are a prosperous and gifted class in India today, influential beyond what their numbers of only about 1.5 million would suggest. Their well-maintained temples are among the most exquisitely beautiful in India.[56]

Sikhism

The Sikh religion, as has already been mentioned, arose early in the sixteenth century on the spiritual boundary between Hinduism and Islam. It answered to the needs of those who, perturbed by the coexistence of two mighty but conflicting faiths, sought a higher truth beyond them both. It taught the simple monotheistic worship of a God who can be called by many names so long as one does not limit him to any of them. Yet Sikhism, over time, became a movement with its own distinctive outlook and its own role in the complex and tumultuous history of India.

According to tradition, Guru Nanak, the first revealer of Sikhism, received his Divine call at the age of 30, when God came to him and charged him to teach humankind the worship of the true name of God through simple prayer, charity, cleanliness, and service. He was lost in the rapture of this experience for three days, and when he reappeared, he said to his companions, "There is no Hindu; there is no Muslim."

Nanak composed many psalmlike poems, such as the one quoted on pages 88–90, which now makeup part of the Holy Granth, the Sikh scriptures. He inculcated in his growing band of followers an inclusive religion focused on the name of one universal, all-powerful, and all-loving God, who makes no distinction among men and women on the basis of caste or creed but who looks into their hearts. The simple worship of God is sufficient; pilgrimage, ritual, or ascetic practices add nothing to it.

As the Sikh ("disciple") movement grew, the idea of the *guru* and of the Sikhs as a distinct community also became more and more important. Nanak was followed by a succession of nine gurus, each appointed by his predecessor, some of whom left distinctive stamps on the character of the faith. The Sikh fellowship, too, came to be clearly defined.

The fifth *guru,* Arjun (1563–1606), did much to make the religion institutional. He compiled the Sikh scriptures, the *Granth,* from the writings of Nanak, Kabir, and other poets and *gurus*. He enshrined the Granth in the famous Golden Temple in Amritsar, which is Sikhism's most venerated site. A strong administrator, he organized local Sikh communities efficiently and pushed for a high measure of self-government for the movement as a whole. Arjun was martyred after he supported the wrong faction in struggles for power following the death of the great Mughul emperor Akbar. This event served virtually to absolutize the reforms of the great leader and to teach the Sikhs they would need to look out for themselves in an increasingly dangerous situation.

That lesson was not lost on Gobind Rai (1666–1708), descendant of Arjun and the tenth and last *guru.* The Mughul Empire in north India, with its many peoples and faiths, was deteriorating under the rule of the fanatically Muslim Aurangzib.

Rai advocated the right of the Sikhs to defend themselves and did much to enhance the military tradition for which Sikhism was to become noted.

In 1699 he inaugurated the *Khalsa,* the Sikh military fraternity. Standing before the great assembly of believers, Rai asked if there were any here, now, today, willing to give their life for the faith. The crowd was astounded by this awesome request. But eventually five brave men came forward. Rai took each into his tent, a thud was heard, and when he came out his sword was dripping with blood. Finally he led the five out before the terrified assembly. They were unharmed, the blood had been that of a goat, but the men were now accounted heroes and the first members of the *Khalsa.* Though of different caste background, they drank *amrit,* sacred nectar, together and were to wear five tokens: uncut hair covered by a turban, a comb, a steel bracelet, a special pair of undershorts, and a *kirpan,* or two-edged dagger. They took the surname Singh, "lion." Others rushed to join the *Khalsa,* pledging never to turn their backs on an enemy. Rai took to the field with some success but died of wounds inflicted in battle in 1708. Before he died, he said that he would be the last *guru* in human form; after him the Granth itself would become the *guru,* and so it has been. In time, Sikh rulers governed states in the Punjab region until subjugated by the British in the Sikh wars of the nineteenth century.

The Sikhs have no formal priesthood. Their worship, reminiscent in some ways of Protestant Christianity, may be conducted by any qualified Sikh. It consists of hymns, prayer, scripture reading, sermons, and the sharing of food together, both in a sort of communion rite at the end of worship and in communal dinners afterwards. Private worship in the home morning and evening is also emphasized. In its mainstream form, Sikhism gives little place to asceticism or celibacy, though it teaches simplicity of life.

Sikhism, then, can be characterized as a monotheistic religion with a strong sense of community, a devotion to family life, a tradition of ethical and military virtues, and a belief that it worships a universal God beyond sectarian divisions.

Sikhism has spawned several further religious movements, typically based on belief that the lineage of authentic *gurus* is still living. Among them are Radhasoami and Eckankar, popular in the West.

Hinduism in America

India Comes to America

The World Parliament of Religions at the Chicago World's Fair in 1893 marked the introduction of Hinduism to America. Prior to that there were an insignificant number of Hindus in America, although Hindu philosophy had had a profound affect on Emerson, Thoreau, and others, which greatly influenced their writings and, thus, had an impact on the American religious landscape. The charismatic Swami Vivekananda took the Parliament by storm with the introduction of Advaita Vedanta, based on the teachings of the Indian saint Ramakrishna (1836–1886), to the West. This was at once an exotically foreign religion for late nineteenth-century Americans, yet at the same time welcome because of its openness toward all religious views. Swami Vivekananda soon established the Ramakrishna or Vedanta Societies in the United States, the first in New York in 1896. By the time of his untimely death in 1902, the Vedanta Societies he established had solid footing in the United States and elsewhere. Their blend of devotion, service, meditation, acceptance of all forms of piety, and a harmonious view toward the religious life, along with a style of worship that brings together Protestant-style services imparting Vedanta philosophy with Hindu *puja* worship, has attracted many followers in America of both Indian and Western descent. Vedanta in America thus paved the way for other varieties of Hinduism to follow, including the Self-Realization Fellowship and the International Society for Krishna Consciousness (also known as the "Hare Krishnas"), as well as many others.

Early twentieth-century America displayed an interest in Eastern philosophy and religion, including Hinduism, but at the same time showed an ambivalent attitude toward Indian immigrants themselves who found the immigration door alternatively opened, then closed, then opened again in 1965.

Hindus of Indian descent in America have had to strike an uneasy balance between their religion and Indian cultural identity and the pressures to Westernize. The establishment of a significant number of Hindu temples constructed in America in the architectural style of northern or southern India and dedicated by Hindu priests from India have become centers of Hindu worship and culture for Hindus of various Indian backgrounds. The temples, in effect, create oases of purity for the orthodox in the midst of the various pollutions that threaten in a modern America where eating meat, class and racial intermarriage, considerable mobility in society, and rapidly transforming family structures are commonplace. Still, Hindu temples generally welcome the serious seeker of non-Indian descent as well as the merely curious, creating a congenial atmosphere for all visitors that speaks well for Hindu hospitality.[57]

Other Hindu Influences in America

Hinduism has had a wide influence on American religion and culture since it was first introduced. As previously mentioned, even before Vivekananda set foot on American soil, it was a presence in the influential writings of Emerson and Thoreau. Hindu ideas have almost imperceptibly become woven into American culture at places where there is concordance. For example, Vedanta's tolerant universal view of religion has found a kindred spirit in certain forms of liberal Christianity and Judaism, no doubt enriching each. And so-called "New Age" religious movements and the Theosophical Society have also benefited from the wisdom of India. Even certain words, such as *mantra, yoga,* and *chakra* have been incorporated into the American lexicon as quasi-religious practices permeating American society. Yoga practices have become so widespread in America today that it is even probable that new generations will perceive them as entirely "American."[58]

We see, then, that Hinduism has been a substantial contributor to the American religious melting pot, as well as to America's rich diversity.

✾ Summary

India has been the cradle of several religions: Buddhism, Jainism, Sikhism. But the great majority of its people follow Hinduism, which can be taken to mean simply "the religion of India." As such, it embraces a vast diversity of gods, practices, and spiritual paths. It includes the worship of God through images and concepts and by taking those images and concepts away. It strives to reconcile the following of *dharma,* the cosmic law and the way of righteousness in this world, and the quest for *moksha,* or liberation from all that is limiting in the attainment of God-realization.

Hinduism has roots in the religion of both the indigenous agricultural peoples of India and of the ancient Aryan or Indo-European invaders. From the former, it probably received such features as fertility cults, mother goddesses, and yoga; from the latter it received the *Vedas,* its classic scriptures, and the rites of the *brahmin* priests. Beginning with *brahmin* sacrificial religion and its cosmic gods, such as Indra and Varuna and Agni, the *Vedas* end with the "interiorization of sacrifice" in the *Upanishads,* with their message that Brahman, the universal Absolute, is one with Atman, the true Self of each individual. Brahman, taking many shapes, is all that is, and only in knowing him is there joy.

During the period of the *Upanishads* (the last few centuries B.C.E. and the turn of the first millennium), other spiritual teachings were arising as well. The Buddha and Mahavira of the Jains taught inward paths to liberation not dependent on the *Vedas.* Patanjali and others taught the essence of yoga: self-control attained through virtuous life, postures, and ordered breathing, then withdrawal from the outer senses to reach mastery and freedom within. The *Bhagavad-Gita,* the great Hindu classic of this era, showed the direction religion was taking by beginning with teachings like those of the *Upanishads* and culminating in a great revelation of Vishnu that established the foundations of *bhakti.* In the process it also gave the *karma-yoga* teaching (which much later greatly influenced Mohandas K. Gandhi) that one can know liberation through work in the world if that work is done selflessly. A little later, *Advaita Vedanta,* the philosophical teaching that speaks of the sole existence of Brahman, and Tantrism, the path to liberation through radical initiations and paradoxical sexual and other practices, added their flavors to Hinduism. In the sixteenth century, the Sikh faith sought to worship the God above Hinduism and Islam.

Hindu deities are numerous, but the major ones fall into two great families: the Vishnu family and the Shiva family. Vishnu represents the forces working for good in the cosmos; from time to time he comes to earth in the form of *avatars,* such as Rama and Krishna, to restore righteousness. Shiva, though also ultimately good, represents the life force or the totality, and Shakti, the great goddess who goes by many names, such as Kali, Durga, and Parvati, is the power and manifestation of the phenomenal universe. She is a powerful religious force in her own right.

Home and family are all-important centers of Hindu religious life. In a devout home, the head of the family offers daily devotions. In traditional India, one's caste was an important determinant of spiritual life; however, the power of caste (now illegal) is weakening. Many Hindus worship in the colorful temples as well as at home, presenting garlands of flowers or other offerings to the Divine images, perhaps with the help of a priest; temples are especially associated with pilgrimage and festival. Some Hindus, especially toward the end of life, become *sadhus,* renouncing the things of this world for the sake of the spiritual quest. They, like others serious about spirituality, may become disciples of a *guru* or spiritual teacher.

Modern Hinduism has made vigorous efforts to relate its ancient tradition to the modern world. Ramakrishna and his followers in the nineteenth century endeavored to show that the philosophical basis of the religion has universal value. In the twentieth century, Mohandas K. Gandhi drew from it to pioneer nonviolent methods of political and social change, which greatly influenced Martin Luther King, Jr., in America.

The development of the ideal of the Hindu wife in the *brahminical* period led to religio-cultural practices, such as child marriage, *purdah,* dowry, and *sati,* together with attitudes such as those toward widows, that greatly restricted women's lives and led to abuses. These became the subject of reform in the nineteenth century. Today the role of women in Indian society is very much a subject of debate, in which Hindu women are vocal participants.

The great majority of Hindus practice some form of *bhakti,* or devotion toward the gods. *Bhakti* devotees believe that love for one's chosen deity is the easiest yet most supremely effective road to liberation. *Bhakti* was subversive to caste and to the restrictive roles for women in Hindu society and so has permitted much greater participation by those in the lower castes, as well as women—many of whom have become recognized saints.

Hinduism has had a profound influence on the American religious landscape. American Hindu temples are centers of worship for Indian immigrants, who strike an uneasy balance between Hindu culture and Western values. Hindu practices and ideas have been almost imperceptibly woven into aspects of American life. There are numerous Hindu-based religious movements in America, including the Vedanta Society, the Self-Realization Fellowship, and the International Society for Krishna Consciousness.

Jainism is an ancient Indian religion emphasizing life in everything and the liberation of the *jiva* or soul from bondage to *karma* or matter through self-denial.

Sikhism, emerging on the border of Hinduism and Islam, presented a simple monotheism taught by a lineage of true *gurus.*

❋ Questions for Review

1. Explain how Hinduism has reconciled the "affirmative way" in religion—the way of moving toward unconditioned reality through devotion to Divine images and ideas—and the "negative way"—the way to God by taking away all that is not God, all lesser images and ideas. See what persons, concepts, and practices are on each side and where they meet.

2. Explain how Hinduism reconciles the following of *dharma,* the Divine social order in accordance with *rita,* the Divine cosmic order, and the way of righteousness in the world, with the pursuit of *moksha,* liberation into Divine infinity.

3. Interpret the view of human life indicated by Hinduism's four goals and four stages of life.

4. Present the main features of *Vedic* religion: its worldview, its gods, the inner meaning of its sacrifices, and how it set the stage for the development of later Hindu philosophy and religion.

5. Talk about the central message of the *Upanishads.*

6. Explain what is meant by Brahman.

7. Discuss the Buddha in the context of his times and how the reaction to Buddhism led to changes in Hinduism.

8. Understand the theory and practice of *yoga.*

9. Show how the thought of the *Bhagavad-Gita* moves from the insights of the *Upanishads* to those of *bhakti,* Hindu devotionalism.

10. Explain the philosophy of *Advaita Vedanta.*

11. Describe some features of the thought and practice of Tantrism as a path to liberation.

12. Describe the two main families of Hindu gods, as well as the mythology and worship of two or three deities in detail.

13. Explain how home and family are the main centers of Hindu worship for a large number of Hindus.

14. Interpret the fundamental meaning of the Hindu caste system.

15. Discuss the meaning and role of *sadhus,* or holy men.

16. Briefly describe typical worship in a Hindu temple.

17. Discuss the development of the model of the ideal Hindu wife from the early *Vedas* to the *Upanishads* and how it had an impact on women's lives.

18. Discuss the reform movement of the nineteenth and twentieth century in India and its relationship to the Indian Independence Movement, as well as the role of women in it.

19. Explain how Ramakrishna and Gandhi, each in his own way, related Hinduism to the modern world.

20. Talk about the insight of Hinduism that you found of most value for yourself.

21. Using the chart on page 73, summarize the fundamental features of Hinduism. How does it answer the great questions about God and the meaning of human life?

22. Give the fundamental features of Jainism.

23. Describe the Sikh religion.

24. Describe Hinduism in American, including the Hinduism of Indian immigrants and Hinduism's influence on the American religious landscape.

❈ Suggested Readings on the Religions of India

General–Ancient

Basham, A. L., *The Wonder That Was India*. New York: Grove Press, 1959. A masterly survey of classic Indian society with much attention to religion.

———, *The Origins and Development of Classical Hinduism*. Kenneth G. Zysk, ed. New York: Oxford University Press, 1991.

Brockington, J. L., *The Sacred Thread: Hinduism in Its Continuity and Diversity*. Edinburgh: University of Edinburgh Press; and New York: Columbia University Press, 1981. A highly regarded introduction to Hinduism in all its periods and forms.

Chapple, Christopher, *Karma and Creativity*. Albany: State University of New York Press, 1986. Helpful essays on an important problem in Hinduism.

Coomaraswamy, Ananda, *The Dance of Shiva*. Bombay: Asia Publishing House, 1948. A brilliant insight into the classic Indian mind through the gateway of art; invaluable for an understanding of the Hindu religion in depth.

Danielou, Alain, *Yoga: The Method of Reintegration*. New York: University Books, 1955. A concise and useful summary of the basic yoga texts.

Deutsch, Eliot, *Advaita Vedanta: A Philosophical Reconstruction*. Honolulu, HI: East-West Center Press, 1969. A splendidly readable introduction to India's most prestigious philosophical tradition.

Dumont, Louis, *Homo Hierarchicus: The Caste System and Its Implications*. London: Paladin, 1972. A brilliant exposition of caste and its meaning in Hinduism.

Eck, Diana L., *Banaras: City of Light*. New York: Knopf, 1982. Brilliant insight into Hindu religion and culture through a study of its most holy city.

Eliade, Mircea, *Yoga: Immortality and Freedom*. New York: Pantheon Books, 1958. An invaluable overview of yogic concepts and literature.

Herman, A. L. *A Brief Introduction to Hinduism: Religion, Philosophy, and Ways of Liberation*. Boulder, CO: Westview Press, 1991.

Hopkins, Thomas T., *The Hindu Religious Tradition*. Belmont, CA.: Wadsworth, 1971. A useful introductory text; particularly valuable for its treatment of Vedic ritual.

Kinsley, David R., *Hinduism: A Cultural Perspective*. Englewood Cliffs, NJ: Prentice Hall, 1982. A vividly written introductory textbook.

Kramrisch, Stella, *The Hindu Temple*. (reprint). Columbia, MO: South Asia Books, 1991. A classic study of the temple's architecture and meaning.

Lanroy, Richard, *The Speaking Tree: A Study of Indian Culture and Society*. London and New York: Oxford University Press, 1971. A substantial, valuable interpretation, particularly for its psychological insights.

Lingat, Robert, *The Classical Law of India*. Berkeley: University of California Press, 1973. Standard study of the Laws of Manu and other ancient legal codes basic to Hindu civilization.

Morgan, Kenneth W., ed., *Religion of the Hindus*. New York: Ronald Press, 1953. A collection of papers by Hindus written on a nonspecialist level; a good introduction to Hinduism.

O'Flaherty, Wendy P., ed., *Karma and Rebirth in Classical Indian Traditions*. Berkeley: University of California Press, 1980. Basic papers on a very important Hindu topic.

———, *The Rig Veda: An Anthology*. Harmondsworth, U.K.: Penguin Books, 1982. An accessible and well-introduced entry into the oldest religious literature of India.

Prabhavananda, Swami, and Christopher Isherwood, *How to Know God: The Yoga Aphorisms of Patanjali*. New York: Mentor Books, 1969. An easy-to-read version of basic yoga text with commentary.

———, *Shankara's Crest-Jewel of Discrimination*. New York: Mentor Books, 1970. The most accessible text of the nondualist tradition and a good introduction to the classic Indian metaphysical mind.

———, *The Song of God: Bhagavad-Gita*. New York: Mentor Books, 1951. The most readable translation of this classic text, with an introduction by Aldous Huxley. Oriented toward an Advaita interpretation.

Prabhavananda, Swami, and Frederick Manchester, *The Upanishads: Breath of the Eternal*. New York: Mentor Books, 1948. A splendidly poetic and readable introductory translation of the most important of these basic texts. Oriented toward an Advaita interpretation.

Zimmer, Heinrich, *Myths and Symbols in Indian Art and Civilization*. New York: Harper Torchbooks, 1962. A rich study; myth and symbol are as important as philosophy for understanding India.

———, *Philosophies of India*. New York: Meridian Books, 1956. A brilliant and readable work by a scholar who understands the Indian tradition in a profound, if romantic, way.

Hindu Gods and Goddesses

Babb, Lawrence A., *The Divine Hierarchy: Popular Hinduism in Central India*. New York: Columbia University Press, 1975. A brilliant field study that provides insight into the workings of popular Hinduism everywhere.

Carman, John B., *The Theology of Ramanuja*. New Haven, CT: Yale University Press, 1974. Excellent insight into bhakti theological thought; aimed at interreligious understanding.

Chandra, Suresh, *Encyclopedia of Hindu Gods and Goddesses*. New Delhi: Sarup & Sons, 1998.

Coomaraswamy, Ananda, and Sister Nivedita, *Myths of the Hindus and Buddhists*. New York: Dover, 1972. An elementary retelling; well written and cumulatively gives a good insight into India.

Danielou, Alain, *Hindu Polytheism*. New York: Pantheon Books, 1964. A massive summary of data about the gods, mostly through selected translations of classic texts. Well illustrated.

Hawley, John Stratton, ed., *The Divine Consort*. Berkeley: University of California Press, 1982. Studies of Radha and other consort-goddesses of Hinduism.

Hawley, John Stratton, and Donna Marie Wilffieds, eds., *Devi: Goddesses of India*. Berkeley: University of California Press, 1996.

Kinsley, David R., *Hindu Goddesses*. Berkeley: University of California Press, 1986. An intriguing account of the major Hindu goddesses and their place in the Indian pantheon.

———, *The Sword and the Flute*. Berkeley: University of California Press, 1975. An excellent study of Kali and Krishna.

O'Flaherty, Wendy P., *Asceticism and Eroticism in the Mythology of Siva*. London and New York: Oxford University Press, 1973. A landmark study of an important and complex deity, illuminating fundamental themes of Hindu mentality.

———, *Hindu Myths: A Sourcebook*. Harmondsworth, U.K., and Baltimore, MD: Penguin Books, 1975. An authoritative introduction to Hindu mythology by a leading scholar in the field.

———, *The Origins of Evil in Hindu Mythology*. Berkeley, CA: University of California Press, 1980. A brilliant study that sheds much light on the whole of Hinduism.

Ramanujan, A. K., *Speaking of Siva*. Baltimore, MD: Penguin Books, 1973. A readable and enlightening collection of hymns to Shiva.

Singer, Milton, ed., *Krishna: Myths, Rites, and Attitudes*. Chicago: University of Chicago Press, 1968. A good, scholarly collection of papers on Krishna and his cults.

Whitehead, Henry, *Village Gods of South India*. (reprint). Columbia, MO: South Asia Books, 1986. A classic study giving much insight into the gods of Hinduism and their popular worship.

Tantrism

Bharati, Agehananda, *The Tantric Tradition*. Garden City, NY: Doubleday, 1970. A splendid, if sometimes technical, exposition of this often murky field.

Bhattacharyya, Narendra Nath, *History of the Tantric Religion: A Historical, Ritualistic, and Philosophical Study*. New Delhi: Manohar, 1992.

McDaniel, June, *The Madness of the Saints*. Chicago: University of Chicago Press, 1989. A fascinating field study of contemporary Tantrics.

Rawson, Philip S., *Tantra: The Indian Cult of Ecstasy*. London: Thames and Hudson, 1973. A lavishly illustrated popular treatment emphasizing the Hindu tradition.

Modern India

Blank, Jonah, *Arrow of the Blue-Skinned God*. Boston: Houghton-Mifflin, 1992. An unusual, readable account of the Ayodhya temple controversy in light of the ancient legends of Rama; imparts much understanding of both classical and contemporary India.

Bonner, Arthur, *Averting the Apocalypse: Social Movements in India Today*. Durham, NC: Duke University Press, 1990. A gripping and important account of current conditions in India, with much on religion.

Brent, Peter, *Godmen of India*. New York: Quadrangle Books, 1973. A fascinating picture of the role of "God-realized" holy men in India today.

Isherwood, Christopher, *Ramakrishna and His Disciples*. New York: Simon & Schuster, 1965. A very sympathetic picture of the influential saint of the last century, who through his followers continues to shape modern understandings of Hinduism.

Iyer, Raghavan, *The Moral and Political Thought of Mahatma Gandhi*. London: Oxford University Press, 1973. A masterful survey of the ideas of India's most influential man of the twentieth century.

Jaffrelot, Christophe, *The Hindu Nationalist Movement and Indian Politics: 1925–the 1990s: Strategies of Identity-Building, Implantation and Mobilization*. London: Hurst, 1996.

Juergensmeyer, Mark, *Radhasoami Reality: The Logic of a Modern Faith*. Princeton, NJ: Princeton University Press, 1991. Excellent study of a new Indian religious movement of Hindu and Sikh background.

Larson, Gerald James, *India's Agony Over Religion*. Albany: State University of New York Press, 1996. An authoritative picture of the contemporary situation in the light of tradition.

Sharma, Arvind, *The Concept of Universal Religion in Modern Hindu Thought*. New York: St. Martin's Press, 1998.

Zavos, John, *The Emergence of Hindu Nationalism in India*. New York: Oxford University Press, 2000.

Women and Hinduism

Allen, Michael, and S. N. Murkherjee, eds., *Women in India and Nepal*. Canberra, Australia: Anu Printing, 1982. A key work based on field research.

Devendra, Kiran, *Status and Position of Women in India: With Special Reference to Women in Contemporary India*. Delhi: Shakti Books, 1986. A study of the Indian post-independence legislation and its effect on the lives of ordinary Hindu women.

Dietrich, Gabrielle, *Reflections of the Women's Movement in India*. New Delhi: Horizon India Books, 1992. A good survey of the subject.

Falk, Nancy Auer, *Women and Religion in India: An Annotated Bibliography of Sources in English, 1975–1992*. Kalamazoo, MI: New Issues Press, 1994. A comprehensive bibliography of sources that includes an index permitting a researcher to find sources readily on topics regarding women and religion in India.

Harlan, Lindsey, and Paul B. Courtright, eds., *From the Margins of Hindu Marriage: Essays on Gender, Religion and Culture*. New York: Oxford University Press, 1995. A series of essays about Hindu women and domesticity, marriage, divorce, widowhood, and women outside the marriage context at points where the Hindu ideal breaks down but nevertheless remains an important influence.

Jacobson, Doranne, and Susan S. Wadley, *Women in India: Two Perspectives*, 3rd ed. Columbia MO: South Asia Publications, 1995. An enlightening series of essays presenting a balanced perspective on the status, role, and participation of Hindu women in various social contexts in India.

Kinsley, David R., *Tantric Visions of the Divine Feminine: The Ten Mahavidyas*. Berkeley: University of California Press, 1997.

Mitter, Sara S., *Dharma's Daughters: Contemporary Indian Women and Hindu Culture*. New Brunswick, NJ: Rutgers University Press, 1991. An intriguing account of the lives of contemporary urban Indian women.

Mukherjee, Prabhati, *Hindu Women: Normative Models*, rev. ed. Calcutta: Orient Longman, 1994. A thorough analysis of normative models of ideal womanhood in Hindu scriptures, prominent works of various schools of Hindu thought, and popular myth.

Ramabai Sarasvati, Pundita, *The High Caste Hindu Woman*. New Delhi: M. C. Mittal Inter-India Publications, 1888, reprinted in 1984. A heart-wrenching, first-hand account of the status of women in the nineteenth century, written by a brahmin woman whose father, against custom, educated his wife, who then educated her daughter. The book was written as an appeal to Western women for funds to educate Indian women.

Robinson, Catherine A., *Tradition and Liberation: The Hindu Tradition in the Indian Women's Movement*. New York: St. Martin's Press, 1999.

Young, Katherine K., "Hinduism" in *Women in World Religions*, Arvind Sharma, ed., Albany: State University of New York Press, 1987, pp. 60–72. A wonderful summary of the subject from a historical perspective.

———, "Women in Hinduism" in *Today's Woman in World Religions*, Arvind Sharma, ed., Albany: State University of New York Press, 1994, pp. 77–135. A not-to-be missed discussion of contemporary Indian women and their attitudes about religion, politics, and the role of women in society.

The Jains

Dundas, Paul, *The Jains*. New York: Routledge, 1992. A recent comprehensive study.

Jaini, P. S., *The Jaina Path of Purification*. Berkeley: University of California Press, 1979. A useful summary.

Stevenson, Mrs. Sinclair, *The Heart of Jainism*. London: Oxford University Press, 1915. A readable overview, although dated; written from a Christian perspective.

Tobias, Michael, *Life Force: The World of Jainism*. Fremont, CA: Jain Publishing, 1991. A simple and appreciative interpretation by a Western enthusiast for the religion.

The Sikhs

Cole, W. Owen, and Piara Singh Sambhi, *The Sikhs: Their Religious Beliefs and Practices.* London and Boston: Routledge & Kegan Paul, 1978. An excellent introduction to the religion.

McLeod, W. H., *Guru Nanak and the Sikh Religion.* Oxford: Oxford University Press, 1968. A valuable modern historical study of the faith's origins.

————, *The Sikhs: History, Religion and Society.* New York: Columbia University Press, 1989. A comprehensive overview by a leading scholar in the field.

————, *Sikhs and Sikhism.* New York: Oxford University Press, 1999.

Singh, Trilochar, et al., *Adi Granth: Selections from the Sacred Writings of the Sikhs.* London: George Allen & Unwin, 1960. A readable translation.

Hinduism in America

Crawford, S. Cromwell, *Dilemmas of Life and Death: Hindu Ethics in North American Context.* Albany: State University of New York Press, 1995.

Ellwood, Robert S., and Harry B. Partin, *Religious and Spiritual Groups in Modern America,* 2nd ed. Englewood Cliffs, NJ: Prentice Hall, 1988, Chapter 7. A good general overview of Hindu-based religious movements in America.

Ellwood, Robert S., *Eastern Spirituality in America.* New York: Paulist Press, 1987, Chapter II. Extended selections from talks and writings of American Hindu leaders.

Jackson, Carl T., *Vedanta for the West: The Ramakrishna Movement in the United States.* Bloomington: Indiana University Press, 1994.

Richardson, E. Allen, *East Comes West.* Cleveland, OH: The Pilgrim Press, 1985, Chapter 1. Addresses the Hindu religion of Indian immigrants and their descendants in America.

CHAPTER FOUR

Wisdom Embarked for the Farther Shore

The Journey of Buddhism

CHAPTER OBJECTIVES

After studying this chapter, you should be able to

✻ **Outline the traditional life and essential teaching of the Buddha.**

✻ **Discuss the major schools of Buddhism and how they spread to various parts of Asia.**

✻ **Present the importance of practice, especially meditation, in Buddhism.**

✻ **Talk about why Buddhism can be thought of as a particularly "psychological" religion.**

✻ **Discuss the role of and attitudes toward women in the major schools of Buddhism.**

A Religion of Transformation of Consciousness

Buddhism is many things. On the flat Ganges plains east of Benares, it is an ancient enshrined tree, said to be a descendant of the very tree under which he who is called the Buddha, on the night of a full moon, ascended through the four stages of trance and attained full, perfect, and complete enlightenment. In Southeast Asia, it is steep-roofed temples, rich in gold and red, that house conventionalized images of the same Buddha, perhaps standing to teach, perhaps in the seated meditation posture of enlightenment, perhaps reclining as he makes his final entry into Nirvana. The images will probably be gilded, gleaming with transcendent golden light, and the figure's eyes will be half-closed and enigmatic. Around his head may be a many-pointed crown or a simple burst of flame. Outside the temple, saffron-robed monks of the Blessed One (as the Buddha is called) walk with begging bowls, seeking alms.

In the snowy Himalayas, Buddhism is a prayer wheel, a cylinder on an axle inscribed with a mantram such as "Hail the Jewel in the Lotus" and set up on a roadway or around a temple to be spun by passing pilgrims. In Japan, it is an old Zen monk making tea or contemplating the rocks in his monastery garden, as well as vigorous, dynamic young people organizing rallies that combine Buddhist chanting with marching bands and rock concerts.

Lotus, a popular symbol of Buddhism or Hinduism

What is it that ties this tradition together? Buddhism is not rooted in a single culture or area, as is Hinduism, but is an international religion, a movement introduced in historical time into every society where it is now at home. It has deeply pervaded these cultures and deeply identified with them. But the perceptive observer never quite loses awareness that, on the one hand, this religion is not identical with all of the spiritual life of the culture, and, on the other hand, it is a movement wider than the culture and has brought in gifts from outside.

All of this gives Buddhism a somewhat different atmosphere than the Hindu context out of which it emerged. Buddhism always combines something of the Indian spiritual tradition with very different cultures. However, instead of the rich, heavy "biological" flavor of Hinduism, of which we have spoken in the preceding chapter, Buddhism has a more psychological thrust.

What is distinctive about Buddhist altars is that, instead of portraying the archetypal hero, mother, or cosmic pillar, as do Hindu altars, the image communicates a unified psychological state—profound meditation, warm compassion, or even unambiguous fury against illusion. Buddhist practices, too, are focused on strong and clear states of unified consciousness. Either they produce clear states, or they draw power from beings who have achieved unfettered clarity.

Given this fundamental psychological thrust, let us briefly look at Buddhism in terms of the three forms of religious expression. We shall examine them in reverse order.

The basic sociological fact in Buddhism is the **samgha**, the order of monks. The monastic order is not a unified organization throughout the Buddhist world, and its structure and role vary. In modern Japan it is often no longer celibate. But almost always, where there is Buddhism, there are men and women who have given up "natural" life and its goals to take formal vows that orient life in another direction, the realization of a different state of consciousness from the ordinary. Inseparable from this purpose, they are teachers and bearers of Buddhist tradition; and by their distinctive garb, monasteries and temples, and way of life, they make the Buddhist presence unavoidably visible in the midst of society.

Buddhist practice is, as has been indicated, immensely varied. But it centers around three foci: the imaged ideal of the Buddha, the transformation of consciousness, and the transformation of *karma* or practical destiny. The Buddha is revered and presented to the world as the fully realized being who teaches and epitomizes the true nature of all other beings. He attained realization through profound psychological self-analysis and self-control. Buddhist practice for transformation of consciousness works in the same way and so is most fully expressed in meditation, but it also includes chanting and ritual. Interaction with the Buddha, with his symbols, with the *samgha,* and following the ordinary moral teachings exposes even people not yet ready for full enlightenment to *karma* that shapes destiny for good; theirs may be equanimity here and a better rebirth later as a king or god.

Buddhist theoretical expression is concerned with the meaning of the Buddha, how consciousness is transformed, and *karma.* Above all it is psychological in point of departure, for it is concerned with the analysis of human perception and experience. Buddhist thought is not a vague diffuse mysticism but a sharp precise intellectualism that delights in hard logic and numerical lists of categories. It holds that ordinary life is unsatisfactory, for it is based on ignorance and desire, resulting in the inability to realize that there is no real "self." All entities within the universe, including human beings, are impermanent compounds that come together and come apart. The answer is a different kind of mind, a "wisdom mind," which finds the "middle way" between all attachments, uniting all opposites—being, like the Buddha, free of partiality toward any segment of the cosmos—and is therefore, in its unclouded clarity, open to all omniscience, all skill, and all compassion.

We shall now look at the life of the Buddha, to see how these themes are expressed in the traditional account of his quest and achievement.

The Life of the Buddha

At the beginning of the tradition of which all these forms and much else are branches lies the life of one man, Siddhartha Gautama of the Sakya clan, called the Buddha, dated by modern scholars to have lived between approximately 563 and 483 B.C.E. The Buddha was born, according to tradition, at Lumbini, about where the border of India and Nepal now lies, north of Benares. His father was ruler of a tiny state in the foothills of the Himalayas.

Tradition has it that a wise old *brahmin* came to the court and, observing certain remarkable signs on the infant's body, predicted the wonderful child would become either a world emperor or a Buddha, that is, an Enlightened One and

World Savior. The father, being more political than spiritual in orientation, preferred that his son follow the world emperor option. Realizing that if the gifted boy saw the suffering of the world he would be so moved by compassion that he would prefer to save humankind from pain rather than rule it from a throne, the king determined to shield the prince from any sight of ill. He built Siddhartha Gautama glorious pleasure palaces, equipped with everything from chariots to dancing girls to delight the heart of a young prince. All was surrounded by a high wall.

There, the future Buddha matured, married, and had a son. But even unbroken amusement palls eventually, and the prince persuaded his charioteer to take him down the road toward the nearby city. He took four trips in all and, despite his father's previous efforts to shield his eyes, saw four thought-provoking sights: an aged man, a man suffering in agony from a hideous disease, a corpse, and finally an old wandering monk who appeared content. After this, Siddhartha saw even his dancing girls in a different light, and large disturbing issues clouded his mind.

What is the meaning of life, he asked himself, if its initial promise of joy ends long before its dreams can possibly all be fulfilled, in the old age in which one totters backward into infantilism again, or in sickness and pain that can reduce a man or woman full of zest and hope to the state of a howling animal, or finally to the apparently blank extinction of death? How can one be delivered from this ghastly condition of birth, fancy, and pain?

Siddhartha did not know; but he knew that until these questions were answered, he could no longer live for anything else than finding the answers. The last sight, the itinerant monk with his staff and begging bowl, inspired him with the idea of a life wholly dedicated to finding the answers he sought. Not long after, in the middle of the night, the prince kissed his wife and son farewell without waking them and slipped off with his faithful charioteer to the banks of a river. There he exchanged his fine raiment for the coarse garb of a renunciant. He then proceeded alone on the great quest.

In his search, he sampled the web of paths to realization that crisscrossed the spiritual map of India. He talked with *brahmins*. He worked with teachers of trance meditation and went the route of extreme asceticism, getting to the point where he was eating only one grain of rice a day and becoming so emaciated that his ribs and spinal column stood out as if he were a walking skeleton. But he found that neither philosophy nor fasting and self-control alone brought what he desired. He gave them up and went back to a moderate diet.

Then, late one afternoon, as he wandered not far from the banks of a river, he felt that the time had come. Purchasing a pallet of straw from a farmer, he seated himself on it under a huge fig tree. He placed his hand firmly to the ground and swore by the good earth itself that he would not stir from that spot until he attained complete and final enlightenment. All night he remained there, sunk in deeper and deeper meditation. Mara, an old god, buffeted him with furious storms and sweet temptations, but a wave of the Blessed One's hand was enough to dispel them. His consciousness refined itself by moving through four stages of trance, beginning with the calmness of the passions that concentration brings and ending with transcendence of all opposites. He also passed through several stages of awareness. First, he saw all of his previous existences. Then, he saw the previous lives, the interlocking deaths and rebirths, of all beings, and he grasped at the *karmic* forces at work; the universe became like a mirror to him. Finally, he saw with full understanding what principles underlay this web and how extrication from it is possible. He saw the mutual interdependence of all things and how ego-centric ignorance leads sentient beings inevitably through desire to suffering, death, and unhappy rebirth. **The Four Noble Truths** (to be discussed later) appeared in his mind: All life is suffering; suffering is caused by desire; there can be an end to desire; the way is in the **Eightfold Path**.

Siddhartha Gautama was now a Buddha, an "Enlightened One," or "One who is awake." He is also called the **Tathagata**, an expression difficult to translate, meaning something like "He who has come thus and gone thus," in the sense of "He who passed beyond all bounds; one cannot say where he came from or where he is but can only point in the direction he went," referring to his overcoming of all conditioned reality in his enlightenment to become "universalized." He was one with the universe itself and not any particular part of it in principle. And after death and entry into **Nirvana**, he no longer continued to have a physical body. (Another title commonly used in Asia is *Sakyamuni, Shaka* or *Shakamuni* in Japanese, meaning "Sage of the Sakya Clan.")

After remaining in meditation many days, he arose and went toward Benares. On its outskirts, in Sarnath, the "Deer Park," he met five ascetics with whom he had been associated before and who at first mocked him for giving up the austere life. He preached to them about the **Middle Way** and the Four Noble Truths. They were converted and became his first disciples.

As he wandered about teaching, other disciples came to join him, until there was a band of some 60 accompanying the Enlightened One. Upon entering the Buddha's order, each accepted the **Three Refuges** or **Three Jewels**. These refer to three fundamental points of orientation in Buddhism, three things that a Buddhist affirms. They are expressed in the form of these assertions: I take refuge in the Buddha; I take refuge in the *dharma;* I take refuge in the *samgha*. The *dharma* here means the Buddha's teaching; the *samgha* is the order of monks.

Thus, the Three Jewels affirm that the Buddha is the supreme embodiment of the potential of human life; his teaching tells how he can be emulated and what his wisdom is; the order is the custodian of the Buddha and *dharma* for future generations and the social context in which the potential can best be reached. We see here Buddhism taking the three forms of religious expression: an intellectual teaching; an emerging object of worship and the practices prescribed by the Eightfold Path, meditation being a central practice; and a sociological expression, the *samgha,* which today is probably the oldest continuing nonfamilial social institution in the world.

The life of monks was strictly governed by rules, of which the basic ten are prohibitions against (1) taking life; (2) taking what is not given; (3) sexual misconduct; (4) lying; (5) taking intoxicants; (6) eating after noon; (7) watching or participating in dancing, singing, and shows; (8) adorning oneself with garlands, perfumes, and ointments; (9) sleeping in a soft bed (taken to represent living luxuriously); and (10)

Large carved Buddhist figure in Oya, Japan.

handling money. (These rules are still followed by Buddhist monks, although they are sometimes interpreted in an allegorical sense in northern traditions. Devout lay people often undertake the first five.)

The Buddha's ministry, which lasted 45 years after his enlightenment, was generally successful. Of those to whom he preached, many were said to have become **arhants**—fully liberated beings who will suffer no more rebirths. Since being a Buddha is unique, the *arhant* state is the spiritual goal of the Buddha's disciples. When the band of disciples reached 60, he sent them out as missionaries. Thousands came to the Buddha or his disciples seeking lay or monastic initiation, many from the highest ranks of society. Sometimes whole tribes or ascetic orders were converted at once. In time, an order of nuns was established, which we will discuss later. Valuable pieces of land were given to the order.

There was, of course, opposition. Certain *brahmins* murmured against the Buddha's doctrine. One disciple, Devadatta, egged on by a hostile king, became a

"Judas" and tried to kill the Buddha, but his plots were foiled by the sage's perception. The Buddha's end finally came from eating tainted food; he died meditating in great peace surrounded by his disciples, passing again through the stages of trance, imparting final wisdom to the *samgha*, such as "Be ye lamps unto yourselves," "All compounds are transitory," and lastly, "Work out your own salvation with diligence." Breathing his last, he then transcended all particularized existence and joined Nirvanic consciousness.

This is the story traditionally told of the Buddha. Much of it is legendary or a reading back of later Buddhist developments, but it is nonetheless important, for it presents the image of the Buddha that has shaped the 2500 years of Buddhist history.[1]

Basic Buddhist Teaching

The Middle Way

When the Buddha returned to preach to the five ascetics in the Deer Park after his enlightenment, he preached to them the Middle Way. When they first saw him and recognized him as one who had been with them but had left, they mocked him as a pleasure lover who had gone back to soft living. But when he opened his mouth to speak, they could not resist a wisdom that went beyond their mere pride in denying the flesh.

Of the Middle Way he said:

Those foolish people who torment themselves, as well as those who have become attached to the domains of the senses, both these should be viewed as faulty in their method, because they are not on the way to deathlessness. These so-called austerities but confuse the mind which is overpowered by the body's exhaustion. In the resulting stupor one can no longer understand the ordinary things of life, how much less the way to the Truth which lies beyond the senses. The minds of those, on the other hand, who are attached to the worthless sense-objects, are overwhelmed by passion and darkening delusion. They lose even the ability to understand the doctrinal treatises, still less can they understand the method which by suppressing the passions leads to dispassion. So I have given up both these extremes, and have found another path, a middle way. It leads to the appeasing of all ill, and yet it is free from happiness and joy.[2]

The Middle Way becomes on its deepest levels an attitude that seeks to find the delicate, infinitely subtle point of absolute equilibrium between all extremes and polarities, from the obvious balancing off of asceticism and self-indulgence, to the recondite metaphysical reaches of eschewing attachment either to life or death, to desire for being or desire for nonbeing. Everything comes in pairs of opposites, the Buddha taught, in our world of partialities, multiplicity, and conditioned reality. The senses, the desires, the unexamined life get hung up on one side or the other in these pairs of opposites, thinking one side or the other is better. The way of wisdom is to find a balance in the totality that includes them both—and so have the permanence and invincibility of the totality. The person of wisdom is stable like the sky, not like clouds now blown this way, now that, and finally dissipated.

The Four Noble Truths and "No Self"

The Four Noble Truths go deep into the psychological analysis behind the Middle Way idea, and the process to attain perfect equilibrium and totality. In his Deer Park sermon, the Buddha went on to say:

> *What then is the Holy Truth of Ill [Suffering]? Birth is ill, decay is ill, sickness is ill, death is ill. To be conjoined with what one dislikes means suffering. To be disjoined from what one likes means suffering. Not to get what one wants, also that means suffering. In short, all grasping at any of the five Skandhas involves suffering.*
>
> *What then is the Holy Truth of the Origination of Ill? It is that craving which leads to rebirth, accompanied by delight and greed, seeking its delight now here, now there, i.e., craving for sensuous experience, craving to perpetuate oneself, craving for extinction.*
>
> *What then is the Holy Truth of the Stopping of Ill? It is the complete stopping of that craving, the withdrawal from it, the renouncing of it, throwing it back, liberation from it, nonattachment to it.*
>
> *What then is the Holy Truth of the steps which lead to the stopping of Ill? It is this holy eightfold Path, which consists of right views, right intentions, right speech, right conduct, right livelihood, right effort, right mindfulness, right concentration.*[3]

These Truths can be summarized as consisting of two pairs. The first is:

> *All life is suffering (or ill, or pain, or anxiety, or bitter frustration).*
> *Suffering is caused by desire (or craving, or attachment).*

This pair is the analysis of the ordinary human condition: a mad circle dance, fueled by ignorance, of suffering and desire chasing each other. The more we suffer, the more we want things to assuage or distract. The more we get, the more we suffer anxiety that we shall lose it, and frustration at the transience of all things, build up further suffering. And so around and around.

Thus, the good news in the second pair:

> *There can be an end to desire.*
> *The way out is the Eightfold Path.*

Buddhism is sometimes thought of as a pessimistic religion, but that is so only in its assessment of the ordinary life governed by the suffering and desire of the first two Noble Truths. Buddhism is one of the most optimistic of religions in its vision of the ultimate potential of humankind once that syndrome is broken.

For the third of the Noble Truths says suffering can be ended by the stopping of craving; at this point the vicious circle can be halted. One can throw sand in its gears and pull the plug on its turbulence.

Desire, then, is the vulnerable point at which the circle can be broken. It is vulnerable because there is something we can do about it. Craving, or desire, the Buddha said, is like a fire, and any fire requires fuel. If fuel is taken away, the fire must die down. The fuel of the fire of desire is the many things to which the senses are attached. How does one pull back the senses from these attachments? By concentration or meditation, the last and culminating point of the Eightfold Path, which focuses one's awareness on something other than objects of desire and so lets the senses quiet down from burning for things they can never really have.

One of the fundamental points of Buddhist psychology, and a key to understanding the whole system on a deep level, is **Anatman**—"No Self." This Buddhist teaching can be compared to the Upanishadic doctrine that the Atman, the innermost self or soul, is really identical with Brahman. The Buddhist negative expression Anatman, or "No Self," is a difference of emphasis rather than a contradiction, for if the "Self" is simply the one universal Brahman, it is also "No Self" in any individualistic sense. But the difference points to the Buddhist tendency to psychological analysis rather than **ontological** statement (that is, a statement about reality).

Reflection on the idea of No Self provides a line of insight into the meaning of the Four Noble Truths, the Middle Way, and the Buddhist experience. This is because the fundamental craving, or desire, that keeps us in the suffering-desire syndrome, ultimately, is the desire to be a separate individual self.

The first Noble Truth—that all life is suffering—tells us that there is something unsatisfactory, something anxious, frustrating, incomplete about all life as it is ordinarily lived. It does not mean that all life is excruciating pain or that there are no pleasant moments. The Buddha, who supposedly lived his first 29 years in a round of extravagant pleasure, could hardly have said that. But what he does say is that there is something frustrating and unsatisfactory in life, and it can get worse and worse.

The second Noble Truth tells us the reason for this sense of inadequacy in ordinary life is that we are always trying to cling to things—objects, persons, ideas, experiences—that are partial and not permanent, and so keep us in anxiety lest we lose them, as sooner or later we shall. Yet, nonetheless, we want to grasp.

The conclusion can only be that somewhere we have acquired a distorted idea about the whole nature and possibilities of human life, that we are basing life on a false premise. And, just as when you try to do a complex mathematical problem with the wrong formula, sooner or later everything will begin to come out wrong, so it is with human life. According to Buddhism, the false premise that underlies all other delusion, suffering, and grasping is that one is a separate, independent, individual self—rather than a transitory compound of several elements that is completely interdependent with the whole universe.

Buddhism teaches that instead of being a "Self," in the sense of a separate enduring "soul" stuck in a body, we are all compounds made up of several different constituents. The five parts that make up a human being are called **skandhas**; the word "*skandha*" means "bundle" and reminds us that these constituents themselves are collocations of *dharmas,* the pointlike primary particles that flash out of the void. The human *skandhas* are the form (the physical shape), the feelings, the perceptions (the "picture" the mind forms out of data transmitted by the sense organs), the inherent impulses (*karmic* dispositions), and the background consciousness. Note that both physical and psychological entities are brought together.

The problem is that when these five entities get together, they interact in such a way as to make the "person" think of him- or herself as a separate individual "Self." Actually, although understandable, according to Buddhism this is a misreading of the data.

Consider what happens when you, as a collection of the five *skandhas,* walk down the street and meet another such collection. You interpret everything in terms of reinforcing the illusion that you are a "Self," yet a moment's analysis would show how false this premise is.

As you walk, you could think, "I must be a separate individual self, for my physical body gives me the impression of being a detached unit, self-propelled and separate from other objects as I walk past them." (Not really true, for even the physical body is in continual and necessary interaction with the environment in the course of breathing and eating. It is only a certain perspective that makes me include the stomach when I say "myself," but not the field that grows the food it digests or the sun that makes that food grow.)

As you see the other person, you could say to yourself, "I must be a separate individual self, or else why would I perceive that unit out there as other than myself?" (But it is not really "I" who sees the other; it is just a phenomenon of light waves hitting sensitive nerves. The *skandha* of the feeling senses then stimulates the *skandha* of perception to form a mental picture on the basis of this data.)

You may react emotionally to the person you see—with joy and desire if it is a person you love, with anger if it is someone you dislike. You may say, "I must be a separate individual self, for if I were not, who would be feeling these emotions of joy or anger?" (But these feelings are not a "self"—they are just something that comes and goes like billowing waves in response to data fed in by the senses, interpreted by the perception, and probably conditioned by the *karma* of patterns of behavior toward that person, or similar persons, carried over from the past along with much else.)

Finally, you may say, "I must be a separate individual self because I am aware of all this." (But the human capacity for self-consciousness is not itself a "self." It is just the *skandha* of consciousness that accompanies physical form, feeling, perceptions, and impulses—for it can neither generate nor erase the latter four; it is only a mirror in which they reflect as they act and react.)

Through such analysis as this, Buddhism concluded that we are not separate individual selves, but collections of elements temporarily brought together and bound to break apart. A life that disregards this fact is basing itself on a false premise and can experience only the syndrome of anxiety and craving as it faces old age, sickness, and death.

Nonetheless, this collection perversely wants to be a separate individual self. From birth on, a human being asserts selfhood as the real reason for most of what he or she does. The newborn baby cries as if to say, "I must be a separate individual self, or else who would be crying, and who would be hungry?"

Through life, one wants to learn, to achieve, to be loved, to accumulate goods, to acquire fame, to become a saint, to win life in heaven—all for oneself, all as though to say, "I must be a separate individual self, for if I were not, who would be learned, famous, beloved, immortal?" Nevertheless, all these dreams bring their own syndromes of anxiety and craving, and the body and perhaps the mind fall apart before they more than begin to be fulfilled.

The Buddhist would put the question another way: Who is rich, famous, wise, holy, immortal? A name? A process? A set of memories? None of these is a "Self." Is there any one who can be abstracted from the round of rising and falling feelings and forms of a human life, who is independent of the continual flux of the universe? If there is no one, then we cannot properly think of anyone as being the recipient of wealth, fame, wisdom, or as experiencing perception, anger, joy, and so forth; there is only wealth, fame, wisdom, perception, anger, and joy, and so forth. But these are not things to be grasped, and there is no one to grasp them. For the Buddha's final words are reported to have been, "All aggregates are transitory." Every compound, including the human, is unstable and will come apart.

The reason is *karma,* the force of universal action and reaction that keeps everything moving and changing. Your activities, mental images, and thoughts, even your desire to perpetuate yourself as a separate individual self, set up "waves" in the cosmos around you as you try to gain this object or fulfill that dream. No energy is lost, and sooner or later the waves based on the false premise will come back to afflict and finally shatter the compound.

If there is no separate individual self, one might ask how Buddhism can talk as it does of reincarnation. What is there to reincarnate?

In one sense, of course, the answer is nothing. But *karma* also means that you get what you want; or rather, you continue to be what you think you are. Every cause, including the illusion of being a separate individual "Self," has an exactly corresponding effect. The illusion then becomes self-perpetuating, life after life.

It might be called a kinetic view of reincarnation. There is nothing solid taken out of one body and put in another. Rather a deceased person's *skandhas* are dispersed into the universe. But the *karmic* waves that one has generated continue to operate until the precise kind of energy they bear has been appropriately transferred, just as ripples may continue to spread on the face of a pond even after a dropped stone has hit the bottom. The *karmic* waves will move until they have put together another set of five *skandhas* having shape, circumstance, and dispositions that are what they are because of the *karmic* energies left by the previous person. In energy terms, then, if not actual substance, this person can be spoken of as the "reincarnation" of the other person.

Nirvana

What is the goal of meditation? Ultimately, it is Nirvana, the state absolutely transcending all pairs of opposites, and so all conditioned reality, by the blowing out of all flames of attachment. In Nirvana, all conditioning and, therefore, attachment, including the notion of being a separate individual self, is gone utterly beyond.

It must not be supposed that Nirvana is simply a state hardly distinguishable from annihilation. It is rather the opposite—universalization, the falling away of all barriers so that the mind becomes undifferentiated from horizonless infinity. The full, attractive, positive nature of Nirvana must be stressed. The word "Nirvana" is said to mean "extinguish" or "blow out," like blowing out a flame, yet it does not mean disappearance in a negative sense, but rather the blowing out of all the fires of desire that constrict us. It does not mean extinction of consciousness but extinction of desires that cage and enslave consciousness. Our present consciousnesses are usually bound up with relishing sensory input and the accompanying mind-fogging cravings and self-delusions. It is virtually impossible for us now to know what Nirvanic consciousness, genuinely free of all this, would be like. Nirvana is truly the opposite of life as we know it. But for all that, or rather because of that, in Buddhist literature it is portrayed as the Otherness that is utterly desirable, a sparkling and golden light, calm beyond all imagining.

Nor is the quest for Nirvana escapist. Far from being less alive, active, or useful, the person who passes into it (if one can so speak), or is brought near to it, is far more—infinitely more—of all of these, as well as blissful to an unlimited degree. For, freed from the shackles of self, one can live purely on the level of universal compassion and oneness with the joy of all beings. But one simply cannot express in any words the full meaning of such statements. All language comes out of making distinctions and so is bound up with the pairs of opposites that rack the conditioned world. Nirvana is beyond all opposites; it is what is left, so to speak, when the last of them are surpassed. Therefore, although we know from the unsatisfactory nature of life within attachments, contraries, and conditions that nirvanic transcendence would be supremely desirable and glorious, words cannot tell what it is, only what it is not, and those who have been there can only smile.

Nirvana is not merely an enhanced personal existence, as if it were just a heaven gained by good merit. As we have seen in both Hindu and Buddhist philosophies, personality or separate existence are finally viewed not (as those in the West tend to think) as vehicles for expanding awareness and joy but as limitations. However much one may learn, see, and experience, infinitely more is unlearned, unseen, and unexperienced. For the separate self is conditioned by being in some particular time and place, has a limited life span, and even the most brilliant human mind can comprehend only so much—a few grains of sand on the beach of the sea of the infinite universe.

So the method of meditation leading to Nirvana does not involve the mind trying to comprehend through the senses and reason, but the awareness breaking through their finitude. This can be done; sense and reason are a ring of fire whose fuel lines can be cut. Meditation does not destroy the mind but opens it up completely by breaking down the barriers, so that one simply is the nirvanic ocean that rides the tides of the infinite like a surfer riding the waves. No longer is one cut off from infinity. Now one sees, thinks, knows, does to an unlimited degree.

This is the state claimed for the Buddha after his enlightenment. He still walked the earth, but in a Middle Way manner, making no *karmic* waves; and at the same time his infinitely attuned mind was able to know all and see all. Although an ordinary-sized human being, so perfect was his equilibrium that he could, like the operator of a perfectly adjusted lever, work incalculable results. It is said that, deep in meditation late at night, his mind would move like a searchlight through the world, find people in spiritual need, and he would transport himself through his power over matter to that point, or even to several points simultaneously, to help.

According to Buddhist belief, when the Buddha died, or rather attained Nirvana absolutely, an effect occurred that can only be called an implosion on the spiritual level. An implosion is the opposite of an explosion; it is what happens when a vacuum is suddenly created and all surrounding molecules of matter rush in to fill the void. The Buddha made no *karmic* waves, as we do trying to grasp at things to fulfill desires. But his passing was like an implosion in the *karmic* field— suddenly there was nothing there—and a stream of *karmic* force (good *karma*) is still rushing in, striving to enter the gateless gate through which he had passed.

The best way to go in the direction he went, of course, is to meditate, emulating the means he used to get there. Next best, if one must act, is to act in ways that harmonize one with the onrushing waves of this stream flowing into the implosion void and let them bear one along. This is the meaning of being a Buddhist who accepts the Three Refuges. It is the meaning of the ordinary acts of kindness that follow the four "unlimited" virtues—unlimited friendliness, unlimited compassion, unlimited sympathetic joy, unlimited even-mindedness. It is the inner meaning of the merit-making acts of lay people toward the meditative monks, such as giving them food, clothing, and donations. It is the meaning of acts of pure devotion that win good merit, like having **sutras** read, gilding images of the Buddha, burning incense, and offering flowers at shrines.

Theravada Buddhism

The Buddhist world is now divided into two great traditions. **Theravada** ("Path of the Elders") Buddhism[4] is found in the nations of Sri Lanka (formerly Ceylon), Myanmar (formerly Burma), Thailand, Cambodia, and Laos. **Mahayana** ("Great Vessel") Buddhism has spread throughout China, Korea, Japan, Tibet, Mongolia, Nepal, Bhutan, Vietnam, and corners of India and Russia.[5] Let us look first at Theravada Buddhism.

Theravada Buddhism grew out of a perceived need in approximately the third century B.C.E. (more than 200 years after the death of the Buddha) to reassert an authoritative Buddhist teaching in the face of growing divergences in the movement.

FUNDAMENTAL FEATURES OF BUDDHISM

THEORETICAL

Basic Worldview	Reality is an indescribable unity. Humans find themselves in a realm of suffering governed by *karma*.
God or Ultimate Reality	Unconditioned reality beyond all opposites: Nirvana, the Void.
Origin of the World/ Destiny of the World	While the cosmos may go through cycles, it has no known beginning or end.
Origin of Humans	An individual is a process of cause and effect rather than a self; to this there is no beginning.
Destiny of Humans	Unending lifetimes in this and other worlds, good or bad according to *karma* and merit. One then breaks through to attain the Nirvana state.
Revelation or Mediation between the Ultimate and the Human	Through the Buddha, who attained full enlightenment, and the scriptures attributed to him.

PRACTICAL

What Is Expected of Humans; Worship, Practices, Behavior	To do good. Religious and moral works that gain good rebirth. To seek Nirvana by meditation or related practices.

SOCIOLOGICAL

Major Social Institutions	Temples; the *samgha,* or order of monks.

The Buddha's teachings had been transmitted throughout the centuries by oral tradition, and they continued to be so even after this development for another 200 years when, sometime during the first century B.C.E., they were compiled as what has been known as the **Tripitaka** or "Three Baskets." The *Tripitaka,* written in the Pali language (a variation of Sanskrit) held to be the language in which the Buddha taught, deals with the Buddha's life and his basic teaching in three parts: the rules of monastic conduct, the Buddha's discourses, and doctrinal principles.

To the present, Theravada Buddhism holds that it is the original form of Buddhism, which emphasizes individual enlightenment and the monastic community. Significantly, it claims an unbroken lineage of monks that extends back to the *sangha* established by Buddha, himself. It is no surprise, then, that Theravadists (the "Elders") believe themselves to be following the Buddha's teachings more literally than do other Buddhist traditions, and place greater emphasis on the historical Buddha.

If you were to visit one of the Theravada countries, it would not be long before the practical and sociological expressions of Buddhism were evident to you, and through them you would perceive the wide and deep influence of Buddhism in these lands. You would be struck by the great number of temples dotting the cities and lush tropical hills of the countryside. The temples are ornate and elaborate. Curved eaves mount up to pitched roofs. Soaring spires, in the case of large and lovely edifices such as the Shwe Dagon Temple in Rangoon, seem to catch the very soul of the East. Guarding the temple gates are fierce-looking mythological beings; these, like the sculpture and murals one may see of epic heroes, such as Rama and Hanuman, are gods borrowed from Hinduism. Shrines to indigenous spirits of nature and weather, *nats* in Burma and *phis* in Thailand, lurk in the temple shadows. Like the borrowed Hindu gods, they are pupils of the Buddha on another plane than the human.

Within the cool temple, however, it is the Buddha who is supreme; his image gleams richly amid lamps and delicate offerings of incense, flowers, fruit, and water. He may be seated, standing, or reclining; these three postures represent, respectively, the Buddha's enlightenment, teaching, and entry into Nirvana. Worshippers come and go doing worshipful acts of merit, which will benefit them in this and coming lives and prepare them for ultimate release into Nirvana.

On the streets walk monks in their saffron-yellow robes, their heads shaved and arms bare in the warm humid air. If it is early morning—Theravada monks do not eat after noon—each may be holding a begging bowl. At the door of a house he will stand silent, head lowered and hands upraised, accepting whatever the indulgent householder places in his dish.

Most of the monks are young, for in all the Theravada countries except Sri Lanka it is a custom (not always observed today) for every young man, from prince to peasant, to spend a year of his life as a monk. This experience serves to stabilize one's religious life and is an initiation into manhood. A youth will not marry until after he has served as a monk, and his closest lifelong friends are likely to be those with whom he shared this experience. But the great majority of men, of course, do not remain in the cloister. However, among the morning mendicants will be a few gentle old veterans of the monastic path, and they are afforded great respect.

If you followed one of the monks, you would return after him to a neighborhood temple with its attached monastery. Here the monks gather after begging to consume the simple meals they have garnered. During the afternoon they will rest, study, and meditate.

The temple may be just a village or town **vihara**, rustic and no tourist attraction, but a center of community life. Here, traditionally, children go to school, festivals public and private are celebrated, and the dead are remembered. For the plain people of the town, monks are counselors, healers, exorcists, and friends.[6]

Or the temple might be one of the popular places of pilgrimage, where the faithful hope to win merit by gilding the Buddha's image or burning incense before the Buddha's giant footprint—that significant and popular shrine that suggests that the Enlightened One was here, is no longer, but we can follow in the direction he went.

Or the monk you followed might be one of the many who throng the great national temples of the Theravada lands—the Temple of the Emerald Buddha in Bangkok, the Shwe Dagon Temple in Rangoon, the Temple of the Tooth in Kandy, Sri Lanka. The skyward-curved towers of these splendid buildings, their pitched roofs and carved beams, their brilliant gold and color, their inner atmosphere of incense and contemplation, all murmur something of the sense of wonder and glory at the heart of Buddhism—and remind us it is far more than just a philosophy.

In theory, the main task of the monk in the monastery is meditation, for he is to emulate the Buddha himself, and it was through meditation that the Awakened One went thence. That the young novice is emulating the Buddha is shown by the procedure through which he enters the monastery, if only for a few months. He goes to the monastery dressed as a prince, accompanied by a friend who plays the role of the Buddha's charioteer. At the monastery, he will have his head shaved, don his coarse monkish robe, and, kneeling before the abbot, take refuge in the Three Jewels.

The monastic initiation of young men in some Theravada countries shows evidence of being a continuation of archaic pre-Buddhist initiations: The women weep as the boy departs; his teeth are scraped or blackened, suggestive of the ritual knocking out of a tooth of older rites; he is often jostled and ridiculed as he tries to put on his unfamiliar robes.[7]

But the high point is movement in another direction. Upheld by the Three Jewels, the monk knows he is to emulate the silent image of the Buddha in the temple, with its serene and inward gaze. He is to explore and know through meditation the inward realm, and finally he is to break through it into the Unconditioned—Nirvana. He is to become an *arhant,* a perfected and enlightened one who has attained nirvanic consciousness.

First, the monk must recognize that there are many worlds besides this one. Except for the animal world, the others are generally invisible, but they are accessible to inner organs of vision and are places of possible reincarnation. Like the shaman of old, the monk plunges into them through meditatively altered states of consciousness.

Hinduism and Buddhism speak of six *lokas,* possible "locales" or places where one can be reborn. These are, starting with the lowest:

The Hells
The Realm of Hungry Ghosts
The Animal World

The World of the Asuras or Ogres
The Human Realm
The Heavens of the Gods.[8]

The upper reaches of the heavens, although still part of conditioned reality and so not Nirvana, correspond to very rarefied states of consciousness. Attaining them is considered excellent spiritual exercise. Theravada Buddhism, then, has two basic kinds of meditation: **samadhi meditation** (which explores the *jhanas,* or higher states above matter and form) and **vipassana meditation** (which breaks through directly to Nirvana).

Samadhi meditation must begin with the practice of *sila,* ordinary morality and simplicity of life. It then moves to the technique of "one-pointed" meditation, focusing on one thing to concentrate the mind. There are 40 traditional topics for this concentration, ranging from discs of various colors to Buddhist virtues to grisly objects such as the repulsiveness of digested food and gnawed corpses— these last considered salutary for those overattached to the lusts of the body. After learning to focus entirely on the object, one can then leave it behind to enter the calm of formless realms of thought.[9]

Nirvana itself requires a more direct thrust. The way is through *vipassana,* the meditation of insight. Instead of 40, it employs only three hard-hitting topics: the impermanence of all things, that all is "ill" or unsatisfactory in conditioned reality, and that one is not a real ego or self. *Vipassana* gets back to the fundamental Buddhist outlook of the Four Noble Truths and *Anatman. Vipassana* meditators analyze themselves until they realize the truth of these three points. Then, as it were, in the gaps left by the breakdown of the ordinary ego-centered way of handling experience, flashes of nirvanic consciousness break through. The meditator is now "entering the stream" and continues in it until becoming an *arhant,* one who has full continuous nirvanic realization and will not be reborn.[10]

Nirvana, the other shore, or the transformation of consciousness, is the goal of Buddhism. Yet it must not be forgotten that Nirvana, for most, is far away, and the life of the religion is something quite other than a direct quest for Nirvana or *samadhi.* Even among the monks, the great majority are perhaps more interested in passing exams, in community affairs, and in the daily monastic round than in assiduous meditation.

Theravada laity do not generally expect to make formal meditations in the manner of monks. Rather, for them the tableau of the Buddhist map of the invisible world—its temples, pilgrimage places, and cosmic lore—become ways they can align themselves with streams of good karmic force set in motion by the implosion of the Buddha's Great Departure. Buddhism, for them, comes as a noble instrument for making merit, which will transform destiny to bring good things in this and future lives.

It must not be supposed, however, that the layperson's Buddhist orientation toward merit-making means a diminished Buddhist vision. It may well be richer than that of many monks. The splendors of the temples that the layperson loves offer a hint of Nirvana itself, which illumines the mind on deep levels. The observant visitor

*Theravada Buddhist monks
in Thailand.*

often is made aware that popular attitudes toward time, human relations, and good or bad fortune in Theravada cultures reflect such basic teachings as "No Self," *karma,* and the Four Noble Truths. But the layperson relates to the Buddhist vision differently: through what he or she does rather than what is experienced in meditation.

The layperson tries to follow, as well as possible, the five precepts: not to take life, steal, engage in sexual misconduct, lie, or take intoxicants. He or she tries also to exemplify the four unlimited virtues: unlimited friendliness, compassion, sympathetic joy, and even-mindedness. Through the four unlimiteds, one can be reborn in a divine heaven.

Merit can also be made by donations of robes and food to the monks, building **pagodas** and making monastery improvements, undertaking pilgrimages, sponsoring a candidate entering a monastery or a formal scripture-reading, working for community good, or giving food to the poor and to animals. The relation of monk and layperson is mutually profitable in merit terms: The laity win merit by donations to the monks; the monks, by preaching and teaching to the laity and by giving them the opportunity to win merit through gifts. The relation of monks and laity exemplifies one of the deepest Buddhist doctrines, the interdependence of all things.

In Theravada countries, there are services in local temples four times a lunar month at the four main phases of the moon. The chief annual festival is Wesak in the spring, commemorating the Buddha's birth, enlightenment, and entry into Nirvana. In various places on this day, trees are watered, candles and incense wave in processions, and rockets blaze through the sky—all aimed in part at producing the rain that will be so critical in the coming growing season.

A month later, the rainy period (May through July) begins in Southeast Asia. During this time, following the example of the Buddha himself, the monks remain in retreat in the monasteries. Many of the laity, in this Lentlike season, make a special effort to keep the precepts, or even enter the monastery temporarily themselves; for just the state of being a monk gives merit and benefit.

The monks and monastic life are like a reservoir of merit. The Buddha, the teaching, the order, and the laity are like concentric circles going around the absolute center, nirvanic consciousness. Every ring profits through interaction with its neighbors, especially the one next in.[11]

In the twentieth century, Theravada Buddhism was caught up in the crises of nationalism, modernization, and ideological conflict that have tormented its corner of the world. In Sri Lanka and Myanmar, some monks played a vigorous role in the movement for independence from Great Britain; and postindependence leaders, especially U Nu in Myanmar, made much of Buddhism, in part as a symbol of the national non-Western culture. Other Buddhist monks have endeavored to reconcile Buddhism with modern science and democracy. In Thailand, the government has made the rural monasteries centers for official programs in health and agricultural improvement. In Cambodia and Laos, Buddhist life has been disrupted by war and political instability.[12] In the 1970s, the Khmer Rouge nearly wiped out the *samgha* in Cambodia, which was especially targeted. There was some recovery under the Vietnamese occupation that followed. Today there is somewhat of a Buddhist revival in Cambodia; however, this has been difficult because so many of the elders were assassinated or fled during the communist takeover. In Laos, the transition to communism did not result in the extreme suppression that was experienced in Cambodia. Rather, the Buddhist monks were enlisted in support of the communist regime. Today the Buddhists in Laos are expected to participate productively in their communities, and the government oversees Buddhist doctrine and practice, purging it of subversive elements.

Yet despite the incursion of modern problems, visitors to the five Theravada countries will still find cultures deeply shaped by centuries of Buddhism. The temples still gleam, and yellow-robed monks still walk the streets.

Worshippers outside a Buddhist temple in Rangoon, Burma.

Mahayana Buddhism

Generally

The northern tier of Buddhist countries, including the great and distinctive Buddhist cultures of Tibet, China, Japan, Korea, and Vietnam, are in the Mahayana tradition. This style of being Buddhist, and of exploring the meaning of the historical Buddha's experience, is different from that of the Theravada Buddhism we have just discussed. It is a tradition almost as old as Theravada, although not as conservative.

The first appearance of what was to become Mahayana was the school called the Mahasamghika ("Great Monastic Order"), which arose within the Buddhist order about a century after the Buddha's death. The points of difference with the Theravadins lay in the Mahasamghika's insistence that monastic meetings be open to all practitioners, that popular religious practices be reconciled with Buddhism, and that the Buddha was really a supramundane and perfect being who came into our midst as a teacher. These are theoretical points that led directly to Mahayana's universalism, accommodation, and transcendence, although it should be recognized that by the time it became the popular Buddhism of several countries, Theravada had made its own adjustments in the same directions.

But through the early centuries of Buddhism, a consistently liberal and innovative group was pushing for more flexible forms of the tradition. By the first century C.E., this group appeared as a distinctive tradition marked off by the fact that they accepted not only the *Tripitaka,* but also a growing body of Sanskrit scriptures called **sutras**. Acceptance of the body of *sutra* literature, rather than any particular **doctrine**, is the formal test of a Mahayanist.

A broad consensus of attitude and doctrine runs through the Mahayana *sutras,* although they were written over several centuries and add up to a hundred times the bulk of the Christian Bible. (In theory, the *sutras* are put into the mouth of the historical Buddha and ascribed by commentators to various stages of his life; many are said to have been "hidden" for hundreds of years to await times when they would be most needed.)

These scriptures start from a universal rather than a historical perspective, holding that there is a universal true reality everywhere—known variously as the Void, Nirvana, Buddha-nature, **dharmakaya**—that is capable of being realized by anyone. Gautama Buddha realized it at the moment of his enlightenment, and so he manifests it and comes from it—but there are an infinite number of other Buddhas, too, and in a deeper sense everyone is actually an unrealized Buddha. Any means of attaining this realization is acceptable insofar as it works; the gradated practice of Theravada may be dispensed with, and techniques of devotion, chanting, even quasi-magic, brought in from *bhakti,* Tantrism, and folk religion, can be employed.

In all of this the key figure is the **bodhisattva**, who becomes for Mahayana the ideal in place of the Theravadin *arhant,* and in many ways sums up the Mahayana vision. The *bodhisattva* is on the way to Buddhahood but holds back at its very threshold out of compassion for the countless beings still in ignorance and suffering; the *bodhisattva* dwells both in Nirvana and in the phenomenal world, having the power and reality of both. As a borderline figure, he or she also imparts grace and receives devotion.

All of Buddhism is built on the Buddha's experience of infinite consciousness at the moment of his enlightenment. Buddhism is all the various methods of getting at the way he saw the universe at that moment, which is the way it really is. All other methods are partial and thus erroneous. Buddhism is also the various ways of interiorizing the same experience insofar as one can. In Theravada, this means "entering the stream" left by the historical Buddha. In Mahayana, there is more emphasis that the world perceived by the Buddha at enlightenment is the true reality everywhere present at all times, and so it can be apprehended directly by a number of different means and through a number of mediators. The historical Buddha, although respected, is relatively deemphasized in Mahayana. In the final analysis, all reality is full of Buddhas and is one's teacher of Buddhahood, just as all reality is one's parents—everywhere one can see sages, gods, and Buddhas who are essentially aspects of one's enlightened mind, and the Buddha-nature is in every blade of grass and every grain of sand.

Visiting a Mahayana country, one is immediately struck by a difference in Buddhist tone from Theravada countries. There is still the great splendor and peace of the Buddhist temple. But now, instead of a single, solitary Buddha image on the altar, attended by mere gods and men, one will see radiant Buddha after Buddha, *bodhisattva* after *bodhisattva,* all transcendentally aware, but all in different moods and poses, from serene meditation to explosive wrath, and from deep withdrawal to many-armed compassionate activity.

This reflects that Mahayana is, in effect, a "multimedia" way to Buddhahood. The "turning of the head" needful to see one's true Buddha-nature is not something that must be done only one way. Because it relates to the ungraspable, it cannot be put into a box. Thus, Mahayana has many methods, some very complex and some so simple as to seem insulting until one realizes that the simplicity is the point. Mahayana disdains none of the senses and no "level" of religion—from peasant folk faith to the most advanced metaphysical system.

Thus, Mahayana is **Zen** monks in Japan in long and immensely calm rows, "sitting quietly doing nothing." It is followers of **Pure Land** Buddhism chanting "Hail, Amitabha Buddha" and hoping to be brought into the "Pure Land" or Paradise of the Buddha of Infinite Light and Life from where attainment of Nirvana is sure—or perhaps just experiencing the "beingness" of doing the chant. It is Tibetan Tantric Buddhists blowing on trumpets of human thighbones and evoking, through chanting and intense visualization, the form of one's patronal spiritual ideal. Mahayana is finally the great peace of massive temples, the brazen images of supernal figures glowing dimly in incensed air.

The ultimate experience of Mahayana is ineffable, and so can be "turned on" by many different means: meditation; the numinous wonder of a temple that causes one to forget oneself for a moment; the quasi-hypnotic rhythm of chanting; the magical concentration of evocation. The very fact that its view of nirvanic realization is so tremendous makes it accessible in seemingly easy and multitudinous ways, for it is already here; everyone is already a Buddha.

The **Lotus Sutra**, one of the most important of all Mahayana texts, tells us that a simple offering of flowers or of a tiny clay *pagoda,* presented by a child to a Buddha, is of far more worth than all the proud efforts of an aspiring *arhant.* For any distance we can advance toward Buddhahood by our own self-centered efforts would be only as an inch to a thousand miles, but if one just forgets oneself in a childlike sense of wonder and giving, one is already there, for in that moment one's high walls of ego have vanished away. True, the temples and gilded images of Buddhist temples are meaningless from an ultimate point of view, but it is they that can bring us across, for they work with the natural effectiveness of bright baubles.

The *Lotus Sutra* also tells the parable of a father who, returning home to the house in which his children were waiting, was appalled to see it on fire and the children apparently unaware of the danger. Thinking quickly, he realized that if he shouted a warning, they might panic and be in a worse state. So instead, he cried out that he had new toy carts outside for them. Laughing and skipping eagerly, they ran from the house and were saved. Images, rites, devotion are like toys that draw us from the flames of desire and begin the process of self-transcendence.

The Buddha acts in a manner consistent with this view. The *Lotus Sutra* pictures him as like a rain cloud over all the earth that waters vegetation of all sizes and shapes equally. He is universal, ineffable reality, who appears on different levels of reality in different forms, in countless worlds over and over again—as godlike heavenly Buddhas and *bodhisattvas,* and in the human worlds as teachers like Gautama. He is, in the climax of this astounding document, portrayed as descending in a tremendous, bejeweled temple to turn the wheel of his teaching in this universe.[13]

Nagarjuna's Two Basic Principles

The greatest philosophical force in the emergence of Mahayana was the teaching of Nagarjuna (c. 150–250 C.E.). His two basic principles are that *samsara* (the phenomenal world) and Nirvana are not different, and that the most adequate expression for this totality is "Void."[14]

That *samsara* is Nirvana and Nirvana is *samsara* means that one does not "go" anywhere to "enter" Nirvana. It is here and now; we are all in it all the time, and so we are all Buddhas. Experiencing getting up, walking down the street, or washing dishes as Nirvana rather than as *samsara* is simply a matter of how it is seen. The way to see it as Nirvana is with complete nonattachment and nonegotism, which means making nothing within the web of our experience more important or more prior than anything else. Neither self, nor any god, nor Buddha, nor the *skandhas,* nor any concept or idea or principle, are to be made into a basic upon which reality is constructed. None of these exist or persist of its own power. All are "hollow"— impermanent, part of the flux of entities and ideas out of which the cosmos is constructed. All exist not of "own being" but only in their interrelationships.

The nirvanic vision, then, is to see all things, including (and this is perhaps the most difficult angle to get) oneself, the observer, equally and as an endless series of interdependencies and interrelationships. This universe neither starts nor stops anywhere. In it all things are continually rising and falling and moving in and out of each other, and nothing is stable except the totality itself, the "framework" in which this frameless and endless moving picture is situated.

Because the cosmos has no pivot or foundation or point of reference within itself (no starting or ending line), Nagarjuna believed the only adequate word for it is "Emptiness" or "Void." To say the cosmos is "Void" is not to say that nothing exists. The term "Void" is only a metaphor. But Emptiness or Void are the only appropriate words for Nagarjuna's cosmos, because any other word would imply some standard or "reality" to be grasped in order to understand it, and he taught that there is none. Void or Emptiness communicates the ungraspable quality of conditioned reality. Like the inside of a dewdrop or a soap bubble, Mahayana reality is, so to speak, done with mirrors—it is full of light and color, but everything is just a reflection of everything else, and there is nothing to seize. One who tries will be like a person who attempts to lasso a rainbow or bring home a sunset in a bucket.

The secret is the insight-wisdom called *prajna.* It is able to see things as they are without being attached at the same time to any structure of thought or theoretical concept. Theories try to make it possible to see things by interpreting them, but the use of such tools also twists them out of shape.

Chinese Bronze Buddha Amitabha, savior in Pure Land Buddhism.

The importance of *prajna* came about in this manner: Mahayana began in part in discussion of the six *paramitas,* or areas in which one could attain Buddhist perfection: donation (giving of gifts), morality, patience, zeal, meditation, and *prajna* or wisdom.

The supreme *paramita* is **prajnaparamita**: It must be built on the foundation of perfection in the other *paramitas.* But it is *prajna* that gives the lightning flash of final insight uniting one firmly, invincibly through every corner of one's subjectivity with the marvelous Void itself, and so makes one as secure as it. This is *prajnaparamita,* the "wisdom that has gone beyond" or the "perfection of wisdom." The earliest distinctive Mahayana literature deals with it. Indeed, in devotional Mahayana, *prajnaparamita* (like wisdom in the biblical Book of Proverbs) came to be personified as an initiating maiden greatly to be desired.[15]

The Bodhisattva

The great key figure in Mahayana thought is the *bodhisattva* ("enlightenment being"). *Bodhisattvas,* almost endless in name and number, dwell rank on rank in Mahayana heavens and flame out from countless Mahayana altars; there are also many of them, known and unknown, at work in this world. Virtually everything that is distinctive and of general interest in Mahayana is related to the *bodhisattva* and the *bodhisattva's* path. To understand this class of being, his or her meaning and methods, is to have the surest key to understanding Mahayana teaching, symbols, and practices.[16]

First, the *bodhisattva* epitomizes the ideal of *samsara* and Nirvana being not different, for the *bodhisattva* lives in both simultaneously. The *bodhisattva* is in the world, but without attachments, and therefore is able to see everything as it really is and to work with all power. Thus, the *bodhisattva* lives on the level of Void-consciousness.

Mahayana lore tells us that the *bodhisattva* is one who has taken a great vow to attain supreme and final enlightenment, however long it takes and at whatever cost, but at the same time to practice unlimited compassion toward all sentient beings, remaining active in this world without passing into absolute Buddhahood until all other beings are brought to enlightenment. Its fulfillment requires great sacrifice and suffering on his or her part. The *Lotus Sutra* portrays the *bodhisattvas* as superior to the Theravada *arhants* and "private Buddhas," who allegedly attain enlightenment for themselves only, falling short of the ideal of universal compassion.

In the *bodhisattva's* work in the world for liberation of other beings, the *bodhisattva* is activated by two principles, skill-in-means and compassion. Both of these derive from unconditioned awareness of the total interrelatedness of all things. Compassion is the ethical consequence of this knowledge; it is merely stating the fundamental Buddhist realization of "dependent cooorigination" in ethical terms. If one truly realizes that everything in the cosmos is dependent on everything else, and nothing and no one can exist apart from the rest of it, the only logical consequence for behavior is love, which negates all egocentricity; for interdependency shows up the error of centering life around private goals. The *bodhisattva*—like the historical Buddha in a previous life—would think nothing of giving his or her physical body to feed starving tiger cubs, for the *bodhisattva* knows that body and time are all transitory and mean nothing, whereas compassion is affirming the basic truth of existence, and any holding back would be basing life on a false premise.

The *bodhisattva's* compassion is not merely a vague, diffuse force, well intentioned but capable of doing almost as much harm as good because of a lack of knowledge of all factors in a situation, as is the "compassion" of some. The *bodhisattva's* compassion is instead a sharp, precise instrument, for it is combined with the accurate insight that the *bodhisattva's* freedom from "thought-coverings" allows. This is what is conveyed in the attribute "skill-in-means." He or she is able to see all the *karmic* factors in a life situation and thus to know just what changes can be wrought to set a person's steps in the right direction.

Moreover, the same deep awareness, undistorted by any egocentricity, gives the *bodhisattva* a control of appearances in the world, which seems magical but is actually based on a deeper awareness of subtle forces than the ordinary person has. The *bodhisattva* is able to take any apparition-body he or she wants, or, rather, that compassionate knowledge provides the insight as to what would be most beneficial in a particular situation. *Bodhisattvas* have worked in the world, according to Mahayana scriptures and stories, as monks, abbots, orphans, beggars, prostitutes, rich men, and gods.

In his or her work in the world, the *bodhisattva* is able to make those small but precise adjustments in a situation that will achieve maximum effect. Even a *bodhisattva* or Buddha cannot change *karma*. No power whatsoever can do this. None can change the lot a person has earned by past deeds or convert the entire world, groaning as it is under the weight of eons of dark *karma,* at a single stroke. But the *bodhisattva* can work with subtlety and skill to bring one to make new resolutions through wise teaching, edifying experiences, and a whiff of the wonder of complete Nirvana.

Above all, the subtly skilled and compassionate *bodhisattvas* impart a sense of sublime serenity, save in some of the wrathful manifestations of the **Vajrayana** tradition (which we will be discussing later). Whether the transcendentally tranquil princes of the Ajanta caves of India, crowned and holding flowers, or the many-armed and enigmatic-eyed Kannon of Japan, the *bodhisattvas* impart a feeling of attainment so perfect as to be effortless and exude mercy like the perfume of a lotus. The concept of the *bodhisattva,* whose beauty has moved hundreds of millions, is the supreme achievement of Mahayana Buddhism. It superbly exemplifies the ultimate meaning of the Middle Way by dwelling at once in *samsara* and Nirvana.

"Mind Only" (Yogacara)

Further developments in Mahayana thought and practice were in store. Some Mahayana thinkers, probably influenced in part by the developing nondualist Vedanta tradition in Hinduism, came to feel that merely to call the fabric of reality a "Void" was inadequate. A new tradition, found in the *Avatamsaka* and *Lankavatara*

Sutras and the thinkers Asanga and Vasubandhu (c. fourth century C.E.), said that what Nagarjuna had called Emptiness or Void is more like mind, like pure consciousness in which particular forms or thoughts rise and fall. This position, called *Yogacara* or *Vijnanavada* and best labeled in English "Mind Only" or "Consciousness Only," was immensely influential.[17] Most important, subsequent schools of Mahayana, including Zen and Vajrayana (both discussed below), are exponents of the Mind Only philosophy and are intellectually grounded on it as well as on Nagarjuna's Middle Way.

Buddhist Mind Only is comparable to idealistic philosophies of the West, such as that of George Berkeley. Mind Only holds that fundamentally only one clear mind or field of consciousness exists, the Buddha-nature or Nirvana. It is the basis of each person's own existence—we are therefore all Buddhas. But we do not realize this because we each "project" an apparent world of many different things, which we think we see outside of us but which actually is in our heads. It is really like an illusion made by the preconceptions and habitual but false modes of perception in which our individual *karmas* have bound us up and blinded us.

One can understand this by thinking of a movie projector. The screen is the one mind, the clear universal consciousness. The bulb in the projector is the one mind within, which is our own true nature. The reel of film is the "movie" put into the head by *karmic* forces reaching out of the past through preconception and habit to make us see and experience the kind of world they have made for us. We think we see forms—mountains and trees, cities and people, pleasure and suffering, joy and sadness—marching across the screen and invading our lives. But actually they are moving pictures cast by the reel running through our heads.

One might ask why, if each of us projects an individual "movie," we all seem to see the same world. Actually, this is not strictly the case; the world appears different to a child and to an adult, to people of different language and culture, and in subtle ways even to brothers and sisters. Yet admittedly there is general consensus about the "lay of the land." Mind Only philosophy says that this is because we carry over shared past impressions from collective as well as individual experience. This is called "store consciousness." Perhaps it would not be too much amiss to translate the concept by saying that the way we "see" the world is formed basically by human and community input, such as the common experiences of birth and having parents, language, education, and culture. What is added by individual *karma* is only like frosting—although it may be very important for individual destiny.

Mind Only, like most Eastern philosophies, is not just a theory. It is also a practice, as it is a path to transformation of consciousness. It describes the projections and store consciousness as a prelude to teaching how to get beneath them and live without coverings on the unstained mirror of the One Mind. One method, developed by **Chan** or Zen, is found simply through still meditation—"sitting quietly, doing nothing"—settling down until one lives beneath the coverings and projections.

Another method, developed by Vajrayana, is a kind of experiential shock therapy where one experiments with different "reels of film" by putting in one after another. This is the role of the psychic experiments and the visualizations of Buddhas and bodhisattvas, characteristic of the Tantric-influenced "esoteric" tradition in Mahayana. Through sacred and powerful words, gestures, and hard meditation, one creates before oneself alternative realities in which unlikely things are as real as rain. One may create a world in which one is a tree, or in which magic works, or where armies of gods battle in the sky, or—and this would be the goal—where Buddhas and *bodhisattvas* appear visibly on one's altar. Then one would "merge" with an evoked Buddha or *bodhisattva* and so share his or her bliss and enlightenment.

To do this, of course, one needs to have a good idea of what the universe of innumerable Buddhas and *bodhisattvas* envisioned by Mahayana—in countless worlds, in aspects of one's mind, in great lineages—is like: what they look like, how they are organized, how one goes about contacting each one. Furthermore, in Mahayana, each Buddha and *bodhisattva* may have his or her own heaven, a sort of aura around the *bodhisattva* from which entry into Nirvana through his or her aid is possible; these are different from the *karmic* heavens, also accepted by Mahayana, the highest of the six *lokas*. By devotion to a particular figure, one might enter the *bodhisattva's* Buddha-heaven.[18]

The Three Forms of Buddhic Expression (The Three "Buddha Bodies")

We see that the Buddha-reality (reality as seen by the enlightened eye) is encountered in so many different "styles"—in the Void, One Mind, Nirvana, in the many transcendent Buddhas and *bodhisattvas,* which seem more like gods in heaven than people of this earth, and finally in this world, where the historic Buddha and the *bodhisattvas* did their works of teaching and mercy. Accounting for these many "styles" led to yet another development in Mahayana, one that seems to have emerged in Mind Only circles. It is the **trikaya** concept, the idea of three "Buddha bodies."

The three "Buddha bodies" or forms of Buddhic Expression are the three ways or levels in which the Buddha essence is expressed. First there is the **dharmakaya**, the "truth body," what the universe ultimately is, the one mind through which the atoms and galaxies dance. It is the way the universe looks to a Buddha at the moment of enlightenment and entry into Nirvana, when all distinctions disappear and the universe and the Buddha's mind are absolutely one. This absolute nonduality is the Buddha-nature, the unstained mirror of the One Mind, the Void, Nirvana.

The second form of expression is the **sambhogakaya**, the "bliss body." It is the *dharmakaya* expressed in paradisal heavens ruled by radiant Buddhas, and it is represented in art and altar as golden Buddhas surrounded by gilded lotuses. But it must be remembered we are not talking about Buddhas or heavens literally "out there," but of the floating world of Buddhist reality, which is both (and neither) subjective and objective. In a profound sense, the *samboghakaya* is the absolute Buddha-nature insofar as it can be put into form—so it is now represented by the most luminous "otherness" kinds of forms possible, those that come out of the realms of dream, vision, and artistic creativity.

Buddhist monks at the royal temple in Bangkok, Thailand, beneath the figure of a giant mythological guardian.

The Great Buddha of Kamakura, Japan. The figure represents Amida, the Buddha of the Pure Land.

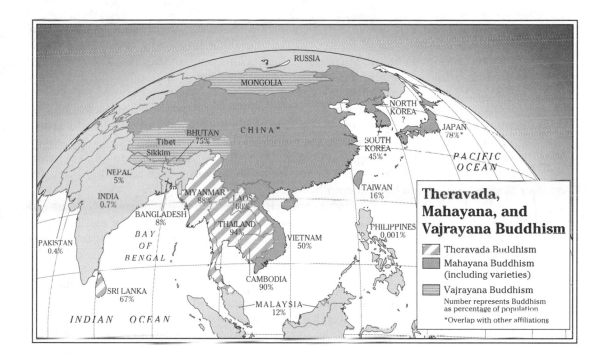

The *samboghakaya* centers around the radiant cosmic or meditation Buddhas, which are important in esoteric meditation. They are not Buddhas who were at one time historical human beings like Gautama, although sometimes legends about human lives in the remote past were given to them. Essentially, they are subjective–objective aspects of reality, which come into being in meditation and visualization as embodiments of aspects of the mind and the universe in their highest ratios. Above all, they are forms that give shape to the wonder of the Buddha-nature, and by bringing them into being in meditation, one provides bridges to it.

The **nirmanakaya**, the "marvelous transformation body," is the Buddha-nature expressed in this world of ordinary, "waking" reality. Because it is a world of seeing people and objects as separate, here the Buddha-nature comes to us as other persons—Gautama the Buddha and all the other Buddha-figures. This is only a development of the mighty concept of the *Lotus Sutra* that the Buddha-nature is really a universal reality without beginning or end, which comes into the world from time to time in apparent, apparition bodies.

Vajrayana (Tantric) Buddhism

The form of Mahayana that most developed these kinds of things is Vajrayana—the "Thunderbolt Vessel" or "Diamond Vessel." Today this is the Buddhism of Tibet, Nepal, Bhutan, and Mongolia, and it has much affected some schools in

China and Japan. But like so much else, it originated in old India. It stems from a confluence of Mind Only Buddhism with the same forces that went into Hindu Tantrism, and it can be thought of as Buddhist Tantrism. In the end, Vajrayana produced colorful art, potent devotional techniques, and philosophy no less deep than that of any other Buddhism.

As we have seen, Tantrism had its roots in the adaptation of obscure indigenous rites by questing persons who hoped, in their secret conclaves, to attain greater power than the *brahmin* and Buddhist "establishments." These practices centered around magic spells, mighty initiations, and usages that sought to generate the power of a kind of shock therapy by deliberately defying ordinary caste, ritual, sexual, and dietary conventions.

Buddhist Tantrists took very seriously the dictum that *samsara* is Nirvana. To them this meant that nothing in the *samsaric* world is intrinsically evil and that everything can be used as a means to liberation. Above all, this is true of the passions, and the most potent among them is clearly the sexual. Rather than seeking to circumvent the passions, which only leaves them lurking behind in one's psyche as potential depth charges, adherents to Vajrayana hold that one should wrestle with them, master them, and then deliberately arouse and direct their energy as dynamos of force for the breakthrough to the ultimate goal.

But the Tantric scriptures warn that this is a dangerous tack and that what the adept does would cost the ordinary bumbler eons in the hells. But Tantrists were nothing if not bold, and they prided themselves on their skill at dangerous occultism. Indeed, if *samsara* is Nirvana, it is necessary to bring all polarities together in the perfected human. The defiance of cultural prohibitions is a way of expressing this.

The dangers meant that secrecy was necessary, and much Tantric literature is veiled in a code called "twilight language." It meant also that only the qualified, or those supposed to be, were admitted, and that the student of these techniques had to work under the close supervision of a master, or *guru*. The one absolute in the Tantrist's world of inverted values was strict obedience to the master,[19] even if the master commanded, as some deliberately did, the most puzzling or perhaps shocking things—presumably to teach lessons about the emptiness of the universe.

By the early Middle Ages, Buddhist Tantra, as Vajrayana, had attained a literature and scholastic exponent. It became the prevailing form of Buddhism in some areas. Inevitably the rough edges were smoothed off; practices that violated conventional Buddhist morality were (because mind is all) translated into subjective meditations, restricted to marriage, or otherwise legitimatized, save in fringe groups. But it never quite lost its wildness either. Tantric adepts have always tended to be fierce, vivid, shamanlike characters, given to heroic spiritual strife deep in mountains or jungles, shunning the more staid academic and religious circles, and leaving behind beguiling tales of wizardry.

In Vajrayana thought, the *dharmakaya* is made equivalent to *prajna* (wisdom) and is regarded as feminine, the supreme mistress, the cosmic womb. Often Tantric practice is described in the texts and by teachers from the male point of view. When so described, the adept, from novice to Buddha, is masculine and personifies skill-in-means, seeking to penetrate and unite with *prajna*. But there are also descriptions of the sexual union as occurring between male and female adepts, where each envisions the other as a Buddha—male or female, respectively. Thus, in Tibetan art, the cosmic Buddhas and *bodhisattvas* are often shown locked in sexual embrace—as a "father-mother deity"—with their respective personifications of *prajna*. This represents the supreme enlightenment achievement. The great Vajrayana *mantrum* of Avalokiteshvara, *Om Mani Padme Hum,* "The Jewel in the Lotus" expresses all this, the union of Nirvana and *samsara,* of the male and female principles. In Vajrayana lands, it is chanted continually by priest and peasant alike and is the message of a million prayer wheels and prayer flags.

A novice being brought into the Vajrayana path will be given by his or her *guru* a particular deity or *yidam* (a male or female Buddha or *bodhisattva,* such as Green Tara, who is active compassion) as patron, from out of the vast Vajrayana ranks that crowd the *mandalas.* The novice will then seek to evoke the patron's presence through concentrated means and will study the deity's conventional picture, until it appears in the mind even when not looking at it. The novice will seek to unify with the deity's lines of spiritual force by repeating an assigned *mantra* and making *mudra* (ritualized hand gestures). Stemming from the Mind Only presuppositions, the practice strives to create for the adept a new universe revolving around the adept's "god." Finally, it is hoped that the deity will appear visibly on the altar to accept the adept's worship. The student will then pull closer and closer to the deity until the ultimate goal is attained, and the student becomes one with the assigned deity and shares the deity's intimate, Divine embrace and Buddha-enlightenment.

In the process, there is no lack of powers of sorcery the Tantrist can wield, generated as byproducts of the *mantras* and supernormal friendship that is possessed. But the true goal is enlightenment—realizing that all is mind—all gods, *bodhisattvas,* and Buddhas, and all souls and phenomena, arise out of mind and sink back into it. In this respect, far from being credulous, Vajrayana is psychologically both sophisticated and boldly experimental. It knows that the numerous celestial beings and forces it calls into service exist only in mind. They are projected out of it and then, once isolated and confronted, called back into it to reign over a liberated mind equal to their power. This is the Vajrayana expression of Mind Only philosophy. It is as if one were taking out one reel and putting in another, until forced to recognize that one can in fact create any universe one wants; and so one knows that no reel is more "real" than any other, and only the One Mind is "truly real." To learn this is to attain the true liberation.

Vajrayana Buddhism in Tibet

Tibet, "Land of Snow" and "Root of the World," has long had a very particular place in the imagination of the other peoples who dwell in lower, more prosaic places. For India, the realm behind the white ramparts of the highest mountains on earth, out of which the sacred Ganges flowed, was the abode of mystic Shiva and of mighty *siddhas,* wizard-adepts. For China, it was roughly Shangri-La, a paradise where the Queen-Mother of the West presided over a happy nation of Daoist immortals. For many in Europe and America, Tibet has been no less a land of magic and mystery, a cloudland of abominable snowmen and lost monasteries where occult lore is the specialty and weird psychic phenomena are everyday occurrences. Today, traditional Tibet has been severely disrupted, indeed nearly destroyed, by Chinese Communist rule, which began in 1951. The tradition is maintained by Tibetan exiles, like the country's monk-ruler, the Dalai Lama, in India and elsewhere.

Although many stories about religious Tibet may be romanticized, there is no doubt that it would seem a very strange place to those of contemporary Euro-American Western culture. But it also is significant, for the real Tibet represents a unique and often profound interpretation of Buddhism and of the human experience.

In Tibet, as much as a quarter of the male population wore the reddish robes of monks, and the great thick-walled monasteries were centers of trade, finance, and government; there were even monk-soldiers who battled with each other. Other monks concerned themselves with complex meditations calling up the visible presence of strange, colorful deities of fierce or benign countenance, or perhaps with the casting of spells or the writing of histories.

Tibetan monk painting a mandala that is used for meditation purposes. ■

The religion of the common people was equally colorful. Houses, as well as the squat, domed temples, were decked with bright prayer flags—pennants with brief *mantras* inscribed on them, flapping in the mountain wind. Prayer wheels—large drums around the outside of a temple, small ones held in the hand, each containing strips of paper inscribed with *mantras*—turned everywhere, sending out auspicious vibrations into the thin, crisp air. On holy days, particularly New Year's Day, brilliant dance pageants were enacted by the local priests and villagers wearing masks of grotesque demons and radiant heroes. Life in old Tibet was hard, and doubtless the ordinary people were, from a Western point of view, backward and exploited by their nobility and monk-rulers. But they were sturdy, immensely proud of their country and its religion, and, according to travelers, a cheerful folk.

The unique Tibetan spiritual culture was essentially a combination of indigenous shamanism with Tantric Vajrayana Buddhism imported from India and allowed, by the unusual degree of isolation Tibet's geography afforded, to develop in its own way. From shamanism came the desire of the adept of power to undergo initiation, demonstrate courage and vision, explore the infinite new worlds of the psychic plane, and manifest accomplishments through preternatural talents. From Buddhism came a sophisticated philosophical framework by which to explain these things. One has acquired unlimited full power because one has become one with the universal, invincible void; one travels to strange realms because one is realizing that one creates all one sees out of the *karma*-twisted mills of one's own mind.

This combination, and something of the profound Tibetan point of view, is made evident in the well-known *Bardo Thodol,* or **Tibetan Book of the Dead**, which is Tibet's most famous contribution to the world's religious thought.[20] The *Tibetan Book of the Dead* is essentially an account of the experience of a deceased person between death and, if destined by *karma* to be born again, the next entry into a womb. In it all levels of the Mahayana Buddhist cosmos are touched. The deep Vajrayana teaching that we create our lives, and our own heavens and hells, out of "Mind Only" is expressed.

The newly deceased entity first starts with the "highest" level to encounter the "Clear Light of the Void," the *dharmakaya,* or absolute essence of the universe. It is of "terrifying brightness," and out of it comes a roaring louder than a thousand thunderclaps at once, the light and vibrancy of an entire cosmos. If the pilgrim recognizes the *dharmakaya* as one's own true nature, however, the pilgrim can merge with it and attain the ultimate liberation immediately. Most, though, will be insufficiently prepared, shrink back, and lose the priceless moment of opportunity.

Still, other opportunities present themselves. The pilgrim next faces, one at a time and then all together, a *mandala* of five great cosmic Buddhas in their "peaceful" aspects. They are like heavenly forms of Universal Reality—the cosmic meditation Buddhas of the *samboghakaya*. Each of these corresponds, among other things, to one of the five *skandas*. It is as though form, feeling, perception, *karmic* dispositions, and consciousness are not merely inside human beings but reflect attributes or potentials that come into a lower level of manifestation in humans and a higher one in this realm. If the traveler in this **Bardo** realm recognizes them as "Mind Only" projections, that individual will merge into one of them and be liberated. But if that test is failed, the pilgrim will be frightened and pass quickly by. The next encounter is with the same deities in their horrible, terrifying aspect, full of wrath but with the same opportunity for recognition. If it is missed, the process of rebirth now firmly takes hold. The pilgrim is propelled by winds of *karma* reaching hurricane force and the entity experiences flash visions of judgment and of his or her future parents in copulation, and finally swoons, forgetting all on a conscious level, all that has transpired between the worlds, to awaken in the womb of whatever animal or human that is fated to give birth to him in the upcoming life. But even in these last stages the process can, with tremendous spiritual effort, be cut short and redirected. The most effective way is to meditate on the "father–mother" *guru,* the union of Buddha and Wisdom as male and female locked in erotic/ecstatic embrace, which is a popular subject of Tibetan sacred art. For the greatest power comes from the union of all opposites. And, psychologically, the deepest polarity that needs to be rejoined is our partiality toward the male and the female.

This account of the experience after death really expresses what Buddhism is about, for in the end all of its language, symbols, and practices are expressions of the union of opposites, the reconciliation of all polarities. From the Buddha's proclamation of a Middle Way, which finds infinite bliss in keeping a breathtakingly delicate balance between indulgence and asceticism, life and death, being and nonbeing, to the Tibetan vision of coupled father–mother gods in the *Bardo* sky, we have met with pointers to an experience of oneness. That experience makes one aware that it is a self-made shell of ego encrustations that keeps one from full consciousness; out of this egg one has to break with a shout of awakening.

Chan or Zen Buddhism

Chan is a form of Buddhism that developed in China, but the tradition is known better under its Japanese name of Zen. Chan means the school of *dhyana,* Sanskrit for "meditation."[21] For Chan and Zen, enlightenment arises unexpectedly, often suddenly, in the course of "sitting quietly, doing nothing" in meditation, or perhaps in response to an unconventional teaching gesture by a master. This is the Chan or Zen expression of Mind Only philosophy where one's goal is to embrace the Void that is the Really Real underlying all projections.

Chan teaching and practice is a "therapeutic" means of bringing people to inward realization of the basic ideas of Mahayana, especially the Void teaching of Nagarjuna and the Mind Only insight of Yogacara. What is distinctive about Chan is the fierce and direct means used to shake aspirants into inward realization of basic Mahayana truth. That was the truth of nondualism—that getting entangled in making distinctions keeps us from realizing that we and all else are the indivisible Buddha-nature now and forever. Chan masters claimed that their tradition was one of getting at the truth by "direct pointing" and that it was transmitted "outside the scriptures," in that it did not depend on words and letters but on immediate experience passed from master to disciple.

The experience, tradition said, began long ago when the Buddha silently handed a flower to a disciple named Kashyapa and smiled. The disciple smiled back and knew—the flower and smile conveyed a universe of wisdom indefinable by any words or books.

After Kashyapa, the secret of the smile was passed down through a lineage of "patriarchs" in India, until the twenty-eighth, a sage from India called **Bodhidharma** brought the tradition to China, where it became Chan in 520 C.E. To exemplify it, Bodhidharma spent years meditating in front of a brick wall and did not hesitate to tell an emperor to his face that all the temples he had built, all the scriptures he had ordered copied, and all the monks and nuns he had supported, had won him no merit whatsoever.

In several ways this account is fictitious and misleading. The line of patriarchs in India is undoubtedly an invention, and Chan was well on the way to formation in China even before the time of Bodhidharma. The claim of Chan to be "outside the scriptures" requires qualification, for the *Heart Sutra* and others are chanted and expounded in its monasteries, and Chan is nothing more than a means toward realization of the central Mahayana concepts that these *sutras* proclaim. But Bodhidharma does dramatize that Chan is interested not in learning for its own sake but in hard, sharp, direct realization—and that colorful stories and exaggerated making-of-points are among its armory of techniques.

So it is that the idea of Emptiness or Void and of the Buddha being found only in one's own consciousness (for all sentient beings are Buddhas and need only to be awakened to realize it) is shown in Chan disparagement of conventional Buddhist piety. In some places Buddha-images were chopped up periodically. In the earlier days of Chan, monks worked in the fields like peasants. A disciple once went up to his master, who was apparently weighing out a harvest of flax, and asked him, "What is the Buddha?" The master, continuing with his work, answered, "Three pounds of flax."

Another master had a habit of remaining silent and merely pointing up his thumb when asked a question like this. A disciple, seeing this and thinking cleverly to himself that there was some occult significance to this gesture, began to imitate his mentor by holding up his thumb in the same way. One day the master saw the boy do this and, quick as a flash, he whipped out a knife and cut the thumb off. When the disciple had recovered himself, he approached the master once more and brought himself to ask again the question, "What is the Buddha?" As though nothing had happened, the master held up his thumb. At that, the disciple attained enlightenment.

Perhaps this anecdote is related to the Chan saying, "When a finger is pointing at the moon, do not look at the finger." Scriptures, practices, and a good master may indeed point to the moon (a Buddhist symbol of Nirvana). But the idea is not to look at them but at where they are pointing. For the reality to which Chan points is prior to words and cannot be reduced to them. A Chan master was once asked what the "First Principle" is. He replied, "If I told you, it would become the Second Principle!"

Once again, the truth prior to words, which Chan and Zen radiate, is that one is the Buddha and in Nirvana now, in the "unborn mind" before thought, and that this realization is attained not by effort but by "doing nothing" and seeing who one is when one is not oriented toward doing anything. That "empty-handed" truth is well presented in a legend of Huineng (638–713), called the Sixth Patriarch of Chan in China, author of the *Platform Scripture,* and the man most responsible for the development of the Chan tradition.

Huineng came as a youth to the monastery of the Fifth Patriarch, Hongren. Only a poor obscure novice from the far south, then considered on the fringes of civilization, Huineng was set to such menial tasks as pounding rice. One day the Fifth Patriarch called the monks together and announced that he would make the Sixth Patriarch whoever of them could write a poem evidencing deep understanding and true enlightenment. One promising monk, Shenxiu (who later became patriarch of the now extinct "Northern School" of Chan), wrote:

> *Our body is the tree of Perfect Wisdom*
> *And our mind is a bright mirror.*
> *At all times diligently wipe them,*
> *So that they will be free from dust.*

The Fifth Patriarch said that these lines showed understanding. But he perceived that this rather pedestrian and moralistic approach did not come near the great breakthrough possible in Chan. The next night, an anonymous verse was posted for all to see. It read:

> *The tree of Perfect Wisdom is originally no tree.*
> *Nor has the bright mirror any frame.*
> *Buddha-nature is forever clear and pure.*
> *Where is there any dust?*

Here was the insight Hongren had been looking for. True enlightenment cannot consist of obsessively trying to wipe away symbolic dust particles, but it is the marvelous freedom of realizing that one's mind, one's self, and the dust are all equally "empty," and so unbounded. The Fifth Patriarch grasped that Huineng had written this poem, secretly called him in from the rice-pounding room, and made him his successor as Sixth Patriarch.

How was the realization of one's true nature to be attained? By not striving to attain it. How does one reach a state of nonstriving? Chan masters used several means. The most important is meditation: just sitting, doing nothing, striving for nothing, attaining nothing. However, Chan sitting does mean a definite posture and long hours. It produces a situation of nonstriving in which something can happen.

Many masters found that other techniques could hurry along the process of reaching nonstriving in their pupils. Some would fiercely scold, strike, and beat the disciples when they showed signs of trying too hard while missing the point, like the pupil who got his thumb sliced off. All this was intended as shock therapy to knock the novice out of the rut his thinking and into a different perspective.

Many masters used the enigmatic Chan anecdotes, riddles, and sayings (known in the West by the Japanese name **koan**), such as "What is the sound of one hand clapping?" or "Where was your face before you were born?" While these puzzles can be answered in terms of the Void and Mind Only philosophies, the real point is that such conundrums bring the ordinary, rational "monkey mind" to a stop. They stop its perpetual chatter by feeding it something it cannot handle in its usual way. Perhaps, Chan says, if the relentless mental process can be quashed for just a moment, the mind will have a chance to see what it is when it is not chattering and chewing.

But liberating what is genuinely free and spontaneous within is not easy. Unlike some shallow romantics, Chan does not confuse true spontaneity with mere self-indulgence. Liberation is not doing what you want to do, for the tradition is well aware that what the ordinary, unenlightened person thinks he or she wants to do is merely the operation of those attachment-rooted desires that, fulfilled or not, can only enslave one in the bitter syndrome of craving, anxiety, and despair. The life of a well-ordered Chan or Zen monastery is very much the reverse of a hedonistic life; through the deprivation techniques of celibacy, scanty food and sleep, hard work, long meditation in freezing halls, and on top of that sometimes physical and verbal abuse, it is hoped that the monk would find out who he is apart from the desire-wrought illusion of being a separate person.

When success comes, then the seeker is truly free —for he lives on the level of spontaneous enlightenment and Buddhahood everywhere, even in the most trivial aspects of life. One master, Huihai, when asked if he did anything special to live in the *Dao* (the Way of the Universe), replied, "Yes; when hungry I eat, when tired, I sleep." When asked how this way differed from what ordinary people did, he replied in effect that ordinary people do not just eat when they eat, but they use eating as an occasion to let the desire-stimulated imagination run wild, thinking of what food one would like or having conceits of how the food one is eating symbolizes one's prosperity, lifestyle, and the like; similarly, ordinary people do not just sleep when they sleep, but they lie on their beds awash with waves of restless worries, fancies, and lusts. The goal of Chan, however, is just to eat when you are hungry and sleep when you are tired—nothing more.

In the same vein, another master, Qingyuan, said that before he had studied Chan for 30 years, he saw mountains as mountains and waters as waters. When he had made some progress, he no longer saw mountains as mountains and waters as waters. But when he got to the very heart of Chan, he again saw mountains as mountains and waters as waters.

Pure Land Buddhism

The other important East Asian style of Mahayana Buddhism is Pure Land. While the scriptures that describe the Pure Land derive from India, it was only in China, Korea, Japan, and Vietnam that Pure Land became an important and distinct form of Buddhism. Like Chan, Pure Land evokes the freedom of nonstriving and nondependence on one's ego-self. A highly seminal early Chinese Buddhist philosopher, Daosheng (d. 434), spoke for both Chan and Pure Land when he argued that enlightenment has to be a sudden leap. Because it is a leap into the indivisible, he said, one can no more go through gradual stages of partial enlightenment than one can jump across a chasm in several steps.

But, in Pure Land, the structure is different; one has freedom from gradualism, striving, and self by dependence on the marvelous help of another, **Amitabha Buddha**, who can instantaneously and effortlessly give, out of his endless store of merit and grace, assurance to all who call upon his name that they will be reborn in his Pure Land where full enlightenment is easily available.

Amitabha, called Emiduo in Chinese and **Amida** in Japanese, is the Buddha in the West of the esoteric *mandala* and *The Tibetan Book of the Dead,* and his Pure Land is also called the Western Paradise. It was said that countless ages ago he was an aspirant who, in setting foot on the path, vowed (the "Original Vow") that if he attained full and perfect enlightenment, out of compassion he would bring all who called upon his name into his Buddha-paradise (an enlightenment world that surrounds a Buddha like an aura, in which his devotees can dwell; not to be confused with the desire-heavens among the six *lokas*). Amitabha's paradise is described in marvelous terms. There are jeweled trees linked by gold threads, fields of lapis lazuli, and perfumed rivers that give off music.

In China and Japan, Amitabha became, for vast numbers of worshippers, virtually the only Buddha (assisted by **Kuan-Yin**, also known as Guanyin, and as Kannon in Japan), who as mercy-working *bodhisattva* has generally been closely linked to Pure Land Buddhism. Amitabha came to be, in effect, the universal Buddha-nature, and placing trust in him is an act of release that negates the individual ego in favor of harmonizing it with Nirvana or the universal. The Pure Land experience, then, ideally is not really different in character from the enlightenment experiences described in quite different words by other Buddhists.

Women in Buddhism

The Dharma: Opening the Door to Women's Enlightenment

Arguably, Buddhist philosophy supports a more egalitarian role for women than previously had been known in Hinduism. The concepts of "no-self," "codependent origination," and the illusory nature of distinctions and polarities provide a fundamental basis upon which to argue that "maleness" and "femaleness" are illusory categories. To contend otherwise is to be ego-attached—valuing one over the other. Still, the practical and sociological manifestations of Buddhism over the centuries have perpetuated feminine stereotypes to greater and lesser degrees, making true equality as yet unachieved.

But Buddhism must be taken in its historical context. For its time it provided a tremendous shift in attitudes toward women. Most significantly, it acknowledged that women, too, can attain Nirvana. Interestingly, this gave rise to the "woman question." No longer were the role and status of women deemed settled questions by the religiously orthodox. Instead, Buddhism opened the door for consideration of such questions as: What are the proper role and status of women? What capacities and qualities are attributable to women? What goals are appropriate for women? The "woman question" has been a much debated topic in Buddhism from the very beginning of its history and remains so today. Consequently, when contemporary feminists raise it in the Buddhist tradition, it is not an innovation. Rather, feminists enter a long-standing debate for which many resources may be found in Buddhist writings.[22]

Women in Early Indian Buddhism and Theravada Buddhism

As we have seen, Buddhism arose out of the social and religious context of old India. Hinduism was a religio-cultural vision of an entire social-cosmic structure. Buddhism, on the other hand, did not provide an alternative vision for society. Instead, it offered an alternative life—the life of the *samgha* and the *dharma*—to those willing to leave behind the conventions of Hindu society. This was a life focused on the goal of overcoming the suffering attachments of ordinary conditioned existence and realizing the bliss of Nirvana.

Thus, Buddhism moved the locus of religion outside the sphere of the home. Instead, the *samgha* became the center of religious life. Consequently, Buddhism provided an opportunity, an option, not available to women before. Women could become or continue in their roles as wives and attempt to exemplify the Hindu ideal; or women could reject convention, live outside the constraints of society, and follow the Buddha's *dharma*.

It is important to recall that early Buddhism developed in India at a time when Indian women led lives that were severely restricted by the dictates of Hindu religious law and custom. Women were focused on (and in many cases bound to) the home and generally were uneducated. Consequently, when the Buddha decided to include women in the *samgha,* it was nothing less than radical. Although the Buddha's *dharma* supported an egalitarian view toward women and men, these ideas were in conflict with an existing cultural bias in favor of female subjugation to male authority. The tension between the *dharma* and socio-cultural attitudes toward women was, therefore, present from the beginning.

The story of the founding of the order of nuns (*bhiksuni-samgha*) and debates surrounding its authenticity illustrate the uneasy compromise between the egalitarian dharma of the Buddha and the socio-cultural views toward women at that time. The story, as told in the *Vinaya (The Book of Discipline)*, is that, approximately five years after the Buddha's enlightenment and the founding of the order of monks (*bhiku-samgha*), women who had been following the *dharma* sought recognition in the new religion. **Mahaprajapati**, the Buddha's aunt and foster mother, approached the Buddha, asking that she and 500 women followers be permitted to join the Buddha in the life of the renunciant. The Buddha rejected

Mahaprajapati's request, but she was not easily dissuaded. Twice more she approached the Buddha with her request, and twice more she was denied.

At the third rejection of Mahaprajapati's request, however, the Buddha's attendant, Ananda, successfully argued the case of the women to the Buddha. He asked: Did not the Buddha hold that women could attain enlightenment? Accordingly, they, like men, would benefit from living the life of the renunciant, Ananda reasoned. Buddha agreed and thereby assented to the founding of the order of nuns on the condition that the nuns were to accept being subjected to eight special rules (*garudharma*).[23] The eight rules were the following:

> *(1) Any nun, no matter how long she had been in the order, must treat any monk, even the rudest novice, as if he were her senior; (2) Nuns should not take up residence during the annual rainy-season retreat in any place where monks were not available to supervise them; (3) Monks would set the dates for the biweekly assemblies; (4) During the ceremony at the end of the rainy-season retreat, when monks and nuns invited criticisms from their own communities, the nuns must also invite criticism from the monks; (5) Monks must share in setting and supervising penances for the nuns; (6) Monks must share in the ordination of nuns; (7) Nuns must never revile or abuse monks; and (8) Nuns must not reprimand monks directly (although they could and did report one monk's offensive behavior to another, who then might take the appropriate actions to correct it).*

In addition, according to the Buddhist monastic rule, nuns were to be teachers of women, but were not permitted to teach monks, although monks could teach nuns.[24] Moreover, the Buddha is reported to have said that because women were allowed to participate, the *samgha* would be weakened and, therefore, the *dharma* would last only 500 years instead of the 1,000 it would have without the nuns. The effect of these rules and the account of the weakening of the *samgha* was to place the nuns in a subordinate position to the monks, keeping authoritarian power in the *samgha* under male control.

As Nancy Falk has written, however, women were likely to have found their situation to be greatly liberating as compared with their previous positions in traditional Hindu society. More important, the eight rules did not interfere with their main purpose for participating in the *samgha*—the pursuit of those practices that would lead them to enlightenment. Also, it has been noted that the rules may have been, at least in part, for the protection of the nuns from violence by the monks and from being treated as servants by the monks who might wrongly think it appropriate for nuns to clean and prepare food for them. Or, possibly, the Buddha may have wanted to preserve the order of nuns against the condemnation of Hindu householders. Keeping the nuns in check under male authority may have mitigated against the arguments of those who viewed the inclusion of nuns in the *samgha* as leading to societal decay in that women were not upholding the Hindu social order by remaining at home.[25]

On the other hand, the lower status of the nuns as compared with monks limited the development of the order of nuns and probably adversely affected their ability to obtain sufficient charitable support for their activities.[26] The monks were more renowned because they were more numerous and more visible, and the nuns could not develop commensurate prestige because they were not permitted to teach men. As Nancy Schuster Barnes has said, "Women were there, are there, but most often seem to remain on the shadowy fringes of the religious life, not at the creative, influential center of religious activity."[27] This is thought to have been a major contributing factor in the decline and eventual demise of the order of nuns in those countries in which it first developed (i.e., India, Sri Lanka, and Burma), and a possible explanation for the fact that the order of nuns never developed fully in other Buddhist countries, such as Thailand, Cambodia, Laos, or Tibet. It is significant to note that by the thirteenth century, no order of Theravada nuns remained in these countries. Today the only unbroken existing lineages of nuns are in China, Korea, Japan, and Vietnam, where nuns have been more visible and influential as teachers of laity and spiritual guides to emperors and their families.[28]

The historical accuracy of the story of the founding of the nuns' order is itself in much dispute. Some scholars hold that because Buddhism always has been egalitarian at the core of its teachings, it does not follow that the Buddha would have distinguished nuns from monks in the manner represented in the story. The Buddha is said to have acknowledged that women could be, and were in his time, exemplary adepts. Moreover, the **Therigatha** (*Psalms of the Sisters*), which has been preserved, contains beautiful accounts of the enlightenment of over 70 women who are believed to have been among the first nuns. This leads such scholars to contemplate whether the foundation story was, rather, a later writing that reflected the continuing tension between the *dharma* and cultural attitudes toward women.[29]

This tension is further illustrated in writings that contain misogynistic passages, particularly from the later period of early Buddhism. One passage in the Pali canon states: "Even when . . . stricken or dying, a woman will stop to ensnare the heart of a man."[30] And the Buddha is reported to have said that "[w]omen folk are uncontrollable...envious . . . greedy . . . weak in wisdom. . . . A woman's heart is haunted by stinginess . . . jealousy . . . sensuality."[31] As in Hinduism, such passages may be attributed to the biases of unenlightened male renunciants who view women as obstacles to attaining Nirvana. As a consequence, these male renunciants project their frustrations with themselves onto the objects of their lust. There are countervailing passages that support this view in which the Buddha himself is reported to have cited men's lust as the problem.[32] The Buddha is credited with many positive statements about women as well. Nevertheless, such misogynistic passages were likely to have contributed to attitudes that resulted in or reflected the tendency to relegate the nuns to a lower place in the *samgha* despite the obvious egalitarian doctrine of the *dharma* and, as Theravada Buddhism developed, to the tendency to exclude women from the *samgha* entirely.

In addition to the *samgha,* the Buddha established an order of laywomen (*upasika*) and laymen (*upasaka*). The lay disciples did not leave behind their conventional lives but practiced a Buddhism that accommodated their worldly vocations. The records reflect a measure of ambiguity regarding early Buddhist laywomen. On the one hand, these women, even more than the nuns, presented a temptation to the monks who would meet them while the monks obtained daily offerings of food.[33] On the other hand, laywomen constituted some of Buddhism's most ardent benefactors. The many passages praising the exemplary qualities of certain laywomen can be attributed, in part, to their substantial economic support of the *samgha*.[34]

In general, laywomen fared reasonably well under Buddhism. They were given the same instruction that the laymen received. And both men and women were encouraged to contribute to the well-being of their communities by upholding the traditional social order more in the sense of a partnership than was so in Hinduism. Significantly, the status of wives seems to have improved considerably under Buddhism, probably due to Buddhist recognition of women as being able to reach the highest spiritual achievements and, therefore, being given the option of the renunciant life, making marriage a choice and not merely a social and religious obligation.[35]

When the Theravada and Mahayana schools split, one central issue was the proper role and status of women. Theravada tended toward a negative view of women and their capabilities. Mahayana, on the other hand, tended to develop a more positive and egalitarian view toward women.

Women in Mahayana Buddhism

It is important to recall at this point that Mahayana Buddhism is the "Great Vessel," a vehicle for an all-inclusive notion of the *samgha*. In this view, all have the universal Buddha nature and are capable of realizing Nirvana now. As a consequence of this altered view of the *samgha* and the belief that enlightenment is not only for renunciants, there is not the sharp division between the renunciants and the laity that is seen in Theravada Buddhism. Householders, both men and women, are recognized as advanced and capable of attaining Buddhahood. This shift in doctrine made Mahayana Buddhism more accessible to all, which resulted in a tendency toward an egalitarian approach toward women not only in theory but in practice.

Nevertheless, the Mahayana order of nuns remained subject to the eight special rules as in Theravada Buddhism, and some Mahayana Buddhist texts reveal a continued ambivalence toward women. This ambivalence is revealed in the writings questioning whether one can reach Buddhahood while remaining in female form. Many texts claim that the "highest levels of wisdom and insight" can be attained by women who are able to espouse the "highest truths and most complex philosophical arguments of Mahayana thought."[36] Other texts argue, however, that it is only after one ceases to be reborn in female form that Buddhahood can be attained. Some Mahayana texts claim that the Buddha himself ceased female rebirths even before he ceased rebirths as animals.[37]

There are many stories of exemplary women adepts being challenged by men on this point. Often such stories recount that, when challenged, the woman transforms herself into a man, revealing that she has attained Buddhahood. One such story is the *Lotus Sutra* account of the miraculous feats of the Naga Princess. She was challenged by Sariputra (who symbolizes conservative Buddhism) because, he claims, the female body is unsuited to the five ranks of existence that one must pass through on the way to Buddhahood. Upon being so challenged, the Naga Princess's "female organ disappeared and the male organ became visible" and she became a *bodhisattva* and then, immediately thereafter, a Buddha.[38] In another story, when asked why she does not change her female sex, the woman transforms her challenger into her own form and herself into his and then asks: "Why don't you change your female sex?" The story concludes with the man realizing that "[t]he female form and innate characteristics neither exist nor do not exist."[39]

There is some dispute regarding the significance of these stories for women. Some, such as Diane Paul, argue that the accounts of a woman's transformation into male form, in effect, derogate the female body, implying that it is inadequate for the enlightened state of complete wisdom and compassion.[40] However, Rita Gross's interpretation probably is more to the point. She concludes that the sexual transformation stories do not show the superiority of the male body, but that the woman already had the power of enlightenment and was unattached to any particular form. Thus, she exemplifies the wisdom that "gender, like every other phenomenon, has no fixed essence and so does not limit those who bear its illusory outward signs."[41] This view is supported by stories of women in other texts who teach the *dharma,* are recognized as having achieved enlightenment, and are not challenged regarding their female form. The story in *The Sutra of Queen Srimala Who Had the Lion's Roar* (i.e., was enlightened) is a notable example. As Nancy Schuster Barnes puts it: "The Mahayana sutras demonstrate dramatically that the man who clings to his maleness is not an enlightened being, and the women who does not worry about changing her sex is genuinely enlightened. This is a dramatic demonstration of the meaning of emptiness."[42]

The *bodhisattva* ideal of wisdom and compassion also supports the view that Mahayana Buddhism, in general, promotes an egalitarian approach regarding women. While a few texts claim that one cannot become a *bodhisattva* in female form, in general, there are numerous references to female *bodhisattvas* in Mahayana Buddhism. Kuan-yin or Guanyin (Kannon in Japan), the *bodhisattva* of mercy, is one of many. Although she originated in India as Avalokitesvara, who was male, in China and Japan she became the Goddess of Compassion and is a central figure, considered a goddess, and is nearly always given a prominent place on the altars of Mahayana temples and homes. And *Prajnaparamita* (the Perfection of Wisdom) is the primordial female principle—the universal expression of absolute wisdom and the mother of all buddhas and *bodhisattvas. The Perfection of Wisdom in 8000 Lines,* an early example of Mahayana literature, beautifully expresses the centrality of this feminine principle:

> *The Buddhas in the world-systems in the ten directions*
> *Bring to mind this perfection of wisdom as their mother.*
> *The saviours of the world who were in the past, and also are now in the ten directions*

Have issued from her, and so will the future ones be.
She is the one who shows this world (for what it is), she is the genetrix, the mother of
*   the Buddhas.*[43]

We can see then that while Mahayana Buddhism continued to exhibit some ambivalence toward women, its texts presented a significant move toward an egalitarian Buddhism.

Women in Vajrayana (Tantric) Buddhism

At the core of Vajrayana or Tantric Buddhism is a recognition of the apparent duality of the universe in male and female forms, which is seen as the most profound fact of existence. Thus, ultimate realization requires the merging of both into an all-encompassing unity—devoid of such distinctions as male and female. *Prajna* (discussed earlier) is the feminine principle, which represents primordial infinite space—that emptiness that is also ultimate wisdom out of which the phenomenal world manifests. The masculine principle, **karuna**, represents "form, activity, compassion"—that which is manifested. Yet, ultimately space and form are not separate for, as is said in the *Heart Sutra:* "Form is emptiness but emptiness is also form."[44]

The central symbol of this unity is the sexual embrace of male and female *yidams* or Buddhas, as we have said. Accordingly, unlike in many other religions (including other forms of Buddhism) where the human body is eschewed as an obstacle to spiritual perfection, in Vajrayana Buddhism the body is celebrated as the vehicle through which one may realize Nirvana in this lifetime, and this results in praise for the female body. Tantric texts are replete with passages describing in detail the wonders of the sacred lotus (symbol of the female sex organ—*bhasa* or *yoni*) through which ultimate wisdom may be sought and received. And female symbolism is pervasive—as the masculine must always appear with its counterpart in what Rita Gross calls a "dyadic unity."[45] This appreciation of the female body, together with abundant female symbolism, makes Vajrayana especially hospitable to women, who in some texts of Vajrayana Buddhism are venerated as goddesses.

Women have many options in Tantric Buddhism. They may be nuns and laywomen practitioners as in other forms of Buddhism. Unique to Tantric Buddhism, however, are the *yoginis* or *tantrikas* who live their lives neither as monastics nor as laywomen, but rather as full-time practitioners who wander the countryside alone or in groups, teaching the tantric methods to both men and women. Tantric texts include stories of extraordinary *yoginis* who were gurus of renown, such as the story of Yeshe Tsogel, the famous and revered eighth century *tantrika,* who, together with her tantric partner, is believed to have established Buddhism in Tibet.[46]

Tantric Buddhism in some of its forms, like Tantric Hinduism, attempts to work against social conventions, which are considered to be obstacles to attaining ultimate wisdom. It is not surprising, therefore, to find the traditional subjugation of women to be reversed. Consequently, one can find many passages requiring men not only to overcome their prejudices against women (which is evidence of their own ignorance), but also to worship women because the veneration of women is the surest path to enlightenment.

An especially beautiful passage from the *Candamaharosana-tantra* instructs a man how to worship his Tantric partner:

> *The man [sees] the woman as a goddess,*
> *The woman [sees] the man as a god.*
> *By joining the diamond scepter and lotus,*
> *They should make offerings to each other.*
> *There is no worship apart from this . . .*
>
> *Then the yogi lovingly*
> *Makes a mandala in front [of himself],*
> *And the woman enters that.*
> *As the embodiment of Perfection of Wisdom,*
> *He continuously worships [her] with flowers,*
> *Incense, butter lamps, and other articles.*
> *After uniting the five mandalas,*
> *He should prostrate to her,*
> *Circumambulate [her] clockwise, and*
> *Worship the ardently passionate yogini.*
> *The man worships the woman in that way,*
> *With a mind full of reverence.*[47]

As we have already seen, Vajrayana Buddhism has an elaborate pantheon of Buddhas and deities, which include many in beautiful, powerful, and wrathful female forms. A central and formidable female cosmic Buddha is Vajrayogini—the liberator. She appears as a blood-red goddess in Tantric art with flowing black hair, dancing with passionate abandon on the corpses under her feet and offering a skull cap full of ambrosia to the Tantric seeker. Another central female cosmic Buddha is Tara—the giver of wisdom. Tara appears as a beautiful emerald green, nurturing goddess, sitting on her lotus flower, inviting the seeker with joy and peace into the calm assurance of her maternal embrace. Both are *yidams* (or deities that exemplify pure enlightenment) on which the adept (male or female) meditates, and that can be visualized in Tantric sexual embrace with a male *yidam*.

There are also many *dakini*. These are enlightened beings who represent the female principle and can be in human or nonhuman form. They surround the *yidam* or *yidam* couple, providing insight and enhancing passionate energy that is evoked to bring about spiritual ecstasy, which leads to enlightenment.[48]

One might expect that a religion so imbued with female imagery—whose very essence requires the presence of the feminine—would be devoid of patriarchal characteristics. Unfortunately, here too in the institutions of Tantric Buddhism we find a tendency toward male control of authority, less education and support of female adepts, and a suspicion of such women for stepping outside the norms of conventional society.[49] And there is evidence that women have been sexually exploited by men who used them as objects in the attainment of their own spiritual goals.

The Tantric Buddhism of Tibet illustrates this discrepancy. There the subjugation of women is inherent in the very word for "woman" in the Tibetan language. It means "born low."

> *This word carries a conscious social status that Tibetans everywhere recognize as low. Yes, they say, a woman is not as capable as a man; she cannot enter into new areas of development; her place is in the house; she lacks a man's intellectual capacity; she is unable to initiate new things; and finally, she cannot become a Bodhisattva until she is reborn as a man.*[50]

As a consequence of these prevailing attitudes, women do not participate equally in the religious practices of Tibet, where male authority is nearly absolute. Tibetan sexual Tantric practices tend to be "right-handed" (i.e., symbolic). Thus, the male adept can perform the rites in meditative trance, visualizing the unity of the male *yidam* and *prajna,* without the aid of actual physical contact. Apparently, the irony of the incongruence of the unabashed acceptance, even reverence, of women in the Tantric texts and the socio-cultural attitudes that severely limit women's actual involvement is not recognized by Tibetans. Even the women themselves accept with resignation the misfortune of their female births and validate the belief that women's subjugation is a matter of the natural state of their existence, rather than something that can be overcome through the sharing of power by and with men.

Nevertheless, there are roles for women in Tibetan religious practice. There is, for example, an order of nuns. Because there is no ordination lineage, however, the nuns remain novices with all of the implications of a reduced status that one would expect from such a situation, leaving all institutional power in the hands of the monks or lamas. A woman also can choose to become a *yogini.* Clearly, however, there is much to overcome when a woman decides to walk the path of the *tantrika.* It is important to note, however, that most of the women who have been honored as exemplary adepts and teachers throughout Tibet's history have been those who have made it "through the maze of negative socialization and gender stereotypes" to become *yoginis,* although an unsuccessful practitioner most certainly would be shunned by society for having broken convention.[51]

Women in Chan (Zen) and Pure Land Buddhism

It is important to recall here that Chan or Zen Buddhism and Pure Land Buddhism are specific developments within the Mahayana tradition. Consequently, what has been said already with respect to women and Mahayana Buddhism applies here— for example, with respect to the continuing ordination lineage for nuns in China. It is important to note specifically, however, a couple of additional things with respect to Chan (Zen) and Pure Land Buddhism.

The ideas and practices of Chan (Zen) Buddhism are grounded in *Prajna-paramita,* which, as we have already seen, is the expression of the ultimate primordial source as the feminine divine. Not surprisingly, then, many issues surrounding femaleness that are found in other forms of Buddhism, including other forms of Mahayana Buddhism, are not present here. Femaleness does not present a bar to enlightenment or Buddhahood in Chan. Significantly, women in Chan Buddhism have been permitted to teach both men and women, and there is historical evidence that there were great women teachers at court with considerable influence. However, this certainly was contrary to the prevailing customs of the host cultures of China and Japan. As a result, the institutions of Buddhism in Japan and China remained male-dominated.

In Pure Land Buddhism, on the other hand, femaleness is treated as problematic because it is deemed to be an unfortunate birth. Buddhism in general was not concerned with changing the social order. Therefore, in its Pure Land form it merely was acknowledging a fact of society—women's lot was indeed unfortunate. The good news in Pure Land is that there are no unfortunate rebirths in the Pure Land. Accordingly, it is believed that all who reach the Pure Land are reborn there as males!

Women in Contemporary Buddhism East and West

The "woman question" in Buddhism continues to be debated to this day, and contemporary women East and West are considering the degree to which Buddhism, in its many forms, is in need of reconstruction in order to give effect to what is perceived by them as its egalitarian core. Feminist Buddhist scholars, such as Rita Gross in *Buddhism after Patriarchy: A Feminist History, Analysis, and Reconstruction of Buddhism,* have made convincing arguments that negative stereotypical attitudes toward women are due to socio-cultural encrustations from Buddhism's various host countries.[52] They point to the problem of the record-keepers nearly always being men, which results in the effective erasure of the history of women's participation and an androcentric point of view that minimizes women's experience within the traditions of Buddhism. As a result, important information about women's own processes and practices in the quest for enlightenment and their contributions to the tradition generally have been lost.

Significantly, Buddhist women scholars have uncovered many nearly forgotten texts that do recount the lives and practices of exemplary Buddhist women. And such scholars have uncovered evidence showing how the failure to tell women's stories has obscured what may have been a more prominent role for women than the majority of texts seem to indicate. For example, in recent times a male Tibetan university student, Namkhai Norbu, who had studied with the *yogini* Ayu Khandro (d. 1953), wrote a biography of his teacher. As feminist scholar Rita Gross surmises, "Without this almost accidental preservation of her biography, we would probably have no idea that such a woman had lived so recently. She may not have been as rare as the impression given us by the records that were preserved."[53]

A significant issue for contemporary Buddhist women is the ordination of nuns. This is an especially difficult issue in Theravada Buddhism where, as noted earlier, no ordination lineage for nuns is extant. Southeast Asian Theravada monks are especially resistant, some say even hostile, to the reinstitution of a nuns' ordination lineage. They argue that because there has been no nuns ordination tradition for centuries in some areas and in others none has ever existed, to have one at all at this point is not in accord with the Theravada tradition. Interestingly, some nuns oppose it as well, arguing that ordination makes them subject to the eight rules and, therefore, subjects them to control by the monks.

There is, however, an unbroken ordination lineage for nuns in China's Mahayana tradition. Contemporary Buddhist women have argued that Theravada nuns' ordination could be reestablished through that lineage. Despite the fact that the monastic tradition is virtually the same for both Theravada and Mahayana, Theravadists argue against conflating their tradition with that of the Mahayanists and conclude that Mahayana ordination is not valid for Theravada. However, some Theravada monks with more exposure to the West support the reinstitution of the nuns' ordination.

Nuns' ordination has support on other fronts as well. Significantly, the Dalai Lama has ordained nuns and thus supports nuns' ordination in the Tibetan tradition, which since the Chinese invasion of Tibet in 1959 continues in India and the West. But as Nancy Barnes has noted, the overwhelming majority of monks worldwide in traditions without a nuns' ordination do not support women's struggle for institutional recognition and support.

Part of the problem in restructuring Buddhism (or, as some would say, reviving the original intentions of Buddhist thought) is that Buddhism has tended to be focused on spiritual advancement and not on the social problems of this world, including the relative status of women. Hence, women arguing for "equal rights" can be criticized as being "attached." The result is that their efforts to better their lot in life can be maligned as evidence of ignorance of the Ultimate Reality, which knows no such distinctions.

Still, Buddhist women have made tremendous strides in the twentieth century. In modern times there have been and are many women teachers of renown. Among them are Ayu Khandro (Tibet), Sister Sudharma (Sri Lanka), Achan Naeb (Thailand), Daw Panna (Burma), Venerable Bhiksuna Tae-heng se Nim (Korea), and Venerable Bhiksuni Hiu Wan (Taiwan). Jiyu Kennett Roshi (1924–1996), who was the head of a Zen monastery in Northern California, was especially esteemed by the several women who have become prominent Buddhist leaders in the West.

The main issue for Buddhist women is that, despite the fact that most schools of Buddhism today espouse an egalitarian doctrine, there is continued reluctance on the part of Buddhist institutional establishments to provide opportunities for women's leadership, and, therefore, Buddhism remains androcentric and patriarchal. Yet, Western influences have resulted in a rethinking of Buddhist values and vice versa, in particular with respect to the role of women. Western feminist scholarship has brought attention to the discrepancy between Buddhism's egalitarian doctrine and its institutional practices, while Buddhism's vision of a nondualistic universe has contributed to an examination of the West's tendencies to see polarities as oppositional rather than complementary. Anne Klein, Rita Gross, and Nancy Barnes see this interplay as a potentially positive development in the modern world, particularly in efforts toward women's equality. Perhaps it will lead not only to a more egalitarian Buddhism but to a more egalitarian Western perspective as well.[54]

Buddhism in America

Buddhists in substantial numbers first came to the United States in the form of Chinese laborers brought to California just after the Gold Rush of 1849. By 1880 more than 100,000 Chinese were to be found in the country, largely on the West Coast. To this day there are Chinese temples in San Francisco and other northern California cities, which, in a characteristically popular Chinese way, combine Buddhist and Daoist (to be discussed in Chapter 5) deities and are important historical momentos of that era. Japanese Buddhists came to work in the sugar fields of Hawaii even before the islands' annexation to the United States in 1898. The first strictly Buddhist temple in what is now the United States was built in Hilo, Hawaii, in 1889. It was in the Japanese Jodo Shinshu (Pure Land) tradition, and this form of Buddhism has been most active among Japanese Americans. A little later, however, temples of other schools of Buddhism—Nichiren, Shingon, and Zen particularly—appeared in the Japanese-American community.

At the same time, interest in Buddhism was growing among American intellectuals. The way had been prepared by the oriental concerns of New England Transcendentalism. Sir Edwin Arnold's poetic story of the Buddha, *The Light of Asia* (1879), had a considerable impact. Also, the 1893 World's Parliament of Religions was a catalyst for the development of Western Buddhism, just as it was of Western Hinduism. One of the Asian speakers at the Parliament, the Japanese Zen monk, Soyen Shaku, returned to the United States in 1905 with several followers to establish the beginnings of Western Zen. A student of his, the layman D. T. Suzuki, wrote and spoke extensively on Zen in English up through the 1950s. By 1930 the first continuing Zen center for Westerners had been founded in New York.

Zen Buddhism was something of a vogue in the 1950s, influencing the art and letters of "Beat" writers like Jack Kerouac and Gary Snyder. At the end of that decade and in the 1960s a number of Western Zen centers were organized in the United States. Another form of Japanese Buddhism, the Nichiren Shoshu school, then promoted by Soka Gakkai, also became widely popular among non-Asian Americans in the 1960s and after.

Other styles of Buddhism also reached American shores in midcentury and after. The devastation of Tibet by the Chinese Communists sent many Tibetans, including learned *lamas,* into exile. Some taught in American universities, some established centers where Tibetan Buddhism was presented to the general public. Helped by the immense prestige of Tibet's spiritual leader, the Dalai Lama, Vajrayana or Tibetan Buddhism, seen as a difficult but rewarding spiritual path by many Westerners, became popular in the second half of the twentieth century.

Those years also saw substantial immigration from other traditionally Buddhist countries: Korea, Vietnam after the fall of Saigon in 1975, and the Theravada nations of Southeast Asia. They brought their religion and monks to teach it with them. The presence of Theravada as well as Mahayana Buddhism in the New World is now shown by the graceful and colorful architecture of Thai, Burman, Cambodian, and Sri Lankan temples in several U.S. cities.

Some Americans of non-Asian descent have taken up the study of Theravada spiritual practice, especially the quiet but deeply penetrating *vipassana* form of mediation. There are Western-oriented centers and teachers of it as well as Asian. It may be mentioned that Chinese Buddhism has also flourished in America. The supreme symbol of this prosperity is undoubtedly the vast and spectacular Hsi Lai temple outside of Los Angeles.

Buddhism, though very much a minority religion in America, has taken root there in two forms: temples ministering largely to Americans of traditionally Buddhist ethnic background, and Buddhist centers geared chiefly to the requirements of persons of non-Asian culture who are interested in Buddhism as part of their personal spiritual quest. These two wings of the Buddhist movement are slowly coming together as a distinctive Buddhism gradually emerges in America, just as it has in every other country to which the *dharma* has spread. That may be a task of centuries, and Buddhist centers catering to national, cultural, and religious interests will understandably also remain important for some time to come. Buddhism is now, however, a significant part of the United States' highly pluralistic spiritual community.

❋ Summary

Buddhism can be thought of as a religion with a psychological emphasis. It teaches the transformation of consciousness from attachment to ego, suffering, and objects of craving to the unattached bliss of Nirvana. Its fundamental teaching is that the Buddha, through his enlightenment, showed the way out of the wheel of rebirth or conditioned reality created by ignorance and attachment; its fundamental practice is meditation and comparable methods of transcending attachment; its fundamental sociological expression is the *samgha,* or order of monks in the succession of the Buddha's disciples.

The Buddha, among the first of the great religious founders, according to Buddhist tradition attained a state of perfect enlightenment after a spiritual quest. He then taught that liberation comes by following a Middle Way between all attachments; he taught the Four Noble Truths that there are suffering, attachment, and freedom from suffering in Nirvana through the Eightfold Path, culminating in Right Meditation. He taught that the ego is the supreme delusive object of attachment, for we are really not egos but impermanent collections of parts called *skandas*.

Theravada Buddhism, the "Way of the Elders," predominant in the Buddhist parts of South and Southeast Asia, adheres closely to these teachings and views itself as standing in the tradition of the historical Buddha. For monks, who claim a lineage that extends back to the Buddha's original *samgha,* it emphasizes meditations leading to spiritual agility and nirvanic consciousness. For the laity, it emphasizes acts and attitudes that will lead to merit and good rebirths.

The Mahayana Buddhism of North and East Asia stresses the presence of the "Buddha-nature," the essence of the universe as the Buddha saw it in his enlightenment, in all beings. Thus, the universe is spoken of as Void and as one with Nirvana, for there is nothing within it to be grasped. The *bodhisattva,* an "enlightenment being" who realizes this and is at once in the world and Nirvana, is a key Mahayana figure. Because liberation is a matter of realizing one's own Buddha-nature, Mahayana teaches the accessibility of salvation to all and offers many diverse paths to the final goal. An important later Mahayana school is "Mind Only" or Yogacara, which holds that one creates reality out of one's mind. It led in turn to teaching about the three "bodies" or forms of expression of the Buddha-nature, in the cosmos (*dharmakaya*), in the heavens (*sambhogakaya*), and on earth (*nirmanakaya*). And it led to Vajrayana, the Tantric school of Buddhism, which presents rigorous initiation and training, leading one to evoke or visualize helping Buddhas and *bodhisattvas,* among other techniques.

Vajrayana, Chan (Zen), and Pure Land are particular developments in the Mahayana tradition. Vajrayana is the Buddhism of Tibet, a land that traditionally had a unique Buddhist culture. The Tibetan text best known in the West is the *Bardo Thodol,* or *The Tibetan Book of the Dead,* which describes after-death experiences and emphasizes that in all one meets there is a manifestation of one's own nature. Chan began in China and later became an important Buddhist sect in Japan. It is the Buddhism of meditation—"sitting quietly and doing nothing." Pure Land is the Buddhism of Amitabha, also known as Emiduo in Chinese and Amida in Japan, who vowed that he would bring all who called upon his name to his Buddha-paradise—the Western Paradise of jeweled trees and perfumed rivers where there are no unfortunate rebirths and everyone can easily attain enlightenment. It is an important Buddhist sect in China, Japan, and Korea.

Early Buddhism offered new opportunities for women. For the first time, women were able to adopt the life of the renunciant. Significantly, Buddhism offered a more egalitarian worldview than did Hinduism at that time. Still, prevailing societal attitudes toward women have held sway throughout Buddhism's history. As a consequence, the women's *samgha* generally has been under the authority of the monks. Theravada Buddhism developed a more socially conservative doctrine toward women, resulting in a limitation of their role in that form of Buddhism, where the ordination lineage for nuns has died out. On the other hand, the many forms of Mahayana Buddhism tended toward the more egalitarian view of women and men that Western and Eastern feminist scholars see as the core of the Buddhist teachings of "No Self" and nonattachment. The debate as to whether the female body can be a vessel for enlightenment is still continuing and is dealt with variously by the many Mahayana sects.

Buddhism has come to the United States in both traditional ethnic forms and in forms designed to appeal to Western seekers. There are now a number of beautiful Buddhist temples and centers in America.

❋ Questions for Review

1. Interpret Buddhism in terms of the three forms of religious expression.
2. Show through what forms a religion ultimately focused on individual liberation also functions as a religion for society. Point to the significant contrasts between Theravada and Mahayana Buddhism in both respects.
3. Talk about the meaning of the Buddha's quest and enlightenment, as presented in traditional accounts of his life.
4. Explain basic Buddhist teaching: the Middle Way, the Four Noble Truths, the Eightfold Path, No Self, Nirvana.
5. Explain why meditation is so important in Buddhism.
6. Understand and be able to put into simple words the fundamental teachings of Nagarjuna that underlie Mahayana Buddhism: *Samsara* is Nirvana, Void, or Emptiness, and is the best metaphor for what we call reality.
7. Discuss the distinctive features of Mahayana: the Buddha-nature in all things, the *bodhisattva* concept, the "multimedia" approach to salvation, the *sutras*.
8. Mention some features of Mind Only (Yogacara or Vijnanavada) Buddhist philosophy and discuss its influence, especially its impact on spiritual practice as well as theory.
9. Explain the three "bodies" (trikaya) or forms or expressions of the Buddha-nature as presented in developed Mahayana thought: the universal essence, heavenly, and earthly (or transformative).
10. Discuss some features of Vajrayana, the Tantric Buddhism of Tibet, Mongolia, and elsewhere, especially its use of initiation and evocation, and its foundation in the Mind Only philosophy.
11. Discuss the scenario and deeper meaning of *The Tibetan Book of the Dead (Bardo Thodol)*.
12. Explain how the advent of Buddhism in India affected women's lives.
13. Discuss the issues surrounding the advent and development of the nuns' *samgha*.
14. Discuss the role of women in Buddhism, especially the issues surrounding the appropriateness of the female body for Buddhahood.
15. Using the chart on page 134, explain the fundamental features of Buddhism. How does it deal with the great questions of the nature of ultimate reality and the goal of human life?
16. Talk about the aspects of Buddhism that seem most meaningful to you.

❋ Suggested Readings on Buddhism

General

Bahm, Archie, *Philosophy of the Buddha*, rev. ed. Fremont, CA: Jain Publishing, 1993. The basic principles in easy language.

Bechert, Heinz, and Richard Gombrich, eds., *The World of Buddhism: Buddhist Monks and Nuns in Society and Culture*. New York: Facts on File, 1984. A good survey for the general reader.

Becker, Carl B., *Breaking the Circle: Death and the Afterlife in Buddhist Thought*. Carbondale: Southern Illinois University Press, 1994. Excellent summary of an important area of Buddhism.

Burtt, E. A., *The Teachings of the Compassionate Buddha*. New York: Mentor Books, 1955. A valuable set of excerpts from translated scriptures.

Byrom, Thomas, *Dhammapada: The Sayings of the Buddha*. Boston: Shambhala, 1993. One of several translations of this ancient collection of simple and moving aphorisms attributed to the Buddha; the Dhammapada is very popular in Southeast Asia.

Chang, Garma C., *The Buddhist Teaching of Totality*. University Park: Pennsylvania State University Press, 1974. A competent introduction to the Yogacara or "Mind Only" philosophy.

Ch'en, Kenneth, *Buddhism: The Light of Asia*. Woodbury, NY: Barron's Educational Series, 1968. A good introductory text, particularly for its country-by-country historical survey and its treatment of Buddhist cultural influence.

Conze, Edward, *Buddhism: Its Essence and Development*. New York: Harper Torchbooks, 1959. A masterful and vivid essay emphasizing Buddhist doctrine. Especially good on Mahayana.

————, *Buddhist Meditation*. New York: Harper Torchbooks, 1969. A collection of texts on this topic; good editing.

————, *Buddhist Scriptures*. Baltimore, MD: Penguin Books, 1959. Another useful collection.

————, *Buddhist Thought in India*. New York: Harper Torchbooks, 1962. A brilliant intellectual history, written with feeling, insight, and style.

————, *Buddhist Wisdom Books*. London: George Allen & Unwin, 1958. Translations of two basic texts, the Heart and Diamond Sutras.

Coomaraswamy, Ananda, *Buddha and the Gospel of Buddhism*. New York: Harper & Row, 1964. A sensitive essay from a Hindu point of view.

De Bary, William Theodore, ed., *The Buddhist Tradition in India, China, and Japan*. New York: Modern Library, 1969. A useful collection of translated texts with good introductions.

Gard, Richard, *Buddhism*. New York: G. Braziller, 1961. A good introductory collection of translated texts and excerpts from studies.

LaFleur, William, *Buddhism: A Cultural Perspective*. Upper Saddle River, NJ: Prentice Hall, 1988. A good introductory textbook.

Morgan, Kenneth, *The Path of the Buddha*. New York: Ronald Press, 1956. Reprint ed., Columbia, MO: South Asia Books, 1986. A series of interesting essays by modern Buddhists written for the general reader.

Queen, Christopher, and Sallie B. King, eds., *Engaged Buddhism: Buddhist Liberation Movements in Asia*. Albany: State University of New York Press, 1996. An overview of contemporary Buddhist social activism.

Robinson, Richard H., and Willard L. Johnson, *The Buddhist Religion*. Belmont, CA: Wadsworth, 1982. A vivid introductory textbook.

Snelling, John, *The Buddhist Handbook: A Complete Guide to Buddhist Schools, Teaching, Practice and History*. Rochester, VT: Inner Traditions, 1991. A useful and generally reliable summary for Western students and practitioners of the many forms of expression Buddhism has taken.

Williams, Paul, *Mahayana Buddhism: The Doctrinal Foundations*. New York: Routledge, 1989. A good introduction.

Chan/Zen and Pure Land Buddhism

Amstutz, Galen Dean, *Interpreting Amida: History and Orientalism in the Study of Pure Land Buddhism*. Albany: State University of New York Press, 1997.

Blofeld, John, *The Wheel of Life*. Berkeley, CA: Shambala Press, 1972. An autobiographical book that offers, through the author's exploration of Buddhist China, rare insights into its manifold variety.

Bodhidharma, *The Bodhidharma Anthology: The Earliest Records of Zen,* Jeffrey L. Broughton, trans. Berkelely: University of California Press, 1999.

Ch'en, Kenneth, *Buddhism in China: A Historical Survey*. Princeton, NJ: Princeton University Press, 1964. An authoritative introduction.

Dumoulin, Heinrich, *Zen Buddhism: A History,* James W. Heisign and Paul Knitter, trans. New York: Prentice Hall Macmillan, 1994.

———, *Zen Buddhism in the Twentieth Century*. New York: Weatherhill, 1992.

Faure, Bernard, *The Will to Orthodoxy: A Critical Genealogy of Northern Chan Buddhism*. Stanford, CA: Stanford University Press, 1997.

Hoover, Thomas, *The Zen Experience*. New York: New American Library, 1980. Zen through the perspective of its great masters, both Chinese and Japanese.

Kapleau, Philip, *The Three Pillars of Zen*. Boston: Beacon Press, 1967. A fascinating introduction to Zen methods and thought. Contains accounts of modern Zen experience.

Suzuki, D. T., *Zen Buddhism*. Garden City, NY: Doubleday, 1956. One of many books by this well-known writer who has successfully communicated much of the Zen spirit to the West.

Welch, Holmes, *The Buddhist Revival in China*. Cambridge, MA: Harvard University Press, 1968. Buddhism in modern China prior to 1949.

———, *The Practice of Chinese Buddhism 1900–1950*. Cambridge, MA: Harvard University Press, 1967. An excellent account of Chinese Buddhism before the Communist revolution; especially good on the actual life of monasteries and temples and on popular devotional practices.

The Buddha

Griffiths, Paul. J, *On Being Buddha: The Classical Doctrine of Buddahood*. Albany: State University of New York Press, 1994.

Karetzky, Patricia Eichenbaum, *The Life of the Buddha: Ancient Scriptural and Pictorial Traditions*. Lanhma, MD: University Press of America, 1992.

Percheron, Maurice, *The Marvelous Life of the Buddha*. New York: St. Martins Press, 1960. A popular account of the traditional story.

Rahula, Walpola, *What the Buddha Taught*. New York: Evergreen Press, 1962. A competent summary for the general reader by a modern Buddhist monk.

Thomas, E. J., *The Life of the Buddha as Legend and History*. London: Routledge and Kegan Paul, 1924. A scholarly evaluation.

Warren, Henry C., *Everyman's Life of the Buddha*. Finnimore, WI: Westburg, 1966. A readable account put together from scriptural accounts.

Buddhism in Southeast Asia

King, Winston L., *A Thousand Lives Away*. Cambridge, MA: Harvard University Press, 1964. A fascinating description of Buddhism in modern Burma.

Lester, Robert C., *Theravada Buddhism in Southeast Asia*. Ann Arbor: University of Michigan Press, 1973. A clear, competent summary.

Ray, Himanshu Prabha, *The Winds of Change: Buddhism and the Maritime Links of Early South Asia*. New York: Oxford University Press, 1994.

Tibetan Religion
Bernbaum, Edwin, *The Way to Shambhala: A Search for the Mythical Kingdom Beyond the Himalayas*. Garden City, NY: Doubleday Anchor, 1980. An unusual book combining mountaineering and scholarship as it explores on several levels the meaning of the Tibetan traditions concerning a paradisal land called Shambhala.
Blofeld, John, *The Way of Power*. London: George Allen & Unwin, 1970. A very clear statement. Sympathetic; emphasizes the Tibetan usage.
Dalai Lama, The, *The Buddhism of Tibet*. Ithaca, NY: Snow Lion, 1987. An exposition of the tradition by its most distinguished voice and winner of the Nobel Peace Prize.
Goldstein, Melvyn C., and Matthew T. Kapstein, eds., *Buddhism in Contemporary Tibet: Religious Revival and Cultural Identity*. Berkeley: University of California Press, 1998.
Hoffmann, Helmut, *The Religions of Tibet*. New York: Macmillan, 1961. A particularly useful survey.
Kapstein, Matthew, *The Tibetan Assimilation of Buddhism: Conversion, Contestation, and Memory*. Oxford and New York: Oxford University Press, 2000.
Lopez, Donald S., *Religions of Tibet in Practice*. Princeton, NJ: Princeton University Press, 1997.
Snellgrove, David, and Hugh Richardson, *A Cultural History of Tibet*. New York: Praeger, 1968. A standard resource.
Thurman, Robert A., Jr., *The Tibetan Book of the Dead: The Great Book of Natural Liberation through Understanding in the Between*. New York: Bantam, 1994. A remarkable new translation with extensive commentary.

Women in Buddhism
Arai, Paula Kane Robinson, *Women Living Zen: Japanese Soto Buddhist Nuns*. New York: Oxford University Press, 1999.
Barnes, Nancy Schuster, "Buddhism" in *Women in World Religions*, Arvind Sharma, ed. Albany: State University of New York Press, 1987, pp. 105–33. A good summary of issues regarding women in the various forms of Buddhism.
———, [Schuster] "Striking a Balance: Women and Images of Women in Early Chinese Buddhism" in *Women, Religion and Social Change*, Yvonne Yazback Haddad and Ellison Banks Findly, eds. Albany: State University of New York Press, 1985, pp. 87–112. An often-cited treatment.
———, [Barnes] "Women in Buddhism" in *Today's Woman in World Religions*, Arvind Sharma, ed. Albany: State University of New York Press, 1994, pp. 137–69. A survey of the role of women in contemporary Buddhism.
Boucher, Sandy, *Opening the Lotus: A Woman's Guide to Buddhism*. Boston: Beacon Press, 1997. An important new work.
———, *Discovering Kwan Yin, Buddhist Goddess of Compassion*. Boston: Beacon Pess, 1999.
Cabezon, Jose Ignacio, ed., *Buddhism, Sexuality, and Gender*. Albany: State University of New York Press, 1992.
Campbell, June, *Traveller in Space: In Search of Female Identity in Tibetan Buddhism*. New York: George Braziller, 1996.
Falk, Nancy Auer, "The Case of the Vanishing Nuns: The Fruits of Ambivalence in Ancient Indian Buddhism" in *Unspoken Worlds: Women's Religious Lives*, Nancy Auer Falk and Rita M. Gross, eds. Belmont, CA: Wadsworth Publishing, 1989, pp. 155–65. A pivotal work in the study of women and Buddhism.
Gross, Rita M., "Buddhism" in *Women in Religion*, Jean Holm with John Bowker, ed. London and New York: Pinter Publishers, 1994, pp. 1–29. A good introductory summary.

————, *Buddhism after Patriarchy: A Feminist History, Analysis, and Reconstruction of Buddhism.* Albany: State University of New York Press, 1993. A comprehensive study and critique of the patriarchal aspects of Buddhism and the possibilities for constructing a nonpartriachal Buddhism by an oft-cited Western feminist scholar who is a practicing Buddhist.

————, *Soaring and Settling: Buddhist Perspectives on Contemporary Social and Religious Issues.* New York: Continuum, 1998.

Macy, Joanna Rogers, "Perfection of Wisdom: Mother of All Buddhas" in *The Book of the Goddess: Past and Present,* Carl Olsen, ed. New York: Crossroad, 1983. An oft-cited article for its argument regarding the positive image of the feminine Divine in Mahayana Buddhism.

Paul, Diana, *Women in Buddhism: Images of the Feminine in Mahayana Tradition.* Berkeley, CA: Asian Humanities Press, 1979. A particularly critical view of patriarchal attitudes toward women in Mahayana Buddhism—a view that is questioned in part by Rita Gross in *Buddhism after Patriarchy,* cited above.

Ray, Reginald A., "Accomplished Women in Tantric Buddhism of Medieval India and Tibet" in *Unspoken Worlds: Women's Religious Lives,* Nancy Auer Falk and Rita M. Gross, eds. Belmont, CA: Wadsworth Publishing, 1989, pp. 191–200. An important, if brief, study of women and tantrism.

Shaw, Miranda, *Passionate Enlightenment: Women in Tantric Buddhism.* Princeton, NJ: Princeton University Press, 1994. A wonderful account of the role of women in early Tibetan Buddhism, showing that Tantric sexual practices can be a path to enlightenment in which the female partner plays a leading role.

Tsomo, Karma Lekshe, ed., *Buddhist Women Across Cultures: Realizations.* Albany: State University of New York Press, 1999.

Willis, Janice D., "Nuns and Benefactresses: The Role of Women in the Development of Buddhism" in *Women, Religion and Social Change,* Yvonne Yazback Haddad and Ellison Banks Findly, eds. Albany: State University of New York Press, 1985, pp. 59–86. A significant historical article.

Buddhism in America

Coleman, James Wilson, *The New Buddhism: The Western Transformation of an Ancient Tradition.* New York: Oxford University Press, 2001.

Fields, Rick, *How the Swans Came to the Lake.* Boulder, CO: Shambhala, 1986. A lively and fascinating narrative story of Buddhism in America.

Friedman, Lenore, *Meetings with Remarkable Women.* Boston: Shambhala, 1987. A fascinating and informative series of interviews with American women Buddhist teachers.

Kapleau, Philip, *The Three Pillars of Zen.* Boston: Beacon Press, 1967. A classic presentation of all aspects of Zen for westerners; includes accounts of experiences of enlightenment by westerners.

Layman, Emma McCoy, *Buddhism in America.* Chicago: Nelson-Hall, 1976. A helpful history to date of publication, emphasizing ethnic traditions.

Morreale, Don, ed., *The Complete Guide to Buddhist America.* Dalai Lama, foreword. Boston: Shambhala, 1998.

Prebish, Charles S. and Kenneth K. Tanaka, eds., *The Faces of Buddhism in America.* Berkeley: University of California Press, 1998.

Prebish, Charles S., *Luminous Passage: The Practice and Study of Buddhism in America.* Berkeley: University of California Press, 1999.

Seager, Richad Hughes, *Buddhism in America.* New York: Columbia University Press, 1999.

CHAPTER FIVE

Dragon and Sun

Religions of East Asia

CHAPTER OBJECTIVES

After studying this chapter, you should be able to

❋ Cite the major religious traditions of China and Japan.

❋ Explain the different roles of Confucianism and Daoism in China.

❋ Interpret the relation of these spiritual traditions to East Asian societies today.

❋ Discuss the role of women in traditional Chinese and Japanese society, as well as the impact of Buddhism and Daoism on women's lives.

❋ Present the religious traditions of Korea and Vietnam.

The East Asian Spiritual World

Some years ago, I* encountered for the first time a non-Western religion in its homeland. That religion was **Shinto**, and the country was Japan. I saw Japanese Buddhist temples on the same visit, of course, but it was Shinto shrines I saw first and which for some reason buried themselves most deeply in my memory.

I could not forget the **torii**, the gently curved archway that led into the precincts of a shrine, separating the noisy bustle of the street from the quiet shrine with its ancient architecture. The *torii* was like a mystic portal between one age and another, and even one dimension and another. In the midst of a modern industrial city, these plain but graceful sanctuaries of the **kami**, the Shinto gods, are set amidst sacred groves of gnarled old trees, and they communicate just a touch of the past, the natural, and the wondrous. In the countryside, where shrines grace mountaintops, clear rushing streams, or inlets of the sea, they lend an aura of the Divine to vistas already beautiful.

I felt strangely stirred by these wooden shrines, simple and rustic in construction, with their pitched roofs and heavy doors. The porticos presented such understated but effective symbols of deity as zigzag strips of paper, immense rope lintels, and gleaming eyelike mirrors. I liked the way the shrines seemed never to clash with nature, but only to embellish it. If a Divine *kami*-presence dwelt within the shrine, one felt, he or she was a deity who knew and respected the old trees in the parish down to their deepest roots and the insides of the ageless stones, as well as the grandmothers, young people, and babies who lived in the streets around his shrine-home. While musing on dreams of the mythic past, the *kami* watched with spirit-eyes the frenetic life of a modern nation.

Nor were these *kami*-presences easily forgotten. Once the official religion of Japan, Shinto, since World War II, is no longer under state control. Now shorn of its once ultranationalistic overtones, it nevertheless retains its shrines under local and democratic administration. It has not withered away as some thought it would, but rather has prospered as a popular religion intermingled with other theological, practical, and sociological expressions. To be sure, few of those frequenting the shrines would call themselves exclusively Shinto. Most are also Buddhist, at least nominally, or members of one of the "new religions" of Japan (to be discussed later). And many would hardly think of themselves as religious at all. Yet they may pause for a moment as they pass a shrine.

At a shrine of any importance, the visitor will not wait long before seeing a Japanese individual or family pass through the *torii,* wash hands and mouth in a basin, approach the shrine, clap twice, bow, murmur a prayer, and leave a small offering in a grill.

The fortunate observer may have the opportunity to be at a shrine festival, or **matsuri**. Then he or she will notice a dramatic change in the atmosphere of the shrine. Instead of a quiet, shy deity in a leafy refuge, the *kami* now becomes a dynamic presence in the midst of the people, calling explosive festivity into being.

*Robert Ellwood.

First, pure offerings of rice wine (*sake*), vegetables, and seafood are very slowly presented to the *kami* by white-robed priests, together with green boughs of the sacred *sakaki* tree brought forward by leading laypeople.

Then, suddenly and startlingly, this mood of classical dignity breaks. Sacred dance in vivid and fantastic costume is performed. A carnival may be held on the grounds of the shrine, with everything from cotton candy to sumo wrestling. The *kami*-presence is carried through the streets in a palanquin (*mikoshi*) by running, sweating young men, who shout "*Washo! Washo!*" as they zigzag down the ways and byways of the *kami's* parish.

Shinto has a highly distinctive personality of its own, yet it also illustrates several characteristics of the religion of East Asia in general. In Shinto shrines, and also in Chinese and Japanese Buddhist and other temples, one senses a close harmony of the human and natural orders. The gods and guides of humankind dwell in virtual symbiosis with woods, streams, and mountains, suggesting that in a larger sense society is a part of nature, and *kami,* immortals, Buddhas, and humans are all parts of a greater cosmic unity.

Very often, then, the Divine is finite and tied to particular places. There may indeed be an indefinable universal Divine principle that underlies all particular manifestations of the Divine and is infinite. But the individual gods one can know are limited, although impressive, as if no more than glorified human beings. Indeed, in China for the last 2,000 years, nearly all deities except Heaven and Earth themselves were conceived of as having once been humans who acceded to Divine status by exemplary merit. Their ranks and titles were confirmed by the emperor as though they were simply another class among his subjects—and the emperor alone was permitted to worship Heaven and Earth directly. In Japan, although only occasionally designating a god, the government did assign the status of the various shrines.

East Asian religion has tended to see a world in which gods and humans both have places and interact with each other more by agreement and respect than on the model of master and servant. To be sure, Chinese and Japanese worship is capable of mystery, awe, and wonder. Buddhism, particularly through the Mahayana philosophies and techniques described in the previous chapter, has made spiritual culture aware of mystical and metaphysical profundities oriented toward the infinite. Yet in East Asia, it all finally comes down to a human-centered view of mystery and metaphysics—the Chinese and Japanese are rarely forgetful that these things are important to humans insofar as they enrich human life and help validate its central institutions, the family and the state. Religious style is likely to be more restrained and pragmatic than the ecstatic abandon of the Hindu *bhakta* or the hard surety of the Christian crusader. Religion is not that kind of commitment; rather, it is part of a ring of relativistic commitments whose real center is inflexible norms or propriety for human and Divine relations: These are the true obligation. The value center, in other words, is one's proper place in society and, therefore, one's means of integration into family and community.

The sociological expression is extremely important in understanding religion in East Asia. In particular, "natural" sociological units—family and community—for most East Asians are one's link with the infinite. It is through worship of one's particular ancestors that one expresses filial relation to the primordial infinite ancestors, Heaven and Earth. It is through one's particular *kami* or patronal deity that one integrates oneself into the hierarchy of the Divine. It is through reverence to particular Buddhas and *bodhisattvas* that one acknowledges tacitly the unbounded wisdom a Buddha represents.

All these features come together when one thinks of East Asian faith as being centered in a "one world" concept. There is no god or heaven outside the world system of which we are a part here and now. Gods, heavens, hells, society, nature, family, and individual are all parts of a single unity of which humankind is (at least for humans) the pivot. This means the individual has to be a part of the whole; if there is only one unified system, it is absurd to try to opt out of it. On the other hand, it means that one is under no obligation to emphasize one part of the system more than another—heaven more than this world, a god more than family. All are parts of the same thing, so one's approach is according to one's circumstances or bent. Most would probably agree that a balanced outlook is wisest.

Some commentators have so stressed this supposedly "humanistic" and "this-worldly" East Asian attitude as to suggest that religion, life after death, heavens, and supernatural entities are unimportant to the Chinese and Japanese. At least in regard to traditional society, such an assessment is very wide of the mark. Whatever some rationalist philosophers may have held, the popular culture of East Asia certainly has not been behind any other in energy and expense devoted to worship of gods, propitiation of spirits, and the assurance of a good fate on the other side of death.

But it is fair to say that this concern, real as it is, has been given a special quality by an overarching perception that the visible and invisible realms are parts of one unity, like the obverse and reverse sides of a coin, and that what is really important to humanity is the continuation and well-being of individual, family, and societal human life on both sides. Except for the most mystical of Daoists and Buddhists, this perpetuation of the good life for humans is the supreme good. The apparatus of religion is appreciated by the many who accept it for the contributions it can make to the good life here and hereafter. It is an invisible world that interlocks with this world.

In East Asia, as we can readily see, religion is not divided neatly into distinct categories, such as "Buddhism" or "Shinto"—each as a "religion" unto itself. Rather, religion is integrated into the cultural landscape of each East Asian region. Accordingly, we will be looking at religion in East Asia by country: first China, then Japan, and then, briefly, Korea and Viet Nam.

RELIGION IN CHINA

Ancient China

To get a perspective on the specifics of East Asian religion, let us begin with China and at the beginning. One of the most distinctive features of the Chinese mentality is its feeling that the Chinese people and the soil on which they live are inseparable and have been together as far back as tradition goes. In most other major societies, a tradition of having come from some other place and conquered the land in which the people now dwell is a feature of incalculable weight in the national image. Consider the significance of the Exodus and the taking of the Promised Land to the Israelites, the journey of Aeneas from Troy to Italy for the Roman mystique, the importance of Indo-European invasions in both ancient India and Northern Europe, the myth of the conquest of Japan by the first emperor Jimmu for Japanese nationalism, or the immigration and pioneer motifs in America's national consciousness. In China, there is none of this. Instead, the Chinese have felt a quieter but even more secure assurance that they have always been in China, were created there, and belong there as surely as the rivers and mountains and rice fields. Consequently, a sense of place, of the cycles of nature, and of lineage were fundamental to the religious outlook of the earliest known Chinese, as they have been ever since.

The cultural line that led to Chinese civilization began around 4000 B.C.E. in tiny villages in the Yellow River basin where millet, vegetables, and pigs were raised. One of the oldest motifs of Chinese religion is the Earth-god. The central sacred feature was often a stone or mound, like a concentration of the forces of the soil into a central focus. These mounds are the ancestors of the city-god temples of today, as well as the great **Altar of Heaven** in Beijing, built like an artificial mountain where the emperor offered worship at the Winter Solstice.[1] Worship was also offered very early to the spirits of rivers and of rain, the latter immemorially represented as the dragon, for the rivers and rain bless the fertile earth with moisture.

In burial and **ancestrism**, continuity of the three identity-giving factors of family, ancestors, and place was emphasized. Burial, the return of the tiller of the earth to its bosom, has always been very important in China. As the peasant works his fields, he may see on the side of an overlooking hill the site he has selected for his tomb. He knows that from there he will in spirit watch his progeny generation after generation work the same fields. At the tomb, at the family shrine with tablets bearing the names of ancestors, and in the home shrine, his descendants will remember him with offerings of food and drink and with information concerning family events. This reverence may be tinged with awe and dread, for even the humblest family head grows mightily in power when he returns to union with the earth, and he can reach out from the grave to bless those who keep bright the family honor, or to afflict its enemies. From another perspective, perhaps the continuity of life and death made death less feared than it may have been in other cultures. Here, the afterlife was understood to be a continuation of family and community, and to be remembered by one's family through the ages must have been some comfort of itself.

The concern with burial goes as far back as Chinese culture. Neolithic farmers buried children in urns under the house and adults in reserved fields. In the first period of real civilization, the Shang era, great pits were dug in the earth for the burial of a king. In what must have been a scene of incredible barbaric horror and splendor, the deceased monarch was interred brilliantly ornamented with jade, together with the richly caparisoned horses who had borne his hearse, hundreds of sacrificed human retainers and prisoners, and a fortune in precious objects.[2]

The Shang **Dynasty** and its successor, the Zhou Dynasty,[3] lasted from about 1750 to 221 B.C.E. The basic motifs of religion in these eras represent in developing form the fundamental ideas of Chinese religion and philosophy.

The thinkers of those days talked of a supreme ruler or moderator of the universe, Di or Tian, usually translated as "Heaven," who gave rain, victory, fortune or misfortune, and regulated the moral order. All things ultimately derived from **Tian**, but it was more a personification of natural law than a real personality and was not directly worshipped; Heaven was like the high god of many archaic peoples—understood as being remote.

Other gods, lesser but more accessible to worship, were those of sun, moon, stars, rivers, mountains, the four directions, and localities. These were given offerings, some seasonally, some morning and evening. Above all were the ancestral spirits, treated to meals and remembrance and expected to intercede on behalf of the living with Tian.

The dead, in other words, were made a part of life. They could communicate with the living through the lips of shamanesses and oracles, and unpropitiated ghosts of the dead were much feared. There were also myths of culture heroes who combated floods, built irrigation systems, and taught the people agriculture. If not directly worshipped, such figures as Yu and Hou Ji had marvelous births, precarious and miracle-fraught childhoods, and lives of self-sacrifice and superhuman works comparable to those of Divine heroes and saviors elsewhere.

The Shang era is most famous for divination with the "oracle bones." The procedure was that kings would ask their ancestors questions, and the answers would be determined by cracks made in a tortoiseshell when it was heated over a fire. Thousands of these shells, with the questions and sometimes the answers inscribed on them in an archaic form of writing, have been preserved.

Archaic Chinese religion is also noteworthy for the importance it gave to ceremonial elements. Highly stylized and exact rites were performed for each season, for gods and ancestors, and for the major occasions of life. These were done at court and apparently had their parallels among the common people as well. Court ceremonies were elaborate affairs; as we have seen, they sometimes involved grisly but solemn animal and human sacrifices.

Divination, the seasonal cycle, and ceremonialism all suggest one basic principle that has run through Chinese thought from the beginning—that the universe is a unity in which all things fit together. If humanity aligns itself with it, all will fit together for us as it does for nature. On this assumption, traditional Chinese lived with the turning of the seasons, and in their ceremonies strove to make life into an image of their harmony. Divination is based on the same worldview, for it presumes that if the world is a unity, each fragment of it—like a tortoiseshell—must contain clues to what is happening or will happen in other parts.

The Dao—Foundational to Confucianism and Daoism

The unity in which all things fit together harmoniously is called the **Dao** (*Tao*). The word is most often translated "way," and it originally meant a road but can also mean "speak." Among philosophers it came to mean the inexpressibly broad track down which all things roll; in philosophical writing, it has been translated by such terms as "way," "nature," "existence," and even "God."

Dao—how to know it, live it, and construct a society that exemplifies it—is the great theme of Chinese thought and the religious expressions closely related to it. Never was this more the case than in the last two centuries of the Zhou Dynasty, 403–221 B.C.E. Called the "Warring States" period, this was an era when, because the emperor had been reduced to a powerless figurehead, rulers of feudal states battled unceasingly with each other. Although it was a time of cultural and material advance, people felt that all sense of restraint and morality had been lost. Even the rough warrior codes no longer held, and society was caught up in a madness of rapacity, intrigue, and violence punctuated by a depraved brutality in which prisoners were routinely killed by slow and horrible means. The peasants, exploited in the best of times, suffered most.

Yet this was a time of creativity for the human spirit. New concepts that could be the foundation of high civilization emerged, if only because thoughtful people were forced to ask themselves such questions as, "Where did we go wrong? How can we get society back on the right track and find the Dao? How can a sensitive individual find meaning in the midst of so much crassness?"

In asking how to get back on the track of Dao, the Chinese believed there were three realms where Dao could be experienced: nature, human society, and one's own inner being. The question was: How are these to be lined up, with what priorities, and with what techniques for ascertaining the "message" of the Dao?

The answers fell into two categories: Confucian and Daoist. (There were other schools that have not survived or did not develop significant religious expression.) The basic difference was that Confucianists thought the Dao, or Tian (the will of Heaven), as they often called it, was best found by humans within human tradition and society and so was explored through human relationships and rituals and by the use of human reason. The Daoists thought that reason and society perverted the Dao, that it was best found alone in the rapture of merging with infinite nature and the mystical and marvelous.

The difference is comparable to that between rationalists and romantics in the West. Needless to say, Confucianism in China has been associated mainly with moralism and the ruling "establishment" elite together with their education system. Daoism, on the other hand, is linked with sensitivity of feelings, with artists and poets, and with all sorts of colorful, bizarre, "nonestablishment" things—from fairy tales to unusual sexual techniques, from exorcising devils to revolutionary secret societies and esoteric temple rites.

But it is important to recall that relatively few Chinese would think of themselves as exclusively Confucian or Daoist or Buddhist. In the lives of most people, features from all sides would have a place. Confucian attitudes would undergird family and work ethics; Buddhism would help to answer questions about what happens after death; a dash of Daoist color would meet esthetic and spiritual needs in family and personal life. (It has been said that Chinese officials were Confucian at work and Daoist in retirement.)

Confucianism

Confucius (Kung Fuzi) and the Confucian Classics

The Confucian tradition is named after the philosopher **Confucius** (551–479 B.C.E.). We must distinguish Confucius as the man of his time from the almost-deified, impossibly wise, and remote figure of the Confucian educational tradition and state cult. But at the same time, we must remember why this particular man was selected as the symbolic embodiment of that tradition.

First, we must take into account the winsome, wise, persuasive, and utterly sincere personality of Confucius himself. Born in the feudal state of Lu (modern Shantung Province) as the son of a minor official or military officer, Kong Fuzi—to give Master Kong his Chinese rather than Latinized name and title—received an education and sought employment by a prince. He was a member of a class called **ru**, who were specialists in the "six arts"—ceremonial, music, archery, charioteering, history, numbers—and so custodians of what passed in those days for a classical and cultivated tradition. But Confucius had great difficulty in finding a position, apparently because he was too outspoken about proper conduct on the part of rulers and seemed hopelessly to have "his head in the clouds." He had to settle for a role that to him seemed second best but in the long run proved far more epochal than that of government minister. He became a teacher. Among his students were young men who were successful in attaining practical influence and who over the years—and through subsequent generations of students over the centuries—reshaped the values and structures of Chinese statecraft, education, and social organization. It was they who understandably added honor upon honor to Confucius's memory until temples redolent of incense and sacrifice enshrined his name.

Confucius was not revered just for himself but because he was associated with the classical literature that was the real bedrock of the traditional culture. Five books, which existed in early form by the time of Confucius and which were the basic texts of the *ru,* are now often called the Confucian Classics. These are the

Confucius

Book of History, the *Book of Poems*, the *Book of Change* (the famous *Yi Jing* or *I Ching*), the historical *Spring and Autumn Annals*, and the *Book of Rites*. Tradition said, with greater or less exaggeration, that Confucius had written parts of them and edited them all; in any case, he became the symbol of their authority.

Four other books from shortly after the time of Confucius are also canonical and bear the putative seal of the master's authority: the *Analects* (containing the remembered words of Confucius himself), the *Great Learning*, the *Mean*, and the *Book of Mencius*.[4] (Mencius was the next best known philosopher in the Confucian tradition.)

These books are important because they reflect basic Chinese values and ways of thinking. Their tradition went back before Confucius and continued after him. Confucius is not a peerless sage because he created this tradition. On the contrary, he is unequalled because the tradition "created" him, and he reflected it faithfully.[5]

Fundamentals of the Confucian Tradition

It was not unfair to Confucius to honor him as the embodiment of the tradition, for the burden of his teaching was above all to maintain this heritage and apply it fully and properly. He was a creative and deeply principled conservative. He believed that the way to get society on the right track again was to go back to the example of ancient sage-emperors. The basic structures of society, he felt, were adequate. The needful thing was to convince people they must act in accordance with the roles society has given them. The father must act like a father; the son, like a son; the ruler must be a real ruler like those of old, wise and benevolent; the ministers of state must be true civil servants, loyal and fearless and self-giving.

This change to becoming what one "is" (called "**rectification of names**") must first of all be within. One must be motivated by virtue, or **ren**, a typically vague but eloquent term suggestive of humanity, love, high principle, and living together in harmony. It is the way of the **jun-zi**, the superior man, who, as the Confucian ideal suggests, is a man at once a scholar, a selfless servant of society, and a gentleman steeped in courtesy and tradition; as an official and family head, he continually puts philosophy into practice.

Confucius conceded that this noble ideal is enforced by no outside sanctions except the opinion of good men, for it was based on no belief in Divine rewards or punishment after death. Its sincere practice in this life might, as often as not, result in exile and hunger rather than honor from princes. Yet in the end it draws men by the sheer attractiveness of the good and by the fact that it embodies Dao, and so to follow *ren* is to align oneself with the way things are.

There follows a fundamental satisfaction from acting in accordance with the real nature of things that the virtueless devotee of passion and gain can never know and that finally makes such a person's life hollow. For Confucianism has generally believed that the basic nature of mankind is good. It is only perverted by bad external example or bad social environment, and people will turn naturally to the good when good examples and social conditions are present. To make them present is the weighty responsibility of the ruler, advised by Confucian sages.

MAJOR ERAS—CHINA

Zhou (1123–221)

End of Shang (c. 1750–c.1050)

Qin (221–206)

Han (206 B.C.E–220 B.E.)

PERSONALITIES AND EVENTS—CHINA

Court rituals
Laozi (?)
Confucius (551–479)
Zuangzi (c. 300)
Mencius (372–289)
Tung Zhungshu
(179–104) and
Han Confucianism

MAJOR ERAS—JAPAN

Prehistoric   Protohistoric

PERSONALITIES AND EVENTS—JAPAN

Shamanism
very influential

Clan period

1500 B.C.E.   1000 B.C.E.   500 B.C.E.   1 B.C.E./C.E.

Three Kingdoms (220–265)
Jin (265–420)

Yuan (1280–1368)

Ming (1368–1644)

Six Dynasties (420–589)
Sui (589–618)
Tang (618–907)

Qing (1644–1911)
Republic (1912–)
People's Republic on
mainland (1949–)

Song (960–1280)

Han synthesis

High point of Buddhism

Ge Hong (283–343)
Beginning of Chan and
Pure Land Buddhism

Zhu Xi (1130–1200)

Neo-Confucianism dominant

Huineng (638–713)

Wang Yangming (1472–1529)

Taika (645–710)

Kamakura (1185–1333)

Nara (710–784)

Muromachi (1333–1568)
Monoyama (1568–1600)
Tokugawa (1600–1867)
Modern (1868–1945)
Postwar (1945)

Heian (794–1185)

Introduction of Buddhism
(early 6th century)

Honen (1133–1212)

Hakuin (1685–1768)

Zen dominant
Dogen (1200–1253)
Eisai (1141–1215)

Confucianism
dominant culturally

Kojiki (712)

Kobo Daishi
(773–835)

Shinran (1173–1262)

Nationalism

Esoteric Buddhism

Nichiren (1222–1282)

New Religions

500 C.E.   1000 C.E.   1500 C.E.   2000 C.E.

External influences, then, can aid in the inner development of *ren*. This leads to another very important Confucian term—**li**. It indicates rites, proper conduct, ceremonies, courtesy, doing things the right way. Despite a professed lack of concern about ghosts and gods, for Confucius the performance of rituals was extremely important.

It may seem to us excessive that a man, at the height of his career, upon the death of his father would go into retirement for three years, wearing sackcloth, wailing through day and night, eating only tasteless food. It might seem that the government of a nation ought to have better things to do than spend endless hours and money in the preparation and execution of seasonal ceremonies, one after the other. But *li* needs to be understood as Confucius understood it, not as cold or mere "formalism" but as a supremely humanizing act. Animals act out of the lust or violent emotion of the moment, but mankind can rise above this in the societies it creates, and *li* exemplifies this potential. *Li* expresses a society that becomes a great dance and thus incarnates harmony. In ritual, everyone acts out proper relationships and has a structured place. Ritual generates order in place of chaos and nurtures "rectification of names." It can be hoped that if a person acts out, if only ritually, the proper conduct of his or her station in life often enough, in time he or she will interiorize the action, and the inner and outer will become one: the ritual father a true father, the ritual prince a true prince. *Li,* then, is meant to stimulate *ren,* even as melodious music induces calmness and heroic poetry valor.

It is within society that humanity comes to its best, for here the mutual stimuli of *ren* and *li* can be operative. Here is the key point of difference with the Daoists, who contended that society, or at least its regulations and rituals and mandatory relations, obscure the Dao. For Confucius, it was precisely in these social expressions that the Dao became visible and "spoke" to mankind.

Society for Confucius was founded on the "**five relationships**": (1) ruler and subject, (2) father and son, (3) husband and wife, (4) elder and younger brother, (5) friend and friend. In all of these, proper behavior, *li,* was required to give what is simply biological or spontaneous the structure that makes it into human society—calm and enduring for the benefit of all.

The cornerstone relationship is the second—father and son. A son was expected to negate his own feelings and individuality in deference to the wishes and pleasure of his father in **filial piety**.[6] It was in this relationship, which is (at least according to Freudian psychoanalysis) the most feeling-laden and difficult of all, that fundamental attitudes of *ren* and *li* and societal orientation were to be learned. It was as though to say, if love and virtue are to be learned truly, they must be learned at home and by making this difficult but all-important relationship the pivot. Father–son becomes the primal model of an interpersonal relationship, and in Confucianism it is in interpersonal relationships that man is humanized and Dao is manifested. If this relationship can be rectified, then all other relationships will also fall into place.

One might ask: Why is the relation between father and son, rather than that between mother and child, the key? Perhaps it can be looked at in this way: The mother–child relationship is essentially a given as it is biological, fraught with deep feelings and instincts that humankind shares with most of the higher animals. The father–son relationship, on the other hand, is more social in nature. This is not to say, of course, that the father does not have a biological role and some instinctual equipment to go with it. But in many archaic societies, the father's biological role does not in itself establish social responsibility for a child. Rather, the crucial factor is the father's taking responsibility for the child in his social role as head of the household. The role is defined by his picking up the child, giving him a name, and recognizing him as his ward and heir. In other words, the father–son relationship is the most basic relationship, inextricably intertwined with the social as well as the biological components of human culture, such as language (giving a name), moral responsibility, family as a legal entity, and the combination of privilege and repression that makes learned behavior—all that flows into *li* and *ren*—possible. It is therefore significant that in Confucianism, with its emphasis on human society as the key bearer of the Dao for human beings, the father–son relationship—the primal social, structured relationship—should be central. (In contrast, Laozi, whose Daoism, as we shall soon see, emphasized the natural and biological and spontaneous as better than the social for manifesting Dao, several times uses the mother–child relationship as a metaphor for the relation of a person with Dao.)

Needless to say, this perspective has meant that Confucianism, like many another traditional religions and social orders, has presumed and established an essentially male-centered worldview and society. Women, while given a place in the pattern of relationship, have found that place to be distinctly subordinate—something we will be addressing in more detail later. (We have not hesitated to use the terms "man" and "mankind" in the discussion of Confucianism, for this usage certainly conforms to the Confucian outlook.)

Subsequent Confucian philosophers talked about human nature and how society can best be organized to manifest the Dao within it. **Mencius** (372–289 B.C.E.), for example, held that human nature is basically good and is only impeded by an evil social environment, while **Xunzi** (fl. 298–238 B.C.E.) said that man is basically evil in the sense of being self-centered and, therefore, needs education and social control to become good.

We must give more attention, however, to the ways in which Confucianism clearly took the three forms of religious expression, presenting a unified structure of teaching, rites, and sociological forms. In Confucianism, these three forms appeared simply in the "natural" units of family and traditional community. Because Confucius wanted to enhance and sanctify these units, he did not want to establish a center of sacred value elsewhere. His teaching was about the family and community, for which his rituals were performed, and through which they made their own sacred community. The secular was the sacred.

But as Confucianism became a quasi-state religion in the Han Dynasty (206 B.C.E.–220 C.E.) and after, it found it needed a quasi-theology, a quasi-divinity, and a quasi-priesthood with its own rites. Quasi-divinity it found in Confucius himself, and quasi-priesthood in the powerful class of Confucian scholar/bureaucrat elites—the *ru* or **mandarins**—who staffed the bureaucracy of the empire. Confucius, as the peerless infallible sage, was seen as a sort of mystic king, with a true right to rule the inward kingdom of ideas and values upon which the outer realm, administered and educated by the *mandarins,* was based.

The "Han Synthesis" and Yin-Yang

This kind of thinking, which may be called the "**Han Synthesis**" because it generously incorporated Daoist and other traditional motifs into Confucianism, was the work of **Dong Zhongshu** (c. 179–104 B.C.E.) more than of any other individual. His thought is like that of cosmic religion in that it is interested in the total interrelationship of all things rather than free, personal, ethical, and political questioning. Dong presented a doctrine of correspondences, in which humanity and nature are parts of an interwoven web. A portent in heaven may be related to a forthcoming event on earth, and the moral decisions of a ruler may affect the prevalence of rain in his nation's fields.

Yang and Yin

Unlike many moderns, traditional Chinese did not see people and nature as separate, going by different laws. Instead they assumed that humanity, human history, and government cooperate with nature and are controlled by the same laws. It is as though we were to say that perpetual motion is as impossible in the history of a nation as it is in mechanics, if it is a true law. To further the comparison, it would be as though we then said that the nation must have a public ritual once a year to counteract its slowing down and to wind the energy up again.

For Dong, the key to the whole web of correspondences of which life is woven is the **Yin-Yang** concept. This theory had very early origins in occult speculation connected with astrology, alchemy, and *Yi Jing* divination, but it did not emerge fully into the mainstream of Chinese philosophy until the "Han Synthesis" gave it a place.

In this view, the Dao—that is, all the 10,000 things—is divisible into two great classifications: *Yang* things and forces, and *Yin* things and forces. Fundamentally, *Yang* is associated with the masculine and *Yin* with the feminine. But their respective meanings go far beyond gender. *Yang* is what is male, but also day, sky, spring, and all that is bright, clear, hard, assertive, growing, moving out. Its symbol is the dragon. *Yin* is female, and also night, earth, moisture, autumn and harvest, spirits of the dead, and all that is dark, underneath, recessive, pulling in, connected with the moon, mysterious. Its symbol is the tiger, which may be thought of as Blake's "Tyger, tyger burning bright / In the forests of the night"—emblematic of the arcane, inward, unfathomable, yet unescapable in human life.

It must be emphasized that philosophically *Yang* and *Yin* are by no means either "good" or "bad." Neither is "better" than the other. They are both neutral, like gravitation. To keep going, the universe needs both, and they need to interact in a balanced way. Too much of either brings disaster, just as rain and sun are both necessary in their places, but too much of either brings flood or drought. (In popular religion, however, *Yang* is often preferred because of its fertility associations, and no doubt also because of the male predominance in the culture.)

The task of humanity is to keep these two eternal antagonists and partners, the dragon and the tiger, in proper balance, for our place is between them, and we are finally to interiorize them both. An elaborate art called **feng-shui** arose to de-termine, according to *Yang–Yin* "bearings," the most auspicious locations for houses, businesses, tombs, and temples, between, say, a rock considered *Yang* and a tree determined as *Yin*. (Much more was involved in the full system of *feng-shui* and of correspondences, too: the values of the five "elements" or modes of natural activity—fire, water, earth, metal, and wood—each of which corresponded with seasons, colors, tones, and so forth.) Finally, particularly in esoteric Daoism, one sought through alchemical potions and *yogic* practices to bring to equilibrium the two forces within oneself and thus achieve immortality. It is *Yang–Yin* imbalance that results in decay and death: One who has them in as perfect harmony as the great Dao itself will be as deathless as the great Dao. Confucianism has always emphasized finding a balance and keeping away from too much or too little of anything.

The ritual year, both at the imperial palace and in the humblest village, strove to "work" *Yang* and *Yin*. The object was to support what the Dao, through the re-spective force, was doing at that time. The first half of the year, the time of growing and outgoing of nature as it awoke from the sleep of winter, was the time of the dy-namic, rain-giving dragon. The Chinese New Year is marked by a parade through the streets of a gigantic, weaving dragon borne by many men. In midsummer, to consummate *Yang*, dragon boat or horse races are held. Then to inaugurate the *Yin* months of in-gathering and the darkening of days, lion or tiger dances are held. The traditional harvest festival when the dead return (as at Halloween) is full of *Yin* symbolism—it is held at night, and cakes in the shape of the moon, decorated with moon castles where immortals live, are placed in the courtyards.

In the Han period, this sort of ideology also became political as a part of the "Han Synthesis." The emperor was *Yang*, the people *Yin*, and the ruler was to serve as activator of proper response by the ruled. Moreover, the sovereign was media-tor between Heaven and Earth, the midpoint in a triad of Heaven, Earth, and human society. In his lawgiving, he was representative of Heaven, the great origin, to the people; as chief priest in his worship, he represented humankind before Heaven. In all this it was his responsibility to promote the proper working of *Yang* and *Yin*. If deterioration in nature or society became evident, it would be widely said that the sovereign had lost the **Mandate of Heaven**, that is, the right to rule as representative of Heaven.

Mandarins (Ru)

The thinking we've been discussing fit the needs of the *ru*, or *mandarin* class who studied the lore, enacted the rites, and made Confucius the symbol of learning and authority. His **cultus** grew apace. In 56 C.E., sacrifices to Confucius were ordered in all schools. By the end of the empire in 1912, he had (in 1908) been declared co-equal with Heaven and Earth themselves, as though to say the best of human cul-ture was no less a great thing than cosmic nature.

The importance of the *mandarin* scholar class in Chinese tradition can hardly be overemphasized. Three things set them apart: (1) They were bearers of the ongoing tradition as dynasties rose and fell; (2) they were unique as a class in ability to read and write well; and (3) in theory they were not a hereditary aristocracy, but an elite of brains who attained their positions in academic competition. As both teachers and administrators, they were indispensable to generations of rulers who found that sooner or later they had to conform to the values and usages of this class because they could not rule without its support.

The role of these Confucian scholar/bureaucrats meant that the real focus of power was not the sword but the pen, and that the vessel of cultural continuity in this society was a class of refined elites, who scarcely hid their disdain of the rough soldier, but who made the written language and ability to wield it elegantly the supreme symbol of superiority over the toiling masses. This situation involved

Chinese New Year celebration. ■

no small flourishing of class privilege, yet it also enabled a rudimentary democracy, for the means of entry into the privileged class was through education and civil service examinations—ostensibly merit. In nearly all periods there were young men of humble background who managed to succeed in that grueling ordeal to become a *mandarin*.

Dynasties periodically rose and fell, and with the transfer of the Mandate of Heaven, a peasant or outlander might well come to the throne. There was no official nobility, and all families experienced years of bad fortune as well as good. China, then, did not know the domination of intermarrying noble lines like the Bourbons and Hapsburgs of Europe century after century; what lasted instead was the gray-gowned meritocracy of the learned.

The *mandarin* class naturally developed its own internal traditions and style. Its members grew fingernails inches long to prove that they did not do manual labor. Anything in writing, however trivial, was treated by them with respect and would be reverently burned rather than thrown out. They would typically be skeptical of beliefs concerning ghosts, spirits, gods, and an afterlife, but would treat such beliefs among the common people (or even the womenfolk in their own households) with a disdainful tolerance. It was better the masses believe in such things than that their discontent with their lot in this life get out of hand. In this spirit, the *mandarin* scholar who was appointed governor of a city would conduct the rites of the city-god, even to whipping the image of the deity when that Divine protector failed to protect his people from misfortune. He would, however, know that beliefs like this were unworthy of a philosopher.

Confucian followers burning incense at the tomb of deceased great scholars in Korea.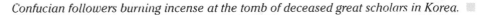

Rituals of the Mandarins (Ru)

On a more serious level, the *ru* would manage the execution of the state ceremonies, culminating in the emperor's worship in the middle of the night at the Winter Solstice and the worship of Earth at the Summer Solstice. The drama of the Midwinter worship of Heaven has been described by many observers prior to its last enactment in 1911. In icy darkness broken only by flaring torches, the sovereign and

---

FUNDAMENTAL FEATURES OF CONFUCIANISM

THEORETICAL

Basic Worldview	The universe a unity under heaven, of which humans are an integral part. For humans, family and society are the most important links to the universe.
God or Ultimate Reality	"Heaven" or *Tian,* regulating the world and moral order.
Origin of the World/ Destiny of the World	Vague, but world originates from heaven and proceeds through interaction of Yin and Yang and the five "principles" or elements.
Origin of Humans	Vague; ultimately from heaven and earth.
Destiny of Humans	No stress on afterlife except in terms of ancestrism. Ideal is to live a good life in this world through family and society.
Revelation or Mediation between the Ultimate and the Human	The teachings of Confucius and the classics; mediated by the educational system.

PRACTICAL

What Is Expected of Humans: Worship, Practices, Behavior	To observe official and ancestral rites; to honor parents and meet other ethical obligations. One works for a good society by exercising benevolence and practicing mutuality with others, especially through the "five relationships."

SOCIOLOGICAL

Major Social Institutions	Great importance of family and of elite class; aligned to state under empire.

his ministers, clad in the heaviest furs, would arrange elaborate presentations of food, wine, and cloth on the huge tiered mountain of masonry in Peking (now Beijing) called the Altar of Heaven, and the emperor would read an elegant prayer. In principle, only the emperor, as mediator, could worship Heaven and Earth, the greatest ultimates; others had to be content with ancestral and Divine intermediaries. For the Confucianist, these rites were of grave importance as expressions of *li*; they were contributory to making society into a vast harmony or dance rather than a mere collection of thinking animals.

Another set of rituals were of special meaning to the Confucian elite. These were the major sacrifices to Confucius himself, held at the Vernal and Autumnal Equinoxes, significantly midway between the two great rites of Heaven and Earth. These would be conducted at the temples of Confucius located in the more important cities. Although formerly they contained images of Confucius, since the Middle Ages they gave tribute to the superior worth of writing in the eyes of devotees of the philosopher by presenting only an upright tablet with the inscription "Confucius the Wise and Holy Sage," flanked by similar tablets to the master's disciples. At these rites, the local scholar-rulers would gather; *kowtow* (kneel deeply so that the forehead touched the floor) before the altar; present offerings of a whole slaughtered bull, pig, and sheep, together with wine and vegetables; offer a tribute; present music and dance supposed to be from the time of Confucius; and finally feast on the offerings.

Understanding this ritual, as enacted by presumably skeptical scholars for one whom no one considered exactly a god, creates difficulty for the Westerner accustomed to quite different styles of thought. Clearly, it was an act of reverence and sacrifice that was less than Divine worship yet more than Western civil ceremonies. It was somewhere between what might be done at the Arlington National Cemetery on Memorial Day and a cathedral service, with the difference that animal victims were sacrificed in a way that Westerners consider barbaric (despite the slaughter of thousands daily with less ceremony in our stockyards).

Apart from their value simply as *li*, the Confucian rites can be thought of best in connection with the ancestral system. The Confucian scholars greatly valued their own family shrines and lineages; yet they were also, as a special called-out class, members of another "family," a spiritual clan of all of their vocation. Of this family of literati the supreme scholar Confucius was the ancestor.

Neo-Confucianism

A word should be said about **Neo-Confucianism**, which began as a movement in the eleventh and twelfth centuries during the **Song Dynasty** (960–1280 C.E.) and became the authoritative interpretation of the Confucian intellectual tradition. Partly in response to the issues raised by Daoist and particularly Buddhist thought, Neo-Confucian philosophers greatly enhanced their tradition's metaphysical foundation. It became a comprehensive worldview concerned with the nature of mind and the ultimate origin of things, and with simple methods of meditation, as well as a social philosophy, although it never lost the ideal that the philosopher finds joy in the midst of family and social life, not in permanent withdrawal from them. Two leading Neo-Confucianists were **Zhu Xi** (also written as Chu Hsi, 1130–1200) and **Wang Yangming** (or Wang Shouren, 1472–1529). Zhu Xi taught that one great ultimate is manifested in the principles of the myriad separate things, as the light of the moon is broken onto many rivers and lakes. Through reflection on particulars, especially human morality, one can know the ultimate. The more idealistic Wang Yangming taught that the principles are actually within the mind itself, and so the supreme requisite is sincerity of mind. Through reflections such as these, the spiritual and intellectual side of Confucianism was given a transcendence that made the practice of Confucian rites and virtues more deeply religious, even developing a sort of mysticism in the midst of a life of service.

Confucian Moral and Social Values

But the most important impact of Confucianism on China was in the area of moral and social values. Although ancestrism, the family system, and the ideal of selfless work for the common good have pre-Confucian roots, Confucianism gave these values ultimate prestige through the civilized centuries. It was of a piece with Confucianism that all important families had ancestral shrines in which the names of parents, grandparents, and great-grandparents were lined up on higher and higher shelves for each generation, and worship was offered them, as it was at the tombs and in the home. Inseparable from ancestrism was the Confucian-based family system in which loyalty and filial obedience were obligations that gave precedence to no others. Confucianism too underlay the Chinese "work ethic," the high regard for diligence and productivity for the honor and prosperity of one's family name. Without the mental image of the wise and sober sage from the state of Lu, and the words from his followers' pens, China would be very different from what we have known it to be for more than twenty centuries.

Daoism (Taoism)

Fundamentals of Daoism

Confucianism, even in its most expansive forms, does not exhaust the spiritual heritage of China. Few people can be wholly devoted to sober virtues all the time, and the Chinese are no exception. There is another side that demands its due. This is the side of human personality that is attracted to what expresses the private fears, fancies, and aspirations of the individual. It is the side that feels for communion with nature and aspirations of the mystic rapture, imaginative works of art and letters, rebellion against social conformity, inward fear of evil, and love for gods. This side affirms the needs of personal life against the demands of structured society, and it affirms the place of the feeling, symbol-making, nonrational side against the cool, word-oriented rational side. In China, all this side has danced about under the broad umbrella of the Daoist tradition.

An eighth-century figure of Maitreya, the future Buddha, a Buddhist monk in Sichuan, China.

The Torii or ceremonial gate of the Miyajima Shinto shrine in Japan, located offshore.

Perhaps we can understand the role of Daoism in China by thinking of the cultural situation in America. During the 1960s and 1970s it was common to think of society as manifesting roughly in two modes. First, there was the "establishment" and its values: the major institutions of business, government, education, and church, upholding the usual values in family life, behavior, and the legitimate organization of society. Second, there was what was called the "counterculture." It consisted of people who had to varying degrees "dropped out" of the establishment. They were preoccupied with a gamut of things—living in the woods, ecology, writing poetry, painting, engaging in new styles of marital and sexual life, or trying to reach "altered states of consciousness" by meditation, chanting, yoga, and drugs. Some got involved in radical politics. If there was a unifying idea to this countercultural movement, it was that one must above all be true to what one is in the depths of one's personal self—one must "get oneself together" and "do one's own thing."

Since then what was referred to alternatively as the "establishment" or the "counterculture" has continued, but not as distinct cultural identities. Now in America the two intermingle. Where once a person might have been identified as an "establishment" or a "countercultural" person, now the very same individual might be "establishment" in one context, for example at work, and, at the same time, do things that were once thought of as "countercultural" in another context, for example, go on a meditation retreat. And even if not merged in any particular individual in this way, these two and other influences interplay in society as a whole.

This is similar to China, where what we have called "establishment" corresponds more or less to what Confucianism has undergirded in China. And parallels in China to the countercultural features have appeared in connection with the Daoist tradition. Yet, as in contemporary United States society, but to even a greater degree, the two interplay and interact in such a way that to an outsider they do not appear as separate religious forms.

As one would expect from this, Daoism has been many things to many different people and has taken an immense variety of forms over the centuries. It has included hermit poets, temples with lavishly robed priests burning clouds of incense before resplendent gods, and "underground" secret political societies. It has ranged from "nature mysticism" to occult quests for immortality to the rites of spiritualists who call up the dead.

Some commentators have talked about a "pure" philosophical Daoism and a "degenerate," "superstitious" religious Daoism. But such presuppositions get in the way of real understanding. It is more instructive to comprehend how all of Daoism forms a unity of experience around a single pole, focusing on the feeling-oriented, nonrational side of life. Here it is simple to move rapidly from mysticism to occultism to revolution and back, and from "nature" to the most elaborate religious robes and rites, so long as they express something imaginative and personal. Daoism in China is really a tapestry of countless strands of folk religion, ancient arcana going back to prehistoric shamanism and private vision.

Laozi and the Dao De Jing

Daoism's supposed founder is the sage **Laozi** (Lao-tzu). Appropriately for such a romantic tradition, he is more legend than fact, and his very name suggests anonymity, for Laozi just means "The Old Man." Stories say that the bearer of this epithet was an older contemporary of Confucius, and indeed that Confucius once met him, found him hard to confront, and said, "Of birds I know that they have wings to fly with, of fish that they have fins to swim with, of wild beasts that they have feet to run with. For feet there are traps, for fins nets, for wings arrows. But who knows how dragons surmount wind and cloud into heaven? This day I have seen Laozi and he is a dragon."

Laozi was, according to tradition, a "dropout." It is said he was an archive-keeper at the Zhou Dynasty court and a popular fellow who kept a good table. But he became disgusted with the grasping and hypocrisy of the world, and at the age

Laozi, the supposed founder of Daoism, riding an ox.

of 80 left his job, mounted a water buffalo, and wandered off to the West. At the Western portals of the empire, the gatekeeper is reported to have detained him as his guest, refusing to let him pass until he had recorded his wisdom. So the Old Man wrote down the book called the **Dao de jing** (*Tao te ching*) and then departed in the direction of Tibet, becoming mysteriously lost to the world.

Other ways may be found to interpret the emergence of the Daoism of the *Dao de jing*. Some have pointed out that at the time of Confucius there were apparently a number of fairly well-educated people around, more than there were government or literary jobs available; Confucius's own difficulty in finding a position may testify to this. Such persons, unable to work at the level of their abilities and too proud to return to the fields, formed a floating intellectual class for whose way of life early Daoism could provide at best an inspiration and at least a rationalization.[7]

Others have noted that, on the other hand, the *Dao de jing* does contain a political philosophy aimed at rulers as well as reflections for the solitary individual; it must not have been intended only for people without place. Still others have seen in it the veiled but rather technical manual of a yogic school.[8] In sum, the origin of the *Dao de jing* is as mysterious as its meaning; each reader must get from it what he or she can.

Let us now look at the message of the *Dao de jing*. It is a book about the Dao, that universal way or track down which all the 10,000 things roll and which is their substratum and the only lasting thing there is; the name *Dao de jing* means something like "*The Book of the Dao and How to Apply Its Strength*."

Although a book about the Dao, it begins with the curious affirmation that nothing can be said about its subject matter:

> *Existence [the Dao] is beyond the power of words*
> *To define:*
> *Terms may be used*
> *But are none of them absolute.*
> *In the beginning of heaven and earth there were no words.*
> *Words came out of the womb of matter.*[9]

There is no word, this means, that is an adequate expression of the Dao. That is obvious when we consider that all human words come out of finite human experience. They do convey something of what really is, but only as human beings with their limited sensory equipment and limited field of experience have known it. When someone says to you the word "tree," certain images pop into your mind. But these images derive only from your own limited experience with trees.

The image you have may be of a tree in your backyard as a child, or one that you saw in a picture book when you learned the word; you let this tree represent for you all the trees theoretically covered by the word. The word says little about all the trees you have not seen, or about how trees are experienced by other people or animals, much less about how a tree experiences itself! The word "tree" is really only a very pale thing, calling up few hints of what "treeness" means to a human being who is alien to a tree's life. It scarcely touches the vast untapped richness contained in the reality of trees "out there"—how they were in ages past before humankind arose, what they may be like on other planets, what they seem like to squirrels and birds who live in them, how they "feel" deep down in their own lives.

If this is true of something that is still only a part of creation, how much more must the limitations of language apply to the infinite whole? Add to the limitations of our experience the fact that language by definition cannot really apply a meaningful label to the whole because the purpose of words is to categorize the particular. We use words to distinguish one thing from another. To call something rice implies there are other things that are not rice from which it needs to be distinguished.

Even to use a word ostensibly for the whole, such as Dao or existence, does not avoid this limitation. All these words can do is point in a certain direction of comprehension, but they cannot make clear that there is really nothing comparable to Dao or existence from which it could be distinguished.

Philosophical discussion like this may begin to open up the kind of realizations that seized the writer of the *Dao de jing*. But for him the book was no mere metaphysical nitpicking—nothing would have won his contempt more.

Rather, these reflections opened up a different, ecstatic mode of being in the world. Once you realize that the Dao, which flows in and through everyone and everything, cannot be labeled and put in a box, you can respond to it in a different way, with simple wonder, turning to it as an infant turns to its mother. The first chapter ends, "From wonder into wonder Existence [the Dao] opens." Elsewhere we read, "Can you, with the simple stature of a child, breathing nature, become, notwithstanding, a man?...Can you, mating with heaven, serve as the female part?" And again, the writer, seeing himself as a misfit in artificial society, although marvelously near the Dao that others miss, says, "All these people are making their mark in the world, while I, pigheaded, awkward, different from the rest, am only a glorious infant still nursing at the breast." In contrast to the Confucian cornerstone—the father–son relationship—the *Dao de jing*, which emphasizes the natural, biological, and spontaneous as being better than the social manifestation of the Dao, makes becoming feminine, or becoming a child in a mother's arms, a basic image for the relationship of the individual with the great Dao.

In the seemingly weak stance of the female or the child is tremendous strength—the strength of water that wears down the hardest rock, or wind and rain that can come and go as they wish. In yielding, bending with the wind like a supple tree and then springing back renewed, is a vital strength that will weave its way subtly through all the permutations of the Dao. But that which is stiff like a man standing on tiptoe will break and fall. We are told that the best ruler is he who guides his people unobtrusively, so that they say, "We did this ourselves."

Making comparisons are inimical to this way of life, for they induce partial views and keep one from seeing life and the Dao whole:

People through finding something beautiful
Think something else unbeautiful.
Through finding one man fit

Judge another unfit . . .
Take everything that happens as it comes,
As something to animate, not to appropriate . . .
If you never assume importance
You never lost it.[10]

This outlook has political implications, and they are quite contrary to the elitism of "getting the best man for the job" of the Confucianists. There is also an attack on the philosophy of advertising: Nothing would be more contrary to Daoist political and economic ideas than our system of choosing leaders through elective competition and creating prosperity by encouraging consumption.

It is better not to make merit a matter of reward
Lest people conspire and contend,
Not to pile up rich belongings
Lest they rob,
Not to excite by display
Lest they covet.[11]

Elsewhere, we are told in the *Dao de jing* that the ideal community would be a village of simple, hardworking, prosperous farmers, so unsophisticated that they did not even use writing but kept records with knotted cords, and so content that even though they could hear the dogs barking and the cocks crowing in the next village, they never visited it.

Needless to say, this approach was quite at odds with the Confucianists' earnest talk of cultivating virtue and their moral norms such as filial obedience. Laozi instead refers back to a primordial paradise where people lived simply in harmony with the Dao spontaneously. Only when deterioration sets in, he thought, did rules and norms appear, and they were both cause and effect of the deterioration.

When people lost sight of the way to live
Came codes of love and honesty.

Learning came, charity came,

Hypocrisy took charge;
When differences weakened family ties
Came benevolent fathers and dutiful sons;
And when lands were disrupted and misgoverned
Came ministers commended as loyal.[12]

In other words, what for the Confucianists was the very essence of true civilization, for the Daoists was the token of decay and hypocrisy. To them, true virtue, like that of nature or of a child with eyes full of wonder, could never be forced by bookish ethics. If we got rid of formalized learning and duty, Laozi said, people would be a hundredfold happier and would do naturally what they now resist just because they are told to do it.

Here we can see clearly the Daoist reaction against ordinary conventions of thought and behavior. It is but a step from this generalized sense of wonder and of the limitations of ordinary words and attitudes to the affirmation of the most extraordinary seeming ideas: the possibility of deathlessness, the reality of fabulous secrets, powers, and worlds. In fact, even the *Dao de jing* appears to affirm that one who is in inseparable harmony with the Dao is as immortal as the Dao is, and that through the way of yielding one can find mysterious powers so great as to seem miraculous. But it remained to subsequent Daoist writers to make this potential of Laozi's vision more explicit.

The Development of Philosophical Daoism

The first and greatest of the Daoist writers to expand on Laozi's vision more explicitly is **Zhuangzi** (Chuang-tzu, died c. 300 B.C.E.).[13] Little is known of Zhuangzi apart from his book, *The Zhuangzi,* but it is enough. Written in a vivid, fanciful, and humorous style, it immediately brings the reader into a world of expanding horizons. One is first told of strange marvels, as though from tales of Sinbad—of an immense fish thousands of miles long that changes into a bird just as large and flies to a celestial lake in the South. The writer then juxtaposes these examples of the fabulously large with mention of the tiny motes in the air that make the sky blue and tells us that to a mustard seed a teacup is an ocean. As the reader's imagination is swung violently from the microscopically small to the immensely huge, from fairy tales to the homey, the reader gets a sense of mental vertigo. One feels that one is spinning and things are coming unfastened.

That is just what Zhuangzi wanted one to feel, for he wanted to shake the reader loose from the ordinary way of seeing things. Zhuangzi wanted a person to be free—above all, free from oneself, one's own prejudices, partial views, categories, and from judging everything in terms of oneself. To this Daoist, man is not the measure of all things. The way the universe happens to appear to a biped six feet tall is no more the way it is than the way it appears to a fish, a mote, an eagle, or a star. Only the Dao itself is the measure.

In the same way, ordinary rational waking consciousness is no more the measure of all things than the world of dreams and fancy and of the improbable. Zhuangzi tells us he once dreamed he was a butterfly, and when he awoke he did not know whether he was Zhuangzi who had dreamed he was a butterfly or a butterfly dreaming he was Zhuangzi. The dream world, in other words, is just as real as any other.

Unlike the sober Confucianist, Zhuangzi delights in the world of fantasy: of rocs and leviathans, wizards who can fly over the clouds, and islands of immortals. The world of the unconscious and the imagination, he is saying, is just as much a manifestation of the Dao as the rational—and may indeed better lead us to comprehending the Dao. At least it opens us to that sense of wonder and infinity beyond all limits that is necessary to comprehend the Dao—for the Dao is precisely the unbounded.

This was the direction in which Daoism went. A later Daoist thinker, Ge Hong (283–c. 343 C.E.), put it even more clearly, both in his life and in his writing. He lived during the three and a half centuries (221–589 C.E.) when division and political confusion reigned in China after the fall of the Han Dynasty in 221 C.E.—a time that nonetheless was culturally quite creative. Buddhism spread extensively, Daoism revived, and brilliant new forms in art and literature emerged to express the visions of these new, and newly personal, spiritual visions.

Confucianism was still accepted as normative, but the collapse of the social order based on its "Han Synthesis" version discredited it for many. In any case, the Confucian view of life oriented toward social usages and interpersonal obligations simply could not "work" well in a time of social confusion. Many were driven to look for more personal paths that promised inner meaning in spite of what is going on around them.

To this effect it is interesting that Ge Hong's book, the *Baopuzi,* contains what are called "Outer" and "Inner" parts. The "Outer" presents conventional Confucian teaching; the "Inner" offers Daoist material centering on the achievement of personal immortality through alchemy and *yogic* techniques. It is as though to say that while Confucianism may still be adequate for social ideology, a new self-consciousness and sense of social failure has made Confucianism hollow without something for the individual as well.

This quest for personal immortality was a basic theme of the new Daoism, and with it came interest in the worlds of miracles and of immortal supernatural beings that the quest implied and almost predicted. It had, as we have noted, philosophical roots in Laozi's implication that harmony with the Dao is immortality, and in Zhuangzi's, that truth is found in unfettered openness to all levels of consciousness and all possibilities, however fantastic.

The consequent distinction between Confucian and Daoist styles of thinking is very clear in a fictional debate that Ge Hong composed between a Confucianist and a Daoist on the possibility of immortality. The Confucianist argues that every living thing that anyone has ever heard of dies and that belief in immortality is therefore untenable nonsense. Baopuzi, the Daoist, responds that there are exceptions to every rule, and that just because things of which we know die, we cannot say that everything in this universe, of which we really know so little, must die. In effect, the Confucianist says, "You can't prove immortality," and the Daoist says, "You can't prove there isn't immortality." Perhaps little is proved in this particular argument except that, for Confucianists, the instinctive response to a query is the safe, rational, common-sense answer, and for Daoists, the romantic, speculative approach open to nonrational, "mind-blowing" possibilities. The cleavage is temperamental and comparable to the gulf between Enlightenment rationalism and the Romanticism that followed it in the West.

Other Daoists of this period of uncertainty followed lifestyles that seemed almost to repudiate the importance of personal immortality (as did earlier Zhuangzi), so much did they emphasize spontaneity. To them, living with the Dao meant a **feng liu** ("wind and stream") life, acting according to the movement of what was happening day by day. Many were artists and poets, or at least aesthetes; the unplanned life, which savored the beauty of each event and the richness of each impulse, well suited the temperament of their callings. Philosophical works that went with this Daoist stance made much of Dao as being **wu-wei**, nonbeing or not doing, in the rather technical sense that the Dao is not a "thing" or a "cause" and does not produce by plan or through work. Instead, all things just flow out of it freely or spontaneously in an endless stream of flux and change; the person who is attuned to Dao lives life in this way.[14]

Religious Daoism

It was religious Daoism with its popular gods and quest for immortality that took lasting institutional form. Its roots are complex, reach far back into the murky past, and are far from adequately traced.[15] We have noted that magical techniques to attain deathlessness, and *yogic* practices to control breath and induce joy, may be reflected in the *Dao de jing* and are very ancient. We have also mentioned that in the Han period, popular religious movements emphasizing healing and revolution were attached to the *Dao de jing* tradition. For example, Zhang Ling in the second century C.E. started a revivalistic healing movement that established itself as a state within a state in mountainous areas. Zhang Ling said that Laozi had appeared to him from the realm of spirits and had given him a sword and other apparatus by which he was able to exercise control over the spiritual world. Zhang was called Heavenly Teacher, and his direct descendants (sometimes misleadingly called the "**Daoist Popes**") have continued the title to the present, the present holder of the title now living in Taiwan. Formerly, they dwelt on Dragon and Tiger Mountain in central China, exercised a tenuous spiritual authority over Daoist priests in the South, and sold mysterious charms that were distributed far and wide.

The popular Daoist religious system, which embraces the "Daoist Pope" and his charms and priests, presents a rich and colorful face. Perhaps no religion in the world has had a vaster pantheon of gods—many said to have once been human beings who became immortal and finally reached Divine status. Some gods are ancient, although many were "appointed" to divinity by **Tang dynasty** (618–907 C.E.) and especially **Ming Dynasty** (1368–1644) emperors.

This recalls the extensive interaction between Confucian and Daoist systems in China. Not only did the emperor, in designating approved worship, act out the role of mediator between Heaven and Earth assigned by Confucian thought, but the pantheon itself exemplified a heavenly reflection of the earthly bureaucracy manned by Confucian officials. Many of the deities, like Kuan Di, a strong military god who is considered a protector against evil forces, were originally earthly officials immortalized in the heavenly court.

The supreme deity in religious Daoism was the Jade Emperor, a personal high god for the masses that were ineligible to worship Heaven directly; he was enthroned in the Pole Star. Around him was his court: the Three Pure Ones—Laozi, the Yellow Emperor (mythical first sovereign of China), and Bangu (the primal man); the Eight Immortals, very popular in art and folk tales; and gods of literature, medicine, war, weather, and so forth. The gods and immortals lived in numerous

FUNDAMENTAL FEATURES OF DAOISM

THEORETICAL

Basic Worldview	The universe is one, yet always moving and changing.
God or Ultimate Reality	The Dao, the great Way down which the universe moves.
Origin of the World/ Destiny of the World	An expression of the Dao, without a known beginning or end.
Origin of Humans/ Destiny of Humans	An expression of the Dao, to share in its never-ending evolution. One may become immortal by mastering the Dao and its power.
Revelation or Mediation between the Ultimate and the Human	The teachings of Laozi and other sages. Benign immortals or gods can be honored and serve as helpers.

PRACTICAL

What Is Expected of Humans: Worship, Practices, Behavior	To live spontaneously and close to nature; in more formal systems, to mediate and perform rites that draw one close to gods and immortals.

SOCIOLOGICAL

Major Social Institutions	Temples, monasteries, the Daoist priesthood.

heavenly grottos, in Islands of the Blessed to the East, and the Shangri-La of the Mother Goddess to the West, deep in the mountains.

The priests of this faith were a varied lot, affiliated with several different **sectarian** strands with differing specialties. Some were celibate and monastic; others, married. Some were contemplative, concerned above all else with perfecting in themselves the seeds of immortality. Some were custodians of lavish temples with huge and ornate images of the Jade Emperor and other worthies; to these temples believers would come to receive divination, have memorial services performed on behalf of their departed, and worship at important festivals, which were also occasions for carnival and feasting. Other Daoist clergy were mediums, male and female, who would deliver messages from the Other Side; some were sellers of charms, perhaps issued by the "Daoist Pope"; some were exorcists who performed dramatic rites of driving demons out of possessed persons and places.

Behind all of this lay the affirmation of immortality and of immortal entities. The panorama of religious Daoism made visible the invisible but deathless realm of gods and sages who had won the priceless secret. Those who would reveal the secret were not lacking, however. Religious Daoism pointed to three main highways to immortality: (1) alchemy, (2) yoga, and (3) merit.

Alchemy referred to the preparation of elixirs supposed, in combination with spiritual preparation, to circumvent death through manipulation of Yin and Yang and the "five elements." Most were based on cinnabar or mercury ore (HgS). Some seven Chinese emperors are said to have died of mercury poisoning as a result of taking this medicine of immortality! Yet, as scholars such as C. G. Jung and Mircea Eliade have pointed out, both Chinese and Western alchemy contain important spiritual and protoscientific insights that cannot be neglected by the serious historian of ideas.[16]

Daoist yoga is equally complex. Its central motif seems to have been the holding of the breath to circulate it throughout the body inwardly, awakening the gods of various physical centers. Finally the breath is to unite with semen to produce an immortal "spiritual embryo," which emerges as new life within the self. As it flourishes, the old mortal shell can fall away like the chrysalis of a butterfly. Diet and sometimes sexual practices of the Tantric sort were important supports of this process.

The hope of attaining immortality for the masses who were not adepts lay in merit. The idea was approached with typical Chinese concreteness. Some popular temples even had a large abacus or calculating machine in full view to recall to the faithful the reckoning of good and bad deeds that will be required. Various texts cite the number and kinds of good deeds—building roads, acts of charity, compassion to living things—that would win immortality at diverse grades; even one demerit, however, would require the aspirant to start at the beginning of his labors again.

Daoism is usually presented as but one of the spiritual traditions of China, and not the most prestigious in the eyes of traditional scholars. But the attitudes of religious Daoism came closest to the spiritual world of the vast majority of ordinary people. Even Buddhism and Confucianism became "Daoicized" in *cultus* though not in doctrine and morals; whatever their origin, most plain people thought of the Buddhas, *bodhisattvas,* and even Confucius himself as immortalized humans now become spirits and able to send down blessings from above. Daoist and Buddhist priests served interchangeably in many localities, but their major functions, such as funerals and exorcisms and village festivals, were Daoist (that is to say, popular Chinese) in style. To be sure, popular Daoism borrowed the use of images and its quasi-monastic clerical organization from Buddhism and the bureaucratic model of its pantheon from Confucianism—but those are historical matters, not at all readily apparent to the person on the street.

Daoism, as the pervasive tone-setter of the nonestablishment side of Chinese life, has contributed to those undying elements of cheerful fancy, fairy tales, colorful festivals, bright pictures, and striking spiritual practices that are as much a part of Chinese life as Confucian common sense.

Buddhism in China

Buddhism first entered China during the Han Dynasty (206 B.C.E.–220 C.E.), spread widely during the three and a half centuries of disruption that followed the fall of that dynasty, and reached its peak of maturity and creativity during the Tang Dynasty (618–907 C.E.).[17] It was chiefly brought in the caravans of traders, not directly from India but from central Asia. The new faith first took root in the major cities and among the aristocrats. In the late Han and post-Han times, as we have seen, many of this class were searching among occult, mystical, and aesthetic possibilities for a richer inner life than could be offered by a decaying social order and its tired Confucian rationale. The wilder side of Daoism naturally appealed to some of them. But the profound mysteries of Buddhism, brought by exotic foreigners and bearing a whiff of the mystic perfume of India, as well as a more substantial philosophical and ethical base, were to many even more appealing. It speaks of both the power of Buddhism and the dissatisfaction of those times, that until the modern Western influence and the subsequent Marxist triumph, no outside cultural force other than Buddhism has ever succeeded in making a major impact on China.

In the period when Buddhism was taking root in China, it was quite fashionable among the upper echelons of society. Aristocrats entertained visiting Buddhist priests, commissioned the translation of scriptures, and built temples in the mountains to which they would retire for genteel retreats. They also built hospitals and orphanages in the cities in accordance with the dictates of Buddhist compassion.

Buddhism opened up a new world of artistic possibilities with its demand for massive sculpture, mystic painting, and temple architecture. Buddhism also broadened ethical horizons more than many were prepared to accept, with its very new (and very controversial) notions of universal compassion, monasticism, and the relative independence of religion from the state *cultus*. These emphases, although suggested in Daoism, went strongly against the Confucian grain, with its feeling that the arts are more frivolous than civil service and that obligation to family and sovereign is primary. In particular, the ideal of the celibate Buddhist monk stood contrary to Confucianism, which put family life and the subordination of self to society at the center of value.

But Buddhism also made its adjustments to China. Indeed, for a long time the Indian religion was considered a variant of Daoism—an illusion promoted by some Daoists who even claimed that Laozi, after disappearing into the West, had gone to India and become the Buddha. In the translation of Buddhist texts from Sanskrit to Chinese, Daoist and Confucian terms were used, with inevitable shifts in connotation. Thus, *dharma* became Dao, *arhant* became immortal, and Buddhist morality was couched in the terms of submission and obedience hallowed by Confucian usage.[18]

Even the monastic system was modified in the direction of supporting rather than challenging the Chinese family unit. Young monks acquired a filial relation to their teachers, in imitation of obedience to father, and moreover were expected to assist their natural families dutifully by devoting much attention to prayer on behalf of relatives living and dead. Sometimes boys were dedicated to the monastery by their families for this reason or in fulfillment of a vow made in prayer, because it was considered beneficial for a family to number a monk among its members. Finally, monasteries were brought under the control of the throne, which licensed them and regulated the number of ordinations they could perform.

On the level of popular religion, Buddhism accommodated itself to China even more thoroughly. As already mentioned, popular Buddhas and *bodhisattvas* came to be regarded as blessing-giving deities little different from indigenous gods, except perhaps more broadly compassionate. The *bodhisattva* Avalokiteshvara in India became Kuan-Yin or Guanyin in China (Kannon in Japan), the Goddess of Mercy who answered prayers for healing, women in childbirth, and wanderers. **Maitreya**, the Buddha of the future who would bring to pass a new paradisal era, was transformed from the lean, elegant, poised contemplative of Indian art to the immensely fat, laughing **Miluo** of China, who suggests a heartier, earthier vision of the joys of the new age. He has also been associated with revolutionary religio-political movements. In fact, even the Indian origin of Miluo, as of other Buddhist figures, came to be forgotten. Folklore identified him with a popular wandering wise-fool monk of the tenth century.

Probably the most important contribution of Buddhism to popular religion in China was in concepts of life after death. Previously, the Chinese had known belief in survival as ancestral spirits, as ghosts, or as Daoist immortals in blissful hermitages. To this Buddhism added the novel ideas of reincarnation and of elaborately gradated heavens and hells. Both these notions, however inconsistent with each other and with indigenous belief, were widely received, even by many who understood little else of Buddhism.

Reincarnation appears as a popular theme in literature. The hells were described in religious tracts, temple paintings, and sculpture displays (such as the well-known Tiger Balm Garden in Hong Kong), with a blood-splattered realism that even the dullest countryman could not ignore. The officials of hell, presided over by Yanluo (originally the Indic Yama, whom we previously encountered in the *Katha Upanishad*), were Confucian bureaucrats. As a reward for years of conscientious service, they were allowed to continue in the same line of work on the other side, where they saw to it that demons administered horrendous (but not eternal) punishments for infractions of both Confucian and Buddhist moralities.[19]

On the intellectual level, a number of different traditions of Buddhist thought and practice were introduced into China. Only the broad, tolerant, and variegated Mahayana had any success, however. But within it, the Void school, Yogacara or Mind Only, and esoteric Buddhism or Vajrayana all had early followings at various monastic centers. On Mount Tiantai, the syncretistic Tiantai school endeavored to reconcile all styles of Buddhist thought into a system that made the *Lotus Sutra* the summit of many planes of accommodation in the Buddha's teaching.

When the dust settled, however, two strands of Buddhism emerged as the most important in China: Chan and Pure Land. The concept of clearly defined denominations, like those of Christianity or even of Japanese Buddhism, is alien to China except for minority sectarian movements. But it has ended up that most monasteries in China proper largely followed Chan teaching and practice, and Pure Land Buddhism was most popular among lay followers.

Historically, the prevalence of Chan and Pure Land is in large part the result of a suppression of Buddhist monks, nuns, and monasteries in 845, under the instigation of Confucian and Daoist rivals who persuaded the court that the persons and institutions of the imported Buddhist tradition were unproductive parasites on society. Chan, because its monasteries were less wealthy and more scattered throughout rural areas than the others, and Pure Land, because it was largely a popular lay faith, best survived the despoilation.

Significantly, both (while having ultimate Indian roots) are highly **Sinicized** styles of Buddhism, owing much to different sorts of Daoist belief. Chan enlightenment is really like following the Daoist concept of *wu–wei*, not-doing, and so letting events happen spontaneously. The assumption is that what is truly spontaneous is the Dao at work—or in this case, one's true Buddha-nature—while what is planned is of human egoistic contrivance, artificial and inauthentic. Pure Land could also easily be related to Daoist ideas—in this case, not only effortless and spontaneous release, but also popular belief in paradisal realms to the West where immortals dwelt amid fairy-tale loveliness. But both Chan and Pure Land embraced the realization, emergent early in Chinese Buddhism's independent development, that true enlightenment is a sudden, spontaneous happening rather than a laborious process.

These two doctrinal traditions, usually working closely together and not seen as inconsistent, formed the basis of Chinese Buddhism in recent centuries. The nation boasted scores of large monasteries. They followed a Chan regimen for the most part, modified by concessions to Pure Land, esoteric practices, and the economic necessity that Buddhist monks perform funeral and memorial rites; for many these rites were quite time-consuming, but they kept monks in touch with the lay public.

Monastic novices were ordained by a rite that included burning incense in several spots on the candidate's shaved head, a painful practice leaving scars intended to exemplify the *bodhisattva* vow to work and suffer at whatever cost for the salvation of all beings. The monasteries were headed by an elected abbot, and they were flourishing economic units busy with administering lands and dealing with pilgrims. The monks would often devote themselves to meditation and work on half-year shifts. Four monasteries on mountains in the four directions were especially important as pilgrimage centers. The roads to them would be lined with colorful shrines and hermitages. Travel to these places for the sake of a vacation, enjoyment of natural beauty, and spiritual renewal all together was very popular. Many monks traveled frequently from one monastery to another in a manner akin to the wandering students of medieval Europe. Others might become hermits.

The majority of those who were students in a major monastery, however, would be receiving training like a seminarian and would sooner or later become priests in village temples. There the priest would live a fairly easy life, unless he were given to much study or spiritual practice. He would keep his temple in order as a place for prayer and performing funerals, memorial rites, and other services as his parishioners required and could pay for them. Although the priest probably had Chan training, the temple would doubtless give principal encouragement to the Pure Land and Kuan-Yin devotions as being more suitable for the laity. However, among more sophisticated urban lay Buddhists, especially of more recent times, many took one or another of the monastic vows, such as celibacy or vegetarianism, as a lay associate of a major temple and received advanced training in meditation or other practices from a distinguished master.

Religion in Traditional China— A Syncretistic Practice

We began by observing that East Asian religion is generally religion of the particular place and social unit, deeply rooted in soil and family. We have, however, devoted much attention to exploring historical tracks made by the Confucian, Daoist, and Buddhist traditions. This has necessitated portraying them as three major traditions extending through time as though they were great independent causes. It is not possible to understand religious China fully without this historical and philosophical background. But in popular religion, the major traditions unite to form a single spiritual world. It is now time to refocus on the particular to see how they are combined in practice.

Consider a single family in old China, the Changs. They lived in a home in the countryside: The setting and ornamentation of the house itself reflected some ideas we have discussed, for when it was built its location was carefully determined so it would be at the meeting point of *Yin* and *Yang* forces in the environment and would be spiritually protected. Open places and straight lines dissipate the benevolent breath of nature and encourage invisible evil forces, so the house was situated between a sunken pond and a bamboo grove, and the road up to it was curved.

The Changs took the veneration of their ancestors very seriously. They were memorialized in three places: in the home at a small shrine with tablets bearing their names; in the chapel of the Chang clan or extended family where large tablets would be set up, rank on rank, rising on higher and higher tiers, the further back in time the generations went; and at the cemetery. A bit of water, incense, and food would be presented daily at the household shrine. Several times a year, the clan shrine and cemetery would be visited, cleaned, and given larger offerings and a report on family events. Ancestrism, combining very old spiritualist beliefs with Confucian filial piety toward departed parents and grandparents, was most important.

The biggest annual holiday was New Year's. At the end of the year, debts would be settled and the house cleaned. On New Year's Eve, the picture of the protective kitchen-god, which had been hanging in the house all year, would have its mouth smeared with honey, to put it in a good mood, and would then be burned—for it was believed that this deity would then ascend to the court of the Jade Emperor to give his report on the merits and demerits of the family for the past year. On New Year's Day itself, members of the Chang family would be gathered from far and wide and extensive offerings of food and drink—plus a plate of soup set outside for lonely spirits without family to care for them—would be placed with bows and prayers before the family shrine, full of ancestors and protective gods. Then the family would join in a feast. Outside, they would hear firecrackers and doubtless see a *Yang* dragon parading down the road, animated by the feet of many men.

The Harvest Festival in the autumn would have a different, *Yin* sort of atmosphere, being oriented toward the moon, night, and returning spirits. Round cakes would be made, and tables set up in the courtyard of the house, both showing the fabulous palaces of the moon where Daoist immortals dwelt.

In the Chang household, sober Confucianism would have its due as well as Daoist fancy. The sons would bow to their father, and if educated, they would study first and foremost the Confucian classics. When the elder Chang died, the sons would mourn for him according to Confucian ritual—although somewhat modified and shortened—kneeling before the father's portrait or tablet, wearing gowns of rough sackcloth, and eating coarse and tasteless food.

For the funeral and subsequent memorial rites, Buddhist or Daoist priests would be called in. They would chant *sutras* or prayers and burn elaborate paper houses and imitation money offerings to be used by the deceased on the Other Side. They would pray to the protecting city-god to serve as his advocate before the dread court of Yanluo. The family might discuss the possibilities for the deceased amid the many hells, heavens, and paths back to reincarnation in this world. They might well consult a medium, of Daoist ties, who would contact the departed spirit to find out what the disposition of his case had been, how he had fared, and what the living could do to help him. There were even shamanistic Daoist priests who cut themselves with knives in order to take on themselves the after-death suffering of their clients.

For answers to problems in this life, the Changs might consult a diviner who would use the ancient *Yi Jing*. He would throw coins or sticks to determine which of the 64 "hexagrams," or sets of six lines (some unbroken *Yang* lines; some broken *Yin* lines) that unfolded the meaning of the situation in question. The text in the *Yi Jing* for that hexagram would suggest, in fairly cryptic language, whether favorable or unfavorable lines of force were in operation, whether it was a time for action or waiting, and the like. This book, now popular in the West, is perhaps the oldest extant Chinese book in its most ancient parts; it is one of the Confucian classics, yet it also expresses a Daoistic philosophy. In its own way it epitomizes a Chinese worldview that underlies both traditions based on a profound sense of the continual, rhythmic interaction of visible and invisible forces within a unified world process to which humankind must gently and wisely accommodate itself.[20]

From time to time a representative of the old Chinese Chang family would go to one of the temples in the locality. The temples vary from tiny edifices with images the size of a doll to huge structures with giant, superhuman gods of awesome countenance. Some would be Daoist, some Buddhist, some mixed. But it should be realized that they were homes of the gods, not generally places of congregational worship. When Mr. Chang or another of the family visited the temple, it was generally to ask a favor or pay respects, as one would to a powerful neighbor. Most frequently the visit would be to ask advice of the deity, done by throwing two wood-blocks, drawing a printed oracle, or perhaps consulting a medium retained by the temple. Sometimes the family representative would make an offering of incense or paper temple money in thanksgiving for a favor or in response to a vow. This worship would be done especially at earth-god shrines—humble but ubiquitous temples to deities of the soil older and closer to the people than any of the major faiths—in the spring for the crops, and in the fall in thanksgiving for the harvest. Food might be presented to the deity, but it would be brought back home for a feast.

At irregular intervals, depending on local custom, the temple would hold a great festival. Brilliant red candles would be burned around the Divine image, priests would perform elaborate rituals, and villagers and visitors alike would throng the temple with offerings and divinations. The temple courtyard would be set up like a fair, with booths and amusements and colorful pageantry. There would be ranks of offerings, particularly pigs, presented by families and businesses. Here the Chang family might be represented, and the family members (except women in traditional middle- or upper-class families) would delightedly attend.

If Mr. Chang were of the *mandarin* class, he would also go to the nearest Confucian temple at the two equinoxes to join with his peers in the old dances and offerings presented to the Wise and Holy Sage by his latter-day disciples. He would probably also take part in the rites of the city-god, the protector of the town, honoring him with thanks for good times and perhaps punishing him when misfortune struck, for his *cultus* was part of the official religion.

Then again, one day Mr. Chang or someone else in the family might become pious, or at least acquire a wanderlust, and go on a pilgrimage to some Buddhist or Daoist monastery on a cloud-wrapped mountaintop or an isolated island. There he would break his routine by living with the monks for a spell, sharing their meals and conversation, and renewing his spirit in a setting of exalted beauty.

The Chang family, then, would be touched by the attitudes and institutional life of all three of the great traditions, and by ancestrism and the earth-gods as well. This combined experience is nowhere better expressed than in the first part of the old Chinese fantasy novel *Monkey*.[21] In it, the Buddha and the Jade Emperor visit and consult with one another. Dragon-kings, *bodhisattvas,* and sages with the secret of immortality move in and out of the narrative—yet the monkey-hero, like the sturdy peasant farmers of China, employs both wiles and wonders to combat authority, even the hosts of heaven itself, to preserve the autonomy of himself and his household.

Religion in the People's Republic of China

Today his tradition has been completely disrupted. To understand how such an immense cultural and religious change could come about, it is necessary to know something of the history of China and the impact of that history on Chinese religion.

During the long, wrenching, and often dreadful hundred years from the middle of the nineteenth to the middle of the twentieth century, China underwent tremendous shock and change, not the least to its traditional ideological and religious systems. The fundamental factor that made the shocks of this era even more climactic and catastrophic than those that accompanied earlier changes of dynasty was the incursion of the Western powers—demanding trade, missionary rights, and often inordinate influence on Chinese affairs.

The impact of these humiliations and of the countless subsequent little humiliations inflicted upon a proud people by the presence of privileged and often insensitive and exploitative foreigners went far beyond the immediate terms of the treaties forced on China by these foreign powers. It resulted in the discrediting of Chinese authority itself; in the eyes of many thoughtful persons, the whole system upon which it was based, down to its ideological and religious roots, seemed anachronistic and discredited as well. A host of alternatives, ranging from reactionary to radical, arose to try to fill the void.

In 1912, after other traumatic vicissitudes, such as the **Boxer Rebellion** of 1900 (with its roots in magical Daoism), the lingering death of Imperial China was finally consummated with the establishment of a republic. Inspired by Western democratic idealism, its history was, in reality, rocky and sometimes ignoble. The central government was rarely able to control either large-scale corruption or the power of avaricious local warlords. Just after it seemed, in the late 1920s, that headway against China's immense problems was being made, the Chinese republic was dealt further staggering blows by Japanese military incursions and then World War II.

During the period of the republic, Confucianism declined in influence with the disestablishment of the state *cultus*; Buddhism experienced a modest revival; there was considerable Christian missionary activity; and the Communist Party of China, full of high dedication and radical solutions, flourished more and more. Then, upon the triumph of Communism in 1949, numerous missionaries and Buddhist monks, together with the "Daoist Pope," fled to Hong Kong and Taiwan. But the bulk of their followers remained behind to contend as best they could with the new regime. That government, the People's Republic of China, did not profess any sympathy for religion, for in accordance with general Marxist theory, Chinese Communism saw religion as essentially the product of feudal conditions and bound to fade away as the circumstances of alienation and exploitation between classes disappeared.

The Communist approach toward religion in China passed through several clearly defined stages. The first (1950–1952) was a period of consolidation of the new regime. All foreign elements were forced out of China. This meant a mass exodus of missionaries together with many Christian Chinese clergy and believers. Religious bodies remaining on the mainland were pressured into forming themselves into "patriotic" organizations with corresponding nationalistic allegiances. While Confucianism was only criticized and Daoism received little consideration, some Buddhist institutions were permitted to survive in the People's Republic, chiefly as showplaces to enhance the new China's image in the rest of the Buddhist world.

The period of 1952 to 1960 was a time of relative cooperation between the new society and reorganized religious bodies. There was an increasing tendency to align religious thought with Marxism. This was particularly true among "patriotic" Buddhists, who did not hesitate to compare the Marxist utopia with Nirvana—because desire is eliminated in both—and the revolutionary struggle was compared with the tortuous quest for enlightenment. But the 1950s were also a time when persecution of uncooperative religionists was harsh. Innumerable churches and temples were confiscated for more productive use as schools or warehouses, and the great majority of monks were defrocked to join the workers in factory and field. In particular, the great Buddhist religious and cultural tradition of Tibet was brutally extirpated.

Nonetheless, in the early 1960s reports came of a resurgence of religion, particularly Buddhism. Accounts of foreign visitors interested in religion between 1960 and 1965 indicated that, at the least, religion of all sorts was ostensibly being practiced routinely and without hindrance; churches and temples, while far diminished in number from before the revolution, were in full swing—but it was the proverbial calm before the storm.

The **Great Cultural Revolution** of 1966 to 1969, with the young Red Guards in its vanguard, swept through China, leaving virtually no locale or institution untouched. They were fired by a drive to suppress all that was old and a desire, perhaps contrived by the aging **Mao Zedong** (Chinese Communism's charismatic leader), to renew revolutionary fervor at the expense of social stability. As a consequence, they disrupted education, harried enemies, defaced monuments of the past, and left nearly all religious places ransacked and closed. Such religious life as survived went deep underground.

Much was made in this period by outside observers of the religious character of "Maoism" itself. Certainly the phenomena suggested such an interpretation. Chinese Communism had a "sacred history" repeated over and over in dramas and monuments. Its great programmatic rallies had a quality little short of sacred ritual. The famous "little red book" containing the sayings of Chairman Mao was read like scripture and, carried constantly about and eagerly held up by the faithful, doubled as a holy talisman. Above all, Mao himself was hymned and praised in language that made him hardly less than deity.

Yet if Maoism was a religion, it turned out to be one of the world's most ephemeral. After the Great Cultural Revolution had run its course by around 1970 and the need for a return to normality was apparent to almost everyone, fervent Maoism was definitely in recession, and more traditional religious practice recovered its foothold. Following the death of Mao in 1976 and the subsequent purging of the "Gang of Four," who allegedly wanted to return to the policies of the Cultural Revolution, little more was heard of it.

Since then, government policy has become more pragmatic and open to the world, and indications are that religion has been generally allowed to flourish openly, though under tight control. However, visitors report that the situation in Tibet remains tense, and new religious movements outside of official control, such as the neo-Daoist Falun Gong, which received much publicity in 2000, have been regarded as subversive and have been harshly repressed.

Only time will tell whether the tradition exemplified by our earlier account of the Chang family has been broken irrevocably or only submerged "underground," waiting for a more welcoming time. It still survives in Taiwan, Hawaii, Singapore, and other Chinese outposts outside the People's Republic of China; but on the mainland, for that vast majority of Chinese who represent a quarter of the earth's population, the situation is unclear but certainly very different.

Women in Chinese Religion

As we already have said, Chinese religion is an amalgamation of many different ideas, myths, practices, and institutions. Obviously, this is so for women in Chinese religion as well, where women play important roles in the syncretistic Chinese popular religion's "little tradition" as shamans, diviners, mediums, and the like. Still, for discussion purposes, rather than an attempt to tackle the subject as a whole, it is easier to ferret out those themes, myths, practices, and institutions by considering the component parts themselves. This is important, too, because some women's lives have been influenced or directed more by one component than another. With this in mind, let us now turn to what is one of the most defining aspects of Chinese culture and, therefore, the most defining of attitudes toward women and their lives.

Women in Classical Confucianism

Confucianism, as we have seen, provided an entire social vision grounded in relationships. In the Confucian worldview, each person is to perform his or her role in accordance with the Confucian idealization of that role. The result of this is believed to be a well-organized, well-functioning society—as if everyone in society were performing a great dance. While the cosmic implications of this were not emphasized by Confucius himself, Confucianism nevertheless related its social vision to the cosmic order. As we shall see, this resulted in the religio-cultural institution of the subordination of women to men, greatly limiting women's participation in and influence on the "dance," while at the same time acknowledging the role of women in Confucian society as a respected and necessary one.

In Confucianism, women's lives were centered in the family. Women were the "inside" members of the family, while the men were the "outside" members. This reflected the ideal of women as homebound and the ideal of men as participants in society-at-large. In particular, the father was the representative head of the family to the world outside the home. In upper-class families this arrangement was reflected in the very structure of the house, which included inside compartments for the women and outside compartments for the men.

As in Hinduism, Confucian women were to remain under the dominion of the men in the home in accordance with the "three obediences" of the *Book of Rites*:

The woman follows (and obeys) the man: in her youth, she follows her father and elder brother; when married, she follows her husband; when her husband is dead, she follows her son.[22]

Moreover, a young girl was not considered to be a part of her natal family and, therefore, was not a part of any ancestral line. It was not until marriage that she attained a recognized place in a family and her name was included on the ancestral tablets on the family altar. It is not surprising then that the marriage ceremony was the most significant and life-transforming event in a Chinese woman's life. She then had a recognized and respected role in the Confucian social order as wife.

Because a female child was not deemed a part of her natal family, the birth of a female child often was not greeted with joy, giving rise to such proverbs as "Raising a daughter is like weeding another man's field" and "The best daughter is not worth a splay-footed son."[23] Not surprisingly, with such attitudes prevalent, female infanticide was a continuing practice throughout the centuries, although discouraged by Confucian authorities.[24]

At birth, the baby girl's anticipated place in society was acknowledged. As the *Instructions for Women* by Pan Chao state:

On the third day after the birth of a girl, the ancients observed three customs: first to place the baby below the bed; second to give her a potsherd with which to play; and third, to announce her birth to her ancestors by an offering.[25]

Theresa Kelleher's interpretation of the passage is: "The first action indicated that as female she should be lowly and submissive, humbling herself before others, the second that she should be hardworking and diligent in the domestic sphere, and the third that she should enter fully into the wife's responsibilities to the ancestors of her husband's family."[26] Thus, at birth, the girl's destiny was fixed, and her education accordingly was devoted entirely to learning the "wifely way" (*fu-tao*)—sewing, meal preparation, how to serve the parents-in-law, the development of a proper demeanor, and the like.[27]

The marriage relationship itself, in accordance with the Confucian ideal, involved very defined roles and much formality between the couple. The couple generally was segregated in the household except for sleeping. A wife was to exemplify *Yin* (passive, pliant) in order to provide the harmonious complement to the husband's *Yang* (active, firm). Thus, instead of a harmonious complement of power and status between husband and wife, the goal of harmony was to be achieved by the wife's submission to her husband. Again, we can return to the analogy of the dance. It is the husband who leads and the wife who follows with movements that complement, that is, harmonize with his. This was perceived to reflect the cosmic order, where Heaven (identified with the husband), which is creative, is superior to Earth (identified with the wife), which is receptive.

Divorce was very limited in Confucian society. Husbands could divorce wives only under seven specific circumstances: incurable sickness, no male heir, talking too much, stealing, disobedience, promiscuity, and jealousy. However, he was not permitted to divorce her if she had performed funerary rites for one of his parents, he had become rich during the marriage, her parents were no longer living, or she otherwise had no home to which to return. On the other hand, a woman was never permitted to divorce her husband. Her filial piety obligations to his (and now her) family would not accommodate that. Furthermore, she was not to remarry after the death of her husband because this would disrupt the family ancestral line of which she was a part.

In Confucian society, as we have seen, parents and ancestors were honored by all. Accordingly, the wife was to join her husband in making the happiness and comfort of his parents their prime focus. But the parent who most shaped the life of the young wife was her mother-in-law whose every wish was to be served by her. Upon marriage, a young woman in effect became the servant of her new mother-in-law and was to be her "shadow and echo" in all things. Moreover, the new wife was the lowliest person in the family hierarchy, and thus was expected to be submissive to everyone else in the household as well. In her *Classic of Filial Piety for Women,* which was an authoritative text for Confucian women through the centuries, Ch'eng wrote (ca. 700 C.E.):

> *A virtuous wife never dares demean the younger concubines, how much more is her solicitation for her sisters-in-law. Therefore they are all happy and get along with each other, and are able to serve their parents-in-law. In managing the household, she never dares mistreat the chickens or dogs, how much more is her care for the servants. Therefore those of all ranks are content with their lot and are able to serve their master well. . . . In these ways, the nine degrees of relatives are kept in peace and harmony, calamities do not arise, nor disorders occur.*[28]

A woman was expected to be completely devoted to her husband—her highest goal being to win his love. "To obtain the love of one man is the crown of a woman's life, to lose the love of one man is to miss the aim in woman's life."[29] Moreover, she was to win her husband's love by exhibiting correct behavior. She was to be obsequious, quiet, demure, and industrious in her work in the home, pure, clean, chaste (although her husband would be permitted concubines, to whom the wife was to be courteous)—such behavior being called the "womanly virtues."

The Confucian ideal for women was set out in several very influential texts, for example, *Instructions for Women* by Pan Chao (?–116 C.E.), the *Classic of Filial Piety for Women,* already mentioned, and the *Analects for Women* by Sung Jo-chao (ca. 800 C.E.). Another important text regarding women is the *Biographies of Exemplary Women,* collected by Lui Hsian (77–6 B.C.E.), which chronicles the lives of exemplary women and their contributions to their husbands. Most involve extreme self-sacrifice for virtue, chastity, and honor. Some recount the woman's choice to commit suicide rather than violate the dictates of filial piety. And the work of Margery Wolf indicates that suicide was indeed the choice made by many young wives who found themselves in family situations that they could not endure in accordance with the ideal.[30]

With marriage as the central focus of women's lives, it is easy to see that women who did not marry were not accorded many options in traditional Confucian society. Prostitution or domestic labor were their only viable options—with their concomitant shame. Women for whom there was an insufficient dowry or who for other reasons were unmarriageable were often sold.

Yet, unlike some other patriarchal social systems in history and in various parts of the world that seem to hold a view that the world would be a better place without women, Confucianism never took so harsh a view. For Chinese ideologies always have had at their core a profound respect for the cycles of life. Accordingly, the greatest joy (and thus duty) of a couple is to bring new life into the world. Hence, the woman's role as wife and mother is not deemed extraneous to something else perceived as central to life (e.g., meditation), but is integral to the family—the center of life. Therefore, regardless of her subservient status, the wife is nonetheless a necessary part of the life cycle. This unfortunately did not undercut the repetition of some of the taboos we see in other cultures, such as those requiring men to avoid the "impurity" of menstruation and childbirth. Still, the arrival of children, particularly sons, greatly increased the status of the wife in the household. All recognized upon the birth of a son that the new mother, herself, eventually will attain to the status of mother-in-law with all its concomitant privileges. And as mother she can develop what Margery Wolf has called the "uterine family"—a network of family affiliations surrounding the mother of married children, which contributes to the enrichment of her own life and those around her.[31]

Women in Confucian society were not without their means of exerting power to influence their situations. One way in which a women could exert power was to work through the other societal relationships. In Chinese society, decorum, proper behavior, and harmony might mean that a wife could not complain directly about improper treatment by her husband. However, if the husband were to drink too much alcohol, shirk his responsibilities, or become abusive, his wife could report it to other women who would then urge their own husbands to take action. The threat of shame—"losing face"—was probably a powerful deterrent to wayward husbands.[32] In addition, the considerable power of the mother-in-law must not be underestimated. On the other hand, because this power was exercised, for the most part, over daughters-in-law, on balance the societal arrangement seems to represent more a control of women in general than an expression of women's power in society as a whole.

Women in Daoism (Taoism)

Filial piety and the role of wife place considerable demands on women in China but also offer status and respect in the Confucian worldview. But Confucianism is not the only religious influence to have shaped Chinese women's lives. There is another side of life to which women could appeal as a spiritual source—that provided by Daoism.

Daoism, as we have seen, has taken an immense variety of forms over the centuries, which include philosophical and religious forms, the latter incorporating mysticism, shamanism, sexual practices, and magic in a syncretistic blend that is virtually indistinguishable in many cases from Chinese popular religion. We can find Chinese women in most all of Daoism's manifestations, perhaps because of Daoism's emphasis on nature and the feminine, which opened the pathway for women's participation.

As we already have seen, the *Dao de jing* makes ready use of feminine symbolism to describe the Dao. The Dao is the creative source, which is potential itself and out of which flows existence—an existence sustained by the Dao "stream," just as a mother gives birth out of her womb to a child, who is then nourished at her breast. As said in the *Dao de jing*:

> *The breath of life moves through a deathless valley*
> *Of mysterious motherhood*
> *Which conceives and bears the universal seed,*
> *The seeming of a world never to end,*
> *Breath for men to draw from as they will:*
> *And the more they take of it, the more remains.*[33]

Because the feminine symbolism is so pervasive in Daoism, some scholars, such as Ellen Marie Chen, have concluded that Daoism has ties to an ancient Mother Goddess and the Dao itself is the Great Mother.[34]

Daoism seeks a balance of the *Yin* and *Yang* just as does Confucianism, but for Daoism that balance is struck by grounding it in the *Yin*. Thus, the way of the Dao is *wu-wei*—going with the flow, which is associated with the "natural" passivity and flexibility of women. Thus, women were deemed to be naturally good Daoists. But Daoism does not appear to have moved women beyond patriarchal norms.[35] Instead, perhaps because Daoism was a reaction to the rigidity of Confucianism and perceived Confucianism as "too *Yang*" in its striving to construct a structured society, Daoism used the patriarchal stereotype of *Yin* as an antidote. Significantly, whatever influence Daoism had, it never had much of an impact on the social order prescribed by Confucian norms, and thus generally did not move women out of their subordinated roles. Still, Daoism's emphasis on the inner self, feelings, and imagination must have provided a spiritual outlet for women—the "inside" members of the family.

Religious Daoism drew from shamanism (which had been central to Chinese popular religion) the belief that women especially are receptive to Divine inspiration. This, together with the perceived need for a complementary balance of *Yin* and *Yang* in all aspects of life, paved the way for an openness toward the participation of women in nearly all levels of religious Daoism, despite the patriarchal norms of mainstream Chinese society.[36]

Yet, early on, Daoism developed a patriarchal leadership with the Celestial Masters, who were the highest administrators, being men. However, even then women held prominent leadership positions equally with men as libationers (who provided the ritual and moral leadership of Daoism) and as officials over the districts. Women were ordained equally with men in all ranks, except the highest rank—that of Divine Lord.[37] Women also founded Daoist sects and were revered adepts, masters, alchemists, and scholars. And convents were founded so that women could be free of ordinary social ties in order to pursue spiritual lives.

Significantly, there are women among the Daoist Immortals, and the Daoist spirit world is filled with many female entities—jade maidens, fairies, spirit-generals, and beautiful, as well as gruesome, female spirits.[38] There are also many female deities, for example, Toumu, a powerful deity who is the Mother of the Pole Star, and other celestial goddesses. And there are goddesses of the household who appear with male deities, such as the kitchen god and his wife, who keep track of the good deeds and indiscretions of members of the household.[39]

As in Tantric Hinduism and some forms of Tantric Buddhism, the participation of women was essential in those forms of Daoism that include sexual practices in the attainment of the spiritual goal. Here the sexual union represents the balance of *Yin* and *Yang,* and the goal is to prolong life—even to achieve immortality by forming an incorruptible embryo as a culmination of the practice. Still in Daoism, as in many other religions, the texts often are written from a male perspective, making it difficult to ascertain the participation and techniques for women in the sexual practices and indicating that sexual practices may, in some instances, have led to the exploitation of women.[40]

On the other hand, there is an interesting contrast here in Daoism to Buddhism. The highest spiritual levels were deemed by Daoists, for the most part, to be achievable only in female form, as opposed to male form as we saw in Buddhism. (See Chapter 4.) As Barbara E. Reed's research has shown: "Pregnancy is a basic [D]aoist model for attaining immortality. A [D]aoist, male or female, creates and nurtures an immortal embryo within the corruptible physical body. According to this model, males must become females, at least metaphorically, to achieve their goal of deathlessness."[41]

Daoism provided an alternative view that venerated women and thus opposed the subjugating tendencies of the primarily patriarchal society. Moreover, it offered significant leadership opportunities for women and provided an option for women outside the strictures of mainstream, patriarchal Confucian society as Daoist priestesses, nuns, and shamanesses. But in all this we must take note that Daoism as a religious institution was marginal at best in Chinese society, relegated to the lowest levels. Consequently, the participation of women, even at the highest levels, did little to raise the social status of the women involved.[42]

The "Golden Lotuses"—Footbinding in China

Any account of women in China cannot be complete without a discussion of the practice of footbinding because of its pervasive impact on women's lives. Partly religio-cultural, partly fashion, partly eroticism, the 1,000-year practice of binding the feet of young girls remains an enigma for those outside of Chinese culture. No one knows with certainty how the practice became tradition, but one fairly credible account has it that it began in the royal palaces in Southern China in the mid-tenth century as an outgrowth of a kind of ballet toe dancing, where the dancer wore silk socks wound with strips of silk.[43]

Although the practice began with royalty, nobility, and the very rich, it eventually worked its way into the entire range of Chinese social strata—even the peasant classes—and became a central feature in the Chinese family, at least for the women, and, therefore, was bound up in the religio-cultural attitudes toward women and their place in society that derived from the Confucian ideal. (However, certain minority ethnic groups, such as the Manchu and Hakka, did not adopt the practice, and it was not as severely performed in some remote areas where "loose binding" was the tradition.)

The main reason that the practice began to spread and become pervasive throughout Chinese society was that it came to be linked to marriage and tradition. Footbinding became a symbol of social status. So, the feet of upwardly mobile girls, even in the lowest classes, were bound in the hopes of better prospects in marriage than would otherwise be the case. Moreover, it was thought that even if those prospects were not realized in this lifetime, the girl would attain to a higher status in the afterlife if her feet were bound.

Footbinding became a kind of art form or craft for women. The binding was sometimes performed by the girl's mother or mother-in-law-to-be (if the girl was betrothed early), but more often it was done by experts in the family or community. A girl was usually between the ages of five and seven when the procedure was first begun, but sometimes it would be started as early as two years old and as late as thirteen.

Upper class women would be more discreet than the women in this photo and would allow long skirts to cover all but the tips of their "Lotus Slippers."

There were many variations on the basic method for binding the feet, and experts were highly regarded and eagerly sought. The goal was to mold the feet into perfect "golden lotuses"—three inches long and shaped like the bud of a lotus flower. A perfectly formed bound foot would appear to extend "naturally" from the leg, rather than veer off at a 90-degree angle as do unbound feet. This was accomplished by binding the feet tightly with cloth to break the arch of the foot and all the toes except the big toe, which was left to protrude forward to create the lotus flower point. The broken toes were curled under the sole of the foot. Sometimes sharp glass or metal shards were included in the bindings, or the girls were required to walk on the glass or metal after the binding was completed. This was to help the skin that would die from the tightness of the binding to slough off. The feet were unbound every so often for cleaning, but also so that they could be rebound in order to tighten the bindings. This extremely painful procedure usually took two years or sometimes longer in order to achieve the desired result. Thereafter, bindings would be worn throughout the woman's life.

We have already seen the central place marriage and its traditions played in the lives of Chinese women under the influence of the Confucian ideal. Tiny lotus feet and the accompanying "lotus gait" that the women acquired because of the bindings were highly desired. As a result, only those with excellently bound feet were marriageable. The tiny feet provided evidence that the girl was obedient, submissive, and able to endure great pain; moreover, her sexuality was controlled because she could not easily "run around."[44] There also is literature showing that bound feet even became an erotic fetish for men. All of this made the young woman with bound feet an excellent selection for a wife. So highly regarded were the "golden lotuses" that they were often the first thing the mother-in-law-to-be inquired after when choosing a bride for her son. Samples of the girl's silk shoes would be sent to her future in-laws for them to inspect for size and shape, as well as for the quality of the embroidery and other workmanship on the shoes, as each shoe was meticulously created by the girl herself. So confined was a young girl's life that the embroidery designs on the tiny silk shoes were often the only outlet for a fertile imagination.

It was not only Confucian ideals that contributed to the religious overtones of footbinding. There was much family ceremony and tradition associated with it. Generally, all of the women in the extended family would come together for the first binding of the young girl's feet. The mother would choose an auspicious day for the event by consulting astrologers, fortune tellers, or diviners. She also would have made the first shoes to be worn by her newly bound daughter and would have placed them the night before the event on an altar to Kuan-Yin, the Goddess of Mercy, or "Little Footed Miss," an obscure goddess associated with footbinding. The hope was that the deities would ensure the success of the binding and a perfect result, so that the daughter would make an excellent match in marriage. In other words, the mother was praying for the future happiness of and good fortune for her daughter.

In the nineteenth century, as China had more contact with Westerners who viewed footbinding as barbaric, the antifootbinding movement began. The Manchus,

Each shoe was meticulously crafted and embroidered by the women themselves, providing one of the only creative outlets for the women's fertile imaginations.

who were in power through 1911 and who never bound their feet, discouraged the practice without much success. Long-held traditions die slowly, but the antifoot-binding movement, which was inextricably linked (for obvious reasons) to women's liberation in China, eventually held sway. The practice was abolished in 1949 when Mao Zedong came to power.

Still, we must remember that while footbinding may seem a horrific atrocity today, it is removed by genre and degree only slightly from some of the practices in the West designed to serve many of the same purposes. For example, corsets worn by women of the eighteenth and nineteenth centuries were designed to cinch in a woman's waist to unfathomable narrowness, often resulting in crushed ribs. And just as a modern American woman may have considerable pride in the beautiful breasts that have been perfectly molded by her plastic surgeon, Chinese women's tiny feet were a source of great pride and perceived beauty for them as well.

Chinese Women in Buddhism

We already have discussed Chinese women in Buddhism in the context of Mahayana Buddhism in Chapter 4. It is important to emphasize here as well, however, that Chinese Buddhism brought with it a pervasive female symbolism for the Divine, including *Prajnaparamita* (the Divine source, which is analogous to the Dao) and Kuan-Yin, the Goddess of Mercy. Chinese Buddhism provided a rich mythology and history filled with female deities, adepts, and laywomen to be woven together with other religious influences into the popular religion practiced by many women.

Buddhism also offered an alternative life for Chinese women as nuns. But because the Buddhist convents operated outside the conventional social order, women's participation in them was viewed by those adhering to traditional Chinese standards as subversive to the social order. Nevertheless, the convent provided women with a viable alternative to the role of wife and mother in traditional Chinese society and a place wherein women could exercise considerable leadership as respected teachers.

Women in the People's Republic of China

As we have already seen, the Communist revolution brought with it a suspicion, even disdain, of religion. As a consequence, Buddhist convents were destroyed, and nuns were moved into the workforce. Daoism and popular religion were suppressed. Hence, the doors were closed to the options these religions offered to women.

In their efforts to purge Chinese society of religion, however, the Communist reformers opened new doors to women as well. They sought to eradicate the oppressions they saw as pervading Confucianism, and this included the oppression of women. Mao Zedong saw in women a great resource for his cause as revolutionaries and as workers in the new Communist economic system. Accordingly, he was a great supporter of the reform of women's role in Chinese society, declaring that "women hold up half the sky." Although the trend had begun in the Republican period, under Communism women were encouraged to find roles "outside" in the economy and in politics, as well as "inside" as participants in family life.

No doubt some hypocrisy obtains in these claims. To be made a part of a regimented and overworked labor force along with men is not necessarily liberation. And few women attained top leadership roles. The hidden history of Communist China includes terrible but long-concealed famines, the result of misguided government policies, in which women and children suffered most of all. Nonetheless, the Party sought to end dowry and expensive wedding ceremonies, made divorce more readily available, and promoted education for women. These social changes have radically altered women's lives. Women now work outside of the home in factories, sales, other business roles, politics, educational institutions—in all aspects of Chinese society, albeit still not to the same degree or level as men.

Women's lives have been altered in other ways as well in Communist China. In an effort to curb the population explosion in China, the Communist Party has imposed a one-child rule on families, which has had a profound impact on women's lives. The preference for sons places women who bear daughters in danger of abuse, and a woman may endure forced abortion if she becomes pregnant after bearing a first child. Moreover, the limitation to one child has undermined the traditional role of women, which was a source of pride and status for some. A woman can no longer look forward to developing a "uterine family."

Still, in many respects women's lives often are better today than in traditional Chinese society. Women are now full citizens, having gained to a large degree equal status with men under the law, if not in practice. Although women have not achieved full equality, they play a much greater role, participating in the political structure at least in some measure and by working outside the home. Infanticide has been curbed, if not eliminated; footbinding has been abolished; and the sale of women is no longer permitted. And in recent years, the Party's hard line toward religion has softened, providing renewed opportunities for women in the religions of China.[45] Yet, there continue to be reports of the repression of women, especially those involved in religiously motivated dissident activity, including Tibetan Buddhists, Roman Catholics, Protestants, and those in banned religious groups.

Today, China remains in transition and, therefore, what this all means now for women under Chinese Communism—a blend of a totalitarian political structure and an evolving capitalist economy, which many in the West argue is repressive for all—remains to be seen.

The Influence of Daoism in America

Daoism in the New World has had two kinds of vehicles: the practice of religious Daoism by Chinese-Americans, and the general cultural influence of Daoist themes. Appropriately, for a spirituality that sees its path as like that of water, which though seeming soft and weak in the end wears down the hardest rock, the Daoist impact has been unostentatious but surprisingly pervasive.

I* once observed the characteristic religious Daoist interaction of mystery and community in Hawaii. I was visiting the annual festival of a large interrelated group that had immigrated in the nineteenth century from a single village in south China. The deity on the brightly decked altar in the community hall was Kuan Di, a stern military god who is considered a strong protector against evil forces. He was a famous general back in the third century C.E., who was so exemplary that after his death an emperor declared him a god. He became known and worshipped all over China.

As members of the community entered the hall, they lit sticks of incense and set them upright before the deity. Spread before Kuan Di were food offerings including a roast pig, paper boxes and houses, and firecrackers. Also on the altar were esoteric symbols of the Daoist craft: scissors, a measuring stick, and the symbol of Dao, the mystic universal unity.

*Robert Ellwood.

Then an old Daoist priest vested in a red and green robe put on a peculiar black cap. He stood before the altar, waved incense, and opened a worn liturgical book. The *jiao* or Daoist service offered by the priest had nothing directly to do with the community. It was essentially a priestly rite, although he performed it in the community's presence. Through chanting occult formulae, the officiant called up a series of high spirits—the spirits of the eighteen stars of the Big and Little Dipper and the Three Pure Ones—hierarchical rank upon rank, a celestial court like the old imperial bureaucracy. Each level contained fewer but more powerful entities than the one below it. Meditatively, then, the adept brought the cosmos into greater and greater unity until *Yin* and *Yang,* the two ultimate polarities into which all other multiplicity is resolved, remained alone. Then the priest merged them and stood before the ritually presented great Dao itself, the endless, incomprehensible stream down which all things visible and invisible flow. He did not become Dao, but he stood before it in awe.

In a real Daoist temple, such as examples still found on Taiwan, this *jiao* ritual might be performed in a great ceremony involving several priests and lasting for days at an important festival—and the ritual would be secret, the temple closed to all but the priests participating. In Hawaii, however, the members of the community were mostly seated in a big half-circle around the priest and altar, many talking and laughing quietly—not out of disrespect, but just because priest, rite, spirits, community, Kuan Di, the Dao itself, are all part of one big family in which one feels at home. The incoming spirits wanted the community to be happy and prosperous, to enjoy the good things of life, good food and good companionship— they were in fact inducing the ripples of merriment and kindly gossip to roll around the room as waves in the tide of Dao.

Suddenly the tempo changed. The esoteric part of the mystery was over. The spirits were dispatched by burning the paper offerings outside in a big fire; firecrackers were set off. The roasted pig was quickly cut up and served. Everyone received a heaping plate of food and turned to enjoying a lavish banquet; a leading community official discreetly handed the priest of Dao the traditional bright red envelope containing payment for his services.

This is one side of Daoism in America. The other side is martial arts studies, surfers wearing emblems with the *Yin-Yang* symbol of the Dao, macrobiotic diets, exercises like *tai chi chuan,* Chinese medicine practices like acupuncture and the taking of traditional Chinese herbs, the practices of *feng shui,* and even important aspects of the thinking that has gone into the ecological movement. Not all of this is Daoist in the strictest sense of the word, but all are based on cultural imports from China or the Chinese cultural sphere and stem from broadly Daoist concepts: the importance of balancing energies; of humans living in harmony with nature, working with nature rather than against it; and of isolating and releasing the inner biological/spiritual energy called **chi**.

A few centers and movements teaching philosophical and spiritual Daoism, sometimes including Daoist yoga and meditation, have appeared in America. Much more widespread have been martial arts studios. While certainly not exactly religious, the martial arts centers often help students prepare for training through meditation and "centering" of consciousness, and above all emphasize the importance of releasing the *chi* and the intuitive direct insight that goes with it—all fundamentally Daoist, whatever the nationality or formal affiliation of the center. Somewhat the same can be said of clinics practicing Chinese medicine. Its premises are that health is recovered through opening clogged channels through which the *chi* should pass, using such techniques as acupuncture, and through restoring a proper harmony of *Yin* and *Yang* and the five elements in the body.

Even more widespread is the influence of a basically Daoist mentality through such instruments of popular culture as *Star Wars*. The combination of myth, fantasy, otherworldliness, and the idea of the mystical Force (analogous to *chi*) in those films is profoundly Daoist in spirit—and their immense popularity makes it difficult to say just how broad an impact the ancient Chinese religion has had in the West. Again, the enigma would be typical of Daoism, the watercourse way of weakness and near-invisibility that is really strength. It may be that Daoism has really had more cultural influence in America than other Eastern religions whose temples and centers are far more visible.

RELIGION IN JAPAN

Shinto in Japan

Shinto and the Four Affirmations

The word "Shinto" actually means "The Way of the Gods," and the *"to"* (i.e., "way") in Shin*to* is the Dao of China. Shinto is a broad path offering a pattern of rites, attitudes, and subtle experiences that harmonize humankind with the many faces of its spiritual environment in the context of an ancient culture.

Comparable to the Chinese city-god and ancestral chapel, the Shinto shrine expresses Japanese religion's rootedness in place and family. But typically the Shinto shrine will have a light, lean construction, contrasting with the heavy and ornate quality of Chinese temples. Shinto shrines, and the Shinto religious complex, have distinctive attitudes and practices to go with the unique architecture. If we were to remain around a Shinto shrine and observe its activity, we would see things happen that would bring out four basic affirmations that are inherent in Shinto: (1) of tradition, (2) of life in this world, (3) of purity, and (4) of festival.

Virtually every Shinto shrine has its unique set of traditions: the festivals that are celebrated, the rituals that are performed. Some are ancient and some less so, but all strongly link the present with the past. They appear in the midst of modern Japan like time capsules from earlier centuries. The traditions of some shrines present brilliant spectacles drawing vast throngs of tourists; others are of only local interest. But in any case, the observer will note that while Shintoists may have little idea exactly why a rite is performed in a certain manner, or what it means theologically or philosophically, the action will be done in a precisely pre-scribed way.

The fire to cook the offerings may be started with a traditional fire drill, a ring of evergreen may be set up in the same way each year for people to walk through to remove pollution. What is really being affirmed is not so much the importance of this or that particular custom as the importance of having tradition itself, of living in the presence of visible carryovers from ages gone by, with all their color and evocative power. For millions of modern Japanese living in a rapidly changing tech-nological world, this role of embodying a traditional past they do not want entirely to lose is the most important function of Shinto and one very precious to them.

Torii

The affirmation of tradition is clearly related to the motif of affirmation of life in this world. Shinto, the religion of clans and their communal spirit, of joyous fes-tivals and bountiful harvests, affirms the good things of this world and natural re-lationships. Its land of the dead is shadowy, and its mystical and intellectual life relatively undeveloped. But in the exuberant festivals of harvest or the stately splendor of ancient dance and ritual, Shinto comes into its own.

This is related to another important Shinto affirmation: the distinction be-tween purity and pollution. Shinto shrines, demarcated by their *torii,* represent pure spaces in the midst of a polluted world. Upon entering the shrine precincts, one washes, and rituals begin with the symbolic sweeping away of impurity with a green branch. What is fresh, lively, and bright is pure; what is stagnant, decaying, sick, or dying is impure. Blood, disease, and death are the most impure things. A dead body would not be brought into a shrine; on the rare occasion of a Shinto fu-neral, the rite is held at another place. Through its avoidance of impurity, Shinto affirms the persistence and superiority of life and joy.

The fourth affirmation is festival. As we have seen, the quiet, inactive shrine in its wood or beside its stream may have an air of still purity, but it is not until the *kami* (the diety of the shrine) is stirred to vigorous life by the drums of a *matsuri* (Shinto festival), that the full color and dynamism of the Divine side of reality is manifested. For one who has been at a *matsuri,* the sylvan quietude of the shrine on ordinary days, when only individual worshippers approach it to clap twice and pray, has a feel of expectant waiting about it. The still drum, plainly visible on the open porch at the front of the shrine, and the dance pavilion remind one of an-other mood.

To fully understand Shinto worship and festival, it is necessary to have a mental picture of the structure of a shrine. After the visitor has entered under the crossbeams of the *torii* and passed the purificatory font, he or she approaches the porch with its drum, **gohei** (zigzag paper streamers), and other accoutrements; this is the **haiden**, or hall of worship, where the laity pray and sacred dance is of-fered. Behind it, but visible from the front, is a second segment with a curious eight-legged table for offerings; this is the *heiden,* or hall of offerings. Behind the table, the observer will note a set of extremely steep steps leading up to a massive, richly ornamented door. It leads to the *honden,* an enclosed room much higher than the rest of the shrine and the symbolic dwelling place of the *kami.* In this room will be a heavily wrapped object called the *shintai,* representation of the god—an old sword, mirror, inscription, or something else—which from ancient times has been the sacred presence of Divinity in this shrine, in a manner somewhat analogous to the reserved sacrament in a Roman Catholic church.

Formal Shinto worship occurs at varying intervals, depending on the importance of the shrine. Some small shrines without a resident priest will enjoy offerings only two or three times a year; others will have services monthly, or every ten days, or daily in a few major shrines. Special rites commissioned on behalf of families and groups are common at larger shrines too. The spring and fall festivals will usually be the most important *matsuri*. However, many shrines also have very colorful and dramatic midsummer rites directed against evil influences. New Year is a time of considerable shrine activity too, especially for private visits.

Shinto Worship

All full Shinto worship follows a basic structure. It can be remembered by a series of four words beginning with the letter P: purification, presentation, prayer, and participation.

First, a priest, dressed in white or perhaps lightly colored garments and a high black hat (derived from ancient court costumes) may, according to local usage, wave a branch or stick with paper streamers on it (the *onusa*) or sprinkle salt or water over the heads of the people gathered in the courtyard as a rite of purification. Then the priest will enter the shrine and present the offerings, very neatly

Shinto ritualist in Meiji Shrine, Tokyo.

arranged, before the *kami*-presence on the eight-legged table—or on very important occasions he will open the great doors and lay the offerings on the floor of the *honden*. The presentation is accompanied by dramatically accelerating drumbeats and perhaps the eerie tones of reed flutes. The offerings, mostly fruit, vegetables, rice, seafood, salt, water, and rice wine, are borne up and arranged with reverent care. Then, all in order on the altar, the priest reads a formal prayer, either silently or in a high chanting voice.

Next follows one of several possibilities, depending on the elaborateness of the occasion and the resources of the shrine. While the offerings are still on the altar, formal dance may be presented as part of the offering and as a representation of the Divine presence to the worshippers. At the close of the service, individuals may present as an offering a small branch, as though to show their participation; and, as a kind of holy communion after offerings have been solemnly removed from the altar, they may partake of a tiny bit of the wine and perhaps other offerings.

As soon as the offerings are removed, it is understood that the solemn part is over. Then a dramatic, Divine change of pace takes place as the *kami*-spirit animates the people with a festival spirit. Particularly at the main annual *matsuri,* vivid local activities occur affording everyone participation in the festivities. These will be as exuberant as the offering and prayer were solemn. The *kami* may be borne through the streets in a palanquin by young men zigzagging and shouting. All over the shrine grounds, booths are set up as for a carnival, with cotton candy stalls and sumo wrestling exhibitions, and crowds throng onto the carnival grounds with laughter and squealing children.

In some great shrines, splendid parades, historical pageants, folk dances, medieval horseracing or archery performances, fireworks, indeed, an almost endless variety of traditional activities, may be parts of the "participation" aspect of the *matsuri*. Some are rustic fairs little known outside the locality; some take months of professional preparation and draw spectators from around the world.

The Kami and Their Myths

So far we have described only Shinto shrines and worship, saying nothing about the particular deities who are the recipients of this worship. This is not inappropriate, for to most Japanese the name and story of a particular *kami* means little; it is the shrine, worship, and festival itself that counts. Partial exceptions are the familiar *Inari* shrines, distinguished by their red *torii* and stone foxes, to which people go to pray for prosperity. But Shintoists are far from having the kind of relation to their *kami* that Hindu *bhaktas* have with Shiva or Krishna. Japanese religion, like the Japanese temperament, is much more reserved and formal.

Nonetheless, the *kami* do have names and myths. Many Shinto *kami* are only local. But many of those of national importance are named in the two great collections of Shinto mythology, compiled by order of the imperial court of the time to present its Divine descent and commission—the **Kojiki** (712 C.E.) and the **Nihon-shoki** (720 C.E.), two of the oldest books in Japanese. They tell the story of creation and give an account of the Sun-Goddess, Amaterasu, believed to be ancestress of the Japanese imperial family. She is worshipped at the grand Shrine of Ise, a sort of Shinto national cathedral.

The national myth in the Kojiki and Nihonshoki tells us that in the beginning the High *Kami* in heaven sent the primal parents, the male **Izanagi** and the female **Izanami**, down from the High Plain of Heaven. They indulged in a virtual orgy of procreation, giving birth to islands and gods, until Izanami was burned to death upon the birth of the fire-god. Izanagi tried to bring his wife out of the underworld, but he was unable to do so because she had already eaten of its food. Izanagi then exchanged boasts with Izanami about the greater power of life over death. He bathed in the ocean to cleanse himself of the pollution of the underworld. From

FUNDAMENTAL FEATURES OF SHINTO

THEORETICAL

Basic Worldview	Universe is pluralistic, having many gods. It is growing and changing. Nature, humanity, and the divine are not sharply separated.
God or Ultimate Reality	Many kami.
Origin of the World	Generated by the gods.
Destiny of the World	Unknown, but historical progress has meaning.
Origin of Humans	Descended from kami.
Destiny of Humans	Unclear; perhaps to become kami or merge with kami.
Revelation or Mediation between the Ultimate and the Human	Myths, traditions, and festivals of shrines where one approaches the kami presence.

PRACTICAL

What Is Expected of Humans: Worship, Practices, Behavior	To remember and celebrate the gods, remain pure and sincere, enjoy life. Support the societies of which kami are patrons.

SOCIOLOGICAL

Major Social Institutions	Shrines, with the ujiko community of each. Family, work, and regional ties with particular shrines important.

his washings were born several great gods, above all Amaterasu, the lovely goddess associated with the sun and ancestress of the imperial house.

In heaven, Amaterasu once hid herself in a cave when her brother greatly offended her at the harvest festival. She was drawn out from the cave when a goddess did a ribald dance and another *kami* held up a mirror to the solar Goddess's curious emerging face. Later, Amaterasu gave the same mirror (now said by tradition to be enshrined as a sacred object in the Grand Shrine of Ise) to her grandson, Prince Ninigi, who was sent down from heaven to establish the line of sovereigns on earth. This brings us to another aspect of Shinto, its relationship to the Japanese state.

Shinto as a State Cultus

During the period of modern nationalism in Japan up to 1945, the mythical Divine descent of the imperial house just described and the accompanying ancient belief that the emperor is himself in a mysterious sense a "manifest deity" was used (often in a rather cynical way) to focus extreme loyalty to the emperor and to justify militaristic policy. The ancient role of the emperor, however, was one of sacred kingship in the priestly sense. In most periods of Japanese history, he has exercised very little real power. He has a special role toward the *kami,* however, which is well expressed in the **Daijo-sai**, the harvest festival as celebrated by the emperor after his accession.[47]

Buddhism in Japan

Nearly as common as Shinto shrines, and also of graceful wooden architecture but without the *torii,* are the Buddhist temples of Japan. However, the Buddhist edifices are likely to be larger than the shrines, with room for throngs of worshippers within. The temple is dominated by imposing Buddhist images, some large and of a deeply glowing gold. These images personify a spiritual force that is not as old in Japan as the *kami,* who go back to misty prehistory, but is as old as history itself. For with the coming of Buddhism to Japan came writing, new models for art and governmental organization, many material boons of continental civilization, the keeping of records, and consciousness of history.

Buddhism arrived in Japan from Korea in the early sixth century. Early Japan long had closer ties with the Korean peninsula than with China proper, even to the extent of maintaining military and trading settlements there. In the sixth century, Buddhism had just come to Korea from Tang Dynasty China, and in China itself it had only been a strong influence for some three centuries. It still was a young and dynamic enthusiasm in that part of the world, and the *Ninonshoki* says a Korean king, anxious to cement an alliance, sent the Japanese emperor a Buddhist image and scriptures.[48]

But we must remember that as new as Buddhism seemed then, that faith already had behind it nearly a thousand years of development. Mahayana, Tantrism, temple architecture, *sutras,* images, *mandalas,* schools such as Chan and Pure

Land—all these had reached mature forms before Buddhism touched the shamanistic and nearly unlettered people of old Japan. Buddhism came, therefore, as a powerfully more sophisticated culture, with splendors of art and subtleties of concept undreamed of before. It was far from well understood, but it was a force and a presence that could hardly be avoided.

As they have done repeatedly since, the Japanese responded initially with debate between the desire to keep their culture intact and the desire to be open to everything foreign that seemed advanced and advantageous. Then as later, they swung between extremes on each hand. But from then on, Buddhism was an increasingly deeply rooted part of Japanese culture.

Tendai and Shingon

Japanese Buddhism has taken several forms. The first major denominations of Buddhism in Japan, which flourished in the Nara Period (710–784) and the Heian Period (794–1185), were elaborate and complex, with temples honoring many Mahayana Buddhas and *bodhisattvas* with colorful rituals. They often verged toward Vajrayana practices. The most important denominations of this type, which stem from the beginning of the Heian Period and still exist in large numbers today, are **Tendai** and **Shingon**.

Tendai, founded by Saicho or **Dengyo Daishi** (762–822), holds that the *Lotus Sutra* is the fullest expression of Buddhist truth. But under that "umbrella" it is tolerant of a great diversity of Buddhist devotions, holding that there are innumerable ways to enlightenment.

Shingon, founded by Kukai or **Kobo Daishi** (773–835), is more Vajrayana-like in style. It emphasized the Great Sun Buddha (Dainichi) who is the universal Buddha nature everywhere, and taught esoteric practices—*mantras* or chants, *mudras* or hand gestures, meditations that visualize the Buddhas—by which one could express one's inner Buddhahood. Its temples and rituals often presented *mandalas* or *yantras,* sometimes three-dimensional, showing the interrelationships of the many Buddhas and *bodhisattvas.*

The Kamakura Reformation: Pure Land, Nichiren, and Zen

In the **Kamakura Period** (1185–1333) the religious picture changes. Politically, the Nara and Heian Periods had centered on the imperial court in the cities of Nara and then Heian (modern Kyoto). The courtiers had appreciated and patronized those many-faceted forms of Mahayana Buddhism. But in the Kamakura Period a new force came to power, the warlords or **shogun**, who established their capital in the city of Kamakura far to the North of Kyoto. With their rise to power came a religious change that has sometimes been compared to the Protestant Reformation in sixteenth-century Europe.

If Heian was dominated by the elegant refined courtier and the esoteric monk, Kamakura was characterized by the simple, direct warrior. Moreover, times

Passerby praying at Buddhist shrine in Tokyo. ▣

were troubled, and pessimism was in the air. People talked of the Buddhist idea of the **mappo**, the last age, when doctrine and morality would deteriorate so much that one could be saved only by faith, if at all. To meet the new age, three new forms of Buddhism arose in Japan—Pure Land, Nichiren, and Zen.

Each in its own way represented a popularization of Buddhism as a path to liberation for the masses. Each also represented a radical Buddhist simplification. Kamakura Buddhism was a soldier's reaction against the deep metaphysics and ostentatious rituals of the Heian Period. The soldier, in a time of disorder and death, wanted assurance of salvation, but his straightforward nature was not attracted by monasticism or beautiful but impersonal rites or subtle philosophy. He insisted on some simple and sure key to salvation, as dependable on the battlefield as in the monastic temple.

Hence, synthesis and mystery gave way to simple faith, popular preachers, and practical techniques. An age can be understood as well or better through the questions it asks as through the answers it gives. The Heian Period (like medieval Europe) had asked, "How can all knowledge and spiritual experience be brought into a great inclusive system?" Kamakura Japan (like Reformation Europe) was asking instead, "How can I know that I am saved?" It was eager to shuck the brain-splitting mysteries of the cosmic *mandala* and the three Buddha-bodies and the rest for a sure answer to this desperate question that anyone could understand. Its new forms of Buddhism—Pure Land, Nichiren, and Zen—can be called products of the Kamakura Reformation.

Pure Land Buddhism was taught in Japan by **Honen** (1133–1212) and his disciple **Shinran** (1173–1262), who founded respectively the **Jodo-shu** (Pure Land) and **Jodo Shinshu** (True Pure Land) denominations.[49] The basic practice is expressing faith in the vow of Amida Buddha to save all who call upon his name through faith by the *Nembutsu*—the chant *"Namu Amida Butsu"* ("Glory to Amida Buddha"). It is a very simple but deep faith in which one loses ego not by meditation, as in some other forms of Buddhism, but by trust in the help of another far more powerful—Amida. Shinran taught an even more radical salvation by faith alone than Honen, and he implemented it thoroughly—demanding married clergy, the removal of all figures in temples, except Amida, and a new "secular" Buddhist way of life. If salvation is by faith and faith alone, he argued, all the rest of the vast baggage of Buddhic rites and rules is unnecessary.

The militant Kamakura spirit in religion is supremely manifested in **Nichiren**. [50] The son of a poor fisherman, Nichiren (1222–1282), an intelligent and perceptive youth, was haunted by two questions. He wondered why, in the struggle between the old Heian regime and the rebellious warlords, the imperial armies had been defeated despite the countless incantations offered on their behalf by the Tendai and Shingon clerics. And he asked, like so many in his day, how one could experience the certainty of salvation. Both of these are serious themes, which were to become pillars of the faith he finally offered the world.

In 1242, Nichiren went to study at Mount Hiei, where he stayed until 1253. Under the influence of Tendai, he became convinced that the answer to his problems lay in the *Lotus Sutra*. Salvation was not only in its teachings, although they are the supreme expression of Buddhist truth, but in the gesture of accepting the *Lotus Sutra* as the sole bearer of Buddhist faith and authority. In 1253, he began a prophetic mission, urging the whole nation to return to the *Lotus Sutra*.

From the beginning, Nichiren Buddhism had a rigorous quality; his disciples did not shrink from using contentious and disruptive means to spread the faith. While for several centuries his faith settled down to become a fairly ordinary denomination, Nichiren's thought was not without its effect on Japanese nationalism and modernization. Since World War II, a new Nichiren movement, the **Soka Gakkai** (actually a lay organization within Nichiren Shoshu, the largest of the Nichiren sects) was founded by persons who suffered persecution from the wartime nationalist regime. Soka Gakkai ("Value-creation Society"), which has grown remarkably, places special emphasis on the power of chanting to achieve results in this life. Following the "this-worldly" promises of Nichiren faith to augur a new age of human fulfillment, this tightly organized order has shown the force of Nichiren as a prophet for the modern world. Thanks largely to the work of Soka Gakkai, Nichiren faith has been a potent force in contemporary Japan.[51]

Because the basic principles of **Zen** have already been presented in connection with its sources in Chinese Chan in the chapter on Buddhism, it will be sufficient here just to make a few comments on its Japanese development. Chan was transmitted to Japan by two men, Eisai (1141–1215) and Dogen (1200–1253). Both were priests educated at Mount Hiei, and both, like many others, were looking for something more. Each went to China, and each came in contact with one of two major traditions of Chan, which in Japan became the Zen Buddhism **Rinzai** and **Soto** schools.

Besides being a denomination that administers temples, Zen in Japan is a distinctive esthetic and cultural influence. Zen cultural expression—in poetry, paint-

Rock garden in Japanese Zen monastery.

ing, the tea ceremony, the garden—suggests the Zen experience of the absolute in the ordinary and in the natural in that perfect simplicity that comes out of perfect control. For example, let us look at the Zen garden. A Zen monastery may possess a garden with raked gravel and moss and gnarled trees. The objects will not be spaced in the geometric patterns of a European formal garden, as at Versailles, but in a seemingly natural and irregular way that nonetheless enchants and satisfies. Like all the other Zen arts, it manifests the truly natural by pruning and control.

Early one mild spring morning, I* sat overlooking the world-famous stone garden of the Ryoanji Zen temple in Kyoto. This garden is simply a large rectangle of raked white gravel in which are set five rough boulders, "islands" of rock, with bits of moss around them. The big stones are in a seemingly random pattern, yet one cannot quite leave them alone. For long periods I gazed at them, torn between the intellect's insatiable desire to make everything into meaningful relationships and the inherent meaninglessness of this, which was yet a work of art. Over and over again, I felt that I had almost, but not quite, seen the meaning of the rock "island" relationships; I seemed to know it but could not quite say it. Finally, like a **koan**, the rocks and their relationships brought me up against the futility of the pattern-making mind in dealing with certain ultimates. In gazing at the garden, I saw now random bits of moss and stone, now a cluster of galaxies in the trackless void of space.

*Robert Ellwood.

Confucianism in Japan

Confucianism is an "invisible" but profoundly pervasive spiritual presence in Japan. With one or two exceptions, it presents no eye-catching shrines like Shinto or splendid temples like Buddhism. Yet its influence on the structures and values of Japanese society can hardly be overestimated. However diverse their metaphysical positions, the practical, this-worldly ethics of all accepted religions in Japan are essentially Confucian in character, stressing family, loyalty, harmony, and fulfilling obligations. More than anything else, Confucian values have made Japan the industrious, harmonious, hierarchical, sometimes repressive, web of intricate loyalties and mutual obligations that it is. And more than anything else, these values lie behind Japan's success as a world-class economic power, even given its recent set backs. It is vital, therefore, to understand something about the Japanese adaptation of Confucianism, which in certain ways is different from what it meant in China.

Confucianism has been taught in Japan since the earliest arrival from the continent, although it rarely took explicitly religious expression in Japan. There was a Confucian university during the Heian Period. Confucianism's Japanese heyday, however, was the Tokugawa Period (1600–1867), when it flourished as the state ideology and also as the main inspiration of several popular or deviant philosophical movements.

Influential popular movements during that time also inculcated broadly Neo-Confucian values. Some embraced worship at both Shinto and Buddhist sites but made central the cultivation of the heart's original purity, holding that human nature is one with the natural moral order. Others taught respect for the social order and its laws, seeing in them human expression of that natural moral order—a characteristic Neo-Confucian perspective and one well calculated to produce a hardworking, law-abiding society.

Still, loyalty and obligation—the two values that have shaped Japanese social character more than any others—are deeply rooted in Confucianism. (Some say they go back even further than Confucianism, to the life of the archaic village and tribe, but certainly they have been articulated in historical times through Confucian language.) Loyalty in Japan goes beyond literal filial piety to apply to anyone who can be seen as being in the place of a parent. Thus, feudal lords and many others have made extensive use of adoption to continue their line when suitable natural heirs were not forthcoming. Moreover, the concept has been extended to include loyalty of students to teachers, workers to their employer or corporation, even gangsters to their underworld bosses, and subjects to state and sovereign. In Japan these obligations could, and often did, take precedence over family. That was because they were based on another key principle, the **on-giri** relationship, that of *on,* or benefaction, and *giri,* the resultant supreme obligation to repay by work and loyalty; this makes the benefactor a parent substitute.

Although outer forms continually change, these attitudes are virtually as alive today as ever. No understanding of contemporary Japanese politics or corporations is possible without a grasp of how Confucian values make such institutions complex networks of loyalties and obligations, or of how the other Confucian-based ideals of harmony and cooperation lead to decision-making as a sort of consensus-seeking process—one often quite mysterious to outsiders. For loyalty does not form an autocrat out of the recipient. Rather, the Japanese way tends to make superiors—including the emperor—figureheads and facilitators and to exalt the collective responsibility and consensus decision-making of the whole family, group, or network involved.

Japan, then, is a fundamentally Confucian society and a very effective one that in many ways displays the tradition's potential for making human life work smoothly in the twenty-first century as well as in the days of the Ancient Sage. But it is Confucianism with a difference, without the *mandarins* or the rituals—save as the former are now captains of industry, and the latter, the interpersonal courtesy for which Japan is famous.[52]

The New Japanese Religions

One of the most fascinating of all contemporary religious phenomena is a set of groups called **shinko shukyo**, "newly arisen religions," in Japan. Although most of them have earlier roots, they grew and flourished tremendously in the post–World War II years of disillusionment with traditional life, including conventional Shinto and Buddhism. The golden age of these religions was the 1950s, when many were growing at fantastic rates and, in some, the original charismatic leader was still alive. But at the beginning of the twenty-first century, they are still very much a part of the Japanese scene.

The new religions have generally been based on revelations given through the lips of their founders, often women. Sometimes they have seemed to be in the tradition of ancient Japanese shamans and shamanesses. Generally, they have emphasized new teachings and practices suitable to the rapidly changing modern world. One example is **Tenrikyo** ("Religion of Heavenly Wisdom"), founded in 1838 by Miki Nakayama (1798–1887), who said that "God the Parent" is seeking to call the human children back to himself through telling them the forgotten story of creation. The main temple of the faith, in Tenri city near Nara, centers around a pillar said to mark the place where creation began and a new paradisal age in the future will be inaugurated. Rituals include beautiful sacred dances acting out the creation story. Other new religions with Buddhist roots, like the Soka Gakkai, already mentioned, or based on other modern messages from the Divine are also found, such as The **Church of World Messianity**, in which adherents channel the "Divine Light of God" through cupped hands to a recipient. Another new religion is **Konkokyo**, in which adherents are given personal spiritual guidance channeled by the priest.

In the 1980s and 1990s, the "classic" new religions just mentioned, while still important, leveled off somewhat in terms of growth. Soka Gakkai was affected in 1993 by conflict and separation between the Nichiren-shu priests, who had authorized or conducted the movement's strictly religious rites, and the dynamic lay organization that had done so much to evangelize Nichirenism. However, some new movements, often called **shin-shin-shukyo** or "new new religions" have appeared, often with a healing, charismatic, and individualistic emphasis, similar to the "New Age Movement" in the West. Examples are Mahikari, a healing faith similar to World Messianity, and Agonshu, a faith of Buddhist background emphasizing ancestrism and the enactment of spectacular *goma* or fire rituals like those of Shingon.

Women in Japanese Religion

As in China, religion in Japan involves a confluence of many diverse elements. In addition to Shinto, which is indigenous to Japan, themes from the religious influences of Buddhism, Daoism, and Confucianism, which were imported from China, were woven into the Japanese social fabric. Due in particular to the influences of Confucianism, Japan has been extremely patriarchal at least since the feudal era (twelfth to seventeenth centuries), during which women were relegated to a lesser status than they had previously known. More important, negative Buddhist attitudes toward women as being obstacles to male enlightenment and being more readily distracted from their own enlightenment were conflated with Confucian notions to bolster the view that women's subjugation was warranted. Prior to the importation of these religious influences (third century C.E.), women were significant religious figures in their own right as shamanesses, who were skilled in trance and able to contact the *kami* and the dead and proclaim their messages to others. Shamanesses, such as Pimiko and Empress Jingu, were charismatic ruler queens, and those who did not rule were nevertheless well-educated, experienced, central, and respected figures in early Japanese culture. The elevated and prominent social role played by shamanesses was nearly eclipsed, however, by Chinese religio-cultural influences eagerly appropriated by the Japanese who were taken with them.[53] However, the shamaness tradition did survive and continues to this day, particularly in rural settings. And it provides the impetus behind the acceptance of the charismatic women leaders of the "new religions," such as Miki of Tenrikyo.

Confucianism provided the foundation of Japanese family life. Confucian ideals regarding the formality of hierarchical relationships of the family prevailed in Japan. As a consequence, family and society became the province of male authority, and the woman's role came to reflect the Confucian ideal of wife and mother, including the importance of purity, chastity, submissiveness, and the bearing of sons. A woman's place was inside the home and her main objective was complete devotion to her husband. As in traditional China, women in Japan joined the families of their husbands and lived under the authority of their mothers-in-law.

Family loyalty plays a considerable role in Japanese life—a confluence of Confucian notions and ancient clan allegiances. This and Buddhist doctrines of selflessness (together with the influence of the Daoist *wu-wei*) merge to make acceptance of one's lot in life, and service to the familial group, the religious ideal. For women this meant accepting their subservient status without complaint.

Shinto retained the distinctly Japanese folk wisdom and mythology of a prior age. The creation myth, as we have seen, provides a prominent place for the female

Divine as one deity in the primal Divine couple. Amaterasu (the Sun Goddess), their progeny, is the patroness and ancestor of the Imperial Family. The many *kami* include both male and female deities.

The shamaness tradition has survived in Shinto's rural folk religion manifestations. However, even here where female symbolism abounds, we find a reiteration of the cosmic order as requiring the submission of women to men. For example, in the creation myth, when Izanagi, the male, is to join with the female, Izanami, the female speaks first. As a result, their first offspring is defective. Clearly, she was to have deferred to her male counterpart. Further, in Shinto, blood is taboo. Consequently, women themselves were taboo during menstruation and childbirth.[54] Yet, it is Shinto's emphasis on the beauty and divinity of nature (bolstered by analogous Daoist thinking and practice) that provides the aesthetic sensibilities so central to Japan. This added to women's vocation the development of elegance and grace in her person and her home. Thus, women, under Shinto influence, combined with Confucian ideal family life, are to serve and beautify.

Daoism did not develop a distinct religious tradition in Japan. Instead, as we have seen, its themes were infused into the social framework as a complement to Shinto's reverence of nature. Daoism also greatly influenced Zen Buddhism, providing it a reverence for "naturalness." Interestingly, some aesthetic aspects of Japan associated with Zen are performed by women—the tea ceremony and flower arranging come to mind.

The role of women in contemporary Japanese religion can only be described as mixed and in flux. Women retain some traditional religious roles from the past, as *miko* or shamanesses, as founders of new religious movements, occasionally as Shinto priests or priests in temples of new religions. Even in religions where the hierarchy is officially male, in a characteristically Japanese way, active women—sometimes as wives or mothers of priests—are expected to exercise considerable influence.

At the same time, the secondary status of women in Buddhism is being increasingly challenged, no doubt under the influence of Japanese and worldwide feminist movements. Recently, Buddhist nuns have been agitating for equality in the *samgha*. The wives of Buddhist priests also have long had an anomalous place. Although most Japanese priests are married, the fact that they are theoretically supposed to be celibate has put many of these women in the position of persons whose role is not supposed to be openly recognized. They are now forming organizations to try to rectify this situation in order to give them the dignity to which they are entitled.

A matter that has attracted much attention recently, and that affects women profoundly, is the burgeoning of *mizuko kuyo* rites, memorial services for aborted fetuses. Abortion is common in Japan, and these services, offered by many Buddhist temples, have provided ways for women to deal with the feelings of loss and guilt evoked by the tragedy in ways consistent with Buddhist beliefs in the afterlife and reincarnation.[55]

Contemporary Japan also is beginning to undergo a crisis of its traditional Confucian family values. One often sees articles in the print media and on television presentations treating, in tones of either enthusiasm or despair, the reality that young people seem no longer to regard elders with the veneration of old, and women are increasingly expecting equal opportunity in business, professions, and politics. At the same time, change is often slow. Many Japanese, women and men both, remain influenced by the Confucian tradition of recognizing the importance of one's integration into larger social units—family, community, corporation—and therefore they are skeptical of the extreme individualism promoted by the West.

Today Japanese women's status in society as a whole remains low. Despite equal opportunity for education and a constitutional provision against sex discrimination, Japanese women do not find equal opportunity in the workplace. Yet, they have not developed a feminist movement quite as strong as those in other modern, developed industrial nations. Perhaps this is because many Japanese women remain family-oriented, consistent with religious ideas, and wield considerable power in the home. Perhaps it is because Japanese women were not subjected to the extreme oppressions of women in other societies. Perhaps it is because the Japanese worldview does not permit a notion of liberation. Everyone is part of the group— the clan—and is not an individual in one's own right. Whatever the reason, women are well rooted in traditional Japanese religion and society and many accept their role without a perceived need to mount a strong resistance. Still, there are those whose voices are beginning to be heard, as Sandra Buckley's recent work, *Broken Silence: Voices of Japanese Feminism,* has shown.[56]

RELIGION IN KOREA

Korea has been called the "Bridge of Asia." This peninsula, reaching from the mainland toward Japan, has long been a melting pot of religious and cultural influences and a pathway by which they have been transmitted to Japan. As we have seen, Buddhism first entered Japan from Korea. At the same time, with a population of some 60 million (now divided between the Republic of Korea in the South and Communist-ruled North Korea), Korea is an important cultural sphere in its own right.

Korean religion may be looked at in terms of five constituents: indigenous shamanistic faith, Buddhism, Confucianism, modern new religions, and Christianity. These are the main ingredients in the contemporary Korean religious melting pot, together with a dash of Daoism from China that is, among other things, represented in the *Yang–Yin* symbol found on the Republic of Korea's flag, but that is less of a definable religious stratum in Korea than the preceding five.

The ancient indigenous religion of Korea is comparable to early Shinto, to which it is probably related. It presents a myth of the origin of the Korean people in the union of a god descended from heaven who made a she-bear into a human and mated with her. Their son, Tangun, was the founder of Korean society. He then worshipped the high god of heaven, Hananim. Shamanism was very important, persisting today in the role of *mudangs,* colorful shamanesses who may perform a rite called *kut* to drive away evil spirits and restore good fortune.

Buddhism came into Korea late in the fourth century C.E. and quickly took hold owing to patronage by rulers of several Korean kingdoms. Buddhist influence was all in the Mahayana tradition; monastic life has come to be predominantly *Son* (Zen), while lay Buddhism has focused on Pure Land faith and the worship of the *bodhisattva* Kwanseum (in Chinese, Kyan-Yin; in Japanese, Kannon), the heavenly bestower of mercy. The great Buddhist temple and monastic centers of Korea tend to be in isolated places, quiet retreats often stocked with invaluable Buddhist libraries and works of art.

The golden age of Korean Buddhism was the early Middle Ages. The Yi dynasty (1392–1910) favored Confucianism and tended to restrict Buddhist activity. National temples performed Confucian rites, and Confucian (especially Neo-Confucian) values deeply affected Korean life. The patriarchal family, filial piety, and the honor of traditional learning among the elite were as absolute in old Korea as anywhere, and the impact of centuries steeped in Confucianism is far from gone today.

But in the nineteenth and twentieth centuries, the closed Confucian cultural world of the Korean "Hermit Kingdom" was harshly violated by Western and Japanese incursions, ranging from extensive Christian missionary activity to bitterly resented Japanese rule, and then to the Korean War and the shocks of modernization. These traumatic events have created an ardent sense of Korean cultural identity and messianism, reflected in several new religious movements. Tonghak ("Eastern Learning") was founded in the 1860s and renamed **Ch'ondogyo** ("Way of Heavenly Teaching") in 1905. It inculcated the worship of the God of Heaven but combined features of shamanism, Buddhism, and Confucianism. It also advocated social change against the anachronistic, ultraconservative Yi Dynasty, and it lay behind a great rebellion in 1894 that nearly toppled that regime and produced in turn the Sino-Japanese War of that year. Another group, which combines Christian, shamanistic, and messianic features, is that founded by the Rev. Sun Myung Moon, known in the West as the **Unification Church**.

Christianity, brought by Catholic and Protestant missionaries, has been more successful in Korea than in most other parts of East Asia except the Philippines, embracing nearly half of the population of South Korea as the twenty-first century began.[57]

RELIGION IN VIETNAM

Situated on the southeast corner of the Asian mainland, Indochina is an area where Indian and Chinese cultural influences meet. Two of the Indochinese countries, Laos and Cambodia, are Theravada Buddhist and traditionally oriented toward the Indian cultural direction. The third and largest, Vietnam, has sometimes experienced Chinese rule and has been more dominated culturally and religiously by its great neighbor to the North. In the early centuries C.E., however, the Southern tip of Vietnam, then the kingdom of Funan, was a center of Indianization.

But China ruled major parts of Vietnam, mostly in the North, for more than a thousand years, from 111 B.C.E. to 939 C.E. Despite ardent Vietnamese resistance to their rule, the Chinese succeeded in sinicizing Vietnamese culture to no small extent. This is reflected in the dominance of Mahayana Buddhism, largely in the form of Thien (Chan or Zen) Buddhism, and in the traditional role of a Confucian *mandarin* elite imbued with the values of that tradition. However, these institutions have adapted to Vietnamese culture; in recent centuries, monk and *mandarin* alike have embodied Vietnam.

Like the other societies of Southeast Asia, Vietnam in the nineteenth and twentieth centuries suffered severe shocks that gave rise to new questions about the nature of its spiritual identity. The decades of French colonial rule, the missionary presence of Roman Catholicism, the demise of the traditional Confucian order in China itself, and some thirty-five years of war and confusion all left traumatic marks. Vietnamese felt caught between a Catholicism frequently benign but associated with alien rule, a moribund Buddhism, and a Confucianism linked to a social order clearly passing away. In this situation it is not surprising that not only did Communism win support, but highly nationalistic "new religions" also gained large followings. The two most important new movements, **Hoa Hao** and **Cao Dai**, both controlled whole provinces and fielded their own armies in the complicated struggles of Japanese, French, and various Vietnamese forces during the 1940s and 1950s. They continued as powerful factors in Vietnamese life until the unification of the country under the Communist Hanoi regime in 1975.

Hoa Hao was a Buddhist movement with Theravada leanings that sought to restore "pure" Buddhism. Cao Dai, on the other hand, was a highly syncretistic church based on spiritualistic communications, reminiscent of Daoist sectarianism. It embraced Confucian morality, such Buddhist doctrines as *karma* and reincarnation, and spiritist mediumship, while possessing an organizational structure under a "pope" clearly inspired by Roman Catholicism.

Since 1975, religious activity generally has been severely curtailed in Vietnam itself, but Buddhism, Catholicism, and Cao Dai continue to be practiced in Vietnamese refugee communities around the world.

✸ Summary

The religion of East Asia has emphasized the unity of the cosmos and the integration of the individual with nature as well as with family and society. Ancestrism has been an important way of meeting both ends. It has, however, also been a religious tradition deeply influenced by outstanding individual teachers and leaders.

Confucianism, deriving from the teaching of Confucius and other philosophers, as well as from ancient Chinese attitudes, is perhaps the most pervasive spiritual force of all in East Asia. It has emphasized the importance of inward virtue, the obligations of the individual to family and society, and rites and forms through which these are expressed. Daoism, with its stress on mystical unity with all of nature and with such nonrational aspects of human life as love of beauty, fantasy, and personal immortality, has provided compensation for the rational and ethical character of Confucianism. Both sought to align human life with the Dao, the universal Way, or with the will of Heaven; for Confucianism it was supremely found in a good society; for Daoists, it is in nature, beauty, fantasy, and mystical experience outside the corrupting influence of society.

Hardly less influential in East Asia has been Buddhism. In China, it was considerably affected by Daoism. Its main forms were Chan (Zen, in Japan; Son, in Korea), emphasizing meditation and nature, and Pure Land Buddhism, emphasizing rebirth in paradise through faith in Amida. In the popular religion of traditional China, Confucianism, Daoism, and Buddhism combined with ancestrism, seasonal festivals, and local deities to make up a colorful complex.

In the contemporary China of the People's Republic, this tradition has been largely broken. Religion, while still practiced, is circumscribed, and China is generally a secular society.

In Japan, Confucian values have been and still are important, but formal religion has been mainly a matter of the indigenous Shinto faith and Buddhism, imported at the dawn of Japanese history. Shinto is the worship of the *kami* or polytheistic gods of clans and places. The *kami* are housed in simple but lovely shrines and worshipped either privately or in community *matsuri,* which stress tradition, purity, and the festive spirit.

Japanese Buddhism has centered more around major leaders and has changed character through the production of new denominations with major changes in historical eras. Its earlier forms, such as Shingon and Tendai, stressed comprehensiveness and often used esoteric forms. The newer denominations of the Medieval Kamakura period—Pure Land, Nichiren, and Zen—moved in the direction of the simplification and popularization of Buddhist salvation.

Women in East Asia have held a centrally important role in the social order prescribed by religious norms regarding family and the social order. Although considered integral to the "good life," women's significance in that regard did not mitigate against patriarchal patterns that required subordination of women to men. A woman's accepted vocation involved only the realm of the home, where she was highly restricted. Buddhism and Daoism offered alternative avenues of religious and personal expression for women. As Buddhist nuns, women may become teachers and leaders, although, for the most part, they are subordinated to monks. In Daoism, East Asian women have found an accommodating theology, and, therefore, more opportunity for significant roles than found elsewhere in these cultures. Yet, religious Daoism itself is marginal in its impact on the great society. Consequently, advancement there does not provide women with social status.

In modern Japan, a number of new religions have arisen in response to times of rapid change, and women have played important roles in them.

Two other important East Asian countries, Korea and Vietnam, also share a heritage of Confucianism and Buddhism in the Chinese Chan and Pure Land styles; and, in the context of a modern experience devastated by upheaval and war, they have generated major new religious movements.

❋ Questions for Review

1. Discuss the main general features of East Asian religion: its stress on cosmic unity, its orientation toward family and society, and its practicality.

2. Interpret the meaning of the important theme of ancestrism.

3. Discuss the thematic chart for Chinese religion, showing how it brings out the aspects of Chinese religion oriented toward society and those oriented toward nature, and how it sorts out those aspects that stress a rational approach to ultimate meaning and those that give vent to the nonrational side of human nature.

4. Talk about the meaning of Dao.

5. Present the main features of Confucianism. Be sure to distinguish the features of philosophical Confucianism and the religious aspects of Confucian worship, but also show how the two fit together in traditional China through the values and role of the *mandarins*.

6. Discuss the "Han Synthesis" and its significance.

7. In the same way, explain the main features of Daoism (Taoism), distinguishing between the outlook of the Daoist philosophers and religious Daoism, but also indicating how they are related.

8. Discuss the main forms and features of Chinese Buddhism, explaining how Buddhism was modified through interaction with Chinese culture.

9. State the major points of popular religion in traditional China, such as ancestrism, the celebration of seasonal festivals, and the relationships involved in family and place.

10. Explain what the attitudes and policies of the People's Republic of China toward religion have been and what has happened to religion under its rule.

11. Discuss the principal features of Shinto.

12. Discuss Buddhism in Japan, stressing the role of the great leaders who have shaped it and how its character has changed with changing historical periods.

13. Interpret the general characteristics of the "new religions" of Japan.

14. Using the charts, explain the fundamental features of Confucianism, Daoism, and Shinto. How do they answer the great questions about the nature of ultimate reality and the meaning of human life?

15. Discuss the role of women in traditional Chinese and Japanese societies.

16. Explain how Buddhism and Daoism offered alternative roles for women in China.

17. Discuss women's aesthetic role in Japanese society.

18. Describe the religious traditions of Korea.

19. Summarize the religious heritage of Vietnam.

❋ Suggested Readings on East Asian Religion

Chinese Religion

Ahern, Emily M., *The Cult of the Dead in a Chinese Village*. Stanford, CA: Stanford University Press, 1973. A good introduction based on field research of this very important facet of Chinese popular religion.

Baity, Philip Chesley, *Religion in a Chinese Town*. Taipei: Orient Cultural Service, 1975. A valuable study based on field research in Taiwan.

Bauer, Wolfgang, *China and the Search for Happiness*. New York: Seabury Press, 1976. A brilliant study of Chinese religion and popular culture, emphasizing the role of paradises and other symbols of ultimate happiness; valuable insights into religion.

Blofeld, John, trans. *I Ching*. New York: Dutton, 1968. The most readable translation of this classic.

Bredon, Juliet, and Igor Mitrophanow, *The Moon Year*. Shanghai: Kelly & Walsh, 1927; reprinted New York: Paragon Press, 1966. A report of Chinese religious and traditional customs centering around the festival calendar.

Eberhard, Wolfram, *Guilt and Sin in Traditional China*. Berkeley and Los Angeles: University of California Press, 1967. Analyzes popular morality books and fiction, together with popular concepts of heaven and hell; invaluable for understanding popular Chinese religious concepts.

Fung Yu-Lan, *A Short History of Chinese Philosophy*. New York: Macmillan, 1960. A sound, well-written summary.

Jochim, Christian, *Chinese Religion: A Cultural Perspective*. Englewood Cliffs, NJ: Prentice Hall, 1986. A fine introductory textbook.

Jordan, David K., *Gods, Ghosts, and Ancestors: The Folk Religion of a Taiwanese Village*. Berkeley and Los Angeles: University of California Press, 1972. An illuminating report of field research.

Loewe, Michael, *Divination, Mythology, and Monarchy in Han China*. New York: Cambridge University Press, 1994.

Lopez, Donald S., ed., *Religions of China in Practice*. Princeton, NJ: Princeton University Press, 1996.

Paper, Jordan D., *The Spirits are Drunk: Comparative Approaches to Chinese Religion*. Albany: State University of New York Press, 1998.

Sommer, Deborah, ed., *Chinese Religion: An Anthology of Sources*. New York: Oxford University Press, 1995.

Thompson, Laurence G., *Chinese Religion: An Introduction*. Belmont, CA: Wadsworth, 1969. An excellent beginner's book that integrates all levels and periods of Chinese religion into a unified picture.

———, *The Chinese Way in Religion*. Encino, CA: Dickenson, 1973. A valuable collection of translated texts and studies, with good introductions.

Wolf, Arthur P., ed., *Religion and Ritual in Chinese Society*. Stanford, CA: Stanford University Press, 1974. A collection of anthropological studies on popular religion.

Yang, C. K., *Religion in Chinese Society*. Berkeley and Los Angeles: University of California Press, 1961. Advanced, but a landmark treatment of the sociology of religion in China.

Confucianism

Bahm, Archie J., *The Heart of Confucius*. New York: Harper & Row, 1971. Simple translations of two basic Confucian texts, *The Mean* and *Great Learning,* with an introduction that gives useful explanations for beginners of basic Chinese philosophical terms.

Ch'u Chai, and Chai Winberg, *Confucianism*. Woodbury, NY: Barron's Educational Series, 1973. A useful introduction to Confucian philosophy from an intellectual history point of view.

Creel, H. G., *Confucius and the Chinese Way*. New York: Harper Torchbooks, 1960. A standard book on the life, thought, and influence of Confucius.

De Bary, W. T., *The Trouble with Confucianism*. Cambridge, MA: Harvard University Press, 1991. Essays on this tradition and its ambiguous position in the modern world by a renowned scholar.

Fingerette, Herbert, *Confucius—The Secular as Sacred*. New York: Harper Torchbooks, 1972. A brief but stimulating interpretive essay.

Nivison, David S., and Arthur Wright, *Confucianism in Action*. Stanford, CA: Stanford University Press, 1959. A classic account of how Confucianism worked as the ruling ideology of imperial China's officialdom and educational system.

Taylor, Rodney, *The Confucian Way of Contemplation*. Columbia: University of South Carolina Press, 1988. Innovative exploration of Confucianism as a personal spiritual path, with exemplary study of a modern Japanese master of this way.

Ware, James R., *The Sayings of Confucius*. New York: Mentor Books, n.d. A readable translation of the *Analects*.

Wright, Arthur F., *The Confucian Persuasion*. Stanford, CA: Stanford University Press, 1960. Masterly essays by a leading scholar on Confucianism in various periods of Chinese history.

————, and Denis Twitchett, eds., *Confucian Personalities*. Stanford, CA: Stanford University Press, 1962. A look at Confucianism through essays by various scholars on important or representative figures in its long history.

Yao, Hsin-chung, *An Introduction to Confucianism*. New York: Cambridge University Press, 2000.

Daoism

Blofeld, John, *The Secret and Sublime: Taoist Mysteries and Magic*. London: George Allen & Unwin, 1973. A personal, anecdotal narrative giving a lively picture of the Daoist world.

Bokencamp, Stephen R. *Early Daoist Scriptures*. Berkeley: University of California Press, 1997.

Bynner, Witter, *The Way of Life According to Lao Tzu*. New York: Capricorn Books, 1962. A free but very readable translation of the Tao Te Ching.

Clark, J. J., *The Tao of the West: Western Transformations of Taoist Thought*. London; New York: Routledge, 2000.

Cleary, Thomas, *Immortal Sisters: Secrets of Taoist Women*. Boston: Shambhala, 1989. Discussion and selections from a number of past Daoist women poets and spiritual teachers; a fascinating work.

————, *The Inner Teachings of Taoism*. Boston: Shambhala, 1986. Introductory passages, with discussion, from the world of esoteric and religious Daoism.

Girardot, Norman J., *Myth and Meaning in Early Taoism*. Berkeley: University of California Press, 1983. An excellent scholarly study.

Goullart, Peter, *The Monastery of Jade Mountain*. London: John Murray, 1961. A vivid, atmospheric account of Daoist life in pre-Communist China.

Kohn, Livia, *The Taoist Experience: An Anthology*. Albany: State University of New York Press, 1991.

Lagerwey, John, *Taoist Ritual in Chinese Society*. New York: Macmillan, 1987. Daoism as it functions in modern Chinese society.

Merton, Thomas, *The Way of Chuang Tzu*. New York: New Directions, 1969. A sensitive mystical interpretation of a seminal Daoist thinker.

Rawson, Philip, and Lazslo Legeza, *Tao: The Eastern Philosophy of Time and Change*. New York: Avon Books, 1973. A groundbreaking explication of Daoist philosophy and its expression in religion, art, and symbolism.

Saso, Michael R., *Taoism and the Rite of Cosmic Renewal*. Pullman: Washington State University Press, 1972. A rare scholarly account of Daoist religious ritual, with much insight into religious Daoism.

———, *The Teachings of the Taoist Master Chuang*. New Haven, CT: Yale University Press, 1977. Religious Daoism through the eyes of the modern practitioner.

Ware, James R., *Chinese Alchemy, Medicine, and Religion in the China of* A.D. *320: The Nei P'ien of Ko Hung (Pao-p'u tzu)*. New York: Dover, 1981. Basic works of Ko Hung (Ge Hong); insight into the world of esoteric Daoism.

Welch, Holmes, *Taoism: The Parting of the Way*. Boston: Beacon Press, 1957. The best general introduction to all sides of Daoism.

Buddhism in China

Blofeld, John, *The Wheel of Life*. Berkeley, CA: Shambala Press, 1972. An autobiographical book that offers, through the author's exploration of Buddhist China, rare insights into its manifold variety.

Ch'en, Kenneth, *Buddhism in China: A Historical Survey*. Princeton, NJ: Princeton University Press, 1964. An authoritative introduction.

Welch, Holmes, *The Buddhist Revival in China*. Cambridge, MA: Harvard University Press, 1968. Buddhism in modern China prior to 1949.

———, *Buddhism Under Mao*. Cambridge, MA: Harvard University Press, 1972. A thorough study of Buddhism in Communist society.

———, *The Practice of Chinese Buddhism 1900–1950*. Cambridge, MA: Harvard University Press, 1967. An excellent account of Chinese Buddhism before the revolution; especially good on the actual life of monasteries and temples and on popular devotional practices.

Wright, Arthur F., *Buddhism in Chinese History*. Stanford, CA: Stanford University Press, 1959. A brief, vivid, and reliable treatment of the introduction and assimilation of Buddhism into China.

Religion in Japan

Blacker, Carmen, *The Catalpa Bow: A Study of Shamanistic Practices in Japan*. London: George Allen & Unwin, 1975. A carefully researched and beautifully written summary of Japanese shamanism.

Davis, Winston, *Japanese Religion and Society*. Albany: State University of New York Press, 1992. Essays on various aspects of modern Japanese religion by a leading scholar.

Earhart, H. Byron, *Japanese Religion: Unity and Diversity,* 3rd ed. Belmont, CA: Wadsworth, 1982. A fine introductory text, historically oriented. Excellent bibliography.

———, *Religion in the Japanese Experience: Sources and Interpretation*. Encino, CA: Dickenson, 1974. A useful collection of texts and examples of modern scholarship.

Ellwood, Robert S., and Richard Pilgrim, *Japanese Religion: A Cultural Perspective*. Englewood Cliffs, NJ: Prentice Hall, 1985. A survey of Japanese religion and its interaction with culture.

Hori, Ichiro, *Folk Religion in Japan*. Chicago: University of Chicago Press, 1968. A collection of readable essays by a prominent Japanese scholar.

Kitagawa, Joseph M., *Religion in Japanese History*. New York: Columbia University Press, 1966. An authoritative historical survey, emphasizing the modern period.

Reader, Ian, *Religion in Contemporary Japan*. Honolulu: University of Hawaii Press, 1991. Highly recommended; a well-written and penetrating look at the current Japanese religious scene.

Smith, Robert J., *Ancestor Worship in Contemporary Japan*. Stanford, CA: Stanford University Press, 1974. The best study of this important aspect of Japanese religion.

Buddhism in Japan

Bloom, Alfred, *Shinran's Gospel of Pure Grace*. Tucson: University of Arizona Press, 1965. A highly insightful interpretation of Pure Land Buddhism.

Dumoulin, Heinrich, *A History of Zen Buddhism*. New York: Pantheon, 1963. A standard work, covering this tradition in both China and Japan.

Eliot, Sir Charles, *Japanese Buddhism*. London: Routledge and Kegan Paul, 1959. An older book but still useful as a reference, especially on the various denominations.

Hoover, Thomas, *Zen Culture*. New York: Random House, 1977. An excellent overview of the interaction between Zen and Japanese culture.

———, *The Zen Experience*. New York: New American Library, 1980. Zen through the perspective of its great masters, both Chinese and Japanese.

Kapleau, Philip, *The Three Pillars of Zen*. Boston: Beacon Press, 1967. A fascinating introduction to Zen methods and thought. Contains accounts of modern Zen experience.

King, Winston, *Zen and the Way of the Sword: Arming the Samurai Psyche*. New York: Oxford University Press, 1993.

Machida, Soho, *Renegade Monk: Honen and Japanese Pure Land Buddhism,* Ioannis Mentzas, trans. Berkeley: University of California Press, 1999.

Saunders, E. Dale, *Buddhism in Japan*. Philadelphia: University of Pennsylvania Press, 1964. A useful historical survey.

Suzuki, D. T., *Zen Buddhism*. Garden City, NY: Doubleday, 1956. One of many books by this well-known writer who has successfully communicated much of the Zen spirit to the West.

Shinto

Breen, John, and Mark Teeuwen, *Shinto in History: Ways of the Kami*. Honolulu. University of Hawaii Press, 2000.

Kageyama, Haruki, *The Arts of Shinto*. New York and Tokyo: John Weatherhill, 1973. A well-illustrated treatment that gives insights into some little-known sides of Shinto.

Nelson, John K., *A Year in the Life of a Shinto Shrine*. Seattle: University of Washington Press, 1996.

Ono, Sokyo, *Shinto: The Kami Way*. Rutland, VT: Charles E. Tuttle, 1967. A basic introduction, representing the point of view of a leading modern Shinto scholar.

Pickens, Stuart D. B., *Essentials of Shinto*. Westport, CT: Greenwood, 1994. An excellent guide to Shinto teachings particularly.

Ross, Floyd H., *Shinto: The Way of Japan*. Boston: Beacon Press, 1965; reprint, New York: Greenwood, 1983. A readable introduction, in some places communicating a personal perspective.

New Religions of Japan

Guthrie, Stewart, *A Japanese New Religion: Rissho Kosei Kai in a Mountain Hamlet*. Ann Arbor: University of Michigan Press, 1988. This study of one small religious group in a small village is done in such a way as to give the reader major insights into religion generally in Japan today.

Hardacre, Helen, *Kurozumikyo and the New Religions of Japan*. Princeton, NJ: Princeton University Press, 1986. Study of the oldest of the "new religions," with general theoretical considerations on the new religions.

———, *Lay Buddhism in Contemporary Japan: Reiyukai Kyodan*. Princeton, NJ: Princeton University Press, 1984. A representative study of one Buddhist-based new religion, utilizing careful field research and good sociological insight.

McFarland, H. Neill, *The Rush Hour of the Gods*. New York: Macmillan, 1967. A well-researched, sometimes critical overview of several of the groups.

Offner, Clark B., and Henry van Straelen, *Modern Japanese Religions*. Tokyo: Ruper Enderle, 1963. A careful study emphasizing healing in the New Religions.

Thomsen, Harry, *The New Religions of Japan*. Tokyo and Rutland, VT: Charles E. Tuttle, 1963. A readable basic report on the major new religions.

Women in East Asian Religions

Andors, Phyllis, *The Unfinished Liberation of Chinese Women, 1949–1980*. Bloomington: Indiana University Press, 1983. An excellent treatment of an important period for women in Chinese history.

Arai, Paula Kane Robinson, *Women Living Zen: Japanese Soto Buddhist Nuns*. New York: Oxford University Press, 1998. An important new work.

Bernstein, Gail Lee, ed., *Recreating Japanese Women, 1600–1945*. Berkeley: University of California Press, 1991. A study of economic and religious influences on gender roles.

Chen, Ellen Marie, "Nothingness and the Mother Principle in Early Chinese Taoism," *International Philosophical Quarterly,* 9 (1969), pp. 391–405. An often-cited pivotal study.

———, "Tao as the Great Mother and the Influence of Motherly Love in the Shaping of Chinese Philosophy," *History of Religions,* 14, 1, (August 1974), pp. 51–64. An important work illustrating the value of the feminine in Daoism.

Cole, Alan, *Mothers and Sons in Chinese Buddhism*. Stanford, CA: Stanford University Press, 1998.

Ellwood, Robert S., "Patriarchal Revolution in Ancient Japan: Episodes from the Nihonshoki Sujin Chronicle," *Journal of Feminist Studies in Religion,* 2, 2, (Fall 1986), pp. 23–37. An account of the patriarchal revolution in 300–318 B.C.E. Japan.

———, "The Saigu: Princess and Priestess," *History of Religions,* 7, 1, (August 1967), pp. 35–60.

Iwao, Sumiko, *The Japanese Woman: Traditional Image and Changing Reality*. New York: The Free Press, 1993.

Jackson, Beverley, *Splendid Slippers: A Thousand Years of an Erotic Tradition*. Berkeley: Ten Speed Press, 1997. A well-written account by a textile scholar, photographer, and collector of "Lotus Shoes." This is a beautiful book with numerous photographs.

Hong, Fan, *Footbinding, Feminism, and Freedom*. London and Portland, OR: Frank Cass, 1997. An excellent scholarly treatment.

Kelleher, Theresa, "Confucianism" in *Women in World Religions,* Arvind Sharma, ed. Albany: State University of New York Press, 1987, pp. 135–59. A splendid summary of the issue of women and Confucianism.

LaFleur, William R., *Liquid Life: Abortion and Buddhism in Japan*. Princeton, NJ: Princeton University Press, 1992. A very detailed, well-written, and engaging study of abortion rites in Japan.

Levering, Miriam, "Women, the State, and Religion Today in the People's Republic of China" in *Today's Woman in World Religions,* Arvind Sharma, ed. Albany: State University of New York Press, 1994, pp. 171–224. An excellent summary of the situation.

McFarlane, Stewart, "Chinese Religions," in *Women in Religion,* Jean Holm with John Bowker, ed. London and New York: Pinter Publishers, 1994, pp. 158–67. A good summary.

Nefskym, Marilun, *Stone Houses and Iron Buildings: Tradition and the Place of Women in Contemporary Japan*. New York: Lang, 1991.

Reed, Barbara, "Taoism," in *Women in World Religions,* Arvind Sharma, ed. Albany: State University of New York Press, 1987, pp. 161–81. A useful overview.

Sered, Susan Starr, *Women of the Sacred Groves: Divine Priestesses of Okinawa*. New York: Oxford University Press, 1999. An important new work on one of the few societies where women priestesses predominate in religious life.

Stacey, Judith, *Patriarchy and Socialist Revolution in China*. Berkeley: University of California Press, 1983. A good perspective on contemporary China.

Yusa, Michiko, "Women in Shinto: Images Remembered" in *Religion and Women,* Arvind Sharma, ed. Albany: State University of New York Press, 1994, pp. 93–119. An interesting account.

CHAPTER SIX

One God, Many Words and Wonders

The Family of the Three Great Monotheistic Religions and Zoroastrianism

CHAPTER OBJECTIVES

After studying this chapter, you should be able to

❋ Understand the unique features of monotheistic religions, and their relation to the historical period in which monotheism as we know it emerged.

❋ Discuss the relation of the major Western monotheistic religions to each other.

❋ Understand Zoroastrianism and its influence on the three great monotheistic religions of the Middle East and the West.

The Nature of Monotheistic Religion

Monotheistic religions are those professing belief in one all-powerful and personal God and in no other gods. The largest and most influential of these faiths today are Judaism, Christianity, and Islam, each of which will be discussed at length in the chapters that follow. Zoroastrianism, small today but of profound historical importance in the development of monotheism, will be presented later in this chapter. Here we are concerned with showing how Judaism, Christianity, and Islam are a family, for they all explicitly go back to one source, the experience of the one God of the ancient Hebrews recorded in the Old Testament. The God of Judaism, Christianity, and Islam is the God of Abraham, Moses and the prophets; these fathers in faith are venerated by all three.

There are other monotheisms too: Zoroastrianism, Sikhism, and in a sense bhaktic Hinduism and Amidist Buddhism. Overtones of monotheism appear in the primal high god and in nondualist Hinduism and Buddhism. But Judaism, Christianity, and Islam are a family, and they are uniquely bound together in origin and history. Even their quarrels have the special bitterness of family fights (and never have other religious hatreds and persecutions matched those among and within these three).

Yet, for all their shared past, we find divergences both among and within the three faiths every bit as great as between one of them and, say, Hinduism or Shinto. Thus, the following discussion of the characteristics of the monotheistic traditions may appear full of qualifications, exceptions, and statements that this or that trait is or is not shared by other traditions too. That is because religious life simply is that way. A distinctive belief, such as belief in one personal God, does not necessarily make the religion different in practice all the way through—and different people may experience the same religion in different ways. There is certainly a distinctively monotheistic style of relation to God, a relation of interpersonal awe, love, and obedience unshared by polytheism or mystical monism. But not everyone in a monotheistic tradition is really concerned with that sort of relationship to God or feels one ought to be. Rather, for many the practical and sociological aspects of a monotheistic religion—worship, law, customs, society, mysticism, the institutional structure of leadership and clergy—are what is important.

Within the monotheistic family itself, the messages communicated by the practical and social forms, including art and architecture, could hardly be more contrasting. Compare the Muslim mosque in the Alhambra in Granada with a Spanish Roman Catholic church. The mosque has clean lines, devoid of pictures or images, the worshippers who pray in it having been oriented only by a bare niche in the wall to the direction of Mecca. Yet far from giving an impression of barrenness, the cool, still arabesque interior of the mosque is in an almost indescribable way symbolic of fullness and light. It turns thoughts to God, for all that is not God is expunged; nonrepresentational designs of arabesque fantasy line the walls and dome, raising the mind beyond image to dimensions of meditation where God is pure spirit.

FUNDAMENTAL FEATURES OF ZOROASTRIANISM

THEORETICAL

Basic Worldview	The universe a battleground between good and evil.
God or Ultimate Reality	The good high God, Ahura Mazda, whose adversary is the evil force.
Origin of the World	Made by Ahura Mazda to entrap the evil force.
Destiny of the World	At the end of the age, to be remade as a new, pristine paradise.
Origin of Humans	Made by Ahura Mazda with free will to help trap and defeat the enemy.
Destiny of Humans	Judgment after death, sentence to paradise or hell; resurrection in the new world at the end of the age.
Revelation or Mediation between the Ultimate and the Human	Revelation through the prophet Zoroaster; mediation by priests.

PRACTICAL

What Is Expected of Humans: Worship, Practices, Behavior	To choose the good, do right, keep pure; to maintain the faith by supporting its rites and institutions.

SOCIOLOGICAL

Major Social Institutions	Temples, priesthood, a close-knit community; now mostly Parsees in India.

The traditional Spanish Roman Catholic church also evokes feelings of wonder and awe, but in a very different way. Here one typically is confronted with richness and diversity of forms to rival a jewel box. The altar is a gleaming shape of gold and brocade; and behind it the reredos, or decorated screen, reaches to the ceiling, an ornate waterfall of gilt, lights, and statues of saints. Indeed, images are not exhausted at the altar but continue around the church, each in its own little chapel—sorrowful and bleeding Christs; the Blessed Virgin Mary, Queen of the Universe in imperial crown and robe; St. James of Compostela on his horse; and so on. Apostles, monks, nuns, bishops, kings, each unique yet each part of a larger

Rooftop view of the old city of Jerusalem. On the left is Al-Aqsa Mosque; on the right is the Mount of Olives. ▪

mosaic, suggest that in this church the power of the beam of monotheistic light is shown by the many different colors and forms into which it breaks as it interacts with the world. This faith appears close to polytheism, though it is not that. Yet neither is it the clear, austere monotheism of Islam, whose simplicity, oddly enough, is matched by the rustic grace of many shrines of that most polytheistic of religions, Shinto.

On the other hand, if one were to compare a New England village Protestant church with a Islamic mosque, one would feel, at least, in the same world. Orders of monks and nuns bring Roman Catholic and Eastern Orthodox Christianity closer to Buddhism, in this particular sociological respect, than to most of their Protestant, Jewish, and Muslim neighbors. So we can see that many different grids can be laid over the religious world to produce different configurations of similarity and difference.

Nonetheless, the three monotheistic faiths have common features, both historically and practically. All have their roots in the period of responding to the awareness of history described in Chapter 1. Human consciousness emerged from cosmic religion into a state in which it was apparent that things change and do not change back—that human history is a process in which the new and more complex is always unfolding. This increasing consciousness of history suggests a force, greater than seasonal natural forces, that governs this larger process.

Awareness of history also makes possible monotheism's central pivot in history—the distinctive revelation, prophet, and scripture—which can give meaning to the new and more complicated historical world.

Each monotheistic religion, then, traces itself back to a historical founder, such as Moses, Jesus, Muhammad, or farther East, Zoroaster and Nanak. Monotheism is never a continuation of something growing out of a timeless past, as we saw, for example, in Hinduism. Nevertheless, it may embrace important elements of cosmic religion. The idea of a special revelation through a known historical figure, who at a known point in time gave an authoritative word from the one personal God, which the monotheistic faith proclaims, seems to be inseparable from monotheistic expression.

Thus, monotheism generally has strong roots in the teaching of great individuals. It tends to stress intense individual commitment and emphasis on verbal expression. This means that the written word, scripture, is of great importance in monotheistic religion. While other religions also have constantly studied and chanted scriptures, in the monotheistic religions, scriptures (characteristically short and clear-cut compared with *Vedas* or *Sutras*) are especially decisive statements of law and belief, as well as mystical hymns, monastic rules, and philosophy. They are to be universally proclaimed and are given through the founder, or at least are fruits of a process started by him, at the pivotal moment. Significantly, the **axial age** of the founders of the three great monotheistic traditions also was the time that writing emerged.

In keeping with its linkage to the discovery of history, monotheism is inevitably tied to what we have spoken of as a linear concept of time. While the idea has played different roles in different times and places, Zoroastrianism and the three monotheisms now under discussion have taught that the world was created by God at the beginning of time and is moving toward a climax at an equally definite end: the coming of the **Messiah**, the final judgment, the making of a new heaven and earth. Monotheisms are, in other words, **eschatological**.

Finally, it can be noted that monotheisms arise or become socially important in periods of rapid cultural change; that is, in conjunction with the emergence of national cultures and political institutions—ancient Israel, the Arabs at the time of Muhammad, Christianity in the flux of the Roman world and subsequently providing a cultural focus for the dying Roman Empire and the new European nations. (Of course, other religions that emerged in this era, such as Buddhism and Confucianism, have done this too.) Monotheism, with its idea of a universal God who can legitimatize one sovereign and one law below, helps greatly in a transition from tribalism to nationhood.

But monotheism also, by its own intrinsic logic, is universalist, for if there is but one God with one message, it must be for all people everywhere. This is modified considerably in Judaism, with its idea of the "chosen people" with a special calling by the one God; but even there, the chosen people are to mediate a blessing to all the families of the earth. In Islam and Christianity, monotheism and belief in one revelation have at various times served as an ideological undergirding for the creation of empires uniting many cultures and people—even though systematic

HISTORY OF THE THREE MAIN WESTERN MONOTHEISTIC FAITHS

GENERAL INFLUENCES

Pyramid texts

Zoroaster

Sumerian decline

Egypt and
Mesopotamia
dominant in
Near East

Cyrus
Persian Empire

Trojan War

JUDAISM

Abraham

Moses

Exodus (c. 1290)

Judges

David (r.c. 1000–962)

Solomon (r. 961–922)

Early prophets:
Amos, Elijah

Exile (586)

Jeremiah, Isaiah

Return from
captitivy in
Babylon (538)

Most wisdom
literature

Apocalyptic
literature

CHRISTIANITY

ISLAM

| 2000 B.C.E. | 1500 B.C.E. | 1000 B.C.E. | 500 B.C.E.. |

Alexander
Hellenistic
Culture
Roman Empire

Renaissance
European
preeminence

Byzantine Empire
Feudalism

French & American
revolutions

Marxism

Maccabees (165)
John the Baptizer
Temple destroyed (70)
Talmud

Jewish dispersion
throughout Europe, Asia
& N. Africa

Maimonids (1135–1204)
Zohar (1275)
Kabbalah

Hasidism
Reform
Conservative
Holocaust
State of Israel
(1948)

Jesus (c. 30)
Gospels (60–100)
Paul (d. 62)

Council of Nicaea (325)
Augustine (354–430)

Conversion of Europe

Rise of medieval papacy
Monasticism
Constantine (r. 312–337)
of Eastern Orthodox
and R. Catholic
churches (1054)
Crusades
St. Francis (1181–1226)

Separation

Aquinas (1225–1274)
Medieval
Catholicism
Medieval
"heretics"
Luther (1483–1546)
Calvin (1509–1564)
English Ref. (1534)

John Wesley
(1703–1791)
American
Christianity

Radical Reformers

Muhammad (570–632)
Muslim conquests
Rise of Sufism
Baghdad Caliphate
(750–1258)
Avicenna
(980–1037)

Al-Ghazali
(d. 111)
Al-Arabi (d. 1290)
Islam spreads to India,
Malaysia, Indonesia
Rise of Ottoman
Empire

Sufi orders and devotion
prominent
Growth of Islam in
Africa
Nationalism

| 1 B.C.E. | 500 C.E. | 1000 C.E. | 1500 C.E. | 2000 C.E. |

polytheism can also serve this function. But an international, universal gospel serves especially well as a dynamic for the vigorous missionary expansion of culture. It is usually personal monotheism, then, or a psychologically similar form of Buddhism, such as that of Kamakura in Japan, that strongly missionizes and spreads cross-culturally.

Monotheism is like a river running through religious history. The obscure springs where it arose are located very far back indeed, doubtless with the primordial high god of archaic hunters. The river flows through the fertile lowlands of the inevitable polytheism of archaic agricultural religion, with its emphasis on the marriage of heaven and earth to produce the Divine harvest-child, and of the ancient empires uniting the local gods of many tribes and towns into an organized composite. Even then, however, monotheism glimmered faintly in the usual concept of a controlling universal principle, associated with an often vague but sovereign deity: Tian, Varuna, Amon, Zeus. In the ancient Judaism of Abraham, Moses, and the prophets, the river first emerges as a distinct current: It is then fed by tributaries such as Zoroastrianism and Greek philosophy, and at the same time it spreads out like a delta to form its three main branches—Judaism, Christianity, and Islam. Sometimes these branches flow torrentially. More often they become slow, amiable, domesticated streams and millponds, which coexist comfortably with diverse landscapes of cosmic religion, folk religion, and local culture. But the river never quite stops moving toward a destination.

We will now look at one important example of a monotheistic faith—Zoroastrianism.

Zoroastrianism

Between Mesopotamia and India lies the vast expanse of the land called Persia or Iran. It is a land of paradoxes: nearly empty, yet the homeland of an ancient and immensely creative civilization; forbidding, with its endless deserts and stony mountain ranges, yet a country incomparably important as the transmitter of goods and ideas between East and West. Persia had, and Iran still has, a distinctive and splendid culture of its own. It has given its own gift of the **magi** to the religious world in Zoroastrianism, a faith now much diminished in numbers, but one which has had immense influence both East and West. Even after Persia formally submitted to the Muslim crescent, its ancient faith made rich contributions to the art, literature, and thought of Islam.

Wherever Persian spiritual influence has been felt, Zoroastrianism has given or reinforced three basic motifs: a battle between light and darkness as respectively good and evil; **eschatology** (or emphasis on an end to history) as a Divine judgment and the making of a new purified earth; and the concept of paradise (a Persian word), an ideal heavenly realm with a divine court and abode of the blessed. In turn, these ideas have impelled religion in Persia and elsewhere toward monotheism, ethics, and a sense of the religious meaning of history. These Iranian contributions have done much to move Western religion away from mystical identification with the forces of nature or states of consciousness and toward "ethical monotheism."

Indeed, while the ancient Hebrews believed in one God who judged and punished those with whom he was angry in this life, it was not until after they had had some contact with Persia that such ideas as **resurrection** of the dead at the end of the world, a final judgment, the making of a new earth, and heaven and hell, became important in the Hebrew scriptures. These ideas, all part and parcel of Zoroastrianism, entered the Biblical tradition after the exile of the Judeans to Babylon, from which they were released by the great Persian king Cyrus; thereafter, contact between Jew and Zoroastrian was frequent. Today, ideas like final judgment and heaven and hell are important to traditional Judaism, Christianity, and Islam. The exact nature and extent of Iranian influence on Judeo-Christian eschatology is a matter of scholarly dispute, and other factors such as Greek and Egyptian influence and indigenous development played a part too. But nowhere in the ancient world, prior to late Judaism, Christianity, and Islam, is there an eschatological scenario with the grandeur of the Persian; one cannot doubt its vision would strongly stimulate those who came to know it.

Zoroaster

The prophet Zoroaster (or Zarathustra; before 600 B.C.E.) was a great son of Persia about whom we have little reliable information, despite all the influence he had.[1] It is said that atop a great peak, he experienced a transcendent vision. He saw **Ahura Mazda**, as he named the High God, in all his splendor and glory above and beyond the old gods. Ahura Mazda was accompanied by six Amesha Spentas, Holy Immortals or Good Spirits, angels or perhaps aspects of God himself. Zoroaster understood then that religion reflects an ongoing universal battle. Ahura Mazda and his forces of light are in combat against the legions of **Ahriman** or Angra Mainyu, the evil spirit also called the Lie, and the *daevas* who are in his following. Boldly, Zoroaster gave the dark army the name *daeva,* meaning *deva* or god in the old polytheistic sense. The great battle was a battle of Truth versus the Lie. Ahura is a god of goodness and morality; Ahriman is the Lie. Humans must choose, out of free will, which side they are going to be on.

The battle of good and evil was the most satisfactory way Zoroaster could explain the ill he saw around him. Ahura Mazda, he believed, is only good; therefore he could create only good things and do only good deeds. Like all who wrestle with the problem of evil and find it very hard to explain its coexistence with an all-powerful good God, Zoroaster and his followers had difficulty explaining theologically the relation between Ahura Mazda and Ahriman—whether they are both eternal realities, meaning that Ahura's power is limited; or whether, as many thought, Ahriman is an offspring of Ahura who rebelled against him. But there is no question of the moral force of what Zoroaster was trying to say: We are combatants in a war of ultimate significance and cosmic dimension. No one can be just neutral; in every area of life, day by day, everyone must decide which lord he or she will side with, the Lord of Light or the Lord of the Lie.

Ahura Mazda, we are told, made this present world as a trap in order that his masterpiece, humankind, might ensnare the enemy. Humans are the bait. By drawing Ahriman, eager to tempt and win over humanity, into Ahura Mazda's world and by then freely choosing the good when tempted, humans weaken Ahriman's force and wear him down so that he can eventually be destroyed.[2] Each person, then, is under judgment. Here the eschatology of Zoroastrianism comes in. While Zoroaster himself undoubtedly had strong eschatological ideas, they have been preserved in a later form. That form centers on reward and punishment (although, in contrast to the Judeo-Christian tradition, punishment in hell is not eternal), and on the making of a new world.

Zoroastrians said that on the fourth day after death, a deceased person had to cross the bridge called Chinvat, which connects humanity with the unseen world. The righteous will find it broad as a highway, and they will take it to enter the House of Song, where they will await the Last Day. Yet to the wicked, the bridge will seem narrow as a razor, and they will fall off it into hell.

But on the Last Day, Ahura Mazda will defeat evil. He will purify the entire world and reign over it. All persons will be raised in a general resurrection. The souls of the wicked, having been purified along with the earth, will be brought out of hell with their sentences terminated. All together will enter a new age in a new world free from all evil, ever young and rejoicing.

Just before the Last Day, it was said, Zoroaster would return in the form of a prophet conceived of a virgin by his own seed, stored in a mountain lake. A prophet would in fact appear in this way at 1,000-year intervals during the 3,000 years between Zoroaster and the renovation of the world.

The Zoroastrian priests, or *mobeds (magi),* were great practitioners of magic as well as being profound philosophers. In the days of the Roman Empire (as the account of the visit of several of them to Bethlehem in the New Testament bears witness), they were a byword for astrologers and wizards. Zoroaster himself was accounted a great magician. However, many of those called *magi* around the ancient Mediterranean were probably only from Mesopotamia, where the occult arts flourished mightily. The Parthian Empire, Rome's great rival, ruled the Persian and Mesopotamian regions from 250 B.C.E. to 224 C.E. It was a melting pot of polytheism, Zoroastrianism, Hellenism, Babylonian religion, and teachings from East and West, out of which mystical and esoteric movements bubbled continually.

How widespread or exclusive a religion Zoroastrianism was in this period is disputed. Its heyday as an official, organized religion in Persia was during the Sasanian dynasty (224–651 C.E.). The **Zend Avesta**, the Zoroastrian scriptures, were then compiled. Although they contain the *Gathas,* hymns ascribed to Zoroaster himself,[3] there is much material of a later and more sacerdotal character.

After the fall of the Sasanian Empire, Persia was converted to Islam, and the minority of Persians who wished to remain faithful to the old religion were under pressure. Some—about 14,000—remain in Iran to this day. Others moved to the more tolerant atmosphere of India. Zoroastrians there, now called Parsees ("Persians") and living mostly around Bombay, number perhaps 150,000.

The Zoroastrianism that survives today in India is life-affirming. It says that the world, having been made good by Ahura Mazda, is to be accepted with thanks. One's basic duties are to confess the religion, take a mate and procreate offspring, and treat livestock justly. Asceticism and world negation are not approved. The main places of worship are the clean, attractive fire temples, where a perpetual flame is kept burning as a symbol of the purity of God, being fed five times a day with prayers. Here the scriptures are chanted and other rituals performed.[4]

The faith of cosmic battle and renewal given us by Zoroaster, once the religion of a powerful empire, has now greatly declined in numbers. But no decrease can erase its immense influence on the history of religions, an influence that reaches us today in the great monotheistic religions that arose out of the Middle East—Judaism, Christianity, and Islam.

✹ Questions for Review

1. Discuss the nature of monotheism.
2. Explain why the present great monotheistic religions have their origin in the period of the "discovery of history."
3. Tell why those religions have given an important place to a single individual founder, to revelation in history, and to scripture.
4. Discuss the relationship of Judaism, Christianity, and Islam to one another.
5. Discuss Zoroastrianism and its influence on the great monotheistic religions of the Middle East and the West.

✹ Suggested Readings on Zoroastrianism

Boyce, Mary, *Zoroastrians: Their Religious Beliefs and Practices*. London and Boston: Routledge & Kegan Paul, 1979. Especially good on the medieval and modern thought and life of the religion.

Duchesne-Guillemin, J., *The Hymns of Zarathustra*. Boston: Beacon Press, 1963. Translation of the oldest parts of the *Zend-Avesta*.

———, *Zoroastrianism: Symbols and Values*. New York: Harper Torchbooks, 1970. A short study by a prominent scholar.

Masani, Rustom, *Zoroastrianism: The Religion of the Good Life*. New York: Macmillan, 1968. An account by a modern Parsee Zoroastrian. Idealizing, but offers an unusual view of the religion from within. Easy to read.

Zaehner, R. C., *The Teachings of the Magi*. New York: Macmillan, 1956. An excellent summary, based on a standard catechism of Zoroastrian doctrine.

CHAPTER SEVEN

Keeping Covenant with God in History

The Unique Perspective of Judaism

CHAPTER OBJECTIVES

After studying this chapter, you should be able to

❊ Present the ancient and modern history of Judaism.

❊ Discuss the uniqueness of the Jewish religion.

❊ Explain the importance of practices and observances in Judaism as a way of life.

❊ Discuss attitudes toward and the role of women in traditional and contemporary Judaism.

Jewish Uniqueness

Every religion is unique in its own way. But none perhaps is as distinctive or has as remarkable a history as that of the Jews. Judaism seems always to be the exception to every rule of history, just as Jewish thought or even the mere presence of the Jewish community has so often pointed up the limitations of whatever "universal" truth and practice someone else has tried to lay out. Toward the ancient empires and polytheisms, toward Eastern mysticism and Christian salvationism, toward modern nationalism, dictatorship, Communism, mass culture, and disbelief, Judaism—or at least some segment of Judaism—has always said "Yes, but . . .".

It has not opposed all of these things: Judaism has had mystical systems that compare with those of India, and it also has its share of skeptics, and it has been and is today expressed in nationhood. But it has always been wary of making an "ism" out of them and then saying that mysticism, or skepticism, or nationalism is the end of meaning and truth. Jews have always had a tendency, fired by centuries of living as a minority "different" from the majority culture of whatever nation they happen to be inhabiting, and honed by centuries of hard study of the bristly legal texts of their law, to say, "Yes, but perhaps there's another side. If the majority worldview leaves us out, it's not the complete and final truth."

Star of David

The questions have not always been put verbally. The mere presence of the Jewish community as an all-too-visible exception to a nation's spiritual and cultural homogeneity has stated them more eloquently than words. Needless to say, such questions, whether verbal or implicit, are not always welcome to those who prefer to leave the waters of mystical or cultural unity unruffled. Jewish "differentness" and the awkward queries it implies for others have given Jews much suffering. But they have persisted in making the question felt and have thereby also pressed human society not to settle for partial truths.

Jews have been exceptions from the beginning of the tradition among the Israelites of the Hebrew Scriptures (which Christians call the Old Testament). They were developing toward the monotheism of a personal God while polytheism became richer and richer among their neighbors.

Why this reliance on one God, and finally the belief that he is the only God and sole king of the universe, developed uniquely among the Israelites is hard to say. It may have arisen in part out of the climatic situation of pastoral peoples wandering over the face of the hard desert. The fact that humans are like aliens in these lands, caring for flocks that would die were they not taken to pasture and well by shepherds, suggests that God in the infinite desert sky above guides his people as a shepherd his flock. That the shepherd, like Abraham, sets up an altar and worships the same God in many different places, wherever his wanderings take him, implies that his God is universal, not tied to place or nature like an agricultural deity. (Yet, although the early monotheists were pastoralists, many pastoralists did not become monotheists.)

The traditional Jewish interpretation is simply that God himself, for reasons of his own, selected this people and made himself known to them. This did not mean that he meant to make their life smooth and easy; the call involved heavy responsibilities and frequent suffering. He established a covenant, or agreement, with them that they would worship him, follow his Law, and be faithful to him. On his part God would preserve them throughout history, even to a consummation at the end of history when the meaning of this relationship would be made known. A core, at least, of Jews have maintained this trust. No people so dispersed as they have been for 2,000 years, so much a minority and so persecuted, has ever kept a faith intact for so long.

This faith has not been centered on belief in an afterlife, or an experience of salvation in personal or mystical terms, or a philosophy, or a technique of meditation, or even a set of doctrines. It has been centered on awareness of this unique relationship with God, but it has taken different forms at different times.

The Ancient Story of Judaism

The ancient religion of Syria and Palestine, and no doubt of the earliest Hebrews, was related to that of the major Semitic civilization, the Mesopotamian. These peoples were all Semitic (except the Sumerians) and believed in common deities, like the Great Mother Ashtoreth (Ishtar) and the dying-rising vegetation god Tammuz or Baal. The account in the Book of Genesis tells us that Abraham, father of the Hebrews, came out of Ur in the Valley of the Two Rivers, affirming still more strongly the common cultural background. This is reinforced by many passages in the Hebrew Scriptures, from the obvious parallels between the flood story featuring Noah in Genesis and that of Utnapishtim in Babylon (though the monotheism of the former and the polytheism of the latter afford quite a difference in tone), to the reference in Ezekiel to the practice in Israel of "wailing for Tammuz" (of which the **prophet** much disapproved). The difference was that the Hebrews were originally herder Semites, like the Arab Bedouins of today, in contrast to the more numerous and prosperous sedentary agriculturalist Semites of Mesopotamia and the fertile regions of Syria and Palestine, who worshipped fertility-giving lords of the land such as Baal.

However, the Hebrews—wandering herders originally on the fringes of the great Semitic civilizations—had their own God. They were familiar with Baal, Ashtoreth, and Marduk, for from time to time they must have come into the cities to trade and could not help but notice the massive temples, the powerful priests, the sacred prostitutes. But for themselves, at sacred stones and mountaintops deep in the desert they knew better than anyone else; they worshipped their own God, Yahweh, who was not tied to one place but could be served wherever the tribe wandered.[1] Moreover, he was not pleased with the offerings from the cultivated field but preferred instead the odor of roasting flesh from the herds of his own poor but free people, as the story of Cain and Abel tells us (Gen. 4:3–5).

It was not until most of the Hebrews themselves became sedentary agriculturalists after settling in the land of Canaan (Palestine) that the issue of Baal, Ashtoreth, and the other gods of neighbors became acute. Should the tribes stay with a god of the desert after they had become people of the soil or go to Baal and their kin, whose province seemed to be the agricultural way of life? Many understandably took the latter option.

But there were always those, led by the prophets, who contended that the Hebrews should continue to worship Yahweh even in the new way of life. This was because Yahweh was particularly connected with basic rules of the nation, the Law of Moses, and with inspiration (originally more or less shamanistic in type) that seized the nonpriestly spiritual leaders called prophets. Because they hearkened back to the nomadic period with its simpler ways, the parties favoring continuing loyalty to Yahweh had a rigid, conservative appearance, and the other side doubtless a suggestion of judicious flexibility.

Ironically, the faith in Yahweh had far more future to it and apparently far more potential for adjusting to various cultural levels, from planting to modern industrial life, than Baal. The desert god of the Hebrews lives today, while the Semitic agricultural religion, which seemed the height of sophistication in 800 B.C.E., did not outlive the cultural level it served.

A statement like this is, of course, only one side of the situation. A deity can keep the same name and become different or change names and remain the same. Although the name of Yahweh was kept among the agricultural Hebrews, his worship evolved to include farming feasts and offerings, and these in turn have been retained among Jews long after they became urban.

A fundamental feature of the Hebrew Scriptures is what we have spoken of as a historical or linear concept of time, in which God himself imparts new revelations in history. A picture steadily emerges of the relation between God and the Children of Abraham as a dialogue in which God's faithfulness is constant; but as his people are more or less loyal to their pledge, the situation takes different forms: reward for obedience and punishment for disobedience. It is a history in which God is himself acting and revealing more of himself. The Books of Deuteronomy and Chronicles in particular interpret the history of Israel in these terms, as do the prophets regarding the events of their day. One can think of it as a "graph," with the high peaks representing the moments when Israel was seen as close to God and the low points the periods of apostasy.

The story begins with a very high point, the creation of the world and the placing of Adam and Eve in the Garden of Eden. But suddenly the graph falls to near the bottom as the primal couple disobey God in the matter of eating the forbidden fruit and are expelled from the original paradise. From then on, the dealings of God with the people of Israel are really a part of his plan to bring humankind back to the original high level of the relationship.

The story of Noah, the ark, and the flood tells us that the process began as God exercised judgment toward the fallen world and also mercy, as he saved one righteous family and specimens of the animals, in the destruction of the wicked. But the plan did not really get underway until Abraham and his family were called to leave Ur of the Chaldees, in order to go to a new land that God promised to give Abraham, where he would make of him a mighty nation. This was not for Abraham's sake alone but was part of a plan for the good of the whole earth, for God said "by you all the families of the earth will bless themselves" (Gen. 12:1–3). An ancient city of Ur has been excavated, which may well have been Ur of the Hebrew Scriptures, and it has been verified that there were people called Hapiru (which are thought by some to have included Hebrews) in Ur, a Sumerian capital, before roughly 2000 B.C.E., when it appears Abraham and his people left for the Promised Land by way of Haran, a city in northern Mesopotamia that was a center of the cult of Sin, the moon-god.

This Covenant of God with Abraham was ratified by Abraham's sacrificing to God, and it was confirmed by God's giving Abraham a son, Isaac, in his old age. The promise then passed to Isaac and to his son Jacob, also called Israel, the name by which the Hebrew people became known. Under Abraham, Isaac, and Jacob, the line on the graph clearly moved upward; for all their human failings, a new relationship was being established between God and humankind in the patriarchs. Indeed, the sharp difference between Hebrew religion and some others could scarcely be more evident than in the personalities of the father of faith, Abraham, and his son and grandson. They are not mystics or meditators, magicians, or philosophers, but shrewd, barely literate, sometimes coarse, obscure wanderers on the edge of civilization, who fought and made love and drove hard bargains and (at least in the case of the young Jacob) were not above trickery to get their ends. In the Bible, however, it is not the self-purification or spiritual achievements of a yogi or adept or Buddha that makes one available to God to advance his work.

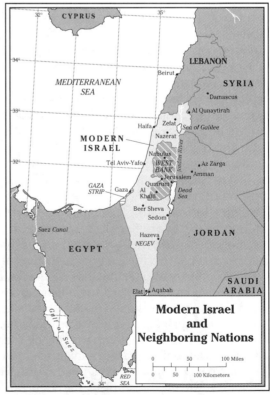

It is rather that the one God, with true omnipotence, is able to reach to the "bottom of the barrel" if he wishes and select whomever he wants, however unpromising.

Very hard times came in the latter days of Jacob, and he went down to Egypt (where Jacob's son Joseph had been taken earlier and risen to power) to try to buy food. But in time the Children of Israel ended up in bondage there, and this was a low point on the graph, for the God of the patriarchs and his worship may have been nearly forgotten.

After 400 years, we are told, this situation was reversed through the labors of Moses, the most outstanding figure in the Hebrew Scriptures. Moses appears as a member of the oppressed Hebrew class in Egypt who nonetheless advanced high in the service of the pharaoh. But he killed an Egyptian he saw beating a Hebrew and was forced to flee to the deserts of Midian (now northwestern Saudi Arabia), where he kept the flocks of distant kinsmen. There God spoke to him in the vision of a burning bush, and Moses returned to Egypt to lead the Hebrew people out of bondage. He succeeded, and the event was fraught with great drama. Moses and his brother Aaron pronounced ghastly plagues upon Egypt to force the pharaoh's hand, culminating in the death of the firstborn, save those of the Hebrews, who marked their homes with sacrificial blood so that this final plague would pass over them. That night, too, they ate a hurried meal in preparation for the flight from Egypt; this is commemorated in the **Passover** (to be discussed more later).

The **Exodus** has been dated to about 1300 B.C.E., although some date it a couple of centuries or so earlier. The narratives of the parting of the Red Sea, so that the escaping slaves could thwart their last pursuers, and of the forty years of wandering in the desert, are well known. At Mount Sinai, in the midst of this trek, the final definition of the covenant, or agreement, between God and Israel was made. Amid the thunder and lightning of a great storm, Moses on the mountain received the Ten Commandments and the rest of the law recorded in the **Torah** (the first five books of the Bible containing the "Law of Moses"). At this point, the line on the graph moves sharply upward.

Moses himself died before he could lead Israel into the Promised Land. This difficult and warlike task was undertaken by his successor, Joshua. Gradually, a nation was put together from an assortment of restless herding and raiding tribes, who were at best a rough democracy under the leadership of the emergent charismatic prophets called "judges." (It must be pointed out here that scholars believe the Book of Judges contains the oldest material in the Bible that can be accepted as history in the ordinary sense. The accounts of the patriarchs, Moses, and the Exodus are of inestimable importance for the Judeo-Christian-Islamic religious outlook and certainly reflect real events, but they reach us in the form of tradition rather than of strictly historical documents.) As the Hebrews adapted to the agricultural way of life indigenous to Palestine, sedentary institutions like kingship came to seem more and more appealing. Finally, it is written that God consented to the anointing of the first king, Saul, though Yahweh expressed only reluctant approval through the prophet Samuel for this development, indicating the conservative nature of the Yahwist and prophetic faith.

Saul, however, proved unworthy of the kingship. He failed to liquidate completely the people and flocks of the Amalek folk, as Samuel said Israel was commanded to do by the Lord. David, who was designated by Yahweh to succeed Saul, began his reign c. 1000 B.C.E. He was succeeded by one of his sons, Solomon.

Under Solomon a great temple to Yahweh was built in which all the ritual prescriptions of the Law of Moses for temple worship could be carried out. From the time of Moses until then, Yahweh had been worshipped in a movable shrine called the **tabernacle**, which contained the written Torah. After Solomon, the kingdom divided into Israel in the North and Judah, around Jerusalem, in the South, and the glory of the people began to decline.

During these times the line on the graph, as read by devout later historians, wavered up and down like a fever chart. In the time of Joshua and the judges, it was presumed that whenever Israel won, the Lord was pleased with them; when Israel lost, it was because there had been sin. But then came the early prophets (such as Samuel, Elijah, Elisha, and Nathan), and after them the writing prophets (Amos, Isaiah, Jeremiah, and the rest), who argued that this was not necessarily the case. The prophets apparently were originally members of a class of seers who entered into some sort of visionary, divinatory trance, not wholly unlike a shaman's, and there gave out the direct word of God for a situation. As in the case of Samuel reproving Saul even as the king stood victorious over the Amalekites, or Nathan reproving David at the height of his glory for having taken Bathsheba, another man's wife, the word of the Lord that came through these envoys could well indicate that God was displeased even when his people seemed successful. It could still happen that they were forgetting the fullness of God's commandments. Even in prosperity, they might, as Amos said, be too much "at ease in Zion" and sell the needy for a pair of shoes.

The low point in this period came in 586 B.C.E., when the Babylonians took Jerusalem, destroyed the temple, and carried off leading citizens to Babylon for a life of exile and servitude. Prophets like Jeremiah blamed this on the failings of the king and nation. When, some decades later (the year 538 B.C.E. is often given), Cyrus of Persia took Babylonia and allowed the exiles to return and the temple to be rebuilt (an event celebrated in Isaiah 40 to 66 and described in Nehemiah and Ezra), it seemed a marvel beyond hope or belief, a victory of God when all was darkest, and is so sung in Isaiah 58:8 and many passages of similar power:

> *Then shall your light break forth like the dawn,*
> *and your healing shall spring up speedily;*
> *your righteousness shall go before you,*
> *and the glory of the Lord shall be your rear guard.*

Or in a Psalm like 126:

> *When the Lord restored the fortunes of Zion,*
> *we were like those who dream.*
> *Then our mouth was filled with laughter,*
> *and our tongue with shouts of joy.*

Yet for all that, the religious experience of Israel was not fully satisfied with the Return from Babylon, for it was also a return, like all such, to the ambiguities of ordinary life in history. There were new problems and new challenges. These were faced by the new temple and, even more significantly, by a new affirmation of Judaism as a religion of the Torah, or Law of Moses, and by new developments in literature and belief. The last centered on a literature of wisdom and the growth of a belief in a Last Day and a Messiah. But first let us look at the story of those times.

From the Second Temple to the Talmud

Some twenty years after the first Jews were permitted to return to Jerusalem by Cyrus the Great in about 538 B.C.E., the foundations of a smaller but nonetheless adequate second version of the temple were laid in the Holy City by Zerubbabel and Haggai. It was completed in 515 B.C.E. But the work of rebuilding Jewish society in the land of Israel—of which the reconstruction of the temple was an important aspect—is epitomized in two men who subsequently were leaders in the religious and political spheres respectively, Ezra and Nehemiah. Each has his book in the Hebrew Scriptures. The promulgation of the Torah, or Law, by Ezra in 444 B.C.E. and the people's assent to it (Nehemiah 8 to 10) is of immense religious importance, for it vividly displays the changes that exile and distance from the site of the temple had wrought in Judaism.* Though the temple was rebuilt, the religion became more and more what it ultimately would become, a religion of **synagogues** ("gathering places"), where worship consisted of prayer and the study of the Scriptures without sacrifices.

Although details are unclear, tradition has it that the text of the Torah and, eventually, all of the Hebrew Scriptures were edited and finalized over these years by an assembly of learned scholars called the Great Synagogue, founded by Ezra. These developments must have been accelerated by exile, when Jews had to make

---

*Most scholars believe that the Law read by Ezra at this time was essentially what is known as the Priestly Code, the legal, ritual, and moral prescriptions contained in the Book of Leviticus and large parts of Exodus and Numbers, or a portion of that code. Much earlier, before the exile, the righteous king Josiah (r. 640–609 B.C.E.) had promulgated a book of the Law, which was probably essentially the Biblical Deuteronomy. Certainly the Law has a long history, much of it now lost, prior to Ezra. But Ezra's recitation and the people's response is of immense importance, for it represents the triumph of the Torah—and so of the Torah's God—as the supreme, unquestioned authority in normative Jewish religion. Before, especially before the purgation of exile, we read much of the admixture of Yahwist religion with various forms of paganism and idolatry. On another level, the charisma of the prophets, profoundly inspiring and disturbing, had reached its height in figures such as Isaiah, Jeremiah, and Ezekiel before and during the exilic era. It had then shared pride of place with the emerging Torah tradition, but now quickly fades also, subordinated to a scriptural text that contained (though in legal rather than poetic form) the Yahwist and Mosaic values for which the prophets had stood and, in time, their own "books." (The poetic tradition was perpetuated in the "wisdom" books of the Bible, such as the Psalms, large parts of which are certainly post-exilic.) After Ezra, we hear nothing of idolatry within Judaism and very little of fresh prophecy. Judaism from this point on was basically the religion of the Torah and its elucidation, and Jewish identity intimately bound up with the life of the Torah.

do religiously without temple rites and were far from their homeland. Instead it was necessary to gather, to pray and to sing what they could recall or had written down, to hear the words of the wise and of the books proclaiming the Law and the words of men of God, to eat and drink and hold festival in accordance with the Law, and to remember. This is the essence of synagogue life to this day. Though the temple was rebuilt, more and more Jewish communities near and far worshipped mainly in the synagogue style, and within a few centuries this form of worship prevailed.

Here is that history. After the Return, the land of Israel remained a province of the Persian empire, locally ruled (no doubt as far as possible under the emerging law) by the chief priests of the restored temple and lay leaders such as Nehemiah, a Jew who had risen high in the civil service and arranged to have himself appointed governor of Judea. In 331 B.C.E., Alexander the Great conquered the Persian empire and, with it, the homeland of the Jews. Alexander's empire, after his early death, was divided among his leading generals, Egypt going to the house of Ptolemy, and Syria to that of Seleucus. Palestine went at first to Egypt but was later transferred to the Seleucids. In 168 B.C.E., the Syrian ruler Antiochus IV, seeking to impose Greek civilization on all his people, desecrated the temple and prohibited the practice of Judaism.

This led to a rebellion much celebrated in Jewish lore. The Maccabee brothers mounted a campaign to drive out the oppressor. Then, in 165, they relit the lamps of the holy temple, a joyous event commemorated in the festival of **Hanukkah** (to be discussed more later). For over a century thereafter (167–63 B.C.E.), Judea existed as a tiny and precariously independent state under first the Maccabees and then their descendants, kings of the Hasmonean house, who increasingly combined high priestly and royal functions in Jerusalem. Rome brought the Holy Land into its empire in 63 B.C.E., ruling sometimes directly, sometimes through client kings such as Herod the Great and his lineage.

During these difficult years, the Jewish religious tradition, based on the now-established Torah, was being consolidated by a succession of distinguished **rabbis**, men such as Hillel, Gamaliel, and those of the school known as the Pharisees. They composed commentaries and case-applications of the law, in part validated by the contention of the Pharisees that there was an oral law given to Moses as well as the written, the former living as Judaism's succession of teachers and giving guidance to their exposition of the latter. These labors were compiled in the **Mishnah** (c. 200 B.C.E. to 200 C.E.), a compilation of stories that fill in the gaps in the oral Torah, and the **Gemara** (c. 200 to 500 C.E.), rabbinical commentaries on the Mishna to connect it to the written Torah; both together make up the great multivolumed text known as the **Talmud**. Jewish scholars prepared out of close argumentation these vast commentaries on the law, which made it both precise and flexible enough to be applicable to the new times in which Jews were more likely to be an urban minority than rural farmers and herders.

Next to the Scriptures, no book is of more importance to Judaism than the multivolumed Talmud. It is a vast and ever-fascinating collection of religion, folklore (**aggadah**), and ethics and jurisprudence (the law, **halakhah**), and it is the text to which all learned Jews instinctively turn first for illumination of the tradition's thought on virtually any issue, though its role is understood differently by liberal and orthodox authorities.*

The new age brought forth other responses too. Jewish tradition divides the Hebrew scriptures into three parts: the Torah; the Prophets, which also includes historical books; and the Writings, containing other books of history, such as Ruth and Esther, as well as the "wisdom" literature (Psalms, Proverbs, Job, Ecclesiastes, and the Song of Solomon). Although the Wisdom Books incorporate much pre-exilic material, they were compiled in their final scriptural form in the days of the Second Temple or even later. These works are often called Wisdom Books because they are primarily concerned with presenting timeless words of devotion, reflection, moral advice, and philosophy. They are remarkably diverse. To one whose view of the Bible is chiefly shaped by those parts concerned with God's law, judgment on sin, or calls to faith, passages in the Wisdom Books may seem amazingly skeptical or speculative.

Belief in the eventual coming of the **Messiah** also has pre-exilic roots, but it flourished most in the atmosphere of extreme alternating hope and disillusionment, and of the precarious national existence that characterized Israel after the Return. Prophetic proclamation of God's judgment led to growing expectation of a final, culminating judgment of the entire world and the making of a new, purified heaven and earth. Related to this idea was the believing hope that, before that great event, a Messiah (the word means "anointed one," because anointing with oil was the way of designating a king in ancient Israel), or sublime hero and king, would be sent by God. He would defeat Israel's enemies and rule in perfect justice and peace. Many expected even nature to be bountiful beyond imagining in the messianic age.

Medieval and Modern Judaism

Just as one sees changes in Judaism from the desert wanderers' religion of Abraham or Moses to the temple of Solomon, spiritual center of a kingdom and of a largely farming society, so has it continually adjusted to new situations through its long

---

*It is important to point out that Jewish Orthodoxy does not mean the kind of direct, unmediated adherence to the scriptural text characteristic of Christian Fundamentalism. Rather (as in the case of so-called Muslim "Fundamentalism," with its insistence on strict adherence to the *shari'a,* the Islamic law developed case by case over centuries by its recognized interpreters), Orthodoxy does not mean individual recourse to the original Biblical Law but acknowledgment both of its Divine inspiration and its legitimate interpretation and application by a recognized succession of rabbis, down to the rabbinical courts operative in Orthodox Judaism today. The findings of this succession are recorded in the Talmud and the later "responsa" of eminent jurisprudents. Rabbinical decisions, like those of any court, are bound to honor and take into account precedent, though variations along accepted lines may be mooted. The "fundamentalism" of Orthodox Judaism, though, lies in the literalistic acceptance of Talmudic and subsequent rabbinical teaching, not directly in scriptural literalism. Though the Hebrew Torah is believed to be literally inspired by God, word by word and even letter by letter, its explication is beyond the power of the unaided individual human intellect and requires the authoritative guidance of the tradition.

subsequent history. As we have seen, there was the destruction of the first temple and the exile to Babylon; but the temple was rebuilt. It was destroyed again by the Romans in 70 C.E., and from then on Judaism survived in **diaspora**—that is, in many widely dispersed communities. During this time, Judaism made its transition to a way based on the home-centered ethical and ceremonial precepts of the Law, without the temple with its bleating animals, its heavy smells of blood and incense, and its richly vested priests. The transition was not as difficult as it might seem, for synogogue practice and study had already taken hold everywhere except in Jerusalem. Pilgrimage to the temple had once been the main bond of worldwide Jewry. Now cohesion lay in the "Fence of the Torah," following the law as interpreted by the Talmud, which gave inwardly, and in the eyes of others, a separate identity in a world of change and confusion. There were other kinds of flexibility, too; Philo Alexandria (first century C.E.), for example, interpreted the Scriptures allegorically in terms of Platonic philosophy.

The "Fence of the Torah" style of Judaism persisted through the Middle Ages and into modern times, as Jews dwindled to very small numbers in their homeland (first ruled by Christians and then by Muslims). But Jews became important minorities in European and Near Eastern cities and spread as far as India and China. When they did not suffer persecution, they generally flourished, and many Jews rose to prominence in Christian or Muslim societies. Their education and diligence, fruits of the careful study that the Law required, were frequently superior to that of their neighbors.

A lone Hassidic Jew prays amid a crowd of schoolboys at the Western or "Wailing" Wall.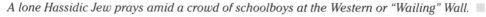

Several new developments colored medieval Judaism. The form of Jewish mysticism called the **kabbala** had its supreme expression in the *Zohar,* or *Book of Splendor,* probably composed within a developing tradition by Moses de León in Spain about 1275.[2] Based on finding deeper, allegorical meanings in the words and letters of the Hebrew Torah that point to metaphysical realities, it held that God in himself is infinite and incomprehensible, but that his attributes provide windows of insight into God as he relates to humanity. As topics of meditation, certain basic attributes of God drawn from the scriptures are arranged into a pattern of male–female polarities and on different levels in the hierarchy of spiritual things called the "kabbalistic tree." Meditation on their dynamic interaction provides a subtle and often profound spiritual path.

Kabbalism had many areas of influence, from magic to messianic movements. The most important is the more popular form of Jewish mysticism called **Hasidism**. This is a pietistic movement that started in Eastern Europe in the eighteenth century through the teaching of Ba'al Shem Tov (1700–1760). Hasidism is a feeling-oriented reaction against rabbinic emphasis on learning and legalism and against stifling social conditions. It teaches Jews to follow the Law but to make it an expression of fervent love for God. (The colorful stories and doctrines with which its venerated teachers explain the meaning of love for God and the symbolism of ritual law are deeply dyed with kabbalistic lore. They emphasize pious love and the wisdom of the person of simple devotion.) Music, dancing, and even uncontrolled ecstatic behavior are frequently part of Hasidic worship. Small but vigorous groups of Hasidic background, such as the Lubavitcher movement, which has done much to encourage a return to Orthodox practice, are still active in Israel and America.[3]

Another strand of modern Judaism, the liberal and rationalistic, has roots both in certain ancient schools and in the thought of the medieval philosopher Moses Maimonides (1135–1204), whose commentaries on the Talmud and law codification made use of Greek philosophy and presented a smooth, logical face to the faith. It was not until the eighteenth-century Enlightenment, however, that this lineage exercised its full influence on Jewish life. Particularly in Germany, Jewish leaders and thinkers, such as Moses Mendelssohn (1729–1786) emphasized acculturation to non-Jewish European life and the critique and defense of Judaism through philosophy. In the end—although this was not Mendelssohn's intention—many Jews in Western Europe became more or less secularized, like countless Christians of the same period, more interested in the mainstream of European culture than the law and the synagogue.

Modern Jewish life is a conflux of several forces. It has been touched by traditional Orthodoxy, Hasidism, and Enlightenment secularization and liberalism, as well as the many cultural milieus in which Jews in *diaspora* can be found. For example, customs and styles of worship of the **Ashkenazi** (Jews from Northern and Eastern Europe) differ from those of **Sephardim** (Jews from the Iberian peninsula) and Eastern Jews. It is influenced also by the bitter effects of persecution in Russia in the late nineteenth and early twentieth centuries, and by a milder but ugly anti-semitism widespread in Europe and America, restricting Jewish participation in many areas of life.

FUNDAMENTAL FEATURES OF JUDAISM

THEORETICAL

Basic Worldview	Universe is made by God but is an arena for humans to live in and enjoy, exercising free will, in cooperation with God's guidance.
God or Ultimate Reality	In traditional Judaism, a sovereign, personal, all-good creator God.
Origin of the World	Created by God.
Destiny of the World	Will be led by God through historical vicissitudes, until finally a messianic age brings it to a paradisal state.
Origin of Humans	Created individually by God.
Destiny of Humans	Chiefly in this world; with Divine help and human cooperation, the human condition can become better and better until a paradisal age is reached.
Revelation or Mediation between the Ultimate and the Human	The scriptures, especially the Torah, or Law, and its traditional interpretation in the Talmud.

PRACTICAL

What Is Expected of Humans: Worship, Practices, Behavior	To honor and serve God by following the Law of Moses in letter or spirit, to maintain the identity of the people, and to promote the ethical vision of the great prophets and humanitarians. Jewish customs are followed in the home as well as in the place of worship.

SOCIOLOGICAL

Major Social Institutions	After the Jewish people as such, the basic unit is the congregation of Jews, forming a synagogue or temple. Jewish family life is also very important.

Most horrible of all Jewish experiences was the Holocaust under Nazism, in which some 6 million Jews perished before and during World War II, and traditional Jewish life in Europe was devastated. All Jewish life since then has been interwoven with sorrowful remembrance of this terrible event and with the attempt to cope with it. It has deeply affected Jewish–Christian dialogue. The determination that it not happen again has immensely strengthened support for an independent Jewish homeland.

Thus, a major force in modern Judaism is the movement known as **Zionism**, which led to the establishment of the state of Israel. Zionism, the effort of Jews to make a national homeland of their own, preferably in Palestine, began late in the nineteenth century as a response to the frustrations of confinement and prejudice in Europe. Palestine, though never without a Jewish community, had been mainly Muslim for 1,000 years and was then part of the Turkish Empire, but European Jews began settling there in the 1890s, often forging out new lifestyles, like that of the agricultural communes called **kibbutzim**. Against all probability, the global vicissitudes of the twentieth century led to the birth of the state of Israel in 1948. This was, of course, just after the Holocaust, and the population of the new nation was enriched by many survivors of that tragedy. They wanted to make it a place of refuge for Jews everywhere facing persecution. Israel includes Jews of all types, from the most secular to the extremely Orthodox and Hasidic. Israel is also a center of Jewish learning. Israel is important today as a cultural and religious focal point for world Jewry; it is also important to many Jews to be able to know there is one small place in the world that is free and definitely Jewish.

Menorah in front of Israel's Parliament.

Judaism in America

Although Jews have certainly experienced antisemitism in America, Jewish immigration provided a reservoir of strength there and they have thrived. Today, America is home to some 6 million Jews—more than contemporary Israel (4.5 million).

American Judaism is not homogeneous but is divided into four main traditions. **Orthodox Judaism** teaches the full following of the law, or Torah, and are quite traditional in Talmudic scholarship, theology, and forms of festival and worship. **Reform Judaism**, which calls its places of worship "temples" rather than "synagogues," has roots in the German Enlightenment experience. It is liberal in attitude, oriented more to the prophets than the Law, and believes the essence of Judaism does not involve following the Law legalistically. Many Reform Jews follow it hardly at all, save for major festivals, though they refer to its underlying principles in thinking about ethical and moral questions. Between Reform and Orthodox is **Conservative Judaism**, which takes Jewish law and history seriously as a guide to life but believes that the Law's provisions can and should be adjusted to suit the conditions of modern living. **Reconstructionist Judaism**, which has roots in humanism and is the most radical in terms of reform, holds that Judaism should be ever-evolving to meet the challenges of the contemporary age, and it rejects "chosenness" in favor of an all-inclusive Judaism.

Today Judaism, like Christianity, is embraced by many as an "American" religious tradition. Politicians, scholars, and others now refer to the "Judeo-Christian" religious tradition of the United States. Therefore, the discussion below of the beliefs, practices, and sociological elements of Judaism reflect American Judaism as much as it does Judaism around the world.

Jewish Beliefs

Judaism is often presented as a religion in which the importance of formal, theological doctrine is minimized. In a real sense this is true. No dogma is as significant to most Jews as adherence to the Jewish community, a relationship many feel better expressed through practice—participation in the **Sabbath** worship, festivals, customs, and observances traditional to the community—and through a living sense of being part of the Jews' long history, than in creedal affirmations. Jewish theoretical and ideological expression, on the part of both theologians and ordinary believers, has accordingly been remarkably free and varied. Practitioners of Judaism as a religion, or as a communal tradition, have ranged from literal believers in God as presented in the scriptures to agnostics and atheists.

Nonetheless, it is fair to say that over the centuries a broad theological consensus has survived among the majority of serious Jews. A conventional touchstone for its delineation has been 13 principles of faith put down by the great medieval thinker Moses Maimonides:

1. God is Creator and Guide.
2. God is One in a unique way.
3. God does not have a physical form.
4. God is eternal.
5. God and God alone is to be worshipped.
6. God has revealed his will through the prophets.
7. Moses is the greatest of the prophets.
8. The Torah was revealed to Moses.
9. The Torah is eternal and unchanging.
10. God is all-knowing.
11. God gives rewards and punishments.
12. The Messiah will come.
13. The dead will be resurrected.

Whether interpreted strictly or liberally, these principles appear to have four main emphases. First, they affirm the existence of a God who is creator and sustainer of the world and who is absolutely one without a second. This expresses the uncompromising monotheism that is Judaism's central religious theme and most distinctive gift to humanity. Second, the principles affirm that this God is an active God, in some way continually involved in human history. He has revealed his will through prophets and scripture in the context of history and is preparing a messianic culmination of history. Third, they affirm the complete religious adequacy of Judaism, its greatest prophet—Moses, and its Torah. Fourth, they powerfully elucidate depth, meaning, and righteous judgment in individual human life, as they affirm that God knows each life thoroughly, bestowing rewards and punishments to each in a manner not fully specified. By speaking of personal resurrection Maimonides avows the eternal significance of each individual life.

Like all creeds, this statement cannot be wholly detached from its historical context. In this case, Judaism lived amid Christianity and Islam. The opening stress on God's oneness, incorporeality, and eternity as metaphysical categories reflects the profound influence of Greek thought on the philosophical expression of all four faiths and so establishes common ground. On the other hand, the principles indirectly distinguish Judaism from Christianity by making no allowance for the Trinity or the Incarnation of God in Christ, insofar as these tenets compromise God's oneness and bodilessness. They also clearly deny both Christian and Muslim assertions that Moses and the Torah were succeeded by greater prophets and more perfect scriptural revelations; and of course they disallow that the Messiah has already come. (Asked about the last point, most Jews will respond that while they much admire the Jew called Jesus as a heroic figure and great rabbi, he was not the kind of Messiah they expected and still anticipate, for after 2,000 years the world is still painfully far from the reign of peace, justice, and abundance that prophecy declared the Messiah's age would bring.)

At the same time, some dimensions of Judaism are not mentioned in the principles. Most conspicuous in its absence is the concept of Jews as a "chosen people" having a special covenant relationship with God. As we have seen in connection with the traditional establishment of that covenant with Abraham, the momentous pact was not made with that patriarch alone but with all his descendants, and it was not for their sake alone but for the blessing of all the human race. For Jews this "specialness" has certainly brought as much or more suffering as blessing by any ordinary worldly measure, though its inner, spiritual worth is immeasurable in such terms. In any case, most Jews are well aware of their peculiar role as the blessers and, often to extreme extents, sufferers of the world, and most religious Jews give this experience special meaning as the product of their Divine chosenness.

The problem of combining existence in historical time, so inseparably intertwined with "chosenness," with Judaism's transcendent monotheism has been a crucial issue in modern Jewish thought. This has been all the more true since recent history has dealt Jews both opportunity and horror to unprecedented degrees—the emancipation of the Jews in early nineteenth-century Europe, the Enlightenment, the movement into the mainstream of Western culture, the immigration to the New World, the massacres and the unspeakable Nazi Holocaust, and the rebirth of Israel as a state. In all this, the God of Israel has been left behind by some, as though irrelevant to such new ways of life or such raw terror. Yet, some would say, never has the heart of Jewish faith been more needed. Here are three examples.

Franz Rosenzweig (1886–1929) insisted that Divine revelation within historical time must be central to any religion that truly revolves around God and is not merely philosophical idealism or moral consciousness. This revelation is a relation between the eternal God and finite, time-bound individuals, a discourse between the Divine subject as (to us) Thou and the dependent and autonomous I.

This "I–Thou" relationship became the key concept of Rosenzweig's friend Martin Buber (1878–1965), who was also heavily influenced by Hasidism. Without diminishing the importance of the Divine–human I–Thou, Buber made the I–Thou concept a keystone of all authentic interpersonal relationships, in which the other is not simply an "it" to be used like an impersonal object, but a "Thou," full of inwardness and subjectivity like that of the "I."

Abraham Joshua Heschel (1907–1972), a Jewish thinker whose ideas often took mystical wing under kabbalistic and Hasidic inspiration, celebrated the holiness hidden in all things and the possibility of an intense, passionate relationship between God and humans. Jewish practices sanctifying the whole of nature and life facilitate both realizations. Yet, as we shall see, Heschel also wrote of Judaism's particular emphasis on the manifestation of the sacred through time, whether in the stream of history or the annual round of festivals and holy days.

We must now turn to such sacred observances in Judaism. Before we leave the company of wise men, however, we might make one final observation: both of the last two, Buber and Heschel, shared to the full the vicissitudes of modern Jewry. Both were raised in the richly traditional, scholarly Jewish culture of Eastern Europe; both were compelled to leave the Europe of Hitler's storm troopers to end their days in two relatively safe havens for Jews—Buber in Israel and Heschel in the United States.

Jewish Life

Let us examine some of the specifics of Jewish life. It should be remembered always that there are various degrees of observance and various attitudes toward the importance of, for example, the dietary laws and strictness of Sabbath-keeping. The differences are not only between the serious and the lax. Jews of equal inner commitment, insofar as this can be gauged, may place the emphasis on different strands of the tradition. (Differences of these kinds are, of course, found between the various traditions of all major religions.)

But throughout all of Jewish life a special chord reverberates. It is made up of a tradition of respect for education, awareness of history, and a sense of being an often-persecuted minority group, as well as the specific festivals, customs, and religious rites of Judaism. The close family and community life of Judaism reflects this tone, through whichever of several possible styles of Jewish life it is expressed. There is always some sense of Jewish identity, too. It has often been commented that every Jew, however nonpracticing and secularized, knows that he or she is a Jew.

The sociological bedrock of Jewish life is the family. With only very few possible exceptions, such as the prophet Jeremiah and perhaps the Essene communities of Hellenistic times, religious celibacy has had no place in Judaism. One of the most consistent themes of all Jewish history, after the theme of being a special called-out covenant people, is that of the holiness of marriage and the procreation of children: a fundamental religious duty for the wisest and holiest rabbi as well as for any other Jew. It is not a concession to the weakness of the flesh but a sacred as well as a joyful way of life and a part of the covenant:

> *The whole world depends on the holiness of the union between man and woman, for the world was created for the sake of God's glory and the essential revelation of His glory comes through the increase of mankind. Man must therefore sanctify himself in order to bring to the world holy people through whom God's glory will be increased. . . .*[4]

It is in the family, then, that religious observances begin. The Sabbath, festivals, and the dietary rules all involve, especially in Orthodox tradition, much more that is done at home than in the synagogue with the community as a whole—the Sabbath meal and prayers; holiday blessings and customs, such as Hanukkah lights and the Passover meal in which the head of the family is the religious leader; the hours spent preparing food according to religious regulation. Beside this, the synagogue is not where religion "happens" so much as where one receives instruction and inspiration to make it happen in its true locus, the home. But under the changed conditions of modern life, the tendency, especially in the more liberal traditions, is to express Jewish identity more through synagogue, temple, or community participation and less through the complicated and time-consuming home actions in their traditional forms. Even so, it must be emphasized that the

The bride and groom under the chuppa, *or wedding canopy.*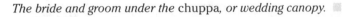

home can still be a place where Jewish identity in its moral and cultural meaning is learned and deeply felt.

The cornerstone of Jewish practice is the observance of the Sabbath. This period of twenty-four hours from sunset Friday to sunset Saturday commemorates the Lord's day of rest after the work of creation, and it is intended for the rest and refreshment of both body and soul. On the Sabbath no work is done, and there is feast and celebration and nourishment for the body and mind and soul at the table and the synagogue. Far from being an onerous burden or a time of negative prohibition, the classical Jewish literature sees the Sabbath as a bountiful gift to God's people, as a lovely bride to be welcomed with eager love.[5]

Traditional Sabbath observance begins with concluding one's ordinary business, bathing, and putting on fresh garments reserved for that festive day on Friday afternoon. After sundown, the previously prepared Sabbath meal is eaten, with traditional Sabbath dishes and prayers and blessings over the food and the full cup of wine.

On the next day there is public worship in the morning and late afternoon. Synagogue or temple worship consists basically of reading from the Torah and the other scriptures, prayers, and chants. But the atmosphere of the worship varies considerably from one tradition to another. In Orthodox synagogues, men and women remain on separate sides; the liturgy is in Hebrew; and the preservation of many ritual customs, as well as in some cases a certain Hasidic exuberance expressed, perhaps, in swaying or dancing to the music, tells us that this is the Judaism most in continuity with that of Old World Europe. In Reform temples, the service will be plain and dignified, with more emphasis on the sermon. Conservative synagogues will follow a middle course. However, Reform and Conservative worship, like that of some once-staid Christian churches, is today in a new way discovering the Jewish heritage of lively music, dance, and chant, especially in services for young people. Reconstructionist services generally adhere fairly strictly to tradition, while, at the same time, being the most liberal of the Judaisms in content.

The most important object in any Jewish place of worship is the Torah, the scroll of the law, in its large ornamented box, called the Ark, at the front of the hall. A lamp continually burns before it. Opening the door and curtains in front of the Torah and finally removing it from the case for reverent reading are major actions in the drama of the service.

Festivals and Practices

Besides the regular Sabbath worship, the Jewish year is marked by several festivals. Although not really as important as the weekly celebration of the Sabbath (only the Sabbath is mentioned in the Ten Commandments), many Jews today observe the **High Holy Days** (Rosh Hashana and Yom Kippur) and the Passover. The holidays can be divided into three groups. Because they follow the partially lunar Jewish calendar, the dates (like that of the Christian Easter) vary from year to year.

First are the High Holy Days, or "Days of Awe," which come in the autumn. **Rosh Hashana**, literally "Head of the Year," is kept as the anniversary of the creation and is the Jewish New Year's Day. Then, after a sacred season of ten days for repentance, comes **Yom Kippur**, the Day of Atonement. It is said to be the day when God reckons up the sins of every person for the previous year and, accordingly, sets their fate for the coming year. For some Jews, God's reckoning is only a metaphor, but it nevertheless sets the tone of Yom Kippur, a day when Jews assess themselves in their hearts and determine how to amend their lives. The customs of the day create a backdrop for this inward strife and turning: fasting for 24 hours and a daylong synagogue service full of haunting, dirgelike music and corporate confession.

Three happier festivals are basically grounded in the agricultural society of ancient Israel and fit the seasonal cycle of all archaic agricultural religion, yet also have meaning as commemorating the mighty acts of God on behalf of Israel recorded in the Bible. They orient the believer to God's work both in nature and in history. These are Passover in the spring, **Shavuot** in late spring or early summer, and **Sukkot** in autumn.

The Passover, or *Pesah,* recalls God's sparing, or "passing over," the firstborn of the Israelites and the hurried meal that the Israelites ate before leaving their enslavement in Egypt for the great events of the Exodus, the parting of the Red Sea, the receiving of the law at Mount Sinai, and the entry into the Promised Land. An impressive family rite, the Passover meal, or **seder**, with its traditional foods (the paschal lamb, which is not actually eaten but is like a sacrifice; unleavened bread; roasted egg; vegetable; bitter herbs; wine; and so forth) and the questions and answers between the youngest son and the father concerning the meaning of the symbols, is deeply loved in Jewish homes and is the Jewish holiday best known to Christians because of its association with the death of Jesus.

Shavuot, or Pentecost, seven weeks after Passover, was anciently a harvest festival for grain and is also commemorated as the anniversary of the giving of the law on Mount Sinai. Traditional Jews mark it by all-night study of the Torah, and it is a customary time for religious confirmation and graduation exercises.

Bright and colorful Sukkot is the autumn harvest festival for fruit and vegetables. When possible, booths are set up on lawns and in temples, gaily decorated with apples, pomegranates, gourds, corn, and the like. The booths are covered with straw, boughs, or palm fronds but with spaces so that one can see the stars. People eat, study, and sometimes sleep in them. Like so much of Judaism, it is the sort of religious rite that children find exciting and unforgettable.

Finally, there are several minor holy days. Two of them are Purim and Hanukkah. **Purim**, in February or March, commemorates the story recounted in the Book of Esther: how the Jews were saved from the wicked designs of Haman, chief minister of the Persian king, by Esther the queen and her cousin Mordecai. Like Mardi Gras or carnival in Latin countries, which comes at approximately the same time, Purim is the time when religion gives sanction to the role of comedy, buffoonery, and "letting go" in human life. Tradition says one may drink until one cannot tell the

Woman lighting candles before a Passover seder. ▪

difference between "Blessed be Mordecai" and "Cursed be Haman." During the reading of the story in the synagogue, children gleefully make a tremendous racket with noisemakers whenever the name Haman is spoken. Strolling players and schoolchildren perform farces in which solemn rabbis and elders might be spoofed most of all.[6]

Hanukkah comes at about the time of the Christian Christmas and has become popular in America partly as a result of this association. It commemorates the rededication of the temple in Jerusalem in 165 B.C.E., as we have seen. The event is too late even to have been included in the Hebrew Scriptures, although the Books of Maccabees do appear in the Roman Catholic Bible and in the "Apocrypha" of some Protestant versions. The celebration is simple and is carried out in the home. An eight-branch Hanukkah **menorah**, or candelabra, is lit, and a Hanukkah song sung, over an eight-day period. On the successive nights cakes and gifts are presented to the children.

Jewish boys undergo certain rites of passage: circumcision, performed as a religious act, when eight days old; **Bar Mitzvah**, when the boy reads from the Hebrew scriptures and begins the entry into manhood. In America, the Bar Mitzvah has often become the occasion of gala celebrations. In the Conservative, Reform, Reconstructionist traditions, and to some extent in the Orthodox tradition, a parallel festival for girls, the **Bat** (or **Bas**) **Mitzvah**, has been introduced. Reform Judaism also has a confirmation rite for young people of high school age, when commitment to the faith is expressed.

The Jewish dietary laws have had an immense role over the centuries in keeping the faith alive and its people together, for the rules of food preparation are so exacting they make it almost a practical necessity—if they are to be kept—for one to eat with, and therefore live in and marry within, his or her own community. Today, however, their observance varies. Some follow them minutely; some give them only token honor such as the refusal to eat pork; some feel they are entirely irrelevant to the modern world and observe them not at all.

No restrictions govern food from plants; the law deals only with killing and eating conscious life. The basic rules are that animals eaten must have a split hoof and chew the cud; this includes cattle and sheep but excludes a vast swarm: swine, reptiles, elephants, monkeys, horses, and all carnivorous beasts, among others. Of sea creatures, only those with fins and scales may be taken; birds of prey and insects are forbidden. Furthermore, meat must be slaughtered and prepared in special ways to be **kosher**, or edible by those keeping the dietary rules. The rules also forbid the eating of meat and dairy products together and expect that separate pots and plates will be used for each. The keeping of two sets of dishes (and a third for Passover) is a sure sign of a quite traditional Jewish home.

The tradition also requires men to pray morning and evening and to give time to Torah study.

In all these observances we see again that Judaism is not primarily oriented toward doctrine as its basis; one finds that ideas about God and such matters as the afterlife vary immensely. Yet the Jewish faith continues to be intensely felt as a way of life here and now. The reason may be that it is oriented toward time and history, rather than eternal ideas, as the source of human meaning and obligation. The law is important because it comes out of past history and now controls present time, making time holy through demands on how it is spent and how biological events in time are sanctified. In turn, the Jewish hope of salvation is chiefly oriented toward future time. The tradition affirms that God will, in his time, send the Messiah, a hero heir to the greatest kings and prophets of old but greater than they, and in his day and through his work all evils on the earth will be rectified and an era of joy initiated. Some interpret this hope literally; others figuratively, in terms of a "Messianic Age."

Judaism is a religion whose centers of value are in time: tradition out of the past and hope for the future. We are beings in time and history, and we are to look to the tradition and our hopes, rather than to new revelation or mysticism alone to find what we need most to know and believe to live this human life as it is meant to be lived.

Women in Judaism

Women in Traditional Judaism

Judaism, throughout its long history, has exhibited a certain ambivalence toward women. On the one hand Jewish women, as wives and mothers, have been celebrated, some say even glorified, in Jewish tradition. Judaism's texts and traditions extol outstanding women as charismatic luminaries, heroines, intellectuals, devoted wives and daughters-in-law, and leaders. Two books of the Hebrew scriptures are named after the exemplary women whose lives they recount. On the other hand, texts and traditions at times also reveal a profound suspicion of women and their sexuality, resulting in restrictive rules and disparaging pronouncements ("The uterus is a place of rot"[7]). And perhaps worse, because education was the purview of men, men traditionally have been the rulemakers and the keepers of the records. This has led to an androcentric perspective resulting in the failure to account for many aspects of women's lives at all; thus, the rules reflect a concern only with the places in which women's lives intersect with men—marriage, divorce, sexuality, the birth of offspring. Other than this, women, in effect, are invisible in the texts. Accordingly, the rules do not deal with such things as relationships among women.[8]

Perhaps unique to the Jewish tradition, however, is its apparent refusal to pin down one idealized conception of womanhood. While Proverbs 31 sets out the characteristics of an ideal wife, the Hebrew Scriptures provide accounts of women who have been significant participants in the unfolding of Jewish history in other ways.[9] For example, the Book of Judges tells us of Deborah, who, in addition to being a wife, was the "judge" of Israel at the time of the account (that is, she was one of a succession of prophets and charismatics who guided the people of Israel). She was instrumental in Israel's success in a significant battle, having advised a military leader before and during the battle. In later lore (*aggadah*) there are stories of clever, saintly, and wise women.

Nevertheless, it is the role as wife and mother that takes center stage for women in traditional Judaism, and most of the traditions regarding women revolve around her role in the home. In particular, Jewish women's fertility was fundamental to her worth. Indeed, the greatest blessing and duty for the husband and wife was the bringing forth of children, particularly sons, to continue the patrilineal line. But this could be a two-edged sword for women because, while the birth of children was a blessing, it was believed that barrenness meant that God had judged a woman harshly,[10] and the failure to bear children was grounds for divorce.

Still, Judaism, at most times in its history, has offered women a greater role than many other traditions. Although their main province has been the home, Jewish women have rarely been restricted to the house, as we see in some other religious traditions. On the contrary, the traditional ideal Jewish wife is industrious in obtaining provisions for the home, strong and capable, and involved in buying and selling in the marketplace in addition to more generally recognized vocations for a wife, such as weaving, sewing, and providing food for the family.

Moreover, a good wife is every bit the blessing for her husband that Eve was for Adam in Genesis. As it says in Proverbs 31:

> What a rare find is a capable wife!
> Her worth is far beyond that of rubies.
> Her husband puts his confidence in her,
> And lacks no good thing,
> She is good to him, never bad,
> All the days of her life.[11]

And the Talmud, which generally advocates moderation, admonishes the husband to spend beyond his means when it comes to his wife and children.[12]

Yet, from ancient times to the present, maleness has been praised while femaleness is discounted. Again and again the importance of the birth of a male child is emphasized, while the birth of a daughter is not even mentioned in the Hebrew Scriptures and is lamented in the Talmud, which includes in a traditional blessing: "[B]less thee with sons, and keep thee from daughters because they need careful guarding."[13] Perhaps most telling of this attitude is the daily prayer recited by traditional Jewish men:

> Blessed art thou, O Lord, our God! King of the Universe who hath not made me a heathen.
> . . . who hath not made me a slave.
> . . . who hath not made me a woman.[14]

These attitudes have been reflected in other aspects of Jewish tradition as well, resulting in the secondary status of women. The laws given by Yahweh to Moses at Sinai (Genesis 20 and 21), and the story of the Levite's concubine (Judges 19), indicate that in ancient Judaism women were considered men's property and not persons in their own right*—a disposition that has had an impact on later attitudes toward women.[15] For example, in Jewish tradition the marriage of a woman to her husband is the transfer of the father's rights in the woman to the husband.[16] Further, the Talmud, the most influential book regarding the status of women in Judaism, is replete with suspicions and superstitions regarding women. One

---

*The story of the Levite's concubine (second wife) is one of the most disturbing stories in the Hebrew scriptures. It is often cited by Jewish and Christian feminists as one of several passages exhibiting a disregard for the humanity of the women portrayed in the Bible and evidence of women's extremely low position in society at the time. The Levite (of the Levi tribe) was traveling with his concubine and was staying in the home of a man who had provided them shelter. While resting there, some men came and threatened the Levite, whereupon he threw his concubine out to them as an appeasement to be abused sexually by them through the night. In the morning, the Levite, her husband, found her dead on the doorstep. This incident was the catalyst for a fierce battle against those who had committed the outrage, but it is clear that the outrage was the offense against the Levite rather than the concubine in her own right. Thus, there was no condemnation of the husband for having thrown her out to the malefactors to a horrific death.

example is the belief that women are prone to sorcery. This reflects the view that women are dangerous if permitted to function outside the accepted institutions as independent persons. Therefore, women are deemed "holy" or "sanctified" when married and potentially "unholy" or "impure" when not.[17]

The emphasis on purity is also reflected in **niddah**—the rules regarding menstruation. These address the taboos that we have seen in other religious traditions regarding the avoidance by men of the blood of menstruation and childbirth. Some of the rituals and regulations concerned with these taboos (which involve avoidance of sexual contact and prohibiting women from entering the temple during proscribed times, as well as ritual cleansings) still are observed today in Orthodox Judaism.[18]

Significantly, the Talmud provides 613 obligations for men, including the obligation to appear at temple and to study the Torah. These obligations relate to the covenant with the God of Israel and reveal the many places in which a man's life touches the sacred. Yet, only three obligations apply to women: lighting the candles for the Sabbath celebration, breaking of the Sabbath bread, and observing *niddah*. Accordingly, women are not required to attend temple services nor to study Torah, because these things are thought to interfere with a woman's first obligation to fulfill her duties as wife, and, significantly, her involvement in them is not necessary for the fulfillment of the covenant with God. The result of this has been a general tendency to exclude women from study and limit their participation and attendance at temple—those things that are the sacred centers of Judaism. As the Talmud says: "A woman may not read from the Torah because of the honor of the congregation."[19] And even when women were included in temple worship, they could not be counted in the *minyan* (the quorum of ten required for public worship). Of course, with such limitations, women were not considered for leadership roles in the synagogue and were not ordained as rabbis.

In traditional Judaism, marriage is a pivotal event for the immediate family, as well as the entire community, as the family is the basic component of the Jewish social structure.[20] The marriage is a contractual arrangement between the man and woman set down in the **ketubah** (the marriage contract). But this not only has legal significance, it also is a profound religious commitment that is analogous to the covenant of Yahweh with Israel. Moreover, unlike in some other religious traditions we have seen, in Judaism sexuality is embraced as a gift from God, and is to be enjoyed fully in the marital union as God's purpose. This sentiment is nowhere more beautifully expressed than in the Song of Songs of the Hebrew Scriptures, where mutual passion is glorified as analogous to the relationship of Yahweh to Israel, which, as Denise Lardner Carmody has said, "places sexual passion near the heart of the covenant."[21]

> *O that you would kiss me with the kisses of your mouth!*
> *For your love is better than wine,*
>
> *your anointing oils are fragrant,*
> *your name is oil poured out;*
> *therefore the maidens love you.*

Draw me after you, let us make haste.
The king has brought me into his chambers.
We will exult and rejoice in you;
we will extol your love more than wine;
rightly do they love you.

Nevertheless, traditionally, while the woman's consent was required for marriage, divorce has been allowed only upon the husband's action (although at certain times and under certain circumstances the wife's consent has been required). Grounds for divorce included such things as the woman's adultery (although tradition had it that the wife could not accuse the husband of adultery), childlessness, vociferousness, indiscretion, or immodesty. Only the husband could prepare and deliver the *get* (bill of divorce). The wife's only recourse should she want a divorce was to persuade her husband to divorce her. When a wife had good grounds for wanting a divorce (for example, the husband's impotence, his refusing sex or staying away from home too much, and severe illness, such as leprosy), the rabbi would be prevailed upon to persuade the husband to divorce his wife, and sometimes the full weight of the Jewish courts would be brought to bear to this end. Unless the wife was involved in a scandal (which usually involved some breach of law or custom, such as not covering her head in public), she would be paid the amount set forth in the *ketubah* as the marital settlement. Once divorced, the man and woman were permitted to remarry others.[22] These traditions are still the practice in Conservative communities today and are enforced by Orthodox religious courts in Israel.

A very difficult situation for a woman is to become an *agunah*—a woman who is not free to remarry either because her husband refuses to provide the *get* or he disappears. This has been a considerable problem for Orthodox women whose husbands have not been accounted for after wars and, more recently, after the Holocaust. Unless a wife can find two witnesses (who must both be men, because women are not permitted to appear as witnesses in court), she is never free to remarry.

Jewish Women Today—Modernity and Feminism

While, as in all religious traditions, women participated in ways unrecognized and unrecorded by the authorities, the Jewish tradition we have outlined prevailed as normative into the nineteenth century when modernity began to have an impact on Jewish culture. When the Jews were emancipated in Europe in the early nineteenth century, there was a move in some quarters to harmonize Jewish faith with reason and ethics. The encounter with Enlightenment ideas, such as democracy and pluralism, and the concomitant development of the notion of civil rights, caused Jews to reconsider the role of women in Judaism.[23]

Out of this ebullition of ideas arose Reform Judaism, which championed women's rights. In 1846, at its Breslau Conference, Reform Judaism spoke out for women's equality—an idea that began a slow unfolding into practice. Gradually attitudes toward women shifted, and the door to greater participation of women began to be opened. Finally, after much debate and obstruction by more conservative forces within the ranks, Sally Priesand became the first publicly ordained woman rabbi in 1972.[24] Today there are women ordained as rabbis and cantors in Reform, Conservative, and Reconstructionist Judaism. Although Orthodox Judaism still does not ordain women, it now permits and encourages their study of the Torah.

Since the 1970s, Jewish feminism has had a considerable impact on the reform of traditions affecting women, and Jewish feminism is now found in every branch of Judaism. Feminists have challenged *halakhah,* pointing out its reflection of historical androcentric biases.[25] They have also unearthed evidence from early Judaism that reveals that some of the practices thought to be age-old traditions—e.g., the separation of women and men in the temple—do not derive from Judaism. Rather, they are practices assimilated from surrounding cultural contexts. Feminists have questioned assumptions regarding the perception of "masculine" and "feminine" roles in Jewish tradition. Moreover, they have sought equality not only in being able to participate in ways that traditionally have been the exclusive domain of men, but also by raising to consciousness the particular ways in which women approach the religious life, perhaps transforming Judaism in the process.[26] Further, they have challenged the use of male-gendered language to describe God, asking: If God is gender-neutral, as traditional doctrine holds, why do we refer to God as He?[27] And Jewish feminists have pointed out that using male metaphors to represent God sets up an impossible situation for women: "If God is male, and we are in God's image, how can maleness not be the norm of Jewish humanity?"[28] Women, and progressive men as well, have worked to reform the language of the liturgy so that it is gender-inclusive.[29]

Jewish feminists have begun a revalorization of the feminine to counter negative stereotypes and unfounded suspicions regarding women found in traditional texts. Some have begun to emphasize the feminine images of the Divine, readily accessible in the mystical tradition, which can be found in Jewish texts and traditions—**Shekhinah** (the spirit of God at the Sabbath, which is feminine) and Wisdom (imaged as female and present with God at the beginning of creation). Women have found that there is much on which to base the equal dignity of womankind with mankind. One example is the Genesis account of creation in which God creates both man and woman in His image and does not blame the Fall on Eve alone as later interpretations would have it. Another is the tradition that one could not be "born" Jewish unless one's mother is Jewish regardless of the father's religious heritage.

In addition, women also are revising old rituals and creating new ones. Now, as we have seen, girls in many synagogues, just as boys, have a rite-of-passage ritual—the *Bat* (or *Bas*) *Mitzvah.* In addition, the wedding ceremony has been revised. Whereas in the traditional ceremony only the males spoke, the revised ceremony includes statements by the bride. More progressive women have begun to create new rituals for other passages in women's lives: childbirth, naming baby girls, marking menopause, and so forth.[30]

But reform has not been an easy task because, as we have seen, the Jewish tradition itself is grounded in a patriarchal pattern of social relations and values.

Jewish feminists must then face the question: How do we transform tradition and still maintain Jewish identity and community? This question has been answered by various feminists in several ways in the distinct branches of Judaism, and inroads have been made by uncovering androcentric biases, reinterpreting texts, including women's experience, and reconstructing Jewish law and tradition by challenging traditional attitudes toward women.

Many in Orthodox and Conservative Judaism contend that Reform and Reconstructionist Judaism have gone too far, resulting in an obscuring of the tradition (although the range of practices among Conservative Jews is quite large, and Reconstructionist practice can be traditional in its form). More important, there is concern among some traditionalists that Jewish feminist critique ultimately is a secularizing force that detracts from the Jewish tradition's religious significance.

Still, the most progressive feminists say that the reforms we see today are only a beginning, and such feminists challenge the patriarchal structure itself, which they say permeates the tradition, making it unwelcome to women.[31] They point out that Judaism traditionally has envisioned its people as "Jews" (i.e., men) and "Other" (i.e., "other than" the norm—that is, women).[32] Thus, Rachel Adler argues, in her article entitled "The Jew Who Wasn't There," that women have been peripheral in Judaism at best.[33] This, Jewish feminists say, must change. As Judith Plaskow has said:

> Once we begin to see women as a class, and gender as a central category for the analysis of any culture or tradition, we are bound to break out of a system which renders women's status invisible. At this stage, in any case, a feminist Judaism must insist on the importance of women's experience and, thus, on shaking up the categories and processes of Jewish life and thought.[34]

Such feminism seeks not only to reform tradition but to re-form it, making it accessible to relational models of leadership rather than hierarchy, and unity rather than separation and distinctions. Yet, the conservative question is not without merit: When is the re-formation so counter to tradition that it results in something that is no longer Judaism at all? This question and the feminist challenge continue to be salient for Judaism in the twenty-first century.

✸ Summary

The pioneers of the tradition of the great monotheistic faiths were the ancient Israelites, the people of the Old Testament. Their self-understanding as a people with a covenant relation to God, who was leading them for his ultimate purposes through suffering and success in historical time, gave them a special attitude toward God and history and a scripture to interpret it. The Hebrew Scriptures contained the Torah, or Law of Moses—its first five books—giving the commandments God had given the people to set them apart and to reveal the covenant relationship; histories, showing the course of the relationship with God; prophetic books, giving the proclamations of Divine spokesmen of what God says in particular situations; and wisdom books, with timeless poetry and philosophy from out of this historical experience.

The center of worship was the temple in Jerusalem. But around the beginning of the Christian era, because of the dispersal of the Jews and the destruction of the temple, worship and learning came to be centered around the synagogue, a gathering of the community for prayer and study. In the Middle Ages, Jews experienced widespread dispersion throughout Europe (*diaspora*), where they were sometimes prosperous and sometimes persecuted. The mystical philosophy called *kabbalism* arose. Since the beginning of modern times in the seventeenth century, Judaism has seen the rise of the popular mysticism called Hasidism in Eastern Europe, trends toward rationalism and secularism in response to the Enlightenment, persecutions culminating in the Holocaust during World War II, further dispersal through immigration, and Zionism—the successful movement to create a Jewish state in the Holy Land.

Judaism has the highest regard for marriage and the family; ideally, Jewish religious life revolves around the home even more than the synagogue. Its chief expression is the Sabbath with its special observances. The High Holy Days and festivals are yearly landmarks of faith. Jewish distinctiveness and faith are also shown through the rites by which persons are brought into the adult community and among some by following dietary laws.

American Jews are divided among Orthodox, Conservative, Reform, and Reconstructionist schools of interpretation. All have in common a sense of a unique Jewish experience and mission in the world and an emphasis on the sacred importance of time and history.

Traditional Judaism has reflected an ambivalent attitude toward women. On the one hand, it glorifies women as wives and mothers, and it recounts the lives of exemplary women and their contribution to Jewish history. On the other hand, it reveals an underlying distrust of female sexuality and independence, which has led to the traditional subordination of women to secondary status in the Jewish community. Enlightenment ideals of modernity and the feminist movement since the 1970s have had a profound impact on Judaism as a whole, particularly with respect to a change of attitudes toward women's equality with men. The question of whether and to what extent Jewish tradition can be transformed and still maintain Jewish identity and community is one of the most significant questions facing Judaism in the twenty-first century.

✸ Questions for Review

1. Show how Judaism has produced both traditionalist and innovative expressions and has shown in various movements both feeling-oriented and rationalistic approaches.

2. Interpret the meaning to Judaism of the Jews as "chosen" or covenant people.

3. Discuss the Jewish Scriptures (Old Testament) as a drama of the relationship of God with humanity.

4. Summarize the history of Judaism from the second temple to the Middle Ages and the emergence of the Talmud, the synagogue, and the rabbinical tradition.

5. Cite the main features of medieval Judaism, such as its dispersion and kabbalistic thought.

6. Cite the main features of modern Jewish history: Hasidism, the Enlightenment and Jewish responses to it, immigration to the New World, persecution and the Holocaust, and Zionism.

7. Discuss basic Jewish beliefs and the perspectives of important modern Jewish thinkers.

8. Talk about the meaning and role in Judaism of the family, the Sabbath, the High Holy Days and festivals, and the dietary laws.

9. Discuss initiation into Judaism through circumcision and the Bar Mitzvah.

10. Interpret the meaning of Judaism as a religion oriented toward time.

11. Think about how the traditional views of women in Judaism resulted in their secondary status, while still glorifying women as wives and mothers.

12. Consider the ways in which traditional views toward women in Judaism must be altered in the Judaisms that wish to incorporate Enlightenment and feminist ideas.

✹ Suggested Readings on the Hebrew Scriptures and Judaism

Hebrew Scriptures/Old Testament

Albright, W. F., *From the Stone Age to Christianity*. Garden City, NY: Doubleday, 1957. A scholarly guide to Palestinian archaeology, emphasizing its relation to the Old Testament and its meaning for the philosophy of history.

Anderson, B., *Understanding the Old Testament,* rev. ed. Englewood Cliffs, NJ: Prentice Hall, 1986. A standard introductory textbook.

Buber, Martin, *The Prophetic Faith*. New York: Macmillan, 1949. A study by a famous Jewish theologian.

Cross, Frank Moore, *From Epic to Canon: History and Literature in Ancient Israel*. Baltimore, MD: The Johns Hopkins University Press, 1998.

Flanders, Henry Jackson, Robert W. Capps, and David A. Smith, *People of the Covenant: An Introduction to the Old Testament,* 3rd ed. New York: Oxford University Press, 1988. A good standard introduction.

Gaster, T. H., *Dead Sea Scriptures*. Garden City, NY: Doubleday, 1964. A semipopular overview of these important finds and their meaning.

Harrison, Roland Kenneth, *Introduction to the Old Testament*. Grand Rapids, MI: Eerdmans, 1969. A standard text written from an evangelical perspective.

Heschel, Abraham, *The Prophets*. New York: Harper & Row, 1962, 1969. A brilliant introduction to the spirit of prophetic religion in ancient Israel by a very distinguished Jewish thinker.

Pritchard, James B., *The Ancient Near East in Pictures*. Princeton, NJ: Princeton University Press, 1954. A fascinating survey by a distinguished archaeologist.

Thompson, Thomas L., *The Mythic Past: Biblical Archaeology and the Myth of Israel*. New York: Basic Books, 1999.

Judaism

Bamberger, Bernard J., *The Story of Judaism*. New York: Schocken Books, 1970. A valuable introduction.

Borowitz, Eugene B., *Liberal Judaism*. New York: UAHC, 1984. An important statement of a non-Orthodox Jewish perspective.

Boyarin, Daniel, *Dying for God: Martyrdom and the Making of Christianity and Judaism*. Stanford, CA: Stanford University Press, 1999.

Bulka, Reuven P., *Dimensions of Orthodox Judaism*. New York: KTAV, 1983. A survey of the Orthodox position and its varieties.

Cohen, Shaye J. D., *The Beginnings of Jewishness: Boundaries, Varieties, Uncertainties*. Berkeley: University of California Press, 1999.

Eisen, Arnold M., *Rethinking Modern Judaism: Ritual, Commandment, Community*. Chicago: University of Chicago Press, 1998.

Elliott, Mark Adam, *The Survivors of Israel: A Reconsideration of the Theology of Pre-Christian Judaism*. Grand Rapids, MI: Eerdsman, 2000.

Finkelstein, Louis, ed., *The Jews: Their History, Culture, and Religion,* 2 vols. New York: Harper, 1949. A standard reference.

Friedman, Maurice, *Martin Buber's Life and Thought,* 3 vols. New York: Dutton, 1981–1984. A comprehensive survey of Buber's contribution.

Glatzer, Nahum N. ed., *Franz Rosenzweig: His Life and Thought*. New York: Schocken Books, 1961. An introduction to this important thinker.

Heschel, Abraham, *Between God and Man: An Interpretation of Judaism*. New York: The Free Press, 1965. The view of a very distinguished, moderately liberal modern Jewish thinker.

Katz, S. T., *Interpretors of Judaism in the Late Twentieth Century*. Washington, DC: B'nai B'rith International, 1993. Schools of thought in contemporary Judaism.

Kaufman, William E., *Contemporary Jewish Philosophies*. New York: Reconstructionist Press, 1976. An introductory survey of current Jewish theology.

Levine, Lee I., *The Ancient Synagogue: The First Thousand Years*. New Haven, CT: Yale University Press, 2000.

McNutt, Paula M., *Reconstructing the Society of Ancient Israel*. Louisville, KY: Westminster John Knox Press, 1999.

Neusner, Jacob, *The Life of Torah: Readings: The Jewish Religious Experience*. Encino, CA: Dickenson, 1974. An anthology; emphasizes discussion of the Commandments.

————, *The Way of Torah: An Introduction to Judaism,* 2nd ed. Encino, CA: Dickenson, 1974. A good introduction; emphasizes Jewish history and way of life.

Novak, David, *Covenantal Rights: A Study in Jewish Political Theory*. Princeton, NJ: Princeton University Press, 2000.

Rosenthal, Gilbert S., *Contemporary Judaism: Patterns of Survival*. New York: Human Sciences, 1986. A valuable introduction to the history and ideology of the major Jewish traditions: Orthodox, Conservative, Reform, and Reconstruction.

Roth, Cecil, ed., *Encyclopedia Judaica,* 18 vols. Philadelphia: Coronet Books, 1994. A comprehensive source on the Jewish world.

Seltzer, Robert M., *Jewish People, Jewish Thought*. New York: Macmillan, 1980. A sensitive interactive treatment of Jewish history and ideas.

A celebration of a Jewish Bar Mitzvah at the Wailing Wall in Jerusalem.

Jews celebrating Succoth at the Lion's Gate in Jerusalem.

Waxman, Meyer, *Judaism: Religion and Ethics*. New York: Thomas Yoseloff, 1953. A clear survey of Jewish practice and moral attitudes today.

Wouk, Herman, *This Is My God*. Garden City, NY: Doubleday, 1959. A popular statement of the meaning of Orthodox Judaism by a well-known novelist.

Judaism in America

Elazar, Daniel Judah, *The Conservative Movement in Judaism: Dilemmas and Opportunities*. Albany: State University of New York Press, 2000.

Karp, Abraham J., *Jewish Continuity in America: Creative Survival in a Free Society*. Tuscaloosa: University of Alabama Press, 1998.

Fishman, Sylvia Barauk, *Jewish Life and American Culture*. Albany: State University of New York Press, 2000.

Jewish Mysticism

Cohn-Sherbok, Dan, *Jewish Mysticism: An Anthology*. Oxford: Oneworld, 1995.

Scholem, Gershom G., *Major Trends in Jewish Mysticism*. New York: Schocken Books, 1961. Quite scholarly; the definitive work, especially on the kabbala.

Weiner, Herbert, *9 1/2 Mystics: The Kabbala Today*. New York: Holt, Rinehart & Winston, 1969. A fascinating, easy-to-read account by a modern rabbi of visits to contemporary centers of Jewish mysticism; provides an incomparable insight into their spirit.

Women in Judaism

Adler, Rachel, *Engendering Judaism: An Inclusive Theology and Ethics*. Philadelphia: Jewish Publication Society, 1998. A highly recommended work.

———, "The Jew Who Wasn't There: Halakhah and the Jewish Woman" in *On Being a Jewish Feminist*, Susannah Heschel, ed. New York: Schocken Books, 1983, 1995, pp. 12–18. An important article in a classical collection on Jewish feminism.

Baskin, Judith R., ed., *Jewish Women in Historical Perspective*. Detroit, MI: Wayne State University Press, 1991. Excellent articles on various aspects of the subject.

Biale, Rachel, *Women & Jewish Law: An Exploration of Women's Issues in Halakhic Sources*. New York: Schocken Books, 1984. A good resource for Jewish Law regarding women.

Cantor, Aviva, *Jewish Women/Jewish Men: The Legacy of Patriarchy in Jewish Life*. San Francisco: HarperSanFrancisco, 1995. A competent survey.

Carmody, Denise Lardner, "Judaism" in *Women in World Religions*, Arvind Sharma, ed. Albany: State University of New York Press, 1987, pp. 183–206. A good summary of women and Judaism.

Davidman, Lynn, and Shelly Tenenbaum, eds., *Feminist Perspectives on Jewish Studies*. New Haven and London: Yale University Press, 1994. A good collection of articles providing various points of view.

Fishman, Sylvia Barack, *A Breath of Life: Feminism in the American Jewish Community*. New York: The Free Press, 1993.

Goldman, Karla, *Beyond the Synagogue Gallery: Finding a Place for Women in American Judaism*. Cambridge, MA: Harvard University Press, 2000.

Gross, Rita M., "Female God Language in a Jewish Context" in *Womanspirit Rising: A Feminist Reader in Religion*, Carol P. Christ and Judith Plaskow, eds. San Francisco: HarperSanFrancisco, 1979, 1992, pp. 167–73. An often-cited treatment of the subject.

Heschel, Susannah, ed., *On Being a Jewish Feminist*. New York: Schocken Books, 1995. A pivotal collection of articles on the subject.

Kaye, Melanie Kantrowitz. and Irena Klepfisz, *The Tribe of Dina: A Jewish Women's Anthology*. Boston: Beacon Press, 1986, 1989. Another pivotal collection of articles on the subject.

Levitt, Laura, *Jews and Feminism: The Ambivalent Search for Home*. New York: Routledge, 1997.

Nadell, Pamella Susan, *Women Who Would Be Rabbis: A History of Women's Ordination, 1889–1985*. Boston: Beacon Press, 1998.

Peskowitz, Miriam and Laura Levitt, eds., *Judaism Since Gender*. New York: Routledge, 1997. A new collection of articles providing contemporary perspectives.

Plaskow, Judith, "Jewish Memory from a Feminist Perspective" in *Weaving the Visions: New Patterns in Feminist Spirituality,* Judith Plaskow and Carol P. Christ, eds. San Francisco: HarperSan Francisco, 1989. A classic article.

Plaskow, Judith, *Standing Again at Sinai: Judaism from a Feminist Perspective*. San Francisco: HarperSanFrancisco, 1990. A highly acclaimed book that is important to read for anyone interested in Jewish feminism.

Sered, Susan Starr, *Women as Ritual Experts: The Religious Lives of Elderly Jewish Women in Jerusalem*. New York: Oxford University Press, 1992.

Trible, Phyllis, "Eve and Adam: Genesis 2–3 Reread," in *Womanspirit Rising: A Feminist Reader in Religion,* Carol P. Christ and Judith Plaskow, eds. San Francisco: HarperSanFrancisco, 1979, 1992, pp. 74–81. A classic paper interpreting the biblical account of Eve and Adam.

———, *Texts of Terror*. Philadelphia: Fortress, 1984. A powerful look at controversial biblical passages from a religious feminist perspective.

Wessinger, Catherine, ed., *Religious Institutions and Women's Leadership: New Roles Inside the Mainstream*. Columbia: University of South Carolina Press, 1996.

Wright, Alexandra, "Judaism," in *Women in Religion,* Jean Holm with John Bowker, ed. London and New York: Pinter, 1994, pp. 113–40. A good summary of women in Judaism.

CHAPTER EIGHT

Spreading the Word of God in the World

The Growth of Christianity

CHAPTER OBJECTIVES

After studying this chapter, you should be able to

❋ **Place the life and teaching of Jesus in a historical context.**

❋ **Explain the historical development of the Christian religion.**

❋ **Summarize the teaching, practice, and institutional life of the major forms or denominations of Christianity.**

❋ **Discuss the position of Christianity in the world today.**

❋ **Discuss the theological views that have shaped attitudes toward women in Christianity and their impact on women's struggle for equality and the twentieth and twenty-first century American debate on the "woman question."**

The Scope of Christianity

For the majority of Americans, Christianity is the most familiar form of religious expression. In fact, it probably shapes unconscious attitudes about what religion "ought" to be like.

In a sense this reaction is appropriate today, for although this is changing as the new century begins, in the twentieth century few countries had more influence on the world's religious history than the United States. Apart from countless indirect American influences on world culture and hence on religion, in the twentieth century, America served as chief bastion, financial resource, and exporter of its various forms of Christianity—from Roman Catholicism to Pentecostalism, the latter originating in America in its present form to become a Christian "third force" worldwide.

But Christianity is also an ancient faith with a long history, the greater part of it transpiring before America was settled by Europeans, and set in cultural environments immensely remote from ours. Most of the other major faiths, except Islam, are closer to 2,500 than 2,000 years old, the age of Christianity. But Christianity is scarcely behind any of them in the sense of antiquity imparted by its oldest shrines in the Old World. The comparatively new brick, glass, or wood churches that dot Christian America by the tens of thousands may give this religion an almost modern facade, but that is not the impression it gives in other places. In Europe the church buildings are often the oldest structures in an old city, giving a feel of the remote past.

The hymns and worship style Americans call the "old-time religion" largely date only from the nineteenth-century American frontier. Before that are eighteen other centuries of Christianity. Some of the forms it took in the past would seem almost as exotic as Tibet to us today, and much of this history is relatively little understood or known by most American Christians.

In the waning days of the Roman Empire, Christians not only worshipped in underground burial tunnels called **catacombs** and met lions in the Colosseum, but wrote, argued, and took the faith to barbarian tribes. These Christians built churches on wagons to follow the barbarians on their wanderings. After the fall of Rome, Western Europe was in what some refer to as the "Dark Ages." During that time, worship in Constantinople—with its opulently robed priests, clouds of incense, and sonorous music—reached a splendor that visiting Russians reportedly said was closer to heaven than earth. In the tenth century, the Nestorian Church of the East, following the caravan routes, was planted from Mesopotamia to the imperial city of Tang China. A Christian church of Eastern Orthodox type has existed in South India since the fourth century at least. At the other end of the world, Irish monks let God guide their flimsy boats to remote islands and promontories, inhabited only by sea gulls, to build rough monasteries.

Then there are somewhat more familiar but no less colorful Christian images: medieval popes in monarchical splendor, crusaders, manuscript-copying monks, Canterbury pilgrims, Protestant reformers, visionaries of the Blessed Virgin Mary at Lourdes or Fatima, and missionaries on tropical islands. Christianity embraces worshippers at high masses and at silent Quaker meetings, people for whom the faith is a liberal charter and those for whom it demands the most rigorous conservatism on both social and theological issues.

Jesus

Like all major religions, Christianity has integrated into itself meanings and practices from many places where it has dwelt. The process begins with the Greek vocabulary of the New Testament itself. But there is only one focal point which brings together all this diversity: the last two or three years of the earthly life of Jesus of Nazareth, called the Messiah or Christ.

Jesus appeared publicly in Roman-occupied Palestine around the year 30 C.E. He was first visible as an associate of a man called John the Baptizer, an ascetic who had lived in the desert and then had come into the Jordan Valley to preach fiery outdoor sermons calling on people to repent and change their ways, for God was about to judge the world and punish the wicked. Such **apocalyptic** expectation was rife at this time, all the more because the heavy hand of Roman tyranny seemed to block all nonsupernatural hope for the Jewish nation or for individuals, except those who curried favor with Rome.[1] The repentance John called for was

Engraving of Jesus healing the sick by Gustave Doré.

marked by a ritual washing, or baptism, which he administered to his converts in the Jordan River.

Among those who received this baptism was a young man from Nazareth called Jesus (Joshua). Not much is definitely known about his background. The stories later told about his descent from David, miraculous conception, birth in Bethlehem, and childhood are difficult to corroborate historically and are generally accepted or not on the basis of one's religious outlook; for Christians, they embody important religious truths about Jesus.

Shortly after Jesus' baptism by John, John was arrested and then executed. This arrest did not give Jesus the leadership of John's movement directly, but it did partly inspire him to gather disciples and start a ministry of his own, which was in some ways parallel to John's, but came to develop distinctive characteristics.

Like John, Jesus began by proclaiming in his preaching that the **Kingdom of God** was at hand. The "Kingdom" meant the paradisal rule of God that would follow the apocalyptic distress and judgment. The Kingdom as a concept was intimately tied up with the work of the Messiah, who would inaugurate it.[2] Jesus also taught that people should repent of their former ways and, in preparation for the Kingdom, live now as though in the Kingdom. The principles for this way of life are assembled in the Sermon on the Mount in Chapters 5, 6, and 7 of Matthew's Gospel. The essence is to practice forbearing love and nonresistance of evil, because God will shortly be dealing with it in judgment, and to be perfect even as the God who is to rule is perfect. By comparison, John's moral message was merely of repentance and following justice.

Unlike John, Jesus did not baptize, although his followers did. His work of healing was the major sign in his ministry of the power of the coming Kingdom, just as baptism had been John's major sign. His miracles of healing the sick, the insane, the blind, and the paralyzed, and his other miracles such as feeding 5,000 people with five loaves and two small fish, are presented as signs of the Kingdom's arrival. Healing was often understood as the exorcism of evil spirits from the disturbed. Jesus said, "If it is by the finger of God that I cast out demons, then the kingdom of God has come upon you" (Luke 11:20). He also performed nature miracles, like walking on water.

The nature miracles and healings bring to light another special feature of Jesus' ministry, his aura of authority, and his mingling with both sexes and with all classes of society. Jesus taught everywhere, not only in synagogues but also by the lakeshore and in open fields. Instead of using close argument or extensive scriptural analysis, he used stories, **parables**, and simple but acute aphorisms to make his points or, better, to catch up the hearer in his vision of the Kingdom's nearness—so near its power is already breaking through and is within reach of those who see its rising light.

Just as the Kingdom was for everyone, but in a special sense for the poor who had so little, so did Jesus bring its message to everyone. He numbered among his associates fishermen, prostitutes, revolutionary zealots, despised tax collectors, and (though he also harshly upbraided them) members of the strict religious party, the Pharisees. He did not inculcate extreme asceticism but rather was

Cross

known as the teacher who came eating and drinking, and his illustrations show a sympathetic awareness of the ways and problems of ordinary life with its sorrows, joys, and innocent festivities.

After only a short year or two of this life, however, the young wandering preacher and charismatic wonder-worker of the Kingdom left Galilee, his homeland, and went down to Jerusalem shortly before the Passover, when Jews traditionally made a pilgrimage to the holy city. He clearly intended this journey, which God had laid upon him, to be a climactic appeal to Israel to accept the incoming Kingdom and to reject perversions of religion. To this end he made certain dramatic gestures: He entered the pilgrim-thronged holy city in a sort of procession (which has come to be commemorated as Palm Sunday), and he caused a disturbance overturning the tables of the currency exchangers and the chairs of the sellers of birds and animals for sacrifice in the temple courtyard. He and his disciples then withdrew for a few days to live in suburban Bethany and to teach in the temple precincts.

But in the edgy political situation, these gestures combined with news of Jesus' popular appeal in Galilee understandably came to the concerned attention of Roman and Jewish authorities alike. They perceived revolutionary political overtones in the young prophet's activities and appeal. How far this perception was justified is much disputed by historians, but there is no doubt there were those among both supporters and opponents of Jesus who expected him to be at least the figurehead in an uprising against Rome, and perhaps against the collaborating Jewish elite as well.[3] This was an upshot neither the Romans nor the Jewish elite wished. Before the end of the week the decision had been taken and carried out to dispose of him.

Jesus was arrested with the help of Judas, a disgruntled radical among his disciples, and hastily but decisively tried by the various authorities concerned, ultimately before the harsh Pontius Pilate, the Roman governor who throughout his tenure had shown no pity to protesters against Roman rule. (Indeed, Rome finally recalled him for excessive cruelty.) On Friday in Passover week, Jesus was executed by **crucifixion**—being nailed to a structure made of two crossed beams set upright—the slow and agonizing death that Rome awarded to rebels. But, of course, the story did not end there.

The Early Jesus Movement

The drama of this tragic death of one so young, beloved, and appealing to many inevitably worked deeply into the minds of those who had been committed to his movement and caught up in his vision of the Kingdom. They tried to find ways to understand the man and the event in categories familiar to them. Some thought of the tradition of a coming Messiah, "Anointed One" or King, and wondered if, as some of Jesus' words and deeds suggested, he were this figure. (The title "Christ" is the literal Greek translation of "Messiah.") In particular, they now conjoined the Messiah image with the poignant passages in Isaiah about the "suffering servant"—the hero who saves his people not by military victory but by undergoing excruciating pain, baring his back to the smiters, his cheek to those who plucked out the hairs.

Some thought of the words "Son of Man," which he had often used, words that his hearers would have recognized as referring to the mysterious judge who would descend on clouds on the last day in the current apocalyptic expectations. It was frequently ambiguous whether Jesus meant the title to refer to himself or another coming one, or if he meant both at the same time. Others, closer to the Greek religious tradition, thought of the titles "Lord" and "Son of God," used of Hellenistic kings and deities alike, or even of philosophical concepts like **Logos** ("**Word**" or "Principle") or Sophia ("Wisdom"), used to describe the creative power of God at work in the world, in connection with the enigmatic and unforgettable man from Nazareth. As to exactly how he thought of himself and his mission, in his own subjectivity, who can say? Almost all we know of him, including the words he is reported to have spoken, comes to us through the hands of those who saw him in light of categories and concepts such as those just mentioned. Beyond all the words, however, there is mystery—the mystery of one whose charm and stern-ness, magic and endurance of torture, empathy and remoteness, combined to make him both unknown and unforgettable. He had the combination of mystery and clarification of all great religious images and symbols.

Soon enough he was a supreme symbol of the ineffable mysteries of life, death, and God, all of which he somehow seemed to bring into focus for many. His form and the instrument of his suffering were reproduced in gold and silver and gems around the world.

This kind of thinking took hold in the community of Jesus' disciples and fol-lowers. Christianity, which has never been a purely individual religion, was com-munal even before the crucifixion. The disciples, leaving job and family, formed a new social group around Jesus, and it was in the context of this group especially formed in expectation of the Kingdom that the teaching about the Kingdom and the wonders that foreshadowed it were imparted. The disciples were always at hand for Jesus' preaching and miracles, and it was they who were told the inner meaning of parables and signs.

On the Friday Jesus died on the cross, this community was dispirited and scattered; Peter went back to his fishing. But on the first day of the next week, word of a new event brought the community together again. It was reported by Mary Magdalene, a woman close to Jesus and the disciples, and then by Peter him-self, that the tomb was empty and Jesus was walking in the garden where he had been interred. More such accounts were quickly bruited about: He had joined two disciples walking to Emmaus, and when they broke bread together he was known to them; the disciples were in a room with the doors shut, and he appeared in their midst; they were in a boat, and he appeared on the shore and cooked breakfast for them. He seemed the same and yet different in these postdeath appearances, as though partly in a different dimension. He ate. "Doubting Thomas" was able to touch Jesus' wounds to assure himself that Jesus was really the crucified one and not a ghost or imposter. Yet this Jesus was able to pass through shut doors and ap-peared or disappeared unexpectedly and by no pattern discernible to mortals.

Finally, forty days after the first appearance in the garden, the resurrected Jesus appeared to them, we are told, in familiar Bethany. There, as they talked, he took them out to a nearby hill, blessed them, and was taken up into heaven.

By now, the nascent Christian community—the disciples, certain women such as Mary Magdalene and Mary the mother of Jesus, and peripheral followers—was vitalized and enthusiastic. The series of mysterious resurrection appearances, which came only to members of the community, greatly reinforced its thinking about who Jesus was along the lines of the categories and concepts discussed above. The supreme event came when, on the Jewish feast of Pentecost 50 days after Passover, shortly after his ascension into heaven, those who were gathered in an upstairs room suddenly felt tremendously shaken by a spiritual force they were certain was the Holy Spirit of God mentioned in the Old Testament and whose coming was remembered to have been promised by Jesus.

After receiving the Holy Spirit, the **apostles**, as the inner core of the group were now called, began preaching in the streets to the many peoples who crowded into the holy city. They preached basically that Jesus who had died was risen from the dead, that this event confirmed that he was and is both Lord and Messiah—the Christ, and so all the scriptural prophecies about both the Jewish and universal roles of the Messiah and the Last Days were fulfilled or will be in him.

Many heard and believed. Most were Jews, but some of the earliest converts to the truth and significance of this new happening in Judaism were Greeks, probably of a class called *proselyte,* who, without undertaking the whole of the Jewish law, admired Judaism, worshipped its God, and accepted as much of its teaching and practice as possible. The incipient universalism of the Christian sect, with its proclamation of a new age when the reign of the Jewish God would be evident everywhere, and was now already present in Christ, must have greatly eased the spiritual plight of such people.

Paul

Presenting Jesus as a manifestation of God who welcomed Jew and Greek alike was given preliminary definition by the council of the apostles described in Acts 15, where only a minimal adherence to the Jewish law was required of non-Jews. But it was in the work of Paul, the most notable convert and missionary in the days of the early fellowship, that this universalism in Christ fully came through.[4]

Paul, a Hebrew who was a Roman citizen, was originally called Saul. He was a strict follower of the Law of Moses and a persecutor of the new Christian sect. But while traveling from Jerusalem to Damascus in his anti-Christian efforts, at one place in the road he unexpectedly fell to the ground in a violent rapture. He experienced a vision of Jesus the Christ appearing to him and saying "Saul, Saul, why do you persecute me?"

Although he did not immediately begin his public missionary work, Paul was a great if controversial advocate of the new faith between about 45 and 62 C.E. and Christianity's first theologian. His labors on its behalf took him through Asia

Minor, Greece, and finally to Rome. More and more he saw himself as the apostle to the **Gentiles** (non-Jews), and his calling was to show that, in these days after Jesus, the Gentiles had been "grafted" into Israel as an alien branch onto an old tree, and so when they prayed in the name of Jesus, they had all the privileges and responsibilities of being God's people that had formerly been Israel's alone. But this did not mean, for Paul, that they had to follow the Jewish Law. They had only to believe the Gospel, or "Good News," about Jesus and have trust in him, and they would be brought into his oneness with God—not on their own merits but as a free gift of God transmitted even as they were grafted into old Israel through Jesus Christ. Jesus' death on the cross, Paul said, broke the sway of sin and death in the world, and his rising again brought new life. By joining oneself to Christ by faith (not only belief, but by a commitment of one's whole self) and by the acceptance of baptism (the ritual immersion in water representing initiatory rebirth), one received new life in Christ and was no longer of this world, which is passing away, but was entered into the everlasting reign of God.

Christianity in the Roman World

By now a number of interpretations of the Christian message and community had become articulated. Some still thought of Jesus primarily as the Jewish Messiah who would soon return to vindicate Israel. Some thought all of this as a continuation—one might say an "export version"—of Judaism, making its promises freely available to all apart from the Jewish social and dietary law. (One can compare the relation of Buddhism to Hinduism.) Others doubtless experienced it as something closer to the well-known Greek mystery religion, the purveyor of a belief and an experience that would give a blissful state after death to one who received it. The death and **resurrection** of Christ provided for them the pattern of such a deliverance, which one needed only to appropriate for oneself. All of these, and other philosophical and religious themes as well, found their way into the newly emerging and varied groups that together made up the early Jesus movement.

These various ideas were stirring in groups that Paul and the other apostles, as well as others, established throughout Mediterranean world in such varied places as Judea, Syria, and Egypt, as well as Rome, itself. They were usually fringe groups to the Jewish community, but they embraced many others as well—rich and poor, slave and free, but more of the dislocated than of the well established in the polyglot, spiritually mobile Mediterranean world. The destruction of the Temple in Jerusalem by the Romans in 70 C.E., mentioned in connection with our discussion of Judaism in Chapter 7, and the dispersion of Jerusalem Jews, had a profound effect on the Jesus movement as well. By severely weakening the Jerusalem church, with its links to Judaism, it spawned the schism between Judaism and the followers of Jesus that has had a profound effect on Middle Eastern and Western history ever since—Christianity eventually becoming more Gentile in its makeup and universal in its teachings than Judaism had been.

As the first century advanced, the many communities of Jesus' followers began to write down and circulate what had previously been orally transmitted accounts of the sayings of Jesus and stories of the life of Jesus. These writings in many ways reflected the views of the various traditions of the communities from which the writings came—some emphasizing the death and resurrection of Jesus and others emphasizing the teachings of Jesus. Eventually, four of these writings became accepted as the four Gospels; there were others that were not. The first three of the Gospels, or lives of Jesus, are called the **Synoptic Gospels**. They obviously go together because long passages are virtually identical. The shortest, Mark, was evidently written first, probably between 65 and 70 C.E. Matthew (c. 70–80) and Luke (c. 80) borrowed much from Mark and added much of their own, emphasizing different aspects of the life of Jesus and his teachings. The fourth Gospel, John (its date is uncertain but is probably late first century), evidently was written from a completely different point of view. Concerned to present Jesus as the light and life of the world, the eternal Logos or principle of God's activity revealed to the eye of faith, it contains much that is religiously beautiful and profound yet is perhaps less close to the historical facts about Jesus than the other three—though matters like this are the subject of continuing scholarly discussion beyond the scope of this book.[5]

Added to this growing corpus of Christian literature were the **Epistles** (letters) of Paul, written earlier than the Synoptic Gospels, only twenty to thirty years after the crucifixion, much treasured in the churches he had founded; the Acts of the Apostles by Luke (probably written 85–90 C.E.); and other writings of varying types, some of which finally became part of the Christian Bible and some of which did not.

At this time we also see the emergence of normative Christian beliefs, rites, and church organization in some localities, while others remained loosely organized groups. This stage, sometimes called "early Catholicism" because it obviously represents the beginning of the course of Christian development that led to the structure of the medieval church, can be found as far back as the New Testament "Pastoral Epistles" (I and II Timothy, Titus) and the Epistles of Peter. There were formulas of belief slowly becoming standardized into creeds (for example, II Timothy 2:11–13); attacks on heretics (such as those found in I Titus 1:10–16); and a quieter, more sober and conventionally moralistic way of life. With the hope of many in the Christian community for an early appearance of the Lord in glory disappointed, the virtues of soundness and self-control were urged, being needed for a long-term sojourn as the children of light in the midst of a dark (but not yet passing away) world. The brilliant apocalyptic colors of the Gospels and the tumultuous early days of Acts fade; concern turns to sorting out true from false doctrine and the proper qualifications and prerogatives of church officers and various classes of members, such as young men and widows.

Yet the churches of those days had an appeal of their own. Each local church came to be headed by an *episcopos* ("overseer"—the word "bishop" is derived from this Greek word), assisted by a council of *presbyteroi* ("elders"—"priests" or "presbyters" in English), and by *diakonoi* ("servers"—"deacons" in English, whose special duty was caring for the needy). The churches apparently had many other categories of roles as well, from readers and healers to widows—each with special duties in worship and otherwise, and perhaps a special place to stand during service. Everyone was to have a definite and important part. The church did extensive welfare work among its membership. Like most such organizations in the Roman world, it was a mutual aid society as well as a religious fellowship.

The church met for worship early in the morning on Sunday (of course, just another ordinary workday then), the day commemorating the Resurrection, and perhaps on other days as well. To avoid legal problems, Christians often gathered quietly and, until late in the third century when churches began to be built, in private homes or catacombs. Worship combined Scripture, prayer, and instruction with the **Eucharist**, the sacred communal meal representing the Last Supper which, as the Mass, **Holy Communion**, or Lord's Supper, remains the principal act of worship of Roman Catholic, Eastern Orthodox, and some Protestant churches.

The evidence suggests that a typical service in those days would have been as follows: At the back of the room, behind a table, sat the bishop, with his presbyters seated on either side. In front of the table would stand the deacons, probably two in number. The service would begin with readings from the Scriptures of the Old Testament, with emphasis on the passages believed to prophesy the coming of Christ, and the Psalms, used as hymns of praise. Many people might take part in these readings. The bishop, and possibly others, would discourse on their meaning. Perhaps letters of the apostles and accounts from the life of Christ would be read too; gradually these came to be more and more a formal part of Christian worship, until they evolved into the normative collection known as the New Testament. The bishop would then pray at some length, and the Kiss of Peace would be exchanged. After this, everyone would bring up to the table a gift of bread or wine. The bishop, standing behind the table with the elders, would raise his eyes to heaven and offer thanks for this food. Then the people would come forward to receive a piece of bread from the bishop and a bit of wine offered in a chalice held by a deacon, believing this to be a sacred meal in which Jesus Christ is mystically known and his grace imparted.[6] Not to be confused with the Holy Communion was the *agape,* or love feast, held afterward as a social communal meal.

The other great service was baptism. This initiation into the Christian life was generally held on Easter Eve. Only those who had received baptism would take part in the communion just described; *catechumens,* or those receiving instruction, and also penitents going through a process of readmission after confessing a major sin would remain at the service only through the first part. Instruction would be very long and thorough, lasting perhaps for two full years, and would be followed by careful intellectual and moral examination. Then during the week before Easter the candidates would be given a final exam by the bishop on Wednesday, would bathe on Thursday, fast on Friday, be blessed and exorcised by the bishop on Saturday, keep an all-night vigil, and finally, early on Easter morning, would be baptized in a font or by having water poured over them, and would immediately afterward receive Holy Communion.[7]

During this period, Christian intellectual life continued to increase the philosophical sophistication with which the faith was presented. Celebrated Christian thinkers such as Clement of Rome, Clement of Alexandria, Origen, Justin Martyr, Irenaeus, Tertullian, and others moved the emphasis from showing the continuity of Christianity with Judaism to showing its compatibility with Greek and Roman philosophy, and its points of difference from it. This is natural, since the non-Jewish Greco-Roman world increasingly became the milieu of Christianity.

The tone of Christian thinkers ranged from the fiery Tertullian (c. 160–225), a former lawyer who thought that everything pagan was alien to Christianity and who deemed faith alone and a very strict moral life the only proper Christian way, to the mild Clement of Alexandria who, with his fellow Alexandrian Origen, emphasized that all truth leads to Christ, who is the Word or creative principle known to philosophy. Some Christians went much further; the Gnostics combined Christianity with more esoteric and mythical elements of Greek and Asian thought. They were countered by the bishop of Lyons, Irenaeus, who emphasized the importance for Christians to follow the traditions passed down from the apostles, particularly the truth of God's taking on human flesh in Christ in order to undo the tangled knot of evil wrought by Adam in the Garden of Eden, and thus to bring the creation back to himself by one who is flesh of our flesh. This was in conscious opposition to Gnostic ideas that, the flesh being evil or virtually worthless, the taking of flesh by God is only illusory or allegorical, and salvation means escape from the world through realization of one's true, Divine nature.

Everyone has heard of the persecutions of Christians under the Roman Empire: of **martyrs** hung upside down on crosses, or burned at the stake, or thrown to the lions in the Colosseum. Indeed, there were ghastly persecutions, although they were sporadic and local until the third century. Often Christians in the empire lived undisturbed lives, and while they were not an officially recognized religion, the general policy was to tolerate all groups, however bizarre, that did not present a clear threat to the government. Tradition has it that the Emperor Nero (r. 54–68) instigated a persecution (in which the apostles Peter and Paul were killed) to deflect blame from himself for the disastrous fire at Rome; if so, such persecution was limited to the capital.

In the third century, however, there were persecutions ordered for the entire empire under Decius (r. 249–251), Valerian (r. 253–260), and Diocletian (r. 284–305). By this time the numbers of Christians had grown quite visible, and troubles were increasing in the Roman state requiring both solidarity and scapegoats. In the face of external invasion and internal dissension, these emperors desperately wanted unity and did not yet realize that the empire and Christianity could converge and be mutually supportive, as they were to do within a century. Ironically, it was generally the most conscientious emperors who persecuted Christianity, for they took most seriously their responsibilities for unifying and strengthening the realm.

Usually the persecution was in the context of a drive for all subjects of the empire to express loyalty to the sovereign, who was nominally regarded as divine. Few took this seriously, but it was expected that patriotism would be expressed by burning a bit of incense before a portrait or image of the emperor, an act regarded as offering Divine honor. At the times of persecution, Christians might be summoned by the authorities and required to make this and comparable gestures or suffer imprisonment and possibly death. Christians, regarding the token gesture as idolatry, frequently refused it. This was taken as proof that they were subversive—and they suffered the consequences.

Greatest havoc was wrought by Diocletian, a dedicated and capable man striving desperately to save a rapidly disintegrating situation but who suffered many problems and bad advice. By his time Christianity had numerous churches, costly possessions, and large numbers. The emperor shrank at first from shedding blood but ordered all Christian buildings, artifacts, and books destroyed, seeking thereby to weaken the obstreperous movement. That did not work, and before long his agents were working torture and death as well among the faithful.

It must be noted that among Christians a certain cult of martyrdom flourished. Those who died violently under the various persecutions were afforded heroic status, and the bones and graves of many became relics and shrines. Here began the veneration of **saints**. There were those who looked to the example of Jesus Christ and the earlier martyrs and were fully prepared for, and even sought out, the martyr's death. Thus Ignatius, bishop of Antioch, was taken to Rome in the days of Trajan (r. 98–117), where he met his death at the jaws of wild beasts in the amphitheater. Thinking no doubt of the Holy Communion, he wrote to the church at Rome while on his journey to death:

> I am God's wheat; I am ground by the teeth of the wild beasts that I may end as the pure bread of Christ. If anything, coax the beasts on to become my sepulchre and to leave nothing of my body undevoured so that, when I am dead, I may be no bother to anyone. I shall be really a disciple of Jesus Christ if and when the world can no longer see so much as my body. Make petition, then, to the Lord for me, so that by these means I may be made a sacrifice to God.

In this vein, he also said:

> The pangs of new birth are upon me. Forgive me, brethren, do nothing to prevent this new life.[8]

The Christian Triumph

Not long in terms of world history was Christianity to dwell amidst the smell of beasts and blood, save in memory. In the early decades of the fourth century, Christianity emerged from its place as merely one of the competitors in the lavish spiritual marketplace of the Roman world to become first the dominant and then the sole official religion of the empire and, in time, of all Europe. This reversal happened with surprising speed. True, the church had done well during the long years of comparative peace since the end of the Decian persecution in 251. In some places, especially in Asia Minor, Christianity was the majority faith, and nearby Armenia had become the first officially Christian nation around 300. In many cities, including Nicomedia in Asia Minor (modern Turkey), to which Diocletian had moved his capital, there stood impressive churches, and members of the emperor's family as well as the lowly supported them until his persecution of the church.

Nonetheless, the reasons for the triumph of Christianity around 312 are not all immediately apparent. The faith of Christ had no greater prestige than the Neoplatonic mysticism favored by philosophers, or the Mithraism popular in the army, or the ancient polytheisms nostalgically upheld by patrician traditionalists. Indeed, it had been only a few years earlier (303) that, at the instigation of his son-in-law Galerius, the aging Diocletian imposed persecution.

But one of Diocletian's commanders, Constantine, who emerged in Western Europe after the former's abdication in 305 as an Augustus or "co-emperor," favored the Christian cause. Another co-emperor, the sadistic Maximin Daza, who continued persecution in the East, was deposed by a rival, Licinius. The latter met with Constantine in 313 to decree toleration, the so-called **Edict of Milan**. Thereafter, Constantine and Licinius ruled together.

Deep psychological currents favorable to Christianity apparently ran through the complex mind of Constantine. His mother, Helena, had become a Christian, and at the famous battle of the Milvian Bridge, where he defeated a rival in 312, it is said he saw a cross in the sky and the letters IHS—the Greek beginning of the name Jesus, or the Latin initials for *In Hoc Signo,* "By this sign."[9]

After 323 Constantine was the sole emperor. He established his capital in Byzantium, later named Constantinople (modern Istanbul), and pursued policies favorable to Christianity, although he was not himself baptized until on his deathbed. In 325 he sponsored a council of bishops at Nicaea, which made most of what is now the **Nicene Creed** the standard of doctrine. But Christianity did not become the official religion, the only one whose open practice was possible, until the reign of Theodosius I (379–395).

During the same period, and largely in reaction to doctrinal disputes, the **canon** of authoritative New Testament scriptures was established. It was not finalized until a council of bishops at Carthage in 419. The final codification of scripture thus was fairly late and came after much of the development of Christian teaching, worship, and social organization. On the other hand, the selection was influenced by the fact that most of those books to be considered canonical were already accepted as authoritative by the most prominent churches. Still, it is thought by many scholars that the inclusion of the four Gospels, each reflecting a different perspective on the life of Jesus and his message (rather than choosing one as authoritative), represented a compromise among the various groups who wanted their account included in the canon. The last disputes over the canon were chiefly about the Pastoral Epistles, Jude, and the Book of Revelation, and whether the Epistle to the Hebrews was actually written by Paul. Many then as now were dubious about its Pauline authorship but accepted it anyway as part of the New Testament.[10]

While the great pagan temples were turned into churches or public buildings, and the centers of **pagan** learning dispersed, **paganism** lingered a long time in the countryside. In the course of becoming the dominant religion of society and sub-suming all the roles that had animated the former faiths—from folk religion to the mysteries to Neoplatonist philosophy—Christianity naturally underwent develop-ment. In church organization, the bishops remained in the cities where the faith had long held sway, becoming more and more the spiritual parallels of governors and magistrates. Successors of the *presbyteroi* of old, parish priests, ordinarily one to a church, strove to Christianize the archaic agricultural religion of the country-side. Festivals such as Christmas and Easter, which borrowed symbols from the in-digenous pagan religions of conquered lands, became colorful public holidays; pagan shrines and temples changed names. Moreover, the new faith spread rapidly among the restless Germanic tribes who were replacing Roman provinces with their rude kingdoms and dukedoms.

The Foundations of Medieval Christianity

Let us look more explicitly at the changes Christianity underwent during the me-dieval period in terms of the forms of religious expression.

Theoretical expression became more and more solidified, particularly in re-gard to an understanding of the **incarnation**—how God became human in Christ. This articulation took place by means of **General Councils**, meetings to which all bishops were invited. They sought to condemn **heresy**, or false teaching, and de-fine correct, or **orthodox**, teaching. The councils had political overtones as well, for they were all held in the area of Byzantium, and the theological issues were often identified with parties or nationalities of political significance within the em-pire. In particular, issues were frequently polarized between Egypt and the north-ern part of the empire. The Bishop of Rome, being an outsider to Eastern squabbles, often could mediate these problems. This increased his authority and helped in the development of his office into the medieval and modern papacy.

There were four important General Councils. The **Council of Nicaea** in 325 af-firmed, in the Nicene Creed, that Christ is of one substance or essence with God the Father. This definition opposed that of others who held that Christ was only "like" God and a lower being sent as his envoy. Constantinople reaffirmed the Nicaean po-sition in 381. The **Council of Ephesus** in 431 affirmed Christ was always God from his mother's womb (and so it called Mary his mother *Theotokos,* "God-bearer"), not a man who had been made Son of God. The **Council of Chalcedon** in 451 affirmed that Christ is both True God and True Man, two natures conjoined in one person.

A similar matter that underwent theological refinement at about the same time, although never the subject of a General Council, was the doctrine of the **Trinity**. Christians had experienced God in three basic ways: as God the Heavenly Father, as the Son of God in Jesus Christ, and as the Holy Spirit who was promised by Christ and who filled the community in the upper room on **Pentecost**. Now it was written that these are three "persons" bound together in infinite love, who nonetheless are but one God.

In the West, Christians were less involved in the General Councils than in the East, but theological work continued there, too. The greatest Western figure was **Augustine** (c. 354–430 C.E.), a North African bishop who taught about the Trinity and about grace, God's free gift or help, among other topics. Concerning grace, Augustine emphasized that God takes the initiative in relations between himself and us. All begins with grace, for we cannot seek God or do things pleasing to him unless he first enables us, because we are naturally self-centered and do not truly seek God or do selfless acts on our own. In such terms as these Augustine explained **original sin**, the doctrine that holds that human beings inherit an inherently sinful nature, and "prevenient grace," Divine grace that must come before we humans can do anything that goes beyond our self-centeredness.

It is too easy, however, to stress the history of ideas in the church and forget that changes of similarly immense consequence were going on in worship and social organization. Indeed, as always, for the uneducated majority what was seen to

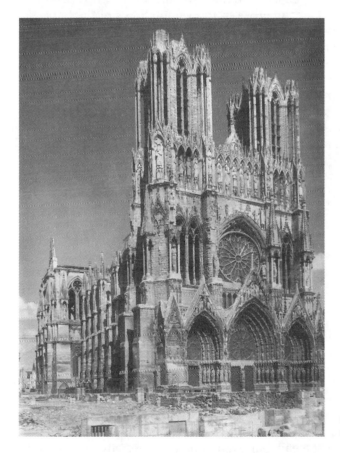

Gothic architecture: Reims Cathedral in France.

be done in worship, and the socio-political role of religious institutions, was much more influential than the discussions of theologians.

As the church moved out of the spiritual underground of the great cities and into spacious buildings, typically modeled on the basilica or Roman court of law, or into the rural world of peasant and lord, the liturgy, or pattern of worship, also changed. It became expressive and ornate. The clergy wore symbolically colored garments and moved with slow ritual, accompanied by music and incense, to present and bless the bread and wine of the Eucharist. In the West, the language of the service was Latin; in the East, Greek. These tongues, especially Latin, quickly became "sacred" languages, like Sanskrit in India, as the vernacular changed and numerous new peoples came into the orbit of the faith.

For the Christian population was rapidly growing and changing. During the fourth century virtually all the peoples of the old Roman Empire were at least superficially Christianized—even those of areas no longer Christian today, such as North Africa, Egypt, Syria, Palestine, and Asia Minor. In the East, missionaries won converts in Ethiopia, Mesopotamia, Persia, and even India. In the West, Visigoths, Saxons, Vikings, Franks, and the like, challenged the new authorities who now ruled the lands only barely brought under the cross in the waning days of the imperial order; the situation was often chaotic. By the year 1000, however, all but a few corners of Europe had been converted, and the rambunctious tribes had begun slow progress toward becoming nations.

Let us look briefly at two examples: England and Ireland. Christianity came to Roman Britain in the third century. Apparently it was brought by unknown soldiers and merchants, although stories were told in the Middle Ages that Paul himself had visited Britain, or that Joseph of Arimathea (he who claimed the body of Jesus) had come there and planted the sacred tree known as the Glastonbury Thorn, a favorite object of pilgrimage. These legends are significant because they typify the believing world of medieval Christianity. The Celtic and Roman settler population had become widely Christian by the time Britain was cut off from Rome early in the fifth century.

Shortly afterward, massive invasions of Danes, Angles, and Saxons, still adherents of the old Germanic religion of Wotan and Thor, had pushed the Christianized Britons back to the far West, to what is now Wales and Cornwall and their vicinity. There they held out; the tales of King Arthur reflect in part the days of these beleaguered people, who still remembered something of Rome and Christ, as well as old Celtic religious motifs. But in 597 a missionary named Augustine (not the North African bishop) was sent out from Rome to Kent, the Saxon kingdom in the extreme southeast corner of England. Its king and people, through the agency of the king's Christian wife, were converted, and not long afterward all the Anglo-Saxon kingdoms—Wessex, Sussex, Mercia, and the rest—had submitted to the faith of Christ.

Ireland's conversion was worked by the famous Patrick, who died in 461. The population was still tribal, and the church followed tribal lines. It was full of zeal and its monks full of wanderlust. Missionaries from Ireland traveled to many parts of Europe. Ireland was Christian while England and much of the continent was not;

in those confused times Ireland was a preeminent center of Christian learning and effort in the West.

The classical pattern of bishops, who governed the church in geographical areas called *dioceses,* and parish priests in each community was perpetuated wherever the church acquired a foothold. The bishops of major cities became known as "archbishops." The Council of Chalcedon made the bishops of five of the most important cities in the ancient empire—Constantinople, Antioch, Alexandria, and Jerusalem in the East, and Rome in the West—**patriarchs**, and the patriarch of Constantinople, the capital of the Byzantine empire, was called the ecumenical or universal patriarch. With this title, he is still the chief dignitary of the Eastern Orthodox Church, though only as "first among equals." On the other hand, the patriarch of Rome came to be called the **Pope**. He had long been looked upon as the chief arbitrator of disputes and heir of the church which, having been associated with the apostles Peter and Paul themselves, had an apostolic tradition of unquestionable soundness. Indeed, it was said by many in the West especially that the Pope, successor to Peter as bishop of Rome, was heir to those promises that Matthew's Gospel records Jesus as having given to Peter:

> *You are Peter, and on this rock I will build my church, and the powers of death shall not prevail against it. I will give you the keys of the kingdom of heaven, and whatever you bind on earth shall be bound in heaven, and whatever you loose on earth shall be loosed in heaven. (Matthew 16:18–20)*

Furthermore, in the confusion that attended the collapse of the Roman Empire, the Popes, particularly strong Popes such as Leo (r. 440–461) and Gregory (r. 590–604), emerged as dominant figures in both church and secular affairs, beacons of stability and hope in a dark and terrifying world. It is not surprising that by the Middle Ages, their sovereignty over the church in the West was firmly established.

One extremely important social development in Christianity was **monasticism**. In order to serve God better, and in search for security and purity in a corrupt and chaotic society, young men—and, not long afterward, women—left society to remain unmarried and form communities focused on the worship of God. The monastic movement started in Egypt in the late third century when men such as Anthony and Pachomius went into the desert to pursue lives of prayer as hermits. Soon they were followed by disciples, and communities grew up. Before long the idea had spread throughout the Christian world. Benedict (c. 529) established the Benedictine monastic pattern, which became normative for the church in the West. Monasteries quickly became centers of both missionary work and the preservation of learning, as well as orphanages, hospitals, and way stations.[11]

Parallel to monasticism was the general idea of celibacy for the clergy. There was a widespread feeling, based both on the examples of the apparently unmarried Jesus and Paul the apostle, and on lingering aversion to the "passions" derived from Greek philosophy, that the celibate life was holier and closer to perfection than the married. The actual situation in the early church was mixed, however. In the East, it was held that bishops should be celibate but the ordinary clergy may be married. This pattern was established at least by the time of the General Councils and prevails in the Eastern Orthodox church today. In the West, partly in response to the social disruptions, regional churches and finally the papacy enjoined celibacy for all clergy, and this was observed (at least officially) everywhere in the West by the Middle Ages.

Patterns of popular Christian worship also evolved strikingly. One feature was devotion to the Blessed Virgin Mary, mother of Jesus Christ, and to other saints. It had roots in the early church's veneration of martyrs and in Christian belief that all who are in Christ, whether in this life or the next, are one family and so able to communicate with and help one another. Now this area of the faith grew and expanded. Shrines and altars to saints and festivals for them appeared in both East and West; statues in the West and icons (sacred paintings) in the East, as well as saints' relics—bones, clothing—came to focus this devotion. The cultus, especially for the vast illiterate masses now Christianized, provided a deeply felt color and warmth. With it also came pilgrimages, journeys for the sake of devotion to Jerusalem and other holy places.

Christian life now had two basic emphases: the winning of eternal life in heaven and the avoiding of hell after death, and following Christian moral teachings while on earth. Although the Last Judgment, typically portrayed on the rear wall of medieval churches, was much regarded, like death it was chiefly seen as a narrow portal to heaven. Heaven was gained through the **sacraments** (baptism, Holy Communion, and the "last rites" especially) and by prayer, penitence for sins, and a moral life. Morality included doing those things that would make earthly society just and stable, a worthy prologue to heaven. Thus Christian moral teaching helped to make the medieval world, which idealized itself as an unchanging human social order lying between the time of Christ and the Last Judgment.

Medieval Christendom

Let us look at the religious life of a medieval peasant, typical of the vast majority of people in Europe between 800 and 1500, and in many places until much later. A peasant's life would center around the village where other peasants lived, the manor or castle of the lord, and the church. In some cases the lord would actually be a bishop or abbot; usually he would be a hereditary feudal lord, who would spend much of his time leading his knights, in combat with other lords and their knights and who would probably name the priest of the church.

Most villagers would be illiterate or virtually so; the peasants and probably the lord and his household would consider reading beyond or beneath them; the priest might have a limited education in theology and would be able to recite the service in Latin. Education grew gradually more prevalent among both clergy and genteel laity as the Middle Ages wore on; but for the most part only bards, monks, lawyers, and Jews had anything that resembled real learning. Their world was beyond the horizon of the peasant.

As serfs, the peasants were bound to the soil of the manor and never would have been more than a few miles from the village where they had been born. They would live and die in sight of its church spire. The village was a shabby affair of mud, wattle, and thatch; above it loomed the imposing but grim castle or manor house of the lord. In theory, the serfs were obligated from birth to the service of the lord in the castle, although they had plots of their own as well as the lord's fields that they worked. The lord could employ them, tax them, and judge them at law as he saw fit. They could not marry without his consent nor leave the estate. In

---

FUNDAMENTAL FEATURES OF CHRISTIANITY

THEORETICAL

Basic Worldview	A world made by God, but fallen far from harmony with his will; Jesus Christ bridges the gap between God and humanity. In this situation faith and love are required.
God or Ultimate Reality	A sovereign, personal, all-good creator God.
Origin of the World	Creation by God.
Destiny of the World	At the end of time, to be judged and then remade as a paradise of God.
Origin of Humans	Created individually by God.
Destiny of Humans	Judgment and resurrection on the last day; eternal life.
Revelation or Mediation between the Ultimate and the Human	Supreme self-manifestation by God in Jesus Christ the mediator; revelation in scripture and, especially in the Roman Catholic, Eastern Orthodox, and Anglican traditions, the tradition and authority of the Christian church.

PRACTICAL

What Is Expected of Humans: Worship, Practices, Behavior	To seek to know God, to worship him, to practice the ethics of love and service.

SOCIOLOGICAL

Major Social Institutions	The Christian church, divided into many traditional denominations; also monastic orders, missionary works, numerous associations.

practice, however, the relationship was complex and mitigated by custom, for the lord was also dependent on the serfs and lived close to them in an isolated community. Lord and peasant shared feasts in the great hall, and all but the greatest lords had to work alongside their peasants at harvest and were hungry with them during the cruel medieval winter if that year's harvest was poor.

The center of this community was the parish church. This stone building was an island of relative grace and color in a drab world. It might have vivid paintings and windows showing supernal things: a radiant saint, the wondrous Mother of God with her warm open arms and compassionate look, Christ judging high and low alike on the dreaded Last Day. At the front would be the richly decked altar, with its hangings, glowing cross, and flickering candles. A scent of incense might hang in the air. This place was different from the cold, heavy castle with its endless fighting, or the drab village, with its often hungry and sick inhabitants. It was clearly the portal of another world of heavenly terror and joy, a magic lens that enabled a richer level of perception.

On Sunday morning bells from this church would ring out, and the lord and his family and knights would gather together with the peasants in the church for Mass, generally at nine o'clock. The priest in his vestments would stand before the altar and, with many bows and elaborate gestures, wavings of incense and strikings of bells, celebrate the Mass. It was the same offering and blessing of bread that the early Christians had done in their catacombs and upper rooms, but the priest would be muttering now in an old and sacred tongue the words that made the wafers of bread and cup of wine the Body and Blood of Christ, for the saving of souls in his parish. He might also give a sermon. Priest and church were supported by *glebe lands,* fields of the manor set aside whose revenues went to this cause.

Besides Sundays, numerous festivals of saints broke the tedium and hard work of village life. Then would come special services, dancing, fairs, and traditional practices; some of them, like the Procession of the White Lady of Banbury (cited in Chapter 2), which brought great delight to the peasants, had clear pre-Christian background.[12]

There were other breaks in the rhythm too. Merchants and tradesmen were able to make pilgrimages to shrines where miracles were said to take place, as Chaucer's pilgrims did, both men and independent women like the Abbess and the wife of Bath, to Canterbury. Some even went as far as Jerusalem. In other ways, too, the pattern of medieval life was often broken, for the Middle Ages were by no means the static "Age of Faith" sometimes imagined. Changes and dissidents were always present. The vicissitudes of war and weather and often disease swept continually through medieval town and countryside.

Rumors of the Crusades—those remarkable combinations of bloodthirstiness, greed, and piety—must have reached almost everywhere. The Crusades expressed the very spirit of medievalism, but they helped to bring that age to an end by opening up contact with new ideas from the East and from the Greek culture better preserved there, as well as leading to deep-seated enmity between Christian Europe and Islam and between Eastern and Western Christianity.

In the year 1054, before the Crusades started (in 1095), came the formal rupture between the Eastern Orthodox and Western (Roman) Catholic churches. The official reason was the *filioque* question, whether the Holy Spirit proceeds from both God the Father and God the Son (as the Western version of the Nicene Creed stated), or from the Father alone (as the Eastern version had it), and a few other theological and ecclesiastical issues of similar quality. But the real issue was the growing authority of the papacy in the West (the word *filioque,* "and the Son," had been added to the Western Nicene Creed by authority of the Pope, not of a General Council), and even more perhaps by wide cultural differences emerging between Western Europe and the Byzantine East. The split was effectively made irrevocable by the Crusades; the sack of Constantinople by soldiers of the cross in 1204 left a bitter legacy that made lasting reconciliation impossible.

The greatest Western religious thinker in the Middle Ages was **Thomas Aquinas** (c. 1225–1274), the major figure of the style of philosophy known as *scholasticism*. Influenced by the Aristotelianism of the Muslim thinker of Cordova, Averroës (whose works had been discovered by the West during the Crusades), Aquinas was concerned to distinguish between the realm of nature where reason holds sway and the realm of faith where revelation adds its gifts. The existence of God, shown by nature, is (he stated) knowable through reason alone. But the way to salvation can only be known by revealed Christian faith. The result of this philosophical and theological labor was a vast synthesis of Aristotelian science and philosophy, Christianity, and medieval experience, which summed up the vision of that age and has been the most important intellectual force in Roman Catholicism down to the present. In it, all beings under God—angels, humanity, matter, sound reason, and sure revelation—have their logical places and reasonable duties in reflecting God's glory, a vision expressed more poetically but no more powerfully in the *Divine Comedy* of Dante Alighieri.

The Middle Ages teemed with new religious movements centering in holy, charismatic personalities, increasingly so as time advanced. The important thing to note is that these were challenges to the medieval order by a new, sometimes cantankerous, but always deeply felt, individualism and a rejection of the old corporate village faith of the parish church and the succession of festivals.[13] It is important also to realize that there were skeptics and religiously indifferent persons in the Middle Ages as today, and that many areas were barely reached by the church.

Most of the new religious movements were reactions to the church in favor of "Gospel simplicity" and "inwardness." They favored asceticism, fervent religious feelings, and freedom of movement for religious persons in contrast to the comparative wealth, objective worship of shrine and sacrament, and rootedness in feudal village and agricultural patterns of the conventional church. The dissident movements were, significantly, strongest among the crafts- and tradespeople of the burgeoning towns, although sometimes they swept through countryside districts on a wave of social protest. They were a combination of the age-old "holy man" ideal (which was sometimes exemplified by women as well) and the modern severing of religion from its rural roots. Both motifs contrast with the medieval alliance of religious and feudal concepts, and of Christianity and agricultural religion.

Some of these movements, like that of Francis of Assisi and his friars, remained within the orbit of orthodoxy. Francis, the "Little Poor Man," lived and inspired many others to live a life of Christian perfection marked by poverty, universal love, and a new personal devotion to the human Christ in the manger and on the cross. His order of friars, or "brothers," wandering, begging, and relatively free from control by bishop or parish priest, transmitted this experience throughout Europe and soon enough to Latin America and the Orient.

Other such preachers, however, were considered heretical. Some, like the Albigensians or Cathari, who were the object of brutal persecution in the thirteenth century, were inspired by the ancient Gnostic-type religion called Manichaeism (which held that matter is the source of evil), as well as by simplicity and inwardness. The Albigensians so honored spirit above flesh that they held self-starvation to be a noble thing. Others, like the Waldensians, Lollards, and Hussites, were more concerned to conform Christian life to the Bible according to their own specific beliefs.

The Reformation and Martin Luther

The next development was the Reformation, which carried all these trends to their natural conclusion—a new style of Christianity. Perhaps the onset of change was abetted by the Black Death, or bubonic plague, which swept across Europe, wiping out something like a third of the population from 1348 to 1350, disrupting traditional patterns of society, leaving many parishes without clergy, and on a deeper level going far toward discrediting the traditional faith and church. (People asked themselves, "Why did good and bad alike succumb to the plague? Why did the prayers of the traditional church not protect us?")

At the same time, the prestige of the papacy as the unifying force in Europe and Christendom was greatly weakened by the abduction of the Pope by agents of the French king in 1309 and the relocation of the papal residence to Avignon, under French domination, from 1309 to 1377. Above all the papacy's image was tarnished by the resultant Great Schism of 1378–1417, when two "popes" reigned, one in Rome and one in Avignon, each claiming to be the true ruler of the church and each holding the allegiance of several nations.

Against this background, groups such as the English Lollards, followers of John Wycliffe, began around 1380 to demand such reforms as abolition of clerical celibacy, the use of images, prayers for the dead, pilgrimages, and elaborate vestments. They demanded that the clergy should chiefly preach and that the scriptures should be freely available to all in the vernacular language. In Bohemia and Moravia, the Hussites, followers of John Hus, made similar demands, particularly asking that the church manifest poverty and that church lands be expropriated. Some, like John Hus in 1415, were executed as heretics by burning at the stake.

It was not until the sixteenth century, however, that new ideas came into their own at a time of the slow decline of feudalism, the rise to prominence of towns, and the corresponding shift of Christian emphasis (even in Catholic mysticism) from churchly and sacramental religion to a preoccupation with inner motivation and experience. It would be an oversimplification to say that these changes caused the Reformation. The modern mind was also shaped by Renaissance businessmen and intellectuals in Catholic Italy who shared many of the new attitudes yet did not become Protestant. But certainly social changes and the Reformation went together.

The Reformation was overtly focused on spiritual and theological issues, however. The man who by far most influenced its course, Martin Luther (1483–1546), was little concerned consciously with these matters of social history. He had been a scholarly friar of the Augustinian order since the age of 21, though his father—a strict, pious, enterprising civic leader engaged in the mining business in the small German town of Eisleben—was typical of the kind of man the Reformation would help to supersede knights, lords, and peasants. Nonetheless, it was Luther's deeply inward spiritual struggles that defined the issues, language, and direction of the Reformation.

In his monastery, Luther experienced grueling anxiety. His problem was that he felt himself a sinner, however blameless a life he had lived as a monk. So long as he thought of it in terms of how much he had to do, what standards he had to meet, what religious acts he had to perform, and what devout feelings he had to feel, he could only live, it seemed, in a cruel uncertainty, which would virtually lead to madness if one were really serious about it—and Luther was nothing if not serious. He felt trapped; he was commanded to love God, but how could one love a God whose demands left one in such anguish? Could he ever know if he had done enough?

Then, in studying the scriptures, Luther struggled with the lines "He who is righteous by faith shall live" (Habakkuk 2:4, Romans 1:17), until this saying provided a sunrise of new awareness that led to his doctrine of *sola fides,* "faith alone." He realized to the depths of his being that what set a person in right relationship with God was not the things he had been trying before, but simple faith—sincere belief, trust, and intention—and this as a matter of inner attitude was available to anyone at any time. In fact, it is not really a matter of what we do at all, for faith is first of all a gift—a grace (from *gratia,* meaning "free") from God—always free, always poured out in love, to which we only can respond with sincerity. When Luther realized this, all else appeared superfluous and likely to confuse. For this reason he insisted also on the principle of *sola scriptura,* the Bible alone as guide to Christian faith and practice, for he felt that salvation by grace through faith was the clear and central message of the scriptures, and that its obscuring had come about through overlays of human philosophy and ecclesiastical tradition.

Luther's new understanding of Christianity first brought him into conflict with its medieval version over the issue of the sale of **indulgences**. Indulgences were related to the doctrine of **purgatory**—a universally held medieval belief that there is an intermediate state between heaven and hell for those who die neither saints nor hopeless sinners. Their souls suffer purging fires for a long or short time, until they have been cleansed of evil and justice is satisfied, and they can then await entry into the presence of God. The Pope, it was believed, held the spiritual key to a "treasury of merit"—the superabundance of merit attained by Christ and the saints. Indulgences were certificates issued by the Pope, the effect of which was to transfer to the penitent some of this merit. This affirmed that because the recipient had done an adequate number of acts of penitence and devotion, so many "days"—or possibly all—of his or her prospective suffering in purgatory had been remitted. Indulgences could be obtained for oneself or even by one person on behalf of another, living or dead.

This profoundly medieval doctrine was not without its attractive side. It was a concrete way of stating the benefits accrued from such extra and innocent religious acts as pilgrimage, and it suggested, in the exchange of merit idea, that Christians deeply share in one another's lives and can bear one another's burdens. It was an implementation of the communion of saints. Indulgences are still made available in the Roman Catholic Church. But in Luther's day, indulgences were being widely distributed in Germany with little consideration but for the donation of money customarily given by the recipient. In effect, they were being used as a means of church fund-raising, and a special drive was on to raise funds for the building of St. Peter's Basilica in Rome. Moreover, the theology behind indulgences went very much counter to Luther's new inner discovery of salvation by grace through faith only. The use indulgences by the Roman Catholic Church at that time also raised the hackles of nascent German nationalism, for many Germans felt that they were being exploited for the sake of interests of Rome.

On October 31, 1517, Luther reportedly posted 95 theses, or points for debate, on the door of All Saints Church in Wittenberg, which served as the university's bulletin board. It was the eve of All Saints' Day, when many relics of the saints (a comparably questionable matter with Luther) would be exposed for veneration in that church. In the famous Ninety-five Theses, Luther spoke against abuses of indulgences, relics, and the like, but the tone was not extreme, nor did he question papal authority or the doctrine of purgatory as such. He stressed the supreme value of inwardness and of sharing the sufferings of Christ more than prematurely trying to take advantage of heaven: a theology of the cross rather than a theology of glory.

This challenge started as a theological dispute but quickly escalated beyond what one would normally expect of such arguments among monks. Luther was engaged in a course that finally led to his rejection of papal authority as its logical outcome, and this in turn produced his excommunication by Rome in 1521.

Public opinion in Germany tended to take Luther's side. Spurred on by his pamphlet "Address to the Christian Nobility of the German Nation," a sense of German national pride and identity, long smoldering under cultural and spiritual domination from southern Europe, was inflamed. When Luther was summoned before the Imperial Diet at Worms to defend himself, he may not actually have used the famous words, "Here I stand; God help me, I can do no other," but that was what he meant, and his defiance of resented authority deeply stirred many a German knight. But this did not please the young Holy Roman Emperor Charles V, who desired to continue the alliance between his throne and that of the Pope.[14]

The test of inward faith, rather than rites, sacraments, or pious deeds, was congruous with a longstanding German mystical bent. The precise theological points at issue may have mattered less to the knights and people at large than to scholars, but the common folk grasped the implication that the new teachings meant all persons were fully equal before God. When Luther's German Bible and simplified services in the vernacular soon appeared, people well understood both the new orientation toward inward faith and the implicit Germanic self-affirmation.

Luther had hoped to see the church purified and Christians everywhere find new inner freedom and peace. It was a cause of grief and bitterness to him that one of the most conspicuous results of reform was conflict—theological, political, and military. In the following century conflict escalated into the devastating Thirty Years' War, finally settled at the peace of Westphalia in 1648. Scandinavia, most of northern Germany, and small minorities elsewhere were thereafter **Lutheran**.

Calvin

The most important reformer after Luther was John Calvin (1509–1564). He was French but is associated mainly with Geneva in Switzerland. As a young man he was a Renaissance **humanist**, but in 1533 he was converted to the Protestant movement that Luther had spearheaded. He immediately wrote his theological masterpiece, *Institutes of the Christian Religion*. The brief first edition was published in 1536, but Calvin kept revising and expanding it until the definitive edition of 1559.

After 1541, Calvin lived in Geneva, which had recently thrown out its ruling bishop and become Protestant. Calvin was invited to take over leadership. Reluctantly (he much preferred a quiet scholarly life), he accepted. During his stay, Geneva became a kind of holy community of the Reformed faith, dominated by Calvin and other clergy, who enforced strict moral rectitude and correct belief in church and city government alike.

Calvin's theology is based on a strong contrast between the infinite greatness and power of God and the sinfulness of humanity. God's glory fills the universe; the division between the sacred and the secular is done away with, for all is sacred. Further, Calvin held to a doctrine of **predestination**—all that happens is due solely to God's will, from life and death to the smallest seemingly accidental events. Nonetheless, humankind is in rebellion against God; God permits this in order that his mercy may be shown in the salvation of those whom he chooses, while Divine justice is affirmed by the punishment of the rest. Those whom God chooses for eternal life do not have any merit of their own; they are recipients of his grace which, as Luther (following Augustine) had emphasized, must come before anything right that humans can do. The "elect," those chosen through grace, will be marked by a righteous life and a seemingly spontaneous and persevering predilection for true religion. Calvin's theology also emphasized the mystical union of the Christian with Christ.

Calvin stressed, like Luther, the importance of the Bible alone as the normative guide for Christians. In church organization, he made greater changes than did Luther. Doing away with bishops, he gave considerable place to local control and boards of elders, or **presbyters**. But like Luther he dealt harshly with dissenters.

The sacraments of baptism and the Lord's Supper were greatly simplified in administration, and the preaching of the **Word of God**, the chief means by which people are called to faith and grace, was given new emphasis.

The theology and style of church life left by John Calvin has been much criticized; and indeed, when **Calvinism** appears without the panoramic world vision and inner piety of its best men and women, it can easily become harsh and rigid. But Calvinism's positive role in the making of the modern world must be appreciated. Calvinism contributed immensely to the development of democracy: indirectly through its new emphasis on the equality of all before God, for the elect might be found in any social station, and directly through the model of its presbyterian or congregational forms of church organization, which gave many sorts of people experience in decision-making responsibilities, and did not fit as well with feudalism or absolute monarchy as did bishops. Calvinists also insisted, as did other Protestants, that everyone should be able to read the Bible, and this gave much impetus to education. Finally, it can be noted that Calvinism appealed especially to the rising business class in Western Europe. Its stress on the elect's sense of inner call, commitment, and righteousness in the midst of work in the world, rather than sacerdotalism or monasticism, and its stern ethics focusing on self-denial, hard work, and individual responsibility contributed to the psychology that made this class prosperous and, in fact, for several centuries second to none in worldwide influence. Sometimes prosperity was seen as in itself a sign of divine election and favor.

Today, churches known as Reformed, Presbyterian, or Congregational are from the Calvinist tradition, although Calvin's original message has been varyingly modified by them over the years. Calvinism became dominant in Holland, Scotland, and parts of Germany and Switzerland. The Puritan movement in England and America was Calvinist as well and has had tremendous impact on life in those countries and in their spheres of influence. Minority Protestant churches in France, Hungary, and some other parts of Europe are also Calvinist in background.

The English Reformation

In England the Reformation took yet another form. It is natural that this country of Wycliffe and the Lollards, and of emerging nationalism as well, should have harbored many people who responded enthusiastically to news of the events in Germany. Yet the English character has always exhibited a sense of pragmatism, moderation, and appreciation of tradition as well as a thirst for reform. All of this is evident in the English Reformation. Significantly, it did not receive its impetus from a wholly engaged reformer such as Luther or Calvin, but from a rather sordid political matter. The king, Henry VIII, had been an enthusiastic defender of the old faith against the reformers, but in the early 1530s he desired to divorce his queen, Catherine of Aragon, because she had been unable to give him a living male heir.

This step required a dispensation from the Pope, which the latter, Clement VII, was unwilling to authorize. Therefore, Henry called upon Parliament to sever relations with Rome and make the king supreme head of the church in England. The resultant Act of Supremacy was passed in 1534. Henry was divorced and married again, not for the last time.

Although strained relations between Rome and England were no new thing, undoubtedly the continental Reformation created an atmosphere conducive to taking this final step. But those who desired a more thoroughgoing reformation were initially disappointed. Monasteries, convents, and pilgrimage shrines were promptly dissolved and their wealth divided among Henry's henchmen, but otherwise little changed. Most of the same bishops remained in their sees, and the same celibate priests in their parishes, saying the same Latin mass. The king rigorously enforced Catholic doctrinal orthodoxy.

But after Henry VIII died in 1546, the dike could no longer hold. Calvinist influence now pouring in from Geneva overbalanced the conservative side. A new form of worship in the English language, the *Book of Common Prayer,* was produced in 1549. Essentially, it perpetuated the basic structure of the old Latin forms but with substantial concessions to Protestantism on sensitive issues, such as its formal elimination of devotion to saints. It was over a century before the religious situation in England was fully stabilized, but the essential outline of its official form, the Church of England, was already apparent: In the Prayer Book of 1549, characterized by continuity of church structure from the Middle Ages; in English-language worship, which was Catholic in outline but designed to be nonoffensive to moderate Protestants; and in a pragmatic mentality (which emerged more slowly), allowing for some divergence of theological opinion among individual clergy and members, especially between the Catholic and Protestant traditions that met in the Church of England's emerging **Anglicanism**.

A minority in England maintained allegiance to the Church of Rome. Over the next two centuries, others separated themselves from Anglicanism into more fully Protestant groups: Puritan (Calvinist), Baptist, Quaker, and Methodist. We shall now examine the story of groups such as these.

Radical Reform

Outside the great movements of Luther and Calvin, and that in England, and generally without the support of rulers, the Reformation stirred up the zeal of many who wanted many more far-reaching changes in the church and often also in society. These movements typically stressed the need for personal conversion experiences, moral perfection, and a close following of the New Testament both in faith and social life. They varied from Anabaptists (indirectly the forebears of modern Baptists in England and America), who rejected the baptism of infants, insisting that Christians should have a personal conversion experience and be baptized only after it; and Mennonites, who were perfectionists, pacifists, and often communalists; to rationalistic Unitarians, such as Michael Servetus, who denied the doctrine of the Trinity and was burned at the stake in Calvin's Geneva.[15]

The non-Anglican Protestant groups in England have been particularly influential in world Christianity. That is because they have flourished wherever the far-flung British people have settled overseas—especially in a nation as large and powerful as the United States—and because they have generally been active in missionary work. Many of these Dissenters or Nonconformists, as they were called in England, emigrated overseas because of discrimination or persecution against them in the homeland.

British nonconformity has its post-Reformation roots in the Puritan movement that began in the Church of England in the latter part of the sixteenth century. It was comprised of highly Protestant-oriented Anglicans who wished to "purify" the church of what they saw as persisting elements of Catholicism. Puritans wanted simple (though long) services emphasizing preaching, Biblical doctrine (with a Calvinist tone), moral earnestness, and an emphasis on the religious life and role of the laity. Some of them preferred the presbyterian or congregational forms of church government to the bishops of the established church.

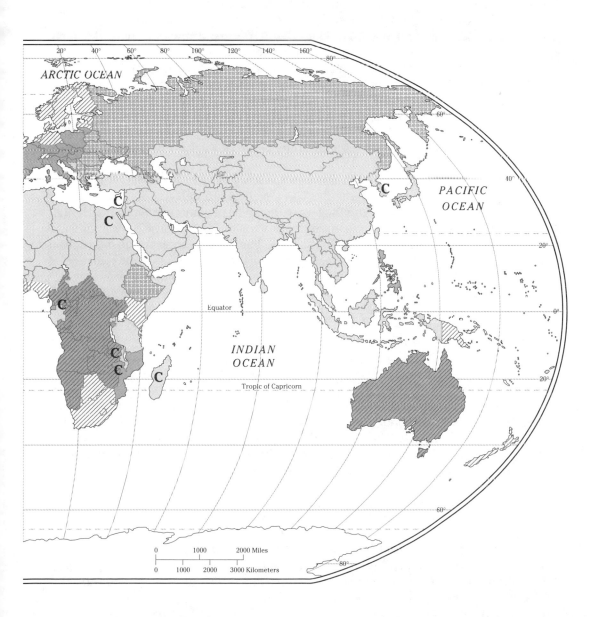

By the 1580s, some Puritans realized that the Church of England was not going to change its basic character (which was based on the Catholic–Protestant compromise known as the "Elizabethan settlement") in the direction they wished. Some of them felt compelled by conscience to worship apart from it with like-minded believers as the "gathered church." They were called "Independents" or "Separatists." These persons were severely repressed; some emigrated, like the "Pilgrims" who established Plymouth Colony in 1620.

In the seventeenth century, the fortunes of Puritanism and dissent rose and fell dramatically, becoming entangled in fierce battles between king and parliament, old aristocracy and rising middle class, as England painfully wrenched itself into the modern world. In general, the Stuart kings of the century strongly supported episcopacy and the Church of England (when they were not Roman Catholic sympathizers), while Parliament and the rising middle class favored Puritanism. Religion was not the only issue, but it was an age when religious positions were taken very seriously and became flags of allegiance of classes and interests as well as passionately held convictions. These struggles climaxed with the civil war between royal and parliamentary forces in the 1640s, the parliamentary Puritan victory and the beheading of King Charles I in 1649, and the subsequent rule of England by the faction controlled by Oliver Cromwell.

The 1650s, the decade of Cromwell's Commonwealth, were rife with radical social as well as religious movements. The Levellers wanted to abolish all hierarchical distinctions in society. The Diggers were agrarian communalists who, though harassed by both the law and violent mobs, endeavored to cultivate common land they said should be made available to the poor. The Ranters showed the interaction of radical political and spiritual protest by bringing to such causes their rejection of all authority of scripture or creed, holding instead only to an inner experience of Christ that makes all equal and free. But hope that this radical decade signaled a new age in which the world would truly be "turned upside down" were dashed by the end of the Commonwealth in 1660. Most of these movements did not survive. One that did, and that has long preserved—though sometimes in rather fossilized form—the spirit of the age of Levellers, Diggers, and Ranters—is the Religious Society of Friends, commonly called the **Quakers**. Founded in the 1650s by George Fox (1624–1691) and others, the Quaker movement carries to one sort of logical conclusion the quest for earnestness, truly inward religion, and the equality of all believers. Quakers reject all "outward" rites, such as baptism with water and ritualistic Holy Communion, wishing instead to be baptized and commune with God inwardly. They consider all persons to be equally ministers, and they were far ahead of their time in accepting the spiritual equality of men and women in the ministry. Quakers also refuse on religious grounds such practices as oathtaking, removing one's hat before anyone but God, and participation in war. Their meetings for worship are conducted in silence unless anyone feels moved by the "Inner Light" to speak or pray.

In 1660, after Cromwell's death, the monarchy was restored, and Anglicanism was once again in the saddle. At first, despite the wishes of the new king, Charles II, for religious liberty, punishment was once again visited upon Dissenters. But gradually, as the bloody events since the Reformation made it clear that national uniformity in religion was a hopeless ideal, a trend toward accepting religious pluralism and liberty set in, culminating in the Toleration Act of 1689. It granted freedom of worship to all Christians except Roman Catholics and Unitarians. Their emancipation was not to come until much later.

These dramatic events had momentous consequences for the emerging denominationalism of the English-speaking world, including America—then a thin ribbon of seaboard colonies on the east coast of the New World. On both sides of the Atlantic, Congregationalism became the successor of the independent Separatist congregations. English and American Baptists came from the same background; they were originally independent congregations who differed little from the others save in their rejection of infant baptism and their insistence that baptism can be given only to believers who have made a mature confession of faith. But as time went on, the general mood of Baptists shifted from Puritan Calvinism toward **Arminianism**—that is, emphasis on the individual's freedom to decide rather than on predestination. This is evident today in the tendency of Baptist preaching to stress the individual's responsibility to make a decision for faith in Christ.

The last great English dissenting movement was Methodism. It did not arise until the eighteenth century under the leadership of the Anglican clergyman John Wesley (1703–1791). After a youthful conversion experience, Wesley became a powerful preacher who took all England as his parish, teaching the necessity of genuine conversion and the possibility of Christian perfection. This ministry made a powerful impact amid the social evils of the early Industrial Revolution (of which Wesley was well aware), in a time when the older churches were at a low ebb after the passions of the previous century. Societies and classes were formed in numerous communities to study and practice the Wesleyan approach. Although Wesley himself never intended that his movement should leave the Church of England, shortly after his death many of these groups, finding they could no longer keep their new wine in old bottles, became independent churches, both in England and in America. At least as many followers of Wesley remained within the Church of England to become the seedbed of a powerful Anglican **evangelical** movement.

The Catholic Reformation

During the period of the Protestant Reformation, far-reaching developments were also taking place in the papal church against which the Protestants had rebelled, the church known—in distinction from Protestantism—as Roman Catholic. These developments are sometimes known collectively as the Counter-Reformation. But there was more to them than mere reaction to Protestant criticism, even though that formidable challenge certainly pressed Catholics to rethink and strengthen their tradition.

Some moves for Catholic reformation had been underway even before the Protestant reformers. The Fifth Lateran Council (1512–1517), on the eve of their Reformation, accomplished little but kept the idea of internal reform alive. Church leaders such as Cardinal Ximenez de Cisneros (1436–1517) in Spain had worked diligently for the improvement of clerical education and standards. But after Luther and Calvin, such efforts cried out for considerably augmented energy and scope. The need was answered by widespread renewed emphasis on Catholic education and discipline, especially among priests, and above all by new religious orders such as the Capuchins (1528) and the Jesuits (1540), dedicated to missionary work abroad and to holding the line against Protestantism in Europe.

The new situation also called for even greater Catholic unity and clearer definitions of the Catholic position, especially in regard to issues raised by the Protestant reformers. In that task the **Council of Trent** (1545–1563) is the centerpiece. At first attempting unsuccessfully to achieve reconciliation with the Protestants, the Council during a second phase beginning in 1551 sought above all to purify and then defend the traditional Catholicism of the Middle Ages and before. The result of the Council's decrees was a church clearly governed by the Pope and his "cabinet," or **Curia**, possessing a high degree of uniformity in doctrine and worship (centered in the Latin Mass); firmly maintaining such controverted teachings as purgatory and the invocation of saints; sure of its own authority based on both scripture and tradition rightly interpreted by its **magisterium**, or teaching jurisdiction; determined to uphold high levels of training and commitment; prepared to win back what it could from the Protestants and to spread itself over the earth. This was essentially the style of Catholicism that was to prevail for four centuries.

Christian Mysticism and Devotion

Before presenting the characteristics of the major branches of Christianity today, let us pause to look at the mystical and devotional side of the religion and its literary expression. Perhaps more than other religions, Christianity makes a clear-cut distinction between theological writing and mystical-devotional literature. Christian doctrine and thought have an objective and a historical quality that makes it possible to understand them, at least superficially, without direct experience of the divine realities that lie behind them. Many would say that one can have saving faith without the sort of experience of God of which mystics and devotees speak. In this respect, Christianity shows its difference from a religion like Buddhism, in which the equivalent of salvation would have to be the ultimate transformation of consciousness represented by Nirvana. But mainstream Christian theology and preaching is generally more concerned with salvation than with mystical experiences to which not every Christian is called.

By mystical experience we mean experience interpreted as immediate contact with the Divine, very frequently expressed in the language of unity: "I felt the oneness of all things," "I was united with God." Mystical writings describe this experience and how to attain it. Devotional writing presents prayers and meditations addressed to God or intended to lead one's mind toward union with him. Since the one who prays or meditates is still speaking to God or thinking about him, a certain distance, however filled with love and feeling, remains between that person and the Divine. Devotion, then, falls short of the mystic's experience of sheer union. That is why mystical experience is often said to be "beyond words," and mystics may shock the conventionally pious when they say that even prayer and meditation are practices to be surpassed.

Though not the same as the theological tradition, there is a Christian tradition of mystical and devotional writing worthy of comparison with that of any other faith and that cannot be neglected if one desires to comprehend the fullness of Christianity as a religion. Moreover, the Christian mystics, while they sometimes say startling and disturbing things, also say things (not infrequently at the same time) that go to the very heart of Christianity's essential meaning—or so many feel who have studied them long and deeply.

The first Christian mysticism after the New Testament was deeply indebted to Neoplatonic philosophy for its terminology and philosophical concepts. But instead of developing categories for laying out the Christian view of God, Christ, Holy Spirit, salvation, and so forth, mysticism was concerned to show how the soul inwardly rises to more perfect union with the One. Classical Christian mysticism was, therefore, less interested in borrowing Neoplatonic terms for theological purposes than in mining the vein of Neoplatonism that instructs that in raising minds and hearts to the infinite we must pass beyond words and concepts.

The most influential Christian mystical writings of this sort are those of the writer who called himself Dionysius the Areopagite—the Greek philosopher of the Book of Acts who heard Paul on Mars Hill (Areopagos) in Athens. The union of Christianity and Greek thought symbolically suggested by this attribution is very apt, but the writings, which include *The Mystical Theology* and *The Divine Names,* are now believed to be by a Syrian monk of the sixth century.

"Dionysius" was a Neoplatonist who believed that God in his fullness and infinity is beyond human knowledge and so is ultimately nameless and ineffable. Nothing we could say about him is adequate to the unbounded mystery of Divine being. God is thus spoken of by Dionysius as a "darkness which is beyond light"—though the darkness is really due to an excess of light beyond that which human faculties can handle, like the shadows that fall across the eyes when we try to look directly at the sun. The way to God, then, is through an "unknowing" by which human intellect and feelings, too frail for this sublimest task, are stilled in mystical contemplation. "We pray," Dionysius says, "that we may come unto this darkness which is beyond light, and through the loss of sight and knowledge may see and know that which is above vision and knowledge." This "Dionysiac" Neoplatonist approach was most influential in the Christian mysticism of the Middle Ages and the Reformation.

But during the same Middle Ages, something else began stirring as well. A Christian mysticism of the affirmation of images was coming to flower. If mysticism of the Neoplatonist, "Dionysiac" type says to take away all that is not God, and so is often called the "negative way," its counterpart is the affirming way of using images in the mind and before the eyes as stepping stones to God.[16] It was not wholly a medieval product, having roots in the piety of Paul and Augustine. One example of an affirmative mystic was Francis of Assisi (1181–1226).

Francis of Assisi fervently promoted devotion to Jesus in the manger and on the cross, both affirmative pictures to which devotion could be affixed in mind and heart. Tradition credits the "Little Poor Man" of Assisi with making the first Christmas crèche and with receiving the **stigmata**, or marks of the nails and crown of thorns and wounded side of Christ on the cross, in his own flesh. The Franciscan order, which burgeoned in the late Middle Ages, eagerly carried his style of devotionalism throughout Western Europe and later to the Spanish and Portuguese New World.

Protestant mysticism began in the age of Luther himself. Lutheran and Calvinist Christianity centered on inward faith and the inner workings of grace, rather than the attainment of spiritual stages or mystical "states." However, others in the Protestant movement took things in a different direction. Sebastian Franck (1499–1542) and his disciple Valentine Weigel (1533–1588) were both Lutherans, the former a sometime preacher and the latter a pastor, and also both Dionysians. They wrote that God is beyond all notions, definitions, concepts, and thought, but is incarnate as the inner essence of humans. Another German, Jacob Boehme (1575–1624), a shoemaker, is widely considered the greatest Protestant mystical thinker. Boehme spoke of the Divine infinity beyond words and concepts as the Original Ground; its expression is through the interplay of opposites. All this is incarnate in humans.

Movements like seventeenth-century Pietism on the European continent and Wesleyan Methodism in eighteenth-century England so stressed the importance of inwardly felt conversion in the believer that they easily led to positive devotional focus on the catalyst of the change—Jesus Christ. The result was a highly Christocentric Protestantism, still immensely powerful, which mentally pictures, prays to, and inwardly relates to Jesus himself. This Christian style is well expressed in such hymns as "O Sacred Head Now Wounded," or "I Come to the Garden" ("He Walks with Me and He Talks with Me").

Roman Catholic mysticism during and after the Reformation era reflected comparable lines of development. The Roman church's greatest mystics and spiritual writers in this period tended also to be great founders or reformers of religious orders who labored on the spiritual, intellectual, and practical levels to enable their church to meet its new challenges. In particular this was true of the great sixteenth-century Spanish mystics: Ignatius of Loyola (1491–1556), founder of the Society of Jesus (Jesuits) and author of the celebrated *Spiritual Exercises;* John of the Cross (1542–1591), monastic reformer and writer of the profound *Dark Night of the Soul,* which explores the stripping away of self and sense one must pass through to reach, through love alone, the unitive state; and Teresa of Avila (1515–1582), also a reformer and spiritual writer of great perception on the stages of gain and loss leading to union, where even God is momentarily forgotten as he is gained.

In the next century, Roman Catholic leadership in exploring the spiritual life passed to France, where a group of devout and learned priests made the practice of meditation move further in the general direction of pietism through emphasis on picturing such subjects as the life of Christ in the mind and in filling oneself with affective feeling toward the savior.

The spirituality of the Eastern Orthodox Church has remained very conservative, long adhering in its essence to the Christian Neoplatonism of the early Christian centuries, yet also long remaining more deeply entwined with the lives of ordinary believers than has often been the case in the West.

Eastern Orthodoxy

The branch of Christianity called Orthodox is the dominant religious tradition of Greece, the Balkans, and Russia. There is a scattering in other parts of the Near East, and of course it is found wherever immigrants from its homelands have come, including the United States. (A Russian Orthodox cathedral was established at Sitka, Alaska, as early as 1794.) The Orthodox churches, about 160 million strong, are often called "Eastern" because their center of gravity is in Eastern Europe, although this faith is of worldwide importance. They are sometimes called Greek Orthodox, since the cultural and historical background is Greek. The tradition took its definitive form in the culturally Greek Byzantine Empire. But the majority of Orthodox Christians are now Slavic rather than Greek. The Orthodox churches of various nationalities commonly go by national names, such as Russian Orthodox, Serbian Orthodox, Rumanian Orthodox.

Orthodoxy likes to speak of itself as the oldest Christian church, and indeed geography makes its churches continuous with those that Paul and other apostles founded or visited in places like Thessalonika, Corinth, and Cyprus. But the ritual and ethos of the present-day Orthodox churches is essentially the form in which it crystallized in the Byzantine period before the fall of Constantinople to the Turks in 1453. Since then, most Orthodox lands have spent long centuries under Muslim or Mongol rule, just as most of them more recently have experienced Communist regimes that were cold toward church and religion. Both under the Byzantine Empire and sympathetic modern nation-states, and in a different way under the Ottoman Empire, the Orthodox Church has been very closely linked to the state and often controlled by it. This history, different from that of Christianity in the West, has inhibited outward development but has given Orthodoxy a deep relation to the national culture of several countries and often a very rich inner spiritual life.

The word "orthodox" has varying uses and connotations in English. For the people of the Eastern churches it is an attractive and strong word, not primarily suggesting rigid and narrow attitudes. They believe, of course, that their churches alone preserve the correct, or orthodox, tradition of Christian teaching and life from earliest times. But they also like to point out that in Greek the word "orthodox" can mean both "right teaching" and "right glory." The combination of these two gives insight into the world of Orthodox life.

A highly conservative mood informs the standard doctrinal teaching of the Orthodox churches. It is held that only a General Council can officially define doctrine, and only those seven councils held in Nicaea, Constantinople, Ephesus, and Chalcedon up to 787 C.E. are recognized. Moreover, Orthodox thought has been deeply influenced by Platonism with its assumption that what is most real and true

Russian Orthodox ceremony.

is unchanging. Thus, central to Orthodoxy is the reality of the Trinity, God as three in one—an eternal mystery that undergirds the world. Next is the eternal reality of the incarnation of God in Christ, not only a historical episode but an eternal involvement of God in the material world, through struggle and suffering, making the children of earth Divine, manifesting true glory.

On the one hand, this attitude has led to an exaltation of timeless contemplation, exemplified by devout Orthodox monks, such as those living virtually out of history on Mount Athos in Greece, whom all serious Orthodox regard as ideals and as unseen givers of life to the church. The goal, the Orthodox say, is to be deified in the sense of becoming "partakers of the Divine nature," actual sharers in God's own life; contemplation raises us to this level.

Yet on the other hand, Orthodoxy greatly celebrates Christ's Resurrection and the anticipated Last Day when God will make the new heaven and earth and be all in all. These events represent the triumph of God's suffering work in the world as he makes visible what the contemplative knows inwardly: it is infused with Divinity.

The worship side of Orthodoxy richly expresses these ideas. For one used to the plainness of much Western Christianity, a first visit to an Orthodox church can be an overwhelming experience. The service is long and may be in an unfamiliar tongue. But few will be untouched by the glowing color and the soaring, exotic music. The Divine Liturgy, as the main Sunday service is called, is also at heart the early church's offering and blessing of bread and wine. The ornate vestments shimmer richly, incense is swung into the music-laden air over and over, the book of the Gospel and the elements of bread and wine are brought out in procession.

Across a partition (the *iconostasis*) before the altar and at the church entry and elsewhere will be seen *icons*—vividly colored stylized paintings of Christ and the saints. These, which the faithful reverently kiss and before which they burn candles, have a very special meaning in Orthodoxy. Made according to holy traditions, they are seen as radiating the Divine Glory of the subjects and so are like peepholes into eternity and the means of raising oneself to it. In fact, the whole Divine Liturgy is seen as an experience of moving up into another plane, or conversely a breakthrough of heaven to earth. The entire intricately wrought interior of the building may be backgrounded in gold, representing eternity.

These experiences of the Divine that the church is believed to make available here on earth help one understand the activity of people in Orthodox worship. People will often be seen coming and going throughout the long service, or getting up on their own to pray and light candles, perhaps with prostrations, at various icons. The sense of individual freedom suggests the church is more like a home than an institution. At the same time, Orthodoxy inculcates a deep sense of community within which this freedom is possible. A sense of simple belonging to the Orthodox community is an interior identity that goes beyond any particular forms of outward expression. There is much that is important and traditional in matters of worship, fasting, and so forth, yet they hardly stifle the homey and spontaneous tone with legalism.

Something of the same feeling permeates the other forms of Orthodox social expression; this was particularly the case in old Russia. No country except India has had as many wandering holy men as Russia before the Communist Revolution. In some ways the Orthodox Christianity of "Holy Russia" was more Asian than Western in religious style. The *startsi,* holy monks or hermits, more often laymen than priests, familiar to readers of Dostoevsky, were venerated counselors and givers of blessing. Some remained in one place; some were perpetual pilgrims who wandered about the vast land—even as far as Jerusalem—with nothing but the clothes on their backs and perhaps a sacred book or two, begging or remaining silent unless pressed to teach. There were also the "Holy Fools," perhaps idiots, madmen by conventional standards, or cripples, who would babble nonsense, meow like a cat in church, or castigate a czar for his sins, yet before whom even nobility might bow with humility, for they were seen as embodiments of the suffering Christ and of the irrational side of God here on earth.[17]

Thus, Eastern Orthodoxy has quite distinctive forms in the three areas of religious expression: theological emphasis on God in Trinity and incarnation as eternally unchanging yet present all through the world, even in the lowliest, and always breaking through in mystery and glory; a worship that expresses that glory; and social forms making room for tradition, homeliness, and spontaneity in individuals within a mystical community.

Roman Catholicism

The Roman Catholic Church, the communion of Christians who recognize the supreme spiritual authority on earth of the bishop of Rome, the Pope, and who share much else as well, is the largest Christian body. A billion people are within its spiritual, or at least cultural, orbit. It is the dominant religious tradition in most of Southern and Central Europe, Ireland, and Latin America, and is an important minority in English-speaking North America, Australia, and parts of Africa and Asia.

Needless to say, there is, and long has been, much diversity, based on various cultures and individual emphases, within a religious institution that large, as well as a common core of teaching and practice. One thing outwardly links this realm together: acceptance of the Pope as symbol and guarantor of Christian unity. Even this sign has varied in appearance through the centuries, with Popes being weak and relatively little noted in some centuries and in others great potentates who played major roles in international politics, lavishly patronized the arts, or exercised near-absolute control over the church. Now understanding of the papal role, like much else, is changing. But its profoundest meaning, as a symbol of the catholicity, or universality, of the church, is likely to abide. With the papacy goes another characteristic that is also changing in nature, yet is deeply ingrained in the Latin past and Catholic present—an acceptance that some uniformity and centralized authority are good in the church, not only for practical reasons, but also because of the opportunity they provide members for spiritual growth through obedience and self-discipline.

The papacy is far from being the only distinguishing mark of the Roman Catholic Church, however, and many today would argue it is not one to be overemphasized, even though in some ways it symbolizes much that is distinctive about Roman Catholic experience. Here are some other general characteristics:[18]

1. *Affirmation of sacramentality and visible forms*. This attitude, shared by Eastern Orthodoxy and many Anglicans and Lutherans, affirms the central importance of the sacraments, or acts by which Divine grace is bestowed through material forms: water in baptism, bread and wine in Holy Communion. The seven sacraments recognized by the Roman Catholic Church are baptism, confirmation, penance (confession of sins and absolution or forgiveness mediated by a priest), the Eucharist (the Mass or Holy Communion), marriage, ordination, and unction (anointing of the sick and dying, part of the "last rites"). The same sacramental and visible

forms also affirm the appropriateness of colorful ceremonies, vestments, and images. They affirm through them the presence of the **numinous** in the church and the necessity of the church appearing to the world as a visible, organized community. The fundamental assumption is that God's work is not wholly invisible and unpredictable, but that God does work through specific matter, people, and institutions; that the incarnation of God in Christ authenticates this experience and God's promises confirm it. For Roman Catholics, the affirmation of appearances and the sacramental principle are ways of emphasizing that the world was created to be good and that the church is a visible and specific work of God on earth by which he comes to the world through the things of the world.

2. *The church as an instrument of mediation and communion between humans, including those departed—whether saints or sinners or mixed—and between humanity and God.* This characteristic interprets the role given the invocation of the saints as heavenly helpers, prayers for the spiritual growth of those who have left this life, and the importance of the church as God's "extended family" to Catholics. The principle of mediation also interprets the importance of ordained priests, who have a definite role as teachers and as mediators of grace through the sacraments. The institution of the priesthood has an objective side. The Roman Catholic Church maintains a clear pattern of doctrine, and priests and bishops are expected to uphold normative standards regarding devotional practices, celibacy of clergy, and moral issues such as abortion and birth control.

A Catholic priest celebrating Mass.

The legal model is an inheritance of Roman law, to which is added the belief that Christ gave to his church a distinctive teaching authority.

3. *The church as an organic and growing institution.* Besides affirming the church's organization and authority, Catholics increasingly harbor another feeling about it too: awareness that the Christian fellowship, the church, is an organic, growing, and so changing institution. The papacy, general councils, and other organs of the church's teaching authority have power to direct this growth, yet it is believed to move under the guidance of the Holy Spirit, who is always helping Christians better understand the truth given to them. Changes in rite and custom, and clearer definitions of what previously had been latent or unclear in doctrine (although doctrine itself does not change), accompany the church's pilgrimage through the ages. For example, the First Vatican Council in 1870 defined "papal infallibility" as the Pope being preserved from error when he exercises this defining function in a formal way. The **Second Vatican Council** (1962–1965), an event of major significance, liberalized the theological, practical, and sociological forms of Catholic expression by such things as authorizing the use of the vernacular (rather than Latin) in the liturgy of the church, authorizing and encouraging greater participation by laity in the church, acknowledging religious freedom and the relationship of each individual to God, and encouraging the adaptation of the church to the contemporary world.

The Roman Catholic Church, then, is an institution highly visible, sacramental, legal, and yet changing. While it certainly claims continuity with the church of the early centuries and the Middle Ages, it is equally not the same in all respects now as then. Let us look at some specific characteristics of present-day Roman Catholicism.

First, some essential doctrines. God is said to be accessible to reason. Faith means intellectual assent. In other words, one can know by reason that there is a God apart from the Christian revelation, and faith is recognizing in the mind that this is so. This is significant, for it indicates the partnership of religion and philosophy, and the belief, important to many Catholic attitudes, that there are basic truths upon which the Christian faith builds. The added revelation that comes through Christ is mediated through both scripture and tradition, the Bible and the church's lore interacting to cast light upon each other. Its basic points are the Trinity and the incarnation of God in Christ.

The Roman Catholic Church makes much of the Mother of Jesus, the Blessed Virgin Mary. This is fundamentally because her role guarantees the incarnation, but also because she is seen—in her acceptance of God's request that she bear his incarnating son—as a representative of the human race as it was before sin came. She is humanity responding perfectly to God's will and receiving the fullness of God's grace and reward. This is the meaning of the papally defined doctrines of the Immaculate Conception (1854): that Mary was herself conceived without original sin (the doctrine of the Immaculate Conception is not to be confused, as it often is, with the doctrine of the Virgin Birth of Christ); and of her bodily assumption into heaven, defined by the Pope in 1950, which makes her an exemplar of the Resurrection and heavenly reward of all the redeemed.

St. Alfonso Liguori (1696–1787) said, "What Jesus has by nature, Mary has by grace." The prerogatives of Mary, distinctively Christian even if corresponding to the paradigm of the pre-Christian Mediterranean goddesses like Isis and Cybele, and answering to the natural desire of many for feminine as well as masculine principles in religion, have made devotion to Mary notably popular. Her power in heaven is held to be immensely great, and her benevolence virtually unconditional. Marian piety has reached a high pitch in the last hundred years or so with the two previously mentioned definitions. They were paralleled by the widespread belief in appearances of Mary to heal and prophesy at such places as Lourdes in France and Fatima in Portugal, now extremely popular pilgrimage centers, with their holy grottos or wells, their appealing statues of Mary appearing to artless peasant children, their dramatic torchlight processions, and their ongoing miracles. After the Second Vatican Council there was a somewhat reduced interest in the Marian complex for a time, but it has revived in traditional form at shrines like Medugorje in Bosnia-Herzegovina and with new perspectives given by liberationist and feminist Catholics who have seen Mary as an ideal. Pope John Paul II avers a special connection to the Holy Mother.

Other significant doctrines include purgatory and the **canonization** of saints, a process by which the Pope (anciently, any bishop) declares that a given person of "heroic sanctity" is in heaven and so able to intercede on behalf of those who call upon him or her before the throne of God.

Worship is centered on the seven sacraments, although by no means is it limited to them. These include the initiatory rites of baptism and confirmation and the Mass. This last, the ancient offering of bread and wine, was always said in Latin until the Second Vatican Council, except in certain churches using rites similar to those of the Eastern Orthodox. The priest stood at the altar in stately vestments, his back to the congregation, and at the supreme moments when the bread and wine became the body and blood of Christ, knelt and then elevated them, to the accompaniment of bells. At a "high mass" there would be a sermon, incense, and chanted music during the rite. Members of the congregation could follow the Latin service in a book with translations. Even if they did not, the rich atmosphere, so expressive of numinous "otherness," and of the contrast between the sacred and the ordinary, was conducive to prayer and meditation. Since the Second Vatican Council, the use of the ordinary language and a rather more informal mood, with the priest standing behind the altar facing the people as the host at a banquet, suggests something different: the church as a family of love, where the talents of all have a place.

Michelangelo's La Pietà: Mary mourning over her son, Jesus.

Another sacrament is penance, the forgiveness of sins. Traditionally, one was expected periodically to make a private confession of his or her sins to a priest, generally in the small boxlike structure in churches called the confessional. The priest has authority to impart a penance—commonly a set of prayers to say—and to give absolution, or impart God's forgiveness for the confessed wrongs. Today, group confessional prayers recited in church are often used instead.

Marriage is another sacrament, for it is a gift of God and a means of grace. The Roman Catholic Church therefore has rules governing its members' marriages. Because the marriage bond is sacramentally permanent, remarriage after divorce is a matter that requires legal procedures within the church, and there is disapproval of abortion and "nonnatural" means of birth control.

Roman Catholicism is abundant in spiritual life apart from the sacraments. Devotion to the Blessed Virgin may take the form of the **rosary** that one uses to count repeated Hail Marys, or *novenas,* special sets of prayers on successive days; or it may take the form of pilgrimages to shrines. Today, creative diversity continues to emerge. The charismatic movement, for example, enriches Roman Catholicism with spontaneity and "speaking in tongues."

Roman Catholic social expression is complex and highly organized. At the head of the church is the Pope, whose seat is in Vatican City, a tiny independent state of which he is sovereign in the heart of Rome. He is elected by the College of Cardinals, an assembly of some seventy prominent archbishops, bishops, and a few others who have been named by a previous Pope to this dignity. The Pope is assisted by the Curia, a cabinet and bureaucracy whose department heads are generally cardinals. Beneath the papacy, the church is divided into provinces, headed by archbishops, dioceses headed by bishops, and local parishes under their parish priests. Today bishops are generally appointed by the Pope, and parish priests by the bishops, although other arrangements (often with the state having a role) have obtained in the past and still do today in some places.

Parallel to this hierarchy are the orders of monks and nuns—persons who have undertaken not only the celibate state but also vows of poverty and obedience. They usually live communally in monasteries and convents; devote much time to worship together and private meditation; and engage in educational, missionary, or charitable work, or, if they are in an "enclosed" order, in a combination of labor, study, corporate prayer, and contemplation. Orders, such as the active Franciscans, Dominicans, Jesuits, the Brothers of the Christian Schools (or "Christian Brothers"), and the more contemplative Benedictines and Cistercians (including the Trappists), and their distinctive traditional garb, are well known. Today the "religious life," as this way is called, is also undergoing considerable modification, but it remains a bulwark of Roman Catholicism.

Protestantism

The term **Protestantism** is generally taken to include all non–Roman Catholic and non–Eastern Orthodox churches that directly or indirectly derive from the sixteenth-century Reformation in Northern and Western Europe. We have already looked at this event and some of its principles. Although the vast collection of Protestant **denominations** may suggest almost chaotic variety, they do have in common certain basic attitudes traceable to the Reformation. Even points upon which they differ tend to fall into certain predictable categories. Churches of the Reformation tradition vary from, on the one hand, some Anglican and Lutheran churches that have worship and doctrinal emphases similar to those of the Roman church to, on the other hand, silent Quaker meetings and **Pentecostalist** groups that stress spontaneous shouts and "speaking in tongues." But apart from a few exceptions, Protestant worship cannot be mistaken for any other.

Let us look at some common themes of Protestantism, recognizing that they have different meanings and applications in different Protestant traditions.

So far as theoretical expression is concerned, the central emphasis alone for most informed Protestants remains justification by God's grace through faith in Christ alone and all that implies. The important thing is that one's consciousness and feelings be centered on God, open to his will and grace. What is of value, then, is what evokes and expresses this centering. Thus, Protestantism in doctrine and story alike is inclined to apply the principle of parsimony—to cut away everything not essential to hearing and receiving the word of God in the scriptures; to cut away all that might distract from one's personal relationship to God.

The other major, but related, Protestant theme—the sufficiency of scripture alone—finds expression in diverse ways. They range from those who stress that the Bible must judge church life to those, particularly some Anglicans, who—like Roman Catholics and Eastern Orthodox—emphasize the importance of interpreting scripture within the context of church tradition.

There also is a difference between fundamentalist interpretations, which insist on a "literal" rendering of such points as the virgin birth and the miracles of Jesus, and "liberal" interpretations, which hold that scripture must be interpreted in a way consistent with present-day historical and scientific knowledge. This distinction means, in effect, that fundamentalism often functions as a vehicle of resistance to modern culture, while liberalism tries to relate Christianity to the current scientific and scholarly worldview. But on some issues, especially political, the roles may be reversed when fundamentalism speaks for a majority culture.

A continuum is also seen in styles of worship. They range from the solemn and formal services of Anglicans, Lutherans, and Reformed to the folksy worship of many Methodists and Baptists, and the often ecstatic meetings of Pentecostals. In mainstream Protestantism, preaching and reading the scriptures are primarily the means to inspiring faith. The power of words to communicate saving concepts, imagery, or emotions is central to Protestants because the scriptures and sermons and hymns are deemed to contain "the words of eternal life."

The response to grace also finds other diverse expressions, ranging from an emphasis on the ethical life and good works (and here there are those who stress personal morality and those who stress Christian responsibility for society as a whole) to an emphasis on spiritual states and their expression through conversion, inward joy, and ecstatic phenomena. In Anglicanism, the sacraments may be equally important as means of grace. Among Pentecostals and evangelicals, charismatics, who speak in "tongues," and revivalists, who manifest God's grace and evoke faith, have a central place. The most formal expression has generally been that of the **state church** Protestants of Europe and their American counterparts. But the recent growth of informal services and charismatic or Pentecostal phenomena all through Protestantism has changed this pattern.

In general, however, a simplification motif is clearly evident in worship. Protestant worship has generally become stylized. The typical service contains an opening hymn, scripture, a prayer, a sermon, the offering, the benediction, and a closing hymn. A simple service of Holy Communion is also offered, though not every Sunday in the majority of Protestant churches. The main participation of the congregation is in singing, although in some churches the people offer prayers as well. Otherwise the minister, as a trained religious specialist, is the principal communicator of the mainly verbal experience.

In social expression, the ideal is generally recovery of the New Testament church, since seldom (except in Anglicanism) is post–New Testament tradition given much authority. However, the New Testament scriptural paradigm means different things to different wings of Protestantism, and there is a considerable variety in modes of government. Some are ruled by bishops, some by boards of presbyters, some by the local congregation. In practice, the historical situation has also influenced structural form.

After the Reformation, Protestantism had state church status in a number of countries, for example, the Church of England or state Lutheran and Reformed churches in Germany, Scandinavia, Scotland, or Holland, or their American branches. This meant that its organization had to fit in with the laws of the realm. As might be expected, then, the types of organization have varied widely between churches that come out of the state church tradition.

On the other hand, there were independent movements that sprang up as alternatives to the state churches and these usually had, at least originally, **sectarian** characteristics: charismatic leaders, local control, strict moral codes, and greater stress on subjective feelings. Such groups (e.g., the separatist Puritans in England, who rebelled against Church of England practices) being small and fairly powerless, had to focus on the local church as the important entity. In America after the Revolution, and particularly on the frontier, Protestantism was independent of the state and highly fluid. This led to a wealth of new forms of expression that usually were rooted in the authority of the local group or the charisma of the traveling evangelist.

With all the differences that can be seen among the many Protestant denominations, however, Protestant social organization has in common the tacit or explicit assumption that the whole of the Christian church cannot be visible and entire in the world today. It is at best only the sum total of many Christian bodies, and its true membership cuts cross all sorts of lines—and is known only to God.

Christianity in America:
A Wellspring of Denominationalism

Because of the special nature of religious history in America, denominationalism is a key to understanding it. Even Judaism, Roman Catholicism, and Eastern Orthodoxy—all very important to American religious life—in practice have had to fall in with styles of social expression that the American context creates.

The basic facts in American religious life are (1) immigration by peoples of numerous religious cultures, (2) the emergence of a new society with a need for cohesion and for a sense of creating a new political and spiritual way of being in the world, and (3) political **separation of church and state**. These facts have resulted in pluralism rather than a single official or heavily dominant religious institution, as obtains in most other societies. Yet they have also meant that most groups have found themselves affirming common American ethical and social ideals—democracy, patriotism, social concern—together with their distinctive doctrines and worship.

The general history of religion in America reflects these centrifugal and centripedal drives. In the colonial period, immigrants of diverse religious backgrounds settled in different areas, often in order to find a religious haven: Puritans in Massachusetts, Baptists in Rhode Island, Quakers in Eastern Pennsylvania, Lutherans in Western Pennsylvania, Roman Catholics in Maryland, and Anglicans in Virginia and along the southern seaboard. From 1720 to 1740, the movement for a deeper, more intellectually serious and also more feeling-oriented Christianity, called the **Great Awakening**, swept across parish, denominational, and colonial lines. The first vital expression of the American centripedal force, it paved the way for the Revolution in that it gave the populations of the thirteen colonies a new sense of being a distinctive American people with their own spiritual concerns, rather than merely transplanted Europeans.

The Revolution, of course, brought the sense of national unity to a high pitch and culminated religiously in the First Amendment to the Constitution, which made the United States of America the first society in the history of the world to mandate full religious freedom and the separation of church and state. It guaranteed freedom and equality for all faiths and the absence at the national level of any official religious endorsement or support. In this situation, there were many who felt that, forced to stand on its own in a new society and shorn of feudal trappings, religion would wither away, or (as the concurrent Unitarian movement in New England suggested) become very "rational." But such was not to be.

Instead, during the period of westward expansion, nation building, and belief in a special American "Manifest Destiny," both geographical and spiritual, religion flourished in a cornucopia of forms. Evangelical revivals swept the frontier. They brought tremendous growth to the Methodist and Baptist churches, and they produced new denominations such as the Disciples of Christ. New movements, such as **Spiritualism** and the Latter-Day Saints, originated in upstate New York. Utopian communes and numerous colleges were planted in the name of religion. In an expansive era, the centrifugal and centripedal drives reinforced each other and showed, despite some tension, that religious pluralism, in the absence of state interference or support, need not weaken religion, but can liberate it to flourish.

But this primal "era of good feeling" was not to last. Just as Eden ended with the discovery of sin, so the optimism of the first decades after independence was darkened by the confrontation with the shadow side of American life—slavery. The middle decades of the nineteenth century were rent by controversy over slavery, and denominations were divided by it on North–South lines, so that we came to have northern and southern Baptists, Presbyterians, and Methodists (the Methodists were reunited in 1939, the Presbyterians in 1984). After the Civil War, most of the freed slaves entered exclusively black churches. For many decades, black churches were the only important institutions controlled by blacks, and their ministry was the only profession generally available to them. Out of the black churches came a distinctive style of religious life characterized by close community feeling, a free spiritual expression in which the important worldwide movement of Pentecostalism is rooted, and leaders in the civil rights movement, such as Martin Luther King, Jr.

During the same years, and up until 1920, new immigration vastly increased American population with a mixed multitude. During the one decade of the 1840s, American Roman Catholicism grew by immigration from a small minority to the largest single church in the nation—a position it has held ever since. Jews, Eastern Orthodox, and German and Scandinavian Lutherans also immigrated in the millions during the latter half of the nineteenth century. All this was in the context of great social change: the growth of cities, industry, widespread education, and life based on modern technology. The older Protestantism tended to react in two ways: conservatism, which came to be known as fundamentalism and which sought to preserve the religious values of frontier revivalism and religious surety in a changing world; and the more liberal "social gospel" movement, which strove to correlate religion to new ideas in science and society and to recover the old dream of making America into a new "people of God" through social reform.

The strands of this history are expressed in the panorama of American denominations. However, they are far from the whole story of American religion. There was also the centrifugal drive toward a **civil religion**—a common American ethic and vision that cuts across denominations. On the other hand, important issues such as fundamentalism versus the **social gospel** have polarized denominations from within and have found expression in distinctive denominations. Yet, "one issue" denominations without concomitant ethnic or sociological roots have not generally been very successful.

But American denominational pluralism is an important phenomenon. Derived from the unique history of colonial settlement, the frontier flux, the slavery controversy, and immigration, it is as distinctive in its way as Tibetan Buddhism. No other society, except to a lesser extent the British Commonwealth nations such as Canada and Australia, which have had a superficially comparable religious history, approaches the particular form of sociological expression of religion found in America.

Stained glass from Chartres Cathedral in France. Note that this medieval work depicts various ordinary occupations, suggesting that everyday work had a place in the Christian view of the world, as well as religious scenes.

The 124-foot high statue of Christ on a hill overlooking the city of Rio de Janeiro in Brazil.

What follows is a glance at important Protestant denominations or traditions. Membership approximations are for 2000. (For comparative purposes, it may be noted that the Roman Catholic Church has 62 million members in the United States; the Eastern Orthodox Churches, about 4 million. There are some 4 million Jews who are members of religious congregations, an estimated 6.8 million Muslims, 1.3 million Hindus, and more than 2 million Buddhists.)

The Methodist family with more than 12 million members includes the United Methodist Church with nearly 8.5 million members; the Free Methodists, which is a conservative group split from it; and the predominantly black African Methodist Episcopal Church and African Methodist Episcopal Zion Church. As we have seen, Methodism stems from the eighteenth-century preaching of John Wesley and others in England. In America, Methodism greatly flourished on the frontier. But in the process of becoming a dominant faith, especially in the small towns of the South and Midwest, it inevitably became more moderate or liberal than in the heyday of frontier evangelism. In reaction to this, groups such as the Free Methodist Church and the Church of the Nazarene broke with Methodism around the turn of the twentieth century to keep intact the original Wesleyan conversion and holiness doctrines as they understood them.

Easter Sunday services at a Baptist church in New York. ▪

The largest single block of American Protestants are the Baptists. The Southern Baptist Church has some 15.7 million members; it is virtually a way of life in parts of the South. The northern-based American Baptist Church has 1.5 million members. Two predominantly black National Baptist churches total some 11 million, and there are other smaller Baptist groups. Baptists in America derive from the seventeenth-century movements in England, inspired by "radical reformation" Anabaptists on the continent, who stressed that baptism should not be given to infants but should be a sign following adult conversion. Baptists have always stood for religious freedom and have opposed state churches; they have tended to be conservative regarding scripture and personal morality.

The largest Lutheran church, the Evangelical Lutheran Church in America with over 5 million members, was formed by a merger in 1987. The Lutheran Church–Missouri Synod (2.6 million), is a more conservative body. Although the Lutherans represent American expressions of European state churches deriving from Luther's wing of the Reformation, unlike Methodists and Baptists who derive from European dissident movements, the Lutheran Churches were in practice heavily influenced by nineteenth-century pietistic movements, which explains differences between European Lutheranism and the sometimes more conservative American Lutheranism. Lutheran worship is generally stately and attractive, with majestic music and learned preaching. Lutheran people in America, largely of German and Scandinavian descent, are conspicuous in their loyalty to the church and its worship.

The Church of England, the state church that separated from Rome in the days of Henry VIII, is represented in America by the Episcopal Church, with some 2.4 million members. It was dominant in much of colonial America, but great numbers of its nominal members were swept away by the frontier Methodist and Baptist movements after the American Revolution. Episcopalianism managed to recover strength and now represents a tradition similar to that of the colorful, rather ceremonial worship of the Church of England.

In 1984, the two major Presbyterian churches in America united to form the Presbyterian Church (U.S.A.) with 3.6 million members. American Presbyterianism represents the tradition of the state Church of Scotland and its affiliates in England and Ireland. Its theological heritage is Calvinist, its worship simpler and closer to the central Protestant structure than the Episcopalian. It has always emphasized a high level of education and preaching among the clergy.

Also in the Calvinist lineage are two groups representing wings of the Reformed Church in the Netherlands: the Reformed Church in America (300,000 members) and the Christian Reformed Church (200,000).

A Calvinist background is also found in the United Church of Christ, with some 1.4 million members. The UCC is a merger of the Congregational Church, whose heritage is the Puritan settlers from England in New England, and the German Evangelical and Reformed Church. By and large, Congregationalism and the UCC have moved away from the proverbial (though often misunderstood) narrowness of the Puritan to a liberal stance that permits no small diversity of expression. Its congregational organization allows each local church to elect its own minister and draw up its own statement of belief.

A numerically small but significant denomination of New England congregational background is the Unitarian-Universalist Church (218,000 members), a union of two very liberal bodies. It professes absolute freedom of belief; most of its members would reject such doctrines as the Trinity and the divinity of Christ, and many would reject belief in the traditional God in favor of religion centered on human needs and ends. Some, although they acknowledge their Judeo-Christian roots, do not identify as Christian, but, instead, as the more universal religion the name implies.

Another small but important tradition is that of the Religious Society of Friends, commonly called the Quakers. Quakers first settled Pennsylvania. Now the several Quaker denominations have about 104,000 members all together.

A number of denominations have originated in America. These are all farther from European traditions, as one would expect, than the churches cited previously. There are the Churches of Christ, 1.5 million; the Christian Church (Disciples), 880,000; and the Christian Churches, 1 million. These emerged out of the frontier "Restoration Movement" to recover the New Testament church and are now moderate to fairly conservative evangelical churches. Other American-born evangelical churches include the Church of the Nazarene, organized in 1908, 630,000 members, which is the largest denomination in the Wesleyan-Arminian tradition, and the Christian and Missionary Alliance, which began in 1887 as an evangelical movement but eventually formally organized, which has 346,000 members. **Pentecostalism,** so dynamic worldwide that it has been called a Christian "third force," started in Los Angeles in 1906 at the famous Azusa Street meeting. It is represented by a variety of churches: several called Church of God, the Assemblies of God, the Pentecostal Holiness Church, and others. They emphasize the value of "speaking in tongues" as a sign of conversion and of receiving the Holy Spirit. Worship life is spontaneous, immensely alive, and full of the expectation of miracles.

When Pentecostalism began in 1906, it was racially integrated, a very unusual achievement for those times. However, it soon formed white and African-American denominations. But in 1994, in a remarkable meeting in Memphis, Pentecostal churches of both races decided to unite in a new movement representing some 11 million members. Pentecostalism is also growing rapidly among Hispanics in the United States.

Other American movements include the Church of Jesus Christ of Latter-Day Saints (the Mormon church), with some 5 million members in America, based on the teachings of Joseph Smith, whom his followers believe found golden plates in upstate New York telling, among other things, that Jesus came to ancient America and provided a new scripture—the *Book of Mormon*; the Church of Christ, Scientist, founded by Mary Baker Eddy, which emphasizes that God is all and therefore there is no disease save in distorted minds; and the Seventh-Day Adventist Church (733,000 members), which stresses that Christ will return again very soon, and also that Christians have an obligation to keep some of the law of Moses, including worship on Saturday, the old Sabbath. There are churches in the New Thought tradition, such as the Unity churches and the Church of Religious Science, theologically liberal and stressing the power of mind to solve problems and bring joy. Spiritualist churches focus on communication by mediumship with the spirits of the departed to assure believers of immortality.

American Protestantism is indeed diverse. Not only do the denominations differ widely, but even within a single denomination one may find some members asserting that God is dead and that our concerns must be entirely secular, while others see visions and find God's hand at work among them in signs, miracles, and tongues. Yet the diversity is not infinite, and what holds it together is really more basic than its diversity: There is everywhere a fundamental belief in the importance of right inwardness, whether one means by that intellectual integrity, powerful conversion feelings, the Holy Spirit giving supernatural gifts, or positive thinking. There is a definite congregation and a weekly worship service (not the case in all religions), which usually focuses on singing, preaching, and prayer. A Unitarian and a Pentecostal church might seem quite different to an outsider, but the outsider would have no trouble in comprehending that they are related in a way that neither is to a Zen monastery, Hindu temple, Muslim mosque, or even a Rumanian Orthodox or Italian Roman Catholic church. American Protestant churches represent numerous fine gradations of doctrine, worship, and sociological grounding, but all these are finally within only a certain portion of the much broader spectrum of human religion as a whole.

The Modern Expansion of Christianity

Christianity calls forth more than the image of established cloisters and churches. It also evokes scenes from its geographical front lines: the Spanish friar building his sun-washed missions surrounded by native people of the Americas; the nineteenth-century Protestant missionary marching into the jungles of "Darkest Africa" or a "Cannibal Isle," Bible in hand.

These are pictures that call forth in us a profound diversity of responses; the missionary's front-line soldiering on behalf of the Cross has usually been controversial, both in the sending and in the receiving countries. He or she has been admired for incredible heroism, and millions have been deeply grateful for the medical, educational, and spiritual benefits they have received. Yet the missionary's calling also has given rise to gnawing doubts about the right of one religion to impose itself upon people of another, about the relation of modern missions to Euro-American expansionism, and about the long-term impact of the missionary upon cultures around the world whose ancient ways have been challenged and sometimes shattered peremptorily.

The story of Christian missions since the days of Columbus is as complex as these responses imply. But one thing is certain: The Christian missionary endeavor together with European immigration in these five centuries has radically changed the religious map of the world. From being mostly the faith of a relatively small corner of the earth—Europe—Christianity has overwhelmed whole continents and islands across vast seas, and it is represented in nearly every nation of the earth; a quarter of the world's population is, at least nominally, under its spiritual sway.

At the time of Columbus's first voyage to the Americas in 1492, Christianity was gradually recovering from a low ebb. In the previous century the faith had been sorely weakened in numbers or morale by the Black Death, the Papal Schism, and Muslim advances in the East. The last culminated in the Turkish capture of Constantinople in 1453 and the final demise of Christendom's bulwark to the East, the Byzantine empire.

But in the fifteenth century new life was stirring. In those years, Spain and Portugal, having just expelled the last of the Muslims, stood proud, robust, full of enthusiastic Catholic faith, facing the broad Atlantic ready to conquer new worlds for king and Christ. Commerce may have been its real dynamic, but kings and seafarers alike sincerely believed that they were acting at the will of God and that the conversion of the infidel was the greatest objective of their voyages.

Santuario de Guadalupe, a Spanish Catholic mission in the American southwest.

Within a remarkable half-century of 1492, brutal but effective Spanish conquests had subdued the great centers of Native American civilization, Mexico and Peru, and had established colonial outposts from Argentina to the northern Caribbean. In the wake of armies, missionaries baptized thousands daily, bringing the native masses nominally under the cross. The Spanish priests built churches in imposing baroque style, often on the location of major pre-Christian temples. They devised ways to inculcate the rudiments of Christian faith to their illiterate charges. Elaborate sacred dramas, simple hymns and chants, and colorful processions, as well as fiery preaching in both Spanish and native tongues, supplemented the mystery of the Mass.

Another example from this period is the remarkable work of Matteo Ricci (1552–1610), an Italian Jesuit, and his companions in China. Coming to the East with the Portuguese, Ricci entered China through Macao in 1583 and finally reached Peking (now Beijing) in 1601, where he remained the rest of his life. Ricci and his Jesuits pioneered a new approach to missions. Rather than imposing European cultural forms on the people, before beginning their work they mastered the Chinese language and studied Chinese culture in depth. Ricci became thoroughly Chinese in all nonessentials, wearing a mandarin robe and ingratiating himself with the intellectual class through his teaching of Western science and geography. While his number of converts was not large, he established the Christian church in China and won intellectual prestige for it through his own example. But his willingness to employ Chinese language and Confucian practices, such as ancestral rites, in Christian worship created a long-standing controversy within the Catholic church. The "Rites Controversy," as it was called, was essentially over the significant issue of to what extent Christianity can adapt itself and its worship to the ways of the various lands to which it travels. The matter was decided against the Jesuits in the eighteenth century, but in 1939 the Vatican adopted a more liberal policy, and the Second Vatican Council expressed a considerable new openness toward local adaptations of Catholicism, in effect vindicating Ricci's position.

The modern expansion of Christianity has come in great waves. The first, essentially Roman Catholic, followed the Spanish and Portuguese movement East and West. By the seventeenth century this wave had crested. In that century and the next, Christianity continued vigorous expansion but far more through immigration than direct missionary activity. Christian Europeans, both Protestant and Catholic (especially from the British Isles, France, Holland, and Germany), settled in North America and South Africa, where their colonies formed the seeds of great nations of predominantly Christian faith.

The beginning of the nineteenth century saw the beginning of a new wave of European imperial and commercial as well as emigration expansion. Even as the old colonies of the New World won independence, this new outpouring centered on Asia, the South Pacific, Australia, and later Africa. Protestant nations such as Britain and the Netherlands, and later Germany as well as the United States, were most involved, as was also Catholic France.

With the loss of the American colonies, British interest turned substantially eastward to India, Australia, Asia, and the archipelagos of the South Pacific, lately visited by Captain James Cook. This interest coincided with the late eighteenth-century rise of the evangelical movement, which fired missionary zeal, as well as with the expansion of Euro-American commerce, emigration, and colonial empires.

Christian missionary expansion in the modern era has been far-reaching, finding itself in all corners of the globe: the London Missionary Society work in the South Seas, beginning in 1796; the work of William Carey in India, beginning in 1794; Anglican and Methodist missionaries in early nineteenth-century New Zealand; the continued work of missionaries in China and Japan; the exploration and missionary work of David Livingstone (1813–1873) in sub-Saharan Africa; and more. It is still a powerful force today. The work of Mother Teresa, which continued in India after her death in 1997, is but one notable example.

The missionary movement spawned numerous new forms of Christian life as Christianity was adopted by native peoples in various ways, whether or not intended by the missionaries themselves. Interestingly, however, it has also contributed immeasurably to Christian unity. It is primarily out of the missionary endeavor that the modern **ecumenical movement**, dedicated to interchurch cooperation, understanding, and ultimately reunion, has arisen. In the nineteenth century various missionary conferences, regional or among allied denominations, were held. These culminated in the World Missionary Conference in Edinburgh, Scotland, in 1910, bringing together representatives of the missionary work of all major Protestant churches. It led directly to the World Council of Churches, the main ecumenical agency, which the Eastern Orthodox churches later joined. In more recent years Roman Catholics have also cooperated with the World Council as nonmember "observers" and have in other ways striven to promote ecumenical understanding.

The missionary enterprise has had a reverse impact on Europe and America, too; one doubtless unexpected at first. Just as missionaries shattered the isolation of countless tribes and nations around the globe, so have their reports shattered the complacency and spiritual isolation of the older Christian nations. They opened up a wide world that many perceived to be far more complex, spiritually as well as otherwise, than anticipated.

First, questions about the moral underpinnings of Christendom slowly began to arise in the minds of thoughtful Christians as a result of experiences such as that of the first Portuguese missionaries in Africa, who found that natives they had brought under the Gospel of love quickly fell away when brutal slavers arrived flying the same flag as they.

Second, questions about the absolute superiority of Christianity were suggested by missionary reports of non-Christian cultures, which the unbiased mind could only see as equal or even in some ways superior to those in the West. In Asian countries such as India, China, and Japan, missionaries encountered civilizations and religions of great sophistication, and they found themselves regarded as barbarians. Missionary scholars were, in fact, among the first to translate and bring West the great spiritual classics of the East, many of which we have already studied, and which some in the West discovered to be as appealing as the Bible. The reports of Jesuits such as Ricci from Confucian China, with its respect for education, its civil service examination merit system, its apparently tolerant and primarily ethical religion, made that ancient empire seem something of a utopia to intellectuals in an early eighteenth-century Europe struggling toward democracy and just emerging from the bloody religious wars of the seventeenth century. The Chinese image had a significant impact on the emergence of the eighteenth-century Enlightenment ideals of reason, deistic religion, tolerance, the civil service, and democracy—much more of an impact than Europe, despite those missionaries, had on China in the same century.

We see then that the missionary expansion of Christianity, together with exploration and economic exchange, resulted in a nascent move toward globalization, the impact of which was as profound then as it is today.

The New Face of World Christianity

By the late twentieth century, the majority of the world's Christians were not in that faith's traditional European and English-speaking North American strongholds, but in Asia, Africa, and long-Christian but rapidly changing Latin America. The Christian center of gravity was decisively shifting toward the Equator and the Southern Hemisphere. Here the cultural and political dynamics for Christians are different than in the Northern lands.

As a result of its missionary expansion, just described, Christianity has grown rapidly in these populous areas. It has been perceived by recently colonialized, then newly independent and "developing" peoples, to present not only its own intrinsic religious appeal, but also opportunities for education and access to the material and spiritual culture of modernity. On another level, belief in one God and a single revelation has offered inner security in often confusing and rapidly changing situations.

The problem was that forms of Christianity introduced by missionaries naturally came in European and North American "packaging" often quite alien to other people. This issue has led to several consequences.

First, sometimes traditional churches have used what is called in Roman Catholic circles "enculturation," adopting the cultural forms of the host country in religious life and worship as far as possible in Christian practices. (This is actually what was done in Europe centuries earlier, as we have seen, where the basilica-style architecture of churches, even a holiday like Christmas, and countless folks customs and sacred sites were adapted from pre-Christian culture for Christian use.) For example, in Africa, worship in Catholic and Protestant churches may incorporate traditional drums, dance, emphasis on healing, and reverence for ancestors. In another dimension of religion, churches in Asia, Africa, and Latin America have frequently emphasized the important role of Christianity in speaking out against economic and political oppression in the host country, and taking the lead in combating it, often under the influence of what is called **Liberation Theology**——a theology originally arising out of Catholicism, but now not exclusively a Catholic movement, that emphasizes the plight of the oppressed and finds in biblical scripture a liberating message for them.

Second, worldwide Christian movements, although not indigenous themselves, sometimes resonate well with indigenous culture and meet current spiritual needs and so have grown tremendously. Of these the best example is Pentecostalism, and, second to it, Christian forms of Spiritualism. Both actually originated in their modern form in the United States, but have been among that nation's most successful exports. Pentecostalism, with its emphasis on ecstatic experience and fluid church structure, has offered emotional and spiritual identity ("I've been saved and have the power of the Holy Spirit in me, personally") combined with opportunities for religious leadership to many diverse people—clergy and lay, men and women. It has also usually offered definite moral values and an emphasis on the family. This often has been particularly important to people who are moving into new and puzzling social settings, as with peasants moving to great cities (which we are seeing more of throughout the world), and taking up new jobs amid myriad new kinds of temptations. Spiritualism, with its emphasis on contacting the spirits of ancestors and Divine beings (saints and angels in Christian form), connects with indigenous religions of trance, ecstasy, and a rich spiritual world.

A good example of all of this is found in Brazil. Although possessing the largest number of Roman Catholics of any country in the world, this vast South American nation also has many huge Pentecostal churches and a flourishing quasi-Christian Spiritualism. By 2000, Brazil was at least 15 percent Protestant, of which three-quarters were Pentecostal. Members of Pentecostal churches were largely recent converts, who experienced in those churches a rich emotional atmosphere and a spirit of growth and enthusiasm. Worship is marked not only by "speaking in tongues," but also by individual testimonies and fervent preaching oriented toward producing conversion and spiritual gifts. Characteristic of Pentecostal discourse is a "narrative style" emphasizing accounts of personal life-changing spiritual events. These churches today also make much use of television and other modern media to spread their messages. In Brazil, as in the United States and elsewhere, Pentecostalism began as a religion of the poor and still has its base there, but is attracting more and more in the middle class. It is also finding that its once-poor constitutents are frequently moving into better economic conditions, perhaps aided by values inculcated in Pentecostal communities, such as the "work ethic," responsibility to family, and abstinence from alcohol.[19]

Contrasting the Pentecostal Brazilian movements are such Afro-Brazilian religions as those called Umbanda and Candomblé. Indeed, rivalry between these spiritualist religions and Pentecostalism is marked among the poor and lower middle-class people who are the base of both. Often the spirits exorcised by Pentecostalists are the deities of Umbanda and Candomblé. Umbanda and Candomblé worship divinities that originally were African gods brought over by slaves, but now are also identified with saints of popular Roman Catholicism. Leaders of the spiritualist religions are possessed by these diety/saints in trance, exhibiting the well-known characteristics of each. Offerings are made to these entities as well, and their power is used in blessings and curses. Kardecism, a form of modern Spiritualism, involving contact with the spirits of the departed through mediumship, is also widespread in Brazil. Although perhaps marginal to mainstream Christianity, these popular religious movements are part of an overall Christian culture. It is not unusual for Umbandan priests, for example, to go to Roman Catholic Mass.

Within Roman Catholicism, Brazil has also seen some important manifestations of the Liberation Theology movement. While controversial within that church, in many places so-called "base communities" have been established. These are Catholic groups under lay leadership that meet to read the Bible together and discuss its application to life-situations. Though originally inspired in part by the great shortage of priests in the country, the groups also represent a post–Second Vatican Council initiative toward the laity, the Bible, and applying faith to immediate social problems.

The third consequence of European and North American missionary work in Asia, Africa, and Latin American has expressed itself there in new religious movements independent of the traditional churches. Let us look at Africa as an example. There are over 8,000 new religious movements in African alone, most of them Christian. They vary widely in particulars, of course, but common characteristics include an emphasis on gifts of the spirit like healing, purification, prophesy, and exorcism of evil spirits, together with ancestrism and contact with God through dance and ecstasy. Like traditional African religion, they give a prominent role to women. There is often a strict moral code, though they may differ from churches imported from Europe and North America in accepting polygamy—common and even looked on with favor in some African societies.

A good example is the Mai Chaza Church. It originated in what is now Zimbabwe, but has spread through several counties in Southern Africa. It is named after the founder, a woman called Mai (Mother) Chaza who, in 1953–1954, became seemingly deranged and had an experience like death. But she recovered, reported that she had met God while in coma, and, after a subsequent retreat in the mountains, was given the power to heal. As she became well known in this work, she also established *Guta ra Jehova,* Cities of Jehovah, centers of healing said to be modeled on heavenly cities revealed through Chaza. These are now impressive places of pilgrimage, where followers of the religion, wearing uniforms, live and worship.

After her death in 1960, Mai Chaza has been religiously exalted to the role of Messiah and mediator with God for her people. Indeed, she has been made into an African female expression of Jesus. A book of her deeds and saying is used in services alongside the teachings of Jesus as scripture. Worship is colorful, with drums, processions, confessions, and exorcisms. At the time of confession, a white sheep with a black head, called John the Baptist, goes around and points out those in the congregation who must confess. Festivals are dramatic and important in the Mai Chaza Church.[20]

It may be added that some features typical of the new movements have often also been adopted by Pentecostalism, Spiritualism, and traditional churches in Asia, Africa, and Latin America. While their leaders and members are not likely to feel free to accept polygamy openly, those now under local leadership probably will offer more than previously of healing, exorcism, and other gifts of the spirit. They will also incorporate more native modes of music and worship.

As the twenty-first century opens, it is clear that much of the future of Christianity lies in Asia, Africa, and Latin America. All interested in the destiny of the world's largest faith will keep their eyes on those parts of the world.

Women in Christianity

We have seen in the many other cultures that we have studied thus far that the dominant religion in large part shapes social conventions, including those regarding women. This is no less the case in the West where Christianity has dominated Western thought from the fourth century to at least the nineteenth century, and some would say even today.

The West has seen an expansion of women's rights and roles in society that is unprecedented in many other countries around the world. Christianity, together with its attitudes toward women, traveled a long road, however, before it reached its current configuration. It is important to explore that road in order to appreciate better the historical context in which the debate on the "woman question" in the West—particularly the United States—now finds itself. As we shall see, "woman's place" in society and its religious institutions has been a much-debated topic in Christianity from the very beginning and is no less so today.[21]

Women in the Early Jesus Movement

There is considerable evidence that the Jesus movement, at its outset, provided a place for greater participation by women than had been the case in much of Greek and Roman society at that time.[22] Significantly, there are many New Testament references to women—this, at a time when most customs and traditions held that women were to remain in the background. Not only do Mary Magdalene and Mary, the mother of Jesus figure prominently in the stories of Jesus, but several other women are referenced as well. The Gospel of Luke 8:1 indicates that highly stationed women—for example, Herod's steward's wife, Joanna—traveled with Jesus. Some women are mentioned as benefactresses of the newly emerging movement. In the parable of the lost coin in Luke 15:8, Jesus used a woman to represent God. Even more significantly, all four gospels present women as the first witnesses to Jesus' resurrection.

In addition, in Luke 10:38, we find the story of Martha and Mary. The travels of Jesus and his followers took them to the home of Martha. Mary, who was Martha's sister, was not helping Martha in the household tasks (which probably included serving the guests). Instead, Mary was sitting with the men, listening to the teachings of Jesus. When Martha complained, Jesus replied: "Martha, Martha, you are worried and distracted by many things; there is need of only one thing. Mary has chosen the better part, which will not be taken away from her." This is remarkable at a time when the custom was to exclude women from study. Here, Jesus was saying that his teachings were the "better part" even for a woman such as Mary.

New Testament books written later reference women in roles of leadership in the newly emerging movement. In Romans 16:1, Paul acknowledges Phoebe as a deacon (i.e., minister) and benefactor (i.e., provider, implying some status) to the church. Later in the same chapter, Paul refers to Andronicus and Junia (or Julia) as apostles. Junia is a feminine name (although often translated as the masculine Junius), which indicates that there were women apostles who were respected members of the early community.[23]

On the other hand, there are the often cited passages of the New Testament indicating that women should be subordinated to men. First Corinthians 14:34 is a case in point. There the author admonishes women to be silent in church and remain subordinate to their husbands. And Titus 2:3–6 expressly directs women to be submissive to their husbands. Other passages state clearly that women are not to hold positions of authority in the church, but are to remain committed only to their husbands and the duties of the home.

Yet, Christianity was expressly open to everyone, including women. The baptismal formula cited in Galatians 3:28 makes this expressly clear: "There is no longer Jew or Greek, there is no longer slave or free, there is no longer male and female; for all of you are one in Christ Jesus." And while I Corinthians sets up a hierarchy—God as head of Christ, Christ as head of men, husbands as head of wives (11:3), it also acknowledges that women "pray and prophesy" in the church (11:5), which is contrary to the I Corinthians passage referred to above that appears to demand their silence.

Biblical scholars have noted these various passages and others, and many explanations have been offered for the seeming inconsistencies. One theory has it that some of the letters regarding women were written pseudonymously (i.e., writing in the name of another, e.g., in the name of Paul the Apostle), a common practice at the time, or certain passages were interpolated by men of a later period. As Elizabeth A. Clark and Herbert Richardson have noted, "[m]ost scholars now believe that Paul himself did not compose the letters to Timothy, Titus, the Ephesians, and probably the Colossians, which are assigned to later decades; this reduction of the traditional Pauline canon eliminates from Pauline authorship some of the more problematic passages about women in the New Testament."[24] Those who hold this theory surmise that perhaps the later writers were concerned that the newly emerging movement, with its greater role for women, would not be accepted in the Hellenistic culture of the time and, therefore, be suppressed. Accordingly, they brought women into line with the customs of the greater society, and its patriarchal social patterns.

Whatever the case, by the second century the Jesus movement retreated from what was probably a liberating trend for women. Significantly, the early church fathers developed a disparaging attitude toward sexuality. Because women were associated by men with sexuality, they were disparaged as well, and by the second century the most influential sects of the early Jesus movement became extremely misogynistic. Tertullian (c. 155–220), considered by many to be the first theologian of the West, is reported to have called women "the devil's gateway," blaming them for the sin of humanity that necessitated the death of the savior.[25]

Not surprisingly, with views such as these prevailing, celibacy became the ideal, marriage being a second, less holy, choice, and women came to be viewed as extraneous at best and dangerous at worst to the spiritual life of men.

By the fourth century, when the church was officially recognized by the Roman Empire and the church patriarchy was well established, women's role was limited in many of the same ways we have seen in the other religions we have studied. A woman's place was in the home; she was to be subservient to her husband; she was to remain chaste; her main function was to produce children, particularly sons, to continue her husband's family line; and she was to keep silent.[26] But in addition to all of this, a misogynistic strain in Christian theology remained that framed the debate about women in Christianity.

Christian Dualism, the Medieval Vision, and Their Impact on Attitudes toward Women

The two most influential Christian theologians who provided the foundations of much of Christian theology and, therefore, attitudes about women, were Augustine (354–430) and Thomas Aquinas (1224–1274). While both wrote works that had an impact on Christianity as a whole, after the Protestant Reformation Thomas Aquinas continued as the greater influence on Catholicism and Augustine as the greater influence on the major Protestant denominations. Martin Luther was an Augustinian monk. However, both developed views that promoted a dualism that greatly influenced both Catholic and Protestant church attitudes toward women.

Augustine's famous treatise, the *City of God,* espoused the view that there are two realms of existence—the City of God and the City of Man. The City of God is the realm in which the faithful are in tune with God's will and are not sinful. The City of Man is the realm of human beings' defective will that resulted from the original sin of Adam and Eve, who had failed to obey God when they ate the forbidden fruit of the tree of the knowledge of good and evil. As Augustine's works were interpreted and incorporated into later church doctrine, the dual realms of the City of God and the City of Man were equated with the realm of the eternal, that is, heaven, and the realm of finite world, that is, the natural world (the world of the "flesh"), respectively. The natural world was considered the locus of temptations to sin and, therefore, everything "natural" became suspect—including the inclinations of the body. Not surprisingly, the natural desire for the pleasure of sex was equated with sin; and women, being associated by men with sex, were, from their point of view, a primary temptation to sin. Moreover, Augustine linked the transfer of original sin to sexual intercourse and birth.

Still, Augustine's views of women were more favorable than those of many others of his time who stressed the evils of women as a justification for the adoption of a celibate life. Many of these men disparaged the body, sex, and procreation altogether and thought that marriage was an evil to be avoided. At the time there were those in the church who believed that bringing more children into the world depleted the spiritual realm; therefore, women were unnecessary to, or even counter to, the good. Augustine's view was different. Although Augustine, too, favored the celibate life, he was a defender of marriage, and he attempted to legitimate sexual relations as part of God's intention for men and women. He held that children are the first "good" of marriage, and women's legitimate purpose is to procreate.

Despite the fact that Augustine's views might have been more favorable toward women than those of many of his contemporaries, the debate that he had joined reveals the generally negative perspective toward women. At this point in Christianity's history, women were not even valued for their place in the home as central to the family, as was the case in Judaism, Confucianism, Hinduism, and Islam. Because celibacy was promoted as the highest ideal, women were seen as temptresses who were the cause of conflicts in men between the life of the spirit and the world of "flesh." Augustine was attempting to modify this view, but the spirit-flesh dualism that he inherited from Greek thinkers placed women on the side of sin.[27]

Thomas Aquinas, adopting for the most part the views of women that had been held by the famous Greek philosopher Aristotle, believed that women are inherently inferior to men and that men represent the full expression of humanity, while women are lesser beings—"misbegotten males"—who should be subordinate to men. Accordingly, women's roles in the church were severely limited; as secondary creatures, they could not appropriately hold any position of authority. The only reason for a woman's existence, it was thought, was for procreation, where her contribution to the child was the lesser part, matter, whereas the man's contribution was to "prepare" the matter to receive the "form" or soul—what made one human—which was provided by God. He further taught that the operation of the soul in a woman was weakened by her inferior body. As a result, she exhibited a defective mind and will.

As in the case of Augustine, however, Aquinas's views represented a softening of especially negative attitudes toward women at the time. Aquinas argued that, although women were lesser beings, they nevertheless contributed to the completeness of the world and, like men, were created directly by God and not by angels, as others had contended. Still, Aquinas fostered dualistic views that have had considerable impact on women's lives in the West to modern times. The sinfulness of the pleasure of sexuality has continued as a dominant theme, and celibacy has remained the ideal for those who kept to the tradition of Aquinas. Women, who always have been associated with sex and childbirth, have been associated with sin particularly because they have been deemed to be inferior to men.

Rosemary Radford Ruether, a well-respected Christian feminist scholar, has argued that dualistic conceptions of reality in Christianity led to theological justifications for the subordination of women to men. Men associated themselves with what they deemed to be the higher pursuits of the mind and spirit, the realm of the sacred, and linked women with the body and the passions—that which they deemed to be the realm of the profane. It followed then that if reason should rule the passions, men should rule women. Otherwise, spirit could not prevail over the profane world.[28]

Christian Women in Europe during the Middle Ages: Wives, Nuns, Charismatics, and Heretics

The Middle Ages was a difficult time for most Europeans. This was a time of insecurity, as many wars between the various lords were fought and the people suffered from disease, including the infamous bubonic plague. The feudal system lent a degree of safety to the masses but brought with it serfdom and the commensurately oppressive existence that went along with it. Women worked alongside their husbands in the fields. Their many pregnancies greatly shortened their lives.

Yet, the local church, even more than the lord's manor, was a center of community life. Because the people were illiterate (the parish priest himself often only semiliterate), the practical expression of religion was a more dominant force than specific applications of high church theology. As a result, many pre-Christian folk practices were assimilated into the many ceremonies and festivals of church life—for example, the egg hunt at Easter, the maypole dance as Spring bloomed, the lighting of the Yule fire at Christmas. Accordingly, the actual lives of women were a confluence of many factors, and religion was more a "little tradition," where women's participation certainly was more prominent than the official tradition would suggest. Nevertheless, official church doctrine still tended toward oppressive ideologies and practices regarding women and, although the practical effect of these depended in large part on the inclinations of the local parish priest, they certainly influenced the attitudes exhibited in the culture.

As a result of the developing dualistic views of early Christianity, as we have seen, women's roles as wife and mother did not receive the high regard in the Christendom of the Middle Ages that it did elsewhere. Women, being always linked with sex and childbirth, were a suspect group. Their main functions in life did not exemplify their participation in the ideal of the religion. Instead, the socio-religious ideal was a rejection of such mundane matters and an embracing of the spiritual life—not as an adjunct to mainstream society as we saw with Buddhism, but as the primary social vision. As the Middle Ages progressed, however, in no small part because of the influence of the writings of Augustine and Thomas Aquinas, the extremely misogynistic views toward women softened to some degree. Marriage became a sanctified institution. By 1439 the Council of Florence included marriage in its definitive list of the seven sacraments of the Church—a means by which Divine grace is transmitted through matter.

In addition, there were exceptions to the prevailing views of the time. The rise of notions of chivalry (which some scholars have argued were instigated by aristocratic women) and the platonic romanticism of the troubadours for married women certainly influenced views such as those of Dante Alighieri (1265–1321), who wrote of his Beatrice: "Her least salutation bestows salvation on this favored one, and humbles him until he forgives all wrong," suggesting that Divine beauty in the female face can be a sacrament of salvation. But recent scholarship has shown that such views did not translate into enhanced status for women in the Middle Ages as had previously been suggested.[29]

Increasingly, Mary, the mother of Jesus, imaged as infinitely compassionate, sexless, and ever-virgin (even after childbirth), became the venerated image of woman. Mary became the Divine mediator, and popularly held beliefs about such things as her immaculate conception and assumption into heaven upon her death (which later became official Catholic dogma in 1854 and 1950, respectively) abounded, as well as ceremonies in her honor. On the other hand, Eve, now blamed entirely for the Fall of humankind in the Garden of Eden, became the symbol of the inherent sinfulness of women. Weak of will and mind, she was easily tempted by the serpent. In addition, during this time the serpent became increasingly associated with Satan, a figure who now began to take on a more prominent role in Christian theology.[30]

Women, too, wished to overcome the sin of sexuality to which they had been linked and, therefore, many gave up marriage, sexuality, and childbirth in an attempt to exemplify the religious virginal ideal. St. Clare (1194–1253), founder of the Poor Clares, a companion religious order to the Franciscans, reminds us that the life of a convent long was a spiritual path available to women. As early as the second century, women's religious communities seem to have existed, and, in the Middle Ages, they became significant institutions.

The early convents were well endowed because women's dowries were given to the religious houses they entered. Accordingly, convents enjoyed considerable independence and power. As a consequence, convents were able to offer an alternative life for women where they experienced a degree of autonomy. There they were well educated, held positions of leadership within the convent, taught, and went on pilgrimages. The story of convents in the Middle Ages is mixed, however. Sometimes they were placed under the authority of the male bishops, their funds distributed to other institutions, and their independence and authority limited. Later in the period, the authorities demanded a more stringent cloistering of nuns, which greatly limited their activities.[31]

Still, exemplary women, whether or not nuns, were able to transcend negative attitudes of the day toward women. In some ways comparable to the shamaness tradition we saw in China and Japan, charismatic women and women mystic ascetics gained credibility by virtue of their experiences of the Divine, which often included claims to special revelations from Jesus or Mary. If such women were deemed by the officials of the church or popular opinion to be authentic visionaries, they were respected members of the Christian community, and some became leaders and teachers. Thus women notable for asceticism, ecstatic visions, or deep spiritual wisdom were highly honored and, like Clare, sometimes recognized in their lifetime or later as saints.

Hildegaard von Bingen (1098–1179), a German nun, was a visionary as well as a woman remarkably accomplished in several spheres. She has today become perhaps the most famous of all medieval women, remembered for the richness of her visions, described in books which she illustrated herself, for her splendid correspondence, and for her musical compositions. She saw men and women as equal before God in the "creative greenness" of Spirit. She was recognized by the church and was extremely well respected in her time, becoming a very popular abbess of an influential convent.

Another visionary was Margery Kempe (c. 1373–1439), an Englishwoman who, unlike Hildegaard, was married and had no fewer than fourteen children. After the fourteenth, she convinced her husband to permit her to live a celibate life. Alone and often on foot, she went on pilgrimages that took her as far as Jerusalem. From time to time she underwent intensely emotional experiences in which she participated in the agonies of Christ on the cross and equally in the joy of her own close relationship to Christ, whom she saw as her heavenly spouse.

Her emotional outbursts brought her to the attention of church authorities, however, who in turn brought her before the archbishop under charges of heresy. The archbishop judged Margery Kempe authentic, and the charges were dropped. Now officially sanctioned by the church, Kempe became a charismatic preacher, developed a very large following, and gained considerable respect and status. She is remembered today primarily because she recounted the events of her life in what was the first autobiography in English literature—*The Book of Margery Kempe* (1426).

Dame Julian of Norwich (c. 1342–1415), an anchoress (enclosed solitary contemplative nun) who had been visited by Margery Kempe, is known for the splendid visions she described in her *Revelations of Divine Love* (sometimes translated as "Showings"). There she put great stress on love and the feminine as well as masculine nature of God and, thus, spoke of Christ as "mother" and of the "motherhood" of God.

There were many other exemplary women. But most women's lives were extremely limited. The contemporary views of the time reflected the dualism we discussed previously. Consequently, women were blamed for the sin of the world, deemed especially vulnerable to the wiles of Satan, had no legal or religious rights, were denied education, and had no options other than the convent or a married life restricted by prevailing views about keeping silent and submitting to their husband's will, which were modified only in part by local practices and folk beliefs.

As we have seen, Christian women in the Middle Ages were involved in the "little traditions" that were practiced alongside the officially sanctioned tradition. But as the Middle Ages came to an end, the consequences of this proved to be disastrous.

Many remnants of the pre-Christian shamanistically based religions continued into the Middle Ages. Observances involved such things as folk medicine, the care of women in childbirth, and magic for such things as finding a husband or wife. These were largely practiced by women—frequently by such village figures as the "wise woman" or the midwife. Furthermore, as we mentioned, many of the pagan folk festival celebrations continued to be practiced by the peasants, and women played significant roles there—in contrast to their limited role in church celebrations. In the late Middle Ages, the tolerance of earlier times for these practices collapsed as church leaders felt more and more compelled to clamp down on folk religious practices, which were increasingly stigmatized as dangerous and diabolical.

The general suspicions toward women came to be conflated with the perceived need to root out these "evils." Because women were the main practitioners of these old ways, and they were thought to be more subject to the temptation of sin, the male clergy sought to bring women under a more stringently imposed authority of the church. Now these poor females were labeled "witches," and many among the clergy sought to purge Christendom of them. A tract of 1486, The **Malleus Maleficarum** ("The Hammer against Witches"), by two Dominican monks did much to spark more than two centuries of vicious persecution by secular and ecclesiastical authorities of alleged witches, mostly women, whose sins generally lay only in the twisted imaginations of the witch-finders. Often a woman labeled as a witch merely had stepped out of line of the authoritative ideal for womanhood. She was too beautiful—and therefore probably not pure; she was too vocal about things she did not like—and therefore not obedient; she was too popular as a "wise woman" of the village—and therefore not subject to male authority.

After unspeakably horrible tortures, many of which were deliberately directed toward the woman's sexuality, such women might confess to pacts with Satan and name others as "witches." Then they were burned at the stake to free their immortal souls from the grips of evil. Undoubtedly, much significance lay in the fact that the persecutors were men (often male clergy) and the victims mostly women, thought to be especially susceptible to the wiles of Satan. The antiwitch campaign was particularly harsh in Spain and Germany, where some towns had very few women left after a visit from the witch-finders (two towns in Germany in 1585 had only one left), but it also reached Britain and Salem, Massachusetts.

There have been many speculations as to the actual number of women accused of witchcraft who were burned at the stake or died in prison during the period from the thirteenth to the eighteenth century when the witches were purged from first the Catholic and later the Protestant churches. Estimates range from a couple hundred thousand to 9 million.[32] Regardless of the actual numbers of women physically persecuted, the threat of being called in to the witch-finder or inquisitor must have provided a strong incentive for women to fall into line with the orthodox position of the relevant church regarding women's place, and it certainly closed doors to alternative avenues of spiritual expression and leadership.

Women and Reform

The most significant change for women under the Protestant Reformation was that Martin Luther proclaimed that marriage, home, and family are the calling of human beings. He rejected celibacy outright, declaring it to be a sin against God who has commanded people to "be fruitful and multiply," and thus Luther called monks and nuns to leave their monastic orders in order to marry. Protestant Christianity embraced family life as the realm of the sacred where virtue is learned, while rejecting the Catholic dogma that marriage is a sacrament. Women were obviously a necessary part of this sacred center, and they gained respect and status for their holy role as bearers and nurturers of children. Sex within the bonds of marriage was, then, something good in the eyes of God and was praised and celebrated by Luther.

These doctrines were well reflected in other Protestant churches as well. The marriage service of the Church of England, adopted in 1549, combined something of the older sacramental idea with the new Reformation valuing of family life. It speaks of marriage as an "honourable estate," and when the groom gives the ring to his bride he says: "With this ring I thee wed; with my body I thee worship; with all my worldly goods I thee endow; in the Name of the Father, and of the Son, and of the Holy Ghost. Amen." This rite clearly sees the woman and man as, in their physical bodies, the sacramental means of love and grace one to another and even implies that sex is a kind of holy communion.

On the other hand, the major Protestant denominations, having adopted, for the most part, the theological underpinnings of Augustine, melded some of the previously held ideas of the Church with the newly configured Protestant church and, therefore, the dualistic thinking that had pervaded Christianity persisted. The natural world was still the world of sin, and while sex was a gift from God, it was considered suspect unless controlled. Women, still equated with the nature and the body, and believed to have whatever reason they possessed clouded over by emotion, were thought to be more tempted to sin and lust. Accordingly, although the authoritative doctrine offered a degree of mutuality between husband and wife, women's main function was as an adjunct to men for procreation, and men were the rulers of their wives. Unmarried women were suspect, having no recognized place in society. Significantly, an alternative way of life for women—the convent—was eliminated in Protestantism, undoubtedly leaving fewer means of fulfillment available than before to women whose bent went more toward education and art than vocations associated with the home life. Women's sphere became the home, and they had no place of authority in church life.

Christianity and Women in America before the Twentieth Century

Early American Christianity primarily was Protestant. In the very beginning, much of it was in the tradition that we have called "radical reform," involving such groups as the Puritans. For the most part, early American Christianity continued attitudes toward women that had prevailed in the European Protestantism we explored previously. Here, as there, men were expected to guard themselves against the wiles of women. The only accepted role for women was that of the good wife. And women who attempted to step outside the prescribed bounds of society to gain any kind of status or independence quickly were reined in or rejected outright. Some were even accused of witchcraft. Anne Hutchinson's story is a case in point.

Anne Hutchinson (1591–1643), born in England, joined the Massachusetts Bay Colony in 1634 and commenced work as a teacher, holding Bible classes in her home. When she began to promote her own teachings regarding the importance of freedom of conscience and individual inspiration based on what she claimed were revelations from God, she was seen by the authorities as a threat to the religious orthodoxy. She was tried as a witch and, though exonerated of witchcraft, was expelled from the Colony in 1637.

Yet there are many stories of distinguished women who had an impact on the landscape of American Christianity through to the nineteenth century. There are the stories of Mother Anne Lee (1736–1784), who founded the Shaker movement, and Mary Baker Eddy (1821–1910), who founded the Church of Christ, Scientist, both having emphasized the motherly and fatherly features of God, an inward and sensitive feeling-oriented approach to religion, and nurturing, healing aspects of spiritual leadership. There also is the story of Mother Elizabeth Ann Seton (1774–1821), founder of the Sisters of Charity, the first American Roman Catholic religious order. She often is called the mother of the Catholic parochial school system and was beatified by the Catholic Church in 1963. Space does not permit the mention of but a few such names.[33]

There is, however, a story of women in American Christianity that exemplifies the American religious spirit of the nineteenth century and that is particularly informative for us as we face the contemporary debate about the "woman question" in America. The debate on this issue, as we see it in our contemporary popular press, has been framed in terms of the goals of feminists, deemed primarily secular, and the goals of the conservative traditionalists, deemed religious. As we shall see, however, religion played a pivotal role in the advancement of feminist causes. Let us now turn to that story.

The eighteenth century was witness to a development in American Christianity that was to have a far-reaching effect on the lives of women—The Great Awakening of the mid-1700s. This, as we have seen, brought a feeling-centered element to American religion. Emphasis on feeling made the central values of religion more accessible than before to women, with their generally limited education—and women felt called to the spirit in a new way. Now, the great authority of religion was not the doctrinal interpretations of church leaders; instead, one's subjective experience of being infused with the spirit of God was the single most important power dictating how one should live.

The Great Awakening only slightly opened the door to a new way of participating in religion, and, therefore, had only a small impact on everyday life for women in general. But it was the precursor to a new wave of awakenings—the **Second Great Awakening**, which began in the early decades of the nineteenth century and was led at first by Charles Grandison Finney (1792–1875). The impact of this movement was to be felt in the depths of the American imagination, which held dear the importance of freedom of individual conscience. And those imbued with the Holy Spirit—especially women—took this to heart as they were called in great numbers to a progressivist-liberal message for society.

Women's participation in this "holiness" movement had vast implications for America. Spirit-led women embraced the new experience-centered theology and felt called by God to participate in public prayer and give testimonies of their conversion experiences. Women began to preach to large congregations of seekers. As Nancy Hardesty and the Daytons have written: "It encouraged, indeed compelled women to burst the cocoon of 'women's sphere,'"[34] and, thus, it broke through the traditional duality that had kept women in the home.

This development was not welcomed by the church leaders of the day, however, who sought to conserve tradition. "The Bible commands women's silence in the church!" such leaders countered. And many women were not inclined to go against the grain of the Biblical tradition in which they had been raised. But the transformative energy of evangelical conversion and the experience of total **sanctification** (that is, experiencing the power of the Holy Spirit to preserve one from sin and realize Christian perfection, often called the "second blessing") was felt by many women and held sway. Infused with that confidence, they began to challenge notions held by church leaders that the Bible justified such things as slavery, the subordination of women, the limitations of women's education, and the refusal to ordain women.

Together with like-minded men, these women became leaders of progressivist causes that disputed church orthodoxy. Strong in the belief that full reception of the Holy Spirit made women and men spiritually equal, they participated in all manner of social justice activities. Phoebe Palmer, an early leader who experienced sanctification on July 26, 1837, and thereafter published several books expounding her newfound faith, such as *The Way of Holiness* and *Faith and Its Effects,* preached to and inspired other women, proclaiming that "Holiness is Power." One of her converts was Catherine Booth who, with her husband William Booth, went on to found the Salvation Army.

Charles Finney (1792–1875), a Presbyterian minister, was instrumental in these developments. Although roundly criticized by mainstream clergymen for his work, he nevertheless encouraged women to play a greater role in American religious life and to work toward the realization of a vision for equality in American social and political life as well. The Quaker Grimke sisters, leaders in the abolitionist movement, and Frances Willard, founder of the reformist Women's Christian Temperance Union, are notable examples.

Significantly, educational opportunities for women had been severely limited, and therefore their ability to gain recognition in religious hierarchies as ordained ministers or as leaders in secular institutions was extremely difficult. It was not until Oberlin College, under Finney's leadership, became the first coeducational college in the United States—the first to admit women to its degree-granting programs—that the doors to higher education began to be opened. Oberlin produced several graduates who became leaders on behalf of reform movements, including Lucy Stone, the abolitionist and suffragist, and Antoinette Brown, the first woman to be ordained (1853).

Sojourner Truth (1797–1883), a former slave, although not directly involved in the holiness movement, was nevertheless inspired by her experience of the spirit to speak out against slavery and was a powerful women's rights advocate. She is remembered for her tremendous oratory skills, although she had no formal education. Her now legendary speech at the 1851 Woman's Rights Convention in Akron, Ohio, stands as but one example of her work. Countering the arguments of the ministers there (who justified the subordination of women by claiming that men have superior intellect and that God meant for women to be inferior because

Christ was a man and Eve took the apple from the serpent), Sojourner Truth, who was a strong presence standing six feet tall, responded:

> *"That man over there."* Her long finger shot toward the minister in question. *"He says women need to be helped into carriages and lifted over ditches and to have the best everywhere."* She smiled, shaking her head gently. *"Nobody helps me into any carriages, over mud puddles, or gets me any best place...And ain't I a woman?"* Sojourner cried out. *"Look at me!"* She bared her powerful right arm and raised it high in the air. *"Look at my arm. I have plowed. And I have planted. And I have gathered in barns. And no man could head me.* And ain't I a woman?"
>
> *"I could work as much and eat as much as a man—when I could get it—and bear the lash as well! And ain't I a woman? I have borne children and seen most of them sold into slavery, and when I cried out with a mother's grief, none but Jesus heard me.* And ain't I a woman?" . . .
>
> *"That little man in black there! He says women can't have as much rights as men, 'Cause Christ wasn't a woman.'"* Her arms stretched wide as if to evoke the cross, and her eyes burned. *"Where did your Christ come from? Where did your Christ come from?"* Her question rolled over the packed, silent pews. *"From God and a woman!"* She looked witheringly at the minister in question. *"Man had nothing to do with him!"*[35]

While African Americans had gained their political freedom during the Civil War, they had not gained an accepted place in society. Amanda Smith, another former slave, who had received sanctification in 1868, challenged religious and social norms by preaching and singing in holiness meetings in America and later in the British Isles and Africa. Her very presence and the felt authenticity of her message inspired many who had held on to racial prejudice to abandon such notions as contrary to the Holy Spirit.

But these movements were cutting against the grain of mainstream conservative Christian religious tradition, which, as we have seen, projected a certain ideal for Christian womanhood. The church fathers (and many women) of several denominations often were the most vocal opponents of women's advancement, as well as opponents of some of the causes that the women of the holiness movement (and like-minded men) promoted, such as the abolition of slavery. These church fathers cited scriptural passages and appealed to the now well-worn dualistic thinking of tradition (i.e., the inherent inferiority of women and their tendencies toward sin) to justify such things as limited roles for women in institutional structures, placing men over women as their rulers, limited education for women, and no legal standing for women (requiring a woman to be represented by her husband, just as if she were a minor). Permitting women a greater voice on their own behalf and in society at large would undermine the social order ordained by God, such clergymen argued.

Pivotal in the controversy was the Bible. How were those inspired by the Holy Spirit to reconcile their real felt experience with the injunctions against women in the Bible? While there were women who acquiesced in their silencing by church leaders because of biblical pronouncements, others found that the Bible itself provided the support they needed for their participation. For example, Phoebe Palmer cited Acts 2:17–18, which restates the promise of Joel 2:28: "In the last days it will be, God declares, that I will pour out my Spirit upon all flesh [or people], and your sons and your daughters shall prophesy. . . . Even upon my slaves [or servants], both men and women, in those days I will pour out my Spirit; and they shall prophesy." Others sought to reinterpret the Bible, arguing that its main message is one of liberation for all peoples. The Quaker Grimke sisters were of this bent. They, too, had been inspired by Finney's revivalism and were major participants in the abolition movement and the women's rights movement, although they later set aside their work for women's rights, having been convinced that linking slavery to women's oppression *might undermine their ability to convince a majority of those in power to abolish slavery!* Others rejected the Bible outright as authoritative, seeing it as a product of writers from a patriarchal time and not binding for their time. This was the approach of Elizabeth Cady Stanton.

Elizabeth Cady Stanton (1815–1902) is well known for being, among other things, the first person to organize women in an effort to obtain the right to vote and to be ordained as ministers in the churches. Having herself been converted by Charles Finney's revivalism, the inspiration for her religious views arose out of a personal religious conviction. But hers was not one that demanded adherence to a text that she found counter to her experience. Instead, she placed much of the blame for the subordinate position of women in society and women's acceptance of subordination squarely on the Bible itself and on clergymen's interpretation of it. Her alternative was the *Woman's Bible,* which she edited and published in 1895. In her introduction to the first edition, she wrote:

> *From the Inauguration of the movement for woman's emancipation the Bible has been used to hold [women] in the 'divinely ordained sphere,' prescribed in the Old and New Testaments. . . . While [women's] clergymen told them on the one hand, that they owed all the blessings and freedom they enjoyed to the Bible, on the other, they said it clearly marked out their circumscribed sphere of action: that the demands for political and civil rights were irreligious, dangerous to the stability of the home, the state and the church. . . . No wonder the majority of women still, and with bowed heads, accept the situation.*[36]

Legal, political, and religious rights that women in America now take for granted can be traced to the work of such luminaries as Phoebe Palmer, Lucy Stone, Francis Willard, Sojourner Truth, Elizabeth Cady Stanton, and the religious movements that stood against the tide of those who wished to maintain the status quo of women's subordination and the slavery of African Americans.[37]

The "Woman Question" in American Christianity in the Twentieth Century and Beyond

After the Civil War, the intensely felt reformist and abolitionist spirit that was present in the years leading up to that war between the states seemed temporarily exhausted. The holiness movement turned more conservative and inward-looking, and the movement for women's rights became more political than explicitly religion-based, perhaps because religious leaders were instrumental in blocking women's advancement. Women's right to vote was not granted until 1920, and the efforts for ordination of women until then had been of only limited success. However, by the 1950s ordination of women again became a major topic of discussion in many Protestant denominations. Methodists and Presbyterians began ordaining women in 1956. As the new feminist movement of the 1960s took hold, women began to enter theological seminaries in large numbers both in those denominations as well as in others that did not yet permit ordination.

From the 1970s on, many more Protestant denominations granted women's ordination, and a few women have been raised to the office of bishop in them: Margorie Matthews in the United Methodist Church in 1984, and Barbara Harris in the American Episcopal Church in 1989. The Church of England began ordaining women in 1992.

The Roman Catholic and Eastern Orthodox churches have felt themselves unable to take this step, although the participation of women in many levels of leadership—educational, leading services in the absence of a priest, pastoral work in parishes and college chaplaincies—has increased dramatically in the Roman Catholic Church since the liberalizing of Catholicism under the Second Vatican Council. Still, as Rosemary Ruether has noted, "Women's presence in world Christianity in all continents can be seen as a broad-based pyramid in which women are present in large numbers at the base and increasingly small numbers as one moves up the hierarchical ladder."[38]

Most interestingly, there is a confluence of trends the outcome of which is not yet determinable. The 1980s witnessed a new Christian spirit moving through America that became a powerful political, as well as religious, force in the 1990s—the so-called "Christian right." While their political power has waned to some degree at the beginning of the twenty-first century, their voices are still prominent in debates about social issues and their views have tempered previous liberal trends. Concerned that American values are at stake, these conservative Christians advocate a return to a literal interpretation of the Bible, including the biblical injunctions regarding women. Contemporary society appears to them to have lost its original moral ground. As a consequence, they are advocating a return to traditional social conventions reflecting the old duality in order to bolster that which is, for them, a religiously legitimate social order. The late twentieth century saw the rise of the Promise Keepers, a movement of men who hold to this view, as well as the 1998 Southern Baptist Convention amendment of its official statement of belief, the "Baptist Faith and Message." It now states that husbands and wives are of "equal worth before God," but that "[a] wife is to submit graciously to the servant

Emergent leadership of women in religion: Barbara Harris became the first female bishop in the history of the Anglican Church in 1989.

leadership of her husband even as the church willingly submits to the headship of Christ" and that a husband "is to love his wife as Christ loved the church. He has the God-given responsibility to provide for, to protect, and to lead his family." This is a very significant statement of faith in that the Southern Baptists constitute the largest American denomination at 15.8 million members.[39]

On the other hand, while the 1960s "second wave" of feminism appeared to many to turn away from religion as an oppressive institution in society, the second half of the twentieth century gave rise to experience of the spirit in another direction. Spirit-led women of a feminist bent have been instrumental in revitalizing worship in the liberal churches, many of which now profess their faith to God as Mother and Father.

While, on the one hand, conservative Christians are holding to the inerrancy of the Bible, on the other hand, the twentieth century saw new archeological finds and considerable scholarship providing insight into the social and political context in which Christianity was born and new information as to how the New Testament came into being. New biblical interpretations have arisen out of that scholarship, and Christian feminist scholars have had a part in it. Elisabeth

Schussler Fiorenza, in her pivotal work *In Memory of Her,* and Karen Torjesen, in her work *When Women Were Priests,* are just two who have contributed to a feminist reinterpretation of the scriptures that runs counter to the interpretations adhered to by traditionalists.

Significantly, womanist and *mujerista* writers (African American and Hispanic American, respectively) have pointed out that feminism has been a movement of white women seeking to overcome the oppressions associated with gender and, therefore, the focus has been too narrow. The work of womanist and *mujerista* women has revealed that oppression is multidimensional, involving not only gender but race and class as well. Their insights have opened up the theological discourse to include, as Linda A. Moody has written, a "theology across the boundaries of difference."[40] United States *mujerista* scholars and Latin American women theologians have been influential in Liberation Theology movements, which have had a long-range impact globally.

Most important, Western Christian woman's scholarship has generated a global discourse about women and religion. Today we find this scholarship having an impact on some aspect of every religion in the world. In Christianity today, no less than in all the major religions of the world, however, the battle for women's rights is made against the backdrop of tradition. What can be retained of tradition while widening the arena of opportunities for women? How can religion provide a place for women's voices in the shaping of theology—the traditionally exclusive sphere of men? What is women's proper role in family and society? How far should women's rights extend when women are the bearers of the future generation? What is the proper relationship of women and men? The outcome of the many discourses these questions have generated will shape the lives of women in every corner of the globe in the twenty-first century.

Christianity in the World Today

As the tumultuous twentieth century drew to a close, Christianity remained in an anxious world, full of strains, paradoxes, and ominous portents almost beyond imagining. In some places a new age of high technology, symbolized by space probes and sophisticated computers, is being ushered in. Yet a third of humankind goes to bed hungry every night, and the bodies and minds of children shrivel for lack of bread. Even as prospects of amazing progress in science, medicine, and all branches of learning gleam, not for centuries has the future been so feared. For beside that glittering computerized future (and what it might do to human values, nobody knows) loom the grim shadows of the new four horsemen of the Apocalypse: tyranny, war, economic disaster, and famine.

Just because of its phenomenal worldwide spread, Christianity finds itself today at all corners of the world's dilemmas. It is the church of wealthy consuming nations and the church of the starving, of countries old and new, of lands and classes with little in common and much reason to see themselves at cross-purposes.

In 1900 the world's most powerful countries were Christian, ruled by professedly Christian emperors, kings, and presidents. Moreover, it was widely boasted that Europe and America's Christianity had something to do with their manifest superiority over the rest of humanity. Not a few Christians prophesied that, since the day of the other religions and their outmoded cultures was clearly past, the whole planet might be converted within a generation.

By the last quarter of the twentieth century, the confidence of those expansive times was long gone. Wars and revolutions toppled ancient Christian as well as Confucian thrones; movements of national independence brought resurgent affirmations of Hinduism, Buddhism, and Islam; in Europe, America, and elsewhere immense social and intellectual changes weakened the grip of the traditional religion, Christianity, on the minds of many.

Yet Christianity, chastened but quite alive, abides. In some places it is in recession, but in others it is growing. In some places it shows quite a different face from 1900; in others it seems to have changed little since 1900, nor indeed since 900. It retains its complex denominationalism, its amazing diversities of forms of worship and theological opinion, and its chronic inability to find a common voice with which to address a problem-ridden world. Yet it is still a major presence to be reckoned with as it faces new challenges in the twenty-first century.

✹ Summary

Throughout its 2,000 years of history, Christianity has achieved a wide diversity of forms. But they all derive ultimately from the person, life, and teaching of Jesus. The teaching centers on the Kingdom of God, Jesus's proclamation of God's reign or rule, which is both present in the world and coming into it. Jesus was executed on a cross by the Roman authorities; reports spread among his followers that he had risen three days later from the dead. For the religious movement that formed around him, whose teachings were supremely articulated by the apostle Paul, Jesus was a Divine savior; through faith in him one could share his life eternally.

For the sometimes-persecuted early Christian church of the Roman Empire, Christian life was arduous. It centered around baptism, the major rite of entry into its fellowship, and the Holy Communion, the sacred meal that repeated Jesus's Last Supper before his crucifixion.

After the triumph of Christianity under the Emperor Constantine, the religion faced new problems and opportunities. Doctrinal differences were resolved by General Councils, which emphasized that Jesus Christ is of one substance with God the Father, truly God and truly human. Christian worship became more elaborate; the church became the official religion of the empire, and over the next few centuries converted most of Europe. The medieval style of Christianity that followed seemed outwardly to express the stable social order with a steady round of festivals and Sunday masses that were the medieval ideal; but beneath the surface were tensions that gave rise to radical movements and set the stage for future developments.

The sixteenth-century Protestant Reformation was sparked by the monk Martin Luther's conviction that salvation was not won by the amount of one's piety or good works but was freely given by God as grace and received by faith. In opposition to medieval church life, he proposed an alternative style centered on scripture, preaching, and the ideal of inward faith. The second great reformer, John Calvin, emphasized the sovereignty of God and his calling of people by grace to his service and salvation. The Reformation in England was more conservative than that on the continent, resulting in a church with both Catholic and Protestant features. On the other hand, England was also a main center of radical reform—movements of more extreme Protestants who favored a simple church of believers, social change, and separation of church and state. From out of the radical wing of the Reformation came such denominations as those of the Congregationalists, Baptists, Quakers, and, later, Methodists.

Christian mysticism and devotion has run deep over the centuries, in two great though sometimes converging channels: the way of the negation of images, which seeks to know God by taking away all words and concepts less than God; and the way of the affirmation of images, using ideas and mental images to lift one to God. Both have expression in each of the three main divisions of Christianity: Eastern Orthodoxy, Roman Catholicism, and Protestantism. But in these and other respects, the three show differences as well.

Highly traditional, the Orthodox church centered in Eastern Europe presents firm doctrine, ornate worship, and a deep affiliation with the cultures of the countries in which it is predominant. Its spiritual life combines freedom with a feeling for the meaning of corporate church life and the resurrection of Jesus.

The Roman Catholic Church is distinguished by the papacy, a sense for the importance of combining freedom with order, and an emphasis on the sacraments in Christian life. In it, traditionalism combines with a capacity for change.

Protestantism displays wide diversity but generally is characterized by relative simplicity of worship, emphasis on scripture and preaching, and often a desire for local and democratic control of church government.

During the last 500 years, Christianity has expanded to become the largest and the most worldwide of religions. Beginning with the work of Catholic missionaries in the wake of Vasco da Gama and Christopher Columbus, Christianity has expanded remarkably through a combination of missionary work and European emigration. The nineteenth century, when Protestant as well as Catholic missionaries were active, was particularly a period of growth. As the twenty-first century opens, much of the future of Christianity lies in Asia, Africa, and Latin America where, as the result of missionary expansion there, many forms of Christianity have thrived, from the traditional, such as Roman Catholicism, to those with ecstatic practices, such as Pentecostalism, to new religious movements, such as the Mai Chaza Church.

The writings of the early Jesus movement reflected more inclusion of women than was the norm at the time; however, this was countered with Biblical admonitions that have provided justification for placing women under the authority of their husbands and silencing them in church affairs. The early institutionalized church made celibacy, rather than home and marriage, the ideal, and limited women's participation. However, women found an alternative in the life of the convent where they could be educated. The Protestant Reformation included women's place in the home as wives and mothers in its sacred center—the nuclear family. But European Christendom from the fourteenth century through the seventeenth century sought to purge many of the folk customs that remained a part of the religious practices of the people, resulting in the removal of women's spheres of influence in the "little traditions" of local church life. This also resulted in the outright persecution of women as "witches." Although conservatism and religion are often thought to go together, religious movements of the nineteenth century, such as the "holiness movement," proved to be fertile ground for the development of women's rights. Today, just as in other religions in the world, Christianity is involved in a debate about women, tradition, and reform, the outcome of which will have a great impact on women in the twenty-first century.

In the late twentieth century, Christianity faced many problems and many prospects. Now, in the twenty-first century it remains a worldwide faith, with much variation in its appearance from one part of the world to another.

✸ Questions for Review

1. Summarize the life and central teaching of Jesus.
2. Summarize the basic teaching of Paul the apostle.
3. Give a description of life in the early church: its forms of worship, way of life, organization, and fundamental beliefs.
4. Explain the reasons for persecution of Christians under the Roman Empire and the Christian attitude toward martyrs.
5. Interpret what the triumph of Christianity under Constantine meant to the religion. What new problems appeared? What new opportunities? What new forms of Christian life arose?
6. Summarize the meaning and teaching of the first four General Councils.
7. Trace the development of medieval Christianity, and outline its major features.
8. Interpret the nature of Martin Luther's basic religious experience, and cite the main points of his teaching.
9. Explain some fundamental features of Calvinism.
10. Outline the course of the Reformation in England, and tell how and why it was different from that on the continent of Europe.
11. Discuss the nature of radical reform, explaining who the Puritans were, and the background of such denominations in the English-speaking world as Congregationalists, Baptists, Quakers, and Methodists.
12. Trace the course of mysticism within Christianity.

13. Summarize the main features of Christian teaching, practice, church organization, and life within Eastern Orthodoxy, Roman Catholicism, and Protestantism. Be sure to include variations within each of these major branches of Christianity.

14. Trace the history of the expansion of Christianity in the last 500 years, referring to the worldwide role given Christianity and the questions it has raised.

15. Explain how Christian dualism has had an impact on Christian attitudes toward women and remains influential in Western culture as a whole.

16. Trace the history of women in Christianity from its earliest times to the present.

✸ Suggested Readings on Christianity

General

Altizer, Thomas J. J., *The Contemporary Jesus.* Albany: State University of New York Press, 1997.

Balston, David B., *From Conquest to Struggle: Jesus of Nazareth in Latin America.* Albany: State University of New York Press, 1991.

Callan, Terrance, *The Origins of Christian Faith.* New York: Paulist Press, 1994.

Ellwood, Robert S., and James B. Wiggins, *Christianity: A Cultural Perspective.* Englewood Cliffs, NJ: Prentice Hall, 1988. An introductory textbook.

Evans, Craig A., *Life of Jesus Research: An Annotated Bibliography,* Rev. ed. New York: E. J. Brill, 1996.

Gerrish, Brian A., *The Faith of Christendom: A Source Book of Creeds and Confessions.* New York: World, 1963. A helpful collection of primary materials on Christian beliefs.

Latourette, Kenneth Scott, *A History of Christianity.* New York: Harper & Brothers, 1953. A massive, well-written history, emphasizing the expansion of Christianity.

Niebuhr, H. Richard, *Christ and Culture.* New York: Harper Torchbooks, 1956. A classic study of different ways Christianity has related to its cultural environments.

Pelikan, Jaroslav, *Jesus through the Centuries.* New Haven, CT: Yale University Press, 1985. A remarkably insightful and informative study of how Jesus has been perceived in art, devotion, and theology in the various periods of Christian history.

Smart, Ninian, *The Phenomenon of Christianity.* London: Collins, 1979. A good phenomenological study of the varieties and commonalties of Christianity.

Tillich, Paul, *A History of Christian Thought.* New York: Harper & Row, 1968. A leading Protestant theologian's view of the topic.

Underhill, Evelyn, *Mystics of the Church.* London: J. Clarke & Co., 1925. A semipopular account by a distinguished scholar; emphasizes Roman Catholic figures.

———, *Worship.* London: Nisbet & Co., Ltd., 1936. A view of Christian worship and its meaning that tries to be sympathetic to all traditions. Written before the modern liturgical movement, but a classic.

Walker, Williston, *A History of the Christian Church,* rev. ed. New York: Scribners, 1984. A standard text.

The New Testament

Bornkamm, Gunther, *Paul*. New York: Harper & Row, 1971. Widely regarded as the best study of the apostle's life and thought.

Brown, Raymond E., *The Birth of the Messiah*. Garden City, NY: Doubleday, 1979. A major work on the birth and infancy stories of Jesus.

———, *The Community of the Beloved Disciple*. New York: Paulist Press, 1979. Study of the background of the Gospel of John by a distinguished scholar.

———, *The Death of the Messiah*. New York: Doubleday, 1994. A major, much-discussed summary of scholarly knowledge about the last days of Jesus.

Casey, Maurice, *From Jewish Prophet to Gentile God: The Origins and Development of New Testament Christology*. Louisville, KY: Westminster John Knox Press, 1991.

Court, John, and Kathleen Court, *The New Testament World*. Englewood Cliffs, NJ: Prentice Hall, 1990. A richly illustrated volume, of special value to students and nonspecialists.

Delling, Gerhard, *Worship in the New Testament*. Philadelphia: Westminster Press, 1962. A useful treatment of the field.

Ehrman, Bart D., *The New Testament and Other Early Christian Writings: A Reader*. New York: Oxford University Press, 1998.

Fredriksen, Paula, *From Jesus to Christ: The Origins of the New Testament Images of Jesus*. New Haven, CT, and London: Yale University Press, 1988.

Grant, Robert M., *A Historical Introduction to the New Testament*. New York: Harper & Row, 1963. A standard overview of the New Testament from the perspective of its setting in time and place.

Hengel, Martin, *The Four Gospels and the One Gospel of Jesus Christ: An Investigation of the Collection and Origin of the Canonical Gospels*. Harrisburg, PA: Trinity Press International, 2000.

Kee, H., *Community of the New Age*. Philadelphia: Westminster Press, 1977. Studies in the Gospel of Mark.

———, *Jesus in History*. New York: Harcourt Brace Jovanovich, 1977. A balanced analysis.

———, *Understanding the New Testament,* 4th ed. Englewood Cliffs, NJ: Prentice Hall, 1983. A standard textbook.

Ladd, George Eldon, *A Theology of the New Testament*. Grand Rapids, MI: Eerdmans, 1974. An excellent presentation of the evangelical perspective; monumental scholarship.

Meeks, Wayne A., *The First Urban Christians: The Social World of the Apostle Paul*. New Haven, CT: Yale University Press, 1983. An important study providing fresh insights on the sort of people who became early Christians and the role of the Pauline church in their lives.

Richardson, Alan, *An Introduction to the Theology of the New Testament*. New York: Harper & Row, 1958. A standard, fairly conservative work by a distinguished scholar.

Vaage, Leif E., and Vincent L. Wimbush, *Asceticism and the New Testament*. New York: Routledge, 1999.

The student is directed as well to the section on "Women in Religion" below for feminist perspectives on the New Testament and the early Christian Church and to the Frontline website entitled "From Jesus to Christ" on the Public Broadcasting System website: *www.pbs.org.*

The Early Christian Church

Cloke, Gillian, *This Female Man of God: Women and Spiritual Power in the Patristic Age, 350–450*. London and New York: Routledge, 1995.

Conzelman, Hans, *Gentiles, Jews, Christians: Polemics and Apologetics in the Greco-Roman Era*. M. Eugene Boring, trans. Minneapolis, MN: Fortress Press, 1992.

Gough, Michael, *Early Christians*. New York: Praeger, 1961. A valuable, well-illustrated survey oriented toward archaeology.

Grant, Robert McQueen, *Heresy and Criticism: The Search for Authenticity in Early Christian Literature*. Louisville, KY: Westminster John Knox Press, 1993.

Ludeman, Gerd Ketzer, *Heretics: The Other Side of Early Christianity*. John Bowden, trans. Louisville, KY: Westminster John Knox Press, 1996.

Meeks, Wayne A., *The Origins of Christian Morality: The First Two Centuries*. New Haven, CT: Yale University Press, 1993.

Pagels, Elaine, *The Gnostic Gospels*. New York: Random House, 1979. A new view of Gnosticism and the early church based on recently discovered Gnostic texts.

Robinson, James M., ed., *The Nag Hammadi Library in English*. San Francisco: Harper & Row, 1977, 1981. Translation of the important recently discovered Gnostic documents.

Stark, Rodney, *The Rise of Christianity: A Sociologist Reconsiders History*. Princeton, NJ: Princeton University Press, 1996.

Waddell, Helen, *The Desert Fathers*. Ann Arbor: University of Michigan Press, 1957. A good translation, with a beautifully written introduction. Gives a vivid picture of the earliest Christian monastics.

Wand, J. W. C., *A History of the Early Church*. London: Methuen, 1937. A well-written work; traditional point of view.

Eastern Orthodoxy

Calian, Carnegie Samuel, *Theology without Boundaries: Encounters of Eastern Orthodoxy and Western Tradition*. Louisville, KY: Westminster John Knox Press, 1992.

Davis, Nathanial, *A Long Walk to Church: A Contemporary History of Russian Orthodoxy*. Boulder, CO: Westview Press, 1995.

Ellis, Jan, *The Russian Orthodox Church: Triumphalism and Defensiveness*. New York: St. Martin's Press, 1996.

Fedotov, G. P., *A Treasury of Russian Spirituality*. London: Sheed & Ward, 1952. A fine anthology of the mysticism of Eastern Christianity.

Lossky, Vladimir, *The Mystical Theology of the Eastern Church*. London: James Clarke, 1957. Fairly scholarly, and a brilliant treatment of the topic.

Prokurat, Michael, *Historical Dictionary of the Orthodox Church*. Lanham, MD: Scarecrow Press, 1996.

Ware, Timothy, *The Orthodox Church*. Baltimore, MD: Penguin Books, 1963. A good, solid introduction.

Zernov, N., *Eastern Christendom*. London: Weidenfeld & Nicolson, 1961. A sympathetic popular introduction.

Roman Catholicism

Adam, Karl, *The Spirit of Catholicism*. New York: Macmillan, 1929. A profound but fairly simple essay, written from a personal point of view.

Bausch, William J., *Pilgrim Church: A Popular History of Catholic Christianity*. Notre Dame, IN: Fides, 1973. A modern treatment.

Brantl, George, *Catholicism*. New York: Braziller, 1969. A useful anthology.

Cunningham, Lawrence, *The Catholic Experience*. New York: Crossroad, 1987. A readable summary.

Flannery, Austin P., *The Documents of Vatican II*. Grand Rapids, MI: Eerdmans, 1981. A knowledge of this council and its products is necessary to any understanding of Roman Catholicism since the 1960s.

Heimann, Mary, *Catholic Devotion in Victorian England*. New York: Oxford University Press, 1995.

McBrien, Richard P., *Catholicism*, rev. ed. San Francisco: Harper, 1994. A good textbook.

McKenzie, John, *The Roman Catholic Church*. Garden City, NY: Doubleday, 1971. A standard resource.

Rahner, Karl, *Teachings of the Catholic Church*. New York: Alba, 1967. A summary by a modern liberal Catholic theologian.

Protestantism

Barnstone, Aliki, et al., eds., *The Calvanist Roots of the Modern Era*. Hanover, NH: University Press of New England, 1997.

Cox, Harvey, *Fire from Heaven*. Reading, MA: Addison-Wesley, 1995. A readable overview of Pentecostalism around the world by a leading theologian.

Dillenberger, John, and Claude Welch, *Protestant Christianity*. New York: Scribners, 1954. A historical introduction.

Dunstan, Leslie, *Protestantism*. New York: Braziller, 1961. A useful anthology of historical material.

Haverstick, John, *The Progress of the Protestant*. New York: Holt, Rinehart & Winston, 1969. A lavishly illustrated popular history of Protestantism.

MacIntosh, Hugh Ross, *Types of Modern Theology: Schleiermacher to Barth*. New York: Scribner's, 1939. A fine introduction to the most talked about modern Protestant theologians.

Marty, Martin E., *Protestantism*. London: Weidenfeld & Nicholson, 1972. A survey of Protestant attitudes on a number of issues; good bibliography.

Nichols, James Hastings, *Primer for Protestants*. New York: Association Press, 1951. A well-done basic introduction to traditional Protestant attitudes.

Niebuhr, H. R., *The Kingdom of God in America*. New York: Harper & Brothers, 1937. A seminal history of the interaction between Protestant attitudes and American history.

Pauck, Wilhelm, *The Heritage of the Reformation*. Glencoe, IL: The Free Press, 1961. An authoritative historical statement.

Tawney, R. H., *Religion and the Rise of Capitalism*. London: John Murray, 1926. A statement of the often-discussed thesis that Protestant and capitalistic attitudes have reinforced each other.

von Rohr, John Robert, *Profile of Protestantism*. Belmont, CA: Dickenson, 1969. A good basic textbook.

Williams, George, *The Radical Reformation*. Philadelphia: Westminster, 1962. The standard book on this aspect of the Protestant Reformation.

Christianity in America

Ahlstrom, Sydney E., *A Religious History of the American People*. New Haven, CT, and London: Yale University Press, 1972. A substantial but readable story of American religion, emphasizing periods and broad themes. Reliable and highly recommended.

Bednarowski, Mary Farell, *American Religion: A Cultural Perspective*. Englewood Cliffs, NJ: Prentice Hall, 1984. A descriptive survey of American religion in its diversity and cultural impact.

Bellah, Robert N., *The Broken Covenant*. New York: Seabury Press, 1975. A study of American "Civil Religion": the use of Christian-derived myths, salvation themes, taboos, and the like in political and social life.

Deck, Allan Figueroa, ed., *Frontiers of Hispanic Theology in the United States*. Maryknoll, NY: Orbis Books, 1992.

Jacobsen, Douglas, and William Vance Trollinger, eds. *Re-forming the Center: American Protestantism, 1900 to the Present*. Grand Rapids, MI: W.B. Eerdsman, 1998.

Miller, William Lee, *The First Liberty: Religion and the American Republic*. New York: Knopf, 1986. Bound to become a classic study of the first amendment to the U.S. Constitution; on religious freedom and separation of church and state, and the story of its interpretation and application.

Raboteau, Albert, *Slave Religion*. New York: Oxford University Press, 1978. Important study of a significant, but in some circles little known, sector of American religious history.

Rosten, Leo, ed., *Religions of America.* New York: Simon & Schuster, 1975. Questions and answers about the basic beliefs and practices and the major American religions and denominations; a good introduction. Valuable statistical information as well.

Roy, Jody M., *Rhetorical Campaigns of the Nineteenth Century Anti-Catholics and Catholics in America.* Lewiston, NY: Edwin Mellen Press, 2000.

Theis, Jeffrey, *Mexican Catholicism in Southern California: The Importance of Popular Religiosity and Sacramental Practice in Faith Experience.* New York: P. Lang, 1993.

Women in Christianity

Barstow, Anne Llewellyn, *Witchcraze: A New History of the European Witch Hunts.* San Francisco: HarperSanFrancisco/Pandora, 1994. An important recent work on the subject, which provides new scholarship.

Blevins, Carolyn DeArmond, ed., *Women in Christian History: A Bibliography.* Macon, GA: Mercer University Press, 1995.

Borresen, Kari Elisabeth, *Subordination and Equivalence: The Nature and Role of Woman in Augustine and Thomas Aquinas,* Charles H. Talbot, trans. Washington, DC: University Press of America, 1981. An interesting work on the subject.

Boyd, Lois A., and Douglas Brackenridge, *Presbyterian Women in America: Two Centuries of a Quest for Status.* 2nd ed. Westport, CT: Greenwood Press, 1996.

Brasher, Brenda, *Godly Women: Fundamentalism and Female Power.* New Brunswick, NJ: Rutgers University Press, 1998.

Braude, Ann, *Radical Spirits: Spiritualism and Women's Rights in Nineteenth-Century America.* Boston: Beacon Press, 1989. An important work addressing the impact of religious experience on the nineteenth-century feminist movement.

Carmody, Denise Lardner, *Women & World Religions,* 2nd ed. Englewood Cliffs, NJ: Prentice Hall, 1979, 1989, Chapters 8 and 10. Good summaries of women in Christianity and women in America.

Chaves, Mark, *Ordaining Women: Culture and Conflict in Religious Organizations.* Cambridge, MA: Harvard University Press, 1997.

Christ, Carol P., and Judith Plaskow, eds., *Weaving the Visions: New Patterns in Feminist Spirituality.* San Francisco: HarperSanFrancisco, 1989. Another not-to-be-missed collection of articles on women and religion.

———, *Womanspirit Rising: A Feminist Reader in Religion.* San Francisco: HarperSanFrancisco, 1979, 1992. A not-to-be-missed collection of articles on women and religion.

Clark, Elizabeth A., and Herbert Richardson, *Women and Religion: The Original Sourcebook of Women in Christian Thought,* rev. ed. San Francisco: HarperSanFrancisco, 1996. An excellent overview of issues regarding women in Christian thought from the New Testament accounts to the twentieth century, including excerpts from original sources.

Cooper-White, Pamela, *The Cry of Tamar: Violence Against Women and the Church's Response.* Minneapolis, MN: Fortress Press, 1995.

Fiorenza, Elisabeth Schussler, *In Memory of Her: A Feminist Theological Reconstruction of Christian Origins,* 10th anniv. ed. New York: Crossroad, 1994. A pivotal work that provides a feminist interpretation of the Scriptures.

Hardesy, Nancy, *Your Daughters Shall Prophesy: Revivalism and Feminism in the Age of Finney.* Brooklyn, NY: Carlson Pub., 1991.

Isasi-Diaz, Ada Maria, *Mujerista Theology: A Theology for the Twenty-first Century.* Maryknoll, NY: Orbis Books, 1996. An important work by one of the pivotal mujerista authors.

James, Janet W., ed., *Women in American Religion.* Philadelphia: University of Pennsylvania Press, 1980. Articles on American religious women in all their diversity, from colonial Quakers to contemporary Roman Catholic sisters.

Johnson, Elizabeth A., *She Who Is: The Mystery of God in Feminist Theological Discourse.* New York: Crossroads, 1992. An often-cited, important work on the subject.

Kraemer, Ross Shepard, *Her Share of the Blessings: Women's Religions Among Pagans, Jews, and Christians in the Greco-Roman World*. New York: Oxford University Press, 1992.

Mabee, Carleton, *Sojourner Truth: Slave, Prophet, Legend*. New York: New York University Press, 1993. A good, scholarly treatment of the life and work of Sojourner Truth.

McLaughlin, Eleanor Commo, "Equality of Soul, Inequality of Sexes: Women in Medieval Theology" in *Religion and Sexism: Images of Woman in the Jewish and Christian Traditions,* Rosemary R. Ruether, ed. New York: Simon & Schuster, 1974, pp. 213–66. A good article on the subject.

Moody, Linda A., *Women Encounter God: Theology across the Boundaries of Difference*. Maryknoll, NY: Orbis Books, 1996. An excellent overview and interpretation of feminist, womanist, and mujerista theology.

Ruether, Rosemary R., "Christianity and Women in the Modern World," in *Today's Woman in World Religions,* Arvind Sharma, ed. Albany: State University of New York Press, 1994, pp. 267–301. A good survey of the subject with statistical information, particularly with regard to ordination.

———, *Sexism and God-Talk: Toward a Feminist Theology*. 10th anniv. Ed. Boston: Beacon Press, 1993.

———, *Women and Redemption: A Theological History*. Minneapolis, MN: Fortress Press, 1998.

——— and Rosemary Skinner Keller, eds., *In Our Own Voices: Four Centuries of American Women's Religious Writing*. San Francisco: HarperSanFrancisco, 1995. A good collection of articles on the subject.

——— and Eleanor McLaughlin, eds., *Women of Spirit: Female Leadership in the Jewish and Christian Traditions*. New York: Simon & Schuster, 1979. A wonderful collection of articles on women in Christianity and Judaism.

Schulenberg, Jane Tibbets, "Women's Monastic Communities 500–1000: Patterns of Expansion and Decline" in *Sisters and Workers in the Middle Ages,* Judith M. Bennett et al., eds. Chicago and London: University of Chicago Press, pp. 208–39. A significant article on the subject.

Torjeson, Karen, *When Women Were Priests: Women's Leadership in the Early Church and the Scandal of Their Subordination in the Rise of Christianity*. San Francisco: HarperSanFrancisco, 1993, 1995. An excellent and thorough account of the subject.

Townes, Emilie M., ed., *A Troubling in My Soul: Womanist Perspectives on Evil and Suffering*. Maryknoll, NY: Orbis Books, 1993. An interesting work addressing specifics.

Trevor-Roper, Hugh, *The European Witch-Craze of the Sixteenth and Seventeenth Centuries*. Harmondsworth, U.K.: Penguin Books, 1969. A classic work on the subject.

Wessinger, Catherine, ed., *Women's Leadership in Marginal Religions: Explorations Outside the Mainstream*. Urbana/Chicago: University of Illinois Press, 1993.

Westerkamp, Marilyn J., *Women and Religion in Early America, 1600–1850: The Puritan and Evangelical Traditions*. New York: Routledge, 1999.

Williams, Delores S., *Sisters in the Wilderness: The Challenge of Womanist God-Talk*. Maryknoll, NY: Orbis Books, 1993. An excellent work by a significant writer in the field.

CHAPTER NINE

Submitting to the Will of God

The Building of the House of Islam

CHAPTER OBJECTIVES

After studying this chapter, you should be able to

❁ Discuss the basic teachings and practices of Islam.

❁ Explain the historical role of the Islamic faith.

❁ Summarize the major schools of Islam.

❁ Interpret the place of Islam in the world of today.

❁ Talk about the role of women in Middle Eastern Islam past and present.

The Meaning of Islam

Over 1 billion, or nearly one-fifth of the world's population adhere to the faith of Islam, the youngest of the world's great religions. Despite important variations within Islam, it is also the most homogeneous and self-consciously an international community of the three giant cross-cultural faiths: Buddhism, Christianity, and Islam.

Islam is a community that does indeed cut across many cultures. Non-Muslims often envision Islam as the faith of romantic (and now tremendously oil-wealthy) Arab sheiks and caravaneers, but only a minority of Muslims are Arab, and only a tiny minority are wandering desert dwellers. The largest single Muslim nation is tropical Indonesia, where the faith of Muhammad is superimposed on an East Asian culture. Other Muslims in great numbers are farmers and craftspeople in India and Pakistan; businesspeople in the cities of Turkey, Iran, or Malaysia; blacks in sub-Saharan Africa, where Islam is growing. Even in the Arab countries, where Islam originated, the population is largely urban or engaged in intensive, sedentary agriculture in fertile strips like those along the Nile and the Two Rivers. Normative Islam, in fact, has historically been preeminently a faith of citified, mobile, internationally minded people, sometimes conquerors but more often urban businesspeople, and through them it has spread from culture to culture.

Partly because of this base, Islamic culture has a quite visible unity as well as a great diversity. From Morocco to Java, the Muslim **mosque** presents a distinctive atmosphere. Few would mistake a mosque for a church, synagogue, or Hindu temple. The mosque, a place of prayer to the infinite Lord, has no picture, image, altar, flowers, or candles—only a vast, clean, cool, austerely beautiful empty space. The floor may be spread with rich carpeting and the walls and ceiling or dome with the delicate, fantastic tracery of arabesque. But nowhere will realistic representational art be found. Only a bare niche in the wall serves to orient prayer in the direction of Mecca; only a modest affair like a seat atop a staircase serves as pulpit.

On the streets of a Muslim country, the pervasive influence of the religion is felt too. Five times a day—sunrise, noon, afternoon, just after sunset, at dark—a crier, called the **muezzin** (nowadays often replaced by a recording and a loudspeaker system), summons the faithful to prayer from the **minaret**, the tower attached to every mosque. His plaintive cry replaces the bells of Christendom. Then believers prostrate themselves in prayer in shops and homes, wherever they are, as well as in mosques.

In the markets, veiled women are not seen as much as formerly, but they are still common in some parts of the Muslim world. Although the Muslim admonition against alcoholic drink is not always strictly observed, it is in coffee shops and teahouses rather than pubs or bars that one sees the men gathered of an evening to discuss the affairs of the day. Finally, if one is at all familiar with the local language, one will be struck by the frequency of expressions such as "If Allah wills" in daily conversation.

The very heart of Islam is submission to the total will of **Allah**, or God. (Allah is not the name of a god, but simply means "The God"—the one and only God.) God's will for humanity, Muslims believe, was most fully given in the **Qur'an**, the book revealed through the prophet Muhammad. The word **islam** means "submission," and the name tells us that the central idea of this faith is simply full and complete submission to the will of God. An adherent of the faith is called a **Muslim**, one who has made the submission.[1] So it is that the *muezzin* in his five-times-daily cry says:

> *God [Allah] is great! God is great!*
> *There is no god but God,*
> *And Muhammad is his prophet!*
> *Come to prayer! come to prayer!*
> *Come to abundance! come to abundance!*
> *(At dawn, he here adds:*
> *Prayer is better than sleep!*
> *Prayer is better than sleep!)*
> *God is great! God is great!*
> *There is no god but God!*

Muslims praying in Afghanistan.

That is the central motif of Islam—the greatness of God alone. Because Allah is great and sovereign, all the world and all the affairs of humankind belong only to him. For this reason Islam does not lavishly embellish the religious sphere with rites and symbols and priesthood; if Allah is truly great, Islam says, he can be worshipped anywhere by anyone in the simple forms prescribed by the Qur'an and tradition. If God is truly sovereign, what he has commanded for all of society—law, ethics, government—is just as important as the religious commandments and inseparable from them. For this reason, Islam is experienced as a total and indivisible way of life. It is deeply consistent with the basic premise of the faith—the absolute sovereignty of God over all situations and over every atom of the universe—that whenever feasible Muslims not only establish Muslim worship but create Muslim societies under Muslim rulers based on Qur'anic law. Modern conditions have often mandated reinterpretations of this ideal. But the Qur'an remains the fountainhead of the true law and true culture and a summons to submission in every area of life, the "secular"—political, economic, and family life—as well as such conventionally religious matters, as how one says prayers.

Muhammad

At the core of Islam lies the experience and faith of Muhammad (570–632) himself. He lived in Arabia and was born and raised in the city of Mecca, a commercial center already sacred to the Arabs. Its holy sanctuary, which drew numerous pilgrims, was the home of many polytheistic gods—of moon, stars, and the days of the year, chiefly—and the resting place of a sacred stone, probably meteoritic, considered to be from heaven. The area around this place of worship was a neutral zone where representatives and merchants of many tribes, often warring, could meet in peace.

Muhammad came from a respected merchant family of modest means that was part of the prestigious Quraysh tribe, custodians of the sacred places of Mecca. According to tradition, he became a camel driver as a young man. When he was 25, he entered the service of Khadija, a wealthy widow much older than he. Before long he married her, and she bore his daughter Fatima.

Muhammad was always a serious, thoughtful, and rather withdrawn man. But until he was about 40, his life was not outwardly much different from that of the other merchants of the sacred city. At that age, however, he found himself going into the mountains more and more to devote himself to meditation.

About the year 611, Muhammad began to have a remarkable series of experiences in these solitary meditations in mountain caves. A mysterious darkness would come over him, then the luminous figure of the archangel Gabriel would appear and recite words to him, which he could remember clearly. These words were first of all about the unity of God—that there is but one single god, "Lord of the worlds," who abominates idolatry and will judge the earth on a day of fire and anxiety; and God calls upon all humanity to accept his sovereignty.

For ten years (611–621) Muhammad implored his fellow Meccans to obey this call to acceptance of the oneness of God, but with little success. Indeed, it seemed to many that his fervent message threatened the lucrative polytheistic cultus, and Muhammad found his position in Mecca untenable. In 622 he accepted an invitation from the city of Yathrib (now Medina) to teach there. His journey to Yathrib is called the **Hijra**. The date of the Hijra is the date from which the Muslim calendar starts; it marks the beginning of Muhammad's public and organizational work on a large scale.

It may be helpful to consider for a moment the context of this work. The Near East in Muhammad's day was dominated by the political, economic, and ideological rivalry of three great powers; the Byzantine and Ethiopian empires, which were Christian, and the Persian, which was Zoroastrian but harbored influential minorities of Jews and non-Orthodox Christians. The Byzantine and Persian empires, archfoes, fought interminable and debilitating wars, which usually ended in standoffs.

In this situation, Arabia was by no means the barbaric backwater sometimes imagined. But it was nonaligned, a no-man's-land between superpowers. There were Christians and Jews in Arabia who were thought to lean, respectively, to Byzantium and Persia. But the merchants of Mecca and Yathrib, well aware of world affairs through trading contacts in the great imperial cities, realized that their well-being required them to avoid overdependence on either side.

Yet many were also well aware that the religions of the great powers were more "modern" than their own polytheism. Belief in a sovereign deity—whether the Christian God or Ahura Mazda or the God of the Jews—was clearly the new progressive thing upon which great civilizations were being built. Moreover, "new occasions teach new duties," and the prosperous, individual-enterprise Meccan merchants found the old sense of identity in the tribe breaking down deep within them. A new doctrine and ethic was called for, emphasizing mercantile values, individual responsibility, and the sacredness of the individual betokened by personal judgment and immortal life. The new teaching might draw from Zoroastrianism, Judaism, and Christianity, or at least parallel them, in its idea of one God and moral choice. But it had to be politically independent of other ideologies. Some, called **Hanifs**, had already moved in this direction; they are not fully understood, but apparently they were a pious though not highly organized people who shunned the worship of idols and affirmed a generalized monotheism. Other Arabs to the north were Christian. But in this situation an Arab prophet was lacking, one who as an Arab would bespeak the common national and spiritual concerns of the Arabs.

That is what Muhammad did visibly in the ten years that remained to him, and he did it so well that his words carried conviction far beyond the Arab world. Using Medina as a base, he brought all Arabia, including Mecca, under his control. He became at once the religious leader of the Arabs, their political ruler, and military commander. Right up to the end of his life, which occurred just after his return from his triumphal progress to Mecca in 632, the Divine revelations continued. Together they make up the text of the Qur`an, the Holy Scripture of Islam.

The Qur`an

Unlike the Judeo-Christian Bible, the Qur`an is not a collection of diverse material from over a thousand years. It was all delivered in a period of no more than twenty-two years to one man in the form of communications from God through his angel. It is not a book of history, or a life of Muhammad, or a philosophical treatise. It is a book of proclamation: proclamation of the oneness and sovereignty of God, of his coming judgment, of the need to submit to him. In passing, it also presents a Muslim view of previous religious history, especially of the earlier prophets such as Abraham, Moses, and Jesus. From time to time it gives instructions to the faithful, upon which Muslim law is based.

To Muslims, the Qur`an is a miracle—the most convincing miracle of all as validation of their faith. It is said to be untranslatable, but to be in the original Arabic of exquisite, incomparable beauty of rhythm and expression. That one man, and he illiterate according to tradition, could be the merely human author of "the Glorious Qur`an, that inimitable symphony, the very sounds of which move men to tears and ecstasy,"[2] seems to Muslims incredible. The Holy Qur`an, they deeply believe, is the full and complete message of the infinite Divine Mind to humanity. Thus, it is not only studied, but chanted, memorized, and recited on all sorts of occasions, venerated both as words and as a book. Even its way of speaking is Divine; it represents the personal style of Allah and so transmits something of God's essence. Its very choice of rhythm, metaphor, and rhetorical method, in other words, reveals something of how God thinks and feels, just as do its contents. So significant is the Qur`an to Islam that it makes a distinction between other religions that have comparable scripture—even if not equal to the Qur`an—and "idolatrous" religions that do not. The former, especially Jews and Christians, are called "People of the Book" and are considered of higher status and closer kinship to Muslims.

It is necessary to bear in mind always the Qur`an's purpose—to proclaim the oneness and sovereignty of God. It does not develop a philosophy or tell a story because those are not its purposes. The Qur`an is intended only to state one basic truth; it repeats itself to reinforce that one simple truth. As A. J. Arberry has put it, it is like being surrounded by a gallery of paintings on the same subject.[3] If the accounts of some matters common to other faiths, such as the lives of Abraham or Jesus, seem twisted to those of such other faiths as they appear in the Qur`an, it must be remembered that Muslims are not, after all, Jews or Christians. They are under no obligation to regard the versions the latter consider authoritative to be fully authentic or complete. In fact, they consider the older Hebrew and Christian scriptures to be incomplete and corrupted by human intervention. On the other hand, they view the Qur`an as being complete because it was dictated directly by God, Muhammad being only, in effect, a scribe.

The Qur`an begins with the following prayer, which well sums up its basic spirit and message:

In the Name of Allah, the Compassionate, the Merciful
Praise be to Allah, Lord of the Creation,

The Compassionate, the Merciful, King of Judgment-day!
You alone we worship, and to You alone we pray for help.
Guide us to the straight path,
The path of those whom You have favoured,
Not of those who have incurred Your wrath,
Nor of those who have gone astray.[4]

The book continues to describe the wonders of creation; how God made humankind from the union of the sexes, out of clots of blood, and through the mysterious development of the embryo. God, it says, created man of ideal form. It exhorts humans not to deny but to show gratitude for this panorama of mercy and marvel, for when the judgment comes, wrongdoers will not be asked about their sins but will be known by the expression on their faces. The deniers of the Lord's blessings then will suffer in hell, but those who have regard for the Divine majesty will find themselves in surroundings fit for heroes: gardens of flowing springs, lush fruits, and dark-eyed damsels. Like the paradises of most religions, this one has the brightly colored, gemlike, antipodes-of-the-ordinary quality of dream, poetry, and sensuous youthful joy. But the deeper meaning of the Qur`an's message is less reward and punishment than the inescapable fact of Allah himself:

Roam the earth and see how Allah conceived Creation. Then Allah will create the
Second Creation. Allah has power over all things;
He punishes whom He will and shows mercy to whom He pleases. To Him you shall be
recalled.
Neither on earth nor in heaven shall you escape His reach; nor have you any beside
Allah to protect or to help you.[5]

And again:

To Allah belongs the east and the west. Whichever way you turn there is the face of
Allah. He is omnipresent and all-knowing.[6]

The fundamental faith of the Qur`an, then, is consistent monotheism. It is expressed in the coming judgment, the absolute sovereignty of Allah over all things, over both the making and the fortunes of the present world, and the issue of who will be brought into joy in the Second Creation. Muhammad is the envoy of God and the last, or seal, of the prophets and this fact is not, for Muslims, an addition to consistent monotheism but the way God guarantees that this truth shall be known.

Muslims believe that Islam is the ultimate religion, the complete religion. It is the religion of Abraham, the primal monotheism of the beginning, come back in finalized form. It is the ultimate form of religion because it is in fact the simplest and clearest. It is just the essence of religion, plain and perfect submission to the absolute God in all areas of life.

The Qur`an indicates that before Muhammad a series of prophets, all to be greatly honored, labored to call humankind back to this perfect islam, or

Students at Qur`anic School, Dakar, Senegal.

submission. They included Abraham, Moses, Ishmael, Idris (Enoch), and Jesus. But it was through Muhammad that the final, complete message came, superseding all that went before—it was the culminating message of God for humankind.

The role of Jesus in the Qur`an and in this series of prophets usually puzzles Christians. The Qur`an makes Jesus the greatest before Muhammad. He was called to preserve the Torah of the Jews and was a wise teacher of deep inward holiness. (This last quality has made him especially beloved of the esoteric mystics of Islam.) Jesus has, to say the least, been far more highly regarded by Muslims than Muhammad has been by Christians.

The Qur`an accepts the virgin birth of Jesus and calls Mary one of the greatest among women, but it says Jesus was born under a palm tree rather than in a stable. It mentions the Last Supper, but it denies that Jesus was actually crucified. It says that people only thought he died on the cross; instead, he was taken directly to heaven. It does not make Jesus the "Son of God," for in Muslim eyes such a concept would be polytheistic and idolatrous.

However different the life and meaning of Jesus may here appear, in looking at Islam and the Qur`an, Christians may, in the words of Seyyed Hossein Nasr, "come to understand how the sun of their own spiritual world is also a shining star in the firmament of another world."[7]

One of the loveliest passages of the Qur`an reads:

God is the light of the heavens and the earth.
The likeness of His light is as a niche,
Wherein is a lamp, the lamp in a glass, the glass like a glistening star, kindled from a
*   blessed tree,*
An olive neither of the east nor of the west,
Whose oil would almost shine had no fire touched it.
Light upon light: God guides to His light whom he will:
God brings similitudes for men and God has knowledge of all things.[8]

In all ways then the light of God is added to light; the final revelation is not inconsistent with what was presented by earlier prophets, even though the other People of the Book may have distorted their heritages. But Islam gives the final luster of a perfect glass to the light of God agelessly hidden in the lamp of the world.

All the way through, then, the central message of Islam is oneness: the unity of the line of true prophets, the oneness of final prophet and book, the oneness of the People of God, the one submission to be made, and finally the supreme oneness of God.

Islamic submission to oneness is expressed in part through avoidance of **shirk**, idolatry, or putting other gods beside the One. It is typified by the avoidance of images and often of any representational art in Muslim religion and culture. This is not a condemnation of the world of created things, for Islam has little asceticism of that sort. It extols the joys of marriage and the table, and paradise itself is described in sensual terms. But these are gifts of God, to be accepted and enjoyed for themselves with gratitude. They are not to be worshipped or even artistically recreated as symbols for God, who needs no such help.

The submission of Islam is not just a private, personal matter. It is not meant to be the sort of following of inner "leadings" that often merely indulges whims and sanctifies self-inflation. To be sure, Islam has not lacked colorful but dubious figures who have claimed special Divine calls. But the tradition has tried hard to combat the human proclivity to mix piety and egotism through the **shari`a**, or law. Islam makes the Qur`an not only a book of God's self-revelation but also a source of practical regulations covering such matters as marriage, almsgiving, relations with non-Muslims, and punishment of criminals.

*Shari`a* is the Qur`an as it is explicated and expanded by recognized jurists who depend in this process upon **hadith**, traditions based on extra-Qur`anic sayings and examples in the life of Muhammad. Through the use of analogy and by determining consensus, legal scholars decide how Qur`anic law is to be applied to concrete cases before them. Muslim law, then, provides an obligatory and objective measurement of whether a person really submits to God or only says he or she does but loves more the idols of his or her own fantasies.

The submission is made even more objective by the concept of the community, or the house, of Islam, a ready-made political, economic, and juridical, as well as purely religious, unit in the world. Insofar as the *shari`a* ideal is actualized in it,

FUNDAMENTAL FEATURES OF ISLAM

THEORETICAL

Basic Worldview	The world is for humans but under the absolute rule of God.
God or Ultimate Reality	God, sovereign, personal, revealing himself and giving specific guidance to humanity.
Origin of the World	Created by God.
Destiny of the World	To be destroyed on the Last Day, the day of judgment.
Origin of Humans	Created by God.
Destiny of Humans	To be judged on the Last Day and receive reward or punishment in the Second Creation.
Revelation or Mediation between the Ultimate and the Human	The revelation in the Qur'an given through Muhammad, the last and greatest of the prophets.

PRACTICAL

What Is Expected of Humans: Worship, Practices, Behavior	To worship and serve God in accordance with his commandments: to observe the Five Pillars and the rest of shari'a.

SOCIOLOGICAL

Major Social Institutions	The whole Islamic community; the local Friday Mosque community; the ulama, or body of teachers and preachers; Sufi orders; the ideal of the Islamic society.

willing participation in the House of Islam and following its norms is one with Islamic submission to Allah. For the ideal of submission in all areas of life logically implies joining oneself to others who make the same submission; doing so is a test of real sincerity. (As the New Testament also recognizes, it is easy to think one loves God but to dislike others who also love God, which is inconsistent.)

Out of the community ideal of Islam comes the concept of **jihad**, or holy war, which is designed to defend Islam and allow its social practice, though not to force individual conversions, which is forbidden in doctrine, if not in actual practice in some places. Since Islam in principle is a community as well as a religion, presumably only an absolute pacifist would be able to reject the theory of *jihad* out of hand, since other communities also fight to defend or expand their ways of life. However, on the deepest level many Muslims interpret the *jihad* as allegorical of the spiritual struggle.

The Five Pillars of Islam

Let us examine some aspects of traditional and normative Islamic life based on *shari`a* as derived from Qur`an and *hadith*. These center around the **Five Pillars of Islam**: the confession of faith, prayer five times a day, giving of alms to the poor, fasting in the month of **Ramadan**, and the **hajj**, or pilgrimage to Mecca.

The first of the five pillars is to say, "There is no god but God (Allah), and Muhammad is the *rasul* (Prophet or messenger) of God." This statement sums up in a few words the simple Muslim faith. The basic concept of the oneness of God has been discussed. When Muhammad is called the **rasul** or messenger of God, it means exactly this—that he is God's appointed spokesman, the mouthpiece through which God chose to deliver his call for submission and his final commandments to the world. True, Muhammad is also considered a paragon of virtue and fountain of wisdom, so that his sayings and acts, as transmitted by tradition, are basic precedents in Muslim law. But he is not a saint, seer, wonder-worker, Divine incarnation, or even a profound mystic like the Buddha or a peerless philosopher like Confucius. It is emphasized that Muhammad's birth was biologically normal and that he performed no miracles except the delivery of the Qur`an itself. The Qur`an attributes virgin birth to Jesus and miracles to earlier prophets—Moses changed a staff into a serpent; Jesus is said by the Qur`an not only to have been taken up into heaven but also to have caused some clay birds to come to life and fly away. These are appropriate to the son of Mary, for he is the prophet of mystic and marvelous holiness; similar powers are recognized, as we shall see, in numerous Muslim *wali,* or saints. But Muhammad's own calling was not to this sort of thing but simply to be the spokesman of God. His miracle is the Qur`an itself; its production by a man like him in enigmatic circumstances, and the wonderful emergence of the Islamic community around him, are considered sufficient evidence of his authority. Muhammad needed dispense no other, more trivial, miracles as calling cards.

The second of the pillars is prayer, done five times a day. In the next part we shall examine how these formal prayers are performed.

The third pillar is almsgiving. The fundamental obligation is to give a relatively small but variable percentage of one's wealth to the needy within the Muslim community; expanded, it covers good works and comradely attitudes in general, a helping hand and friendly smile for one's neighbor. This pillar reaffirms the social and ethical dimensions of Islam. The Muslim faith strives to remember it is a community of submission and service, working for a more just world, not just a personal path to salvation. Strictly speaking, almsgiving should be done out of religious commitment rather than compulsion (although it has been collected, from Muslims only, as a tax in traditional Islamic states). But many modern reformers have seen in the almsgiving principle a rationale for social welfare programs or socialism as an application of the Islamic community ideal under contemporary conditions.

The fourth pillar of Islam is the fast of Ramadan. Ramadan is a lunar month of about twenty-eight days in the Muslim calendar; during this period the faithful are neither to eat nor drink between daybreak and dark, but to give attention to prayer and religion. Commonly, family and friends will gather at night to dine as soon as it is permitted, and there are traditional Ramadan dishes. Often the meal will be combined with reading aloud from the Qur'an and prayer, and will continue far into the night. The daylight hours will be for rest and further prayer. At the end of Ramadan there is, as one might expect, a festive celebration that commences when the first sliver of a new moon indicates the end of the month of fasting and the beginning of the next month.[9]

Because the Muslim calendar is lunar, the occurrence of Ramadan moves progressively through the seasons. When it falls in the short, cool days of midwinter, it is relatively easy to endure, but amidst the long summer days of a hot, dry climate, going without food or even a sip of water provides a stern test of Muslim loyalty. Understandably, some partially successful attempts have been made in recent times to reinterpret Ramadan in view of the exigencies of modern urban life. For innumerable devout Muslims, however, Ramadan remains a strenuous test of faith, softened by support from culture and tradition and the "we're all in it together" mood of a Muslim society's observance. For many, too, the opportunity for a deepening of one's life of prayer and Qur'anic study is genuinely welcome.

The fifth pillar is one known to almost everyone who has heard anything about Islam: the pilgrimage to Mecca called the *hajj*. Mecca, the immemorially holy city and birthplace of Muhammad, is the focal point of Islam. As though aligned along rays to a sun, Muslims at prayer face toward this vale in the Arabian Desert, and once in a lifetime their feet are to take them down that ray to the holy place. Every year a million or more Muslims gather at Mecca in the month of pilgrimage; this assembly affords, like nothing else, that sense of unity and identity for which Islam is justly famous.

Not all Muslims, of course, make the pilgrimage even once. Minors, the elderly, the infirm, and those without financial means are among those exempted from the obligation. For those who do go on the *hajj*, the rewards are substantial, not only in spiritual fulfillment, but in prestige within the Islamic family. Back in the home community, wherever it lies between Mauritania and Indonesia, the returned pilgrim may add the title *hajji* to his or her name and will be afforded special honor.

The pilgrimage is properly made in Dhu-al-Hijjah, the last month of the Muslim calendar. The pilgrimage is thus a meeting of sacred ultimates—a return just before the beginning of a new year to the place where Islamic history began.

Muslim belief about Mecca and the *hajj* combines the city's pre-Islamic role as a sacred center, a sanctuary for combative tribes, and a place of polytheistic worship, with beliefs about Abraham and the revelation through Muhammad. According to traditional Muslim belief, Mecca is the navel of the world, the spot where creation began. Abraham (Ibrahim in Arabic), the primal prophet of the original pure monotheistic religion, was then called by God to proceed from Palestine to the valley where Mecca is now located.

This he did, together with Hagar his wife and Ishmael (Ismail) his son, forefather of the Arabs. On one occasion, Hagar was lost in the desert with Ishmael, and she ran desperately about looking for water for the infant, until she found that a well had sprung up where Ishmael had struck the sand with his heel. Later, Abraham under God's instructions built the cubical shrine at Mecca—the **Ka`ba**—with the help of Ishmael. In the corner of the *Ka`ba* was placed the Black Stone brought from heaven by the angel Gabriel. On another occasion, in a variant of the account of the sacrifice of Isaac in the Judeo-Christian Bible, Abraham was commanded by God to sacrifice his son Ishmael. As they went to the place of sacrifice, Satan three times appeared to Ishmael and tempted him to reject his father's demand, but Ishmael kept faith and refused. At the last moment, a ram was substituted for the boy.

The *Ka`ba* is now the center of the great open-air mosque of Mecca and is the real focal point of all Muslim worship. Other mosques have a niche in a wall facing in the direction of Mecca; this mosque, because it is the focal point, surrounds the *Ka`ba,* or Holy House, which stands at its center. The Ka`ba itself is covered with black-and-gold cloth and has a gold-encrusted door, seldom opened. The sacred black stone is visibly inserted in a corner of the Holy House. Around it is a broad marble pavement, where pilgrims circumambulate the shrine, and beyond this, platforms for prayer.

In Muhammad's day the *Ka`ba* contained 360 images of heathen gods (so far had the faith of Abraham declined). But the prophet had these destroyed. Now the *Ka`ba* holds nothing but a few lamps. Yet for Muslims, whose faith is in the infinite God alone, in its emptiness the shrine is all the more holy. The *Ka`ba* is said to be an exact replica of the house of God in paradise above, around which angels circle as the faithful on earth circle the earthly *Ka`ba.* Heaven, tradition says, is closer to earth at Mecca than anywhere else, so prayers are heard best from there. Nothing comes between the *Ka`ba* and the abode of Allah; airplanes are not allowed to pass over it, and it is said that even birds will not fly above the Holy House. Nearby is *Zamzam,* the well of Hagar and Ishmael, reputed to have curative powers.

Interestingly, Muhammad developed his teaching about Meccan pilgrimage during the time he was at Medina, when it was by no means clear that he would ever be reconciled with his home city. The teaching may, of course, have had political motives aimed at appeasing his kinsmen. Yet it also suggests that for the exile Mecca had the quality of many pilgrimage centers of being "the center out there"— a place remote from the center of present action on the worldly plane, yet a place of access to ultimate origins and ultimate goals. So has Mecca ever been.[10] Indeed, after the time of Muhammad, Mecca's role as a commercial center declined, and the holy city has since depended economically almost entirely on its sacred role.

The carrying out of the *hajj* is marked by many careful rituals. As he (or she, as women also undertake the *hajj*) approaches the city, probably from the seaport and airport city of Jiddah on the coast, the pilgrim stops to separate himself or herself from the ordinary world by ablutions, as before prayer. The pilgrim then

A devout Muslim in Sana'a, Yemen.

Muslims praying at the Juma Masjid (mosque) in Delhi, India.

dons special white garments; thereafter, until the rites are completed he or she must abstain from killing human beings, beast, or plant, from sexual activity, and from cutting hair or nails.

Upon arriving at the sacred site, the pilgrim kisses (or if that is not possible because of the crowd, touches) the sacred Black Stone and then circumambulates the Ka`ba seven times.

Next the pilgrim runs seven times up and down a colonnade between two hills about 450 yards apart. The usual explanation is that this commemorates Hagar's running about looking for water for Ishmael.

Then the pilgrim proceeds outside Mecca to Mina, where he or she probably finds quarters in a vast tent city with a temporary population of a million or so; this gathering in itself gives pilgrims an experience of the power and unity of Islam. The next day the pilgrims all proceed to **Mount Arafat**, upon which they must stand between noon and sundown. There, seated on a camel, Muhammad gave his farewell sermon on his own last pilgrimage to Mecca.

This "standing at Arafat" is the culminating act of the *hajj,* and the one act that cannot be omitted. It is the archetypal assembly of the faithful as a united army drawn out of all kindreds and tongues in submission to God. Like Muhammad's followers, they will listen to a sermon by an eminent Muslim scholar as they stand at Arafat. The assembly is said to bring to mind the gathering of all peoples for judgment on the Last Day, and it repeats the first assembly that Muhammad himself commanded so heroically.

After this, the final rites represent a process of desacralization. Returning to Mina, the pilgrim throws rocks at three stone pillars said to represent devils, recalling the three temptations of Satan that Ishmael rejected.

On the last day of the formal sacred pilgrimage time, the pilgrim will sacrifice a ram or goat in a certain field; part of the meat is supposed to be given to the poor. On the same day throughout the Muslim world, an animal is similarly sacrificed. Its head is pointed toward Mecca, and the Muslim cuts its throat, saying, "In the name of Allah." This recalls the ram substituted for Ishmael in Abraham's rite.

Next, in Mecca, the pilgrim has his or her hair cut. The hair, a token of oneself, is left behind as a sign of dedication. The pilgrim circumambulates the *Ka`ba* a final time.

Most pilgrims will then proceed on to Medina, although this is optional. There, in this second most sacred city of Islam, they visit Muhammad's mosque and tomb. Some Muslims desire to come to Medina to die and be buried there with the prophet and his family.

The *hajj* is a collection of diverse traditional acts. Some may seem very Islamic and meaningful; some, like the running and stoning of the "devils," rather primitive and bizarre. Yet Muslims find them all spiritually significant, though none more so than the mere fact of the pilgrimage itself. Many Muslims, including the most mystical, have found deep inward meanings in all the traditions; stoning the pillars, for example, is made to represent striking down sinful desires within one's self.

Perhaps the best explanation is that of the great medieval theologian al-Ghazali.[11] He pointed out that the *hajj* is meant to be a supreme act of Islam, of submission and self-abnegation. That which is less than rationally appealing or satisfying to refined feeling can do much to purify and eliminate the egotism that easily lingers in a heart that considers itself refined. The *hajj* is an act of sheer devotion and of sheer identification with the inscrutable mind of God and with the Islamic tradition. It affirms that at the center of true religion is the finite human facing the infinite mystery of God, not the satisfaction of human inclinations.

Prayers and Mosques

Hundreds upon hundreds of the faithful line up rank on rank, bowing and prostrating in unison in the mosque at noon Friday and spilling over into the plaza in front of it. This is a common sight in Islamic lands that never fails to impress visitors. It expresses eloquently the unity and devotion of Islam.

Equally impressive, and even more frequent, are the five-times-a-day prayers said regularly by believers wherever they are. The manner of saying these prayers and preparing for them is carefully prescribed by Islamic law; their combination of legalistic form and tenacious, fervent faith is close to the spiritual heart of Islam. Five times a day the faithful Muslim's mind and heart, perhaps prompted by the *muezzin,* turns away from the things of the world to prayer:

1. Early in the morning, when dawn has become bright but before the sun has well risen.
2. Noon or early afternoon.
3. Late afternoon.
4. Directly after sunset.
5. Night, between darkness and dawn; usually about two hours after the sunset prayers.

If the worshipper cannot perform the prayers at the time they are called, they may be done any time until the next prayer is proclaimed.

Before prayers, one must be in a state of purification. This is attained by formal washing: the hands and arms are washed up to the elbows, the mouth and nostrils are rinsed, and the feet are bathed to the ankles, all thrice. Mosques and most homes will have water available in tanks, urns, or fountains for this purpose; one may also wash in an oasis. If sufficient water is not present, sand may be used.

Several further conditions should be met, if possible, out of respect for this sacred action. One should pray in a clean place free of defilement. For this reason, many Muslims use special small carpets, prayer rugs, which they spread over the place of prayer. One must be modestly dressed; for women, this means the body must be entirely covered except face, hands, and feet. Before beginning, one must articulate in one's mind the intention to say the right prayers. Finally, one must pray facing in the direction of Mecca.

The prayers begin and end with the petitioner standing upright but include bowing and prostration. They are said in Arabic, the language of Muhammad and the Qur'an, rather than in the vernacular language of the one who prays.

The Muslim first stands to say *Allahu-akbar*, "God is greater [than all]." Then still standing he or she recites the *al-Fatiha*, or opening verse of the Qur'an, given on pages 381–382, and another short chapter of the scripture. The Muslim then bows and says thrice or more, "Glory to the Lord, the Exalted." He or she stands, saying, "God hears him who praises him. Our Lord praise to you." And then he or she kneels, touching the forehead to the ground, to say, "Glory to my Lord, the most High," thrice or more. Finally the petitioner stands saying again *Allahu-akbar*. This whole procedure is called a *raka*, and it is the basic unit of prayer. It is repeated a varying number of times, depending on the time of day. The whole is concluded by a prayer, not from the Qur'an, asking God to exalt and bless Muhammad and his followers.

We have dwelt in some detail with the prayers and their performance because they provide an intimate perception of Islam as it is lived and practiced day by day and an incomparable view of its spirit. The rules surrounding the prayers may suggest that Muslims are burdened with an onerous task in fulfilling this basic obligation of their religion. Certainly, the prayers are not meant to be a trivial, lightly regarded part of one's life, but a constant punctuation of every day recalling one to his or her first identity and responsibility. But for the devout, they are a welcome expression of faith and an added dimension to daily life. They remind the believer that he or she is a Muslim, one who worships and serves God before anything else.

Furthermore, they remind the person who prays that to be a Muslim means to be a part of the worldwide community, which, like any real community, has its traditions, its rules, and its center. One expresses this identity by doing one's prayers not haphazardly, but at the same time, in the same way, and facing toward the same center, as one's comrades in the community. The prayers, then, rank with the *hajj* in creating a deep sense of Muslim identity. It may be noted that, although one may say the prayers with a special intention for some personal need and may pray at any other time on behalf of one's personal petitions, there is no prayer here for individual needs, such as for daily bread or for personal favors. The Muslim knows that one's relation to Allah should be first of all one of faith, praise, gratitude, obedience, and identity with the Islamic community, and that God knows one's special needs before one can ask.

The prayers may be said individually wherever one is, but Muslims have always preferred to say them congregationally whenever possible. The mosque is the ideal place for corporate prayers, and the noon prayers on Friday are generally recited there. This is the major weekly Muslim service; in it certain additional prayers are offered, and two sermons, separated by a short break, are delivered by the **Imam**, or learned teacher, retained by the mosque.

Women are expected to pray but are exempted from congregational prayers. They may pray in the mosque, in a separate section behind the men, but more often pray at home.

The typical architecture of the mosque was originally inspired by the Arab house with its large courtyard and by the basilica-type Christian churches of conquered lands, some of which were converted into mosques. But the mosque has developed into a unique religious structure that represents sublimely the spirit of Islam. Far simpler in ornamentation than most churches and temples of other faiths, yet imposing and monumental, the mosque well reflects the austerity and majesty of Islam and its God.

The feature of a mosque that will first attract the attention of most visitors to the Islamic world are the **minarets**. These are the high towers beside the mosque proper. They are usually capped with the star and crescent moon, which is the symbol of Islam, said to be derived from the moon and single star that lighted the Prophet's way on his *hijra* (flight) from Mecca to Medina. Great centers of worship may have as many as six minarets standing by the shorter and squatter building of the mosque. As we have seen, it is from the minaret that the *muezzin* cries out the call to prayer five times daily.

Approaching the mosque, the visitor enters a wide courtyard. It will probably contain water to be used for ablutions before prayer, and it is a favorite meeting place of the community. Indeed, mosques with their attached structures have traditionally functioned at once as virtually every sort of public building. Schools and libraries were and are connected with them, and their spacious facilities have

Mother and son praying at Dome of the Rock, in Jerusalem, one of Islam's holiest mosques.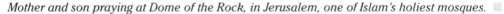

served in the past as a place for gathering armies and as courts of justice. While modern states have felt that separate sites are more appropriate for such activities, their traditional affiliation with the mosque reminds us of the close alliance of Islam with the political, educational, and social life of the community.

The interior of the mosque characteristically possesses a clean, cool, open ambiance, yet the nonrepresentational ornamentation is sufficient to add a note of transcendent richness. The floor is covered with mats or carpets, often highly decorative. The walls and ceilings may be adorned with stunning arabesque designs or calligraphed Qur'anic verses. But one sees no furniture to speak of except the **minbar**, or seat at the top of steps, which serves as a pulpit. Occasionally, a screened box provides protection for a worshipping ruler. A niche, called the **mihrab**, points prayer in the direction of Mecca. By its architecture and appearance, the mosque well expresses the two orientations of Islam—to God and to the community of believers, symbolized by Mecca, which is its earthly center.

The mosque also expresses well an already mentioned feature of Muslim life: its focus in the city or town. The rhythm of Muslim religious obligations; the daily prayers called by the *muezzin*; the ablutions and fasting; the *hajj*, which usually followed trade routes; and the law courts all seem to fit the outlook and pattern of life of the urban trader or craftsperson. Even Muslim farmers have generally wanted to live in villages with mosques. In particular, the Friday noon prayers are supposed to be said in a **Friday Mosque**, a great mosque theoretically large enough to hold the entire community, in contrast to smaller edifices that may be used for daily prayers. The Friday Mosque idea again affirms that Islam is meant to be lived in community, and it perceives the city as the ideal earthly expression of community.[12]

Historic Islam

In 632, the year of the Prophet's death, all these themes were coalescing to form the new faith of the newly unified Arab people. Returning from his triumphal pilgrimage to Mecca, Muhammad preached a farewell sermon and shortly after died with his head in the lap of Aisha, his favorite wife. He was mourned, yet his death came at a propitious moment.

Through a brilliant combination of diplomacy and militancy, Muhammad had united Arabia under his command. He was the charismatic hero of the hour; he died before his hour of supreme glory had had a chance to pall.

His religious mission was apparently fulfilled; the revelations that he delivered were gathered to form the Qur'an within twenty years of his death. Unlike other religious founders, Muhammad died a popular hero among his people, a ruler, a successful diplomat, politician, and general. He was also a mystic visionary, but there was nothing ethereal about him. Instead he seemed to his people a man larger than life in many senses: warmhearted, full of cheerful humor, a planner of stratagems, a marshall who rode into battle with his troops and held his following together by the force of his personality when all seemed darkest—yet also a seer deep in prayer and vision alone in the desert, a rock of convinced faith and principle and of a trustworthy and sympathetic nature. From this complex and extraordinary man came the Islamic faith, a faith that seems at once made for humans as they are, with their needs for politics, laws, wars, and sexual expression—and made for God as he is at his most magnificent: personal, creative, sovereign, and glorious, calling humans to total submission.

Inspired by fresh memories of Muhammad striding through Arabia, the Arabs were ready, at the moment of his death, to carry Islam out of his native land, and this they did under new leadership with a rapidity that ever since has amazed the world. Within a century, the **caliphs** ("deputies" of the Prophet as temporal ruler), who were successors of Muhammad, ruled from Spain and Morocco to the Indus in the East. They came near to conquering Europe, but they were finally stopped by Charles Martel at the battle of Tours in 732. The weary Byzantine Empire reeled before their sway and lost vast provinces—once-Christian Egypt, Palestine, Syria, and part of Asia Minor. The Persian Empire collapsed entirely and passed to Muslim faith and sovereignty. After 750, Baghdad was the seat of the *caliph* who ruled all this realm except Spain. That imperial city typifies the fact that early expansive Islam was fundamentally a faith of urban merchants and men of affairs.

The years of the Baghdad caliphate (750–1258) and of the Cordova caliphate in Spain (755–1236) were the glorious years of early Islamic civilization. In the caliphates, art, science, and philosophy matured—thanks in part to Muslim revival of ancient Greek wisdom and the transmission West of lore from India. Modern mathematics has roots in the Arabic system of numbers and the zero, which the Muslims borrowed from India but whose use they explored. The Greek classics, including the philosophy and science of Plato and Aristotle, came back to Europe in the late Middle Ages and the Renaissance by way of the Muslim world.

After the wars that Christian Europe called the Crusades, which engendered bitter feelings and much misunderstanding between the two faiths (not yet healed), and after the fall of the caliphates, Islam broke down into smaller units. Most of the Arab lands ended up as parts of the Turkish-ruled Ottoman Empire (though the Turks are not Arab). The Turks finally took Constantinople (modern Istanbul) and caused the death of the Christian Byzantium in 1453. Farther East, Persia and the Mughul empire in India became splendid Islamic civilizations.

But gradually, it seemed, the Muslim world grew stagnant. By the nineteenth century most of it was under European influence or direct colonial rule. The reasons for this decline from its brilliant and dynamic early life are complex. In part, it was due to external factors: incursions of conquerors such as Genghis Khan and European advances in technology and world exploration. Internally, the *shari`a* had a stultifying effect, as in case after case it became more and more fixed. The rule of law believed to have Divine sanction inevitably made society static, putting a premium on conformity rather than innovation and new ideas.

In the twentieth century, however, Islam exhibited a new burst of life. It served as a vehicle for identity from North Africa to Indonesia and recovered something of its old dynamic sense of the unity of the diverse peoples who are followers of the Meccan prophet.

Thus, the role of Islam as both a political and spiritual force in the world is by no means over. The new shapes of oil economics and geopolitics, in the last decades of the twentieth century, gave parts of the Islamic world a leverage and comparative prosperity they had hardly known since the Middle Ages. At the same time, in recent decades some Muslim nations have modified Islamic law with legal codes borrowed from elsewhere and have made pragmatic revisions of it in the light of modern conditions—although practice varies from the Republic of Turkey, which was modernized and secularized in the first decades of the twentieth century under the leadership of its first president, Kemal Ataturk, to Saudi Arabia, where traditional law largely remains in force. (For instance, the traditional law that allowed a man up to four wives if he treated them equally and to divorce a wife virtually at will is no longer observed in much of the Muslim world.) Out of this combination of new power, prosperity, and flexibility we may well see creative new forms of Islamic faith and culture emerge in the twenty-first century. At the same time, modernity has also produced a powerful fundamentalist reaction. We shall examine modern Islam in more detail later.

Features of Classic Islamic Civilization

Urban Settings and Family Life

As we have seen, Islamic religious culture comes most fully to flower in urban settings. Never was this more true than in the classical Golden Age of Islamic civilization, when fabled cities like Baghdad and Granada were centers of brilliant culture as well as flourishing political and commercial hubs. Let us examine some characteristics of life in these communities.

A traveler to a great classical (or modern) Muslim city, accustomed to such capitals as Paris, London, or Washington, might first be struck and perhaps a little disappointed by the lack of monumental grandeur and imposing vistas. True, the Islamic city will be dominated by the impressive domes and minarets of its principal mosques and perhaps by a castle or fortress, like the Alhambra of Granada. But streets, especially in residential areas, will tend to be narrow and twisting and often lead to dead ends. Houses, rather than presenting an ostentatious facade, are likely to display only a rough whitewashed wall with a gate and balconies on the upper stories. The main business and shopping section are in the *suq* in many Muslim areas, a covered street lined with shops, displaying a fascinating interior that is not apparent from any outside vantage point.

Star and Crescent

The significant reality about the Islamic city, which interprets its distinctive features, is that the mazelike exterior is, so to speak, full of secrets. Just as Islam tells us that the created world veils and reveals the great secret of the universe—the power and sovereignty of Allah—so the city conceals, while expressing to the discerning eye, its more mundane social structures. Each of the little urban nooks and crannies created by the seemingly chaotic web of streets may house a sub-community of practitioners of a particular craft or trade. Even more important, behind each wall and gate is the intimate world of a family. Beyond the gate is a courtyard and around it the house, with its quarters for women, children, and servants. For in a society in which women have traditionally been veiled and enclosed, and in which the education of young children frequently took place in the home, the house was a private realm with profound meaning for the personal lives of those who resided in it. Much business was conducted in its court; here, at prosperous houses, would arrive merchants, storytellers, wandering holy men, officials, and teachers, bringing the world to the home.

Law and Religion, Trade, and the Development of Islamic Culture

Among the other important motifs that governed classical Islamic civilization already noted was the close relation in Islam between religion and law and the historical role of Muslims as conquerors and then rulers of their portion of the world. This reality had two important, but rather different, effects. First, it meant that Islamic law, with its often benign but ultimately conservative effects, firmly shaped the contours and limits of this civilization. For even the most powerful ruler, whether caliph or Ottoman sultan, was in theory supposed to be only an upholder of the existing law and to innovate nothing.

Second, it meant that the courts of kings and caliphs were immensely influential centers of cultural creativity. The average person thought of them as *Arabian Nights* realms of splendor and wonder. The reality may have been a little less fabulous, but the wealth, power, and entertainments of Baghdad and Granada at their height were the marvel of the world. Courts patronized poets, artists, musicians, philosophers, and theologians, and they drew talent and sophisticated appreciators of culture to their circles. In turn, because lines of trade and communication ran from the capitals like Baghdad, and later Cairo, Delhi, Isfahan, and Istanbul, to the far-flung reaches of the Islamic world, those cities served as centers of cultural dissemination. The fact that Islam was a religious culture of a relatively few great capitals and had relatively great political cohesion during much of its most creative period has much to do with the considerable uniformity of Islamic culture, as does the fact that it was a faith of well-traveled soldiers and traders.

The Role of Nonrepresentational Art, Calligraphy, and Literature in Islamic Culture

The Muslim antipathy to representational art has also played a potent role in creating a highly distinctive Islamic culture. Although not directly Qur`anic, the idea that representation led to idolatry early became almost universal in the Muslim world. Though observed with varying degrees of literalness in various times and places, it has meant that Islamic art has been essentially decorative, and pen and brushwork have been largely limited to calligraphy and book illustration—the latter being the medium wherein representational art has been accepted by all but the strictest Muslims. Islam has also accepted representation in such relatively minor forms as household tiles, figurines, and china, but never in monumental sculpture or painting. However, gifted Muslim artists have explored the acceptable media to the limits and have created a remarkable artistic heritage.

Islamic calligraphy and painting derives its power—and its Islamic validity— from its capacity to reveal the secret that the power and sovereignty of God is everywhere, and so truth and paradisal beauty lurk beneath contrary appearances. Calligraphed lines from the Qur`an join with arabesques to adorn the clean walls and domes of mosques. The latter display the transcendent beauty of the One God; the former add, also through the medium of beauty, that the same God can be known and is known above all through the revealed words of the scripture.

Persian manuscript page painted by Ibn Ishaq el Shihabi, 1557.

For example, Sura 68 of the Qur`an tells us it is "by the pen, and what it writes," that we are blessed and not cursed. But Islam universally holds that it is no sin and much virtue to make those words as appealing to the eye as possible through art and so to impress even more strongly their power.

So also the paintings that illumine the pages of books and sometimes the walls of schools and tombs give more a sense of conveying mystical rather than ordinary reality. They are flat and two-dimensional, with perhaps a gold background suggesting eternity rather than depth perspective. The saints and kings are mythic figures; the birds and gazelles are creatures from paradise. In the same way as the arabesque, these ostensibly representational works actually do not show the world as it is but as it appears to one whose eyes are opened to the presence of the God within and above all that is, and so they preserve a sacred, not a worldly or idolatrous, vision. The famous Persian carpets also often have a comparable sacred message: the spot in the center upon which the elaborate design focuses is an opening from time into eternity.

In Islamic literature, poetry has been of far more importance than prose, for the two most influential literary languages of Islam—Arabic and Persian—lend themselves well to poetry and have highly exalted poetic feeling. Besides religious verse, they both have an exceedingly rich storehouse of secular verse: humorous, amorous, bacchic, and historical, together with odes celebrating the deeds of princes and warriors.

Perhaps because of these associations, poetry has not been well regarded by the most orthodox Muslims. The great exception, of course, is the Qur`an itself, which, though not always strictly poetry, is composed with unique and powerful patterns of rhythm and rhyme. But the position of the Qur`an in Islamic letters is paradoxical. As the text from which traditional Muslims learned to read, of which they had memorized long passages, and which they constantly heard recited, its majestic cadences must have been deeply embedded in their conscious and unconscious minds. Yet the Qur`an has been held to be beyond either imitation or criticism; to attempt either was presumptuous sacrilege. Thus, save in commentaries and pious treatises where it is directly quoted, one does not see an immediate influence of the Qur`an on literary theme or style.

For these reasons, one finds little good religious poetry associated with mainstream Islam. Rather, it is in the mystical tradition, above all in Persia, that the spiritual verse of Islam flowers. As much influenced by the secular poetry of wine and love as by the Qur`an, these songs of the spirit boldly use the language of intoxication and carnal passion to speak of the relation of the soul to God, the supreme Friend and Lover. They celebrate the "inebriate of God" beside himself with Divine love, yet still able to express that love in soaring verse.

Islamic mysticism came also to express itself in elegant books. The most famous example is *The Conference of the Birds* by Farid ad-Din Attar (1119–1230), an allegory relating the quest of thirty birds for the Simurgh, a mythical bird who represents God. When they finally found that splendid being, the questing avians asked him to explain the mystery of the unity and multiplicity of reality. The Simurgh answered (in a mystical image that would be questioned by orthodox

Islam) by saying that his form was a sunlike mirror. He who looks at God sees himself reflected there in all his many parts, yet the mirror is one.

Philosophy, Science, and the Intellectual Life of Islam

Another very important motif, intrinsic to Islam and related to court and mosque alike, is the prestige given to scholarship because of the importance of the law and so of its right interpretation. Members of the **ulama**, or body of learned men, adorned courts and presided in mosques; they also founded universities and searched out the philosophical underpinnings of faith. Because the language of scripture and its legal commentaries was Arabic, in whatever part of the world they dwelt, they had to work in that language. The immense authority of Arabic scholarship also worked powerfully on behalf of Islamic cultural homogeneity. For although popular religion and culture might vary considerably, this factor meant that the "great tradition" of learning and "correct" interpretation would diverge far less, even when the Islamic world was not politically united.

The scientific work of the Golden Age of Islamic civilization has rightly been much acclaimed. Learned Arab men of the Baghdad caliphate and the Spanish caliphate preserved classical Greek and Roman scholarship and transmitted to Europe much of importance from farther East, such as the already mentioned concept of the zero in mathematics (which had been developed in India). They also made substantial advances in such varied fields as astronomy, optics, medicine, geography, and chemistry. All this, as we have said, occurred during the Middle Ages of Europe. Had it not been for the world of Islam, ancient learning would undoubtedly have been lost to a much greater extent than it was, and important advances that set the stage for modern science would not have been possible.

Although the highest intellectual life for the Muslim remained the Divine sciences (understanding the mystery and majesty of God and the application of his revealed law), the openness of the conquering Arabs toward what remained of Greek natural science in the Middle Eastern countries they ruled was remarkable. As one might have expected, conservatives were highly dubious of such foreign and unrevealed lore. Yet more than enough people were of the opinion that all learning about the creation of Allah was good and to his glory, and that science and logic could assist in the understanding of God. For them natural and theological queries were complementary rather than at odds. A story tells us that the ninth century Caliph al-Ma'mun had a dream in which Aristotle appeared to him and, after some philosophical discourse, told him to treat scientists as gold and to hold to the Oneness of God—the fundamental Muslim doctrine. The great philosopher al-Ghazali, although he also emphased mystical intuition, strongly affirmed that the study of Greek logic was a necessary preliminary to the study of doctrine and religious law.

Islamic philosophy had to deal with the impact of Greek thought, to find what it could use of Plato, Aristotle, and the Neoplatonists, and what seemed no longer applicable in the light of new revelation. Interestingly, the Islamic appropriation of

Greek ways of thinking followed the sequence of the Greek's own development, from rationalism to Neoplatonic mysticism.

Rationalism and Mysticism in the Development of Islamic Thought

A very significant early school of Islamic thought was the **Mu`tazila**, founded by Wasil ibn Ata (699–749). It exhibited a strong rationalist tendency. What God does is always what is best according to reason, and reason is equal to revelation and superior to tradition as a source of truth, according to the Mu`tazila thinkers. They explained away anthropomorphic language about God in the Qur`an and contended that scripture was created in time, in opposition to the view of those who considered themselves more orthodox that it is the eternal Word of God. The Mu`tazila were supported by the same Caliph al-Ma`mun (r. 813–833) who entertained Aristotle in his dream. But their supremacy was short-lived.

A reaction that was to condition all subsequent mainstream Islamic theology came through the writings of Abul-Hasan al-Ash`ari (873–935), from which **Ash`arism** developed. He taught that Divine actions cannot be explained in terms of human reason. God is simply absolute power and grace, mysterious rather than reasonable on the human level, to be adored and obeyed. This view won the allegiance of both political and spiritual leaders, and it set the stage for more and more emphasis on the basic Islamic concepts of God's oneness and sovereignty. It led toward determinism or predestination in theology and **pantheist** tendencies in mysticism—in either case, the sole controlling reality in the creation is God, whether viewed in terms of his ever-present will or of his ever-present being.

In the eleventh and twelfth centuries, two scientist-philosophers at opposite ends of the Muslim world labored vigorously to revive the rational approach and in the process profoundly affected European thought. Both ibn-Sina (980–1037) in Persia, known to the West as Avicenna, and ibn-Rushd (1126–1198) in Spain, known as Averroës, were deeply influenced by the Greek tradition. Both wrote important scientific and medical works, as well as pure philosophy, and both strove to assert the primacy of reason and science over revelation, although toward the end of his life Avicenna moved more and more in a mystical direction. But that thinker provocatively held to such assertions as the eternality of the universe and that only the soul survives death. Believing the Greeks had conclusively proved these matters by reason, he required that the Islamic doctrines of creation and resurrection be interpreted in a nonliteral way.

Al-Ghazali, following in the Ash`arism tradition that the ways of God are beyond searching out, attacked these positions in such works as *The Incoherence of the Philosophers,* in which he tried to show that the notion of matter as eternal and uncreated does not even stand up to reason and furthermore that reason itself is a poor guide to ultimate things. Averroës responded with, among his many books, The *Incoherence of the Incoherence,* strongly reasserting reason, though he was able to find a position somewhat more closely approximating orthodoxy than Avicenna's on the resurrection at the end of the world, whereof he contended that while reason and science make it incredible that one's literal physical body could be resurrected, God could supply a new likeness of it on the Last Day.

Averroës's mind, though, was wide-ranging and free. He asserted the superiority of Islam over Plato's idea state because the former seeks the happiness of all, not just a philosophical elite; but he also showed himself unorthodox when he regretted that Islam did not afford women the same equality he thought that Plato did in his *Republic*.

However, such a liberal outlook was not to be characteristic of subsequent Islamic thought. Instead, the devout antirationalism of Ash`arism and al-Ghazali, more and more colored by Sufi mysticism (which will be discussed later in this chapter), was predominant in the last great classical school—that of Shihab al-Din al-Suhrawardi (1155–1191), ibn al-Arabi (1165–1240), and Sadr al-Din al-Shirazi (d. 1640), which pursued a high Neoplatonism, influenced also by Zoroastrian concepts of light and darkness, portraying a multilevel reality within the sole being of God.

Classical Islamic civilization, then, created a world of rich diversity and brilliance but all constrained by the sometimes flexible parameters of a worldview whose touchstone was the Qur`anic revelation.[13]

Sunni Islam

We shall now examine some of the variations of belief and practice within Islam. The most important division today is between the Sunni and Shi`a traditions. **Sunni Islam** is the normative Islam of most places except Iran. Shi`a Islam is the official Islam of Iran, is dominant in southern Iraq, and is represented by minorities in Lebanon, Pakistan, India, Yemen, and elsewhere.

Sunna means "well-trodden path," and it refers to the consensus of traditional legal and social practices, as well as referring to the majority Islamic community that claims to be founded on the authentic and correct consensus tradition. It is a tradition given to accommodation of differences and tolerance within the overall Islamic perspective, often citing as its precedent the Prophet's saying, "Differences of opinion within my community are a blessing." The 85 percent or so of the world's 1 billion Muslims who are Sunni nonetheless maintain considerable overall homogeneity of belief and practice without a centralized organization or authority, for while some nostalgia for the caliphate remains, Sunni Islam today is self-governing in each Muslim country.

In Sunni Islam the fundamental authority, after the guidance of the Qur`an, is Muslim law. It is interpreted not by a single individual but by a consensus of learned men who base their decisions on tradition, *hadith,* and analogy. Although al-Azhar University in Cairo has long been considered the most venerable repository of such learning, Sunni interpretation is decentralized. Its emphasis is on the basic Five Pillars of Islam and on a rather formal—though deeply felt—style of devotion. Its legal bent stresses putting all of life under God and the Qur`an. Different schools of law interpretation obtain within Sunni Islam, though they are not competitive but recognized alternatives. Sunni Islam also embraces some sub-movements; one is the Wahhabi movement, dominant in Saudi Arabia, a conservative, puritanical reform dating from the eighteenth century.

Shi`a Islam

**Shi`a Islam**, the Islam of Iran, southern Iraq, and minorities elsewhere, is different in tone and more complex. Shi`ites believe that after Muhammad there was intended to be a succession of Imams, Divinely appointed and authoritative teachers of Islam, to guide the faithful. The first was Ali, Muhammad's cousin, and after him Ali's eldest son, Hasan, and then Ali's second son, Husain. There were then nine others in family succession, down to the twelfth, who was born in 869.

All of these, except the last, died mysteriously and are said by Shi`ites to have been killed at the instigation of various caliphs. From the Shi`a point of view, the caliphates represent dark usurping powers seeking to destroy the true spokesman in each generation of the house of the prophet of God. The twelfth Imam, the Imam Zaman, or **Mahdi**, the Imam for All Time, is said to be still living but invisible. In the fullness of time he will reappear to bring justice to the earth. Subsects of the Shi`a recognize only part of the lineage, or variations on it. Understandably, colorful claimants to the title of Mahdi have appeared from time to time in Muslim history.

Shi`a devotion puts most emphasis on Husain, the third Imam and the most worthy and tragic of all. In the sixty-first year after the *Hijra,* he and his companions were killed by the forces of the Caliph Yazid in a great battle at Karbala, in southern Iraq. The death of this splendid young hero has been made by Shi`a into an event that demands eternal recompense by fervent mourning and reenactment. Husain's shrine at Karbala is a mighty place of pilgrimage.

The death of Husain is commemorated by Shi`ites in the first ten days of the Muslim year, the festival of **Muharram**. During these days Shi`a communities exhibit great religious fervor. At the end of the old year, black tents are set up in the streets with memorial arms and candles to remind passersby of the martyr. On the first day of Muharram, the devout cease from bathing or shaving. The story of Husain is vividly recited from pulpits in the tents; the listeners respond with wailing and tears. Occasionally, groups of men roam the streets venting their anguish by inflicting sword wounds on themselves, dragging chains, dancing wildly, and pulling out their hair.

The climax of this remarkable commemoration of a hero's death is on the tenth day of Muharram. The battle of Karbala and the death of Husain are enacted in a colorful passion play, with horsemen in bright costumes charging and recharging each other, battering their comrades in sport with wooden staves. The crowd becomes more and more excited; finally, Husain is taken and is seen to suffer excruciatingly from thirst while the cruel foemen make sport of him. At last he is beheaded.[14]

The atmosphere of Shi`a Islam, as reflected in the Muharram and the beliefs about the mysterious martyred or hidden Imam, is clearly different in tone from that of Sunni Islam. The Shi`a world, far from being one in which submission to the revelation of Allah steadily and progressively triumphs, is a darker sphere where treachery and cruelty are all too likely to prevail on the outer plane. Heroes and true prophets of God suffer and die in anguish, while ruthless imposters sit upon thrones; the number of true faithful is small compared to that of frauds; and the faithful are known chiefly by the fervor of their righteous wailing for the evils of this hard world and the keenness of their hope in God's inward, invisible plans.

The Shi`a mentality is conditioned by centuries of experience of being almost always a religious minority within Islam, save under the Fatimid dynasty, which ruled medieval Egypt and surrounding areas in the tenth and eleventh centuries, and in Iran since the Safavid dynasty made it the official faith early in the sixteenth century. But history as old as Islam itself lies behind the Shi`a experience.

When the Shi`a movement began, it appeared on the surface as more of a political than a religious caucus. It was the party (*shi`a* means "party" or "faction") supporting Ali and his descendants for the caliphate over against the line recognized by the Sunni majority. According to the Sunni tradition, Muhammad left no designated successor. Upon his death, the community selected Abu Bakr, the Prophet's closest companion and father of his wife Aisha, to be its leader. He died after only two years, but he appointed as his successor Umar (r. 634–644), the real organizer of the Arab empire. From then on, the control of the empire by Meccans, of the Umayyad and later (after 750) of the Abbasid house, was clear, despite a brief and challenged caliphate by Ali himself from 656 until his assassination in 661.

According to the Shi`a account, Muhammad appointed Ali as his successor before his death, but while the latter was still mourning the Prophet's passing and before he could assume active leadership, a clique within the companions of the Prophet had advanced the elderly Abu Bakr to the fore, and Ali's party felt compelled to accept him temporarily in order to prevent division at this critical juncture for Islam, despite knowing it was contrary to Muhammad's wishes. The bitterness of the Ali party was only increased by the attack during Ali's caliphate mounted against him by Mu`awiyah, governor of Syria, an exceptionally able ruler to whose banner the majority of Muslims turned as Ali's rule appeared weak and precarious. But the Ali party won sympathy from the discontented, especially the Bedouin tribesmen, with its demands for social justice and its opposition to the increasingly luxurious aristocracy of the empire. Further, the movement's emotional tone was, as we have seen, deepened when Ali's son Husain was cut down trying to raise a revolt against the Umayyads with a small, ragtag but heroic army in 680. The Shi`a faction also had roots in ancient antagonism on the part of South Arabians and their powerful allies in Iraq and Iran where Ali found support—regions where Shi`a is still strong—against the North Arabian Mecca-Medina power base of the ruling Islamic establishment in the caliphate era.

As Shi`a Islam persisted despite failure in the military and political arenas, its theoretical concept of the Imam grew more and more exalted. The Sunni caliph was viewed as "successor" to Muhammad only in the latter's role as administrative leader of the Islamic community. No caliph presumed to share the Prophet's unique religious vocation as mediator of Divine revelation. But Shi`a concepts of the Imam

made his a unique and sacred spiritual office, though they varied from conservative doctrines in which he was little more than a Divinely blessed caliph to extremist theologies that saw him as virtually an incarnation or manifestation of God himself on earth and so even greater than Muhammad. What might be called the Shi`a mainstream was satisfied to hold that, by Divine grace, the Imam is without sin, has various sorts of superhuman wisdom and power, and is able to interpret the Qur`an infallibly. However, since the "hiding" of the Imam, these extraordinary functions have been exercised by him through the visible spiritual leaders of Shi`a sects and

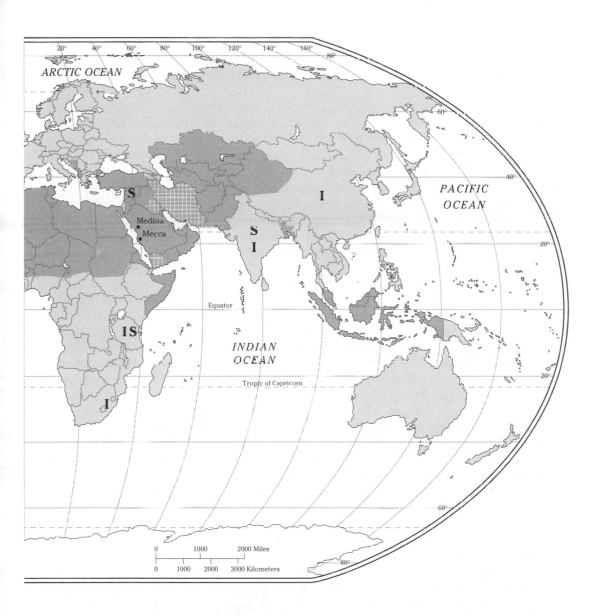

nations who participate in some way in the Imam's prerogatives. The basic difference between Sunni and Shi`a Islam on the question of authority is clear: for Sunni Islam it derives from *ijma,* consensus of the community; for the Shi`a it is entirely centralized, in theory, in the Imam or his deputies, whom the faithful are to hear and obey. But the upshot has been somewhat paradoxical. The Sunnis, through the consensus principle, tend toward rigid adherence to tradition and support of established Muslim rules. Shi`ites, who as we have seen were more often than not an oppressed minority, tend in following their almost-Divine leaders to accept considerable innovation if it is believed to be specially revealed through the Imam. They are predisposed to mistrust and sometimes oppose the state, and they are inclined to partisan factions under leaders believed to be the Imam or Mahdi, or his envoy or precursor.

We are not surprised to find, then, that most sectarian movements within Islam have been Shi`a. The considerable majority of Shi`ites accept the standard list of twelve Imams before the hiding of the twelfth, and they are therefore called **Twelvers**, Ashariyah. Like the Shi`a of Iran, they hold to the moderate position concerning the Imam outlined above. But a smaller faction, generally called **Ismailis**, though sometimes also "Seveners," accept only the first seven and differ on the identity of the last. The Twelvers contend that the younger son of the sixth Imam inherited his dignity because the elder son, Ismail, was guilty of the sin of drinking wine. But Ismailis assert that the succession did pass to Ismail, and moreover they claim that he was the last visible Imam, and that his son Muhammad at-Tamm will return as the Madhi.

The Ismaili system of belief has been deeply influenced by esotericism of Gnostic and Zoroastrian background. It holds that the Qur`an contains veiled doctrines in which concepts of the Neoplatonic sort of emanations, levels of reality, and the mystic significance of the number seven are important. Ismailism takes a cyclical view of history and views all actual, public religions relativistically.

Ismaili history is fascinating, for it shows how easily the sort of radical social attitudes engendered by Shi`a move from idealism to fanaticism and from anarchy to absolutism. In the ninth century, an Ismaili order called the Qarmatians arose in southern Iraq and Bahrain. The Qarmatians practiced communal living, holding all things in common and serving one another's needs. But they also defied the caliphate, engaging in terrorism against those they regarded as their foes. They achieved such exploits as sacking Mecca and temporarily carrying off the Black Stone of the *Ka`ba* in 930 C.E.

The Qarmatians prepared the way for something even greater: the rise of the Ismaili Fatimid dynasty. At once imperial and revolutionary, this house perceived its mission in highly ideological terms. Its ruler was himself the quasi-divine Mahdi, or coming Imam, and his task was to destroy the hated usurping caliphate in Baghdad, convert Sunni Muslims to the true faith, and establish a world empire under the world's true sovereign. Originating in North Africa (though claiming descent from Muhammad's daughter Fatima), the Fatimid house conquered Egypt in 969, making Cairo their capital and building there a great university and mosque. Besides armies, which tried to press ever closer to Baghdad, the Fatimids sent out missionaries to spread subversion and terror as well as to make converts in the lands of the enemy. But after reaching a high point in 1059, when they actually held Baghdad for a year, the Fatimids went into decline, harried not only by the caliphate, itself in decline, but also by the rising power of Turks and Christian crusaders. Their regime was also made ultimately untenable by the fact that the majority of Muslims simply could not accept Ismailism or the legitimacy of Fatimid claims. Ismaili believers themselves came to lose faith in them, and the dynasty ended in 1171.

It left a grim progeny in the order called Assassins, which flourished in the mountains and, through secret agents, in the cities of Iraq and Iran and adjacent areas from 1099 to 1266. Founded by a fervent Ismaili missionary and a deposed claimant to the Fatimid throne, the Assassins lived by raiding and terrorism, believing that the murder of those considered enemies was a religious duty. The name "Assassins" derived from the hashish they allegedly took to steel themselves for their bloody deeds. They were finally put down by invading Mongols, who also took Baghdad in 1258, ending the caliphate there and indirectly allowing Islamic culture to flourish all the more elsewhere—in Persia, India, Egypt, and later Turkey. (A strictly religious, nonpolitical caliphate was set up in Cairo, where it remained until 1517. Thereafter, the title was taken by the sultans of the Ottoman Empire who held it till 1926, when the ancient dignity of Commander of the Faithful and Successor of the Prophet vanished from the earth.)

The Ismailis today survive in several groups. The Druzes, a people of highly esoteric and initiatory faith centered in southern Syria, believe their creed was founded by al-Hakim, the sixth Fatimid ruler, who in 1017 proclaimed himself the latest incarnation of God. In 1021 he disappeared. Though others opine that he was deranged and murdered, the Druzes ever since have taken him at his word and regard him as the hidden Imam. Other Ismaili sects are centered in India and Yemen. The best known, with a following in the millions, is the Nizari movement, whose spiritual leader is now known as the Aga Khan. Aga Khan III (1877–1957) was much celebrated in this century as a philanthropist, sportsman, and Indian statesman.

But despite its wide dispersal and political origin, undoubtedly it is no accident that Shi`a Islam has its oldest roots in the Valley of the Two Rivers, where anciently New Year's (which Muharram really is) included rites of battle with chaos by the hero Marduk and wailing for the dead Tammuz. (One is reminded of the enacted battle and wailing for Husain.) Shi`a is also strong in formerly Zoroastrian Iran, with its belief in a cosmic battle of good and evil, a hidden coming prophet, and an apocalyptic reversal to which the faithful looked forward. Christian and Manichaean influences on Shi`a cannot be excluded either, for Husain emotionally becomes virtually a suffering savior. Shi`a attitudes undoubtedly had some part in setting the stage for the Iranian revolution of 1979, under the leadership of ayotollahs whose authority is believed to be conferred by the hidden imam.

Islamic Mysticism

A discussion of Islam would be superficial if it dealt only with its outward, official history and practices and left out the mystical wing, which has frequently given the faith of Muhammad another face. This tradition is known to the West as **Sufism** and its practitioners as Sufis. Their God is the same God as that of the Qur`an and the tradition. But they seek not only to follow his external commandments but to know him intimately and even to lose themselves in love into the depths of his being.

Around the Sufis' mystic quest have clustered a number of auxiliary practices, many of great beauty: spiritual masters, parables and wisdom tales, spiritual fraternities, schools of meditation, and techniques of attaining ecstasy through music, chanting, and dance.

Sufis believe their approach is grounded in the inner experience of the Prophet himself. Muhammad clearly prayed deeply and knew God intimately, even experiencing trance and rapture. Certain verses of the Qur`an, such as this one already cited, support the quest for mystical awareness of God everywhere: "To Allah belongs the East and the West. Whichever way you turn there is the face of Allah."[15]

Another suggests the esoteric side of things: We are told that Allah took his servant from a holy mosque to a farther mosque to reveal certain Divine signs.[16] According to some traditions, this last passage refers to God's mysteriously transporting Muhammad in a single night from Mecca to Jerusalem, and then taking him up into heaven to show him sights not seen by other mortals. Second-hand accounts of this journey probably helped inspire Dante's *Divine Comedy*.[17]

Thus many Sufis believe not only that their way is that of Muhammad himself, but also that Sufism is really a timeless path known to the wise in all generations, just as in a sense Muhammad's declaration was but a restoration of the true primordial faith of Abraham and of Eden. Doubtless there is truth to this, represented historically by the parallels and possible influence between Sufism and Asiatic shamanism, Greek Neoplatonism, Christian monasticism, and the lore of Hinduism and Buddhism. But within Islamic history, Sufism became visible as a movement about a century after Muhammad. Like Shi`a but in a different way, Sufism was a reaction against the luxury and corruption, the loss of original desert simplicity and pure faith, which many serious Muslims saw overtaking the newly triumphant Islamic world of the caliphates.

The origin of the word *"sufi"* is disputed, but the majority of scholars attribute it to the Arabic word for wool, *suf,* alluding to the coarse wool garments worn by ascetics seeking a more inward way, as a mark distinguishing them from those content with outward conformity to Islam.

Sufi inwardness made of greatest importance one's personal relationship of faith and love to God, a love which was its own reward. Never has this attitude been more eloquently expressed than by the mystic Rabi`a al-Adawiya of Basra (?713–801), a former slave who had been trained as a flute player. At night she would pray thus:

> *Oh my Lord, the stars are shining and the eyes of men are closed, and kings have shut their doors, and every lover is alone with his beloved, and here am I alone with Thee.*

She said also:

> *I saw the Prophet in a dream, and he said to me, "O Rabi`a, dost thou love me?" I said, "O Prophet of God, who is there who does not love thee? But my love to God so possessed me that no place remains for loving or hating any save Him."*

And again:

> It is a bad servant who serves God from fear and terror or from the desire of a
> reward. . . . Even if Heaven and Hell were not, does it not behoove us to obey Him?[18]

This is a pure Sufi spirit echoing down through the ages. As time went on,
this sheer love of God came to be more and more organized, with particular practices and doctrines and societies shaping the lives of those who followed its path.

Thus, Abu Yazid al-Bistami (d. 874) described the stages of the spiritual life
leading up to **fana**, complete passing away of the separate individual self into God.
The fana state was often manifested in ecstatic spiritual intoxication. In that state,
al-Bistami, hardly knowing whether it was he or God in him whose words they
were, did not shrink from such expressions as "I am your Lord," "Praise be to me,
how great is my majesty," or "My banner is greater than that of Muhammad." The
conventional were duly shocked.

Finally in 922, one of these God-possessed persons of uninhibited rapture,
al-Hallaj, was executed at Baghdad for saying "I am the Truth"—"Truth" being an
attribute of Allah. The tragic al-Hallaj had taken Jesus, in Islam the exemplar of the
inward mystic, as his model of the God-incarnate man, and he was sentenced to
the same fate as Jesus: crucifixion.

At the same time, a reaction in favor of a more orthodox Sufism set in. Junayd
of Baghdad (d. 911) emphasized that the claims of mystical experience cannot be
given priority over normative moral and customary demands of religion, and that
the nature of love itself demands that, even in the mystic's "identity" with God,
there be also a difference between him and God.[19]

The great al-Ghazali (1058–1111), who had been a conventional Muslim scholar
until he experienced and then sought to interpret the mystic path, made Sufism a
respectable part of Islam. He interpreted Sufi inwardness as an attitude to accompany the outward acts and bring them to life, as we have seen in his treatment of
the *hajj*.

The philosopher and Sufi master ibn al-Arabi (1165–1240), a spiritual follower
of al-Ghazali, moved in the direction of a pantheist philosophy as the intellectual
expression of what the Sufi "knows" and enacts. For him God was not only the
source of all but the sole reality. Within the Divine, however, are gradations; between the human and the Divine is a realm of images that reflect in the human
imagination—angels, the Day of Judgment, and so forth—and on these images religious visions and events are grounded.

The Sufi way has made much of **shaykhs**, spiritual teachers and masters, and
wali, saints. Drawing initially from Shi`a sources, Sufis also have talked of hidden
holy ones and of a coming Mahdi, or apocalyptic teacher-savior. According to
Sufism, the saints are different from the prophet Muhammad but are in their own
way nearly as great. For a Sufi to attain *wilaya*, sainthood or being a "friend of
God," was as good a goal as outward Islam's submission.

Indeed, by the tenth and eleventh centuries the twin goals of sainthood and
submission came together, as the notion gained force in Sufi circles that one

should submit to one's *shaykh,* or spiritual guide. The *shaykh,* called farther East around India a *pir* or *murshid,* was more or less an Islamic parallel to the Hindu *guru.* The very self-abnegation of submitting to his commands "as a dead body in the hands of its washers" was an experience of egolessness and bore its own spiritual reward, whether the guide was wise or not.

Many were wise, and their wisdom was often expressed in peculiar tales and gnomic wisdom. We are told, for example, that a certain man fell down in a seizure on a street of perfume sellers. People tried to revive him with various of the sweet odors of the tradesmen, but to no avail. Finally someone thrust sharp, pungent, ammonious ordure before his nose, and he arose. The implication is that only by the different, even the disconcerting, can the walking dead be brought to life.[20] *Shaykhs* have employed the methods of differentness with their paradoxes and their chanting, dancing, and trances.

Since the labors of al-Ghazali, Sufi masters generally have emphasized doing the normative devotions of Islam but with a special mind to the inward as well as the outward aspects. But beyond that, there are particular ecstatic techniques for knowing God that the *shaykhs* taught: practices such as *dhikr* (or *wird*), reciting the beautiful names of God on beads; or even whirling dances like those of the **dervishes**, or feats of shamanistic fervor like rending garments, eating glass, or cutting oneself without pain to show one's Divine absorption.

Practices such as these were developed by the great Sufi orders that spread across Islam after the tenth century. They still exist, although since around 1900 their power has diminished. For the most part they were not celibate monastic orders, although in some instances an inner core of devotees or leaders might—whether officially married or not—exemplify a level of commitment comparable to that of monks or abbots in other faiths. But for the bulk of lay adherents, the orders were more like lodges: One would receive a formal initiation by a *shaykh* or *pir* of the order and then would practice its devotion corporately at periodic meetings and otherwise privately. Some Sufi orders, especially in the Turkish empire, had political and revolutionary overtones. Some have been suppressed by modern Islamic governments because the whole Sufi attitude was considered by modernizers to inculcate a medieval, superstitious, nonproductive mentality; ironically, at the same time Sufism has been discovered and much appreciated by many outside of Islam.

Sufi orders with their saintly masters were and are a great proselytizing force for Islam. It was primarily in their gentler, more mystical form that Islam entered India and Indonesia. It is easy to speculate that, apart from its empathetic presentation by such mystic Sufi saints, Islam might have had but little success in these cultures. Today, Sufi orders are having success in spreading Islam in Africa.

The prestige of the *shaykh* made much of Islam into a cult of personalities. *Shaykhs* became saints who had cosmic as well as temporal meanings. It was said to be the saints who kept the world together generation after generation. In an invisible hierarchy were varying degrees of saints: "successors," "pegs," "pillars," and finally the *qutb,* the "pole" or "axis" of the universe. There is only one *qutb,* according to a popular tradition, in every generation, and when one dies he is replaced by another. The members of this hierarchy are the true pivots upon which the world in its inner life turns. They may not be known to the general public—indeed, a saint in his humility may not even know himself that he is a saint, much less an axis of the world—but should he fail in the mysterious work his inward sanctity enables him to do, the social order and the earth itself would fall apart. Finally, *sufis* spoke of the enigmatic leader of the saints themselves, al-Khidr, "the Green One," a generally invisible but immortal and ever-youthful guide who appears at time of need in the dreams or waking sight of the sincere questor on the mystic path.[21]

The Muslim public knew well the reputations of the more visible saints. It flocked to their presences and, after their deaths, to their tombs. In the heyday of popular Sufism—the twelfth through nineteenth centuries—legends of saints were rife, and pilgrimages to their holy places rivaled Mecca in popularity. Many of them are still much frequented. In Shi`a areas, the shrines of *imams,* like that of Husain himself at Karbala in Iraq, are thronged. Countless village mosques contain tombs of local saints, unmarked by image or picture but well known and visible because of their coffin shape, inscription, and the many colored flags on buildings.

In the valley of Bamian in Afghanistan, famous for its ancient Buddhist monastic caves, but whose population is now strongly Muslim, I* came across a shrine of an "ice-burning saint." According to the local legend, this mystic had once come with his disciples into the valley and begged for fuel with which to cook food for himself and his band. But the villagers, not recognizing him for what he was, hardened their hearts against his request. The saint then sent a disciple into the nearby mountains to get some ice, and by a miracle he caused the ice to burn and used it for firewood. Thereupon, the awestruck villagers believed in him and besought the holy man to stay, which he did. When he died, the shrine was built over his tomb, a modest domed edifice of mud with a wall around it, all festooned with red banners. I saw bearded men of the village circumambulate the tomb inside the walls muttering *dhikr* as they went; in setting out, each stooped to pass under a table holding the Qur`an.

I* sensed here both the devotional power of popular Islam and the basic similarities of the central Asiatic myths and *culti* of men of power, whether in shamanistic, Hindu, Buddhist, Muslim, or Christian forms—for the "wizard saint" has been a constant in all the many faiths that have swept across the wild mountains, deserts, and forests of that vast area of the earth.

Islam generally believes that the saints have power to perform miracles. Muhammad did none, except the miracle of the Qur`an itself. But the saints have a different calling from that of the public envoy of God, one at once more arcane and more popularly appealing. They must work wonders to show the transcendence of spiritual attainment over the material and do works of mercy that help hold the universe together. They are masters of the realm of archetype and dream that lies above this world and below God, as written in the philosophy of al-Ghazali and ibn al-Arabi. The *baraka,* or numinous power of the saints, rests eternally over their tombs and relics, and for this reason pilgrims to these sites are often healed and blessed.

*Robert Ellwood.

Islam in the World Today

At the beginning of the twenty-first century, Islam finds itself second only to Christianity in number of active members among the religions of the world. The devastation of Buddhism and the traditional religions of China by Communist revolutions leaves no doubt about that status. Moreover, as we have seen, Christianity today appears to be shorn of the overconfidence with which it began the twentieth century, though it still possesses much strength. But Muslims would have little hesitancy in viewing the position of their faith and of Islamic culture at the beginning of this century as being far stronger than at the beginning of the last.

In 1900, the Muslim world was notoriously in decline compared to Europe and America. It was sunk in poverty and technologically backward. Much of it was subject to humiliating European colonial rule: The Dutch controlled Indonesia; millions of Indian Muslims as well as Hindus lived under the British flag; France ruled vast reaches of Muslim North Africa. The only large sovereign Muslim states were the Ottoman (Turkish) and Persian empires, which sprawled over much of the Middle East. They were anachronistic and corrupt regimes, if anything more oppressive than colonial rule to their long-suffering subjects; and moreover, despite nominal independence, subservient to Europe in many ways. Finally, Islam in 1900 was only beginning to get in touch intellectually and spiritually with the modern world.

But by the last quarter of the twentieth century this situation changed dramatically. Rarely since the stunning spread of Islam in its first century have the fortunes of a religion changed so remarkably in so short a time. Virtually all Muslim nations have attained independence. The old Ottoman and Persian empires are now Turkey (much diminished in size) and Iran. With the new names have come new regimes and far-reaching changes. Some Muslim countries have achieved great wealth, mostly from petroleum. Kuwait and Saudi Arabia have reached levels of *per capita* income that are among the highest in the world. Islam is growing rapidly, both through a high birthrate in many places and through missionary efforts. Emigration and the establishment of Islamic centers have given the religion a new visibility around the world. Islam is also experiencing vigorous intellectual ferment and powerful movements for simplification and purification of the faith and its practice.

Change is uneven, of course. The House of Islam includes not only some of the richest nations in the world, but also some of the poorest, such as Bangladesh. Some aspects of its resurgence have seemed, at least to outsiders, as more like rampant nationalism accompanied by religious zealotry than real spiritual awakening. But such matters are not always well judged by outsiders, and they require considerable perspective in time before their ultimate meaning can be discerned. However one assesses it, Islam seems in a period of religious ferment and renewal associated with nation-building and expanding confidence, perhaps comparable to the Protestant Reformation in the Christian world. As did the Protestant Reformation, the Islamic resurgence has also produced much war and bigotry. Yet nonetheless, the Reformation helped wrench Europe into new stages of historical development. What Islam will generate remains to be seen.

Not infrequently, the resurgence of traditional Islam has been associated with the self-assertion of underprivileged classes in Muslim countries, whether rural peasants or urban masses. These resisted the Westernized elite who typically dominated the governments and economies of these countries in their early period of modern nationhood, especially during the first three decades after World War II. While those elites have often done much to promote nation-building and the development of modern (that is, Western-type) industry, transportation, education, and political institutions, these benefits have not always been readily available to those not of the elite class, whereas their disruptive effect on traditional village, family, and Islamic moral and spiritual values have been all too apparent. Moreover, the elites are commonly perceived as inwardly contemptuous of traditional values and unduly eager to cultivate the ways and friendships of non-Muslim Europeans and Americans. All of this has been exacerbated because economic globalization, touted by many such elites, is thought by many to further threaten traditional life.

The political and social upsurge of traditional Islam that became so evident in the late 1970s, most conspicuously in the Iranian revolution of 1979, was the explosive outburst of long pent-up hostility by nonelites against the dominant class. Often led by fiery Muslim fundamentalist preachers and mystics, the dispossessed understandably seized upon pure Islam as the symbol for what they stood for and stood against; Islam was their faith and culture, the true life-soul of a land that was truly theirs. They insisted that Islam, far from being an awkward roadblock to modernization, is as good (indeed better) an ideological framework for building a more just social and economic order than is Western socialism or capitalism, and at the same time it was seen as a sure rampart against the corroding influences (chiefly from the West) that traditionalists saw threatening family life and pride in one's land and culture. Four principles have been fundamental to the Islamic resurgence since the late 1970s:

1. The *shari`a,* or systematized code of Islamic law based on the Qur'an and the traditions, must be the fundamental law of the state.
2. To ensure that state policies and actions are consistent with the *shari`a,* Muslim teachers and scholars should have an important role in government, thus achieving what in the West would be called a union of church and state.
3. Wealth must be fairly distributed in accordance with Islamic ideals of justice and brotherhood.
4. Outside (non-Muslim) influences in society must be resisted, and the lifestyle of the people should conform to Islamic rules and values, as in matters of dress, family life, education, and the role of women.

These developments have had varying results around the world. To illustrate, we will begin with two countries that are in stark contrast—Saudi Arabia and Turkey. Then we will survey the situation for Islam around the world.

Saudi Arabia is an Islamic **theocracy**. This nation incorporates the land where the faith began and contains its holy cities of Mecca and Medina. The strict Wahhabi sect, which rejects mysticism of the Sufi sort and demands a state based on literal interpretation of the Qur`an and *shari`a,* dominates it. Under its influence, plays, cinema, alcoholic drinks, and excessive intermingling of the sexes are forbidden. Yet Saudi Arabia, convulsed by new wealth and inevitable social change, is striving to become both a modern and a conservative Muslim state at the same time, while resisting the incursions of the Western military since the 1993 Gulf War and the globalizing economic forces of the West. The final result of this experiment remains to be seen.

On the other hand, Turkey was given over to **secularization**. Turkey lies to the North of the Arab world. It is the homeland of the Turks, the non-Arab race whose sultan long ruled most of the Arabic-speaking peoples in the days of the Ottoman Empire and who fostered Islam wherever he ruled. By the nineteenth century this sprawling imperial state was slipping from the sultan's grasp. Turkey was the "Sick Man of Europe." Despite reforms, culminating in the "Young Turks" *coup d'état* of 1908, conditions only seemed to worsen in the empire's internal and external position. But after World War I, Turkey lost its empire and set off in a radically new direction under the iron rule of Kemal Ataturk (1881–1938). The sultans of the Ottoman Empire had claimed the ancient title of Caliph of Islam, but Ataturk sought to establish a Westernized and militantly secular state. Ataturk ended religious courts and schools, put secular law in place of the *shari`a,* abolished the *caliphate* and Sufi orders, and forbade religious garb outside places of worship. Secularization dealt with matters large and small; Sunday was made the weekly holiday instead of Friday, and the wearing of the *fez,* a hat traditionally associated with old Turkey and with Islam, was outlawed. The substitution of the Roman alphabet for the Arabic in the writing of Turkish further detached the nation from the world of Islam and aligned it with the West.

Ataturk's style of wholesale secularization and Westernization as a solution for the problems of Muslim lands was initially embraced by many in the Islamic world. Ataturk, regarded as the "father of modern Turkey," was a hero to some, and the fathers of several other major Muslim countries, such as Pakistan and Indonesia (which gained independence or underwent transformation in mid-century), paid him the tribute of emulation. They too made no pretense of being orthodox believers. While appealing to the general ideal of Islamic nationhood, they favored "progress" at whatever cost to the particulars of the tradition.

However, after Ataturk's death, the deislamicization program in Turkey was gradually relaxed, and the continuing support of the religion by the peasantry showed the persisting strength of faith. Nevertheless, the pro-secularization factions remain in control of the government in Turkey today. For example, in June 2001, Turkey's high court banned the "Virtue Party" for advocating views that contradict the secular government. In addition, those who wish to don traditional Islamic garb are barred from becoming civil servants or students. Needless to say, Turkey remains divided between secular and pro-Islamic parties. While the secular political factions remain dominant in the government, pro-Islamic parties are gaining force.

It is important to recognize, however, that it was against the policies of "progressive" secular leaders, such as Ataturk and those who followed his lead, to which the Islamic fundamentalist reaction in the late 1970s and 1980s was largely directed. This resulted in the resurgence of Islam and, in some places, considerable conflict.

The movement often labeled Arab Socialism, represented in several countries by the Ba`ath Party, seeks to combine Arab nationalism (aimed at eventual unification of the Arab peoples into one nation) with Qur`anic concern for justice and fair distribution of goods expressed through modern forms of governmental social activism. But progress in this direction has been uneven and its implementation diverse in character. In Iraq, for example, Saddam Hussain rose to power through the Ba`ath Party to become president in 1979. Initially, he sought to improve the economic status of the Iraqi people through socialist reforms and was somewhat successful. However, Iraq's military aggression, first against Iran and then against Kuwait (ostensibly to work toward "nationalizing" the Arab World), ended in defeat. The result was to further divide, rather than unite, the Arab World; the much-resented ongoing Western military presence in the region having been a result of the 1991 Gulf War defense of Kuwait.

In Syria, Arab Socialism is on the decline as radical Islamic elements resist its program as being a secular threat to traditional Islamic values. Moreover, Syria's new president, Bashar al-Assad, continues to support the Hezbollah (Party of God), the Shi`ite militia in southern Lebanon that opposes Israel.

In Libya, the regime of Muammar al-Qaddafi has conjoined ideological socialism with strong nationalism and support of Islam to the extent that, in 1994, Qaddafi declared that the *shari`a* would become the law of the land, rather than the pre-existing secular law, and local government there is now in the hands of *imams*.

In neighboring Tunisia, on the other hand, the government, while nominally socialist and Muslim, has taken a far more moderate stance. Indeed, it has pioneered finding ways to adapt Islamic usages to modern conditions. Still, these efforts have led to a resurgent Islamic fundamentalist reaction in that country the outcome of which is yet to be seen.

After independence, Algeria was on a course in the tradition of its French colonial rulers, holding to the idea of separation of church and state, and fostering socialist reforms. However, in the 1990s, Algeria was rent by civil war between a fundamentalist Islamic political movement, the "Islamic Salvation Front," which hopes to create a theocracy there based on Islamic tradition, and the military-backed secularists. The conflict has been bloody and gruesome. While today the full-scale civil war has abated, battles continue, largely in rural areas. And in June 2001, a large-scale demonstration in Algiers turned violent, proving that the conflict shows little sign of peaceful resolution in the near future.

To the East of the Arab world, Iran presents the most dramatic example of Islamic resurgence. Under the leadership of the **Ayatollah** Khomeini, the Shah Muhammad Pahlavi was toppled in 1979 and an Islamic republic was established, in which the *shari`a* was proclaimed to be normative, and clergy like Khomeini took a decisive role. The resplendent monarchy had lost popular support to a large extent because of its "Westernizing" tendencies. In its place came the classic revolutionary scenario of ecstatic mobs, reprisals, serious economic and social disruption, and the emerging outlines of a state more egalitarian, more isolationist, and more founded on Islamic law than what had gone before. Enforcement of traditional values was effected with much religious fervor. However, more recently, moderate reformers have gained considerable political power. The reelection of Mohammad Khatami as president in a landslide victory has provided a strong mandate in this direction. Nevertheless, the animosity between the reformers and the fundamentalist clerics remains high and the latter's institutional power continues to thwart liberalizing reforms, such as freedom of the press, due process in the court system, and curtailing of the work of the "morals police" over which the current Ayatollah retains considerable control.

In the Indian subcontinent, the same resurgence of strict, traditionalist Islam has brought comparable problems and prospects to its multitudes. Pakistan, founded as an Islamic state at the time of the independence and partition of the former British Indian empire in 1947, retained a legal system based on English law and followed the "progressive" course for a while. But in 1979, the *shari`a* also became law under pressure of the Islamic resurgence. Prayer rooms were set up in factories and cinemas, and radio and television programs were censored to free them of anything obnoxious to Muslim faith and morals—a pattern similar to that elsewhere. In the Republic of India, the ten percent Muslim minority, influenced by the spirit and literature of the resurgence, has become more assertive, and this has perpetuated tensions and riots between Muslims and the Hindu majority, as noted in Chapter 3 in connection with the Ayodhya temple/mosque controversy.

Nowhere, however, is the resurgence of strict, traditionalist Islam more pronounced than in Afghanistan, which borders Pakistan to the South and Iran to the West. Afghanistan's history is one of political and economic instability. Due in part to its strategic location at one end of the famous Khyber Pass (gateway to India through what is now Pakistan), it was invaded in the nineteenth century by the British and in the twentieth century by the Soviets. Between invasions, internal struggles for power left the country's people with economically poor and insecure lives, while at the same time those in power promoted secularization and Western-style developments. With such a history, perhaps it is no surprise that, after the nineteen-year war with the Soviet Union ended with the Soviet withdrawal in 1989 and the several years of civil war that followed, a promise of peace and stability, and a return to Islamic fundamentals, was welcomed by the majority of the people.

Thus, came the rise of the Taliban ("students of Islamic studies"), a fundamentalist Islamic sect, which now controls approximately 90 percent of the country. Soon after gaining power, the Taliban introduced repressive policies based on narrow interpretations of Islamic law, even from the perspective of those in other Islamic nations. Under Taliban rule, contact with the world outside of Afghanistan was severely curtailed. Television and the internet were banned, travel was limited, and, in general, censorship reigns. Taliban policies are especially severe for women and minorities. Under them, women were prohibited by law from obtaining an education, working for pay, driving a car, even leaving their homes without approved male escorts. And when they were permitted to leave the home, they were required to be covered from head to toe, so that no one could gaze upon them. Hindus were required to wear yellow identity patches. Violations of such requirements received the severest of penalties, including execution. Although American Muslims, as well as other Muslims around the world, condemned the Taliban, decrying the Taliban's policies as contrary to the Qur`an, there has been considerable support for the Taliban elsewhere, for example in Pakistan.

Afghanistan first came especially to world attention in March of 2001, when the Taliban ordered and accomplished the destruction of two famous Buddha statues located in Bamiyan, which have stood since the third century C.E., when they were carved into the side of a mountain during the region's pre-Islamic past. The larger of the two statues is believed to have been the world's tallest standing Buddha statue (181 feet tall; the smaller statue, 110 feet tall), and both were considered to be important world artistic treasures.

Needless to say, Afghanistan and its Taliban leadership had continued to be a source of concern for many around the world even prior to the September 11, 2001 attacks on the United States. Its growing influence, particularly among fundamentalists in Pakistan, did not bode well for stability in the region or, as has become evident, the rest of the world. This was all the more apparent because the Taliban harbored militant Islamic groups and their leaders, including Osama bin Laden, the wealthy Muslim militant. Bin Laden has been linked to the World Trade Center bombing in 1993 and the United States Embassy bombings in Kenya and Tanzania in 1998. Apparently, there is now considerable evidence that bin Laden is linked to the September 11th attacks on New York and Washington that resulted in the destruction of the World Trade Center and in significant damage to the Pentagon. The United States responded with military action in Afghanistan against bin Laden and the Taliban.

Farther East, in Malaysia, the Islamic resurgence threatens the delicate racial balance that has held that nation together. Malaysia is 50 percent Malay Muslim, 35 percent Chinese, and 15 percent Hindu and others. Since independence from Britain, its government has been controlled by a wealthy, sophisticated urban class of Malays who have held their Muslim faith in moderation and maintained good relations with the Chinese, who dominate the economy. But a fundamentalist movement, with its own militant political party inspired by zealous preachers, has arisen among the poorer Malay peasants of the countryside. It gives voice to the simple, devout peasant's resentment of both Chinese and worldly urban Malays, and it calls for a rigorously Islamic state on the puritanical model of others we have already discussed. This would, of course, provoke strong opposition from the large Chinese minority, who are not Muslim at all and have no desire to live under such a regime but whose economic life is bound up with Malaysia.

On the other hand, Islam in Indonesia has long been regarded as somewhat superficial. It came late to the vast island nation and sat lightly on top of a spiritual culture still deeply permeated by the Hindu and Buddhist influences that preceded it and above all by an indigenous bent toward spiritism and shamanism. It was the mystical, Sufi side of Islam, most congenial to the Indonesian temper, that won clearest support at first. Here too, however, a strict Muslim party and movement have been gaining support, and some have begun to challenge the secular state. Muslims now make up eighty-seven percent of the population, a large majority of whom believe that Islamic values should dominate society, while, at the same time, many hold to democratic rule, eschew the idea of an "Islamic state," as such, and embrace the possibilities of economic globalization. It will be of much interest to the world to see how the religious climate in Indonesia, the world's fourth most populous nation, develops.

Following the collapse of the Soviet Union in 1989, six traditionally Muslim republics in that union declared full independence. They have been beset by many problems, however, and it is not yet clear what form Islam will take in them and how much influence it will have.

Islam has been part of a turbulent history in the southeastern European region known as the Balkans, which includes largely Muslim Albania, half Muslim Bosnia-Herzegovina, Croatia, Macedonia, and what remains of Yugoslavia—Serbia (including the province of Kosovo, with its large Muslim ethnic Albanian population) and Montenegro. Violence there has been fueled by religious conflict, which dates back many centuries to the years surrounding the famed battle of Kosovo in 1389, which remains legendary in the region today. Around the time of the battle of Kosovo, the region, which had been in primarily in Eastern Orthodox and Roman Catholic hands, came under Islamic Ottoman control. Ottoman rule lasted, with much resistance and brief periods of uneasy independence, into the nineteenth century. The weakening hold of the Ottoman Empire during the nineteenth century led to much instability and periods of violence in the region with the eventual rise of Christian regimes. Then, after the Second World War, the region came under rule by unsympathetic communist governments. For example, in communist Albania, all places of worship were closed and all religious observances prohibited, the most extreme antireligious policy anywhere in the world. In 1992, however, a non-communist government came into power, and these policies were reversed. Due to weakening support from the faltering Soviet Union (which broke up in 1991) and economic decline, nationalism began to rise in the Balkans at the beginning of the 1990s. Civil war ensued and hostilities broke out in the region largely along religious lines. Bloody battles between Muslim and non-Muslim populations in Bosnia-Herzegovina wracked that new nation, and Slobodan Milosevic, who later was removed to the international tribunal in the Hague to be tried for his atrocities, led the Serbs in the ethnic cleansing of the Muslim ethnic Albanians in the Kosovo province of Serbia. The Balkans remain an unstable area.

Elsewhere in Europe, the population of Muslims has grown considerably since World War II as a result of immigration. Turks work in German factories, Pakistanis have settled in England, and Algerians have come to France in great numbers, reversing former lines of European expansion. Muslims also maintain a presence in Greece and Bulgaria. All of this, together with a greatly increased business and diplomatic presence from Islamic countries, has dotted Western Europe with mosques and Islamic centers, even though Muslims do not, of course, represent more than a small minority there.

Despite its sometimes troubled past, then, Islam enters the twenty-first century full of vigor and faith, with its strong Qur'anic egalitarian values, variously interpreted, and often standing against the secularizing and materialistic tendencies of the West.

Islam in America

Islam is a minority but a growing religious presence in the United States. Immigration, important diplomatic and commercial relationships between the United States and the Islamic world, and conversion have all contributed to the remarkable growth in numbers and visibility of this faith in the United States since the middle of the twentieth century. Impressive mosques and Islamic centers have been built in many major American cities, their minarets now joining the spires and domes of Christian churches and Jewish temples. These edifices have enabled American Muslims and visitors from Islamic lands to worship in familiar ways, and have enabled non-Muslim Americans for the first time to observe the practice of Islam, and engage in dialogue with Muslims, without leaving their homeland.

For immigrant Muslims, the experience of being Muslim in America has been challenging and often rewarding. Sometimes they have suffered suspicion, prejudice, and abuse because of negative stereotypes of Muslims held by many other Americans—caricatures no more true of all Muslims than are similar stereotypes of other racial and religious groups true of all their members. Sometimes American Muslims, especially women, have felt conspicuous because of the traditional dress they have chosen to wear. Practices such as regular prayer five times a day and the fast of Ramadan have not always been easy in the context of work and life in the United States.

At the same time, learning how to be a Muslim in America has helped many Muslims to understand their religion in new and exhilarating ways. They have come to discriminate between what they now hold to be the essentials and what they hold to be merely cultural. Most Islamic centers serve Muslims from many parts of the Islamic world—Arabs, Africans, Iranians, Pakistanis, Indonesians, and others—contributing to a fresh and vital sense of Islam as a world community. Like religionists of all other faiths in the United States, they have learned to hold to it without any sort of state support in a pluralistic and open society.

American Muslims have been of different strands. The majority of immigrants, though from many different countries, have been Sunni Muslims, and most immigrant-based mosques have been of this style. Shi'a Muslims from Iran and elsewhere have often worshipped at them, there being no discrimination, though occasionally they have established separate centers. There have also been a smaller number of immigrants (or converts) of sectarian Islamic groups: Ismaili, Druze, Ahmadiyya, and others who have organized their own denominations.

A number of movements that have appealed to Westerners not of Islamic background have their roots in Sufism. Sufism, with its sacred dance, its wonderful poetry, and its rich sense of the immediate presence of God, has a universal appeal that many have discovered. Groups range from the Western followers of various Sufi *shaykhs* or spiritual leaders to those that have become quite independent of normative Islam. The cultural influence of Sufi poetry, like the famous *Rubaiyat* of Omar Khayyam, must also be mentioned.

Many converts to Islam in the United States have been African American. The most influential force in this activity has been the work of Elijah Muhammad (1897–1975), founder of the "Black Muslims" or Nation of Islam, as they were called. The movement originally possessed unorthodox doctrines and staunchly advocated the separation of African and white Americans, but since Elijah Muhammad's death it has moved closer and closer to normative Islam. Its best known adherent, Malcolm X, supported this move toward the end of his life. Today the mainstream of African-American Islam no longer has a distinctive organization and strives to be simply Muslim. Some splinter "Black Muslim" groups, of which the most prominent is the Nation of Islam of the controversial Louis Farrakhan, have maintained the separatist mentality.

The multiracial Baha`i faith, previously mentioned, though it does not identify itself as Islamic, has roots in the Muslim culture of Persia and also has a presence in the United States.

American Islam, like the faith, generally, has a varied and colorful history. It is bound to have a gradually increasing influence on American life.

Women in Islam

In the West it is common for the uninformed to think of Islam as one monolithic religio-cultural phenomenon. Instead, as we have seen, just like Christianity, Islam has taken many forms. While all have the Prophet Muhammad and the Qur`an at their core, Islam's many sociological expressions, theoretical interpretations, and practices have been greatly influenced by the cultural contexts in which Islam is found. Accordingly, the Islam of Egypt differs from that of Saudi Arabia, just as both differ from Islam found in the United States.

In no area are these differences more profoundly revealed than in the attitudes, customs, practices, and laws that involve the role of women. Hence, it is extremely difficult to say anything much that would serve as a generalization for all of the half billion Muslim women all around the world and for all times.[22] Still, in an effort to provide a context for the contemporary discourses on women and

Islam, we will provide some background information regarding Islam in the Middle East, which has provided the foundation for Islam.

Islam and the Question of Women's Role

It is often said that the founding of Islam improved the status of women in its time. I† remember a lively conversation with an American Muslim man in which he stated that Islam proclaimed the equal status of women at a time "when Christians were still contemplating whether women were fully human beings with souls!" Yet, there is considerable contemporary debate about this issue. On the one hand, the Qur`an provides much support for the equality of women and men. It is of no small account that the Qur`an addresses women explicitly, making clear that women as well as men are equally significant in God's eyes. For example, the Qur`an states:

> *Those who believe, men and women, befriend one another, and enjoin what is right and prohibit what is wrong. They observe their devotional obligations, pay the zakat [alms], and obey God and His Apostle. God will be merciful to them, for God is all-mighty and all-wise.*[23]

In addition, there are sayings of the Prophet included in the *hadith* that make clear that equality is a central message of Islam: "All people are equal, as equal as the teeth of a comb. There is no claim of merit of an Arab over a non-Arab, or of a white over a black person, or of a male over a female, Only God-fearing people merit a preference with God."[24] On the other hand, however, certain passages in the Qur`an and *hadith* appear to modify this, indicating that men are superior to women (e.g., one male witness is equal to two female witnesses in court) and that men are to be women's protectors.

More important, the interpretation of passages in the Qur`an can lead to very different conceptualizations of Islamic law respecting women. Take, for example, the following two translations (i.e., interpretations) of Qur`an 4:34—a passage that is often invoked when the subject of women's position in Muslim society is discussed:

One translation makes clear that women are to be subordinated to men:

> *Men are in charge of women, because Allah hath made the one of them to excel the other, and because they spend of their property (for the support of women). So good women are the obedient, guarding in secret that which Allah hath guarded. As for those from whom ye fear rebellion, admonish them and banish them to beds apart, and scourge [i.e., beat] them. Then if they obey you, seek not a way against them. Lo! Allah is ever High Exalted, Great.*[25]

†Barbara McGraw.

Another translation of the very same passage reflects a completely different interpretation. Here, men are admonished to treat women well—even women they find "averse":

> *Men are the support of women as God gives some more means than others, and because they spend of their wealth (to provide for them). So women who are virtuous are obedient to God and guard the hidden as God has guarded it. As for women you feel are averse, talk to them suasively; then leave them alone in bed (without molesting them) and go to bed with them (when they are willing). If they open out to you, do not seek an excuse for blaming them. Surely God is sublime and great.*[26]

Throughout the centuries and in different localities, the ambiguities arising from seemingly conflicting passages and different interpretations have resulted in various views of Islam's injunctions with respect to women. One thing is clear, however, like Buddhism, Islam took the "woman question" to heart in its primary texts. Unlike Buddhism, however, Islam addressed the role of women in society at large, providing an adjusted vision of women's rights and role in society from that which had preceded it.

Early Islam after Muhammad: The Continuation of Patriarchal Patterns

Whatever may have been intended regarding the status of women, soon after its founding, Islam adopted most of the patriarchal patterns of the monotheistic religions—Judaism, Christianity, and Zoroastrianism—that prevailed in the Middle East and the Mediterranean at the time of Islam's founding.[27] It also supplanted the polytheistic religions that had remained, along with their goddesses and the priestesses who served them.

There are accounts of women of considerable independence, education, and wealth who lived prior to the founding and popularization of Islam, some of whom, like Muhammad's sponsor and wife Khadija, were involved in commerce. Islam itself, however, moved away from this toward a more restricted role for women in the home in the years following Islam's founding when it became feudalistic. The patriarchal family structure with the male as head of the family, the woman leaving her natal home to join her husband's family, and the female family members being placed in subordinate positions replaced the variety of family structures that were found outside the monotheistic norms of the time, for example, matrilineal families where the woman remained in her natal family tribe and the husband visited her there.[28]

Still, in many ways, Muslim women were provided with rights unavailable to other women of the same time and place. For example, marriage was not to occur without the bride's consent, and women were given the right to negotiate the terms of their marriage contracts, including the amount of the bride price to be paid by the groom (marriage being a contractual matter and not a sacrament in Islam). The bride price was paid to the bride herself, as a token of love and sincerity on the part of the groom, rather than to her father. Women were permitted to keep the bride price after marriage and, in most cases, even after divorce. Women also were permitted to maintain and manage their own finances, and the husband was to support his wife in accordance with his means regardless of his wife's own wealth. If special provisions were negotiated into the marriage contract regarding divorce or there were other sufficient grounds (e.g., desertion, abuse), a woman had access to divorce (although for men divorces were much easier to obtain). Divorced and widowed women were permitted to remarry, and women were given rights to their children. Under the Qur'an, women could own and inherit property, although a woman could only inherit one-half that of a man because she was not expected to provide for a family as was he.[29] In addition, women's religious obligations were the same as men's, reflecting the Qur'anic teaching that men and women are equally worthy in the eyes of God.

Attitudes and taboos regarding menstruation and childbirth, which we have seen in other religions, were greatly curtailed in Islam.[30] Sex within marriage was not stigmatized, as a good marriage relationship was considered ideal, as opposed to celibacy, which is more highly regarded in most of Hinduism and some forms of Christianity, as well as elsewhere. Further, the Qur'an and the Prophet Muhammad spoke against certain common practices regarding females that had prevailed among pre-Islamic Arabs, such as the inheritance of women as "property" and the practice of burying female infants alive.

In addition, polygyny (marrying many wives), which was a common practice in pre-Islamic society, was severely limited. In some pre-Islamic tribes, each man had numerous wives—over seventy-five in some cases. However, the Qur'an permitted men to marry only up to four wives, and then only if the wives could be treated equally by the husband. The Qur'an also states that it is unlikely that wives can be treated equally and so urges the husband to choose only one.[31] Moreover, many Islamic scholars have argued persuasively that the main reason Islam permitted polygyny was to provide for women who did not otherwise have husbands in a world that offered no acceptable alternative to marriage and childbearing for women. In other words, marrying additional wives was a charitable thing to do. This was exemplified by Muhammad, who after Khadijah, his first wife, died, married, in addition to Aisha, unmarriageable women, for example, an older widow and a woman who had come from a family of non-Muslims and was later abandoned by her husband through divorce.[32]

However, many of these developments were, in practice, greatly diminished as Islam developed. By the third century of Islam, despite the rights granted in the Qur'an, practices and customs of the localities prevailed. The father or other male head of household arranged the marriages of the daughters and, while nominally hers, the wife's property generally was administered by her husband. Despite Qur'anic passages to the contrary, sons were preferred over daughters due to economic considerations—the son being perceived as more able to add to the wealth of the family.[33] Divorce, which had always been easier for a husband to obtain than a wife, became even more readily obtainable for men. A practice evolved that required only that the husband proclaim three times that his wife was divorced.

Thereafter the divorce was irrevocable. Equality in religious obligations was also undermined. Women were admonished to pray in the home rather than in the mosque, and the general practice was that when women did attend services at a mosque, they were to remain in the rear.[34]

In addition, the apparent sanctioning of polygyny in the Qur`an provided religious justification for those men who wished to continue the practice. Regardless of what may have been intended by the Qur`an, its express acknowledgement that men can marry several wives led, not to reform (as many have argued was the original intention), but to abuses, including the development of the harem system.

Many restrictive Islamic practices with respect to women were originally customs of neighboring peoples and conquered peoples that were assimilated into Islamic society. In *Women and Gender in Islam,* Leila Ahmed contends that the Islamic practice of segregating the sexes was not endemic to Islam but came from the practices of the Christians and Jews of the Middle East. Similarly, she contends that the practice of veiling women (which, in some countries even today involves

Several veiled Muslim women ride in a donkey cart with a solitary man walking along on a street in Cairo, Egypt. ■

covering the woman from head to toe with a veil called the **chador** or *burqua* in its more severe version) came from the people of Sasania (Persia) who were conquered by the Muslims.[35]

Most significantly, until very recently, the Qur'an was interpreted by men who were in authority and, because women's education was limited, women generally were ignorant of Qur'anic teachings that might have mitigated against the restrictions placed on them.[36]

Whatever the source of such restrictive practices for women, religious sanctions for them were soon found by those interpreting the scriptures, and such practices have prevailed to such a degree that they have become identified inextricably with Middle Eastern Islam. By medieval times, the *shari`a* was codified and many customs and traditions of the times regarding women were included, despite dubious authority for them in the Qur'an.[37]

Significantly, interpretations favoring restrictive practices regarding women reflected a Muslim ideal of womanhood that we will recognize as mirroring the ideal we have found in many other religions, including Christianity, at times in their various histories—as well as the same suspicions and negative stereotypes. Here, as there, motherhood, chastity, purity, fidelity, obedience to the father and husband, beauty, and modesty became the watchwords of the lives of women. A woman was to be self-sacrificing, being concerned only with the well-being of her husband and children, and she was to be agreeable and sexually available to her husband.[38]

Motherhood always has held a highly respected place in Islamic society, however, providing mothers with considerable status in the home—one that could be a source of great pride and self-esteem. Still, a woman was valued primarily for her ability to produce sons for her husband's family—the bringing forth of girls being a discredit to her. Because polygyny was expressly permitted in Islam, a woman's failure in this regard was a threat to her status in the home. If she did not produce sons, another wife could be brought into the home to serve that purpose, or a wife might be divorced.

Furthermore, women were considered to be ignorant—unfit for high learning—and in many ways inferior to men, and they generally were disparaged as untrustworthy. Accordingly, control of women was considered justified. Many *hadiths* reflect these attitudes.[39]

As we have seen elsewhere, virginity was highly valued in Islam. A woman who was found not to be a virgin on her marriage night was considered a grave dishonor to her family. Sometimes she was killed in order to remove the disgrace. To guard against such shame and dire consequences, woman were kept secluded from the outside world in the home (a practice known as *purdah*); thus, her association with others was highly guarded and her education was restricted to her domestic vocation.

Islam continued the common practice of circumcising male children. In addition, the practice of female circumcision was adopted in many places, and continues today, despite there being no authority for it in the Qur'an. The circumcision of females is much more involved than that for males because it involves a clitoredectomy, usually without anesthesia when the girl is between 7 and 8, and in some areas the operation is even more involved. It apparently was a widespread cultural practice in the Arabian peninsula, as well as other areas in the world, at the time of the rise of Islam. According to Nawal al-Saadawi, it was even practiced in Europe and could be found there as late as the ninteenth century.[40]

Saadawi (b. 1931) is an Egyptian woman who overcame her religious and cultural circumstances to become a doctor and is today a leading Islamic feminist, activist, and prolific writer. In her book *The Hidden Face of Eve: Women in the Arab World,* Saadawi provides a graphic account of her own circumcision. She recounts that she was taught that it was necessary in order to purify her of an offending and shameful organ on her body and to make her a more suitable and chaste wife.[41] Today the practice seems to be limited for the most part to countries in Africa such as Egypt and the Sudan. It has been outlawed officially in Egypt with the highest court there upholding the ban in December 1997 after a three-year battle between reformists who opposed the practice and traditionalists who wished to continue it. However, despite the ban, it is extensively practiced in Egyptian villages. Female circumcision has been raised as a social and legal issue in the United States and elsewhere when families from African countries who continue the practice settle in those countries.

Veiling, segregation, seclusion, and female circumcision (where it has been practiced) can all be seen as the strategies adopted by Islam to achieve the same goals we have seen in nearly all of the preceding religions we have studied—the control of women's sexuality for the preservation of chastity and the reproduction of sons for the husband's family. In medieval times, when the *shari`a* was codified, such restrictive practices were rigorously followed. Significantly, such practices became symbols of a family's social status and have continued into modern times in many Islamic lands, particularly in urban environments in the upper and middle classes, despite the call for reform by those who argue that these traditions have no place in an authentic Islam.

Interestingly, throughout Islam's history, rural women generally have not been segregated, secluded, or veiled. Consequently, such women may have had more opportunity to participate in social situations in which they found themselves; however, this should not be overstated because rural peoples, who tend to be poor, are limited in other ways related to their economic conditions. Moreover, because such practices have been symbols of status, a family that becomes upwardly mobile is likely to adopt them as a reflection of the ideal.

Muslim Women: Leaders, Saints, and Practitioners

These extremely restrictive practices and the severe limitations they placed on women's lives do not tell the whole story, however. From the beginning there have been women who have figured proudly in Islamic heritage and have served as models. One especially notable example is the Prophet Muhammad's first wife, Khadijah, who was considerably older than he. She was a wealthy and independent trader who hired merchants, such as Muhammad, to trade for her abroad. She married Muhammad and provided him with financial support, making his religious vocation possible. It was she who assuaged his doubts about his first revelations and convinced him to make them known. Some argue that Khadijah's independence and wealth reflect more the attitudes toward women of pre-Islamic culture, which permitted more expanded roles for women than did Islam. Nevertheless, Khadijah figures prominently in the development of Islam and is honored for the part that she played.

After Khadijah's death, Muhammad married several women (because polygyny was common at the time), including Aisha, who became his favorite wife after Khadijah. Unlike Khadijah, Aisha lived a more secluded and protected life in the home. It is reported that she was required to speak to others from behind a partition. (Some Islamic interpreters have used this as a justification for the veiling of women.)[42] Nevertheless, Muhammad prized Aisha for her wisdom and insight, and it is reported that he received some of his revelations in her presence and died in her arms.[43] She lived for over forty years after Muhammad's death, and her accounts of the household have provided Islam with a wealth of information about the Prophet which, in turn, has been one of the most important contributions to the *hadith* and a significant influence on interpretation of the Qur`an.[44] It is said that the Prophet told his followers to take half of the knowledge of his revelations from Aisha and the other half from all the rest of his companions.[45] More important, Aisha apparently had considerable authority in the early fledgling Muslim community.[46] (Some reformers have argued that this provides evidence that women held high status in the early Medina community, and, therefore, that it should be so today.)[47]

Another important female figure in the early history of Islam is Fatima, Muhammad's third daughter. She is today a highly revered saint of Islam who has been referred to by one scholar as "the fountainhead of female spirituality in Islam."[48]

We have already encountered one of the most revered women in the history of Islam, Rabi`a al-Adawiya (?713–801), a mystic poet who lived a life as an ascetic in total submission to Allah. The great Muslim reformer Al-Ghazali cites Rabi`a, who was a considerable influence on him, as an important Islamic saint. Rabi`a, who never married, is especially known for having expressed her pure devotion to God as love. Her poems are prominent in Sufi literature, and many legends regarding her abound in Islamic lore. As Charis Waddy has pointed out, Rabi`a's acceptance as a saint, as well as the reverence for other women as saints, makes it clear that women could be as saintly as men, although this fact often seems to have required additional explanation because of the generally disparaging attitudes toward women.[49]

In general, Islamic women have proven to be as resourceful as other women, around the world and throughout history, who have been forced by custom and religion into living narrow lives. Here, as we have seen elsewhere, a "little tradition" has evolved. Many Islamic women seek out and provide access for others to the world of spiritual powers involving warding off evil, healing, good omens, and the like. Viewed as heretical by the authorities, such practices nevertheless inhere in Islam whether or not officially sanctioned.

As for the official practice, again, women are restricted, being admonished to pray in the home. Nevertheless, women are significant participants in certain ways. One primary obligation of Muslims is to give alms. Generally, it is the women who actually perform this duty for the household. Moreover, Muslim women are frequent visitors to the shrines of saints such as Fatima. There, women have the opportunity to meet with other women outside of the seclusion of the family home; there women pray to saints for the good of the family, asking for help in matters pertaining to health, marriage, economic benefits, and the like.[50] Women also participate in the *hajj*. The custom is that the pilgrims dress in a manner that does not distinguish them from others on the basis of wealth, class, and, to some degree, sex.[51] This is to reflect the basic equality of all peoples before God.

Today's Middle Eastern Muslim Women and the Winds of Change

Today economic considerations are influencing changes in many Islamic countries. Women have moved out of the home and into the workplace. While this may be viewed by some as an advance because it opens doors to greater choices for women, others point out that often the opportunities provided are not nearly those provided to men. In those countries where segregation of the sexes is still the norm, segregation is the norm in the workplace as well. As a result, women generally are limited to what becomes "women's work." Not surprisingly, these are the lower-level tasks. Many work in the domestic, food, and textile fields.[52] Still, in some countries, such as Egypt, Pakistan, Turkey, Bangladesh, and Jordan, many Muslim women hold important positions in leadership. Women are governmental officials, doctors, and professors, and hold positions in other professions as well. As these women shatter the mold of the stereotypes of women, there is an increasingly loud call to shatter the religious justifications for restrictive practices as well. On the other hand, the Islamic resurgence we spoke of earlier has led in some places, such as Iran and Afghanistan, to a return to strict tradition.

Women and men who favor women's rights are reinterpreting the Qur`an and the *shari a* and pushing for reforms that they contend are consistent with the original egalitarian spirit of Islam. There has been a revival of the principle of *ijtihad* (creative original interpretation) that was used by the early interpreters of the Qur`an but was abandoned when the *shari`a* became codified in the twelfth century.[53] Reinterpreted texts through *ijtihad* have provided fodder for a feminist critique and reconsideration in modern times of Islamic practices regarding women.

Interestingly, today, the veil has become a significant symbol for both the reformers and the traditionalists. Those who seek reform view the veil as a symbol of oppression and the act of casting it off as the claiming of women's autonomy and rejection of oppression. On the other hand, the traditionalists view the veil as a symbol of a strong and clear Islamic tradition. For them, taking up the veil is a moral act and a rejection of Western mores and practices, which are held by them to be corrupting influences.

It is important to recall that the reformist/traditionalist conflicts with respect to women are inextricably intertwined with nationalist sentiments in parts of Islam. Almost the entirety of Islam had been colonized by the British, Dutch, French, or

Italians over the course of the nineteenth century. British and Dutch rule left the indigenous culture largely intact. On the other hand, the French and Italians required assimilation into European cultural and religious norms, placing additional stress on those cultures. Those countries where the indigenous culture was most threatened have, for the most part, a less favorable attitude toward reform. Understandably, they want to return to their own ways, including practices pertaining to women. In countries such as Iran after the Ayatollah Khomeini came to power, many women have willingly taken up the veil as a symbol of the return to tradition after it had been denied, while others who oppose it are nevertheless subjected to the laws enforcing a return to tradition. In countries such as Egypt, where the indigenous culture was not as threatened, the social environment is more conducive to change, and because of this Egypt has been a primary generator of ideas regarding reform for women. There nationalism has supported reforms for women as the people sought to move away from practices they view as "backward," and that were used as justifications for colonial paternalism by the British.[54]

Modern feminism in Islam formally began with the publishing of *The Liberation of the Women* by Oasin Amin, a male Egyptian lawyer, in 1899. Badran and Cooke contend, however, that an "invisible" feminism existed from the mid-1800s, when middle- and upper-class women's publications were read by women in the harems. From the 1920s, however, feminism very much became visible as women began to organize public movements—first in Egypt and later in Lebanon, Syria, Iraq, and the Sudan. Women organized the Egyptian Feminist Union in the 1920s, the Arab Feminist Union (a pan-Arab organization) in 1944, and the Arab Women's Solidarity Association (also a pan-Arab organization) in the mid-1980s, among others.[55]

Today it is argued by reformists that the Qur`an must be read in the context of its time. This means that the egalitarian spirit held by such reformists to be at the core of the Qur`an is what should hold sway, particularly with respect to women, rather than applying the law in contemporary situations as it was applied then. The law as applied then, they argue, has more to do with acknowledging the social circumstances at that time rather than establishing set rules for all time.[56] For example, they argue that when the Qur`an states that men are to be women's "protectors," it is acknowledging the precarious position that women experienced in the Prophet's time; it did not establish a permanent paternalism that should apply in all times and places.

Contemporary Islam is replete with contradictions that reflect the competing winds of reform and tradition. These competing forces are playing themselves out in various ways in different contexts in the vast and varied forms of Islam found, not only in the Middle East, but all around the world. Where women stand within these various contexts depends on many things: the traditional customs of each area in which Islam is found, the degree to which such customs have been assimilated into Islam, the resolution of the reformist/traditionalist debate in each society, the degree of acceptance or rejection of Western ideas of modernity, and the contributions of Islamic feminism. Consequently, Islam is likely to remain ever-varied as it continues to spread throughout the world in the twenty-first century, and its attitudes and practices with respect to women will be just as widely varied as well.

✸ Summary

Islam is a religion with a highly distinctive cultural and spiritual atmosphere. The word *islam* means "submission"; the faith centers on the submission of individuals and communities to the absolute sovereignty of Allah, God, in all areas of life.

Muhammad, the Prophet of Islam, was a trader from Mecca who began at the age of 40 to receive lines of powerful and beautiful Arabic while meditating in a cave. These lines included words of warning to repent, moral admonishments, and above all revelations of God's greatness. They were recorded by scribes and after the Prophet's death were compiled into the Qur`an, the book believed by Muslims to be the last and greatest Divine revelation to humanity, just as Muhammad is seen as the last and greatest in a line of prophets sent to restore the simple, primal religion of justice and pure monotheism. Muhammad's spiritual purification movement also became a political movement. This is understandable because the Qur`an emphasizes that while conversion to Islam should never be by force, its faith and moral strictures should be practiced in a society that abides by them and seeks to implement them in all human spheres of activity, including the political and economic. By the time of Muhammad's death, most of Arabia had been united under his banner; within a century Islamic forces had spread across much of Africa and Asia to create an empire ruled by a caliph, or successor to Muhammad in the political realm. The caliphs reigned over a brilliant Islamic civilization for several centuries, but finally their realm was replaced by several regional Muslim empires, such as the Moghul, Persian, and Ottoman. Still later, after the experience of European colonial rule in some places, these were succeeded by the numerous Islamic nation-states of today.

The practice of Islam centers on what are commonly called its Five Pillars: reciting the creed that states that there is no God but Allah, and Muhammad is his Prophet; praying five times daily; giving alms; keeping a fast during the month of Ramadan; and once in one's life, if possible, making the pilgrimage to Mecca. The daily prayers are said according to certain set procedures, facing in the direction of Mecca; thus, like the pilgrimage, they reinforce the communal sense of Islam. On Friday noon, prayers are customarily said congregationally in a mosque, accompanied by sermons. The mosque, with its austere ornamentation and its niche pointing in the direction of Mecca, together with its traditional role as community, educational, and judicial center, is a beautiful expression of the spirit of Islam.

Islamic culture has been shaped by several factors: the predominance of the city, the court, and trade in its social and economic world; and the discouragement of representational art and of religious poetics imitative of the Qur`an. Its art has therefore emphasized ornamentation and calligraphy; within these limits it has developed splendid forms that well suggest the universal presence of God. Its poetic and prose literature has been chiefly developed within the mystical traditions; it often borrows boldly from verses of love and intoxication to describe the relation of the soul to God. During the Golden Age of the Caliphate, science, philosophy, and theology were extensively cultivated. Learned men not only preserved the best of classical thought but made important advances, which were finally transmitted to Europe.

Islam is divided into two main groups. Sunni Islam emphasizes the traditional path of Islamic life as interpreted by the consensus of scholars and the community. Shi`a Islam, while following the traditional path, also puts its faith in the authority of Imams who are Muhammad's hereditary successors. Now, the true Imam is said to be in hiding but expected to emerge at the apocalyptic moment. Shi`a Islam has been productive of most sectarian movements within Islam; it predominates in Iran and southern Iraq.

Islamic mysticism, called Sufism in the West, focuses on the presence of the Divine oneness everywhere and offers paths to the attainment of union with God. Several great orders of Sufis are spread across the Muslim world. Their practices include chanting, dancing, whirling, and meditation. The role of the *shaykh*, or spiritual mentor, is very important. Great mystics have often been venerated, in life and after death in their tombs, as great saints capable of working miracles. The literature of Sufism is often of remarkable beauty and has won much admiration both in the Islamic world and outside it.

In the world today, Islam is experiencing much vitality, particularly in comparison to its situation in the nineteenth century. It is growing, Muslim nations are becoming wealthy and important, and there are many signs of spiritual revitalization. Early in the twentieth century, Muslim countries such as Turkey sought to meet the demands of the modern world by secularization, but later, as in the Iranian revolution of 1979, a militant and fundamentalist Islam sought to impose conservative values and an alternative Islamic social order to capitalism and communism. This resurgent Islam is a major force in the world today.

It is very difficult to make generalizations about women in Islam as its practices differ in the many places it can be found around the world. Moreover, there is considerable debate about the "woman question" in Islam, and the answers to that question, differ based on various interpretations of the Qur`an and *hadiths*. In general, it can be said that, when founded, Islam provided women with greater rights than had been experienced by women before. Yet, just as we have seen in many other religions, attitudes and customs from the social context in which Islam has found itself have been assimilated into Islamic culture and religious justifications have been found for them. Although motherhood always has held a place of high esteem for women in Islam, practices such as seclusion (*purdah*), veiling, segregation, and, in some places, female circumcision have limited women's lives greatly. Nevertheless, there have been prominent women in Islam's history who have provided alternative models for women. Today there is much tension between reformists and traditionalists. The reformists take a progressivist stance toward the role of women in Islam and seek to reinterpret the Qur`an in order to return, in their view, to Islam's original intention. After suffering the travails of European colonialism, the traditionalists wish to return, in their view, to the core of Islamic tradition, including the return of women to their traditional place in the home. Casting off or embracing the practice of veiling women has become a major symbol in this struggle.

❈ Questions for Review

1. Describe the "feel" and characteristics of Islamic society.

2. Discuss ways in which Islam relates to the individual and to the community, and ways in which its legalistic and mystical (or sainthood) aspects are expressed.

3. Summarize the life of the prophet Muhammad, placing his life in the context of his times and assessing the nature of his immense impact on both religion and history.

4. Talk about the Qur`an as a book of revelation, referring to its style, content, message, and meaning.

5. Outline the faith and practice of the Five Pillars of Islam: the statement of faith, the prayers, the giving of alms, the fast of Ramadan, and pilgrimage to Mecca.

6. Describe how the Muslim's five daily prayers are done and what they mean.

7. Describe the characteristic architecture, the interior arrangements, and use of the mosque.

8. Describe the history and main features of such principal areas of Islamic culture as art, poetry, prose literature, science, philosophy, and theology.

9. Explain the difference between Sunni and Shi`a Islam, and summarize the history of the Shi`a movement.

10. Discuss Islamic mysticism or Sufism, explaining where it has been in tension with mainstream Islam and in what ways it has deepened and widened Islam's life.

11. Survey the position of Islam in the modern world, giving special attention to its varied responses to the changes wrought by modernization, including the resurgence of Islamic fundamentalism.

12. Discuss the prospects of dialogue among the three great monotheistic faiths: Judaism, Christianity, and Islam.

13. Discuss the impact on differing interpretations of the Qur`an on Islamic women.

14. Describe how customary practices of people of the surrounding regions were assimilated into Islamic law.

15. Talk about the role of women and the ways in which it is discussed as a central topic in contemporary Islam.

❋ Suggested Readings on Islam

General
Christopher, John B., *The Islamic Tradition*. New York: Harper & Row, 1972. A brief introduction covering all cultural aspects of Islamic civilization.

Cragg, Kenneth, *The Call of the Minaret*. London and New York: Oxford University Press, 1956. A brilliant and empathetic treatment of Islamic theology, with frequent comparisons to Christian concepts.

———, *The House of Islam*. Belmont, CA: Dickenson, 1969. A splendid introduction.

Denny, Frederick M., *An Introduction to Islam*. New York: Macmillan, 1985. A very good introductory textbook.

Esposito, John L., *The Islamic Threat: Myth or Reality?* New York: Oxford University Press, 1992. A balanced, valuable summary by an experienced scholar of the issues surrounding Islam's role in the contemporary world, especially as it confronts the West.

———, ed., *The Oxford History of Islam*. New York: Oxford University Press, 1999.

Hovannisian, and Georges Sabagh, eds., *Religion and Culture in Medieval Islam*. New York: Cambrige University Press, 1999.

Martin, Richard C., *Islam: A Cultural Perspective*. Englewood Cliffs, NJ: Prentice Hall, 1982. An excellent shorter introduction to Islam and the Islamic cultural world.

Morgan, Kenneth, *Islam: The Straight Path*. New York: Ronald Press, 1958. A collection of popular papers by contemporary Muslims; a good introduction to the Islamic faith.

Nagal. Tilman, *The History of Islamic Theology from Muhammad to the Present*. Thomas Thornton, trans. Princeton, NJ: Markus Weiner, 2000.

Rahman, Fazlur, *Islam*. Chicago: University of Chicago Press, 1979. A solid textbook by a prominent Muslim scholar, oriented toward history.

Schimmel, Annemarie, *Islam: An Introduction*. Albany: State University of New York Press, 1992.

Voll, John Obert, *Islam, Continuity and Change in the Modern World*. 2nd ed. Syracuse, NY: Syracuse Univerity Press, 1994.

Watt, William Montgomery, *What Is Islam?* London: Longman, 1968. An excellent overview by a distinguished Islamicist.

Williams, John Alden, *Islam*. New York: Braziller, 1961. A useful anthology of Muslim literature.

The Qur`an (Koran)
Abu-Hamdiyyah, Mohammad, *The Qur`an: An Introduction*. London and New York: Routledge, 2000.

Arberry, A. J., *The Koran Interpreted,* 2 vols. New York: Macmillan, 1955. Probably the most readable and literary English version.

Cleary, Thomas, *The Essential Koran*. San Francisco: Harper, 1993. A sensitive, poetic translation of selections from the Qur`an, particularly valuable for notes explaining allusions and poetic wordplays in the original but untranslatable into English.

Dawood, N. J., trans., *The Koran*. Baltimore, MD: Penguin Books, 1968. Also recommended; a sound and accessible translation.

Hawting, G. R., and Abdul-Kader A. Shareef, *Approaches to the Qur`an*. London; New York: Routledge, 1993.

Pickthall, Mohammed, *The Meaning of the Glorious Koran*. New York: Mentor, n.d. An interesting translation by an English convert to Islam.

Islamic Mysticism

Arberry, A. J., *Sufism*. New York: Harper Torchbooks, 1970. A brief, authoritative, and well-written introduction.

Knysh, Alexander D., *Islamic Mysticism: A Short History*. Boston: Brill, 2000.

Schimmel, Annemarie, *Mystical Dimensions of Islam*. Chapel Hill: University of North Carolina Press, 1975. A definitive work on the subject.

Shah, Idries, *The Sufis*. Garden City, NY: Doubleday, 1964. Attractive, moving, readable, much influenced by the author's own point of view.

Smith, Margaret, *Readings from the Mystics of Islam*. London: Luzac, 1950. Beautiful translation of original sources.

Trimingham, J. Spencer, *The Sufi Orders in Islam*. London and New York: Oxford University Press, 1971. Scholarly; gives an incomparable insight into an important aspect of Islamic life.

Islam in America

Haddad, Yvonne, *The Muslims of America*. New York: Oxford University Press, 1991. The standard work.

Haddad, Yvonne, and Jane Idleman Smith, *Mission to America: Five Islamic Sectarian Movements in North America*. Gainesville: University of Florida Press, 1993. A pioneering study of such groups as the Druze, Ahmadiyya, and Ismaili in the U.S. and Canada.

———, eds., *Muslim Communities in North America*. Albany: State University of New York Press, 1994.

———, ed., *Muslim Communities in North America*. Albany: State University of New York Press, 1994. A collection of sociological papers on Muslim groups.

Koszegi, Michael A., and J. Gordon Melton, eds., *Islam in North America: A Sourcebook*. New York: Garland, 1992.

Lincoln, C. Eric, *The Black Muslims in America*. Boston: Beacon Press, 1961. A classic study of this movement as it was at the time it began to attract nationwide attention.

McCloud, Aminah Beverly, *African American Islam*. New York: Routledge, 1995.

Smith, Jane I., *Islam in America*. New York: Columbia University Press, 1999.

Turner, Richard Brent, *Islam in the African-American Experience*. Bloomington: Indiana University Press, 1997.

Women in Islam

Abu-Lughod, Lila, ed., *Remaking Women: Feminism and Modernity in the Middle East*. Princeton, NJ: Princeton University Press, 1998.

Afkhami, Mahnaz, ed., *Faith and Freedom: Women's Human Rights in the Muslim World*. Syracuse, NY: Syracuse University Press, 1995.

Ahmed, Leila, *Women and Gender in Islam: Historical Roots of a Modern Debate*. New Haven, CT, and London: Yale University Press, 1992. A good overview, providing historical perspective.

Aili, Azra Asghar, *The Emergence of Feminism Among Indian Muslim Women, 1920–1947*. Oxford and New York: Oxford University Press, 2000.

Badawi, Leila, "Islam," in *Women in Religion,* Jean Holm with John Bowker, ed. London and New York: Pinter Publishers, 1994, pp. 84–112. A useful summary.

Badran, Margot, and Miriam Cooke, eds., *Opening the Gates: A Century of Arab Feminist Writing*. Bloomington and Indianapolis: Indiana University Press, 1990. Women in Islam from an inside perspective.

Duley, Margot I., "Women in the Islamic Middle East and North Africa" in *The Cross-Cultural Study of Women: A Comprehensive Guide,* Margot I. Duley and Mary I. Edwards, eds. New York: The Feminist Press, 1986, pp. 406–37. Provides valuable information, although a somewhat dispirited treatment.

Engineer, Asghar Ali, *The Rights of Women in Islam*. New York: St. Martin's Press, 1992. Valuable treatment of the legal aspects.

——, *The Qur'an, Women, and Modern Society*. New Delhi: Sterling Pub., 1999.

Fernea, Elizabeth Warnock, *In Search of Islamic Feminism: One Woman's Global Journey*. New York/London/Toronto/Sydney/Auckland: Doubleday, 1998. An intriguing narrative.

Haddad, Yvonne Yazbeck, and John L. Esposito, eds., *Islam, Gender, and Social Change*. New York: Oxford University Press, 1998.

Hekmat, Anwar. *Women and the Koran: The Status of Women in Islam*. Amherst, NY: Promentheus Books, 1997.

Nasir, Jamal J., *The Status of Women under Islamic Law and under Modern Islamic Legislation*, 2nd ed. London/Dordrecht/Boston: Graham and Trotman, 1994. Useful legal perspective.

Roded, Ruth, ed., *Women in Islam and the Middle East: A Reader*. New York: I. B. Tauris; St. Martin's Press, 1999.

al-Saadawi, Nawal [El Saadawi], *The Hidden Face of Eve: Women in the Arab World*, Sherif Hetata, trans. and ed. Boston: Beacon Press, 1982. A not-to-be-missed work by the renowned Islamic feminist.

Schimmel, Annemarie, *My Soul Is a Woman: The Feminine in Islam*, Susan H. Ray, trans. New York: Continuum, 1997. Treatment by an outstanding western Islamicist.

Smith, Jane I., "Islam" in *Women in World Religions*, Arvind Sharma, ed. Albany: State University of New York Press, 1987, pp. 235–50. A good summary.

Smith, Margaret, *Rabi`a: The Life and Work of Rabi`a and Other Women Mystics in Islam*. Oxford.: Oneworld, 1994. Classic study of Islam's most famous woman.

Stowasser, Barbara Freyer, *Women in the Qur`an, Traditions, and Interpretation*. New York: Oxford University Press, 1994.

Waddy, Charis, *Women in Muslim History*. London/New York: Longman, 1980. Detailed and informative survey.

CHAPTER TEN

Spirits Rising

New Religious Movements

CHAPTER OBJECTIVES

After studying this chapter, you should be able to

❋ Discuss circumstances in which new religious movements
   are particularly likely to arise.

❋ Cite and explain the seven types of new religious
   movements discussed in this chapter.

❋ Explain the features of new religious movements.

❋ Give a few good examples of new religious movements.

The World of New Religions

The worldwide religious scene is like the weather; change is always in the wind. As much as purists throughout the centuries may have wished to maintain tradition, religion's thought, practice, and institutions are always changing shape—sometimes in almost imperceivable increments and sometimes by leaps and bounds. One important aspect of religious change is the rise of new religious movements. It is essential, obviously, to know the main features of the major religions, and that is what we have studied thus far in this book. But we must also realize that every one of them once was a new religion and now is steadily challenged by other new religions. Some "new religions," such as Buddhism, Christianity, and Islam, have gone on to become major world religions themselves. Many other new religions have not become large or have not survived at all. But often they have left traces in their cultures and have played a part in world history. Most important of all, they have met the religious needs of people of their times and places, frequently needs that the major, established religions on the scene could not meet or perhaps did not even recognize.

New religions may arise under many circumstances. They may be a way of dealing with extreme disruption of a traditional society, when the former religion seems powerless or discredited, and only a new revelation can offer hope. They may be the result of rapid social change, even if sometimes equated to "progress," which seems to require a new religious worldview. They may even appear in a society that from the outside appears full of hope and doing well, like the United States in the 1840s (Spiritualism), the 1960s (Nichiren Shoshu and many, many other new religions from East and West), or the 1980s (the New Age Movement), but which is experiencing internal, maybe intergenerational, dislocations. Whatever the case, the result is that some people within the society find that the old religion has lost authority and doesn't seem to be in touch with "what's happening now" and they require a new religion as a flag of their new, distinctive identities. Or it may be that people feel called by the Divine to a new way of worship and a new way of being in the world—just as others have felt called to the recognized major world religions.

Nothing is automatic about the emergence of new religions in particular times and places. They do not always seem to be the result of stresses greater than the usual, and some moments of crisis in human history have produced a conservative return to a strict and recognized tradition rather than new religious responses. The appeal of a new religious movement is a complex combination of a setting that has produced some deep-level dissonance between religion and people's present experience, together with just the right message or, in some cases, a charismatic prophet, neither too conventional nor too radical, with the right vocabulary to inspire followers.

Types of New Religions

New religions are of varying types. Of course we cannot presume to categorize all new religious movements in the world, and even if we could, few would present characteristics that fall neatly into only one category. Nevertheless, it is useful to speak in terms of "ideal types," while recognizing many variations in practice.

First are what we shall call here "Reactive Movements"—those are movements that involve a response to stress, usually social or political. Take for example the Mansren-Koreri movement in Irian Jaya (then Western New Guinea, part of the Dutch East Indies). This religion is commonly regarded as the first of the modern "cargo cults" that have swept particularly through such areas of Melanesian culture as this one. Like most new religions, it is based on older traditions. In West Irian Jaya, natives had long believed in a paradisiacal future state called *Koreri,* and in prophets called *konor* who were its heralds. The golden age was, like many in world mythology, really a return to an ideal state at the beginning. It had been ruled over by a beautiful young king called Mansren. Then, when his people rebelled against him, Mansren left and went to the West. But, it was believed, he would return someday to reestablish the realm of happiness, peace, and abundance.

In 1867, while Irian Jaya was under Dutch colonial rule, a *konor* had a vision that led him to call on the people to gather every night to sing new songs and enact dramatizations of the Mansren story; regular work was disrupted. By the 1880s the imminent arrival of the golden age was being prophesied, and in 1886 another *konor* declared that a ship loaded with cargo for Mansren's people was on the way. The enthusiasm took many forms, not a few of which obviously reflected tensions between the natives and their Dutch overlords. It was said that, since Mansren would soon establish a new and better society, it was no longer necessary to pay taxes or grow crops. These provocations caused some *konor* to be arrested and imprisoned for their trouble. Tension also arose between natives and white missionaries. Many of the former were nominal Christians, and their Mansren rhetoric came to include themes obviously inspired by the Bible, but some believers claimed that Mansren was greater than Christ and abandoned the mission churches.[1]

Many movements like this one swept through the South Pacific during the colonial era. Often the claim would be made that the whites had taken from the natives what was rightfully theirs but that a native hero or god, like Mansren, would come to restore them to their heritage. With him would arrive a great ship, or later airplane, such as the Europeans used in their trade, but this time loaded with goods for the natives. In many places cargo cultists ritually built docks or airstrips expressly for these vessels. At the same time, as a sign of the coming of a new age they would stop work on things of the old and perhaps abandon or give away all their goods.

Similar movements have occurred in North America. The words quoted on pages 42–43 are attributed to a leader of the Ghost Dance, a Native American movement of the 1890s at the very end of independent native culture, when prophets said that if certain dances calling back the ancestors were performed, the whites would be driven away and the vast buffalo herds that had once ranged the plains would return. Native Americans would then be able to hunt freely across the immense prairies instead of being cooped up on reservations, where they would need to break the soil and farm to survive.

Second, there are what we shall call here "Accommodationist Movements"—movements that arise out of well-established religions that have been introduced into a new cultural context. The Church on Earth by the Prophet Simon Kimbangu, the Kimbanguist Church in the Democratic Republic of the Congo (Zaire), formerly the Belgian Congo, is a Christian movement of this type. It was founded by Simon Kimbangu (1889–1951), who was converted in 1915 by Baptist missionaries and was at first a lay evangelist. But recalling a childhood vision of a man "neither black or white" appearing with a Bible, he became more and more an independent prophet, performing, it was widely rumored, many miraculous healings like Jesus himself. When he was imprisoned by the Belgian colonial authorities, the Christ-like drama of his life, as it was seen by his growing number of native followers, was further advanced, and he was viewed as a living martyr and special prophet called to bring Christ to the Africans. His church is now a flourishing institution with widespread religious, educational, and social service works. While avoiding any direct political involvement, it played a part in the development of the modern African consciousness that led to independence and nationhood in the Congo and elsewhere.

Third, there are what we shall call here "Spirit Movements"—movements in which the participants claim a special connection with beings from the spiritual realm—angels, ghosts, ancestors, nature spirits, and the like. These groups tend to emphasize a feeling-centered approach to religion and sometimes have been associated with reformist social causes, especially in their early years. The United States has been host to many of this type. One example is Spiritualism, a religion based on belief in communication with the spirits of the dead, primarily through mediumship. Its birth as a movement can be pinpointed quite precisely to the evening of March 31, 1848, in the home of John Fox, a farmer at Hydesville, New York, near Rochester. The family had two daughters at home, Margaretta, 11, and Kate, 8. They had been hearing strange noises in the house, rappings that sounded like the recently invented Morse Code. That evening Kate is said to have snapped her fingers at the rappings and said, "Here Mr. Splitfoot [the devil], do as I do," and commenced to work out a code with them. The mysterious sounds then identified themselves, not as the devil, but as coming from the spirit of a peddler who had been murdered in the house several years before the Foxes had moved in.

Reports of these goings-on created an immediate sensation in upstate New York and soon across the country. Committees investigated, newspapers presented long accounts, and, most important, countless other people tried communicating with spirits. Soon voice-mediumship—the spirit speaking through the lips of a "medium" in trance—proved to be much more efficient than raps or other means.

By the 1850s, Spiritualism was a vogue in the United States, and it quickly spread around the world. Popular mediums and Spiritualist lecturers drew large crowds, and "home circles" wherein people gathered of an evening to experiment with the new phenomena were popular. In some places like the Western Reserve section of Ohio (around Cleveland) regular churches were reported nearly empty as crowds thronged to meetings of the new faith. Persons as prominent as Horace Greeley, Abraham Lincoln, and Queen Victoria were said to be interested in it.

The spirit faith also made connections with contemporary developments, like science and current social thought, and in its concerns for slaves, women, and prisoners certainly showed sympathy for those who were oppressed within the orbit of what was called civilization. It met the needs of some in a new American generation born since the birth of the republic, hopeful of a new world through science, democracy, and social reform, open to new ideas and testing them directly.

Popular enthusiasm faded as some mediums were found to be fraudulent or unreliable, and as national attention was swallowed up by the Civil War. But Spiritualist churches can be found in America to this day.[2]

Some of the groups that are loosely referred to under the rubric "New Age" fall within the "Spirit Movement" category. Contact with Divine beings of one sort or another—angels, spirits, UFOs, biblical figures (although not in any sense recognized by mainstream denominations)—is a popular topic in New Age literature and practice. Some of the other groups described below also speak of contact with the spirit world, and mainstream religions always have a component that is in many ways like the "Spirit Movements." Sometimes the "Spirit" spoken of by a group is not a particular entity like an angel or ancestor. Instead, it is Spirit in a general sense.

A comparison also can be made to similar groups arising out of mainstream religions. The holiness revival discussed in the section "Women in Christianity" in Chapter 8, like Spiritualism, was an experience-based, feeling-oriented religious movement in which people were moved by the Holy Spirit to work for liberal social goals such as abolition of slavery and the rights of women.

One category that includes a great number of new religious groups is the fourth type, which we shall call here "New Revelation Sects." A new religious movement of this type is like a "sect"—a group that represents very strict, demanding adherence to the normative religion of the society—but differs in that it offers new revelatory teachings as well. At its outset, Christianity was a movement of this type. As we discussed in Chapter 8, Christianity arose out of Judaism, Jesus having provided the new revelations. But many others have arisen as well—some that have survived and become mainstream religions in their own right, or at least large denominations within a religion, and some that have remained small or have died out.

Mother Anne Lee (1735–1784) was the first leader of the United Society of Believers in Christ's Second Appearance, an American group commonly called the Shakers. The Shakers falls within the "New Revelation Sect" category. The Shakers' theology is Christian based, but Anne Lee's revelatory visions led her to teach that people should live in harmonious equality and that God was both male and female. The Shakers held to a life of simplicity and celebacy. After her death her followers claimed that Anne Lee's presence on earth was Jesus' Second Coming in female form. The Shaker movement declined after the Civil War, and today the only remaining active Shaker community is in Sabbathday Lake, Maine.

The controversial Family of Love, formerly known as the Children of God, also falls within this type. The Family of Love arose out of the Jesus Movement in the United States in the early 1970s and is still active today. Its founder, David Berg, was considered by the adherents to be a "prophet" of the end times. He had received revelations about the need to abandon worldly institutionalized structures, including traditional religious ones, and establish pure Christian communities.

Another example is the Church of Latter-Day Saints, also known as the Mormons, discussed in Chapter 8, which has become a major worldwide Christian denomination, today boasting 11 million members worldwide.

An all-encompassing version of this type is the Baha`i faith. Baha`i adherents regard Baha`ull`ah (1817–1892), upon whose ideas the faith is based, to have brought forth a new revelation—the oneness of all the major religions of the world and of humanity. Although it arises out of Islam, its founder an Iranian Shi`ite, it claims to fulfill Islamic, Zoroastrian, Jewish, and Christian prophesies and to be the ultimate expression of Divine faith. Baha`i now has 6 million members worldwide and 700,000 in the United States.

A relatively new movement of this type is Mai Chaza Church in Africa (discussed in the "New Face of World Christianity" section in Chapter 8), whose founder Mai Chaza established healing centers in the *Guta ra Jehova,* the "Cities of Jehovah."

In 1999–2000, much worldwide attention was attached to one new Chinese movement of this type, the Falun Gong, because of its persecution, as a dissident group, by the Chinese government. This movement in the Chinese Buddhist/Daoist tradition is based on the authority of the founder, Li Hon Zhi. Li's charismatic power is said to enable people, using certain meditation and movement practices, to arouse spiritual energy, maintain radiant health, and become enlightened. The authoritarian government of the People's Republic of China, in banning the fervent and rapidly growing group, has alleged that its unconventional healing actually has

Oil painting by woman devotee of Hare Krishna.

caused death, and the government no doubt is also threatened by the Falun Gong's independence from their control.

Another category, the fifth, is what we shall call the "Import Religions." Import religions are those that demonstrate the transcultural nature of many new religious movements as they are new to one country but are established religions elsewhere. The International Society for Krisha Consciousness (the Hare Krishna Movement) is in the *bhakti* tradition of India but was an entirely new religious movement for the United States when it was founded there by A. C. Bhaktivedanta Swami Prabhupada in 1966. Similarly, Christian groups are of this type when they are introduced in counties dominated by another world religion, for example, when Christianity was introduced to Japan. The Pentecostal movement in Africa (discussed in the "New Face of World Christianity" section in Chapter 8) is also of this type.

Several years ago I* attended a chapter meeting of Nichiren Shoshu of America (NSA), as it was then called, another example of this type, in a modest one-story frame house in a suburban California city. This group was essentially an American branch of Soka Gakkai, the Nichiren lay movement discussed in Chapter 5. Often counted as one of the "New Religions" of Japan, it has been a dynamic force in that nation since 1945. Far from a stereotypical Buddhist group with an air of monks and unworldly meditation, modern Japanese Nichiren Buddhism is an up-to-date religion with youth rallies, marching bands, and an emphasis on chanting to receive this-worldly as well as spiritual benefits.

The living room of the bungalow where this chapter of NSA met had been converted into a shrine room. At the end opposite the door a cabinetlike box had been set up, with the doors open to display a rectangular sheet of heavy paper crowded with characters. When I* arrived at seven in the evening, four or five young people were already seated on the floor, chanting. Others kept coming in, until 35 or 40 were present. The rapid chant went on and more and more people joined it, humming and bouncing along with the energy of an express train, using the words of the *Daimoku, Nam Myoho Renge Kyo* ("Hail the Marvelous Teaching of the Lotus Sutra").

Then came time for testimonials. I* heard people talk about how chanting had helped to sell a house, reconcile a daughter with her parents, enabled someone to land a good job and another to get into a closed college class in ceramics. One person even said that chanting will find one a parking place when it seems hopeless. But everyone also emphasized that the benefits of chanting are not just materialistic; the spiritual change within that comes from it are really more important and profound. It's just that, as Nichiren Buddhism says, *esho funi,* the inner and the outer are not separate. Change the inner through chanting, and your outer circumstances will also change for the better; put good things into your outer life, and your inner state of mind will improve too.[3] Nichiren Shoshu is no different from most new religions in claiming that, unlike conventional faiths, it can produce visible benefits here and now in the real world.

*Robert Ellwood.

A sixth type involves what is believed by the adherents to be a return to the faith of a prior Golden Age where people were closer to the Divine. We shall call this type the "Golden Age Movements." Such groups often draw from existing religious traditions in the development of their practices but do not identify themselves as being a part of or derived from such existing religions. Two subgroups of this type that are especially expanding in Europe, the United States, Canada, and places such as Australia, are the Feminist Spirituality Groups and the Neo-Pagan Groups. Often the two are intertwined and therefore not readily distinguishable, although we will attempt to discuss them separately here for clarity.

The Feminist Spirituality Groups are loosely aligned as a conglomerate often referred to as the "Goddess Movement." A foundational belief of most of the groups within the Goddess Movement is that prior to the Patriarchal Revolution men and women lived harmoniously with each other and with nature in egalitarian agrarian communities and worshipped a Goddess as Mother of all in her many aspects. There, art proliferated, and all was beauty. The adherents seek to return to the practices and social situation of this time. Some groups consist of men and women working together toward this goal. Others are "separatists"—all men or all women—who believe that a return to equality is not possible until each separately works through biases that have been assimilated from the patriarchal culture in which they now live. Such groups may draw syncretistically from other contemporary or older sources to develop their practices—sometimes Neo-Pagan sources. The ceremonies often evolve out of an artistic creative process involving many of the members and often are not ritually repeated but recreated anew each time.

The Temple of Isis in California is a Goddess Movement group that involves both men and women. It is part of The Fellowship of Isis, an international group with headquarters in Clonegal, Ireland, founded by Olivia Lawrence and Pamela Durdin-Robertson in 1976, and it has about 15,000 members in the United States, Great Britain, Ireland, and Nigeria. While the adherents call their group the Temple of Isis, for them Isis incorporates all manifestations of the Goddess around the world. In the words of one adherent: "We support the resurgence of the Goddess and the realization of a sustainable and peaceful future."

Several years ago I[†] attended a Temple of Isis celebration on a beach outside of Los Angeles at dawn. There gathered men and women dressed in colorful robes and bedecked with flowers to celebrate the "Sisters of the Sea." The ceremony began with the blowing of a conch shell horn to call the participants to the ceremony. All formed a circle, sand at their feet and the sea breeze blowing in their hair as the sun rose, casting streams of brightly colored light across the peaceful ocean. Then the priestesses called to the four directions of the world and asked that the Goddesses corresponding to the directions join the circle for the ceremony.

A slow, deep drumming commenced, and one of the priestesses led the circle into a procession, dancing rhythmically to the music of chimes and bells that had joined the beating drum. The group gathered in turn at each of four altars for the

---

†Barbara McGraw.

four "sisters of the sea"—Isis (Egypt), Aphrodite (Greece), Mari (or Mary in her many aspects around the world), and Yemaya (Yoruba)—and received blessings from the priestesses there. In succession the participants tasted the sweetness of chocolate at the altar for Aphrodite, received a blessing of scented oil placed on the forehead at the altar for Mari; and at the altar of Yemaya received a blessing of cool waters sprinkled over their heads and were given copper pennies, which were then cast into the ocean by each person as an offering to the Goddess. The ritual culminated at the altar of Isis, where the participants gathered around a small boat that had been made by the priestesses out of willow branches and leaves. Each person placed flower petals, shells, herbs, or feathers into the boat as he or she made a prayer wish. The boat was then launched into the sea to send the wishes to the Goddess.

The other subgroup, the Neo-Pagan, also wishes to return to a prior "Golden Age." For them, however, it involves a return to the pre–Judaeo-Christian roots of a prior faith. The prior faith is usually the shamanistically based indigenous religion of a particular place, such as one of the Native American religions of America or the folk religions of Old Europe, now known as Wicca or Witchcraft (not to be confused with the negative images of fairy tales). Usually such groups' thought and practices involve the reverence of nature as sacred and full of Spirit (as we saw in the discussion of animism in Chapter 2), the celebration of seasonal festivals, the use of magical means to experience the Divine and to effect positive changes in one's own life or in the world, and the celebration of the Divine as both God and Goddess. Because of their belief in the sacredness of nature, such groups are often involved in the ecology movement, which itself often has religious overtones.

The seventh, and last, category involves groups that have assimilated ideas and practices from mainstream world religions into an indigenous shamanistically based religious tradition. We shall refer to these as the "Hybrid Religious Movements." For example, many new religions, like Voodoo in Haiti and New Orleans; Santería in Cuba, Puerto Rico, and Florida; Umbanda and Candomblé in Brazil (discussed in the "New Face of World Christianity" section in Chapter 8); and others are syntheses between African religion and Roman Catholicism. A couple of years ago I[†*] went to a Voudou temple in New Orleans. Brightly colored altars were filled with figures sacred to the priestess there, including Jesus, Catholic saints such as Mary, and Africa deities, such as Ezili and Papa Legba.

A good example of this type is Santería. Santería, "the way of the saints," is a religious movement combining African and Roman Catholic features. It arose among the African population in Cuba, but spread to other parts of the Caribbean and, especially after the Cuban exile of 1959, to the United States. Now Santéria can be found in most large North American cities but it is strongest in Florida. It has many similarities to other non-Protestant Afro-American religions, such as Voudou in French Creole-speaking Haiti and Umbanda and Candoble in Brazil.

Santería is fundamentally the traditional religion of the Yoruba people of West Africa. But in the New World setting, their gods, called Orishas, are also identified

†*Barbara McGraw and Robert Ellwood.

Members of Wicca group perform a ritual in the woods, beginning with the forming of a circle—a symbol sacred to them.

with Roman Catholic saints, so that Chango, a great king and warrior who also represents fire, thunder, an lightning, becomes Saint Barbara, associated with thunder and lightning and a patron saint of soldiers; and Yemaya, lovely black mother Goddess, whose power derives from the sea, is also the Blessed Virgin Mary, Mother of Jesus and Star of the Sea. In worship, sacrifices (most commonly chickens) are offered, and devotees often go into ecstasy and are possessed by their patronal *orisha*. Divination, done by priests called *babalawos,* is frequently practiced. The rituals, costumes, and altars of Santéria are very colorful and filled with fascinating symbolism.[4]

There are other ways to categorize new religions as well. Examples include: Millennialist (or Millenarian), emphasizing the coming of a paradisiacal age; Thaumaturgical, emphasizing magical powers; Healing; Prophetic; Communalist, in which members live together, perhaps without personal property; Legalistic, emphasizing strict adherence to rules; Mystical, emphasizing methods of meditation and inner realization; Initiatory, like the Greek "mysteries" emphasizing programmed transformative experiences; Devotional; and Philosophical. And it is important to remember that many new religious movements exhibit characteristics of more than one category.

In addition, as we have mentioned, there are groups that represent a very strict, demanding adherence to the normative religion of the society, like the Amish or Jehovah's Witnesses in America, which are called "sects." Those centered on a new or imported teaching are often called "cults." But these terms should be used with great caution because they have become highly pejorative and stereotyping, although not intended as such by the sociologists of religion who originally coined the terms.

New Religions around the World

The few examples given here have barely begun to suggest the wealth of religious experience and diversity found in new religious movements around the world. It should be remembered that new religions are increasingly mobile, no longer likely to be confined to just one cultural area. In preceding chapters and above we have already looked to some degree at new religions of Japan, Korea, Vietnam, Brazil, Africa, and China.

In the United States and Canada several hundred new religions, many of indigenous, occult, or Eastern background, can be found of nearly every type, some of which have been named in the previous section. They reflect the pluralistic nature of religion in this society and the tendency of some people to be seekers and spiritual experimenters. Asian and Latin American immigration has also brought many new religions to the United States and Canada.

In Europe, new religions comparable to those in the United States and Canada, in fact often the same ones, are plentiful. They can be ascribed to some of the same factors and also to the spiritual vacuum left by relatively low conventional church attendance. In Russia and in the former Soviet bloc nations, the collapse of communism has left a situation of social confusion and seeking that has spurred the growth of new religions too.

The Islamic world has produced a number of new religious movements, some of them arising out of Sufi mysticism. Sufism in many forms has been brought to North America as well. Perhaps the best-known new religion to appear out of the Islamic world is the Baha`i faith, already mentioned previously.

India also has a host of movements, often based on particular spiritual masters like Ramakrishna, whom we have mentioned, and typically presenting not only his or her charisma and spiritual authority, but also a certain method of yoga, meditation, or devotion. One from the twentieth century, the Brahma Kumari movement, allows only female leadership, although both men and women may join as ordinary members. The Sai Baba movement is burgeoning in India and has a large presence in Europe and a smaller one in North America.

Africa has been estimated to host no less than 8,000 new religious movements, and Latin America is rife with them as well.

An interesting phenomenon is the wealth of new religious movements of many types in Japan, which exemplify the vividly diverse panorama of doctrines and practices that new religions throughout the world may exhibit. Tenrikyo ("Religion of Heavenly Wisdom") members perform sacred dances with gestures of sweeping movement to symbolize clearing away spiritual dust. Members of Perfect Liberty, believing that "life is art" and that all aspects of life need to be integrated into a total work of art, emphasize sports and when possible have a golf course near their church. The Church of World Messianity offers *johrei,* in which the "Divine Light of God" is channeled through the cupped hand of one who administers it to a recipient. Most were founded by strong shamanists such as Miki Nakayama (1798–1887), foundress of Tenrikyo, one of the oldest and most prototypical of the new religions, and Bunjiro Kawate, founder of Konkokyo, who had a shamanistic vision in which a folk religion deity revealed himself to be actually a monotheistic high god.

In all the new Japanese religions we see evidence of syncretism, which is often the case with new religious movements around the world that are not of the sect type, although even new religious movements of the sect type may exhibit syncretistic elements as well. Ideas from East and West are combined into new mixes in the new Japanese religions; Jesus is quoted in literature along with the Buddha. Seicho-no-Ie, for example, a group teaching that "all is perfect," draws both from the Western "New Thought" positive-thinking tradition, which places full responsibility for one's condition in the individual—a ramification of the modern isolation of the individual in contrast to archaic village or tribal society and religion, and from the Mahayana Buddhist belief in the universal unstained One Mind.

Communal life in the new Japanese religious movements is especially represented in the Sacred Center. Like Tenri City of Tenrikyo, and Soka Gakkai's new glorious temple on the slopes of Mount Fuji, and the headquarters of Perfect Liberty with its super golf course near Osaka, the new Japanese religions tend to have gorgeous centers, often large communities, which are places of pilgrimage and show what the world will be like when the "new age" comes in. And the new Japanese religions have closely knit organizations. Everyone is taken seriously and given a part. This makes them appealing to the dislocated millions moved far from ancestral shrines to impersonal industrial cities by modernization.

Of course, it is not possible here to discuss all of the individual new religions in detail; only a taste of the multitude of flavors can be given. However, some perspective may be provided by noting that, although there is great diversity represented in the new religious movements, they all have some characteristics in common. Let us then look at some general features of new religious movements.

Features of New Religious Movements

We shall look at features of new religious movements in terms of the three forms of religious expression presented in Chapter 1. What are they likely to have in each of them?

First, in the theoretical or "What do they say?" form of expression, a new religion will probably show enough continuity with the religion of the environment that ordinary people can recognize it as religion. But they will then go on to put a new face on it, one that appeals to vague uneasy feelings that may have that the old religion is outmoded or irrelevant to the crucial problems of the present. Thus, in the Mansren movement, an old story was renewed in contemporary terms when the folk hero was said to be returning to supersede colonial rule and bring a modern ship full of goods like those of the Europeans. Current American new religions of Eastern background speak of God, as do Judaism and Christianity, but tend to mean by it something more impersonal, inward, and universal, like Brahman or the Dao, than the personal God of the traditional religions; some find that approach better.

At the same time, another common feature of the beliefs of new religions, suggested by Spiritualism, is a tendency to fill up the "intermediate" range of the sacred cosmos between the human and ultimate transcendence, with a range of finite but supernatural beings: spirits, angels, gods, goddesses, ascended masters, and the like. These are of course no more than the gods and spirits of animism and polytheism, or the equivalents of Hindu gods and goddesses or Buddhist Buddhas and *bodhisattvas,* in modern dress. But while much modern religion has downplayed or eliminated them, human beings nevertheless claim to encounter them.

In addition, new religions usually offer something the adherents feel is new in the way of its thinking about the social structure of society. This generally takes two forms: a progressivist/reform message or a purist/reform message. Both are messages of change. The first expresses a desire to change the world in new ways not formerly recognized by mainstream faiths. The Neo-Pagan groups and Spiritualist groups are of this form. The second expresses a desire to change to a more "pure" form of a mainstream faith that is perceived by the adherents to have lost its way. The Family of Love and the Amish are of this form. Often the rights and roles of women become central issues in either form.

In terms of practices, worship, or "What do they do?" new religions tend either to center on one repeatedly taught and emphasized practice that is like a single, simple, sure key to a personal encounter with the sacred, like some of the

Groups such as the Amish are called "sects" rather than "cults" because they represent strict adherence to the normative religion of the society, rather than new or imported teaching. ▪

New Japanese religions, or to develop a community worship practice in which the creative process of developing unique ceremonies, as in the Feminist Spirituality Groups, is part of the particular movement's religious mystique. Recall again that a new religion must have a draw strong enough to counter the natural appeal of conventional faiths, which have the support of family, ethnicity, and community. Because they have been around for a long time, established religions may have a variety of services, practices, and emphases, from celebrating popular holidays to ways of private prayer and meditation, but involve activities that strike the sort of person drawn to a new religion as lukewarm and too compromised with the culture. Yet it is difficult to make the break unless the alternative presents a definite experience of greater intensity and more immediate reward, spiritually and perhaps also materially, than the conventional.

The sociology of new religious movements, on the one hand, may be like the practical form of expression in that it must offer enough to compensate for breaking one's "natural" ties—familial, ethnic, and communal—to a birthright religion. The appeal of a highly charismatic spiritual leader, a "guru" or prophet, may have this effect on some people; they want to be near him or her and get far more from that person and the technique than they do anywhere else. The same may be said about the group—intense, fervent, committed, ideally also loving and sharing—that forms. It is not a "natural" group in the above sense, but one made up of people who have made a self-conscious, intentional choice to enter it. This makes it a group with a highly different "feel" from the conventional, which, for some, provides a chosen "family" that overcomes the perceived failures of the birth family. Such a group also is more likely to be more demanding of its adherent's time and energy.

The other way new religious movements can operate sociologically is as very diffuse influences that do not compete directly with conventional religion or make the same kinds of demands. While often there is an "inner circle" of adherents who are dedicated practitioners of their faith, others do not attend formal services so much as they attend lectures and classes, read books and pamphlets, or nowadays listen to tapes and videos sold through the mail. In America today many conventional churchgoers may also take a yoga or meditation class during the week, or read and reflect on a Spiritualist-type or New Age book once in a while. These are examples of what one means by the diffuse type of influence new and unconventional religious movements can have.

❀ Summary

New religious movements have been found worldwide and throughout history and are very numerous today. They appear under many conditions but especially in times of social stress and rapid social change or in answer to new ideas and visions in the air. New religions are of various types, although in practice none fit neatly into only one type. The types we have discussed in this chapter are: Reactive Movements, Accommodationist Movements, Spirit Movements, New

Revelation Sects, Import Religions, Golden Age Movements, and Hybrid Movements. Basic features of new religious movements are likely to be: a different but recognizable doctrine; a practice centered on a single, simple, sure technique or a creative group process and practice; a charismatic founding and leadership and/or an intense, highly demanding group. On the other hand, they may involve a diffuse type of influence that is not directly competitive with mainstream religion. In every case, though, a new religious movement must offer inner rewards sufficiently effective and convincing to compensate for a break with the conventional faith.

✸ Questions for Review

1. What are some circumstances in which new religious movements might be particularly likely to appear?
2. Discuss the common features of new religious movements in terms of the three forms of religious expression.
3. What are the different types of new religions we have discussed in this chapter, and what are the characteristics that define them?
4. What are some common features of new religious movements?
5. Give some examples of new religions from different parts of the world.

✸ Suggested Readings on New Religious Movements

Native American, African, and Oceanic Movements
Aberle, David F., *The Peyote Religion among the Navaho*. Norman: University of Oklahoma Press, 1982, 1991. Excellent study of a particular Native American religion.

Barrett, Leonard E., *The Rastafarians*. Boston: Beacon Press, 1988. Fine study of a new religion based in Jamaica.

Burridge, Kenelm, *New Heaven, New Earth: A Study of Millenarian Activities*. Oxford: Blackwell, 1969. A careful study of millennialist movements and their context.

Fernandez, James W., *Bwiti: An Ethnography of the Religious Imagination in Africa*. Princeton, NJ: Princeton University Press, 1982. An excellent example of a study of a particular African movement.

Lawrence, Peter, *Road Belong Cargo: A Study of the Cargo Movement in the Southern Madang District of New Guinea*. New York: Humanities Press, 1964. A classic study, emphasizing understanding of the native worldview.

Metraux, Alfred, *Voodoo in Haiti*. New York: Schocken, 1989. The best book on this subject.

Simpson, George E., *Black Religions in the New World*. New York: Columbia University Press, 1978. An authoritative survey of African-American religions in the Caribbean, South America, and North America.

Truner, Harold W., ed., *Bibliography of New Religious Movements in Primal Societies,* 5 vols. New York: Macmillan, 1977–1992. A basic resource for further study in this area.

Wilson, Bryan R., *Magic and the Millennium*. New York: Harper & Row, 1973. A seminal and important sociological study of new religions in Africa and the Americas, with extensive bibliography.

New Religions in Asia
(See also the Bibliography and Notes for Chapter 5 for Japan, Korea, and Vietnam)

Asby, Philip H., *Modern Trends in Hinduism*. New York: Columbia University Press, 1974. Classic study of new movements in relation to social change.

Babb, Lawrence A., *Redemptive Encounters: Three Modern Styles in the Hindu Tradition*. Berkeley: University of California Press, 1987. Three important movements: Radhasoami, the Brahma Kumaris, and the following of Satya Sai Baba, a contemporary holy man.

Brooks, Charles R., *The Hare Krishnas in India*. Princeton, NJ: Princeton University Press, 1989. Fascinating scholarly study of this movement and its Western devotees in India.

Chan, Wing-Tsit, *Religious Trends in Modern China*. New York: Columbia University Press, 1953. Though now somewhat dated, a classic study of modern movements and their relation to Western influence.

Elliott, Allen J. A., *Chinese Spirit Medium Cults in Singapore*. London: Royal Anthropological Institute, 1955. A fascinating study based on careful field work.

Jordan, David K., and Daniel L. Overmyer, *The Flying Phoenix: Aspects of Chinese Sectarianism in Taiwan*. Princeton, NJ: Princeton University Press, 1986. A systematic study of modern Chinese new religious movements.

Religious Movements in the United States

Bednorowski, Mary F., *New Religions and the Theological Imagination in America*. Bloomington: Indiana University Press, 1989. Innovative study of the ideas basic to new American religions.

Eller, Cynthia, *Living in the Lap of the Goddess: The Feminist Spirituality Movement in America*. Boston: Beacon Press, 1995. The first thorough treatment; an excellent and insightful resource.

Ellwood, Robert S., *Alternative Altars: Unconventional and Eastern Spirituality in America*. Chicago: University of Chicago Press, 1979. Interpretive study centering on three examples, Spiritualism, Theosophy, and American Zen.

———, and Harry B. Partin, *Religious and Spiritual Groups in Modern America*, 2nd ed. Englewood Cliffs, NJ: Prentice Hall, 1988. Survey of the history, teaching, and practice of all major types of American new religions.

Lewis, James R., and J. Gordon Melton, *Perspectives on the New Age*. Albany: State University of New York Press, 1992. A very helpful resource.

Melton, J. Gordon, *Biographical Dictionary of American Cult and Sect Leaders*. New York: Garland, 1986. Reliable source for fundamental information on new religions through their leaders.

———, *Encyclopedia of American Religions*. Detroit, MI: Gale, 1992. Essential reference work, far more complete than any other in the area of new and unconventional religions.

Miller, Timothy, ed., *America's Alternative Religions*. Albany: State University of New York Press, 1995. An excellent collection of descriptions by leading authorities on alternative religions.

Moore, R. Laurence, *Religious Outsiders and the Making of America*. New York: Oxford University Press, 1987. Excellent study of the importance of alternative religions in American history.

Rochford, E. Burke, *Hare Krishna in America*. New Brunswick, NJ: Rutgers University Press, 1985. A lively participant-observer report; one example of many available studies of particular new religious groups in the United States.

Tweed, Thomas A., *The American Encounter with Buddhism, 1844–1912.* Bloomington: Indiana University Press, 1992. Important study of the significance of this import religion in American culture.

Zaretsky, Irving I., and Mark P. Leone, ed., *Religious Movements in Contemporary America.* Princeton, NJ: Princeton University Press, 1974. Although now somewhat dated, excellent essays on a number of groups.

Women in New Religions

Puttick, Elizabeth, *Women in New Religions: In Search of Community, Sexuality, and Spiritual Power.* New York: St. Martin's Press; Basingstoke, U.K.: MacMillan, 1997. A significant new contribution to scholarship about women and their roles in new religious movements.

CHAPTER ELEVEN

Looking Over the Spiritual Horizon

Religion Today and Tomorrow

CHAPTER OBJECTIVES

After studying this chapter, you should be able to

✸ Present an overview of contemporary religious trends.

✸ Discuss perspectives on the future of religion.

Things Old and New

We have surveyed the religions of humankind past and present. We have encountered a remarkable diversity among them, and we have noted what they all have in common.

Some of what we have looked at seemed very much rooted in the past, if not irrevocably locked there. The past may give religion a romantic patina or sprinkle it with the blood of grisly sacrifices that we are glad are gone. In wistful moods, we may wish we could sit with the Buddha under the bodhi tree or hear Jesus or Muhammad speak. Yet, those of us of this bent hope that their like will be seen again, for perhaps all things do recur in infinite time and, as a poet says of the wonders of Mycenae:

> *It may be that no splendor passes evermore from Earth,*
> *But that, through endless incantations—subtle, strange, divine—*
> *It knows in far-off time and space a new resplendent birth:*
> *In what age, in what world, shall this proud lion find again—*
> *Deep in the sea of stars—his race of gods and godlike men?*[1]

For religion to appear today as something from the past and somewhat out of joint with the present is nothing exceptional in itself. The great world religions, as well as many of the new religious movements, come into the present as something out of the past. Both the temple and the voice of the prophet, in differing ways, point to a world simpler and more pristine than the ambivalent world of the day. In this simpler world of mythic time or of scripture or vision, the works of the gods are more evident and moral values clearer.

On the other hand, it is nothing new for prophets to appear who proclaim that the extant religion is ready to be superseded. So spoke the Buddha, in effect, of the old brahminism and its rites, and Muhammad of the old gods of stars and moon, and so to some of those whose charismatic message spawns new movements today. In all the countless religious changes earth has seen, the religious quest has been renewed, but it has often changed course and set out in unexpected directions. Its new forms have sometimes at first hardly seemed like "religion" at all, compared with the older elaborate structure. At first the Buddha's methods may have seemed more like an ancient version of psychotherapy, and the cause of Muhammad more like a radical political movement than like institutions that would in time show equivalents to heavens full of gods and temples of the Nile. These and other new movements may seem more like breaths of fresh wind, which sweep away all the old gods and clean the skies.

But on a shorter scale, it may indeed seem that much of human religion is trapped beyond renewal in the past, and that even living religion is a carryover from the past into the present that attempts to relate modern experience to ancient maps.

Since the eighteenth century certain intellectuals have predicted the withering away of religion—the "Death of God." But God or the gods have died many times, and even so a new God or new gods have soon been born and have arisen to fill the vacuum. Their names may hardly yet have the glow of the old and holy, and they may come from segments of society little involved in the religious commerce of the previous age. The Buddha was of *kshatriya* rather than *brahmin* caste; Muhammad was from Arabia rather than one of the main religious powers; Jesus was from Galilee. But it is only when such movements become "noncompetitive" to the power structure of the day that they bear the future, like the obscure tiny furry mammals in the age of giant reptiles.

Religion is changing today. Conservative as well as innovative forces are at work in all faiths. Even the vaunted modern technology, which some have said will create a new secular world in which religion can no longer have a place, works both sides of the street. The urbanization and industrialization it has brought have indeed disrupted the traditional religion-based lifestyles of millions, but technology has also greatly facilitated such traditional religious practices as pilgrimage (now via jumbo jet) to Rome or Mecca, the publishing of scriptures for a mass readership, and mass preaching by means of radio and television, as well as providing a new means of communication—the internet—for the faithful of every creed, both new and traditional.

Factors Affecting Religion Today

As our survey of the history of the world's religions has tried to make evident over and over, the shape and strength of religions can be much affected by the social, political, and economic worlds in which they live. What are some of those factors in the world at the beginning of the twenty-first century?

Technology, Ecology, and the Population Explosion

The technological innovations of the last 200 years have changed the lives of most people more than any change since the discovery of agriculture some 10,000 years ago. From the steam engine to the computer, from railways to jets and telegraph to television and the internet, they have transformed not only how we live but how we work, how we relate to the world, and also how we understand what the world is. The contemporary electronics engineer, computer programmer, or technology-assisted businessperson or farmer is very different from the archaic agriculturalists in terms of how they interact with the physical universe.

This immense change has pluses as well as minuses for religion. Religious persons and institutions have been able to make much use of technological aids, especially those of the transportation and communication revolutions, to advance their causes. Most religious language, however, comes out of a pre-technological world. Religion often comes to the present as something out of the past, judging the present in terms of earlier and presumably simpler and purer values. This is tacitly expected, so it gives religious relevance a "grace period" or time-lag. Many people are not bothered that religious language reflects a world of shepherds, kings, and wandering holy men rather than multinational corporations, democracies or dictatorships, and television evangelists. They will argue, no doubt rightly, that the fundamental human problems and spiritual realities are the same in both worlds. Yet, some may question whether the "lag" in some faiths can persist in the face of the development of radically new religious languages and forms of religion that do take account of these changes. Will traditional religions shift and new religions arise to form radically new religious language and theologies as far-reaching as those that accompanied the agricultural revolution millennia ago?

In some respects religion is beginning to engage technology, its language, its underlying driving ideologies, but perhaps in unexpected ways. Some new religions, as well as new theological trends in traditional faiths (e.g., process theology), have evidenced a focus on the relationship of human beings and the natural world. Some are concerned that in the journey into cyberspace one may lose a fundamental tangible, real, felt connection with others and even the earth herself. This focus becomes central in "nature religions"—new (e.g., Wicca) and old (e.g., Native American). But nowhere is this more pronounced that in the international religio-philosophical and environmental movement known as the "Deep Ecology" movement. Deep Ecology espouses the sacred relationship of all living beings and the earth and promotes ecologically sustainable technology and ecocentric approaches to living, as opposed to the anthropomorphic focus that has dominated traditional Western thinking.

Nevertheless, the effort to earn profits for the well-placed by such means as cutting tropical rain forests to graze cattle and using ever-increasing amounts of hazardous agricultural chemicals—is devastating the ecology of the earth. Together with other effluvia of an industrial and technological age, it is killing the oceans and warming the air, melting polar ice, sinking cities, and turning fields into deserts. Yet, it is only those at the margins who call for the massive conversion to nonpolluting fuels.

At the same time, the earth's population has been growing at an astounding rate, from 1 billion to more than 6 billion, since 1850. The world would be hard-pressed to feed this many even with optimal use and distribution of resources. But that has been far from the case, with the wealthy quadrant of the earth's nations consuming much more than their share. Thus, millions—perhaps billions—are doomed to subsistence living at best and face the continual threat of famine.

It seems that humans, no differently than all other animal species, insist on filling their ecological niche to the maximum, not for quality of life but for the quantity that can be gained, even if at the most marginal level. If the world today with all its technological marvels had only the population of 1000 C.E.—about 250 million—or even the billion of 1850, it could be a veritable paradise for all. Instead, we have 6 billion in 2000, and a projection of nearly 8 billion by 2025, with famine, plague, and death as near as they were a thousand years ago for a good many.

While prophets calling for a new environmental-ecological ethic—prophets desperately concerned like those of old who warned humanity of doom to come unless they repented—can be found in all religions, the large-scale response of religion has been far more mixed. Prophecy has been mingled with religion serving other roles: offering otherworldly escape to people oppressed or overwhelmed by the battered world in which they find themselves, even aligning itself with those perpetrating the battering of the planet and its impoverished masses for the sake of gold. In fairness, it must be said that the majority of religious leaders are well-meaning. But they are as baffled by the unprecedented situation as everyone else and find it as hard as anyone to change customary attitudes and styles of living. Many hold that religion is supposed to offer meaning and goals to human life that are not just limited to this world but go beyond it. So they can say, "If this world passes away, all is still not lost." But this attitude still faces the challenging task of fitting in with an ethic of compassionate responsibility toward the earth, the world as the community of human beings inhabiting it, and those enmeshed in its toils. It would seem, instead, that the major religions of the world, with their proud claims to be the moral voices of humanity, would have much to say about resolving this with compassion rather than with a callous market-driven expansion or the cannon.

Globalization

Euro-American expansionism has always been, to some degree, accomplished through trade. However, the primary carrier of Euro-American thought in the past has been missionaries, following soon after explorers and conquerors. Today, however, it is trade, itself, that has become the carrier of Western cultural expression, and, in the late twentieth century and the beginning of the twenty-first century, it is ever more an American capitalist culture that is being exported by trade throughout the world—but not without considerable tensions.

Many extol the positive potentials of a globalized market economy for raising the standard of the living of nearly everyone around the world by providing resources, both in terms of technological aid and necessities. In this regard, many see new hope in the technologies and innovative ideas of multinational non-government organizations (NGOs) for raising the standard of living of the poorest regions of the world. For example, there are NGOs that have developed simplified, but useful products, together with distribution and marketing systems, for the poorest regions of China and India. One involves the manufacturing, marketing, and distribution of laundry soap in a manner that has begun to create a miniature market economy, raising the standard of living for those involved. The manufacturing is accomplished in small regional factories, which employ local workers. The distribution system utilizes locally available human and other resources, such as people on bicycles and in small vehicles. Marketing involves signs painted on the sides of people's huts or vehicles, which have been leased for the purpose. At the same time, each village is equipped with a cell phone and a computer, and the villagers lease time, thus connecting them not only to the company, but to the world. It is believed by those promoting these products and markets that individual and small community economic empowerment will serve as a bulwark against famine and disease, and even perhaps authoritarian regimes, by eventually making available to all the resources of the more developed nations of the world.

Ecological crisis: Sahara Desert sand dunes blanketed with grass to prevent sand from shifting to nearby acres of fertile land. ▪

On the other hand, there is considerable resistance due to the desire on the part of certain peoples and their leaders to preserve their home country's religion and culture. The question becomes, then, whether such preservation is possible in the face of the Western economic onslaught of mass marketing and consumerism, whose ideology is based in a self-centered individualism of satisfaction and preferences that runs counter to most religious impulses.

If, as it appears, the United States will take the lead in the globalization of a capitalist market economy, its policymakers will need to recognize their own approach to the global political economy as having an ideological bent that is potentially undermining to others' conceptions of themselves—an approach that is anything but "neutral." More significantly from a Western perspective, that ideology may even run counter to certain underlying beliefs, originally religious, that once provided the foundation for such central concepts as "human rights." Many hold that the failure to recognize that foundation risks undermining the benefits for the people of the world's future that the proponents of "globalization" promise.

Gender Inequity

Bound up with these problems is a growing sense that the relative roles of women and men in society, including their roles in religious life, need to be profoundly rethought and reordered. The role of women in religion has been a continuing theme in this book. In Chapter 1 we referred to the quite justified insistence of critics dissatisfied with a purely descriptive approach to world religions with respect to the role of religion in the oppression of women. Looking first at religion itself, they correctly point out that the teaching and institutional power of the major religions are almost exclusively male, from their founding to the present. All of the religious founders, saviors, and authoritative teachers are male, and the chief God is generally designated male as well. Virtually all the scriptures and creeds are penned by men or were received by men, and it goes without saying that religious power structures—priesthoods, the ministerial profession, the office of the religious teacher or jurist, even the role of prophet—have been effectively controlled by men, though women have sometimes been given a certain place within them or have served as shamans.

Furthermore, in their views of God, nature, and society, the major world religions stand accused of promoting teachings that effectively put and keep women in subordinate roles, concerned with home and family, while men concern themselves with the larger affairs of public and religious life. One way or another, all major religions have traditionally said that God, the gods, heaven, or *dharma* intended women and men to have distinct roles, with men in the position of dominating public life and exercising leadership and women structurally in a place of greater dependence and obedience, especially within the all-important arena of family life. The reader must decide whether she or he believes this is as it should be. But one cannot deny that in most societies these traditional religious precepts are bound up with social, political, and economic patterns that have given women little more than minority decision-making representation in the worlds of culture, business, government, and religion.

Yet it is also clear that in the matter of gender inequity, discontent is reaching critical mass in both religion and society, and change is in process. How far it will go, and what the ultimate product will look like, is impossible to say at this point. Probably there has never been a society, or major religion, with real gender equality in decision making or access to the sacred, though some tribal societies may have come closer to it than has "civilization" and some new religions incorporate gender (and sometimes sexual orientation) equity into their core beliefs. Yet, we have no working model for large-scale gender equality in either religion or society, and those who labor for such institutions will need to work toward a future that rejects the absolute authority of the past and looks instead to the future.

Sexual Orientation

Not only did the role of women in religions arise as a crucial argument in the late twentieth century, but by the beginning of the twenty-first century, the role of homosexuals, lesbians and gay, is no less hotly contested. This debate has bitterly divided several major denominations in the United States. At issue are two points: first, whether "practicing" homosexuals of either gender can be ordained to the rabbinate, ministry, or priesthood; and second, whether marriages or the equivalent, sometimes called "holy unions," between persons of the same sex should be performed by clergy or in church or synagogue.

Debates involve such matters as (1) religious authority, (2) whether sexual orientation is something one is born with and cannot truly be changed or is acquired and so can be changed, (3) the role of the clergy and of marriage in society, (4) the religious meaning of human love and integrity, and (5) questions as to what can and should constitute "family." These deeply felt questions go to the core of religious identity and community and, consequently, are bound to continue to be contentiously debated in the coming years.

Religious Trends Today

Liberalism

A "liberal" approach to a religion may be defined as one that contends that its traditional formulae need not be interpreted literally or solely in terms of their interpretation in previous eras but rather must be understood in light of the best current standards of reasonable thought and scientific truth. Religious liberals are also characteristically concerned about social justice issues as much as those of personal experience or salvation, and they are inclined to take positions similar to those of political liberals—though of course exceptions do occur.

Religious liberalism is nothing new. Thinkers who have tried to put their religion in language that is harmonious with that of the leading philosophy and science of their day have no doubt existed as long as religion. We have mentioned such schools as the Mu`tazila in Islam, the medieval Christian scholastics with their recovery of Aristotle as a philosophical foundation, and the Neo-Confucians in China. But in the late nineteenth and twentieth centuries the movement was especially forceful because of the unprecedented array of new scientific ideas, from evolution to psychoanalysis, that religion must deal with. It also was more forcefully concerned with social reform than in most periods in the past.

Yet, in the first years of the twenty-first century, the picture of religious liberalism is unclear. Powerful liberalizing forces have been at work. Despite some opposition in high places, the Roman Catholic Church is far more liberal than before the Second Vatican Council. Major movements such as "feminist theology" and "liberation theology," liberal by our definition though they go beyond conventional liberalism, have made profound and probably irreversible changes in religious consciousness in Christianity, Judaism, and elsewhere. Under the influence of persons such as Gandhi, Hinduism in some places has taken steps to liberalize the roles of castes and of women.

At the same time, liberal Protestant denominations are in decline, and new spiritual movements around the world seem little concerned with the conventional philosophy-science-reform liberal program. They are more likely, one way or another, to push for radical (that is, "striking-at-the-root") changes in theology or society than the thoughtful but often fairly comfortable way of the conventional liberal. The latter, after all, have been seen in highly respectable "mainline" churches, universities, or *brahminical* circles more often than among those actually suffering from the way things are, however genuine their compassion is toward them. Moreover, the world of the conventional liberal is in disarray as society fragments and people seem less sure what "conventional wisdom" is, with science plagued by ecological guilt and the politics of both liberals and conservatives thrust into an unfamiliar new stage by the precipitous collapse of Marxism as a credible force in the late 1980s. All this has cut some ground from under the conventional liberal in favor of radical—or radical conservative—options.

Traditionalism and Fundamentalism

"Traditionalism" and "fundamentalism" are both terms used to designate people who do not believe that religion should be reinterpreted to fit prevailing views but rather that its authority is independent of the world in which it lives and must be presented in the same language in season and out. Change in a religion believed to be true is a contradiction in terms, and it must therefore be denied symbolically by allowing little if any change in religious language, moral values, or practice. Traditionalism is the stance of those who adhere to a religious form still living and continuous with a long past but perceived to be beleaguered today, as among Roman Catholic traditionalists. Similarly, fundamentalism puts additional stress on the infallibility—as true now as ever—of the religion's written sources; today they also tend to see their world under siege.

The appeal of traditionalism and fundamentalism in a world of confusing change and uncertain prospects is obvious. For many, it is important that at least one area of life seem secure, linked to one's roots in the past and able to stand still while everything else is reeling. Indeed, many people in this camp argue vehemently that the only sure answers to the complexities of modern life lie in "traditional values," and that by returning to them and building society on them we can reverse those trends that have made the world a dismaying place. Thus, as we have seen, Islamic fundamentalists, as in the Iranian revolution, have determined to resist pernicious outside influences by restoring the authority of Islamic law in all areas of life. In the West, many Christian fundamentalists call for a return to strict Christian morality to counter the moral chaos in the world. (It is often less clear, however, what fundamentalists would do about the technological revolution, from which they have greatly benefited around the world, or its demographic and ecological spawn. These, critics say, will require more than the exhortations to personal morality and the focus on issues such as sexuality or abortion with which fundamentalists tend to feel most at home.)

Much has been made of the late–twentieth-century revival of traditionalism and fundamentalism in several religions, and certainly they have been highly visible forces. However, careful analysis has sometimes revealed that this is not because those groups have been successful in winning over large numbers of "liberals." They have been much better at retaining the numbers they have long had, and they have acquired a new confidence manifesting in a conspicuous political and media presence in many countries. But the real size and staying power of their following in the difficult years ahead in the twenty-first century remains to be seen.

Secularization

One of the big topics of discussion in contemporary sociology of religion is "secularization," that is, whether religion is losing force in society and, on a more subjective level, as a real power in the minds of people. Some say it is obvious that it is, pointing to the dramatic fall in recent decades in church attendance and other religious participation in places like Western Europe and East Asia, and the fact that religion no longer has the near-monopoly it once had in the educational and artistic worlds. Skeptics of secularization point to the persistence of high levels of religious activity in other places, such as the United States and the Islamic world, and say that religion may not really have been quite as powerful in the past as is commonly supposed either.

Whichever side is right, plain secularism—the replacement of religious ideals in the political arena with nonreligious humanistic ideal—is yet another powerful option in the complicated current religious scene, which some contend leads to a lack of interest in religion. Sheer indifference will limit the gains of liberals, traditionalists, fundamentalists, and new religionists alike; and secular values—saying that what is important is what gives people a good life here and now as measured by worldly relationships and assets—will be there to challenge religious values based on heaven, hell, and sacred experience. Secularism could, in fact, point to one possible religious future.

Another possibility is not that people will become entirely indifferent to religion, but that they will be so individualist and private, or small-group oriented, in their religious life that large religious institutions as we now know them will have little social or political influence or even become obsolete. Some observers have detected trends in this direction.

Religious Futures

We will end our discussion with a glance at such possible religious futures in this first decade of the third millennium C.E.

Secularism

It may be that the secularism described above will increase to crowd out religious values thoroughly, especially on the higher levels of education and culture, leaving us with a lingering folk religion at best. Some indications point in this direction. Even in the United States, where local religious participation remains high, faith is not the part of intellectual, economic, and national cultural life it once was and is less a factor in education than in the past. Yet this scenario must contend with the oft-demonstrated power of religion to revive itself and the prospect that the ecological and other crises of this new century could create the kinds of tensions and yearnings that go into religious revivals.

New Religions and New Religious Founders

Could one of the new religious movements become a new world religion? Could a new religious founder in the pattern of the Buddha or Jesus arise to proclaim successfully a new religion for our time? The age of originating great founder religions, and of their faiths sweeping nations and continents as of old, seems to have come and gone. Undoubtedly many people will be converted from one religion to another in the future as they are today. But the very individualism and pluralism that is so much a feature of contemporary faith ought to suggest that not all will go the same direction at the same time. Our news media, with its TV cameras and investigative reporters, create different sorts of images than in days when news traveled more slowly and easily adapted itself to mythic models before it was finally written down. For any one religious leader to capture the imagination of an entire population would be difficult, if not impossible, in this context. Still, a confluence of similar religious messages from many such leaders might constitute a "new world religion" in a way we previously have not considered.

Syncretism

Some have suggested that world religion might become syncretic, that is, taking the best elements of each to form a new universal religion. To be sure, as the world becomes more of a global village, more and more exchanges of ideas and even practices may occur between faiths, as they have in the past. The rosary, for example, is a practice that seems to have originated in the Middle East and been picked up by several faiths. To see this happening wholesale, though, so that all religions are caught up in a "super-religion" is to overlook the integralist and exclusivist drives in all religions that counterbalance that tendency. There are always those who believe strongly—as the traditionalists and fundamentalists exemplify—that their faith must maintain its own purity and integrity. Moreover, in difficult times the trend is usually toward that mentality or toward the emergence of equally rigorous new religious movements—each pulling in different directions.

On the other hand, new syncretistic movements might form a loose conglomerate that becomes a powerful religious force at the level of a world religion. In this regard, many have noticed the similarity in the messages of some of the syncretistic new religious movements around the world such as those in Japan and the New Age Movements in the United States and Europe.

Pluralism

A possibility for the religious future that seems to be emerging more and more is the acceptance of pluralism—the coexistence and multiplication of different religions and cultures in the world and within most countries—as a good in itself. Perhaps pluralism will be seen, as it already is by many today, as a positive influence on society, enriching the lives of all while, at the same time, countering religious strife by offering in its place an opportunity for love, understanding, and learning between people of different worldviews.

Of course there can be tensions, too, because the pluralistic mentality requires looking at each individual religion as part of a spiritual mosaic rather than as absolute truth in itself. This is a difficulty for those who believe deeply in the truth of one—and their views are to be respected. Nevertheless, as many of the world's societies become more and more pluralistic, pluralism itself seems to be indicating a new way to be religious—or, perhaps it is not all that new. At various times and places in the world's religious history that we have encountered in these pages, we have seen religious movements that sought to take under a wide "umbrella" the various beliefs, practices, and sociological structures of different religious views as many "paths" to one Universal Truth or Being, as did Hinduism and Tendai Buddhism to varying degrees. Perhaps it is here that the world's religions will find their future.

Religion's Future

The religious future, then, may be not too different from the past, with its indications every which way. Then again, it may not. Something totally surprising and unexpected may happen. We will see.[2]

In the present book, however, our task has been the fascinating historical and descriptive one. We have traced out some of the paths religion has followed through the years, and some of us may have found that just to be in the presence of all this variegated richness is in itself an awareness-expanding, even a religious, experience. To feel this way before the past and present is a good prelude for turning to the future.

❋ Questions for Review

1. What is your view of the current religious scene? Is religion in permanent decline; is it undergoing radical change; is it returning to traditional thought, practice, and values?

2. What understandings have you gained from your study of diverse faiths that will aid you in your own spiritual development?

APPENDIX: STUDYING THE WORLD RELIGIONS

I. Writing a Term Paper

One assignment you may have in a class on world religions is to write a paper on a selected topic in this area. Here are some ideas on how to go about it.

Topic

Unless the topic is assigned, be sure that you select one that is neither too broad nor too specialized for a student at your level. Attempting to write about all of Buddhism or Hinduism in one paper could result in only extremely superficial coverage. On the other hand, a specialized subject more suitable for a Ph.D. dissertation would usually not be recommended. For the typical 6–12 page research paper something in the middle range would be best, like the life and teaching of a major religious figure—Shinran, Confucius, Luther, Muhammad. So also would the story of a religious group or denomination within a major religion—Nichiren Buddhism, Southern Baptists. One could also select a particular text, like the Diamond Sutra or the Gospel of Mark; or a particular rite or practice, like Zen meditation or the Roman Catholic mass. A few special religious sites, the Ise shrine or Mecca and the pilgrimage to it, would also be suitable. You could write about one of the Hindu gods or Buddhist *bodhisattvas* or something comparable. Those who are philosophically minded might wish to take a basic concept like Nirvana or *karma* or Redemption and study it. On the other hand, don't overlook the importance and fascination of popular religion, like the celebration of festivals such as Durgapuja, Christmas, or Passover; or pilgrimages; or how weddings and funerals are done; or beliefs and practices toward the dead.

These are only a few ideas; the possibilities are almost endless.

Sources

When you select your topic, be sure that adequate resources are available to you on it. I would suggest you first read about the topic in a good encyclopedia, such as the *Britannica,* the *Encyclopedia of Religion,* or the *Abingdon Dictionary of Living Religions,* to get an overview and to look at its bibliography. For more bibliography, look in this textbook, and bibliographies in textbooks on the religion, and in sources like Vol. 4 of *The Reader's Adviser.*

Then use at least four good scholarly books or articles. They should be as specialized as possible; if you are writing about Krishna, use books about him, or at least about Hindu deities generally or Hinduism, not only encyclopedias or general world religion textbooks. There is always material in good scholarly journal articles too; ask your librarian to help you find them. In many cases you will not need to read all of a book; learn how to skim, and use the contents and index to locate what you need. Be careful with the spelling of non-English names and terms.

Notes

In your paper, be sure to use a proper format for notes. Footnote or endnote all quotes and sources of particular, specialized information. If you use computerized sources, either discs or information networks, they must be fully cited the same as any other source. Remember that in most schools plagiarism, or the unacknowledged use of material other than your own in a paper, is grounds for expulsion.

Organization

Your paper should be organized around the three forms of religious expression to which we have referred several times in this book. Here is a proposed outline:

1. *Introduction.* Short introductory paragraph to the whole paper.
2. *History.* Here give the history and background of the subject—for example, if a person like Shinran, the story of his or her life; if a teaching or school, how it came into being and developed over time. Be sure not to confuse myth and history here.
3. *Teaching.* Here present the most important teachings about Ultimate Reality and the nature of human life, its ethical duties, and its meaning and destiny as given by the person, text, or school associated with the deity or practice. Some will be obvious; some, like the teachings behind a rite or festival, will require a little digging, but they are there. Important myths, such as those about a deity or festival, come in here; analyze what they are saying about God, nature, and human life.
4. *Practices.* What forms of worship, meditation, or activity are associated with the subject? How is the god worshipped, what practices did the leader himself follow and teach his or her followers, how is the rite actually done, how is the text used in real worship, or what worship does it imply? Be as specific as possible. Don't just say, for example, meditation, but describe just what method of meditation is used in this context.
5. *Sociology.* Here describe such things as the social role of the teacher, the role of disciples, the organization of a school or denomination. And answer questions, such as: Who does a particular rite or worships a particular god? What does that mean socially? Who makes the pilgrimage and why? What is "leadership" or "authority?" The discussion should include relevant material on the nature of leadership, social and institutional

structures, the interaction of leaders and members of a group, the place of women and other particular classes, and the relationship of a religious group or practice to the larger society.

6. ***Conclusion.*** Here you may, but need not, give your own critical reaction to the topic.

Final Words.   Be sure to proofread very carefully, double-checking the spelling of technical and non-English names and terms. (Although there are different methods of transliteration from some languages, try to use one method consistently.) Take care of all typos, misspellings, bad grammar, and messiness. At the end put a bibliography of all the sources you used, in proper form.

II. Writing a Religious Visit Paper

Another assignment you may have in a class like this is to visit a place of worship, presumably one that is new to you, and write a report on it. In most cases, this will be a visit to a service.

Here are some ideas on how to organize this paper, also based on the three forms of religious expression. It is assumed that this is intended to be a descriptive or "phenomenological" account of the religious activity, neither laudatory nor critical; on this particular occasion the purpose is just to observe carefully and empathetically, in the way discussed in Chapter 1, what is actually done. It is assumed also that this report is to be based on first-hand observation, deliberately avoiding the use of secondary sources, so notes and bibliography are not needed. However, in some cases you may need to get a little background, through prior reading or through material available at the religious site, the better to understand what you see. Interviews may also be helpful as well as perusing the website for the group, if available.

Most religious places welcome sincere students as visitors. Remember to be quiet, respectful, appreciative, and appropriately dressed.

Here is the outline:

1. ***Field information.*** Give the full name, exact address, and religious affiliation of the group (don't just say "a Buddhist temple"; be sure to specify the school or denomination, and the national background); give the exact date and time of the visit; give the name and type of service (if any) attended.

2. ***Preliminary placing information.*** Describe the outside and inside appearance of the building, the way visitors are greeted, and the sort of people in this group, that is, their apparent social class, lifestyle, ethnic background, gender, average age, number present, and so forth.

3. ***Description of activity or symbolism.*** If you attend a service or formal presentation on the religion, describe what happened from beginning to

end. Try to give some sense of the emotional tone and subjective spiritual meaning of the scenario, for example, was the opening dramatic or casual, is congregational participation emotional or reserved, is much of the service spontaneous or ritualized?

If you did not attend a regular service, discuss in detail the significance of the art, architecture, and symbolism in and around the site.

4. ***Analysis.*** Analyze the topic in terms of the three forms of religious expression: theoretical (teaching), practical (worship), sociological. At least one-third of the paper should cover these topics.
   a. ***Theoretical.*** What, essentially, does this religion teach? As far as you could tell from this one experience, what is the main message this religion gives through its sermons, practices, symbols, etc.?
   b. ***Practical.*** What is the basic nature of the worship? Formal or informal? Ancient or modern? Structured or spontaneous? What message about how this group conceives of the role of religion does the nature of the worship communicate?
   c. ***Sociological.*** What kind of group is it? Close-knit or diffused? Mostly people drawn to the religion by family or ethnic ties, or mostly committed converts of different backgrounds? What role does the priest or leader play? What message about religious experience and meaning is communicated by the nature of the leadership and the group?

This should be an interesting experience. Best wishes!

NOTES

Chapter 1

[1]Different terms are used in most traditions for this category; the following are only examples. It should be made clear that these "conditioned" categories are not necessarily evil; they are just arenas of ignorance and separateness and therefore where evil or sin is possible.

[2]Joachim Wach, *Sociology of Religion* (Chicago: University of Chicago Press, 1944), pp. 17–34.

[3]See, for example, Nancy Auer Falk and Rita M. Gross, *Unspoken Worlds: Women's Religious Lives* (Belmont, CA: Wadsworth Publishing, 1989).

[4]A book on ethics in world religions, which combines description and critique, is Denise Lardner Carmody and John Tully Carmody, *How to Live Well: Ethics in the World Religions* (Belmont, CA: Wadsworth Publishing, 1988).

[5]In this book B.C.E. (Before the Christian or Common Era) and C.E. (Christian or Common Era) are used rather than B.C. and A.D.

[6]For a wonderful discussion of postmodernism, see Pauline Marie Rosenau, *Post-Modernism and the Social Sciences* (Princeton, NJ: Princeton University Press, 1992).

[7]Laurence Freeman has expressed this view in his introduction to *The Good Heart: A Buddhist Perspective on the Teachings of Jesus by His Holiness the Dalai Lama,* trans. by Geshe Thupten Jinpa (Boston: Wisdom Publications, 1996), pp. 1–32.

Chapter 2

[1]For the meaning of the term cosmic religion, see Mircea Eliade, *Cosmos and History* (New York: Harper & Row, 1959); and *The Sacred and the Profane* (New York: Harper & Row, 1961).

[2]For further anthropological discussion of the American Halloween, see Victor W. Turner, *The Ritual Process* (Chicago: Aldine, 1969), pp. 172–74.

[3]"'Internal Conversion' in Contemporary Bali," mimeographed, 1961, p. 3. Cited in Robert N. Bellah, *Religion and Progress in Modern Asia* (New York: The Free Press, 1965), p. 176.

[4]James G. Frazer, *The Belief in Immortality* (London: Macmillan, 1913), Vol. 1, pp. 72–73, quoting A. J. Kruijt.

[5]Paul Schebesta, *Among the Forest Dwarfs of Malaya* (London: Hutchinson, 1927), pp. 185–87.

[6]Frazer, *Immortality,* pp. 250–54.

[7]Rita M. Gross, "Tribal Religions: Aboriginal Australia," *Women in World Religions,* Arvind Sharma, ed. (Albany, NY: SUNY Press, 1987), p. 43, citing Catherine H. Berndt, "Women and the 'Secret Life,'" *Aboriginal Man in Australia,* R. B. and C. H. Berndt, eds. (Sydney: Agnus and Robertson, 1964), p. 154. The other information on Aboriginal women for this segment was obtained from Rita Gross's article as well.

[8]Mircea Eliade, *Shamanism: Archaic Techniques of Ecstasy,* trans. by Willard R. Trask, Bollingen Series LXXVI (New York: Bollingen Foundation, 1964), pp. 190–97. © 1964 by Princeton University Press. Reprinted by permission of Princeton University Press.

[9]Peter Freuchen, *Book of the Eskimos* (New York: Fawcett World Library, 1965), pp. 168–71.

[10]See, for example, Peter T. Furst, ed., *Flesh of the Gods: The Ritual Use of Hallucinogens* (New York: Praeger, 1972); Michael J. Harner, ed., *Hallucinogens and Shamanism* (London and New York: Oxford University Press, 1973); and Barbara G. Myerhoff, *Peyote Hunt: The Sacred Journey of the Huichol Indians* (Ithaca, NY: Cornell University Press, 1974).

[11]Mircea Eliade, *Shamanism: Archaic Techniques of Ecstasy,* pp. 60–61.

[12]See Eliade, *Shamanism;* and Andreas Lommel, *Shamanism: The Beginning of Art* (New York: McGraw-Hill, 1967), pp. 11–12.

[13]Franz Boas, *The Religion of the Kwakiutl, Columbia University Contributions to Anthropology,* 10, part 2 (New York: 1930), pp. 1–11. Summarized in Claude Lévi-Strauss, *Structural Anthropology* (Garden City, NY: Doubleday, 1967), pp. 169–73.

[14]Ichiro Hori, *Folk Religion in Japan* (Chicago: University of Chicago Press, 1968), pp. 203–6.

[15]Frank G. Speck, *Naskapi* (Norman: University of Oklahoma Press, 1935), pp. 83–94.

[16]See John Batchelor, *The Ainu and Their Folk-Lore* (London: Religious Tract Society, 1901), pp. 483–95; and Joseph M. Kitagawa, "Aimu Bear Festival (Iyomante)," *History of Religions,* 1, no. 1 (Summer 1961), pp. 95–151.

[17]For a critical assessment of hunting ritual and its relation to hunting reality, see Jonathon Z. Smith, *Imagining Religion* (Chicago: University of Chicago Press, 1982), pp. 57–65.

[18]Margaret Ehrenberg, *Women in Prehistory* (London: British Museum Publications, 1989), pp. 50–62.

[19]James Mooney, "The Ghost-Dance Religion and the Sioux Outbreak of 1890," Annual Report of the Bureau of American Ethnology, 14 (1896), no. 2, pp. 721, 724. Cited in Eliade, *The Sacred and the Profane,* p. 138.

[20]Ehrenberg, *Women in Prehistory,* p. 84.

[21]Mircea Eliade, *Myth and Reality* (New York: Harper & Row, 1963), pp. 104–5.

[22]T. C. Hodson, *The Naga Tribes of Manipur* (London: Macmillan, 1911), pp. 104–5.

[23]Michael J. Harner, *The Jivaro: People of the Sacred Waterfall* (Garden City, NY: Doubleday, 1972), p. 147.

[24]Mircea Eliade, *Patterns in Comparative Religion* (New York: Sheed & Ward, 1958), pp. 344–45.

[25]Gimbutas, Marija, *The Civilization of the Goddess: The World of Old Europe* (San Francisco: HarperSanFrancisco, 1991).

[26]Ehrenberg, *Women in Prehistory,* pp. 63–65.

Chapter 3

[1]Betty Heimann, *Facets of Indian Thought* (London: George Allen & Unwin, 1964).

[2]Robert S. Ellwood and Harry B. Partin, *Religious and Spiritual Groups in Modern America,* 2nd ed. (Englewood Cliffs, NJ: Prentice Hall, 1988), pp. 180–81.

[3]See A. L. Basham, *The Wonder That Was India* (New York: Grove Press, 1959), Chapter 2.

[4]R. Gordon Wasson, *Soma: Divine Mushroom of Immortality* (New York: Harcourt Brace Jovanovich, 1969). See also R. Gordon Wasson, "What Was the Soma of the Aryans?" in *Flesh of the Gods,* Peter T. Furst, ed. (New York: Praeger, 1972), pp. 201–13.

[5]There is a collection of similar words, confusing at first, that are built on this root. Brahma is the creator god in some Indian mythology. Brahman (the neuter form) is used in philosophical writing from the *Upanishads* on to refer to the impersonal Absolute. The Brahmanas are sacred ritual texts that are a part of the *Vedas.* Brahmans are the priestly caste, presumably so-called because they possessed mysterious and magical power like that by which the world is sustained. For the sake of clarity, in this book the common spelling brahmin will be used for the priests.

[6]Mircea Eliade, *Yoga: Immortality and Freedom* (New York: Bollingen Foundation, 1958), Chapter 3.

[7]Swami Prabhavananda and Frederick Manchester, trans., *The Upanishads: Breath of the Eternal* (New York: Mentor Books, 1957), pp. 123–24. Copyright © 1957 by The Vedanta Society of Southern California. Reprinted with permission.

[8]Ibid., pp. 18–19.

[9]On this period and the following, see Basham, *The Wonder That Was India.*

[10]Swami Prabhavananda and Christopher Isherwood, *How to Know God: The Yoga Aphorisms of Patanjali* (New York: Mentor Books, 1969); Eliade, *Yoga;* and Alain Danielou, *Yoga: The Method of Reintegration* (New York: University Books, 1955).

[11]Swami Prabhavananda and Christopher Isherwood, *The Song of God: Bhagavad-Gita* (New York: Mentor Books, 1951), p. 37. Copyright © 1944, 1951 by The Vedanta Society of Southern California. Reprinted with permission.

[12]Ibid., pp. 40–41.

[13]Ibid., p. 79.

[14]Ibid., p. 67.

[15]Ibid., p. 69.

[16]Ibid., pp. 91–93.

[17]On Shankara and Advaita Vedanta, see Eliot Deutsch, *Advaita Vedanta: A Philosophical Reconstruction* (Honolulu: East-West Center Press, 1969); Eliot Deutsch and J. A. B. van Buitenen, *A Source Book of Advaita Vedanta* (Honolulu: University of Hawaii, 1971); Y. Keshava Menon and Richard F. Allen, *The Pure Principle: An Introduction to the Philosophy of Shankara* (East Lansing, MI: Michigan State University Press, 1960); and Swami Prabhavananda and Christopher Isherwood, *Shankara's Crest-Jewel of Discrimination* (New York: Mentor Books, 1970).

[18]See Rai Bahadur, *Siva Samhita,* trans. by S. C. Vidyarnava (Allahabad, India: Lalit Mohan Basu, 1942); Eliade, *Yoga;* and A. Bharati, *The Tantric Tradition* (Garden City, NY: Doubleday, 1970).

[19]Swami Prabhavananda, *Srimad Bhagavatam: The Wisdom of God* (New York: Capricorn Books, 1968), pp. 199–200. Copyright © The Vedanta Society of Southern California. Reprinted with permission.

[20]See Milton Singer, "The Great Tradition of Hinduism in the City of Madras," *Anthropology of Folk Religion,* Charles Leslie, ed. (New York: Vintage Books, 1960). The spirit of Krishna devotion is evident in the "Hare Krishna" movement in America with its fervent bhaktic singing and dancing. This movement derives from a Krishna devotional tradition started by Sri Chaitanya (c. 1486–1533) in Bengal. He and the movement regard Krishna as the supreme, personal God, and not as just an avatar of Vishnu or an expression of an ultimately impersonal Absolute like Advaita Vedanta.

[21]See Wendy O'Flaherty, *Asceticism and Eroticism in the Mythology of Siva* (London: Oxford University Press, 1973).

[22]See Ernest A. Payne, *The Saktas* (Calcutta: YMCA Press, 1933); and John G. Woodroffe, *Shakti and Shakta* (Madras: Ganesh, 1951). See also David R. Kinsley, *The Sword and the Flute: Kali and Krsna, Dark Visions of the Terrible and the Sublime in Hindu Mythology* (Berkeley: University of California Press, 1975).

[23]Rabindranath Tagore, trans., *Songs of Kabir* (New York: Macmillan, 1917), pp. 45–46. Hari is a name for Vishnu. Karim means a Muslim wonder-working saint. Ram is, of course, Rama. A *pir* is a Muslim Sufi teacher comparable to a Hindu guru.

[24]Trilochan Singh and others, *Adi-Granth: Selections from the Sacred Writings of the Sikhs* (New York: Macmillan, 1960; London: George Allen and Unwin, © 1960; reprinted New York: Samuel Weiser, Inc., 1974), p. 24. Reprinted by permission of George Allen and Unwin, Ltd., and Samuel Weiser, Inc.

[25]On ancient Hindu women, see Katherine K. Young, "Hinduism," in Arvind Sharma, ed., *Women in World Religions* (Albany, NY: SUNY Press, 1987), pp. 60–72; Paul Thomas, *Indian Women through the Ages* (Bombay: Asia

Publishing House, 1964); A. S. Altekar, *The Position of Women in Hindu Civilization* (Delhi: Motilal Banarsidass, 1962).

[26]Sharada Sugirtharajah, "Hinduism," in Jean Holm, ed., *Women in Religion* (New York: Pinter Publishers, 1994), p. 61.

[27]Young, "Hinduism," p. 70.

[28]Basham, *The Wonder That Was India,* p. 182; Prabhati Mukherjee, *Hindu Women: Normative Models,* rev. ed. (Calcutta: Orient Longman, 1994), pp. 10–11; see generally, also, Pundita Ramabai Sarasvati, *The High Caste Hindu Woman* (New Delhi: M. C. Mittal Inter-India Publications, 1888, reprinted 1984), especially Chapter 4.

[29]Young, "Hinduism," p. 69.

[30]G. Buhker, trans., *The Laws of Manu, Sacred Books of the East* (Delhi: Motilal Banarsidass, 1964), pp. 195–97; Manu, vol. 5, pp. 147–65.

[31]Ibid., pp. 327–330; Manu, Vol. 9, pp. 2–16.

[32]Denise Lardner Carmody, *Women & World Religions,* 2nd ed. (Englewood Cliffs, NJ: Prentice Hall, 1989), p. 42; Sugirtharajah, "Hinduism," p. 74.

[33]Young, "Hinduism," p. 64; Ramabai Sarasvati, *The High Caste Hindu Woman,* Chapters 3 and 4. See also Mukherjee, *Hindu Women: Normative Models,* rev. ed. (Calcutta: Orient Longman, 1994).

[34]Carmody, *Women & World Religions,* p. 47.

[35]Mary Daly, *Gyn/Ecology: The Metaethics of Radical Feminism* (Boston: Beacon Press, 1978), pp. 120–21.

[36]Ramabai Sarasvati, *The High Caste Hindu Woman,* p. 109.

[37]Ibid., pp. 82–85.

[38]Benjamin Walker, *The Hindu World: The Encyclopedic Survey of Hinduism* (New York: Praeger, 1968), Vol. 2, p. 464, quoted in Daly, *Gyn/Ecology,* p. 117.

[39]Young, "Hinduism," pp. 85–86.

[40]Michael Allen, "The Hindu View of Women," in Michael Allen and S. N. Mukherjee, eds., *Women in India and Nepal* (Canberra: Australian National University, 1982), pp. 16–17.

[41]See Doranne Jacobson, "Golden Handprints and Red-Painted Feet: Hindu Childbirth Rituals in Central Indian," and Susan Wadley, "Hindu Women's Family and Household Rites in a North Indian Village," both in Nancy Aver Falk and Rita M. Gross, eds., *Unspoken Worlds: Women's Religious Lives* (Belmont, CA: Wadsworth Publishing, 1989), pp. 59–71 and 72–81, respectively; reprinted in Doranne Jacobson and Susan S. Wadley, *Women in India: Two Perspectives,* 3rd ed. (Columbia, MO: South Asia Publications, 1995), pp. 137–55 and 157–70, respectively.

[42]Lindsey Harlan, "Abandoning Shame: Mira and the Margins of Marriage," in Lindsey Harlan and Paul B. Courtright, eds., *From the Margins of Hindu Marriage: Essays on Gender, Religion and Culture* (New York: Oxford University Press, 1995), pp. 205–6.

[43]Sugirtharajah, "Hinduism," pp. 67–68.

[44]Young, "Hinduism," p. 91.

[45]Carmody, *Women & World Religions,* p. 49.

[46]See June McDaniel, *The Madness of the Saints* (Chicago: University of Chicago Press, 1989).

[47]For an excellent discussion of the reform movement and its impact on the independence movement in India, as well as the status of women in contemporary India, see Katherine K. Young, "Women in Hinduism," in Arvind Sharma, ed., *Today's Woman in World Religions* (Albany: SUNY Press, 1994), pp. 77–135. This subsection and the next are based in part on this essay.

[48]Ramabai Sarasvati, *The High Caste Hindu Woman,* p. 78; Kiran Devendra, *Status and Position of Women in India: With Special Reference to Women in Contemporary India* (Delhi: Shakti Books, 1986), p. 9.

[49]Joanna Liddle and Rama Joshi, "Gender and Imperialism in British India," *Economic and Political Weekly,* Vol. 20, no. 43, 1985, WS-77, quoted in Young, "Women in Hinduism," p. 83.

[50]Kiran Devendra, *Status and Position of Women in India: With Special Reference to Women in Contemporary India,* p. ix.

[51]Committee on the Status of Women in India. *Towards Equality: Report of the Committee on the Status of Women in India* (New Delhi: Government of India, Ministry of Education and Social Welfare, 1974).

[52]Young, "Women in Hinduism," p. 86.

[53]Sra S. Mitter, *Dharma's Daughters: Contemporary Indian Women and Hindu Culture* (New Brunswick, NJ: Rutgers University Press, 1991), Part 3.

[54]*NIBWA,* 5 (1985), pp. 20–22; *NIBWA,* 11, (1987), p. 30, quoted in Young, "Women in Hinduism," pp. 121–22.

[55]Smriti Vohra, "Woman MP No Sanyasin," [sic] *Times of India* News Service (New Delhi, December 21, 1989), p. 19, quoted in Young, "Women in Hinduism," p. 98.

[56]See Mrs. Sinclair Stevenson, *The Heart of Jainism* (New Delhi: Munshivam Manoharlal, 1970; Oxford University Press, 1st ed., 1915); William de Bary, *Sources of Indian Tradition* (New York: Columbia University Press, 1958, 1966), Chapters 4 and 5; and P. S. Jaini, *The Jaina Path of Purification* (Berkeley: University of California Press, 1979).

[57]See E. Allen Richardson, *East Comes West* (Cleveland: The Pilgrim Press, 1985), pp. 17–50.

[58]On American Hindu religious movements, see Robert S. Ellwood and Harry B. Partin, *Religious and Spiritual Groups in Modern America,* 2nd ed. (Englewood Cliffs, NJ: Prentice Hall, 1988), Chapter 7, and Timothy Miller, ed., *America's Alternative Religions* (Albany: SUNY Press, 1995), Chapters 17, 18, and 19.

Chapter 4

[1]On the life of the Buddha, see E. J. Thomas, *The Life of the Buddha as Legend and History* (London: Routledge and Kegan Paul, 1927); and the shorter summary in Richard H. Robinson, *The Buddhist Religion: A Historical Introduction* (Belmont, CA: Dickenson, 1970).

[2]Edward Conze, *Buddhist Scriptures* (Harmondsworth, U.K.: Penguin Classics, 1959), pp. 55–56. Copyright © Edward Conze, 1959. Reproduced by permission of Penguin Books Ltd.

[3]Conze, *Buddhist Scriptures,* pp. 186–87.

[4]In some sources this tradition is called Hinayana ("Little Vessel"). That term, however, originated as a derogatory label used by Mahayanists for the other camp in debate, and is not used by Theravadins themselves. It seems more courteous to keep to the word Theravada.

[5]In early centuries c.e., Mahayana was strong in the areas of central Asia that are now Kashmir, Afghanistan, and surrounding regions; from this part of the world it spread to China. But it has been replaced there by Islam. It was also strong in medieval times in much of Southeast Asia, including the Khmer Empire centering in present Cambodia, with its great Buddhist temples of Angkor Wat (originally Hindu, then Mahayana, then modified to Theravada), and in present Indonesia (where it has been replaced by Islam). The story of the interaction of Hinduism, Theravada, and Mahayana in Southeast Asia up to early modern times is a very complex one.

[6]On the role of the monk, see Jane Bunnag, *Buddhist Monk, Buddhist Layman* (London and New York: Cambridge University Press, 1973); Robert C. Lester, *Theravada Buddhism in Southeast Asia* (Ann Arbor, MI: University of Michigan Press, 1973), Part 2; Richard F. Gombrich, *Precept and Practice: Traditional Buddhism in the Rural Highlands of Ceylon* (London: Oxford University Press, 1971); and Melford E. Spiro, *Buddhism and Society* (New York: Harper & Row, 1970), Part 4.

[7]A stimulating discussion of monastic initiation is found in Paul Levy, *Buddhism: A 'Mystery Religion'?* (London: The Athlone Press of the University of London, 1957).

[8]The order of some of the lokas varies in different sources; this list follows Lester, *Theravada Buddhism,* pp. 39–41.

[9]The techniques of samadhic meditation are vividly described in B. A. Maitreya, "Buddhism in Theravada Countries," in *Path of the Buddha,* Kenneth Morgan, ed. (New York: Ronald Press, 1956), pp. 113–52. Original texts are found in Edward Conze, *Buddhist Meditation* (New York: Harper & Row, 1969).

[10]For a personal account of the practice of vipassana meditation, see Eric Lerner, *Journey of Insight Meditation* (New York: Schocken Books, 1977).

[11]On the concepts and practices of popular *Buddhism in Theravada lands,* see Bunnag, *Buddhist Monk, Buddhist Layman;* Lester, *Theravada Buddhism;* Gombrich, *Precept and Practice;* Spiro, *Buddhism and Society;* Maitreya, "Buddhism in Theravada Countries"; and Winston L. King, *A Thousand Lives Away* (Cambridge, MA: Harvard University Press, 1964).

[12]See Jerrold Schecter, *The New Face of Buddha* (New York: Coward-McCann, 1967).

[13]A scholarly translation of the Lotus Sutra is Leon Hurvitz, *The Scripture of the Lotus Blossom of the Fine Dharma* (New York: Columbia University Press, 1975). See also *The Lotus Sutra,* trans. by Burton Watson (New York: Columbia University Press, 1994).

[14]On Nagarjuna and his philosophy, see T. R. V. Murti, *The Central Philosophy of Buddhism* (London: George Allen & Unwin, 1955); and Frederick J. Streng, *Emptiness: A Study in Religious Meaning* (Nashville, TN: Abingdon Press, 1967).

[15]On prajnaparamita thought, see two books by Edward Conze: *Buddhist Thought in India* (Ann Arbor: University of Michigan Press, 1967), pp. 198–204; and *The Prajnaparamita Literature* (The Hague, Netherlands: Mouton, 1960). These books contain references to the author's more technical scholarship in this area.

[16]There is no general introductory book in English on the bodhisattva. For easily accessible summaries, see Robinson, *The Buddhist Religion,* pp. 54–63; and Edward Conze, *Buddhism in Essence and Development* (New York: Harper Brothers, 1959), pp. 125–30.

[17]On Mind Only, see Conze, *Buddhist Thought in India,* pp. 250–60; and D. T. Suzuki, *Studies in the Lankavatara Sutra* (London: Routledge, 1930). On a closely related school based on the Avatamsaka Sutra, see Francis D. Cook, *Hua-yen Buddhism: The Jewel Net of Indra* (University Park: Pennsylvania State University Press, 1977).

[18]For an account of most of the Buddhas and bodhisattvas of practical importance in Mahayana art and devotion, see Alice Getty, *The Gods of Northern Buddhism* (Oxford: The Clarendon Press, 1928). See also Walter E. Clark, *Two Lamaist Pantheons* (Cambridge, MA: Harvard University Press, 1937).

[19]Fascinating accounts of Tantric apprenticeships can be found in Herbert V. Guenther, *The Life and Teaching of Naropa* (London: Oxford University Press, 1963); and W. Y. Evans-Wentz, *Tibet's Great Yogin Milarepa* (London and New York: Oxford University Press, 1969).

[20]Translations include Francesca Fremantle and Choguam Trungpa, *The Tibetan Book of the Dead* (Berkeley and London: Shambhala, 1975); W. Y. Evans-Wentz, *The Tibetan Book of the Dead* (New York: Oxford University Press, 1927, 1960); and Robert A. Thurman Jr., *The Tibetan Book of the Dead: The Great Book of Natural Liberation through Understanding in the Between* (New York: Bantam, 1993).

[21]The standard treatment is S. J. Heinrich Dumoulin, *A History of Zen Buddhism* (New York: McGraw-Hill, 1965). For a readable history presented through the lives of the great Chan/Zen masters, see Thomas Hoover, *The Zen Experience* (New York: New American Library, 1980).

[22]Rita M. Gross, *Buddhism after Patriarchy: A Feminist History, Analysis, and Reconstruction of Buddhism* (Albany: SUNY Press, 1993), p. 23. This book is a must for those interested in women in Buddhism, especially with respect to exploring the patriarchal dimensions of Buddhism and how it might be reconstructed in nonpatriarchal form.

[23]Rita M. Gross, "Buddhism," in Jean Holm with John Bowker, ed., *Women in Religion* (London and New York: Pinter, 1994), pp. 3–4; Nancy Schuster Barnes, "Buddhism," in *Women in World Religions,* Arvind Sharma, ed. (Albany, NY: SUNY Press, 1987), pp. 105–33, an excellent summary of the role of and attitudes toward women in the various forms of Buddhism.

[24]Nancy Auer Falk, "The Case of the Vanishing Nuns: The Fruits of Ambivalence in Ancient Indian Buddhism," in Nancy Auer Falk and Rita M. Gross, eds., *Unspoken Worlds: Women's Religious Lives* (Belmont, CA: Wadsworth Publishing, 1989), pp. 158–60, a pivotal work on the subject. See also Barnes, "Buddhism," p. 107.

[25]Falk, "The Case of the Vanishing Nuns," pp. 159–60; Gross, *Buddhism after Patriarchy,* p. 37; Gross, "Buddhism," p. 6.

[26]Falk, "The Case of the Vanishing Nuns," pp. 159–60.

[27]Barnes, "Buddhism," p. 109.

[28]Ibid., p. 124; K. A. Cissel [Kathryn A. Tsai], *The Pi-ch'iu-ni chuan: Biographies of Famous Chinese Nuns from 317–516* (Ann Arbor, MI: University Microfilms, 1972).

[29]Ibid., p. 161; Barnes, "Buddhism," pp. 107–109.

[30]*Book of the Gradual Sayings,* trans. by F. L. Woodward and E. M. Hare. 5 vols. (Pali Text Society, 1932–1936). Reprint. (London: Luzac and Co., 1952–1965), Vol. III, pp. 56–57, cited in Barnes, "Buddhism," p. 108, n. 1.

[31]Aguttaranikaya iv. 8.10, quoted by Cornelia Dimmitt Church, "Temptress, Wife, Nun: Woman's Role in Early Buddhism," *Anima: An Experiential Journal,* 1, 2 (Spring 1975), p. 55.

[32]Diana Paul, *Women in Buddhism: Images of the Feminine in Mahayana Tradition* (Berkeley, CA: Asian Humanities Press, 1979), pp. 27–59.

[33]Denise Lardner Carmody, *Women & World Religions,* 2nd ed. (Englewood Cliffs, NJ: Prentice Hall, 1979, 1989), p. 71.

[34]Falk, "The Case of the Vanishing Nuns," pp. 162–63.

[35]Barnes, "Buddhism," p. 109; Carmody, *Women & World Religions,* pp. 73–74; Rita M. Gross, "The Householder and the World Renunciant: Two Modes of Sexual Expression in Buddhism," *Journal of Ecumenical Studies,* 22, 1 (Winter 1985), pp. 81–96, cited in Carmody, *Women & World Religions,* pp. 73–74.

[36]Gross, "Buddhism," pp. 8–9.

[37]Gross, *Buddhism after Patriarchy,* p. 10.

[38]Diana Paul, *Women in Buddhism,* pp. 187–90.

[39]Ibid., p. 230.

[40]Ibid., pp. 190–99.

[41]Gross, "Buddhism," pp. 10–11.

[42]Barnes, "Buddhism," p. 121.

[43]Cited in Joanna Rogers Macy, "Perfection of Wisdom: Mother of All Buddhas," in *Beyond Androcentrism: New Essays on Women and Religions,* Rita M. Gross, ed. (Missoula, MT: Scholars' Press, 1977), p. 318.

[44]Cited in Gross, *Buddhism after Patriarchy,* p. 103.

[45]Ibid., p. 102.

[46]Ibid., p. 92; Gross, "Buddhism," pp. 16–17.

[47]Cited in Miranda Shaw, *Passionate Enlightenment: Women in Tantric Buddhism* (Princeton, NJ: Princeton University Press, 1994), p. 153.

[48]Gross, *Buddhism after Patriarchy,* p. 108.

[49]Ibid., pp. 80–81.

[50]Barbara Aziz, "Moving Toward a Sociology of Tibet" in *Feminine Ground: Essays on Women and Tibet,* Janice D. Willis, ed. (Ithaca, NY: Snow Lion, 1987), p. 79, cited in Gross, *Buddhism after Patriarchy,* p. 81.

[51]Gross, *Buddhism after Patriarchy,* p. 87.

[52]Ibid., p. 39.

[53]Ibid., p. 88.

[54]Nancy J. Barnes, "Women in Buddhism," in *Today's Woman in World Religions,* Arvind Sharma, ed. (Albany: SUNY Press, 1994), pp. 137–69. This is an excellent review of issues with respect to women in contemporary Buddhism and was used throughout this section as a resource.

Chapter 5

[1]Marcel Granet, *Chinese Civilization* (New York: Meridian Books, 1958), pp. 170–79.

[2]See Judith M. Treistman, *The Prehistory of China* (New York: Natural History Press, 1972), pp. 111–16.

[3]In this chapter, the Pinyin System of transliteration of Chinese into the Roman alphabet is used. This system, adopted by the People's Republic of China, is quite phonetic for English if one remembers that q = ch and x = sh, approximately. In some cases, the older Wade-Giles form is given in parentheses. It will be the one found in many books.

[4]The standard translation of the complete set of nine books is the nineteenth-century work of James Legge (Oxford, U.K.: The Clarendon Press, various dates), although, of course, its scholarship has now been superseded in various particulars.

[5]See Harlee G. Creel, *Sinism* (Chicago: Open Court, 1929).

[6]For translations of the Xiao Jing, the "Classic of Filial Piety," see James Legge, *Hsiao King* (Oxford, UK: Oxford University Press, 1899); and Sister Mary Makra, *The Hsiao Ching* (Annapolis, MD: St. John's University Press, 1961).

[7]Creel, *Sinism.*

[8]Arthur Waley, *The Way and Its Power* (London: George Allen & Unwin, 1934), Introduction.

[9]From *The Way of Life: According to Lao Tzu,* trans. by Witter Bynner (New York: The John Day Co.). Copyright © 1944 by Witter Bynner (renewed 1972). Reprinted by permission of The John Day Co. © 1998 HarperCollins. Reprinted with permission.

[10]Ibid., pp. 25–26.

[11]Ibid., pp. 26–27.

[12]Ibid., p. 35.

[13]See Burton Watson, *Chuang Tzu: Basic Writings* (New York: Columbia University Press, 1964); and A. C. Graham, *Chuang Tzu: The Inner Chapters* (London: George Allen & Unwin, 1981).

[14]Fung Yu-Lan, *A Short History of Chinese Philosophy* (New York: Macmillan, 1960), Chapters 19–20, contains a good brief summary of the Daoism of this period.

[15]The best introduction to religious Daoism, as well as to other aspects of Daoism, is Holmes Welch, *Taoism: The Parting of the Way* (Boston: Beacon Press, 1965). See also Michael R. Saso, *Taoism and the Rite of Cosmic Renewal* (Pullman: Washington State University Press, 1972), which provides a striking description of modern religious Daoism, together with useful and informed comments on the history and meaning of religious Daoism. Peter Goulart, *The Monastery of Jade Mountain* (London: John Murray, 1961), offers a vivid if uncritical picture of Daoist life in mainland China in the decades before the Communist revolution. The same can be said of John Blofeld, *The Secret and Sublime: Taoist Mysteries and Magic* (London: George Allen & Unwin, 1973). Two older multivolumed works, J. J. M. de Groot, *The Religious Systems of China,* 6 vols. (Leiden: E. J. Brill, 1892–1910; reprinted Taipei: Literature House, 1964); and Henri M. Doré, *Researches into Chinese Superstitions,* 13 vols., in English (Shanghai: Tusewei Press, 1914–1938; reprinted Taipei: Chéngwen Publishing, 1968), provide an immense wealth of material on the Daoist pantheon and related rites and beliefs, as well as on other matters, although the scholarship and attitudes are dated.

[16]See Mircea Eliade, *The Forge and the Crucible* (New York: Harper and Brothers, 1962), Chapter 11.

[17]The best general book on Chinese Buddhism is Kenneth Ch'en, *Buddhism in China* (Princeton, NJ: Princeton University Press, 1964). Also useful is Arthur F. Wright, *Buddhism in Chinese History* (Stanford, CA: Stanford University Press, 1959). For the actual life of Chinese Buddhist monasteries and popular devotion, see Holmes Welch, *The Practice of Chinese Buddhism, 1900–1950* (Cambridge, MA: Harvard University Press, 1967); and J. Prip-Møller, *Chinese Buddhist Monasteries* (New York: Oxford University Press, 1937, 1967).

[18]See Wright, *Buddhism in Chinese History,* pp. 36–37.

[19]This area is well portrayed in Wolfram Eberhard, *Guilt and Sin in Traditional China* (Berkeley: University of California Press, 1967).

[20]The most useful translations are John Blofeld, *I Ching* (New York: Dutton, 1968); and Richard Wilhelm, *I Ching, or Book of Changes* (New York: Pantheon Books, 1950).

[21]Arthur Waley, trans., *Monkey: Folk Novel of China by Wu Ch'eng-En* (New York: Grove Press, 1958); Anthony Yu, trans., *The Journey to the West,* 4 vols. (Chicago: University of Chicago Press, 1977–1983).

[22]Stewart McFarlane, "Chinese Religions," in *Women in Religion,* Jean Holm with John Bowker, eds. (London and New York: Pinter Publishers, 1994), p. 161, citing James Legge, *Li chi, Book of Rites,* 2 vols., C. C. Chai and W. Chai (New York: University Books, 1967), 1:441.

[23]Cited in Denise Lardner Carmody, *Women & World Religions,* 2nd ed. (Englewood Cliffs, NJ: Prentice Hall, 1979, 1989), p. 71.

[24]McFarlane, "Chinese Religions," p. 163.

[25]Theresa Kelleher, "Confucianism," in *Women in World Religions,* Arvind Sharma, ed. (Albany: SUNY Press, 1987), p. 144, citing Nancy Lee Swann, *Pan Chao: Foremost Woman Scholar of China* (New York: Century Co., 1932), p. 83.

[26]Ibid.

[27]Theresa Kelleher, "Confucianism," p. 140. This article was particularly helpful to the author throughout this section.

[28]Cited in Kelleher, "Confucianism," p. 148.

[29]Ibid., p. 145.

[30]Margery Wolf, "Women and Suicide in China," in *Women in Chinese Society,* Margery Wolf and Roxane Witke, eds. (Stanford, CA: Stanford University Press, 1975), generally, cited in Kelleher, "Confucianism," p. 146.

[31]Margery Wolf, *Women and the Family in Rural Taiwan* (Stanford, CA: Stanford University Press, 1972), pp. 32–37, and Margery Wolf, *Revolution Postponed: Women in Contemporary China* (Stanford, CA: Stanford University Press, 1985), pp. 9–12, cited in McFarlane, "Chinese Religions," p. 162.

[32]Carmody, *Women & World Religions,* pp. 95–96.

[33]Witter Bynner, trans., *The Way of Life According to Laotzu.* (New York: John Day, 1944, 1972), p. 34.

[34]Ellen Chen, "Nothingness and the Mother Principle in Early Chinese Taoism," *International Philosophical Quarterly,* 9 (1969), pp. 391–405, cited in McFarlane, "Chinese Religions," p. 165 and Kelleher, "Confucianism," pp. 162–63.

[35]McFarlane, "Chinese Religions," p. 166.

[36]Carmody, *Women & World Religions,* p. 101.

[37]Barbara Reed, "Taoism," in *Women in World Religions,* Arvind Sharma, ed. (Albany: SUNY Press, 1987), pp. 167–68.

[38]Ibid., p. 175.

[39]Ibid., p. 179–80.

40Ibid., p. 176–77.

41Ibid., p. 173.

42Ibid., p. 168–69.

43This section is based on the work of Beverley Jackson in *Splendid Slippers: A Thousand Years of an Erotic Tradition* (Berkeley, CA: Ten Speed Press, 1997). See also Fan Hong, *Footbinding, Feminism, and Freedom* (London and Portland, OR: Frank Cass, 1997).

44Mary Daly, *Gyn/Ecology. The Metaethics of Radical Feminism* (Boston: Beacon, 1978), p.136. This is one of Mary Daly's classic works in radical feminism and is an especially critical assessment of footbinding and other mutilations of the female body.

45Miriam Levering, "Women, the State, and Religion Today in the People's Republic of China," in *Today's Woman in World Religions,* Arvind Sharma, ed. (Albany: SUNY Press, 1994), pp. 171–224.

46The best translations are Donald M. Philippi, *Kojiki* (Tokyo: University of Tokyo Press, 1968); and W. G. Aston, *Nihongi* (London: George Allen & Unwin, 1896, 1956).

47See Daniel C. Holtom, *The Japanese Enthronement Ceremonies* (Tokyo: Kyo Bun Kwan, 1928; Tokyo: Sophia University, 1972); and Robert S. Ellwood, *The Feast of Kingship* (Tokyo: Sophia University, 1973).

48See Aston, *Nihongi,* Part 2, pp. 65–67, for the traditional account.

49Harper Havelock Coates and Ryugaku Ishizuka, *Honen the Buddhist Saint* (Kyoto: Cholnin, 1925); Alfred Bloom, *Shinran's Gospel of Pure Grace* (Tucson: University of Arizona Press, 1965).

50Masaharu Anesaki, *Nichiren the Buddhist Prophet* (Cambridge, MA: Harvard University Press, 1916)

51See James W. White, *The Sokagakkai and Mass Society* (Stanford, CA: Stanford University Press, 1970).

52See Robert N. Bellah, *Tokugawa Religion* (Glencoe, IL: The Free Press, 1957); Warren W. Smith, *Confucianism in Modern Japan* (Tokyo: Hokuseido, 1973).

53Denise Lardner Carmody, *Women & World Religions,* pp. 116–17.

54Ibid., p. 121.

55See, generally, William R. LaFleur, *Liquid Life: Abortion and Buddhism in Japan* (Princeton, NJ: Princeton University Press, 1992).

56Buckley, Sandra, ed., *Broken Silence: Voices of Japanese Feminism* (Berkeley: University of California Press, 1996).

57Material on Korean religion can be found in C. A. Clark, *Religions of Old Korea* (New York: Garland, 1981; 1st ed., 1932); and Byung-Kil Chang, *Religions in Korea* (Seoul: Korean Overseas Information Service, 1984). But no English source is equal to Frits Vos, *Die Religionen Koreas* (Stuttgart: Verlag W. Kohlammer, 1977). On special topics see Roger Janelli, *Ancestor Worship in Korean Society* (Stanford, CA: Stanford University Press, 1982);

and two highly readable books by Laurel Kendall, *Shamans, Housewives, and Other Restless Spirits* (Honolulu: University of Hawaii Press, 1985) and *The Life and Hard Times of a Korean Shaman* (Honolulu: University of Hawaii Press, 1988).

Chapter 6

[1]See R. C. Zaehner, *The Dawn and Twilight of Zoroastrianism* (London: Weidenfelt & Nicolson, 1961).

[2]See R. C. Zaehner, *The Teachings of the Magi: A Compendium of Zoroastrian Beliefs* (London: George Allen & Unwin, 1956; New York: Macmillan, 1956), pp. 53–55.

[3]Jacques Duschesne-Guillaume, *The Hymns of Zarathustra* (Boston: Beacon Press, 1963), is a good translation of the Gathas. The bulk of the Zend Avesta is translated in *The Sacred Books of the East*.

[4]Rustom Masani, *The Religion of the Good Life* (New York: Collier Books, 1962), gives an account by a Parsee of their present-day beliefs and practices.

Chapter 7

[1]Transliterated into Roman letters, the name of God, called the tetragrammaton, is *YHVH*. The pronunciation must have been something like Yahweh or Yehveh. The name Jehovah of the King James Bible is an older attempt at pronouncing the same name by supplying the vowels of the title *Adonai,* "The Lord." Devout Jews, of course, would not make the attempt to pronounce the name; as in the Bible, God is spoken of not by name but by terms like *Adonai.*

[2]See Gershom G. Scholem, *Major Trends in Jewish Mysticism* (New York: Schocken Books, 1961), pp. 156–204.

[3]Colorful accounts of Hasidism can be found in the writings of Martin Buber and in Herbert Weiner, *9 1/2 Mystics* (New York: Holt, Rinehart & Winston, 1969).

[4]Rabbi Nahman of Bratslav (1772–1811), cited in Arthur Hertzberg, ed., *Judaism* (New York: George Braziller, Inc., 1961), pp. 91–92. Reprinted with the permission of the publisher. Copyright © 1961 by Arthur Hertzberg.

[5]The meaning of the Sabbath is vividly described in Herman Wouk, *This Is My God* (Garden City, NY: Doubleday, 1959), pp. 55–66. See also Abraham Joshua Heschel, *The Sabbath: Its Meaning for Modern Man* (New York: Farrar, Strauss, and Giroux, 1951).

[6]Wouk, *This Is My God,* pp. 96–99, contains a particularly colorful account of Purim.

[7]Cited in Denise Lardner Carmody, "Judaism" in Arvind Sharma, ed., *Women in World Religions* (Albany, NY: SUNY Press, 1987), p. 204.

[8]Ibid., generally pp. 183–206. This is an excellent summary of the subject and was helpful to the authors throughout this section.

[9]Alexandra Wright, "Judaism," in Jean Holm with John Bowker, ed., *Women in Religion* (London and New York: Pinter Publishers, 1994), p. 114.

[10]Carmody, "Judaism," p. 187.

[11]*The Writings—Kethubim.* Copyright by The Jewish Publication Society of America, 1982.

[12]Denise Lardner Carmody, *Women & World Religions,* 2nd ed. (Englewood Cliffs, NJ: Prentice Hall, 1979, 1989), p. 146.

[13]Ibid., p. 147.

[14]*The Form of Daily Prayers: According to the Customs of the German and Polish Jews,* trans. by Joseph Guns (Budapest: Jos. Schlesinger Library, 1938).

[15]See Phyllis Trible, *Texts of Terror: Literary-Feminist Readings of Biblical Narratives* (Philadelphia, 1984). See also Susan Niditch, "Portrayals of Women in the Hebrew Bible," in Judith R. Baskin, ed., *Jewish Women in Historical Perspective* (Detroit, MI: Wayne State University Press, 1991).

[16]Carmody, *Women & World Religions,* p. 139.

[17]Ibid., p. 145.

[18]See Rachel Biale, *Women & Jewish Law: An Exploration of Women's Issues in Halakhic Sources* (New York: Schocken Books, 1984), Chapter 6. This is a good resource for Jewish law regarding women.

[19]Cited in Susannah Heschel, "Preface," *On Being a Jewish Feminist,* Susannah Heschel, ed. (New York: Schocken Books, 1983, 1995), p. xi.

[20]Originally, Judaism permitted polygyny. The practice is recounted in the Hebrew scriptures and was continued into the Talmudic period, although it appears that no rabbi referenced in the Talmud had more than one wife. See Wright, "Judaism," p. 125. Polygyny was abolished by Rabbenu Gershom (960–1028) who propounded a takkanah (new ruling). The practice was then discontinued in countries in the West. See Rachel Adler, "The Jew Who Wasn't There: Halakhah and the Jewish Woman," Susannah Heschel, ed. *On Being a Jewish Feminist* (New York: Schocken Books, 1983, 1995), p. 16.

[21]Carmody, "Judaism," pp. 187.

[22]Ibid., p. 198

[23]Carmody, *Women & World Religions,* p. 135.

[24]A woman named Regina Jonas was ordained privately as a reform rabbi in 1935 in Germany. She was put to death at Auschwitz in 1944. See Katharina von Kellenbach, "'God Does Not Oppress Any Human Being': The Life and Thought of Rabbi Regina Jonas," *Yearbook of the Leo Baeck Institute,* vol. 39 (1994), pp. 213–26, cited in Susannah Heschel, "Preface," *On Being a Jewish Feminist,* p. xiii.

[25]See Cynthia Ozick, "Notes toward Finding the Right Question," in *On Being a Jewish Feminist,* Susannah Heschel, ed. (New York: Schocken Books, 1983, 1995), generally.

[26]See Judith Plaskow, "The Right Question is Theological," in *On Being a Jewish Feminist,* Susannah Heschel, ed. (New York: Schocken Books, 1983,

1995), pp. 230–31 and Susannah Heschel, "Preface," *On Being a Jewish Feminist,* pp. xii–xvi, generally.

[27]See Rita M. Gross, "Female God Language in a Jewish Context," in *Womanspirit Rising: A Feminist Reader in Religion,* Carol P. Christ and Judith Plaskow, eds. (San Francisco: HarperSanFrancisco, 1979, 1992), pp. 170–71, and Judith Plaskow, "The Right Question is Theological," p. 229.

[28]Plaskow, "The Right Question is Theological," p. 228.

[29]Heschel, "Preface," *On Being a Jewish Feminist,* p. xxii.

[30]Ibid., p. xxiii.

[31]It is important to note that Jewish feminists have written about the problem of Christian feminists' tendency to depict Judaism negatively as a backdrop for the "innovations" of Jesus in his time. They are quick to point out that Jesus was very much a part of the Judaism of that era. As Susan Heschel has written: "The more appropriate evidence from first century Palestine indicates that women served as synagogue leaders and maintained positions of social and financial importance, suggesting that Jesus' behavior was no different from that of other Jews in his day." Heschel, "Preface," in *On Being a Jewish Feminist,* pp. xviii–xix.

[32]Plaskow, "The Right Question is Theological," p. 224.

[33]See Adler, "The Jew Who Wasn't There: Halakhah and the Jewish Woman," generally.

[34]Judith Plaskow, "The Wife/Sister Stories: Dilemmas of the Jewish Feminist," in *Speaking of Faith,* Diana L. Eck and Devaki Jain, eds. (Philadelphia: New Society, 1987), pp. 125–126, cited in Carmody, *Women & World Religions,* p. 156.

Chapter 8

[1]See Robert M. Grant, *A Historical Introduction to the New Testament* (New York: Harper & Row, 1963).

[2]See John Bright, *The Kingdom of God* (Nashville, TN: Abingdon Press, 1953).

[3]For a presentation of the theory that Jesus was involved with political revolutionaries, see S. G. F. Brandon, *Jesus and the Zealots* (New York: Scribner, 1967).

[4]See Gunther Bornkamm, *Paul,* trans. by D. M. G. Stalker (New York: Harper & Row, 1971); John Knox, *Chapters in a Life of Paul* (London: Adam and Charles Black, 1954); and Richard Longenecker, *Paul: Apostle of Liberty* (New York: Harper & Row, 1964).

[5]See John Marsh, *The Gospel of St. John* (Harmondsworth, U.K.: Penguin Books, 1968); and Oscar Cullmann, *The Johannine Circle* (Philadelphia: Westminster Press, 1975).

[6]See Dom Gregory Dix, *The Shape of the Liturgy* (London: Dacre Press, 1945), pp. 36–45.

[7]J. W. C. Wand, *A History of the Early Church* (London: Methuen & Co., 1937), p. 97.

[8]From the *Epistle of St. Ignatius of Antioch to the Romans,* Vols. 4 and 7. Francis X. Glimm and others, *The Apostolic Fathers* (New York: Christian Heritage, 1947), pp. 109–10.

[9]See Hermann Dorres, *Constantine the Great,* trans. Roland Bainton (New York: Harper & Row, 1972).

[10]See Robert M. Grant, *The Formation of the New Testament* (New York: Harper & Row, 1965).

[11]See Helen Waddell, *The Desert Fathers* (Ann Arbor: University of Michigan Press, 1957); Justin McCann, *Saint Benedict* (Garden City, NY: Doubleday, 1958); and David Knowles, *Christian Monasticism* (New York: McGraw-Hill, 1969).

[12]See George C. Coulton, *Medieval Panorama* (New York: Macmillan, 1938); and two works of readable history by H. Daniel-Rops, *The Church in the Dark Ages,* trans. Audrey Butler (New York: Dutton, 1959); and *Cathedral and Crusade: Studies of the Medieval Church,* 1050–1350, trans. John Worthington (New York: Dutton, 1957).

[13]On spiritual dissidents in the Middle Ages, see Steven Runciman, *The Medieval Manichee* (Cambridge: Cambridge University Press, 1960); and Norman Cohn, *The Pursuit of the Millenium: Revolutionary Millenarians and Mystical Anarchists of the Middle Ages* (New York: Oxford University Press, 1976).

[14]A readable life of Luther is Roland H. Bainton, *Here I Stand* (New York: Abingdon-Cokesbury Press, 1950). For the entire period see Harold J. Grimm, *The Reformation Era 1500–1650* (New York: Macmillan, 1973).

[15]See George Harrison Williams, *The Radical Reformation* (Phiadelphia: Westminster Press, 1962).

[16]See Charles Williams, *The Figure of Beatrice* (London: Faber, 1943). Williams describes the longstanding distinction between two kinds of mysticism and devotion: that of "negation of images" and that of "affirmation of images."

[17]Two books that provide real insight into the soul of Eastern Orthodox spirituality, especially in old Russia, are Jon Gregerson, *Transfigured Cosmos* (New York: Ungar, 1960); and *The Way of a Pilgrim, and the Pilgrim Continues His Way,* trans. R. M. French (New York: Seabury Press, 1974).

[18]These characteristics are based in part on those in the article by Richard p. McBrien, "Roman Catholicism," in The *Encyclopedia of Religion,* vol. 12 (New York: Macmillan, 1987), pp. 437–39.

[19]Harvey Cox, *Fire from Heaven: The Rise of Pentecostal Spirituality and the Reshaping of Religion in the Twenty-First Century*. Reading, MA: Addison-Wesley, 1995; and André Cortin, *Pentecostalism in Brazil*. New York: St. Martin's Press, 1949.

[20]David B. Barrett, *African Initiatives in Religion*. Nairobi, Kenya: East African Publishing House, 1971, pp. 110–20.

[21]For an excellent overview of issues regarding women in Christian thought from the New Testament accounts to the twentieth century, including excerpts from original sources, on which this segment is based in part, see Elizabeth A. Clark and Herbert Richardson, *Women and Religion: The Original Sourcebook of Women in Christian Thought,* new ed. (San Francisco: HarperSanFrancisco, 1996).

[22]See note 31 under Chapter 7.

[23]See generally, Elisabeth Schussler Fiorenza, *In Memory of Her: A Feminist Theological Reconstruction of Christian Origins,* tenth anniversary ed. (New York: Crossroad, 1994).

[24]Clark and Richardson, *Women and Religion,* p. 11.

[53]Denise Lardner Carmody, *Women & World Religions,* 2d ed. (Englewood Cliffs, NJ: Prentice Hall, 1979, 1989), p. 171, citing De Cult. Fem., 1:1.

[26]For a discussion of how the original church turned from a more egalitarian view of women to subordination of women, see Karen Torjeson, *When Women Were Priests: Women's Leadership in the Early Church and the Scandal of Their Subordination in the Rise of Christianity* (San Francisco: HarperSanFrancisco, 1993, 1995).

[27]These views probably were derived from Gnostic and Manichean theologies, which were eschewed by early church leaders but nevertheless found their way into the institutionalized views of the church. See Clark and Richardson, *Women and Religion,* Ch. 2.

[28]Rosemary Radford Ruether, "Motherearth and the Megamachine," in *Womanspirit Rising: A Feminist Reader in Religion,* Carol P. Christ and Judith Plaskow, eds. (San Francisco: HarperSanFrancisco, 1992), pp. 43–45.

[29]Clark and Richardson, *Women and Religion,* pp. 90–91, citing Barbara A. Hanawalt, "Golden Ages for the History of Medieval English Women," in *Women in Medieval History and Historiography,* ed. Susan Mosher Stuard (Philadelphia: University of Pennsylvania Press, 1987), p. 17.

[30]Clark and Richardson, *Women and Religion,* p. 121.

[31]Ibid., p. 92.

[32]See Anne Llewellyn Barstow, *Witchcraze: A New History of the European Witch Hunts* (San Francisco: HarperSanFrancisco/Pandora, 1994); Joseph Klaits, *Servants of Satan: The Age of the Witch Hunts* (Bloomington: Indiana University Press, 1985); Hugh Trevor-Roper, *The European Witch-Craze of the Sixteenth and Seventeenth Centuries* (Harmondsworth, U.K.: Penguin Books, 1969).

[33]For a wonderful collection of articles on women in Christianity and Judaism, see Rosemary Ruether and Eleanor McLaughlin, eds., *Women of Spirit: Female Leadership in the Jewish and Christian Traditions* (New York: Simon and Schuster, 1979).

[34]Nancy Hardesty, Lucille Sider Dayton, and Donald W. Dayton, "Women in the Holiness Movement: Feminism in the Evangelical Tradition," in Rosemary Ruether and Eleanor McLaughlin, eds., *Women of Spirit,* p. 244. The authors found this article to be especially helpful in this segment.

[35]The accounts of Sojourner Truth's Akron, Ohio, speech vary. This version is based primarily on the report of Frances Gage as given in Jacqueline Bernard, *Journey Toward Freedom: The Story of Sojourner Truth* (New York: The Feminist Press at The City of New York, 1967, 1990), pp. 165–67, with some modifications based on other accounts. See also Carleton Mabee, *Sojourner Truth: Slave, Prophet, Legend* (New York: New York University Press, 1993), pp. 67–78 and Nell Irvin Painter, *Sojourner Truth: A Life, A Symbol* (New York/London: W. W. Norton & Company, 1996), pp. 167–68.

[36]Quoted in Denise Lardner Carmody and John Tully Carmody, *Exploring American Religion* (Mountain View, CA: Mayfield Publishing Company, 1990), pp. 121–22.

[37]Nancy Hardesty, Lucille Sider Dayton, and Donald W. Dayton, "Women in the Holiness Movement: Feminism in the Evangelical Tradition," pp. 225–54.

[38]Rosemary R. Ruether, "Christianity and Women in the Modern World," in *Today's Woman in World Religions,* Arvind Sharma, ed. (Albany: SUNY Press, 1994), p. 285.

[39]Larry B. Stamer, "A Wife's Role Is 'to Submit,' Baptists Declare," *Los Angeles Times,* 10 June 1998.

[40]Linda A. Moody, *Women Encounter God: Theology across the Boundaries of Difference* (Maryknoll, NY: Orbis Books, 1996).

Chapter 9

[1]Formerly, the religion was often called Muhammadanism and its followers Muhammadans by Occidentals, in analogy to Buddhism or Christianity. But Muslims object to this label and never use it themselves, saying that they do not worship or idolize Muhammad but rather submit to God's will as revealed in his prophetic ministry. Today these feelings are rightly respected, and the proper terms Islam and Muslim are generally used.

[2]Mohammed Marmaduke Pickthall, *The Meaning of the Glorious Koran* (New York: Mentor Books, n.d.), p. vii.

[3]A. J. Arberry, *The Holy Koran* (London: George Allen & Unwin, 1953), pp. 26–27.

[4]N. J. Dawood, trans. *The Koran,* (Penguin Classics 1956, 5th revised edition 1990), p. 15. Copyright © N. J. Dawood, 1956, 1959, 1966, 1968, 1974. Reproduced by permission of Penguin Books, Ltd.

[5]Ibid., p. 194.

[6]Ibid., p. 336.

[7]Seyyed Hossein Nasr, "Jesus through the Eyes of Islam," *The Times* (London), 28 July 1973.

[8]Kenneth Cragg, trans., *The House of Islam* (Belmont, CA: Dickenson, 1969), p. 39. Reprinted by permission of the publisher.

[9]A vivid account of Ramadan, and of much else of Islam in an Iraqi Shi'a setting, may be found in Elizabeth Warnock Fernea, *Guests of the Sheik* (Garden City, NY: Doubleday, 1969).

[10]For an illuminating discussion of pilgrimage, which indirectly casts much light on the meaning of the hajj, see Victor Turner, "The Center Out There: Pilgrim's Goal," in *History of Religions,* 12, 3 (February 1973), pp. 191–230.

[11]G. E. von Grunebaum, *Muhammadan Festivals* (New York: Henry Schuman, 1951), pp. 44–47. The entire discussion of the hajj in this book, pp. 15–49, is very useful.

[12]See Xavier de Planhol, *The World of Islam* (Ithaca, NY: Cornell University Press, 1959), pp. 6–7.

[13]For useful overviews of many aspects of Islamic culture, see Bernard Lewis, ed., *Islam and the Arab World* (New York: Knopf, 1976).

[14]See the account in von Grunebaum, *Muhammadan Festivals,* pp. 81–94. Fernea, *Guests of the Sheik,* contains a colorful firsthand account of the first ten days of Muharram, pp. 216–66.

[15]Dawood, *The Koran,* p. 336.

[16]Ibid., p. 228.

[17]See J. R. Porter, "Muhammad's Journey to Heaven," *Numen,* 21, fasc. 1 (April 1974), pp. 64–80.

[18]From Margaret Smith, *Rabi`a the Mystic* (New York: Cambridge University Press, 1928), pp. 22, 99, 100. Reprinted by permission of the publisher.

[19]See the discussion of Junayd in R. C. Zaehner, *Hindu and Muslim Mysticism* (New York: Schocken Books, 1969).

[20]Idries Shah, *Tales of the Dervishes* (New York: Dutton, 1970), p. 143.

[21]See the discussion of Muslim saints in Fazlur Rahman, *Islam* (Garden City, NY: Doubleday, 1968), pp. 162–65; and in von Grunebaum, *Muhammaden Festivals,* pp. 67–84.

[22]Jane I. Smith, "Islam," in *Women in World Religions,* Arvind Sharma, ed. (Albany: SUNY Press, 1987), p. 235; Margot I. Duley, "Women in the Islamic Middle East and North Africa," in *The Cross-Cultural Study of Women: A Comprehensive Guide,* Margot I. Duley and Mary I. Edwards, eds. (New York: The Feminist Press, 1986), p. 407.

[23]*The Qur`an,* trans. Ahmed Ali (Princeton, NJ: Princeton University Press, 1988), 9:71.

[24]Quoted in Charis Waddy, *Women in Muslim History* (London/New York: Longman, 1980), p. 28.

[25]*The Qur`an* 4:34, cited in Denise Lardner Carmody, *Women & World Religions,* 2nd ed. (Englewood Cliffs, NJ: Prentice Hall, 1979, 1989), p. 193.

[26]*The Qur`an,* trans. Ali, 4:34. See also Asghar Ali Engineer, *The Rights of Women in Islam* (New York: Saint Martin's Press, 1992), p. 46, regarding different interpretations of this passage.

[27]Carmody, *Women & World Religions,* p. 186.

[28]Leila Ahmed, *Women and Gender in Islam: Historical Roots of a Modern Debate* (New Haven, CT, and London: Yale University Press, 1992), p. 4.

[29]Jane I. Smith, "Islam," pp. 239–40; Engineer, *The Rights of Women in Islam,* pp. 30–37.

[30]Engineer, *The Rights of Women in Islam,* p. 45.

[31]Ibid., pp. 21–22.

[32]Carmody, *Women & World Religions,* p. 189.

[33]Engineer, *The Rights of Women in Islam,* p. 36.

[34]Leila Badawi, "Islam," in Jean Holm with John Bowker, ed., *Women in Religion* (London and New York: Pinter Publishers, 1994), p. 109.

[35]Ahmed, *Women and Gender in Islam,* p. 5.

[36]Smith, "Islam," p. 240.

[37]Engineer, *The Rights of Women in Islam,* p. 36.

[38]Ibid., p. 57.

[39]Smith, "Islam," p. 242; Carmody, *Women & World Religions,* p. 195.

[40]Nawal al-Saadawi [El Saadawi], *The Hidden Face of Eve: Women in the Arab World,* trans. and ed. Sherif Hetata (Boston: Beacon Press, 1982), p. 40.

[41]Ibid., pp. 7–10, 33–43.

[42]Smith, "Islam," p. 240.

[43]Badawi, "Islam," p. 89.

[44]Waddy, *Women in Muslim History,* pp. 18–25.

[45]Engineer, *The Rights of Women in Islam,* p. 43.

[46]Ahmed, *Women and Gender in Islam,* pp. 43, 73.

[47]Smith, "Islam," p. 240.

[48]Saadia Khawar Khan Chishi, "Female Spirituality in Islam," in *Islamic Spirituality: Foundations,* S. H. Nasr, ed. (New York: Crossroad, 1987), p. 207, quoted in Carmody, *Women & World Religions,* p. 197.

[49]Waddy, *Women in Muslim History,* pp. 59–60.

[50]Smith, "Islam," pp. 244–45.

[51]Carmody, *Women & World Religions,* p. 190.

[52]Smith, "Islam," p. 248.

[53]Engineer, *The Rights of Women in Islam,* p. 6.

[54]Margot Badran and Miriam Cooke, "Introduction," *Opening the Gates: A Century of Arab Feminist Writing,* Margot Badran and Miriam Cooke, eds. (Bloomington and Indianapolis: Indiana University Press, 1990), pp. xxii–xxiii.

[55]Engineer, *The Rights of Women in Islam,* pp. 41–45.

[56]Ibid., pp. 41–45.

Chapter 10

[1]Friedrich Steinbauer, *Melanesian Cargo Cults,* trans. by Max Wohlwill (St. Lucia, Queensland, Australia: University of Queensland Press, 1979), pp. 5–9. Peter Worsley, *The Trumpet Shall Sound* (New York: Schocken Books, 1968), pp. 123–46.

[2]See Ann Braude, *Radical Spirits: Spiritualism and Women's Rights in Nineteenth Century America* (Boston: Beacon Press, 1989).

[3]Based on the account in Robert S. Ellwood, *The Eagle and the Rising Sun: Americans and the New Religions of Japan* (Philadelphia: Westminster Press, 1974), pp. 69–74.

[4]Joseph Murphy, *Santería: An African Religion in America*, 2nd. ed. (Boston: Beacon Press, 1992); Migene Gonzalez-Wippler, *The Santería Experience* (Englewood Cliffs, NJ: Prentice Hall, 1982), a well-written first person account of the Santeria world; and Isamur Flores-Peña and Roberta J. Evanchuk, *Santería Garments and Altars* (Jackson: University Press of Mississippi, 1994), with beautiful color illustrations of the altars and vestments.

Chapter 11

[1]"Golden Mycenae," in Donald S. Fryer, *Songs and Sonnets Atlantean* (Sauk City, WI: Arkham House, 1971). Reprinted by permission of the publisher.

[2]For further discussion of these possibilities, see Robert Ellwood, *The History and Future of Faith* (New York: Crossroad, 1988).

LOSSARY

Aquinas, Thomas (c. 1225–1274) Priest and great Western religious philosopher of the Middle Ages in the scholastic tradition of the Catholic Church; influenced by the Aristotelian philosophy of the Muslim thinker Cordova (Averroes), whose works had been discovered by the Christians during the Crusades.

Adept Highly skilled practitioner of religious techniques for enlightenment.

Advaita Vedanta Philosophy emphasizing non-dualism; teaches that all is really Brahman; what appears as other than Brahman is maya, or Brahman's appearance in forms not absolute in themselves.

Aggadah The part of the Talmud devoted to folklore.

Ahimsa Literally, harmlessness. A main principle standing behind the nonviolent resistance by noncooperation movement of Mohandas Gandhi, who led the movement for Indian independence, and, following Gandhi's example, Dr. Martin Luther King, Jr., who led the civil rights movement in the United States during the tumultuous 1960s.

Ahriman (Angra Mainya) In Zoroastrianism, the evil spirit, also called the Lie, who opposes Ahura Mazda, the High God, who is righteous.

Ahura Mazda In Zoroastrianism, the High God, who is righteous and who combats Ahriman, the evil spirit, in a universal battle—a battle between Truth and the Lie.

Allah "The God." The Muslim title for the one sovereign God.

Altar of Heaven A huge tiered mountain in Beijing (Peking) where the emperor of China would worship Heaven and Earth at the Winter Solstice and the Summer Solstice, respectively.

Amida Buddha See Amitabha Buddha.

Amitabha Buddha The Buddha of Pure Land Buddhism; the Buddha of the Western Paradise. It is said that countless ages ago he was an aspirant who, in setting foot on the path of enlightenment, vowed (the "Original Vow") that if he attained full and perfect enlightenment, out of compassion he would bring all who called upon his name into his Buddha paradise. Also known as Emiduo in Chinese and Amida in Japanese.

Anatman No self or no ego. The Buddhist teaching that there is no separate individual human self; humans are instead an impermanent collection of parts, the five skandhas (form, sense, perception, karmic impulses, consciousness).

Ancestral spirits The souls of ancestors, believed by many peoples to continue to take an active interest in their communities, and capable of great harm if displeased.

Ancestrism The veneration of ancestors as semideified figures to whom offerings and worship are presented.

Androcentric/Androcentrism Man-centered/man-centeredness, as opposed to human-centered/human-centeredness, which includes women.

Anglicanism The post-Reformation term for the Church of England and its daughter churches throughout the world, such as the Episcopal church in the United States; it retains both Catholic and Protestant features.

Animism   Belief that everything in nature has a soul or spirit and, therefore, all of existence involves the widespread presence of spirit beings, both of the departed and of animated natural objects.

Apocalyptic   From the Greek for "disclosure" or "revelation"; refers to teachings that characteristically claim to be a special revelation and predict a time of troubles, followed by dramatic action by God to defeat evil and establish righteousness.

Apostle   From the Greek for "a person sent forth," one of the twelve disciples of Jesus and Paul, who began their missionary work subsequent to the life of Jesus on earth.

Arhant   One who has obtained complete enlightenment, without becoming a savior of others as a bodhisattva or Buddha; the term especially characteristic of Theravada Buddhism, where the latter vocations are seen as unique to the one Buddha of a world or age.

Arminianism   Belief that one has free will to decide for or against faith in Christ, in contrast to a strict Calvinist view of Divine election and predestination.

Ascetic/Asceticism   One who denies oneself the pleasures of the world; in religion, in order to prepare oneself for receiving enlightenment, God's will, God's love, etc. Asceticism is the institutionalization of ascetics' practices.

Ash`arism   The immensely influential school of Muslim theology that emphasizes that the ways of God are beyond human understanding; human knowledge of God, it says, can only be based on revelation.

Ashkenazi   Jews from Northern and Eastern Europe. Originally, "Ashkenazi" referred to Jews of Germany and France. However, in 1182 the Jews were expelled from France. Many moved to Spain and Poland, as well as Germany. Their special language, Yiddish, developed primarily in Germany and Poland, and their religious practices also were influenced by the cultures of those countries. While Ashkenazi Jewry is gener-

ally considered to be of German descent, the real center became Poland, but eventually spread throughout Europe. Most Jews in the United States are Ashkenzi.

Ashrama   In Hinduism, a stage of life, or a retreat under the guidance of a guru.

Atman   The soul or essence of one's self, said to be actually nothing other than Brahman.

Augustine   A North African bishop of the late fourth and early fifth centuries. He converted from Roman paganism to Christianity and became one of the most influential Christian writers. He was later beatified as a saint. His work had particular influence on Martin Luther and, therefore, Protestantism specifically.

Avatar   An animal or human form taken by a god on earth; an incarnation of God, like Rama or Krishna.

Axial Age   Term originally coined by historian Karl Jaspers but used differently by others following him, which denotes a period of many parallels among the civilizations of the world, especially in religion, during the period of approximately 900 B.C.E. to 600 C.E. The term itself is controversial as, originally at least, it was claimed that Jesus was the "axial" (i.e., the center around which all else turns) and, therefore, the term implied a particular Western perspective on world history not necessary accepted by others.

Ayatollah   In Shi`ite Islam, a legal and religious teacher regarded as possessing very great learning and righteousness, whose authority is believed to be backed by that of the infallible hidden Imam.

Bardo   The dharmakaya plus the heavenly or transcendent-but-with-wondrous-forms expression of the Buddha-nature in Tibetan Buddhism.

Bar Mitzvah   In Judaism, the rite of passage for a young man, when he is able to read the Hebrew scriptures in synagogue or temple, thereby undertaking the obligation of the Law.

Bat (or Bas) Mitzvah   In Reform and Conservative Judaism, the rite of passage for a young woman equivalent to the Bar Mitzvah for young boys.

Bhagavad-Gita   Classic quasi-scriptural text emphasizing karma-yoga and bhakti.

Bhakti   Spiritual path, which developed in India and is based on love for one's chosen deity.

Bodhidharma   The sage from India who brought the Buddhist "tradition of the smile" from India to China where it became Chan Buddhism and, later, Zen in Japan.

Bodhisattva   "Enlightenment being." In Mahayana, a being on the path to enlightenment who has taken a vow to help all other beings and who works through wisdom and compassion for them in the world. In Theravada, a Buddha in a past lifetime when he is on the way to Buddhahood. In both, a future Buddha.

Boxer Rebellion   The "Boxers" was the name given by foreigners to members of a secret society in China known as the Fists of Righteous Harmony, practitioners of martial arts. The Boxers were recruited by the Empress Dowager Tsu Hsi to rid China of foreigners and foreign influences, which had forced the Chinese government to make humiliating concessions in furtherance of foreign trade. In 1900, this resulted in a "rebellion" during which foreign diplomats and their families were placed under siege by the Boxers and repeatedly attacked for two months. The foreign diplomats and their families were rescued by international Western military forces, which subdued the Boxers and the Chinese imperial forces and destroyed the power of the Ching Dynasty.

Brahman   The universal being; God, understood to be not so much personal as the source and essence of all existence.

Brahmin   The priestly caste.

Buddha   An enlightened or awakened one.

Caliph   Leader of Islam regarded as successor of Muhammad in his capacity as temporal (political, this-worldly) ruler of the faithful.

Calvinism   The Reformation teaching and practice of John Calvin, who emphasized God's sovereignty in calling whom he will to salvation—a concept often called Divine predestination.

Canon (of Scripture)   The proper selection and order of books to make up a scriptural authority; in the case of Christianity, the books of the Old and New Testaments.

Canonization   In the Roman Catholic Church, the procedure by which the pope officially recognizes a person as a saint.

Cao Dai   A spiritualistic and syncretistic new religious movement in Vietnam.

Caste   Social group traditionally believed to be an expression of dharma and based on relative purity; caste may determine with whom one may eat, and one's residence, marriage, and occupation.

Catacombs   Underground cemeteries, such as the early Christian catacombs of Rome.

Chador   A covering from head to toe worn by women in Islamic countries with strict practices. The practice of wearing the chador is called "veiling." The *burqua* is a more severe version.

Chakras   In some yogic teaching, centers of spiritual power along the spinal column, which can be opened by raising the kundalini.

Chan   Chinese Buddhism, influenced by Taoism, emphasizing meditation, interaction of master and disciple, and nature; Zen in Japan.

Chi   Chinese word for the inner biological/spiritual energy of nature, including that found in human beings. It is chi that is invoked in martial arts and is manipulated in acupuncture.

Ch'ondogyo   An important new religious movement in Korea that has advocated worship of the God of Heaven, a combination of features of all major Korean spiritual traditions, and of social reform.

Church of World Messianity   A new Japanese religion.

Civil Religion   A term used to encompass the symbols, ideas and myths, and ritual-like practices of a society that legitimize social and political institutions. In a society such as found in the United States, this may include religious and secular elements.

Conditioned reality   Reality as we ordinarily experience it, limited and constrained by space, time, and the patterns of thought and feeling that shape our response to it.

Confucius (Kong Fuzi in Chinese)   One of the most influential men in Chinese history and philosophy. His name is associated with the Confucian Classics, and in his name there evolved a whole system for organizing and conducting Chinese society, based on the idea of *li* (ritual).

Conservative Judaism   School of Judaism teaching that the principles of the law are important, but practice may be modified to meet contemporary conditions.

Cosmic religion   Religion centered on nature—the turn of the seasons, sacred places such as holy trees and mountains, etc.

Council of Chalcedon   In 451 C.E., the fourth ecumenical council of the Catholic church, which was held to oppose the heresy that Jesus was of two natures or personalities, one Divine and one human, and to reassert the orthodox doctrine of the church that Jesus is both Divine and human in one unified personality and nature.

Council of Ephesus   In 431 C.E., the third ecumenical council of the Catholic church, which was held to oppose the heresy that Jesus was not God when born of Mary and to reassert the orthodox doctrine of the church that Jesus was both God and man when born of Mary, and, therefore, that Mary can be called *Theotokos*, God-bearer.

Council of Nicaea   In 325 C.E., the first ecumenical council of the Catholic church, called by Emperor Constantine, to resolve certain doctrinal matters that were in dispute in the Catholic church; the result was the Nicene Creed, which sets out the standard doctrine that, among other things, Jesus was the only begotten son of the Father (God), is of the same substance as the Father, and suffered and died for the sins of humankind.

Council of Trent   In 1545–1563 C.E., the nineteenth ecumenical council, which was held to address the heresies of the Protestants and to reform the Catholic church.

Crucifixion   The common method for executing dissidents in Rome; involved nailing the condemned's hands and feet to a structure made of two crossed beams set upright in the ground, thereby leaving the condemned to die a slow, agonizing death.

Cult   A term used by sociologists to denote a minority religion characteristically centered on a charismatic leader, who requires strict adherence to the beliefs and practices of the group. Generally, the cult combines teachings and practices from several sources and often requires adherents to sever ties with people who are not a part of the cult.

Cultus   A particular form of worship or devotion.

Curia   The "Roman Curia" consists of the people who assist the Pope of the Catholic church; they are from a consortium of departments and institutes, including the Secretariat of State, congregations, tribunals, pontifical councils, and other offices.

Daijo-sai   In Japan, the harvest festival as celebrated by the emperor after his accession to the throne.

Dao (Tao)   Way, Existence, Nature, or God; the Chinese term for infinite Reality.

Dao de jing (Tao te ching)   The book purportedly written by Laozi, the legendary founder of Daoism. "Dao de jing" means something like "The Book of the Dao and How to Apply Its Strength."

Daoist Popes   The direct decendents of Zhang, called "Heavenly Teacher," who said that Laozi, the legendary founder of Daoism, had appeared to him from the realm of spirits and had given him a sword and other apparatus with which he was able to exercise control over the spiritual world. In the past, they exercised a tenuous spiritual authority over Daoist priests in the southern part of China.

Dengyo Daishi   Originally Saicho (762–822), he brought the teachings of the Tiantai school of Buddhism in China to Japan, which became Tendai Buddhism there and which holds that the Lotus Sutra is the culminating expression of the Buddha's teachings.

Denomination   In Protestant Christianity, a church organization comprised of a number of local churches, having a distinctive and autonomous structure and probably some distinctive doctrines and forms of worship, while recognizing itself as only a part of the larger church of Christ on Earth; e.g., the Methodist, Baptist, or Presbyterian churches.

Dervish   Literally, "doorway." The "whirling dervishes" (the Mevlevi Order) were founded by Jelaluddin Mevlana Rumi, who was a mystic and a poet. Wearing long white robes with wide skirts, the dervishes do a whirling dance, which is believed to bridge the material and spiritual worlds.

Deus otiosus   "Hidden god"; term used for a creator god who, after making the world, withdraws from it, leaving day-to-day affairs in the hands of secondary gods and spirits.

Devotionalism   Emphasis on deeply felt prayer and meditation, i.e., devoting oneself to the Divine, however conceived in various religions.

Dharma   In Hinduism, the social order, which works for righteousness in accordance with *rita,* the cosmic order, and to which the righteous adhere; also one's own duty. In Buddhism, the Buddha's teachings, which are related to the cosmic order.

Dharmakaya   The expression of the Buddha-nature as the essence of the universe, a term and meaning really identical in Mahayana with Nirvana or the Void. Called the Clear Light of the Void in The Tibetan Book of the Dead.

Diaspora   Literally, "dispersion." Refers to many widely dispersed communities as opposed to having a center location for a people. In

Judaism, specifically, it refers to the Jewish people who have been dispersed throughout the world because of persecution; however, the term is also applied to others with similar fates, e.g., the Tibetan Buddhists, whose leader, the Dalai Lama, has met with Jewish leaders to discuss ways to continue religious and cultural identity in "diaspora."

Doctrine   A statement expressing basic beliefs of a religion in propositional form.

Dong Zhongshu   A very influential Chinese thinker (c. 179–104 B.C.E.) who developed the Han Synthesis, which combined aspects Daoism and Confucianism.

Dynasty   A family of rulers in succession, especially in China.

Ecstasy   In religion, a state of powerful rapture, trance, or alteration of consciousness believed to open one to spiritual experience, inspiration, or possession.

Ecumenical Movement   The modern movement for mutual understanding among the branches of Christianity, striving for increasing cooperation among them, with the hope of eventual Christian reunion.

Edict of Milan   The edict of Constantine in 313 C.E., which declared that it was no longer legal to persecute Christians.

Eightfold Path   Right understanding, thought, speech, action, livelihood, effort, mindfulness, and concentration or *samadhi*—the fundamental ideals of Buddhist life and practice as taught by the Buddha.

Epistles   Formal letters.

Eschatology   Doctrines concerning the "last things": death, heaven, hell, judgment, resurrection of the dead, the end of the present world.

Eucharist   The sacred communal meal representing the Last Supper, which remains the principal act of worship of Roman Catholic, Eastern Orthodox, and some Protestant churches. See Holy Communion.

Evangelical   Term widely used to refer to those forms of Protestantism that emphasize the supreme authority of Scripture and salvation by faith—sometimes expressed by a powerful conversion experience—in the atonement of Jesus; also, sometimes connotes "evangelizing," that is, spreading the "good news" of the Gospels to others.

Exodus   The journey of the Israelites under Moses out of Egypt to the Promised Land.

Fana   Sufi term for mystical absorption in the Divine.

Feng liu   In Daoism, "wind and stream;" a metaphor for spontaneity, acting according to the movement of what is happening day by day.

Feng-shui   An elaborate art that involves determining the Yang-Yin "bearings" of locations for houses, businesses, tombs, and temples, as well as the arrangements of rooms and the objects within them.

Filial Piety   Important aspect of Confucian society. It refers to the obligation of a son to negate his own feelings and individuality in deference to the wishes and pleasure of his father.

Five Pillars of Islam   The confession of faith, prayer five times a day, giving of alms to the poor, fasting in the month of Ramadan, and participating in the *hajj* (the pilgrimage to Mecca).

Five relationships (The)   In Confucianism, society is believed to be based on these five relationships: (1) ruler and subject, (2) father and son, (3) husband and wife, (4) elder and younger brother, and (5) friend and friend.

Four Noble Truths   The truth of suffering; the truth of attachment as the cause of suffering; the truth of the end of attachment; and the Eightfold Path as the way to end it—the basic Buddhist teaching as presented by the Buddha in his first sermon.

Friday Mosque   A mosque large enough to hold the entire population of a community, designated as the place for its Friday noon service.

Gemara   The part of the Talmud that is a collection of rabbinical commentaries (c. 200 to 500 C.E) on the Mishna in order to connect it to the written Torah.

General Council   A meeting of bishops recognized as authoritative by the Eastern Orthodox and Roman Catholic churches; the former accepts only the first seven General Councils, the latter a longer list, including the Second Vatican Council. See, e.g., Councils of Chalcedon, Trent, Ephesus, and Nicaea, and the Second Vatican Council.

Gentiles   The name given by Jews to people who were not Jews. Saint Paul saw himself as the apostle to the Gentiles.

Gohei   In Shinto, zigzag paper streamers (sometimes made of hemp) that are waved over a person's head for purification.

Great Awakening   Also known as the First Great Awakening, it was an intellectually serious and more feeling-oriented Christian movement in America during the period from 1720 to 1740 than what had been the case just prior to it. It crossed parish, denominational, and colonial lines and paved the way for the American Revolution in that it gave the people of the 13 colonies a sense of being a distinctive American people with their own spiritual concerns, rather than merely transplanted Europeans. See also the Second Great Awakening.

Great Cultural Revolution   From 1966 to 1969, was fired by a drive to suppress all that was old and a desire, perhaps contrived by the aging Mao Zedong himself, to renew revolutionary fervor at the expense of social stability. Its cohorts disrupted education, harried enemies, defaced monuments of the past, and left nearly all religious places ransacked and closed. Such religious life as survived went deep underground.

Guru   In Hinduism, a spiritual teacher or guide; the disciple's relation to the guru is generally considered sacred.

Hadith   Traditions of what Muhammad did or said which, in Islamic law and traditional scholarship, are believed divinely inspired and have great authority, together with the Qur'an, in establishing orthodox teaching and practice.

Haiden The hall of worship in Shinto where the laity pray and sacred dance is offered.

Hajj The Muslim pilgrimage to Mecca.

Halakhah The part of the Talmud devoted to the Hebraic Law.

Han Dynasty A period (206 B.C.E.–220 C.E.) in Chinese history, which paralleled the contemporary Roman Empire in cultural sophistication, and during which China became a Confucian state.

Han Synthesis A way of thinking about Chinese religion and culture, which combined aspects of Daoism and Confucianism, and which it developed a quasi-theology, quasi-divinity, and quasi-priesthood for Confucianism and Confucius. Confucius was seen as a sort of mystic king, with a true right to rule the inward kingdom of ideas and values upon which the outer realm, administered and educated by the *mandarins*, was based. The universe was viewed as a web of correspondences, and the *Dao* and *Yang-Yin* were central ideas.

Hanifs Believers in one God who predated Muhammad, including Abraham and some pre-Islamic Arabs.

Hanukkah Minor Jewish holiday. A joyous event commemorating the relighting of the lamps of the holy temple in the year 165 C.E, during the campaign of the Maccabee brothers to drive out the oppressor.

Hasidism Popular Jewish mystical and devotional movement, which began in eighteenth-century Eastern Europe.

Hatha-Yoga The yoga of physical postures.

Heresy From Greek, meaning "a choosing." It came to mean, however, doctrines or opinions at odds with orthodoxy.

High God A sovereign deity who created the world or humankind, and who may sustain the moral law, but who may not be involved in everyday affairs.

High Holy Days In Judiasm, Rosh Hashana and Yom Kippur.

Hijra Muhammad's flight from Mecca to Medina in 622 C.E.; the date from which the Muslim calendar begins.

History History is not just the story of what has happened. It is also a perspective on what it means to be human. It involves two key assumptions: that we can isolate some past events as far more important than others and that human life in this world is moving along an irreversible time-stream. These realizations began to shape people's attitudes at the time of the **Axial Age**. That was a time which, in turn, had immense consequences for religion.

Hoa Hao A new religious movement in Viet Nam with roots in Buddhism with Theravada leanings.

Holy Communion The rite of consecrating and consuming bread and wine in remembrance of Jesus' Last Supper with his disciples before the crucifixion; the principle service of worship in Roman Catholic, Eastern Orthodox, and some Protestant churches; also called the **Eucharist** (an ancient and sometimes Anglican term, now often used in ecumenical contexts), Divine Liturgy (Eastern Orthodox), Mass (Roman Catholic), and Lord's Supper (Protestant).

Honen The founder of Amidism in Japan, known as Jodo-shu or Pure Land sect.

Humanist One who adheres to humanism, a movement which has roots in the Renaissance and which centers on the well-being and values of humans here and now, that is, their secular well-being and values as opposed to their spiritual well-being and values.

Imam A trained Muslim teacher and preacher; in Shi`a Islam, a supernaturally endowed supreme teacher and leader of Islam who is a hereditary successor of the Prophet.

Incarnation   Becoming flesh. In Christianity, the doctrine that in Jesus Christ, God (i.e., God the Son, the second person of the Trinity) took on flesh and became a human being. In Hinduism, the avataras or descents of Vishnu or other Hindu gods.

Indulgences   Certificates issued by the pope, the effect of which is to transfer to the penitent some of the grace or merit attained by Christ and the saints and "stored" by the Catholic Church. The perceived abuse of the issuances of indulgences by the pope was one of the main causes of the Protestant Reformation.

Ijtihad   In Islam, the creative original interpretation of the Qur`an, as opposed to strict adherence to traditional interpretations.

Initiation   A process, often arduous, through which a person passes, usually in a traditional programmatic way, to acquire spiritual power and social status within a community, whether as adult member or as shaman.

Islam   "Submission" in Arabic; name of the religion.

Ismailis or **"Seveners"**   A minority within Shi`a who differ from the "Twelvers" on the identity of the seventh Imam, who, they believe, is the last and hidden one. Ismailism has incorporated many esoteric elements into its beliefs.

Izanagi   The male primal parent of the national myth of Japan, which is set out in the Kojiki and Nihonshok.

Izanami   The female primal parent of the national myth of Japan, which is set out in the Kojiki and Nihonshok.

Jainism   Ancient Indian religion emphasizing the attainment of freedom from karma and material existence, as taught by sage-ascetics.

Jihad   In Islam, holy war; also allegorical of the spiritual struggle.

Jodo-shinshu   "True Pure Land" Buddhism, a denomination founded by Shinran (1173–1262), the "Martin Luther of Japan."

Jodo-shu   "Pure Land" Buddhism, a denomination founded by Honen in Japan (1133–1212).

Jun-zi   The superior man, who, as the Confucian ideal suggests, is a man at once a scholar, a selfless servant of society, and a gentleman steeped in courtesy and tradition; as an official and family head, he continually puts philosophy into practice.

Kaaba   The cubical temple of Mecca that is the focus of pilgrimage.

Kabbala   Medieval system of Jewish mystical philosophy.

Kamakura Reformation   The Kamakura was a period in Japanese history (1185–1333), during which several new forms of Buddhism emerged (e.g., Pureland, Nichiren, and Zen), all of which represented a radical Buddhist simplification in which there was to be a simple and sure key to salvation, as dependable on the battlefield as in the monastic temple. Parallels can be drawn to the Protestant Reformation in Europe.

Kama-sutra   A Hindu text, which describes the ways to sensuous and sexual pleasure.

Kami   Shinto deities.

Karma   Cosmic and personal cause and effect by which one's thoughts and deeds determine what happens to one, whether good or bad, including one's future rebirths. In *moksha,* one transcends *karma.*

Karma-yoga   Attaining liberation through selfless work in the world and following one's own *dharma.*

Karuna   In Vajrayana Buddhism, the masculine principle, which represents form, activity, and compassion.

Ketubah   In Judaism, the marriage contract. It is often an elaborately decorated work of art as well.

Kibbutzim   Agricultural communes in Israel.

Kingdom of God or **Kingdom of Heaven**   The reign or rule of God, where God's will is done and his power is evident. Jesus said this reign or rule is both present and coming through his ministry.

Koan In Chan or Zen, an enigmatic riddle or saying intended to challenge ordinary rational thought and help one realize one's true nature.

Kobo Daishi Originally Kukai (773–835), he was the founder of Shingon Buddhism and wrote a book trying to synthesize Daoism, Confucianism, and Buddhism.

Kojiki One of two texts that sets out the national myth of Japan. (See Nihonshok.)

Konkokyo A new Japanese religion.

Kosher In Judaism, keeping "kosher" is adherence to the Hebraic dietary laws.

Krishna Originally, an indigenous folk-god, but later one of the principal devotional deities of bhaki in India. His worship is now worldwide.

Kuan-yin The "Goddess of Mercy" or "Goddess of Compassion" in Pure Land Buddhism in China. Also known as Guanyin, as Kannon in Japan, and as Kwanseum in Korea. Originally this *bodhisattva* was the male Avalokiteshvara in India.

Kundalini In some yogic teaching, coiled power at the base of the spine that can be raised for spiritual growth.

Laozi (Lao-tzu) The legendary founder of Daoism.

Li Confucian term for rites, propriety, courtesy; suggests that doing things with correct form has religious and cosmic meaning.

Liberation Theology A theological movement that began in the Latin American Catholic Church; it holds that the primary message of the Gospels is one of a "view from below," which provides one with the perspective needed to liberate the oppressed.

"Little tradition" The name given to beliefs, practices, and social institutions that are outside of the official orthodoxy of a religion. Although historically women have played only minor roles in the authoritative institutions of the various world religions, they often played a great role in the "little traditions" that often emerged alongside the official tradition. See also Popular Religion.

Logos Literally, "Word." The principle of God's activity revealed to the eye of faith. See Word of God.

Lotus Sutra A sutra of Indian origin extremely influential in Chinese and Japanese Buddhism, especially Tian tai, Tendai, and Nichiren. It emphasizes simple devotion and the universal grace of the Buddha.

Lutheran The Reformation teaching and practice of Martin Luther, who emphasized the sole authority of scripture and "justification by faith," the receiving of God's saving grace through inward faith, as cornerstones of Christianity; the term is used more in America than in Europe.

Magisterium The teaching jurisdiction of the Catholic Church; it bestows the authority to teach doctrine.

Mahdi In Islam, the Imam for All Time.

Magi Order of priests or seers in ancient Persia and the Hellenistic world.

Mahaprajapati The Buddha's aunt and foster mother. She asked the Buddha to permit herself and 500 women to join the Buddha as his followers. When he finally agreed, the order of Buddhist nuns was created.

Mahayana The "Great Vehicle," Buddhism of the northern tier of Buddhist countries, including China, Tibet, and Japan; emphasizes the bodhisattva, the Buddha-nature in all things, and the use of many methods and paths to enlightenment.

Maitreya The Buddha of the future who will bring a new paradisal era. See also Milou.

Malleus Malificarum A book published by two Dominican monks in 1486; it sets out the methods for discovering witches and obtaining confessions from them, usually through horrific tortures.

Mandala   In Buddhism or Hinduism, a meditation diagram showing arrangements of buddhas and bodhisattvas or deities.

Mandarins   The quasi-priesthood of Confucianism; a class of scholar/bureaucrats who administered and educated society. (Also known as the *Ru*.)

Mandate of Heaven   In China, the right of a sovereign to rule as representative of Heaven.

Mantra   A set of sacred words or syllables chanted or meditated in order to bring spiritual power or to unite one with the deity they represent. Plural: mantram.

Mao Zedong (1893–1976)   The founder and the first chairman of of the People's Republic of China. Nearly deified by many, historians have likened his leadership and following to that of a religious cult. His charismatic leadership and ideas led to the Great Cultural Revolution. Transliteration also spelled Mao Tse-Tung.

Mappo   In Buddhism, the last age, when doctrine and morality will deteriorate so much that one can be saved only by faith, if at all; concept of considerable importance during the Kamakura Reformation.

Martyr   From Greek for "witness," one who dies for a faith or cause.

Matsuri   Shinto festival.

Maya   Brahman manifest in the world of forms; illusion when these forms are seen as other than Brahman.

Mencius   Next to Confucius himself, the greatest philosopher of Confucianism (372–289 B.C.E.), who held that human nature is basically good and is only impeded by an evil social environment.

Menorah   In Judaism, the eight-branch candelabra which holds candles that are lit successively during the eight-day Hanuka celebration.

Messiah   The "Anointed One." In Judaism, an expected deliverer and Sublime King that will establish a Divine reign of righteousness. In Christianity, Jesus the Christ. The word "Christ" is a direct Greek translation of" Messiah."

Middle Way   The Buddha's path, understood as avoiding attachment to all extremes or conditioned, partial realities; conceived of as coming in pairs of opposites.

Mihrab   The niche indicating the direction of Mecca in a mosque.

Miluo   The Buddha of the future, depicted in China as the fat, laughing Buddha surrounded by playing children. See also Maitreya.

Minaret   The tower beside many mosques from which the muezzin calls out the times of prayer.

Minbar   The seat atop a short flight of steps in a mosque from which the imam delivers sermons.

Ming Dynasty   A period in Chinese history of commercial and literary prosperity; known for its invention and perfection of the art of porcelain-making, as well as the construction of the Imperial Palace in Peking, now Beijing (1368–1644 C.E).

Mishnah   A compilation of Hebrew stories (c. 200 B.C.E to 200 C.E) that fill in the gaps in the oral Torah.

Moksha   Spiritual liberation.

Monasticism   The way of life of the monk or nun, a person who characteristically is celibate (unmarried for religious reasons), has no or few personal possessions, and lives a regulated life of prayer, work, study, and service in a community of such persons. The residence may be called a monastery or convent and is under a superior (abbot, prior, father superior, mother superior) to whom the others owe obedience. Distinctive garb is usually worn by monastics.

Monism   The philosophy that the universe is one unitary whole.

Monotheism   The doctrine that there is only one God.

Mosque   Place of Muslim public worship.

Mount Arafat The hill outside of Mecca where Muhammad gave his farewell sermon in that city and where the faithful on pilgrimage stand throughout the afternoon.

Muezzin One who calls the faithful to prayer at the proper times from the minaret of the mosque.

Muharram The Shi`ite festival which commemorates the death of Husain, the third Imam and the most worthy and tragic of all.

Muslim Those who adhere to Islam; of or relating to Islam, as in "Muslim art."

Mu'tazila An early rationalist school of Islamic thought.

Mysticism Experience or teaching about direct inward experience of divine reality.

Myth A story that expresses in narrative form something of the fundamental worldview of a society.

Neo-Confucianism Refers to the Confucian movement and philosophy of the twelfth century, and after which stressed its metaphysical aspects.

Neolithic "New Stone Age"; the period of the development of archaic agriculture.

Nicene Creed The standard doctrine of Christianity; written at the Council of Nicaea.

Nichiren The founder (1222–1282) of Nichiren Buddhism, which focuses on the Lotus Sutra.

Niddah In Judaism, the rules regarding menstruation.

Nihonshoki One of two texts that sets out the national myth of Japan. (See Kojiki.)

Nirmanakaya The expression of the Buddha-nature as ordinary, "waking" reality.

Nirvana Unconditioned reality, experienced without form or limit when all attachments have been negated and the fires of craving blown out; the ultimate Buddhist goal.

Numinous Spiritual or supernatural.

On-giri Relationship In Japan, the relationship between a benefactor and the recipient of benefaction, which results in the benefactor becoming a parent substitute.

Ontological From ontology; the philosophical study of being or reality. Also, the reality of a thing or person, or the universal whole.

Original Sin The Christian doctrine that human beings are inherently sinners because they are descendants of Adam, who failed to obey God. It was fully developed in the writings of Saint Augustine.

Orthodox Correct in doctrine; the name of the ancient Christian churches of the East, which recognize the first seven General Councils.

Orthodox Judaism School of Judaism that emphasizes a strict following of the Law as traditionally interpreted.

Pagan/Paganism Originally referred to all non-Christian religions of the Roman Empire, and today is used pejoratively to refer to nonmainstream religions. In recent decades, the term has been claimed by those in the Neo-Pagan movement of the United States and Europe to refer to a collection of new religions based on or derived from the pre-Christian folk religion roots of Old Europe, as well as from religions of indigenous peoples around the world.

Pagodas Religious temples and other religious structures in India, China, and Japan, usually associated with Buddhism, but not necessarily so.

Paleolithic "Old Stone Age"; the cultural stage of hunting and gathering before agriculture.

Pantheist One who holds that the universe itself is the Divine being.

Parables Allegorical stories, which are used to convey an idea. Jesus used parables to make his points.

Passover The Spring holiday of Judaism that commemorates the freeing of the Hebrew slaves from Egyptian oppression and the Exodus from

Egypt of the Hebrews to the promised land. God "passed over" the dwellings of the Hebrews when he smote the first born of the Egyptians.

Patriarch A title given the bishop of certain ancient and important cities; in particular, the Patriarch of Constantinople (Istanbul); the senior official of the Eastern Orthodox Church.

Patriarchy Literally, the "rule of the fathers." Term used by feminists and others to denote a society where all of the authority is held by men.

Pentecost In Judaism, the "Feast of Weeks," which celebrates the receipt of the Law by Moses on the fifteenth day after the Exodus from Egypt. In Christianity, the celebration on the seventh Sunday after Easter, commemorating the descent of the Holy Spirit on the apostles, also known as Whitsunday.

Pentecostal/Pentecostalist Related to Pentecost in that it involves emotional and ecstatic practices as evidence of the Holy Spirit.

Phenomenological approach Looking at religion in a way that tries to set aside one's own prior beliefs and biases in order to see the phenomena just as they are.

Pluralism The condition, especially apparent in the modern world, in which many different options for belief and lifestyle exist together in the same society.

Pope The Bishop of Rome who, as successor of St. Peter, is believed by Roman Catholics to be head of the Church on earth and the representative of Christ.

Popular Religion "Religion of the people" as opposed to "official" or authoritative religion. See also "little tradition."

Practical form of religious expression A religion's form of worship, prayer, meditation, pilgrimage, and the like. To find a religion's practical expression, start by asking yourself, "What do they do?"

Prajna Intuitive wisdom in Hinduism and Buddhism.

Prajnaparamita "Wisdom that has gone beyond"; the highest intuitive-enlightenment wisdom in Mahayana; also, the name of a goddess who personifies it.

Predestination The Christian doctrine that all that happens is due solely to God's will, from life and death, including the smallest seemingly accidental events.

Presbyters Members of a local board of elders of a Christian Protestant sect; refers to lay governance as opposed to governance by ordained priests.

Prophet In the Biblical tradition, one who speaks on behalf of God in the context of a particular historical situation.

Protestantism Christian sects that developed in "protest" to the practices of the Catholic Church during the sixteenth century.

Puranas Books deriving from the early Middle Ages, which set out accounts of the folk gods of the indigenous traditions of India. Many of these gods became the devotional gods of bhakti, e.g., Sarasvati and Durga.

Purdah The practice of secluding women by confining them to the home, thus isolating them from society and limiting their education to domestic vocations.

Pure Land Form of Buddhism strong in China and Japan emphasizing the believer's entry into paradise (the Pure Land) through faith in the vow of the Buddha Amitabha (Emiduo or Amida) to save all who call upon his name. Called Jodo in Japanese.

Purgatory In Roman Catholic teaching, an after-death state in which sins insufficient to warrant eternal punishment in hell are purged away, so that the soul can eventually enter heaven.

Purim The Jewish holiday in February or March that commemorates the story recounted in the Book of Esther: how the Jews were saved from the wicked designs of Haman, chief minister of the Persian king, by Esther the queen and her cousin Mordecai.

Quakers Religious sect, also known as the "Society of Friends," founded in the 1650s in England by George Fox and others. They were called "Quakers" because they would "quake" when they communed with God inwardly.

Qur'an (sometimes Koran) The sacred scriptures of Islam.

Rabbi A Jewish scholar or teacher, particularly the spiritual leader of a congregation.

Ramadan The month of the Islamic calendar during which Muslims fast from sunrise to sundown.

Rasul Muhammad's calling in relation to God; means prophet, envoy, messenger, apostle, ambassador, or spokesman.

Reconstructionist Judaism School of Judaism that has its roots in humanism and is most radical in terms of doctrinal reform.

Rectification of names Becoming what one *is*. In other words, fulfilling one's proper role (e.g., father, son, wife, mandarin) in society to the fullest, motivated by *ren* (virtue) so that one contributes to the harmonious "dance" of society.

Reform Judaism Liberal interpretation of Judaism that emphasizes ethics over following the Jewish Law legalistically.

Reincarnation The religious doctrine of several religions, including Hinduism and Buddhism, that after death human beings are born again in this world or in other worlds as humans or as animals.

Ren Confucian term for virtue; a vague but eloquent term suggestive of humanity, love, high principle, and living together in harmony.

Resurrection A raising from the dead.

Rinzai School of Zen Buddhism that developed in Japan during the Kamakura period (1185–1333), which taught that the way to enlightenment is through spontaneous insight.

Rita The Vedic term for the cosmic law or order.

Rosary A string of beads with a crucifix hanging on it, which one uses to count repeated "Hail Marys," or novenas, special sets of prayers on successive days. Also, it refers to the sets of prayers themselves.

Rosh Hashana In Judaism, the New Year holiday, commemorated by fasting and solemnity.

Ru See Mandarin.

Sabbath The seventh day of the week (Saturday) and Jewish weekly holy day, marked by observant Jews with many special practices and by strict abstention from work.

Sacraments Certain rites believed to convey God's grace directly and to be generally necessary to Christian salvation. Many Protestant churches celebrate the sacraments of baptism and Holy Communion, while Roman Catholic and Eastern Orthodox churches acknowledge five additional sacraments: confirmation, marriage, holy orders, penance, and extreme unction ("last rites").

Sadhu A "holy man" or renunciant who has set aside worldly goals for the sake of the spiritual life.

Saint In Christianity, a person recognized by a church as possessing exceptional holiness.

Samadhi The highest state of concentration or meditation, when the mind is one with the Divine.

Sambhogakaya The expression of the Buddhanature as paradisal heavens ruled by radiant Buddhas and bodhisattvas.

Samgha The Buddhist monastic order.

Samsara The wheel of rebirth; the world.

Samskaras Hindu "sacraments" or "rites of passage" performed at definite stages of life, from birth through entry into adulthood.

Sanctification The receipt of the Holy Spirit in a strong, emotional conversion experience.

Sannyasin A wandering monk who renounces all ties of ordinary life.

Sati (or **Suttee**) In traditional Hinduism, a practice wherein the wife immolates herself on the funeral pyre of her dead husband.

Second Great Awakening A movement in Christianity that occurred during the early nineteenth-century in America; it was characterized by a feeling-centered approach to religion, powerful conversion experiences, an emphasis on individual conscience, religious revival events, and the motivation of individuals to social action on such issues as women's rights and the abolition of slavery.

Second Vatican Council The twenty-first ecumenical council of the Catholic Church, which was convened by Pope John XXIII and, after his death, presided over by Pope Paul VI. The purpose of the council was to renew the Catholic Church for the modern era by implementing significant developments in liturgy (e.g., authorization of conducting the liturgy in the vernacular rather than only in Latin), in theology (e.g., including an openness to religious freedom), in the role of the bishops, and in the relationship of the Catholic Church to the modern world, to other Christian churches, and to non-Christian religions.

Sect A term used by sociologists to denote religious groups related to mainstream religions (e.g. Christianity), but whose adherents believe represent a more intense commitment than the average adherent to the religion to which they are related (e.g., the Amish or the Jehovah's Witnesses in relation to mainstream Christianity).

Sectarian Characterized by sects; may also imply partisanship between sects.

Secular Nonreligious aspects of society; worldly.

Secularization Denotes a shift from the religious orientation of a society, an institution, a person, a symbol, etc., to a worldly one; also often the shift of social institutions from religious authority to civil authority.

Seder The name for the Passover meal, which includes a ritual conducted each year in the spring by Jewish families, which celebrates the Exodus of the Jews from Egypt under Moses' leadership and, therefore, freedom itself.

Separation of church and state A central concept in the development of U.S. government, which seeks to maintain a separation of civil and religious authority in society.

Sephardim Jews from the Iberian peninsula. The word "Sephardim" derives from the word for "Spain" in Hebrew. All Jews who did not convert to Christianity were expelled from Spain in 1492. Sephardi Jewish practices were influenced by their association with Spain, and their special language, Ladino, is a combination of Hebrew and Spanish.

Shakti Spiritual power, often identified with the various female Hindu deities that correspond to male deities.

Shaman A person who in many tribal societies through special initiation has powers of spirit-control, divination, healing, and contacting the gods and spirits, usually exercised through elaborate performances and in a trance state.

Shamanism The experiences and practices of the shaman. It is not an institutionalized religion, but it denotes the use of magic, the entering altered states of consciousness, and the use of techniques to induce lucid dreaming, possession, and out-of-body experiences, all of which may have religious implications.

Shari`a The body of Muslim Law.

Shavuot A happy Jewish festival derived from the agricultural roots of ancient Israel, which takes place in late spring or early summer.

Shaykh A Sufi, or a mystical Islamic, spiritual teacher and guide.

Shekhinah The spirit of God at the Sabbath, which is feminine.

Shi`a Islam The "party" of Ali; the minority, some 10 to 15 percent of all Muslims, who traditionally believe that Islam should be headed by a Divinely guided Imam who is a hereditary

GLOSSARY **505**

successor of the Prophet through Ali, Muhammad's cousin.

Shingon Buddhism The form of Buddhism founded by Kobo Daishi (773–835), who was interested in the synthesis of Daoism, Confucianism, and Buddhism. He studied Tantric Buddhism and the Great Sun Sutra in China and then returned to Japan to establish a great monastery on Mount Koya, where esoteric practices were used.

Shinko shukyo Japanese term for the new Japanese religions; literally, "newly arisen religions."

Shinran Founder (1173–1262) of Jodo Shinshu, True Pure Land Buddhism, in Japan.

Shin-shin-shukyo Japanese term for the "new new" Japanese religions; literally "new newly-arisen religions."

Shinto "Way of the Gods"; the indigenous polytheistic religion of Japan.

Shirk Idolatry, putting anything else in the place of God; the ultimate and unforgivable sin in Islam.

Shiva Hindu god considered a personification of the Absolute.

Shogun In Japan, a hereditary military ruler, ostensibly under the authority of the emperor, but who held nearly complete control over the nation until 1867, when the rule of the Shoguns ended.

Sikhism Indian religion emphasizing monotheism and equality; worship centers on its sacred scripture, the Holy Granth.

Sinicize To make something Chinese.

Skandhas Basic constituents of reality in Buddhist thought; five of them—form, sense, perception, reactions, and consciousness—make up a human being.

Social gospel A movement that strove to correlate religion to new ideas in science and society and to recover the old dream of making

America into a new "people of God" through social reform.

Sociological form of religious expression A religion's forms of group life, leadership, relation to outside society, governance, and interpersonal relations. To find a religion's sociological expression, start by asking yourself, "How do the people involved relate to each other?" and "How are they organized?"

Soka Gakka A new Japanese religion in the Nichiren tradition.

Song Dynasty (1127–1279 B.C.E.) A period in Chinese history whose society was the first to print books. As a result, there was considerable educational development in this era, and the famous civil service examination system was developed, permitting the rise to status in society of men by merit rather than merely by "connections."

Soto School of Zen Buddhism that developed in Japan during the Kamakura period (1185–1333), which taught that the way to enlightenment is through lengthy meditation sessions.

Soul The principle of life and consciousness, commonly believed to have a destiny separate from the physical body.

Spiritualism A religious movement that holds that there is continuity of life and, therefore, there is no death; practices include contact with the spirits of the departed through mediumship.

State church The officially recognized church of the governing authority of a nation. See "Separation of church and state," for an alternative approach.

Stigmata Marks of the nails on the hands and feet, of the crown of thorns, and of the stab-wounded side of Christ on the cross, which have been experienced by some ardent Christians.

Sufism The mystical tradition in Islam.

Sukkot A happy Jewish festival derived from the agricultural roots of ancient Israel, which takes place in autumn.

Sunna   The body of established Islamic faith, morals, and practice, established by the consensus of jurists and the faithful.

Sunni Islam   The majority body of Muslims, who stress sunna and consensus.

Sutra   A Sanskrit text, especially scriptural texts in Mahayana Buddhism.

Svadharma   In Hinduism, one's person dharma; one's place in the "great dance" of the social order.

Synagogue   A Jewish congregation and its meeting place, where worship consists of prayer and instruction rather than the sacrificial offerings of the temple.

Synoptic Gospels   The first three Gospels of the New Testament. Believed by most scholars to have been written between 65 and 80 C.E. They are called "synoptic" (derived from *synopsis,* which in Greek means "view together") because they are thought to be related to each other in terms of sources and meaning in ways that the Gospel of John, the fourth Gospel, is not.

Tabernacle   A moveable shrine in which Yahweh was worshipped by the Hebrews until Solomon built a great temple; it contained the written Torah. Its design and method of construction were given by God to Moses at Mount Sinai.

Taboo   A prohibition, as against eating a certain food, or going to a certain place, or touching certain things (e.g., blood); enforced through fear of anger of gods or spirits, if the forbidden act is done.

Talmud   A vast, authoritative commentary on the Hebraic Law, including *aggadah* and *halakhah,* composed by rabbis and completed about the sixth century C.E. Next to the Torah, it is the most important book in Judaism.

Tang Dynasty   A period (618–907 C.E.) in Chinese history of great learning and cultural sophistication admired by many foreigners; the arts flourished and China had considerable military power.

Tantrism   Spiritual path emphasizing initiation, esoteric rituals, and sexual symbolism.

Tathagata   "One who has gone thus" or "come thus"—a title of the Buddha emphasizing his passing from worldly existence into Nirvana.

Tibetan Book of the Dead   The book that is Tibet's most famous contribution to the world's religious thought. It sets out an account of the experiences of a deceased person after death. Also known as the *Bardo Thodol.*

Tendai Buddhism   The form of Buddhism founded by Dengyo Daishi (762–822), who held that the Lotus Sutra is the final and culminating expression of the Buddha's teaching. Dengyo Daishi studied Tiantai Buddhism in China and then returned to Japan to establish a great monastery on Mount Hiei, which became a most significant influence on the spiritual history of Japan.

Tenrikyo (Religion of Heavenly Wisdom)   One of the modern New Religions of Japan; monotheistic.

Theocracy   A government established and maintained in accordance with religious authority.

Theoretical form of religious expression   A religion's stories, concepts, ideas, doctrines. To find a religion's theoretical expression, start by asking yourself, "What do they say?"

Theravada   The "Way of the Elders." The school of Buddhism emphasizing the historical Buddha and a conservative adherence to his teachings as Theravadins understand them; predominant in the Buddhist countries of South Asia and Southeast Asia.

Therigatha   Translates as "Psalms of the Sisters." This is a collection of beautiful accounts of the enlightenment of over 70 women who are believed to have been among the first nuns of Buddhism.

Three Refuges or Three Jewels   The Buddha as the ideal teacher; the Dharma as his teaching or "gospel," and the Samgha, or order of monks, as the ideal community—three ideals that a person affirms on formally becoming a Buddhist or a Buddhist monk or nun.

Tian Chinese word usually translated as "heaven," but means also the supreme ruler or moderator of the universe who gives rain, victory, fortune or misfortune, and who regulates the moral order.

Torah The most important part of the Hebrew Scriptures. It consists of the first five books of the Bible, which contains the Hebraic Law.

Torii The gently curved archway that leads into the precincts of a Shinto shrine.

Totem An animal or plant believed to have a special spiritual relation to a particular tribe or subgroup.

Trikaya The three "bodies" or forms of expression of the Buddha-nature.

Tripitaka The oldest Buddhist scriptures; written in the Pali language, they are the only ones considered authoritative by Theravada Buddhism.

Trinity The doctrine that there are three "persons," the Father, the Son (Christ), and the Holy Spirit, in the one God.

Twelvers (Ashariyah) The majority of Shi'ites, who accept the first twelve of the Imams in the line of Ali, believing that the Twelfth has gone into hiding to return as the Mahdi, or messianic savior, who will establish a paradisal reign on earth just before the end of the world and the judgment.

Ulama Collective term for Muslim religious scholars and teachers who, by consensus, establish correct teaching.

Unconditioned reality The opposite of conditioned reality; reality in its absolute nature equally present in all times and places and not limited in any way.

Unification Church A group founded by the Rev. Sun Myung Moon, which combines Christian, shamanistic, and messianic features. Its ad-

herents are often referred to pejoratively as "Moonies."

Upanishads The last and most philosophical of the Vedas, centering around the message that Atman is Brahman; one's true self is the universal Divine Reality.

Vajrayana Diamond or **Thunderbolt Vehicle** The esoteric or Tantric school of Buddhism emphasizing initiation, mantras, visualizing, and a special elaborate set of symbols and pictures.

Varnas Major groupings of castes in Hinduism; literally, "colors." The four main varnas are (1) brahmins or priests; (2) kshatriyas or rulers and warriors; (3) vaishyas or craftsmen and merchants; and (4) shudras or farmers and peasants. Harijans or untouchables are not one of the varnas, as they are outcasts.

Vedanta A tradition of Hindu philosophy that has generally been the most prestigious in Indian and is best known outside of that country by this name.

Vedas The ancient Hindu scriptures in Sanskrit comprised of the Rig Veda, Brahmanas, Aranyakas, and the Upanishads. The first three parts are concerned mainly with the words, rituals, and the meaning of the sacrificial rites of the brahmin priests. See Upanishads.

Vihara A center of Buddhist practice and teaching.

Vipassana Theravada method of meditation that aims at analyzing one's experience until one realizes that conditioned reality is impermanent, unsatisfactory, and has no "self."

Vishnu One of the major devotional gods of bhakti. Vishnu is God as the force on behalf of order and righteousness. He descends from the highest heaven in incarnate form whenever righteousness declines, working to restore good in the world. Krishna is a descent of Vishnu.

Word, or **Word of God** (1) Jesus Christ as manifestation of God; (2) the Scripture understood as directly revealed by God. (An emphasis on the "Word" aspect of Christianity usually entails an emphasis on Scripture, preaching, and a relation of inward faith to Jesus Christ.)

Wang Yangming A leading Neo-Confucianist (1472–1529) who taught that the principle of the myriad separate things is actually within the mind itself, and therefore the supreme requisite is sincerity of mind. Also known as Wang Shouren. See also Zhu xi.

Wu-wei In Daoism, nonbeing or not doing; not a "thing" or a "cause," but just the spontaneous flow in an endless stream of flux and change. The Dao is of this nature; person who lives this way is in synchronism with the Dao.

Xunzi A great Confucian philosopher (fl. 298–238 B.C.E.), who said that man is basically evil in the sense of being self-centered and, therefore, needs education and social control to become good.

Yang and Yin From China, the interacting cosmic principles, respectively masculine and feminine, ultimately included in the Dao.

Yantra In Tantric Hinduism and Buddhism, a diagram consisting of lines, with no depictions of dieties, buddhas, or bodisattvas. Used in meditation.

Yoga A spiritual path designed to unite one with God or one's true self; in a more restrictive sense, spiritual exercises involving postures, breathing, and meditation.

Yom Kippur In Judaism, the Day of Atonement, which follows ten days after Rosh Hashana, and which is commemorated by fasting and prayer.

Zen See Chan.

Zend Avesta The scriptures of Zoroastrianism. Although it contains the Gathas (hymns ascribed to Zoroaster himself), there is much material of a later and more priestly character.

Zhu xi A Neo-Confucianist leader (1130–1200) who taught that the one great ultimate is manifested in the principles of the myriad separate things. Also, known as Chu Hsi. See also Wang Yangming.

Zhuangzi The first great Daoist writer (died c. 3000 B.C.E.) to make the potential of Laozi's vision more explicit. In fact, some scholars hold that it is really Zhuangzi who wrote the *Dao de jing* and who also invented Laozi as a fictional, but representative figure. Also known as Chuang-tzu.

Zionism The movement to establish a Jewish homeland in Palestine.

INDEX